MIS MEMORIAS
A True Story of Tragedy, Trials, and Triumph

Armando Flores Jr

Soli Deo Gloria

MIS MEMORIAS
A True Story of Tragedy, Trials, and Triumph
Armando Flores Jr

Copyright © 2021 by Armando Flores Jr

All rights reserved. This book or any portion thereof may not be reproduced or used in any manner whatsoever without the express written permission of the author or publisher except for the use of brief quotations in a book review.

Some names have been changed to keep from possibly bringing unintended embarrassment and/or unwanted memories to the descendants or loved ones of those depicted. Additionally, all accounts are consistent with my recollection and are in no way intended to slander or deride any person.

ISBN 978-1-7358303-6-0

*To my lovely wife, Judith, and my loving children
Armando III and Alisha*

FOREWORD

I'm excited for you to read this book for many reasons. Mondy—Armando Flores—has lived the American Dream. He didn't come from much money and, as you will discover, he suffered many losses and has his fair share of regrets.

No one's life is easy. We experience the deaths of loved ones, betrayals, sicknesses, fights, and trials of all shapes and sizes. What defines us are the choices we make; you can bellyache and complain about how unfair life is and blame everyone else for your mistakes or failures, or you can acknowledge the tough situation you're in and decide to overcome it with every fiber of your body. Mondy chose the latter—time and time again.

During high school, he earned a football scholarship to a big-time SEC school: LSU. You will learn in his book why and how he finished his playing career and graduated from the University of Tampa. He began his business career as a Xerox sales rep in 1969. Afterwards, he held various managerial positions with Xerox in sales, marketing, and administration and in 1977 was named the Branch Manager for South Florida. In 1978, he became a Vice President of Jim Walter Corporation until he retired at the age of 44 in connection with their buyout by KKR.

As an active member of his church and community, he worked during retirement more than many people work in their career jobs. He has served on the boards of the Florida West Coast Chapter of the Fellowship of Christian Athletes and the Board of Trustees of the University of Tampa, along with many other service positions.

I'm honored to write the foreword for Mondy's book because he's the real deal. He loves the Lord, he loves to help others, he loves to serve, and he loves his family and friends. He's one of the good guys, and I'm blessed to call him a brother and a friend.

On a personal note, I've known Mondy since I was eight years old. We both grew up in West Tampa, a mile and a half apart. We both attended Jesuit High School where he excelled in football while I played basketball and baseball. Our friendship never wavered over the years as I played major league baseball and then managed several pro teams while he embarked on a very successful business career. Today, our small circle of friends is as close-knit as can be. By the way, we have each celebrated our 50th Wedding Anniversary.

As a professional baseball player and then a manager, I've been surrounded by some of the most physically talented individuals. I know the good, the bad, and the ugly sides of the highest levels of competition. I've seen many people succumb to the lures of money, power, and fame. The best thing Mondy and some of his friends ever did for me was to introduce me to my Lord and Savior, Jesus Christ.

If you know my career, your first image of me might be of me yelling, red-faced, at an umpire, kicking dirt on his shoes while tens of thousands of people cheer or boo. Mondy is responsible for the softer side of me; a side that doesn't make headlines but that changed my life for the better. While we grew up going to a Catholic school and having a sense of spirituality, my life changed entirely when he told me that God wanted an intimate relationship with me. Being introduced to my Lord and Savior, Jesus Christ, was the single-best thing anyone could do for me.

Through this book, even through the dark days of Mondy's life, you're going to sense the presence of God over him. That same God desires to have a personal relationship with you.

This book was not written for Mondy to brag about his successes or to make himself look good. It has been written in a fresh, honest, and raw manner that I believe will captivate you as you journey through the many sides of Mondy's life. As you begin to read this book, buckle up and prepare yourself for a wild ride. Mondy doesn't do things halfway—he's all-in, all the time.

While the book is about Mondy's life, it's not intended to be an autobiography. This book was written for you. Through the sharing of his life story, you'll come away with two undeniable truths. The first is that the power of hope is indomitable. In every challenging situation you find yourself, there is always hope. The other truth is the biggest of all—Jesus is always the answer.

I'm honored to introduce you to my friend, Armando Flores. I'm sure that by the time you're done with this book, like me, you'll call him a friend.

Lou Piniella

MLB World Series champion as a player and manager.

Retired.

Servant of the Most High God.

ACKNOWLEDGMENTS

I would like to thank my lifelong friend John E Oliva, who encouraged me throughout the process and assisted me by reading and re-reading each version followed by helpful comments and suggestions and for tirelessly leading the photo gallery effort converting an arduous task into a time of enjoyment and fellowship. The many hours he spent in every aspect has greatly enriched *Mis Memorias*. Thank you, my friend.

SPECIAL NOTE FROM THE AUTHOR

Mis Memorias (My Memoirs) are a gift to my wife Judith Kay Flores whom I love and have loved increasingly since we met during the summer of 1961 and to who, in large part, is responsible for the superb quality of life I enjoy and have enjoyed throughout our time together; and to our son Armando Flores III and our daughter Alisha Marie (Flores) Cordova, the loves of our lives and to their families and their progeny.

In addition to scratching the curiosity itch common to all, knowing one's history can be helpful as you face challenges that life indiscriminately delivers and can be beneficial by recognizing the many untold, unrealized, and unearned blessings. Hopefully you will realize that your challenges, as great as they may be, can be dealt with more effectively when viewed from an eternal perspective and mellowed by those blessings that just seemed to appear from time to time. The story represented in "Mis Memorias" continues through you and yours.

As you make your history, it is my hope that you will learn from my mistakes and from the mistakes of my ancestors thus not repeating them and build on the things we did correctly. Take your time in reading my thoughts so as to read "between the lines" and never lose sight of the huge sacrifice made by your ancestors (and mine) in leaving their homeland and crossing the Atlantic Ocean to improve the lives of their families to which we belong.

This story does not exist without the stage that is the United States of America. Freedom, of course, is not free and even with all the abuses brought upon this free land under the guise of freedom, there is no place on earth like the USA.

Above all, I want to thank God for placing me in the family in which I was raised and the one I now enjoy and for providing the friends and acquaintances that helped me shape my life and, mostly, for the promise of everlasting life and joy with Him at the appointed time.

Armando Flores Jr

TABLE OF CONTENTS

FOREWORD V
ACKNOWLEDGMENTS VII
SPECIAL NOTE FROM THE AUTHOR IX

PART ONE: EARLY YEARS IN TAMPA 1

FAMILY 3
CALLE LIMÒN 9
TRAGEDY STRIKES 15
SCHOOL DAYS 19
HOW'D THIS HAPPEN? 29
SUMMER OF 1960 35
JUDY, JUDY, JUDY 45
LEAVING HOME FOR TIGERTOWN 51
CHRISTMAS IN TAMPA 71
DIVIDE AND CONQUER 81
SUMMER OF '64 119
THE UNIVERSITY OF TAMPA 129
WHO IS MONDY FLORES? 177

PART TWO: MIDDLE YEARS-THE BIG LEAGUES (1969-1998) 201

XEROX 203
AN OFFER I COULDN'T REFUSE 217
TAMPA 231
ON THE ROAD AGAIN 263
SICILIAN SISTERS VISIT UPSTATE NEW YORK 269
TURN THE HOSE 275
PALM BEACH STORY 293
ARMANDO FLORES III 301
ALISHA MARIE FLORES 339
COMFORT ZONE MORPHS INTO JWC 343
ST. PATTY'S DAY, 1980 357
THE STROLL 371
COMFORT AT HOME 383
CAN YOU HELP? 389
TEENAGE AND BEYOND YEARS 391

PART THREE: LATER YEARS-FINISH STRONG (1999-THE APPOINTED TIME) 421

THE BEST THINGS IN LIFE AREN'T THINGS 423
(MY) GIRL MEETS BOY 435
THE BOMB 441
CIGAR CITY BIBLE STUDY GROUP 463
THE FOURTH CORDOVA SISTER 465
HELL'S CANYON 475
MERCY AT FLATWOODS 489
BLESSING OF BLESSINGS 493
OBJECTIVES, THEN AND NOW 497
ABOUT THE AUTHOR 507

Part One

EARLY YEARS IN TAMPA

FAMILY

The Spanish explorer Ponce de León first arrived in the Tampa Bay area in 1513, but the development of the region began after the territory became part of the United States in 1845, approximately sixty years before my ancestors arrived in the United States setting the stage for *Mis Memorias* (My Memories).

Tampa was a terrific town in which to be raised. In the 1940s and 50s, nowhere in the South, with the exception of New Orleans and possibly Miami, would you find a city with a diverse cultural and ethnic makeup such as Tampa. The population of Tampa consisted, primarily, of Anglos, Blacks (referred to as "coloreds" in those days), and Latins (made up mostly of Cubans, Italians, and Spaniards). There were distinct neighborhoods for each group, and while the workplace was lightly integrated, the residential neighborhoods were primarily assembled according to ethnicity. The two principal neighborhoods for Latins were Ybor City, and the one in which I grew up, West Tampa.

I was born on the first day of February in the year 1945 to proud parents, Armando and Catarina Flores. My only home growing up was our comfortable middle-class home at 2112 Lemon Street, Tampa, Florida 6, telephone: Red Wood-8113. My recollection growing up in West Tampa is very vivid and includes many fond memories and some not so fond. We knew all of our neighbors on Lemon Street, and some farther away. Everyone had a genuine concern for each other in our neighborhood, or so it seemed through the eyes of a young boy. What would be described as a working-class neighborhood was paradise for any youngster with energy and a keen desire to learn "what was going on." There were plenty of kids to play with, and if the supply was ever a bit thin, West Pines Playground was one block away and the activity there was plentiful.

My family was great. My father, Armando Flores, Sr., was bigger than life to our family and to many others, and it had little to do with the fact that he stood 6 ft. 1. He was the only child in a single-parent family, and try as she might, his mother, Juana, from Burgos, Spain was unable to spoil the object of her life. What she did, unwittingly, was raise a giant of a man, metaphorically speaking. He was a charismatic individual who possessed a strong personality and a charm that attracted many friends, a man to whom many would come to for counsel, help, and the like. Included in the strong image I have of my father was his warm and caring side, which would cause him to stop everything if someone had a problem.

He was born to thirty-four-year-old Juana Camarero Gonzalo in Tampa on February 25, 1915. It was not then the common occurrence it is today for a child to be born to a single mother, but such was the case for my dad. Juana was domestic help for the Florez family, Antonio Andrew and Eva Corral Florez. Antonio Andrew Florez (9/12/1897-10/19/1963) from Oviedo, Spain migrated to Tampa and took a job as a "revisador" (inspector) in the "empaque" (packing) department at the Corral Wodiska Cigar Company in Ybor City. Through that connection, he was introduced to and courted Eva Corral, daughter to the company's owners, who he subsequently married. He rose through the ranks of the company and was the general manager when he fathered my dad in union with the family housekeeper, Juana Camarero Gonzalo.

Juana named the fruit of their union **Armando Flores** ending the spelling of Flores with an *s*. Armando was raised by his mother with the help of a woman named Flora, and in Juana's eyes, he could do no wrong. After all, he was a descendant of the reigning social elite of Tampa's Hispanic community. According to what Flora's daughter, Concha, told my sister in an interview initiated by my sister for the express purpose of finding out what our dad's childhood was like, Antonio Florez wanted Juana to give up their baby and allow his family (with her help) to raise Armando. Señor Florez' argument was based on sound principle and rational thought, but Juana would hear none of it and boldly pledged that Armando was her child and she would raise him. From all accounts, my dad was unaffected by my grandmother's coddling and attention. He learned at an early age to be self-reliant and to not look for any favor from his unintended blood relatives. Doing just that, Armando Flores, "el Flaco" (skinny) to his friends, grew up in an atmosphere where the timid did not prevail. Thus, he became quite adept at providing and fending for himself.

My mother, Catarina DiDio Flores, Americanized to *Katie*, was a fiery woman with a "can do" spirit, which she passed on to each of her four children. She was born of Sicilian parents who, in the early 1900s, made the bold decision to leave their family and roots in the "old country" to seek a better life in America. Her parents, Stefano and Giuseppina Greco Ficarrotta Lucchina DiDio (natives of Santo Stefano, Alessandria della Rocca, Sicily) arrived, with their newborn baby, Angelina, at New York City's Ellis Island terminal where droves of immigrants were processed daily before being directed to the center of the country's melting pot, New York City. They found work and lived in the Italian section of the city which became known as Manhattan's "Little Italy." Life in New York was both difficult and good to Stefano and Giuseppina and their baby Angelina, but from the beginning they sought a warmer climate and a rural life that New York City could not deliver. Following that dream, they again relocated, this time to a small town in West Central Florida named Tampa.

Soon after arriving in Tampa with meager savings acquired while living in New York, Stefano and Giuseppina purchased real estate and opened a grocery store on Howard Avenue in the heart of West Tampa. Before long, they acquired three homes on Spruce Street between Howard and Albany Avenues, which they rented out, thus augmenting the income they derived from their grocery store. God blessed their union with additional children, namely Francesca, Giuseppe, Maria, Catarina (my mother), and Francesca (named after their first American-born child who had died at a very young age).

My mother was raised in a strict, Roman Catholic, hard-working family where children were expected to work instead of play. She nonetheless developed a positive view of what this "new world" had to offer, tempered by parents who maintained a vivid recollection of a troubled "old country." She loved to sing, dance, shop, go to the movies, and make people laugh. She was as tough as they come (a trait that would allow her to manage her family through some tumultuous times ahead). She and my father provided all the love and security a youngster could ever wish for.

My brother Bob is fourteen years my senior. He was mature beyond his years, caring greatly about his family... especially his kid sister. He would consistently yield to her arguments, activities of the day, and even which movies they would attend. He was a solid contributor to Jesuit High School's unheralded, but never to be taken for granted, football team. Always in great physical condition, it was not uncommon to see him walking around our home on his hands. If this wasn't enough of a role model for a younger brother, add to the mix the reputation he had for never disobeying our parents. Well, let's say almost never!

Every person should have a sister, and if possible, an older sister. Frances is both to me. You would think seven years difference in age would have taken us different places as we grew up, but my memories regarding her are abundant. Setting apart for a moment normal brother/sister arguments, and we had our share, Frances was a best friend, confidant, part-time mom, and all around buddy to me. She had many friends, centered on her cheerleading, basketball, and other school activities, and I considered her friends to be my friends. We saw Elvis in person together for the first time and it wasn't at a concert.

What an impact older brothers and sisters have on younger ones without trying. I benefited greatly from mine and I wouldn't trade them, or any of my family members for that matter, for any I have ever seen. I've seen many families—some really good—but not like mine. It wasn't until I was a mature adult that I understood the truth of this statement and I've often thought about the impact I had on my younger brother Gene without knowing or trying. Having the benefit of hindsight, I would do a lot of things differently knowing the affect I could have on him, but I know I'm not going to get that chance.

Gene was an easy guy to impact in a positive manner, and conversely, it would have been quite difficult to get him to focus on anything negative. As a youngster, thoughts of Gene center on a trusting younger brother wanting to do what his older brother was doing. He would give you all his trust and confidence and would expect the same in return and rightfully so. He was a fierce competitor and understood the value of pride in the positive sense of the word. His temper would occasionally get out of check during his youth because of the high standards he set (knowingly and unknowingly) for himself; but on balance, he benefited from the high goals he sought to attain, and as an adult, he experienced the satisfaction of knowing he used his God-given talents to the utmost.

BOY MEETS GIRL

The story of my family began with a young man named Armando Flores who, while traipsing the bustling streets of West Tampa, introduced himself to the mildly flirtatious Katie DiDio, who, against the wishes of her parents, was engaged in the age-old sport of "husband hunting." According to my mother, she was immediately attracted to the handsome and dapperly-dressed "el Flaco's" confident demeanor and by his unabashed outlook on life. However, she was concerned whether their casual relationship would ever develop because she was the divorced mother of a two-year-old boy. El Flaco, of course, had a soft spot for a youngster without a dad and immediately took an unusual interest in young Bob, which would later develop into a bond as strong as any he would have with his natural children who would come later.

That obstacle out of the way, Katie's only concern was that Flaco did not have a steady job, which she feared would bring trouble, as it had in her first marriage. To provide her comfort in this area, my dad took a laborer's job with the city of Tampa, but his focus remained on the lure of "Bolita"—the forerunner of today's lottery. The illegality of Bolita was not sufficient deterrent to an eighteen-year-old with high ambition, minus direction from a proper father figure in his life and with the majority of his experience born and seasoned in the streets of Tampa, a city that in a few years would earn the moniker "Little Chicago" (not a compliment to either city).

Catarina (Katie) DiDio Gonzalez was wedded to Armando Flores in a civil ceremony before a notary public by the name of Howard Garret on February 29, 1936, a leap year. She was twenty-three, and just four days earlier, he had turned twenty. Their wedding day included dinner at the Columbia Restaurant in Ybor City and was capped off by a night at the movies at the Tampa Theatre, featuring *Strike Me Pink* starring Eddie Cantor. They afterwards retreated to her mother's home on Cayuga Street in the Seminole Heights area of Tampa where they would stay for two weeks until moving into the home at 2127 Spruce Street in West Tampa, between Howard and Albany Avenues.

The home was a duplex rental property owned by Katie's mother and had as its other tenants, Katie's older brother, Joe DiDio, and his wife Angelina. The rent was a $1.50 per week, cash. One week after their marriage, el Flaco gave up his career with the city under the ruse of a dispute with his supervisor. He could now turn his undivided attention to the enterprise of Bolita under the guidance and tutelage of his friend and mentor, "Red Italiano."

It was a spartan existence in those days, but they were up to the task because they had hope things would improve, and just as important, they had very limited alternatives. Hand-to-mouth was a way of life, and their variety of meals was generally between pasta dishes and rice dishes or rice dishes and pasta dishes. This generation knew how to stretch a dollar and have a good time doing it.

One of the many stories chronicled in our family goes like this: My brother Bobby, who was seven years old at the time, was unsuccessful at trying to convince his mother that he wasn't hungry when she insisted he eat the fried egg sandwich she had prepared for him. Not being one to argue with his parents, he reluctantly took the sandwich, and when he considered it safe, he did what any obedient boy who wasn't hungry would do—he disposed of it. He had not given enough attention to the manner in which he got rid of the sandwich, and he was soon found out much to his chagrin. The penalty for such an offense in those days was a swift and firm spanking intended to communicate the seriousness of throwing away such a scarce commodity as food. Bob recalls that one swat to the buttocks was all it took for him to wet his pants, thus putting an end to the corporal portion of his punishment. The remaining punishment was listening to the periodic sermon on how "rough" things were and the importance of not wasting food (hadn't he told her he didn't want the sandwich in the first place?)

Nonetheless, the intended lesson to Bobby was delivered—maybe too well. Until this day, Bobby remains very sensitive about wasting food. Some close to him feel he may be too sensitive.

Tampa's Bolita business thrived in the 1940s and my dad advanced rapidly. In 1944, he and my mom were able to purchase their own home, in cash.

CALLE LIMÒN

Our neat and comfortable 3-bedroom, 1-bath home at 2112 Lemon Street was chosen by my mother, and as often was the case, that was all it took for my dad to buy the home. This is the only home I knew (except for two years in a college dorm) until I relocated to Sarasota in 1969 in connection with my Xerox career. That would also be the case for my brother Gene who lived on Lemon Street until he married in 1967. Memories of Lemon Street are plentiful and vivid. A memory that remains particularly vivid to me is weekend breakfasts.

During the week, breakfast generally consisted of *café con leche* and Cuban toast. The weekends, however, were different. On Saturday, we did the traditional bacon, eggs, and pancake routine, but Sundays were special. My mother would rise extra early on Sunday morning to begin the spaghetti sauce. The sauce, made with a *sofrito* of garlic, onions, and green peppers, would simmer for hours while the meatballs, pork, hard-boiled eggs, and Italian sausage, exchanged flavors. Cuban bread was delivered to our home and that rounded around the ingredients for Sunday breakfast.

My brothers, sister, and I would wake up to the smell of that sauce. The aroma permeated every room in the house, and it was truly a delightful way to be awakened. My mother would take the ends off one of the Cuban loaves, leaving the remaining loaf to whoever awakened first. The technique we employed was to cut a piece of Cuban bread about ten inches in length, dig out the dough (consumed after dipping into the spaghetti sauce), line the inside of what is now a Cuban bread "shell" with American cheese, and stuff the shell with meatballs. Each of us would follow this ritual—some would do it twice. If there is a better Sunday breakfast, I have not run across it.

Another culinary delight enjoyed by our family was Tampa's famous Goody Goody hamburgers. People circled the curb service area in hope of finding a space to park for the privilege of having the food brought to your car. Others were inside the restaurant ordering and consuming the premium-priced 40-cent hamburger and, its co-star, the 45-cent cheeseburger, which were the central attraction at this bustling hamburger emporium. If the milkshake and French fries accompaniment allowed room, you couldn't go wrong with a piece of their butterscotch or hot apple pie. If you were not in the mood for pie, you could satisfy your craving for dessert at the Old Meeting House on south Howard Avenue where they served an array of delights prepared with their delicious homemade ice cream. If ethnic food is what you craved, you could indulge in a delicious Cuban sandwich and a deviled crab at Tampa's pioneer Cuban sandwich purveyor, the Silver Ring on 7th Avenue (La Septima) in Ybor City. For dessert, there was homemade *Granita* at Lodato's ice cream parlor just around the corner on 8th Avenue (We, of course, were unaware at this time that Rose Lodato would be my brother Bob's wife some years later).

Growing up in our neighborhood was really quite wonderful. I have many wonderful memories of the things we did to entertain ourselves in those days. We participated in many activities, including football, basketball, baseball, cork ball, Indian ball, hide and seek, marbles, building huts, climbing trees, riding and racing bicycles, tinkering on automobiles, playing tag, fussing, fighting, making up and other things. My first best friend was Sam (Samito [pronounced Sah-me-tho]) Rodriguez who lived across the street with his sister, Nancy, and his parents Big Sam and Delfina, who we called Tota (pronounced Tho-tha). Samito had a fertile and vivid imagination and he used it continuously. It took me a while to discern fact from fable, but I soon became quite adept at it, a skill that has served me well to this day.

My brother Gene became increasingly frustrated with Sammy's stories because he, as any trusting soul, believed Sammy and hardly ever saw the stories come true. A story that typifies the relationship we had with Sammy and one that contributed to Gene's and my developing opinion of Sammy goes like this: Sammy had just begun attending Plant High School and he told us he was going out for football, as quarterback of all things. Each time we quizzed him on how he was doing at practice, he would—categorically and without hesitation—give us glowing reports on his progress as Plant High School's junior varsity starting quarterback. Gene, by this time, was sensitive to the questionable veracity of Sammy's stories and sought my opinion regarding the likelihood of him as Plant's JV starting quarterback. I told him I had serious doubt, but that we would attend the first game and find out for ourselves.

Plant was a "powerhouse" football team in those days, and we would have been shocked (but pleased) if he was, indeed, starting as quarterback. On a Tuesday evening, we rode our bikes to Plant High School to watch our friend and neighbor lead the Plant Panthers to victory over intra-city rival, Jefferson. The game was just about to begin as we arrived, so we quickly found our place in the stands and immediately began searching for Sammy. To our amusement, we found Sammy as one of two players whose uniform was different from the rest of the team's. His helmet was not quite the same shade of gold and his jersey had no numbers. Gene and I made sure Sammy knew we were at the game and were anxious to hear his story back on Lemon Street. Sure enough, he had one. He told us he had hurt himself during warm-ups and was not able to play in the game but apologized if he had disappointed us. We laughed to ourselves then and laughed over that story countless times over the years.

Interestingly, both of Sam's parents were very credible people, and where Sammy picked up his propensity to deal in fable has always been a mystery to us. Even though Sammy had a tendency to tell a story every now and then, I had many good times with him and enjoyed his friendship as a youngster.

Two houses east of our home lived the Martinez family. Roy and Mercedes Martinez were parents to Mary and Richard. Mary was one year younger than my sister and was one of her best friends—and they remain that way today. Richard and I were good friends as youngsters and throughout high school. (Even though we saw each other infrequently after high school, we were reconnected in 2007 via the Cigar City Bible Study Group and our friendship has deepened as a result of the spiritual maturation we have gained as we lean on God for things we can't deal with on our own and which we don't understand.)

Across the street from the Martinez family were the Bozas, Gerald M. and Olivia...the "aristocracy of the block," if you will. The Boza Family co-owned the funeral home in West Tampa by the same name and had a daughter, Norma, and a son, Jerry Jr. The thing I recall most about Jerry Jr. was that his dad's funeral home would provide an ambulance for the University of Tampa football games (it was a common practice for football games to have an ambulance present during the game, which I guess tells you something about the sport). The significance of this is that Mr. Boza would have the ambulance driver come by his home and pick up Jerry and a friend, if he so desired, to go to the University of Tampa games in the ambulance and sit in and around the ambulance during the game—the equivalent of a box seat. Young Jerry was ambivalent about going to the UT games, so I had to put on my best sales pitches to convince him it was the best thing to do on a Saturday evening. He went occasionally but I went every time Charles Roberts, the ambulance driver, offered to take me.

Those memories are quite vivid to me. I'll never forget running up to players such as Fred "Moose" Cason, Don Herndon, Tom Spack, Bill Minihan, Holland Aplin and others while they were in their sweaty uniforms cut, bruised, and bleeding, and asking them for their chin straps (a common practice in those days). I was a Spartan fan way before I ever thought of being a Spartan.

The other noteworthy family on our block was the Fernandez family. The Fernandezes lived on the northeast corner of Howard and Lemon. Their father was a merchant marine and quite a disciplinarian while he was home. It was while he wasn't home that questionable activity took place at their home. The kids consisted of two sisters and three brothers—the most notorious of whom was Frank. Frank was constantly in trouble with the law, generally involving fighting, truancy, and theft. Frank was about five years older than me, and I don't mind admitting I was, as they say, "quite respectful" of him. Why an eighteen-year-old would enjoy playing sand lot football with youngsters ranging in age from twelve to fourteen is still unclear to me, but every time we got a game going, you could count on the fact that Frank would soon be there. We would play wearing what we used to call "rubber shoes," or barefooted, but Frank would always play with his motorcycle boots and smoking a cigarette while educating the group in advanced cursing.

One day, while playing football in the neighborhood, I tackled Frank and the heel of his boot caught the skin on the bone just beneath my left eye. The skin split open and bled profusely. When I could not see out of the eye because of all the blood, I asked my friends what happened. Frank, laughing with pride at drawing blood (even from a twelve-year-old), immediately responded that my eyeball was falling out, and I ran home with my hand under my eye to catch it in case it was to fall completely out. My guess is that most of the kids in the game did not appreciate Frank's perverse sense of humor, but no one was about to argue with him, including me. My mother and one of our neighbors temporarily doctored me and took me to the emergency room at El Centro Español Hospital on Bayshore Boulevard (a facility with which I became quite familiar during my youth) for stitches.

Overall, the activities in which we engaged were great! Kids would come from neighboring blocks and we would play hide and seek and 1, 2, 3 Klee Klee, night after night after night, especially in the summer. Living in our neighborhood presented (some of us) with a distinct advantage because located two blocks away was Fort Homer Hesterly. This National Guard armory was the facility of choice for Tampa's entertainment in those days, hosting such events as auto shows, boxing and wrestling matches, Harlem Globetrotters performances, New Year's Eve celebrations, dog shows, flower shows, and any other event that chose Tampa as its venue.

It was because of our proximity to this facility that Frances and I saw Elvis for the first time. The year was 1955. Frances, her friend Mary, and I were spending a lazy afternoon on the front porch of our home when we noticed a peculiar-looking automobile turn onto Lemon Street from Howard Avenue. As the pink Cadillac convertible traveled in front of our home, Mary and Frances could not contain their excitement as they recognized the driver to be none other than the king himself, Elvis Presley.

Before it registered with me, both Mary and Frances were climbing into our family's Chrysler Windsor to follow Elvis. I invited myself as we tailed Elvis as he drove several streets in our neighborhood before ending his journey in the parking lot of Fort Homer Hesterly. Elvis performed there twice, and I caught both performances. Having spent a lot of time around the facility, I developed a method of gaining entrance without the need of a ticket. On the day of an event, we would fill the receiving end of the lock on a remotely located door with a wad of paper, thereby defeating the locking mechanism and allowing us entrance. It was a surefire technique that served me and my friends well throughout our youth. In addition to serving as an entertainment facility, the armory also served as a motor pool for numerous National Guard trucks and jeeps. This provided us with an unparalleled backdrop in which to carry out an activity enjoyed by all young boys... playing war."

Other than the kids in my neighborhood, my cousins Dennis and Joey were good friends with my brother Gene and me. They lived quite a distance, or it seemed so then, at 3011 Cherry Street between Gomez and MacDill, but because our parents stayed in touch with their parents (Uncle Joe and Aunt Frances [Ci Ci]) we saw each other quite often. I was a husky youngster and my cousin Dennis, though shorter, was huskier than me.

We decided one summer day to ride our bikes to Ralston Beach, which was drastically beyond the area within which we were allowed to travel. Our (parent-dictated) northern boundary was Columbus Drive, and Ralston Beach is a good five miles north of that. Since we only had one bicycle (mine), the arrangement was that I would tote my cousin to Ralston and he would tote me back. When we finally reached Ralston, I was spent, but was soon refreshed after playing in Egypt Lake for a while.

My cousin and I had an interesting experience that day. We met two girls who told us they attended the newly-opened Chamberlain High School. I was inexperienced with girls at this stage of my life, and my cousin was less experienced than was I. Before I knew it, the conversation became friendlier and friendlier and horseplay ensued. After a short time of horseplay, we found ourselves holding these girls' hands, and before we knew it, they had their arms around us and we had our arms around them while we were in the water. The next thing I knew, the girl I was with and I were kissing and as I looked over to my cousin, he and his friend were engaged in the same sport. Without regard for people watching us, our foursome continued entertaining ourselves until they told us they had to leave.

My cousin and I discussed the situation on the way home, and we were both shocked. I was merely a junior high school student and had not engaged in this sort of activity to any degree and certainly not in front of others. The lesson I learned was the power and potential peril of sexual attraction between men and women. I have joked about it with friends and family throughout the years, but the fact of the matter is I'm not completely joking when I say I would have probably driven to Georgia (or anywhere else) that day with those two girls. Fortunately, nothing came of it, and hopefully I was on my way to learning one of many lessons regarding relationships with the opposite sex.

As a result of the refreshing afternoon in the cool lake water with our newfound friends, I was re-energized, and I would need that energy because after about a mere block toward our return home, my cousin broke the news he could not tote me any further. I first thought he was jesting and laughed along until I recognized he was not laughing with me. After getting off the bike and quizzing him on this matter, he just stared me in the face and said: "Mondy, I'm sorry. I can't go any further." Well, I placed his large body on the front of the bike and toted him back as well.

In addition to my cousin Dennis, I had other cousins with whom I enjoyed playing, but the family that stands out most during my growing up years is the Russo family. Vincent and Louise Russo and their children, Tanya and Terry, were part of our family for as far back as I can remember. We referred to Vince and Louise as "Uncle Vince and Aunt Louisa" throughout their entire lives. They were the most generous, selfless, and helpful people I had ever known. We would go everywhere with them—the movies, ball games, activities at their home, activities at our home, and everything in between. There was not a Sunday that went by that they would not come over to our home after church for dinner. Louise was always fixing someone's hair or making a dress or involved in some kind of activity to help someone. The Russo family, in fact, became as close to me and to my brothers and sister as any blood relatives of ours. Vince was a mechanic and race car driver, and Louise was a hair stylist and proprietor of the Palma Ceia Beauty Salon. She continually feared his auto racing would either kill or cripple him and kept pressure on him, which in time, caused him to quit the activity he truly loved. It was none of my business then, and it's none of my business now, but I sure liked going to his races and was disappointed when he decided to race no more. They would always make a big "to-do" for our birthdays and Christmas and other days as well. They loved being around our family, and we loved being around theirs. We would co-rent homes at Clearwater Beach and spend vacations together, and those memories are happy and vivid.

TRAGEDY STRIKES

The year 1951 would test the character of the Flores family. Everything was going great. My older brother was home from college; my sister, my younger brother and I were deep into the summer when the lightning bolt hit. It was a typically hot and humid Monday evening that August 27, 1951, when the sound of sirens heading toward West Tampa aroused a concern in my mother, which she often felt in these circumstances. However, the sounds this evening were not for another family; they were for ours. Soon after the sounds of the sirens ceased, my mother received a visit from Jerry Boza, our neighbor and the local funeral home director, who had informed her that my dad had been shot several times while at the Centro Español Men's club in West Tampa. My dad had lived for a short while after taking three shots to the body, but he died before reaching the hospital. He was 35 years old.

The business of Bolita and gambling was a high-risk business. They say that along with high risk comes high reward, but there was no reward our family would have ever accepted for the loss we had just suffered. My mother often expressed (to my dad) her concerns about these types of risks, and he would always end the conversation by telling her not to worry. She, of course, could have made her concerns known more forcefully, but in reality, my dad was not going to alter a career in which he felt very comfortable and in which he was experiencing success. I'll never forget that Monday evening, because I was across the street at Sammy's house playing when the phone rang. I heard Sammy's mother repeating, "Oh no, oh no, oh no!" Additionally, I noticed cars beginning to arrive, bringing visitors to my home, one by one, until our entire block was lined with automobiles. Then another phone call came, and Sammy's mother responded, "Don't worry, he can spend the night here," and I knew something was terribly wrong. Sammy's mother addressed me with the understatement that my dad had been hurt. I asked, "What do you mean, hurt?" She said that my mother would tell me later. I told her I wanted to go home then to ask my mother, and when I got home everything became quite apparent, even to a six-year-old. All our family was gathered at my home, along with friends, and all I can remember is my mother crying nearly hysterically, as well as were my Aunts Mary, Angelina, Louisa, and Frances (Cici). Many other people were crying, as well. I didn't' even ask my mother if my dad was hurt, because it was obvious to me by everyone's reaction that he was dead. I stayed at Sammy's house for two nights and was scheduled to stay longer, but I asked if I could go home because I yearned to be with my family. It was an awful time for us. Things were in complete disarray. Our pillar of strength had been taken from us. People just kept coming by and telling us how sorry they were and my mother and aunts just kept crying, as well as my older brother and sister intermittently. It seemed like it went on for months, even though I'm sure it was only weeks.

I recall conversations between my brother Bob and my mother about his returning to Spring Hill College in Mobile, Alabama. He, of course, did not want to leave, as he was crushed with the loss of our dad and felt he was needed at home since the position of male head of our household had just been thrust upon him. Nonetheless, my mother convinced him to return to Spring Hill as she explained that would be what our dad wanted. Although hesitant to do so, he returned to his junior year at Spring Hill.

School and kindergarten began for Frances, Gene, and me and it probably was the best thing we could do to ease the pain we were experiencing.

My outlook on things changed dramatically. I still enjoyed having fun, but I no longer felt like I was having fun. I was numb. There would be many lessons learned during the upcoming years.

THE PARTY'S OVER

Our house had always been full of friends and visitors and we always had a spread including cold cuts, fresh fruit, and beverages to entertain our visitors. For the first few months, my dad's dear friends continued to call and come by and bring food and other items to help my mother, but within a year, with one or two exceptions, all that had ceased. I remember asking my mother why people didn't come around like they used to, and I remember her response as if she had given it to me this morning.

"Mondy," she said, "when you have food and drink, and money to give or lend to people, you will always have visitors. But when you do not have these things, the only people you will see are true friends."

I recall considering that a rather harsh statement to make to a seven-year-old, but the years have proven her statement to be not only true, but also biblically based in the Book of Proverbs.

BEGGARS CAN'T BE CHOOSERS

My dad kept a journal of loans to business associates and friends. It was obviously my mother's desire and need to collect these balances, because that would be a tremendous help in running our household. I would listen to her call these individuals and I remember being amazed and dismayed by some of the responses. A common response I found interesting and quite convenient for the debtor was, "I just met with Armando last week (before he was murdered) and paid him in full." Because these loans were given on your word and without legal documentation, there was not much my mother could do and I often would sense her disappointment with these kinds of responses. Nonetheless, we had just entered the real world, and there was a lot more of this to come. There were a couple of individuals who paid their debt immediately, and a handful would make payments to my mother once every month or every two weeks until the debt was cleared. I remember going with my mother to these people's homes to collect, in some cases stringing out payments over years without interest. We gained firsthand experience what was meant by the saying, "beggars can't be choosers."

Things had gone relatively easy for us before that Monday in August, but things were about to change. New struggles emerged, led by finances. The six-thousand dollars my father had stashed away in the attic was a substantial sum in those days, but it would evaporate too soon under the burden of private school tuition for me, my brother and sister, and private college tuition for my brother Bob, not to mention normal household expenses. My mother was forced to re-enter the workforce. She took a job at Sun State Slacks because it was a block and a half from our home, and since she had never learned to drive, she could walk to and from work.

My sister was only thirteen years old, and through a little maneuvering at the courthouse and an "approved falsification" of her date of birth, she was issued a full driver's permit as she was the sole means of transportation for our family while my brother was away at college. Bob and my mother knew of property my father owned (in someone else's name) on Clearwater Beach and of his ownership interest in two bars (Blue Moon in Clearwater, and Peach Bar in Tampa) with his partners but we never received any financial consideration or acknowledgment of this fact by them. Additionally, Dad had told Bob on the very week he was murdered that he was planning on purchasing an additional bar, the Oasis, in Tampa, and had sixty-thousand dollars ($60,000) in cash set aside for that purpose. We never located the money, nor did any partner or friend of my father's ever bring up the subject. My father's partners paid for the funeral and stayed in touch with us for a (short) while.

SCHOOL DAYS

As a result of being double promoted, I was entering third grade when I lost my dad. By the time I was ready to enter the sixth grade, we could no longer afford private school. I transferred from St. Joseph's Catholic School to McFarlane Park Public School and enjoyed the transition for at least two reasons that were attractive to a 12-year-old and for which I would later pay. First, the classwork was significantly less challenging, and second, the standard for discipline was significantly lower than it had been at St. Joseph's. These two characteristics continued as I was promoted from McFarlane Park and began attending West Tampa Jr. High School in the seventh grade. West Tampa had other feeder elementary schools in addition to McFarlane Park, and I soon learned that McFarlane Park's students were among the tamest.

I was in shock after attending West Tampa Jr. High for only one week. Among the things I remember is that Frank Fernandez, who lived on the corner of Howard Avenue and Lemon Street in my neighborhood, had a bevy of like-minded people from whom to choose to conduct his activities, and who also were accustomed to attracting the attention of law enforcement. On the third day of my first week at West Tampa Jr. High, I was walking down the hallway after school when I came across quite a commotion in one of the classrooms. I went over and peeked through the doorway, as many other students were doing, and to my surprise, I saw Manuel Fernandez (Frank's cousin and next-door neighbor), threatening to hit the teacher, Mr. Mansel, with the chair he was holding above his head. Everyone seemed quite stressed about the situation, but I knew Manuel would do nothing of the sort, because I had often seen him make similar vain threats during our football games on Lemon Street. As soon as that thought settled in my mind, Manuel proceeded to hit Mr. Mansel on the head with the chair, causing him to fall to the floor, unconscious, his head bleeding. People immediately started yelling for an ambulance, and someone in the office finally called for one. Mr. Mansel was carted off to the hospital while the local police gave Manuel a ride home.

This account is not atypical and my memories of my two years at West Tampa Jr. High are replete with situations similar in nature to this one.

Sammy from across the street also attended West Tampa Jr. High and we rode our bicycles to the house of his aunt who lived two blocks away from the school. The reason we left our bicycles at his aunt's house was because his mother warned us time and again that if we were to take our bikes to West Tampa Jr. High and put them in the designated area (which was enclosed with a chain-link fence and locked during the day), that our bikes could be stolen. I thought it was pretty much of an overkill statement, but nonetheless, Sammy wasn't about to take the chance, so I parked my bike with his every day and we locked them to a support pole in the carport until the end of the school day.

One day, Sammy did not go to school, but I rode my bike to his aunt's house. As I approached Sammy's aunt's house, I decided it was silly to lock up the bike there and walk the two blocks to school, so I rode my bike for the remaining two blocks, put it in the designated area, which was locked as soon as school began. When school let out, I immediately walked to the bike parking area, and to my disbelief, my bike was missing. I simply could not believe it! I immediately summoned the assistance of my cousin Dennis and he allowed me to tote him (sound familiar?) around the neighborhood as we searched for my bike. A full two hours later, we were riding around McFarlane Park Playground and we saw two colored kids, one toting the other, on a bike that looked exactly like mine. As we approached the two boys—and before I could make positive identification—my cousin began to yell, "Mondy, it's your bike! Mondy, it's your bike!" They did not try to get away, but immediately told us someone had sold them the bike. I was not concerned about the veracity of that statement, but told them it was mine and that I had to get it back. They turned it over without incident. I rode it home and never again took it back to West Tampa Jr. High.

Two recollections stand out to me during my time at West Tampa Jr. High. One involved Sammy, who lived across the street from me. The other involved a broomstick. It seems that during the lunch period he and another friend of mine were arguing, and the other friend was accusing Sammy of—guess what— lying. The argument escalated, and before my very eyes, the individual with whom Sammy was arguing took a knife from his pocket and stabbed Sammy in the leg. About that time, a teacher broke up the skirmish and Sammy was off to the hospital to get his leg sewn up. When discussing the situation with Sammy later at his home, he promised me the situation was not yet over and that his assailant would have to pay for his actions. To the best of my recollection, nothing further ever happened.

The very next day seemed like a normal day until 3rd period PE. As a result of failing several times, Frank Olivero was older than the other kids in my PE class, and because he was a behavioral problem, he was assigned to several PE classes where he could be managed by Coach Tony Urso. That particular day, Frank was entertaining students who had showered and were dressing for their next class. Frank's entertainment was pretty raw, especially for seventh graders, and it was about to get much more so.

Frank had been given the responsibility by coach Urso to squeegee the standing water into the drain in order to minimize the possibility of slipping for those coming in for the next class. What I suspect began as a joke escalated when others challenged Frank's idle threat to insert the squeegee (broom) handle into the next anal cavity which was exposed as a result of someone bending over to dry their feet. Everyone laughed and watched with anticipation at what Frank would do next. Then, to everyone's disbelief, Frank made good on his promise and assaulted the unsuspecting Nicky Guarez in a gruesome manner. Nicky yelled with pain as he tried to understand what had happened. Blood freely ran down Nicky's legs as he dropped to the concrete floor from shock.

A usually quiet locker room became the stage for a very upset coach Urso. The look on his face matched his rhetoric and everyone followed his instructions to leave the locker room even though they tried to get a glimpse of what was in store for Frank Olivero. He concurrently attended to Nicky's injury and ordered Frank into his office until he returned.

Frank was expelled for two weeks and it required the same amount time before Nicky was able to return to school. I'm certain Nicky was concerned about what the other students would say about the incident and his concern was well founded. From that day on, everyone referred to Nicky Guarez as "Broomstick Guarez".

However, the memory that most typifies my West Tampa Jr. High experience involves my friend, Peter Lopez. Peter's uncle, (Baby) Joe Guzman, and dad, (Half-Pint) Tony Lopez, were in the bar business, which essentially meant they slept during the day and worked during the night... a situation all too familiar to me. I was twelve years old in the seventh grade, and for the sake of this story, I am going to assume Peter was thirteen.

Peter kept telling me that one day soon his uncle was going to allow him to drive his automobile to school. I went along with the story, as it was fun and harmless; however, I did not hold much expectation of this actually happening. Then one day, Peter told me he had driven his uncle's black Buick to school. I didn't want him to think I would doubt such a claim, but I asked if I could see the car. He was happy to accommodate me. He asked if I wanted to go home with him for lunch, even though we were not allowed to leave the campus. I, of course, told him "sure," and he drove us to his home for lunch where his mother, Lena, fixed us yellow rice with *picadillo, platanos*, Cuban bread, and *flan de leche* for dessert. While leaving his home to drive back to school, he grabbed a couple of his father's cigars and we smoked cigars on the way back to school while he drove his uncle's black Buick Roadmaster.

(As an aside, Peter's older brother, Tony Jr., better known as "Pico," was quite a gambler, drinker, and ladies' man. He had his own Buick Roadmaster, two-tone green and white. Pico was rumored to have been involved in the drug trafficking trade, and several years after I met Peter, an attempt was made on Pico's life while he was at a local bar. An individual came in broad daylight and sprayed the area where Pico was sitting with bullets. Though hospitalized (under police protection) for some time, he somehow survived this attempt on his life, but several years later, he lost both his legs when his car exploded while he was attempting to start it. Pico lost his life in the mid-1980s to failing health associated with the injuries sustained during the attempts on his life.)

With no dad around to put these situations in perspective, I was developing a somewhat skewed view of life. With the exception of driving around in Peter's uncle's Buick, I did not like most of the things I experienced at West Tampa Jr. High, but I did not know what to do about it. I saw people getting mistreated and I did not like it, nor did I like to be mistreated. I saw people being disrespectful and I did not feel comfortable in that situation, nor did I like being treated disrespectfully. I liked the comfort and security of my home on Lemon Street, and I experienced that security in few other places. I did not like violence, yet it was a common occurrence at West Tampa Jr. High. Things were out of focus for me during this time of my life, and quite frankly, I didn't know where to turn. I did not let on to anyone that things were bothering me, because at West Tampa Jr. High that was considered a sure sign of weakness, and I didn't think anybody at my home could help me, so what was the sense of it anyway? Even though I would discuss almost anything with Vince Russo, I did not feel like I could adequately explain how I felt about these situations to him and my older brother Bob was in Massachusetts serving in the Army. I did what I guess most people do when they find themselves in situations they don't know how to handle—they just try the best they can to cope, and that's what I was doing. I became better at disguising my true feelings and became adept at displaying a "tough guy" image, which definitely was not natural to me. However, I maintained this persona as a survival technique among this group of sharks with which I was swimming.

A WELCOME CHANGE

I was thirteen years old during the summer of 1958, which was an odd time for me because I needed to earn some money, yet I was too young to get a "real" job. So, for that summer my source of income continued to be what it had been in previous summers and on weekends during the school year—working in Aunt Louisa's yard.

Make no mistake about it, my brother Gene and I were overpaid by Aunt Louisa, but we still didn't like yard work and don't until this day. Our distaste was such that we wouldn't answer the telephone when she called on Saturday mornings, but that wouldn't stop her. She would drive over and park right in front of our house and toot her horn until we "surrendered." The scenario was quite similar each and every week. She would pick us up at around 7:30 a.m. and take us to Ayre's Diner for breakfast. We would then go to her home and she would assign us the "task of the day," which could have been anything from mowing and edging to planting, pruning, and of course, the dreaded weeding. She not only told us what to do but got in there and did more than my brother or I ever did—she seemed to be on a mission. Not a weekend would go by that she did not have some kind of project and, as I previously stated, they often included yard work.

The only thing I despised worse than yard work was Aunt Louisa's second choice of activities: painting. She would forever be repainting the bathroom or bedrooms in her home, and then of course, there was the huge job of painting the outside of her house. As we aged, Uncle Vince would use one of us to work with him as he repaired automobiles on the weekends. We looked forward to these opportunities. As I look back, it is obvious the Russos were fond of our family and wanted to do whatever they could to point us in the right direction. At lunchtime, Uncle Vince would take us to eat the sandwich or sandwiches of our choice at DiPerrio's on the corner of Dale Mabry and Grand Central Boulevard (since renamed Kennedy Blvd.), and we would bring back Aunt Louisa's sandwich, as she continued to work during our lunch break.

Believe me when I tell you the woman could work. Once the afternoon work was completed, she would drive us home, always leaving us with the option to join them for dinner at a restaurant (she never cooked and they always ate their meals out…a practice they continued throughout their lives).

UNEXPECTED OPPORTUNITY

In late July, Jimmy LaRussa, former schoolmate of my brother Bob, dropped in on my mother for a visit. I was around the house and heard bits of their conversation, which included the compliment Jimmy always paid my mother about how much he loved her black beans and rice dish. Jimmy had been a star athlete at Jesuit High School in the late

1940s and had just returned from military service after graduating from the University of Miami where he attended on a football scholarship. He had a similar demeanor to my brother Bob's, and it was obvious why they were the best of friends. He never had anything but a good word to say about anyone and everyone always thought very highly of him and Bob.

He posed a question to my mother, and I remember her response as if it were today.

"Jimmy, yes, I would like him to go to Jesuit, but there is no way we can afford it."

"Well, if I could work it out where he wouldn't have to pay to go to Jesuit, do you think he would be interested?"

"I'm sure he would," she said, "but let's ask him."

When they asked me if I would be interested in attending Jesuit High School, I felt like I was being offered an opportunity to leave San Quentin Federal Penitentiary. Don't misunderstand my comments. I had many friends at West Tampa Jr. High, some of whom are still close friends today, but the overall environment there was, to me, depressing. Additionally, I was tired of junior high school and was looking forward to high school, but in the public school system I would have to wait another year because public high schools began in the 10th grade then, but Jesuit High began in the 9th.

I told Jimmy I would be very interested in going to Jesuit, but asked why I didn't have to pay like everyone else. He explained that he had spoken to the principal of Jesuit, Father Curry, and the head football coach, Jack O'Connell, and they were willing to waive the tuition if I was interested in attending.

I had no idea how these people even knew who I was or what he was talking about, but I wasn't about to ask any more questions.

What a wonderful opportunity this represented for me, and later for my brother Gene.

I welcomed the change and, during the remaining summer of 1958, I began going to the new Jesuit High School on Himes Avenue four days a week with Jimmy (Coach LaRussa) as he attended meetings and engaged in general preparations for the upcoming football season.

In the morning, I would do prescribed exercises and running, and in the afternoon, we would split up and play this game Coach O'Connell loved. Each team would pass or kick the ball to the other team and the ball would be downed wherever the receiving team first made contact with the ball. Obviously, it was a game that required running, passing, kicking, catching, and a touch of strategy. I really enjoyed being involved in those afternoon outings, and I can tell you Coach O'Connell, Coach DiCharry, Coach LaRussa, Coach Davenport, and the other coaches became my role models even though I didn't know what a role model was at the time.

August 15th soon rolled around and that was the first day of practice, with school to begin about a month later. I was really enjoying the whole scene. Having been in junior high school just two-and-a-half months earlier, I was in awe around this group of guys who, by the end of the season, would have tallied eight wins and only one defeat (7-13 v Palmetto), including an 85-0 crushing victory over Sarasota Riverview considered an avenging of the 84-0 whipping Jesuit had suffered at the hands of Fort Myers High two years earlier.

There were several outstanding players on that team, but two who stood out the most were John Lastra and John Oliva.

As it worked out, coach LaRussa would pick me up in the morning for practice, but I would have to wait on campus between the morning and afternoon practice sessions because he was in meetings with the coaches and did not go home.

After a few days, John Oliva, who was a junior and clearly a star and leader on the team, engaged me in conversation which I found astounding. Since he was one of the last ones to leave after the morning practice, he noticed I always stayed around the locker room and he asked what I did between practices... about a five-hour period. I told him I just hung around and I would get a ride home after the second practice with coach LaRussa.

He further astounded me when he offered me a ride home after the first practice and to pick me up prior to the second practice. I couldn't figure why a person who was clearly regarded as *special* on our team would make such an offer. But as I had done earlier, I wasn't about to ask any questions.

I took John up on his offer, and within the first week of practice I was being picked up and delivered to my home by All-City, All-County, and All-State tackle John Oliva. What made these rides even more interesting was that John would often hook up with his good friend, John Lastra, at Lastra's dad's pharmacy and we would get a bite to eat before resting. Through that connection, I got a chance to know All-City, All-County, All-State, and Jesuit's Most Valuable Player, John Lastra.

John Lastra was a totally different personality from John Oliva, but you could see why they liked each other. Lastra always kidded me and made comments to John questioning what he was doing riding around in a car with a freshman, but Oliva would always come to my rescue, for which I was grateful, because I certainly didn't know the answer to Lastra's riddle.

John Oliva was part of a well-to-do Tampa family and his parents certainly did an outstanding job of instilling in him the virtues of generosity and hard work.

My experience with John Oliva and John Lastra taught me a lot and those principles have stuck with me through today. For instance, if you "really" want to help somebody, help somebody who **needs** help.

Secondly, it doesn't make any difference what your social or economic status is, everyone wants to be wanted, thought of, and respected.

Even harder for me to believe was, in addition to the rides John Oliva provided, he would occasionally invite me to go with him on weekend social outings. We would meet seniors Pancho Trafficante, Richard Valdes, Al Lopez Jr, and others for the midnight movies at the Florida Theatre, and to really test Lastra's friendship, Oliva would ask Lastra to pick me up since I was on his way to the theatre. I would also go with John Oliva to the Colonnade, his girlfriend's house, and anywhere else he invited me to go. I enjoyed being around him because he was a positive individual and demonstrated very high character. He used no profanity, a rarity in that Jesuit locker room.

While I was bigger and stronger than most ninth and tenth graders, I did not possess the experience, agility, tenacity, or the desire required to make the varsity team, and truth be known, I felt quite fortunate to be on the junior varsity. Throughout my freshman year, I would mature, both in terms of my athletic ability and size, and when my sophomore year came, I was in much better position to compete. However, many of the players from the previous year's 8-1 team returned, and I found myself sitting on the bench and participating in the JV games on Tuesday nights, as allowed in those days.

HE'S NOT KIDDING

A rumor circulating the locker room advertised a party at a Plant High coed's home on Davis Island on a particular Thursday evening and the rumor was so well-traveled that it reached Coach O'Connell's office. After practice on Thursday, Coach forewarned the team that he had heard the rumor and he let everyone know in very clear terms that we were not to attend the party, that doing so would constitute a breach of training. I didn't think much about what he said because I had no intentions of going to the party anyhow.

When I arrived at school on Friday there was another rumor gaining steam which heralded the fact that coach O'Connell had, along with another coach, driven around the party the previous evening and had taken names of those Jesuit players who were in attendance. The rumor also indicated he was furious and was contemplating kicking those involved off the team. Sure enough, by mid-afternoon on that Friday, Coach O'Connell gathered the team and advised us certain persons had not heeded his warning regarding the party and they were no longer part of the team. I could not believe it and thought how stupid these individuals were to risk their membership on the team for a party. I would later realize that it was not the party, but human nature's need to challenge authority that convinced those individuals to attend the party. Nonetheless, several linesmen were included in the group kicked off the team, and while I did not start the game Friday night, I did get some playing time for the first time as a Tiger on the Varsity.

Because I saw there was an opportunity for me to play more, I started working harder, and by the end of the season, I was splitting playing time with the starting tackle. What really motivated me was the fact most of the guys who played my position were graduating, and I would be a starter my junior year unless I broke a leg or got crossways with Coach O'Connell.

STUDENT ATHLETE

While I described my athletic experience during my first two years at Jesuit, there was an academic side to those years that was more challenging.

I knew some of the incoming freshmen and sophomores who had also attended St.

Joseph's Elementary School, including my neighbor and good friend, Richard Martinez, but the majority of students at Jesuit were new to me as they had mostly come from other Catholic and some public schools throughout the county in addition to a small contingent from Clearwater in Pinellas County.

I immediately latched onto three individuals as my close friends, two of whom remain close friends to this day. Gene Rivera was a tough kid from Ybor City, and for that reason alone I was fond of him. From Christ the King School in South Tampa came two individuals with whom I would spend the bulk of my years at Jesuit: Ted Cannella and Steve Malzone.

Ted and Steve were troublemakers from Day One. Steve was the brain of their troublemaking endeavors while Ted supplied both brain and brawn. Steve was always cracking jokes and poking fun with people, and I was amused by him and liked the loyalty displayed by his friend, Ted. They both demonstrated the importance of loyalty in a relationship, and I was always impressed by the fact they would never say anything negative about each other behind their back.

Their duo soon blossomed into three people, of which I was the third. I adopted the same philosophy, and the three of us became close and thick as thieves. We double and triple-dated, spent evenings at each other's homes (mostly Steve's), played sports together (organized and unorganized), went fishing, skiing, boating, and went on trips together; you name it, we did it.

Steve and Ted would both get automobiles when they turned sixteen, an event not viable in my family. For the last two-and-a-half years at Jesuit they would pick me up daily, if not more often, and never *seriously* complained about it.

Ted's dad was a Sicilian immigrant who came to Tampa via New York and New Orleans. At a very young age, Norman Cannella took a position as a tailor and worked his way up to Wolf Brothers' top salesman. He did a very good job providing for his family, and they enjoyed a very nice home a block off Bayshore Boulevard at 410 Richards Court.

Ted's older brother, Norman Jr., was a standout tackle on Jesuit's football team who ended up at Auburn University on a football scholarship. Rounding out Ted's family was his sister, Francine, who was a couple of years younger than Ted, and Ted's mom, Angelina, who was a wonderful woman and the "glue" of the family.

Steve's dad, Armand, co-founded and owned a sports apparel manufacturing business, and whatever was in style, the Malzone's had it! Steve's dad would change cars like neckties, and I remember him driving imported automobiles before it became fashionable.

He purchased his clothing from Wolf Brothers, Tampa's premier haberdashery. He and his lovely wife, Ruth, played golf, ate at restaurants frequently, and went dancing often. He had a large fishing boat with inboard motors, which we occasionally used. Additionally, Steve and his brother, Denis, had a speedboat for their use and use it we did!

At the Malzone's, it was Disney World before Disney came to Florida.

Steve's mom was an angel in her own right. She demonstrated an even temperament and was always kind and attentive to me. Steve also had a sweet and attractive younger sister named Christine. There was always great music, great food, and great activities going on at their home and I was developing a taste for the "good life" without yet developing a way to pay for it. Even though Steve's parents were affluent, they wisely required him (and Denis) to work for their spending money.

Steve's school day was generally extended by an hour of "Penance Hall" (Jesuit High School's long standing tried-and-true remedy at redirecting student insubordination) and going directly to his father's manufacturing plant and work there until after closing and a half day on Saturdays, while Ted and I would practice football, and during the off-season, hang out at all the popular spots like rich kids. Incidentally, Penance Hall had virtually no noticeable remedial effect on Steve. He just viewed it as part of the cost of doing business.

I had another bond with Steve. He and I were both awful students. I realized about halfway through my freshman year at Jesuit the reason my sixth, seventh, and eighth grade years were so easy was because I wasn't required to do anything. Well, I learned another lesson in life, "There is no free lunch." I started to pay, and pay dearly.

POLITICALLY INCORRECT

There was a tradition at Jesuit High School of reading aloud all the students' grades at a general assembly each grading period. To make the situation worse, the grades were read aloud, not alphabetically, but in descending order.

Ted was a great student, and he would often walk up to the stage to receive a plaque or other commendation for exceptional work—and then there was Steve and me. As the grade averages descended from the mid-90s for our friend Ted, we did not pay much attention until the mid-70s were being read, and then we became increasingly anxious when they began reading the low 70s and we were yet to hear "Flores" or "Malzone" mentioned. Throughout our freshman year, we endured that self-inflicted embarrassment each grading period, and though we never discussed the matter directly, we both committed ourselves to improving our academic performance during our sophomore year.

The coasting I had enjoyed in public school was taking its toll. I simply did not know how to study, nor did I have the discipline to do so. However, the priests and the rest of the faculty at Jesuit kept the pressure on, and by the end of our sophomore year, both Steve and I were in a respectable (by comparison), high 70s – low 80s range.

Jesuit enjoys a rich tradition today and it was no different during my years there. Jesuit enjoyed a reputation for graduating its students to the best colleges and universities in the country where they developed into doctors, lawyers, and captains of industry.

Jesuit's sports tradition was and is also outstanding, especially when you consider the number of students Jesuit enrolls versus the public schools against which we competed.

John Lastra, John Oliva, and Dennis Agliano earned football scholarships to the University of Florida, while Norman Cannella earned his football scholarship to Auburn University.

Lou Piniella, whom I had known since our elementary school days at St. Joseph, was Hillsborough County's most outstanding basketball and baseball player who would enjoy a wonderful professional career in baseball as a player and manager winning three World Series titles as both a player and a manager, is a member of the Sports Hall of Fame of the Seattle Mariners and New York Yankees as well as the States of Florida and New York, and in my opinion, is past due for the MLB Hall of Fame.

Ken Suarez was another outstanding baseball player, among many, who would later be inducted into Florida State University's Athletic Hall of Fame for his outstanding contribution as a baseball player which led to a Major League career with the Texas Rangers. Ken also has been inducted into the State of Florida Sports Hall of fame.

Fellow 1962 grad Mike Garcia would earn a diving scholarship to the University of Alabama.

There have been many Jesuit graduates who have had noteworthy college careers in sports and several have taken their craft to the professional level.

HOW'D THIS HAPPEN?

There was a significant occurrence during my sophomore year that affected my entire family. We don't talk about it much because it brings back painful memories, but nonetheless, it was significant and it affected our lives.

In 1959, my mother had been widowed for eight years and a couple of her friends were trying to introduce her to "the right man." Our family never thought much of it until one evening she told us she had been introduced to a man through her good friend, Celia Hiajstron. We had never witnessed our mother speak to another man affectionately, and when she started describing how nice this fellow was, we all developed a suspicious concern. I suspect our concern was rooted in the fact we were spoiled by having 100% of her attention for the previous eight years and were leery about sharing her attention with someone we did not know.

Well, she and Celia arranged to have us meet this man in quick order, and before we knew it—and within two weeks—they were talking about getting married.

My older brother Bob had already married the former Rose Lodato by this time, and while he was against even the consideration of marriage with such shallow knowledge of each other, he was somewhat removed from the shock we were feeling.

Frances, Gene, and I discussed the matter outside of our mother's presence, and we remained befuddled about what was happening.

By this time, I had assumed an adult role in matters such as these at our home, so it was left up to me and my sister to caution my mother about the problems that could result from a hasty decision about something as serious as marriage.

She listened, but didn't hear a word we said.

She had been alone for such a long time that I'm convinced she viewed this opportunity as a chance to gain herself a mate who would be with her long after her children were gone. The concept was valid, but the implementation was fraught with issues.

Our mother married Luis Morejon in the fall of 1959, and there was much tribulation ahead of us.

Luis was a Cuban refugee, and by marrying a U.S. citizen, he would be eligible to stay in the United States. Bringing that fact to my mother's attention meant nothing and she soon developed distaste for such comments. We pleaded with her to wait a while before she married Luis, because, if they were truly in love, they could always get married at a later date. However, she responded that if he wasn't married within a certain number of days, he would have to return to Cuba. That sealed it for us. He was marrying her to gain entry into the United States, and as much as we loved her, we had to admit she was blind to that fact.

We were in for some emotional abuse and were ill equipped to deal with it. The "weirdness" started when Luis would eat his meals in the dining room while the rest of the family ate our meals in the kitchen. Frankly, we preferred it that way, but it did seem odd to everyone except our mother. Then it began. A date would pick up my sister and Luis would blow his stack because the young man parked his car in our driveway. As a result—and only when I was not home—he would chew out our mother and then Frances, too, when she would return from her date, explaining to her that the driveway was for his use and not her date's. We again thought that was a little weird, but we had been raised not to argue with our elders, which turned out to be a mistake in this instance.

I recall my friend Ted visiting our home one day, and while he was waiting for me, he placed his feet on the coffee table. I'm the first one to admit he could have exhibited better manners, but nonetheless, it was not the issue Luis made of it when I returned from having been out with Ted. Ted was a bruising 200 lb. fullback and I suggested to Luis that if he had a problem with the way Ted behaved in our home to discuss it with Ted the next time he was in. Luis did not like my response, but I hadn't expected him to.

Likewise, he would pick on Gene about this and that, and Gene, being the youngest of the group, would take it to heart more than Frances or me.

SU CASA, MI CASA

After a few months, Luis invited his entire family from Cuba to live in our home "until they could get settled."

This was quite a shock, since we only had a two-bedroom home after converting the third bedroom into a large jalousie-windowed Florida room after my brother was married. This is where I slept. The sleeping arrangements before Luis were as follows: my mother and my sister occupied the master bedroom and Gene and I shared the other bedroom. After my mother married Luis, he, obviously, moved into the master bedroom with her, which moved my sister into the bedroom I shared with my brother Gene, which in turn moved me into our family room onto a couch which converted into an uncomfortable and undersized twin bed. This arrangement was already tight enough and what we didn't need was an additional family in our home, which could barely accommodate us.

Surprisingly, Luis' adoptive parents were very nice and genteel people. They brought their daughter, Muñeca, and Luis' son, Rey, by a previous marriage (which was news to us, including my mother). There were cots and beds everywhere, as you might imagine, accommodating this group in our small home.

SU CREDIT, MI CREDIT

An incident that pretty well typifies the situation we were enduring at that time involved Luis purchasing, on my mother's credit card, a $505 camera from Maas Brothers. No one knew a thing about it, except I did notice Luis' adoptive father, Emilio, flashing around a rather impressive-looking camera, but I didn't question its origin. One day, after returning from Jesuit, my mother was crying. When I asked what was wrong, she showed me the Maas Brothers statement which indicated an amount due of $505 for a Nikon camera and accessories, plus tax. She had good reason to be crying because she was earning approximately $50 a week and that kind of a purchase would send our family finances into a tailspin.

Luis only spoke and understood Spanish, and my Spanish wasn't sufficient to articulate my position on this matter, but nonetheless, when he returned that afternoon from the sandwich shop he had opened, I confronted him with the purchase and asked him how he intended to pay for it. He had the gall to tell me my mother was going to pay for it and not to worry. I told him that I was worried, because if my mother were to pay for that camera, it would mean we would be unable to buy groceries, a proposition opposed by Frances, Gene, and me.

Disregarding Luis' command not to involve Emilio in *our problem*, when Emilio returned home that evening, I explained the entire situation. He was very apologetic and so ashamed of what had happened that he immediately assisted me in repacking the camera, which I intended to return to Maas Brothers. Even though I only had a learner's permit, I drove my sister's car to Maas Brothers on Saturday and engaged in an experience I would not wish on anyone, much less someone fifteen years old. The salesman asked if he could help me and I told him he certainly could. I said it was my desire to return this unauthorized purchase on my mother's account. I didn't realize it at the time, but I really had a strong position since Luis had just gone into the store, purchased the camera and signed my mother's name to her account. He was not an authorized signer on her account, and therefore should not have been allowed to do so. Had I known this that day, I would have been more at ease. However, not knowing that, I told the sales person I needed to get a credit slip equaling the amount that was charged on her account. He told me it was impossible because the camera was used, and he could not accept used merchandise back into the store after a certain number of days as a matter of company policy. I explained to him if he did not accept the return, Maas Brothers would not be paid for the camera because my mother had no means with which to pay such a large purchase (five hundred dollars may not seem like an extraordinarily large amount of money today, but I can assure you it was extraordinarily large in 1959 to people in our economic bracket. We would have to pay on this purchase for years in order to pay it off.) The salesclerk called for his supervisor, to whom I explained the situation again. The supervisor told me essentially the same thing the salesclerk did and I was becoming a little agitated. I explained to the supervisor they had no choice but to take back the camera as we were unable to pay for it.

The supervisor then called the store manager and I quickly found out why this person was the manager. After hearing my story, he quickly read in my eyes and my voice that this was an urgent matter and it would be in the best interest of Maas Brothers, and certainly of my family, if he would take back the camera. He did, and I went home with a refund totaling the exact amount that was on my mother's bill. That was the happiest day for me and I think for my mother in 1959.

MI ACCIDENT, SU ACCIDENT

Other situations like this one arose as Luis attempted to impress his family using my mother's (meager) savings and/or credit. He purchased an automobile under her name and asked me to go with him to Miami to pick up merchandise he wanted to sell in his store. I didn't have much interest in going anywhere with him, let alone Miami, but I did so to satisfy the request my mother had made of me in his absence. I drove all the way to Miami and was planning on driving all the way back when Luis suggested I take a little nap while he drove on the Florida Turnpike for a while. It sounded like a good idea until, after snoozing for about five minutes; I felt the station wagon jerking back and forth as if he was attempting to keep it on the pavement. As my eyes focused on what was happening, we were swerving off the right side of the turnpike and had entered the first of three rollovers with a station wagon full of merchandise. We flipped the vehicle two more times before coming to rest on the side of the turnpike and, by the grace of God, other than a couple of bumps and bruises, were unharmed. I wondered why God chose to extend His grace to Luis…what an opportune time to snuff out his miserable existence I thought.

I asked Luis what happened and he gave me some lame excuse that a sheet of newspaper on the windshield obstructed his view, causing him to swerve and go off the road as we did.

The Florida Highway Patrol had just arrived when Luis, in a thoughtful moment, asked me if it would be okay if he told the patrolman I was driving the vehicle during the accident. I told him, "Absolutely not," and he pleaded with me to allow him to do so because, according to him, I only had a learner's permit and therefore had less to lose. I again responded, "Absolutely not."

Other than one of the fenders scraping against the wheel, the car was in running condition, even though it was crinkled and dented from bumper to bumper. A wrecker towed us to a repair shop in Ft. Lauderdale, where, fortunately for us, there was an individual who freed the tire from the fender and in an hour and a half we were back on the road to Tampa. Before the tow truck took us into Ft. Lauderdale, we reloaded the station wagon with merchandise that had fallen out of the vehicle. The merchandise in the car was in complete disarray and much of it was damaged.

I took the wheel in Ft. Lauderdale and drove to Tampa, arriving in the wee hours of the morning. Luis was angry with me because I had not allowed him to report the accident as if I were driving and did not speak a word to me all the way back to Tampa. I must say it made the trip much more palatable. We were unable to travel faster than 50 mph because of the condition of the automobile. Two hours into the trip I pulled into a roadside store to relieve myself and get a coke. As I approached the store, my gracious traveling companion expressed to me his disagreement with stopping because he was tired and wanted to get home without unnecessary delays. I disregarded his comments and told him flipping the vehicle in Ft. Lauderdale was an unnecessary delay. It was amazing to me how much "broken Spanish" Luis understood, and from that point on I decided I would speak to him in English and place the burden of communicating on him. After all… we were in America, not Cuba.

While the man in Ft. Lauderdale freed the tire, he only freed it going straight ahead. Every time I made a turn, it would make a significant scraping noise and I was concerned the tire would rupture, causing us big problems. Nonetheless, we made it home.

When my mother came outside to greet us, she saw the car and asked what happened. I remember Luis responding to her that I would not let him tell the highway patrol officer that I was driving at the time of the accident while he showed her the "reckless driving" citation issued to him. I should have been shocked but wasn't when she asked me why I didn't agree with his suggestion. I simply responded to her, "Because I wasn't driving."

SUMMER OF 1960

After a period of time, Emilio, his wife, and their daughter were able to move out of our home, even though Luis' son, Rey, who was about the age of my brother Gene, remained with us. He was actually a nice kid and had no fault regarding what was going on.

School was about to break for the summer, and I asked my mother to contact a couple of friends of my dad who had businesses in an effort to gain employment for the summer. I had outgrown the desire to sit around and play all summer, but I was not yet sixteen years old making it difficult to get a "real" job. I wanted to work at the Miller High Life Brewing Co.'s Tampa's distributor which was owned and operated by my dad's friend Anthony Italiano. The warehouse was only blocks from my home and I could ride my bike to and from work. However, my mother didn't have the same level of interest and the idea was nixed.

My mother was able to get me a job with a family friend who owned and operated one of Tampa's largest plumbing companies. This man was a very good friend of our family and I looked forward to working in his company that summer because I could kill two birds with one stone... earn money, which I needed desperately, and condition myself for the upcoming football season.

I rode my bike the approximately four miles to his company each morning, arriving before 7am. I was assigned to a work crew and we were off the premises by 7:15, returning at about 5:30pm each day. The crew I was assigned to was working on a county project in northwest Hillsborough County, and if it was hard work I was looking for, I had just hit a bonanza. There was no mechanical digging apparatus employed by this company in 1960, so digging trenches to lay pipe amongst the Palmetto bushes was what I did all day, every day. The other guys on the crew would take breaks about every half hour to forty-five minutes, but lunch and a break in the afternoon was all I required. I enjoyed the hard work and was looking forward to a fat payday on Saturday.

Saturday rolled around and apparently the ritual at this company was the owner would meet the workers around noon with their pay envelopes. The owner pulled up in his big Lincoln Continental, went into the office, and came out with all the envelopes. He called off each person's name, and as they came forward, he gave them their envelope stuffed with money. I had learned from the plumbers that they were earning, with overtime, approximately $125 to $150 per week. I was not expecting that amount because I was a plumber's helper, but I had plans for the $50 I was sure I would be earning. The owner gave the last envelope to the next to the last person in the room as he noticed I was standing there and that he did not have a pay envelope for me. Being quick on his feet, he immediately reached into his pocket, pulled out a couple of bills and placed them into my palm while shaking my hand. I shook his hand, put the money in my pocket and told him the week went well in response to the question he had just asked. He then asked how my mom was getting along and sent me on my way.

As soon as I was out of sight, I stopped my bicycle, reached into my pocket and pulled out the two bills to see how much I had been paid. To put it mildly, I was extremely disappointed when I saw the $5 and $1 bills he had given me. I didn't have it in me to confront adults, so I just got back on my bike and rode home. I felt awful all the way home and cried tears of disappointment, frustration, embarrassment, and disrespect.

As soon as I walked into my house, my mother asked what was wrong. When I told her, she tried to console me by telling me since I was just a young boy, I should not expect to get paid as much as others who had families. I explained to her working was about getting a job done and had nothing to do with families and I was not returning to the plumbing company on Monday. She told me if I intended to quit, I should call our friend and tell him about my decision. I told her I would not call *her* friend and as far as I was concerned, if I never spoke to him again, it would be fine with me.

That afternoon, Sam Rodriquez Sr. from across the street had gotten wind of my distasteful experience from my mother and asked me if I wanted to work construction that summer. He was a manager with Lindsey Lumber Company and told me that if I was interested, he might be able to get me on a construction crew with one of the contractors with whom he did business. I told him I was interested and I would appreciate anything he could do. When he returned from work on Sunday afternoon, he advised me that an individual by the name of Arnoldo Pelaez would be picking me up Monday morning to work on his building crew.

Sam was always a very nice man and I appreciated him doing this for me. I was intent on doing a good job for Mr. Pelaez, thus making Sam pleased with his decision to recommend me.

I was standing on my porch at 6:45 on Monday morning when a truck came by and asked me if I was Armando. I said I was, and he said to get in. I got in his truck where his nephew was already seated and listened to him pout about giving up the window seat. We went to the Fourth of July Café to have a cup of Cuban coffee, some Cuban toast, and even though I had already had some at home, I had some more, just to be cordial with my new employer. Mr. Pelaez was building tract homes in the College Hill area of Tampa, and he had an efficient operation going. Two blocks down the street, the concrete crew was laying foundations, then there was a mason crew behind them laying the block walls, a framing crew behind them, and we would finish behind the framers' work by applying the roof.

Everyone detested carrying shingles up the ladder to the roof for obvious reasons, but I considered it a way to condition myself as well as work. When Arnoldo would leave to check on other sites, the men on our crew would tell me not to carry two bundles of shingles at a time because Arnoldo would expect them to do the same. I thought that was a selfish and shallow request, but I just wanted to get along so I accommodated my co-workers.

Arnoldo's nephew spent half the day goofing off; something Arnoldo was well aware of and really agitated by.

On Thursday of my first week it began to rain at about 11:15, and Arnoldo sent the entire work force home and off the clock. He asked me if I would mind going with him to his home and straightening out his garage while he took care of business matters in the house. I said I would be glad to go with him. When we got to his home it was not raining so he asked me would I mind mowing his lawn. As mentioned earlier, I despised lawn work, but I did not let him know that, and graciously told him I would be happy to mow his lawn. After mowing, raking, and edging his lawn, he asked me to clean up and organize his garage, which again, I was happy to do. He took me home later in the afternoon, picked me up the next morning for work and we completed the work week on Saturday at 2 o'clock in the afternoon.

He also had a ritual of giving out pay envelopes to his workers, but this time I had a legitimate spot on the roster. He handed me my envelope stuffed with money, and I immediately put it in my pocket and shook his hand. He then told me something that made me feel very good. He told me I was a good worker and he was happy to have me on his crew. I didn't know how much was in that envelope, but I was confident it was more than $6. I sensed Arnoldo was a fair man; however, I was going to reserve final judgment until I got home and counted my pay. I jumped out of his truck as he came to a slow roll in front of my house and told him I would see him Monday morning as he pulled away. I ran into my home, pulled the envelope out of my pocket and again was shocked…this time favorably. As I counted $115 in front of my mother, she couldn't believe it. I was, to say the least, ecstatic.

Even though I was thrilled with my new employment, I continued with my paper route since it did not take much time to deliver the papers and I did my collecting on Saturday and Sunday afternoons.

One Saturday morning in July, after delivering (news) papers, I was experiencing a stomachache like nothing I ever experienced before. My mother's response, after conveying this feeling of pain to her, was a terse, "You shouldn't have eaten all those pancakes this morning!"

I was in desperate need of sympathy and I had just gotten "pancaked!" After moaning and groaning for a couple of hours that morning, she instructed my sister to take me to the hospital to check out this matter and to get my stomach pumped to remove the excess pancakes she earlier diagnosed as the cause of my stomach pain. The family warmth regarding my condition was radiating in my home. When my sister responded to her with, "I cannot take him to the hospital. Some friends are picking me up and we're going to the beach." I started to groan with added intensity and frequency in an effort to gain some empathy, and after several bellowing groans, my mother ordered my sister to take me to the hospital before going to the beach. My sister was obviously not a happy camper and she let me know it all the way to the hospital.

After less than five minutes in the emergency room, the doctor told my sister that I had an appendix about to burst and they would have to commence surgery in absence of my mother's written consent. Later that evening, the same people who were complaining about me eating too many pancakes and ruining their day at the beach were at the hospital comforting and tending to my every need.

After recuperating for nine days (four working days considering 4th of July), I was back with Mr. Pelaez, but on a framing crew until the doctor gave me the green light to return to the roofing crew. My cousin Dennis covered my paper route in addition to his own, and in a short time I was back in full swing. All that remained from the surgery was a twelve-inch scar and the memory of a missed payday. Isn't it great to be young?

I helped out my mother financially that summer, even though I felt some of my help was getting either directly or indirectly into Luis' pockets. Regardless, I just wanted her to know that I appreciated her. I worked for Arnoldo all summer and earned good money throughout June, July (appendix episode excepted), and the first ten days of August. Then I had to quit my job to prepare for the upcoming season, which would start approximately August 15th. Arnoldo told me again how much he enjoyed having me work for him and told me I was welcome to come back next summer if I so desired. Again, I had learned a significant lesson in life. People are motivated or de-motivated, at least in part, by compensation. Additionally, a significant factor with regard to one's performance is how they view themselves within the organization. Regardless of what I got paid at the plumbing company, I was obviously an afterthought to the owner, evidenced by the fact he didn't have a pay envelope prepared for me. But on Arnoldo Pelaez' team, I was an integral player who he even took to his home during inclement weather to keep me on the clock.

FLORES VS. O'CONNELL

There were more lessons to be learned as I began practicing for the 1960 season. I always noticed how Coach O'Connell and Coach DiCharry praised John Oliva and treated him with respect. I was now expecting that kind of treatment myself. I was even wearing John Oliva's number. Much to my disappointment, rather than praise me, Coach O'Connell began to chastise me for little things I thought were insignificant. Coach DiCharry was more sensitive with me, but nonetheless, had the same concerns. Coach O'Connell had no stomach for a baby junior tackle who stood 6'1" and weighed 235 lbs. He was expecting me to have the same attitude that John Oliva had demonstrated, and I was expecting him to have the same attitude toward me that he'd had toward John. John was doing well at the University of Florida and Coach O'Connell expected me to assume the leadership role that John had vacated.

I knew nothing about leadership, and while I was developing into a decent player, I was not providing the "extras" coaches expect from their top players. This situation would plague me throughout my football career at Jesuit. Instead of putting our shoulders together toward the same goal, Coach O'Connell and I would butt heads almost daily. I'm not using this as an excuse, but it would have been nice to have a male figure in my life at that time who could have explained to me what was happening. I just perceived the situation as Coach O'Connell not liking me, which I realized later, was far from accurate.

We had a pretty decent team both my junior and senior years, but we were only able to turn out a dismal 3-6-1 record each year. I didn't recognize it, nor would I have admitted it then, but as I reflect, I believe the edge we were missing was leadership.

Things got so bad during my senior year that Coach O'Connell would not start me in some games to keep my name off the starting lineup in the Friday morning sports section of the newspaper. I am sure he thought that would motivate me, but it only made me angrier and more disgusted with our relationship. I had not yet learned that the boss is the boss and that regardless of your talent level, you can accomplish more with less aggravation by having your boss as an ally rather than an adversary. It seems very simple now, but it wasn't then.

THANKS, TED AND LINDA

A bright spot during my junior and senior years at Jesuit was that my grades were consistently improving and I achieved a solid 88% average for the third grading period and was striving to hit 90% as the year ended.

An even brighter spot occurred during the summer between my junior and senior years when I met a person who would greatly influence my life in a positive way and to whom I am forever grateful.

Ted Cannella planned to meet a girl from Plant High School, Linda Saxon, on a particular Saturday at Clearwater Beach and asked me to ride with him to keep him company. After explaining that I did not have much interest in going to the beach and watching him and Linda enjoy the day, we came up with the idea to suggest to Linda that she invite a girlfriend to join her, in which case I would join Ted for the day. Linda was able to work it out and Ted and I were on our way to Clearwater Beach.

I was introduced to this attractive blonde named Judy Kay Stallings that summer day, and my first reaction was she could not have been nicer. We made small talk and went into the water several times to cool off from the scorching Florida sun. I thoroughly enjoyed the afternoon and became increasingly impressed by the niceness of this young lady; a trait that made an already pretty girl even prettier.

As the afternoon advanced, she informed me that she would have to return to Tampa because she had a date that evening. I was very disappointed with this news and attempted to talk her out of going back, but was unsuccessful.

I liked her and I sensed that she liked me also. When I asked if she would like me to call her, I was very pleased to receive her smile as she responded, "Yes."

We were different in many ways, yet we shared common values, as I would later discover. One of the ways we were different became obvious to me as I walked her to her automobile for the trek back to Tampa. As we walked toward the parking area, I noticed a brand new 1961 Impala Super Sport convertible, white with red and white interior, and I kept my eyes fixed on it as we continued walking. As we walked up to the vehicle, she threw her towel and bag into the back seat of the Super Sport and I immediately asked her if the car was her dad's. Being duly confused by her answer, I asked did she mean it was her father's car and she was able to use it. She once again explained it was not her father's car; it was a car she and her brother used jointly. As she pulled away from the parking area and headed toward Tampa, I remember thinking what in the world could have kept someone who had an automobile like hers from even mentioning it during the four plus hours we spent together that afternoon. Knowing the sixteen-year-old I was, I'm certain that fact would have been out of my mouth within the first ten minutes of our conversation. I would learn that this was one of many traits this young lady possessed that impressed me.

After returning to Tampa, I phoned her and learned she not only had a date that evening but also was, in fact, "going steady" with this person. I was really disappointed then and expressed my feelings to her. She told me I shouldn't feel bad and that she would like for me to continue to call her causing my disappointment to transition into confusion. My confusion subsided as I soon figured out that she wasn't crazy about her boyfriend and was interested in getting to know me better. I went to her house to meet her family shortly thereafter, who were also different from anyone I had ever met before, and whom I liked immediately. We had a few casual dates, but things cooled off as school began and I immersed myself in football, and to a lesser degree, schoolwork. We stayed in contact and things began to get serious between us as football season ended, which was perfect timing.

COLLEGE BOUND

During that first semester at school, I was to learn yet another lesson in life that would ultimately become a huge advantage in the future.

While explaining to my mother that my school friends were choosing the university they would be attending the next year, she softly interrupted by saying, "Honey, you know I can't afford to send you to college, so I guess you'll be getting a job after you graduate."

I don't know why I was surprised by that statement, because I knew she could not afford to send me to college, but nonetheless, I was somewhat taken aback by this dose of reality. However, that conversation took place early in the season, and though my attitude left a lot to be desired, the level of my play improved tremendously spurred on by the knowledge that attending college was totally my responsibility.

On the bright side, since my academics had improved, I was now a prospect for universities outside the state such as Georgia Tech, where Ted Cannella ultimately decided to attend.

That conversation with my mother caused me to have a new focus on my class work, as well as my work ethic on the field. I was determined to earn a football scholarship because most of my friends were going away to college the following year and I wasn't ready to enter the work force on a permanent basis.

I had no particular attraction to any of the schools that were courting me (Auburn, Florida, Florida State, Georgia Tech, & Miami) even though I was leaning toward Georgia Tech because of my buddy Ted. However, Georgia Tech specialized in engineering, and even though I enjoyed mathematics and logic, I had little interest in engineering.

Gordon Saussy, S.J. was a superb teacher and it was my good fortune to have him for both Algebra and English Literature. He was preparing to become a Jesuit priest and his dedication to his students was at the highest level. His accent was charming and a dead giveaway that he was from New Orleans. He was a serious Louisiana State University fan and proud of it. He asked if I had any interest in attending LSU on a football scholarship, because if I did, he would forward some film to a priest he knew at Jesuit High School in New Orleans, who in turn would put the film in front of LSU's chief recruiter, coach "Pop" Strange. I was interested in Mr. Saussy's offer, but immediately thought of an earlier incident that gave me pause.

The preceding weekend Ted and I had been guests of the University of Florida for their game against LSU, and as such, we had been seated with other prospects on the sideline by the UF team. This recruitment technique was common in those days and was intended to give the prospects an *up close and personal* experience that would pique the interest of the prospect toward the host university.

Well, *up close and personal* it was.

Ted and I were seated on the first row literally three feet from the playing field for this particular contest. We were watching the teams warm up when Ted made a comment to me regarding a physical trait of one of the LSU players, which was overheard by the prospects seated by and behind us eliciting chuckles from them as well as from me. The chuckles fueled Ted's comments, which became animated and loud to the point that some action had to be taken to curtail a situation headed for nowhere but trouble.

Let me explain: one of LSU's receivers had a serious case of bowlegs and looked like he was chewing tobacco as he occasionally caught warm-up balls in our proximity. That's all that was required to provide immature teenagers with sufficient material to fashion less-than-charming comments which were encouraged by equally-immature UF prospects that were enjoying Ted's sideshow having never purchased a ticket.

When that receiver was catching warm-up balls in our general vicinity, giving us a perspective had by few at Florida Field, Ted made a comment comparing the receiver's physique to that of a bull rider or a ranch hand. As previously stated, chuckles ensued which encouraged Ted to generate additional comments coupled with his portrayal of a western yodeler and offering the player some "chew" he concocted by rolling up a popcorn bag, all at a decibel level attracting the attention of people outside his target audience. The player somehow picked up on this amateur comedy act in which he was unwittingly featured as the object of amusement. He coordinated with the quarterback to toss him a ball at our location, which, when effectively executed, would give him the option of running into our group as he attempted to catch the ball or allowing the ball to sail at us as he attempted to avoid our group, still sending the message it was time to end the party we were having at his expense.

Fortunately for us, he chose the latter with a twist of his own. The ball was thrown a foot out of bounds on a trajectory for Ted's head when out of nowhere the player's hand appeared beneath the ball tucking it under his arm as he gained control of his body by chopping his feet until he came to rest in front of Ted and me delivering this message in a composed but stern voice, "You boys should be alert; you can get hurt out here." The message was clear. We understood what he said, and more importantly, what he meant. From that point on, our group was amongst the best behaved in Gainesville, led by Ted and myself, with the exception of a comment here and there by Ted when LSU's <u>defense</u> was on the field.

Prior to this experience, I had been an LSU fan stemming back to 1958 when they won the National Championship led by two-time All American and Heisman Trophy recipient Billy Cannon and a highly-acclaimed defense called the "Chinese Bandits."

I enthusiastically accepted Mr. Saussy's offer, and after the '61 season, Coach Strange invited me to visit the LSU campus. Coach Strange assigned Billy Truax to show me around for the weekend. I surmised the reason Billy was selected was because he had attended (all-boys) Holy Cross Catholic High School in New Orleans giving us instant common ground.

He was the perfect choice. He was an individual of high character, a leader, an obvious achiever, and on top of all that he knew how to show a guy a good time. I immediately liked Billy and the players he introduced to me, especially Robbie Hucklebridge and Dickie Granier.

I arrived in Baton Rouge at around mid-day on Friday and was picked up at the airport by Coach Strange and Billy. Coach Strange told me, in Billy's presence, that they were very impressed with the film they had seen on me and wanted to get my opinion of their program. Billy, Robbie (who was supposed to be confined to the dorm for the weekend for disciplinary reasons), Dickie, and I had a great weekend, including a trip to New Orleans, which I later learned was not allowed (my kind of guys).

Before our trip to New Orleans, Billy said we would go by Coach Strange's home to get some additional spending money because we were running low. Billy suggested I go to the door even though I told him I felt uncomfortable doing so. He and the other guys assured me that this was a commonplace occurrence, so I took them at their word. Answering my knock at the Strange household was Coach Strange's son, David, whom I later learned was scheduled to enter LSU in the fall of '62.

"Can I help you?" asked the muscular and shirtless David.

After introducing myself and exchanging brief pleasantries, he went to get Coach Strange who returned with a grin on his face and cash in his hand.

"Bet you guys are out of money," he said before I could deliver my request. "Here, this ought to see you through the weekend," he said as he handed me $100.

Coach Strange was quite adept in making one feel at ease and he certainly made me feel comfortable in this circumstance. The guys asked me how much I got when I returned to the car and were pleased with my response.

Spending the weekend in the dorm with the guys was a real treat. Everyone made me feel welcome. I was having lunch with Billy and other players on Sunday and was to meet Coach Strange shortly thereafter to be driven to the airport for my return to Tampa. The only pressing question Billy asked me during my visit was would he see me next season in Baton Rouge? I explained to him I had been looking at a few other schools, but I liked LSU.

However, I told him, no offer had been extended to me as of yet. He assured me the coaches would not have brought me from Tampa to Baton Rouge if they were not prepared to make me an offer. I thought that was very nice of him to say, but I didn't know if there was any substance to his comment. We chatted a little after lunch, and before I knew it, Coach Strange was standing in foyer of the dining hall waving his hand to get my attention.

As we drove to the airport, Coach Strange told me something that made me feel very good. He said that he and the coaching staff thought I would be a real positive addition to their team. Needless to say, I was flattered because LSU had just completed another successful season capped off by an Orange Bowl victory. He told me to go home and think about it, talk with my mother and my coaches, and he would call me late in the week to see if I had any questions.

My mother thought it was a good idea if I thought I would like it, as did Coaches O'Connell and DiCharry, especially Coach DiCharry whose brother, Guy, lived in Baton Rouge.

On Thursday of that week, I was called out of class to take a long distance call in the administrative offices. As I walked toward the offices, I solidified my decision to go to LSU and was praying that they had not changed their mind. Coach O'Connell handed me the phone and Coach Strange asked me how my "return trip" was? I wasn't accustomed to chit chat while speaking long distance, but nonetheless engaged him in conversation which concluded by him saying if I was interested in attending LSU on a football scholarship, he would come to Tampa next week or send the necessary paperwork to Coach O'Connell right away, whichever I preferred. I told him I was interested in attending LSU and explained I had no preference as to how the paperwork was handled. He said if it was okay with me he would discuss the matter with Coach O'Connell and do what works best for all concerned. Coach Strange then instructed me to inform the other schools interested in my services that I had decided to "remain a Tiger" and he would communicate the same to the LSU coaches. I agreed, and within a week I was signing the papers and was excited about the opportunity that had just been laid in my lap.

JUDY, JUDY, JUDY

With that behind me, I focused my attention on Judy. She had ended her relationship with her boyfriend and was focusing all her attention on me. My confidence was high, things were going my way, and with the exception of the situation at home, I liked what I saw.

Judy was unlike any person I had ever met. With most of the people I knew, male or female, it was always a game of wits. But not with her; her heart was an open book. She had no hidden agenda and was as honest as the day is long. I immediately was attracted to her good looks, but soon, the depth of her is what captured me. Selfless is but one of the many adjectives that describe her outlook toward others. Her interest is always what she can do for others, not what others can do for her. She had a highly-developed sense of humor and thought I was the funniest guy to ever come down the pike. We got along famously, and before long we were inseparable.

During the school week it was mostly telephone conversations and an occasional visit, but on the weekends we would see each other every Friday, Saturday, and Sunday evening, and sometimes during the day. She really enjoyed the beach and I didn't, but knowing that she did, I took her often. We went to the movies, parties, single-dated, double-dated, triple-dated, sat home and watched TV, went on walks and rides, visited friends and relatives, ran errands, or just sat on her front porch and talked. We enjoyed being around each other and the activity in which we engaged was of secondary importance. I escorted her to all the Plant High School functions in which she had interest and then we performed double duty by going to most of the Jesuit events as well.

I recall escorting her to Plant's "Sadie Hawkins Night" (where the girl provides transportation and pays for the date), and before the dance, we ate dinner at the Tropics Steak House (which would later be purchased by my good friend Malio Iavarone in 1969, whom I had not yet met). I had eaten at the Tropics a few times before with John Oliva when he was being recruited by Georgia Tech and then later with Ted Cannella as guests of "Dynamite Goodloe," Georgia Tech's recruiter when we were recruits; but those times paled in comparison to the evening I enjoyed with the person with whom I was becoming very fond.

I had experienced a limited amount of serious dating. Most of the girls I dated were interested in making certain they were seen at all the right places. What a pleasant switch it was with Judy. She never cared much where we went, with whom we went, or if we went, and that made it much more fun and relaxed. Most of our conversation centered on things about which we laughed. We laughed all the time, and I'd never had that much fun in my life.

I recall our first Christmas season together when I asked my Aunt Louisa what I should get for Judy. After careful consideration, she took me to a jewelry store and pointed to a watch she was suggesting, which I recall cost $39. Let me remind you this was Christmas of 1961 and my mother was running our household on roughly $55/week. I considered Aunt Louisa's suggestion to be pretty bold, but in retrospect, it was a perfect suggestion and I'm glad I sought her opinion on the matter. Aunt Louisa not only made the suggestion for the gift, but also allowed me the opportunity to work in her yard to earn the $39. You could always count on the Russos.

I presented Judy the watch on Christmas Day and she was thrilled, not so much for the watch, but because I thought that much of her. I could have given her a suitcase full of watches and it would not have come close to representing how I felt about her. She was special and I knew it. Her present for me was three Gant shirts; white, powder blue and yellow, an Izod madras belt and a beautiful monogrammed Dopp travel kit for shaving gear and the like. She had purchased these gifts from Tampa's finest men's haberdashery of the day, Wolf Brothers. When you're sixteen years of age, gifts like that accompanied by the right circumstances can make you feel great—and they did.

Obviously, her former boyfriend was relieved from duty, and I couldn't even recall who I was dating before I met Judy. It would have been the wrong thing to do, considering our age, lack of knowledge of each other, and our inability to support ourselves, but I would have married her and never looked back. But God knew better and we just continued dating.

I suppose there always has to be something in a relationship that doesn't go just right, and I was beginning to become acquainted with ours.

Judy would generally respond to important questions I asked her with a response completely foreign to me. Regardless of the question, the response would go something like this: "If you truly believe it's in God's will for you, then you should do it." My counter response went like this: "Of course, it's His will. If it wasn't, why would I want to do it?" That statement, I am sure, demonstrated a new level of theological shallowness to her, but it seemed right to me. Nonetheless, she never seemed offended, never became angry, it never ruined our outing, but she did keep responding in like fashion every time I had an important question. She liked to talk about religion, and so did I. (I now realize that she was talking about Christianity while I was talking about religion.)

Her family was wonderful, as well. Judy, her parents and maternal grandmother, Edna Brown (Mama Ed), lived in Mama Ed's home at 109 E 26th Avenue in Seminole Heights. The eldest of her two older brothers, Elbert, was married and had a family of his own, and Trent, three years older than Judy, had just married and left home. Her home was warm, comfy, and a fun place to be.

These folks went to church on Sunday morning, Sunday and Wednesday evenings, and occasionally there were special reasons to go, sometimes for a week at a time, for these things they called "revivals." I wasn't interested in going to church more than once a week, and then only as long as it wasn't too early. Consequently, the Sunday and Wednesday evening services didn't hold much appeal for me and these "revival" events were even less appealing.

I thought you had to be unconscious or dying to be revived.

As I reflect on my life, good food has often been employed as an inducement for me to do something, listen to something, or meet someone. Well, these days with Judy and her family were no exception. Intentionally or unintentionally, the trap would be set something like this: "Tomorrow, my mom is making a roast with mashed potatoes, biscuits, corn, and salad. Would you like to come over and eat with us?"

The grin on my face I am sure answered the question, but I would respond anyhow to make it official, "Yeah, that would be nice!"

The hook being set, Judy would follow with, "Why don't you come a little earlier and we can also go to church together."

After being "caught" a couple of times, I came up with a counter tactic. My new response was, "Why don't I go to my church while you are going to your church? Then I can come over for lunch when you get home."

To which she responded: "I want to be with you. Why don't we go to your church earlier in the morning, then my church? Then we can eat together!" Well how do you counter that one and maintain your manners? So that's generally what we did.

When I was feeling comfortable with the morning scenario, this is what I would get for the Sunday evening or Wednesday evening request: "My dad wants to take us to eat at Carmine's after church. What do you want me to tell him?"

Well I couldn't tell her what I really wanted her to tell him, so I often said, "Sure. Let's do it!"

Having a voracious appetite and sparse funds can get one into interesting situations. I did not enjoy going to the church services, primarily because of the culture shock, but how I enjoyed those afternoons at Judy's home and evenings at Carmine's.

Through these visits to Carmine's Restaurant, I was introduced to the Iavarone family, who to this day are near and dear to me. Carmine and Malio Iavarone have been instrumental in many important events in my life. We continue to enjoy each other's company, individually and with our families.

Another thing I considered peculiar at my girlfriend's home was her parents spent a considerable amount of time reading the Bible, and they actually were excited watching the Billy Graham Crusade on television. Short of Father Lashley, Prefect of Discipline at Jesuit High School, I had never seen anyone read the Bible for enjoyment. Not only did Mr. Stallings read the Bible, he would often quote verses to make a point. With the exception of Coach DiCharry, the men I had considered role models before Mr. Stallings wouldn't have felt comfortable being seen with a Bible. Mr. Stallings was a hard-charging, hardworking business owner who had to communicate and negotiate to be successful in his business, and while he was always extremely cordial, a "wimp" he was not! So, I learned another life lesson: Contrary to my previous belief, all these Bible-reading Christians weren't sissies.

Mrs. Stallings was as sweet as sweet could be, and it was easy to see where Judy obtained her demeanor. Mrs. Stallings spent most of her time doing for others, but only after everything was done perfectly for her children. Additionally, she and her children demonstrated the utmost love and respect for Mr. Stallings at all times and under all circumstances. These are but a few reasons why I believe the saying, "The fruit doesn't fall far from the tree," pertains to Judy.

SUMMER OF '62

If going to school and talking on the telephone during the week and dating on the weekend was great; then having no schoolwork to contend with for the summer was super! We saw each other practically seven nights a week and Sunday afternoons.

In two-and-a-half months I was bound for Baton Rouge, Louisiana and a month later, Judy would be attending South Georgia College in Douglas, Georgia. Long range thinking for us back then was about a week, thus, we never considered what it would be like when it was time to part.

I worked on Arnoldo Pelaez's roofing crew that summer and the summer was blissfully advancing when my tonsils began acting up to the point where they had to be removed. What I anticipated would be a simple and painless procedure, was neither.

The surgery took place at the only medical facility I had known up to that time, El Centro Español, on Bayshore Boulevard. Our family had been members there and at its sister location in Ybor City, La Benéfica, since I could remember. It was a forerunner to the Hospital Maintenance Organization (HMO) prevalent today; you paid dues/premiums and all care and procedures within their capabilities were provided at no additional cost.

The doctors and staff at these facilities spoke Spanish primarily augmented by a little broken English, as most had come from Spain. Courtesy and compassion were not their hallmark.

I was 6-foot, 2-inches tall and weighed 245 pounds when I had my tonsils removed and the "ice-collar" they placed on my 18-inch neck to mitigate post-surgery swelling was a "one size fits all" device intended to be used for their normal and considerably smaller tonsillectomy patient.

The collar was essentially a thin piece of stainless steel bent into a circular shape covered with a canvas-type material that contained ice. Its only means of staying on one's neck was the designed tension resulting from the bend of the metal. The normal pain associated with the surgery was exacerbated by this pre-puberty "ice collar" and was the centerpiece of jokes by Steve and Ted when visiting to, ostensibly, provide comfort for my situation.

My family and Judy were made suspicious by the fact I was still unable to take any solid food a full week after the surgery. I existed on liquids, Jell-O, and flan. Another oddity was when I ate Jell-O with fruit; I would begin coughing and continue to cough until I coughed out all the fruit from the Jell-O. This began to concern me and I began to explore the depths of my throat with my fingers first and then very carefully with a fork. Before long I was able to snag the culprit. Lodged in my throat, unbeknownst to me and to the crack medical staff, was a wad of gauze from the surgery, which obviously should have been removed but wasn't and was acting as a strainer to my stomach.

I was released from the hospital, and since there was no one at my home to care for me, Judy suggested that I stay at her home during the day. I thought it was a great idea, and soon found myself having everything done for me, including bowls of ice cream served at my beck and call. What made this situation even nicer was that Judy's home was air-conditioned and mine was not.

As I reviewed my mail, which had accumulated during my stay at the hospital, I came across a letter from the LSU football office. After getting past the warm salutation, the essence of the letter was to introduce me to the prescribed workout regimen, which was enclosed. It basically took our reporting date of August 15 and prescribed increasingly intense training drills each week to prepare us for the day of our arrival. On reporting date, we were to demonstrate our level of conditioning by performing a series of strength exercises, followed by every linesman's nightmare, the mile run. Reading this correspondence caused the strawberry ice cream in my stomach to curdle. The picture was clear in my mind: the players with whom I would be competing were doing sit-ups, pull-ups, chin-ups, gassers, sprints, and endurance runs, while I was alternating flavors of ice cream with chocolate chip cookies. It was obvious to me I could not begin training, but it was equally obvious I could immediately begin eating sensibly, and I did. It was not until the last couple of days in July that I could even attempt the prescription workouts, but by August 15, I was prepared to perform each of the required exercise regimens and complete the mile run under the 6 minutes 30 seconds required for linemen.

The time for me to leave was drawing near and there was much to do. My sister took me to O'Falk's, a fine men's store, and bought me the nicest corduroy parka I have ever seen, before or since. Aunt Louisa was busy as a bee making sure I had everything I would need in college. She sewed labels with my name onto all the underwear I had, plus those she had bought for me, all the shirts I had, plus the many she bought for me, all the socks I had, plus those she bought for me, and everything else I identified that I would be taking. I wondered if she thought I was headed for Louisiana State Penitentiary rather than University; nonetheless, I was very appreciative of all she did. In addition to all the clothes she bought me and labels she affixed, she bought me luggage in which to transport my goods. The Russos are always there when you needed them.

Somebody suggested I take an electric blanket with me, as the winters in Louisiana were very cold. As an indication of how much I knew, I believed them, and on the Saturday before the Friday on which I would be departing, Judy and I went to the downtown Maas Brothers department store to purchase the blanket. We were in my sister's '57 Ford Fairlane, as was often the case, and we parked on the north side of the building just about halfway between Franklin and Tampa Streets. After buying the blanket, I let Judy into the passenger side of the car, gave her the blanket to hold, and walked around the car and got in. As soon as I closed the door and looked at her, it hit us simultaneously; I would be gone in less than a week and we would not see each other for months at a time. We burst into tears, hugged each other, and cried for what seemed like twenty minutes. I'm sure it was closer to ten minutes, but after that moment we were on a totally different consciousness level regarding what was about to happen. We cherished every moment between then and when I boarded that plane on Friday.

LEAVING HOME FOR TIGERTOWN

Friday morning was an interesting occurrence in and of itself. At the old Tampa Airport, there was merely a chain link fence separating passengers, family, and friends from the tarmac on which the aircraft sat. Amongst the people I remember as I was preparing to depart, were (of course), Judy, her mom and dad, my mother, sister, and two brothers, the Russos, George and Lali Garcia (close friends of mine through the Russos) and their daughter Joyce, Coaches O'Connell, DiCharry, and Craven, and my two buddies, Ted and Steve. In addition to all the pleasantries spoken that day, I recall a situation I still consider amusing. George Garcia, while putting his arm around me and shaking my hand to say good-bye, slipped me some money along with a warning not to mention it to his wife, Lali. Then, Uncle Vince moved in and did the same thing, instructing me not to tell Aunt Louisa. Lali later came up to me, hugged me, gave me a kiss and an envelope, the contents of which she told me "I would need later," and asked I please not tell her husband, George. I was expecting Aunt Louisa to complete the foursome, and I was not disappointed. She came to me with a shopping bag containing stationery, magazines, chewing gum, and playing cards, all of which camouflaged several rolls of quarters and half-dollars. She, of course, instructed me not to tell Uncle Vince.

Finances were tight and with all the things Aunt Louisa and Uncle Vince bought for me; it was understandable why they perhaps didn't want each other to know they were doing "a little bit more." George and Lali, I suppose, had their own reasons. What I do know is everyone's heart was in the right place.

Waiting until the last moment, I boarded a National Airlines non–stop flight to New Orleans, where I would connect with a commuter to my final destination, Baton Rouge. Soon after we were airborne, the pilot instructed us that we could unfasten our seat belts and walk about the cabin. After the stewardess had completed her duties, and since I was the only passenger in First Class (ticket, obviously, provided by LSU), she sat down and asked where I was going. I responded, "Baton Rouge." If it was possible, I was already feeling homesick and I was only twenty minutes out of Tampa. I didn't feel like talking much, but I guess I looked sad and she was trying to cheer me up. Her next question, simple as it was, opened the floodgates.

"And what will you do in Baton Rouge?"

As I responded, I was losing the battle of managing my emotions, and by the end of my response, she was supplying me with Kleenex to wipe the tears I was rapidly generating. "I'm going there to play football," I told her as I took the tissues.

All the comfort she offered was to no avail. I wanted something I couldn't have... Judy.

TIGERTOWN

When I arrived in Baton Rouge, an individual who introduced himself as Clifford Duke greeted me. After retrieving my luggage and helping him load it into what I noticed was an

LSU vehicle, we were on our way to Broussard Hall, the dormitory that housed LSU athletes. Clifford was about 5' 7" in height and weighed about 145 lbs. In addition, he didn't have a developed muscle in his body. I was quite curious as to how he fit into the scene, and about that time he satisfied my curiosity by telling me he was the Broussard Hall dorm proctor. I later learned that this was code for "coach's spy."

Broussard Hall was an impressive place to a seventeen-year-old. It was comprised of approximately eighty dormitory rooms, a plush recreation and entertainment center, and a very well operated cafeteria. The lighting in the hallways consisted of a series of chandeliers instead of the commercial lighting one would expect in this environment.

Clifford showed me to my room, and it was difficult not to notice that I was the only person besides him in the dorm. When I asked him why that was so, he explained that if I read my letter closely, I would see that players have the option of reporting any time from noon on Friday (it was about 1:30 PM) until 6 PM on Sunday, and that most of the guys would be coming on Sunday, since almost everyone but me was within driving distance. After thanking him for picking me up, I closed the door to my room and immediately reread my letter to discover he was correct!

With the exception of Clifford coming by my room for the evening meal on Friday and breakfast on Saturday, I didn't see a soul. I sat in my room and reminisced over all the good times Judy and I shared and the more of those I remembered, the worse I felt.

Amongst the items I brought to LSU was a 2-foot by 2-foot wall calendar. I proceeded to do the dumbest thing a person could do. I began on the date Christmas break began and counted backward until I wrote the number 128 on that date in August, representing the number of days before I would see Judy again. I then studied the room carefully, deciding which bed I would choose, trying to derive some benefit from arriving two days early. I unpacked everything I brought, plugged in my radio, and listened to music. The more I listened to music, the more I thought of Judy, and I just lay in bed having a pity party of epic proportions.

Clifford came by the room at 5:30pm and told me he would be happy to take me to supper whenever I was ready. I told him I was ready and hungry, and we departed for a restaurant named Bob and Jake's. As I perused the menu, Clifford correctly assumed the prices were causing me to pause with concern. He then perceptively, or of experience, communicated that he was not only authorized, but instructed, to pay for all my meals. I asked if he would be in trouble if the tab was large, and he responded, "Absolutely not!" I then ordered a Porterhouse steak, salad, baked potato and French-fried onion rings and politely told him if he didn't mind I was going to order a filet and French fries as back up. He grinned as he ordered his filet, and I told him to save room for dessert.

The next morning, I was awake and lying in bed when Clifford knocked on the door and asked if I wanted breakfast. I said I'd be ready in twenty minutes and under the same arrangement I enjoyed a cattleman's breakfast with three extra-large glasses of orange juice and an extra order of hash browns. I almost felt as if Clifford was going to invite me to church! When we returned to Broussard, Clifford offered to show me the campus, so we walked to the stadium, the Student Union, and Post Office, but then I told Clifford I would complete the tour by myself, as I mistakenly assumed he had something better on which to spend his time.

LSU's summer session had just ended, and the fall session would not begin until the third week in September, thus the school was literally vacated. After spending ten to fifteen minutes looking at tennis courts with no one playing on them, pathways with no one walking on them, I started to think how much I missed Judy, so I headed back to my room where I could sulk in privacy. I ate my next three meals at the Broussard Hall cafeteria with Clifford, and a few tables away, Brother Ike Mayhew. Brother Ike was Clifford's boss, but unlike Clifford, who was a student at the university, Brother Ike was a full-time employee of the university assigned to the athletic dormitory and in charge of the training table. Brother Ike, whose name I was certain had to be short for Eichman, as in Adolph Eichman, turned out to be a very peculiar individual on which a separate book could be written.

I moped in my room most of Saturday and Sunday morning, and then about mid-afternoon on Sunday, you could hear a trace of bustling in the dorm.

Most freshman players were transported to campus by their dads. Such was the case with my roommate, Charlie Moore, from Chattanooga, TN.

"It's open" I responded to the knock on my door. Charlie introduced himself and his dad and we engaged in small talk. Within a short period of time, supper was being served and he asked if I wanted to join him and his dad for dinner. I, of course, obliged and we were soon enjoying dinner at the Broussard Hall cafeteria with approximately 150 players, including thirty freshmen. Over dinner, I learned that Charlie's grandfather was a Baptist minister—I don't recall Charlie's father's occupation even though it may have been the same. Nonetheless, Charlie's father was a very nice man and I enjoyed conversing with him over dinner.

Soon, parents started returning to their homes and the rest of us retreated to the combination game room/entertainment area of the dorm. The room was nearing capacity with freshman ballplayers and a sprinkling of upper classmen and soon personalities began to emerge. An unassuming individual, who introduced himself as Pat Screen, asked if I was from Jesuit in Tampa. I said I was, and he introduced me to Rene' Viosca and Kenny Vairin. This trio had gone to Jesuit High School in New Orleans, and, I suppose, knew of me through that connection. Pat suggested we play carpet golf, and we were soon at a carpet golf facility in Baton Rouge. We did not get to the fifth hole before we decided to end the banquet the mosquitoes were enjoying at our expense. Pat was a take-charge type of individual and directed Kenny to head to Hoppers drive-in for a milkshake.

Rene' was about my size and played tackle. He was wrestling champion of the state of Louisiana as a high school senior and was a kind and reserved personality. Kenny was a jokester and reminded me of my friend Steve in Tampa. He was about 6' 3", lanky and muscular, and played end. Pat was about 5' 11", weighed about 180 pounds and was targeted as LSU's star quarterback. Pat was also a jokester and very skilled socially. He possessed the ability to say the right thing, at the right time, to the right person, and was a darling to the media. The guys on the team called him "Pope," reflective of his clean living including the fact that he did not curse...a rarity in any locker room with which I was familiar.

Pat enjoyed his reputation, which was well-deserved, and he played it to the hilt "going to confession" prior to football games as he and a priest walked the sidelines. I had spent my first "official" evening with three of the nicest fellows you would ever want to meet.

Charlie Moore and I deduced that we were paired as roommates because both of us were considered out-of-the-area recruits. On a *prima facie* basis, it made sense; many players could go home on weekends during the off-season, but that would not be the case for Charlie and me, and therefore each of us would have a companion. Well that's a nice theory, but it's not that simple.

In those days, the vast majority of LSU's recruiting was conducted in Mississippi and Louisiana—a formula that proved very successful. Charlie was from the "Lookout Mountain" area just outside Chattanooga and attended prep school after graduating high school. This provided him with an additional year to mature physically—a significant advantage at this age. He was the reigning AAU National Wrestling champion and self-proclaimed "lover boy." Charlie and I had numerous discussions about varied topics, but the topic we discussed mostly was the opposite sex. Charlie had a unique perspective on most things, and this certainly was true as it related to girls. Charlie had a ruddy complexion, as I did (even though I did not realize it), and he was convinced that girls preferred a ruddy complexion to what he called the "beach boy look."

He explained that girls preferred young men who looked like men and not like other girls with smooth faces. He went on and on regarding this topic. When he read on my face that I was unsure of his theory he offered to prove his hypothesis to me the next time we were with a girl together. He took the first opportunity and asked a girl in my presence about his theory. The young lady responded as he had hoped, at which time he turned to me with, "What did I tell you?"

"What did you expect her to say to two guys with ruddy complexions?" I said, acknowledging the girl's manners.

Charlie was a fun guy, but he took fun to a level that was not consistent with our main objective. This presented a potential problem since I possessed the same outlook as did Charlie. As a result, our biggest problems were off the field as opposed to on the field.

Charlie took the fraternity rush program as seriously and intently as I have ever seen prior to or since. We were "rag tired" after practices, but he would manage to attend every rush party to which he'd been invited, and some to which he hadn't. He always invited me to join him, but I would beg off as fraternities are not my thing. Additionally, we had a curfew of 10:30pm, which Charlie totally disregarded. (Don't misunderstand me; I missed many a curfew for reasons that were equally important to me.) Nonetheless, Charlie would often employ the overworked tactic of placing pillows beneath the sheet to affect the look of him sleeping when he was actually being "rushed" to his heart's content. One particular evening—make that early morning—Charlie was returning to the dorm from a party at which he consumed much more than he could handle. Charlie mimicked a football drill as he came down the hallway, jumping up and "intercepting," if you will, the chandeliers, and adding his own touch by smashing them to the floor. This caused quite a ruckus, and soon the entire section of the dorm was awake and aware of what just had happened.

Charlie came into our room and asked me to cover for him before I was awake enough to think clearly. Clifford Duke was up and down the hallway trying to piece together an account of what happened, as he was certain to be assigned the task of determining who the responsible party was. In a group that large, with diverse backgrounds and competing interests, loyalty can become thin and the blame for the incident was soon tagged to Charlie and me. Many of the players whose rooms were close to our room knew I was not involved and offered to say so, if needed, even though they were unsure as to Charlie's involvement.

The coaches were understandably upset with the episode and considered it quite disruptive to the task at hand. Head Coach Charlie McClendon, better known as "Cholly Mac," made the statement at a team meeting that he would get to the bottom of this matter. He urged whomever was involved to turn themselves in. The whole team would not have to be punished in that event and the punishment to the perpetrator would be much lighter. We were given three days to admit to this wrongdoing, and by the third day no one had come forward.

Charlie and I discussed the matter continuously over the three days and were wavering on the position we had taken earlier. We had committed to sticking to our story that we had seen an individual with blue jeans and a white T-shirt do this dastardly deed and run out and away from the dorm. We knew no one would believe the story, but no one would be able to refute it, either. There was one eyewitness, and he gave us his word that he would say nothing. We had been getting counsel from many on the team and, at one point, we were considering admitting to the deed and taking our punishment. I however was less interested in this approach than Charlie since I was sleeping when I heard the crash of the first chandelier.

The coaches, however, were convinced that this offense had been perpetrated by two individuals and wanted no less than two sacrificial lambs. An interesting side note to the situation is that I was enjoying the notoriety of being accused, and at the same time, fearful of the consequences of an action in which I was not involved. I strongly disassociated myself with the event to some who asked and mildly disassociated myself with the event to others as a means of leaving doubt with them as to whether I was capable of such a deed. I wanted it both ways, and I had not yet learned that is a perilous position to take.

Charlie and I emerged as prime suspects and were scheduled for separate meetings with Coach Mac at his office on the final day of the extended period set aside for the repentant soul(s) to turn himself (themselves) in. I had given Charlie my word that I would not rat him out, but I wondered if I could trust him. Nonetheless, as I approached Coach Mac's office located in Tiger Stadium, I noticed Robbie Hucklebridge hanging around the Players Entrance to the stadium. As I drew nearer to him, he gestured to me to come to where he was. He told me he had heard I was meeting with Coach Mac and he wanted to know what I was going to say to him. I was certain he was not a double agent, so I told him that I wasn't exactly sure what I was going to say. Without hesitation, he gave me the following advice.

"You admit to nothing, because they are trying to make an example of someone and this is a perfect opportunity for them. So, look me in the face and tell me you will not admit to any part of the chandelier incident and will not allow Coach Mac or anyone else pressure you into saying anything different."

I told him I would follow his instructions and asked if he would communicate the same to Charlie Moore who had an appointment right after mine. He told me he was meeting a friend and did not care what Charlie Moore told Coach Mac.

It made me feel good that a junior starter on our football team would take the time and interest to meet me as Robbie did. I was already fond of Robbie and this "big brother" meeting led me to like him even more.

I entered the reception area of the coaches' office and was greeted cordially by the receptionist whom I already knew. She asked me to take a seat and Coach Mac would be right with me. I was somewhat nervous about the upcoming meeting, but I was experienced in these matters from my days at Jesuit with numerous incidences in which Ted, Steve, and I were *the usual suspects*. Coach Mac escorted me into his office and was also cordial, but quite serious I might add. He said he thought I knew what happened with regard to the chandeliers and he wanted me to tell him everything. I told him I was sleeping when I heard a crash, and when I came out of my room to see what happened, I saw an individual with blue jeans and a white T-shirt running away from the dorm. He asked if Charlie Moore was the individual in the blue jeans and white T-shirt to which I responded "No." He said I would be making a serious mistake if I did not communicate to him everything I knew, and if I was involved, he was sure I would be able to handle the consequences. I agreed with him, but told him I had no involvement, nor did I know who was involved other than the fellow with the blue jeans and white T-shirt. It was obvious to me he was not satisfied with the outcome of the interrogation, but nonetheless, he had no proof. He said I was free to go, and on the way out of the reception area Charlie Moore whispered to me, "How did it go?" I just nodded as I passed him indicating my displeasure with the venue he chose to ask his question. Charlie went through the same drill and later thanked me for standing firm on my promise to him. We were not found guilty, but in no way were we considered innocent. The coaches and a few of the players resented our alleged involvement in such a deed, but the majority of the guys considered the incident relatively harmless and Charlie and I were thought of as "hell raisers." Curiously, at this stage of my life, I was not embarrassed at all by this dubious distinction and was, in a twisted sort of way, proud. There would be more to come, demonstrating my need for attention but going about it in the wrong way.

Assistant coaches patrolled some of the hot spots in Baton Rouge to ensure compliance with curfew and training. I recall seeing a couple of coaches buzzing Hoppers one evening but thought nothing of it since it was well within curfew and Hoppers served no alcohol. At a subsequent team meeting, Coach Mac called out a list of players who had been seen smoking at Hoppers. I listened intently as I had witnessed several players smoking the same evening that I saw the coaches and I was interested in comparing his list with my recollection. He called the names of almost every player I saw smoking and I was impressed with his surveillance operation until he called my name as the last. I never smoked, and the players chuckled when I adamantly disputed being seen smoking. Coach Mac did not like me questioning the matter in front of the team and told me so later. He also told me something that turned out to have more substance than I gave it credit for at the time. He said "Florees" (the way many in Louisiana pronounce my last name), "if you don't want to be accused of something, don't hang around with people who are doing the very thing you deny doing." I, of course, thought that was a cheap shot, but I had no alternative other than showing up at the "600 Club" drills set up specifically for offenders of curfew and/or training policies. The coaches were alternately assigned to monitor this group, which essentially required the participants to be ready to run the stadium seats at 6 AM each morning for two weeks per offense.

I was experiencing flashbacks of arguing with Coach O'Connell at Jesuit and was frustrated as to why I was getting crossways with my new coaches. Additionally, what they were doing to try to make me better was making me bitter. I wanted to be wanted, but I didn't know how. Adding to the complication of the matter was that I maintained two sets of friends: leaders of the team and troublemakers. I maintained my friendship with Billy Truax and I quickly became close friends with other leaders on the team, including Pat Screen, Doug Moreau, David Strange, and Remi Prudhomme (the latter two represented both groups). The troublemaker group included David Poché (pronounced Poh-shay), Joe Labruzzo, and of course, David Strange and Remi Prudhomme. What I found interesting about this group was, with the exception of David Poché, that they were troublesome off the field, but knew how to interact with the coaches in a positive manner on the field—a skill I had not yet developed. I was drawn to the daring nature of guys like both Davids, Joe, and Remi, but I was also impressed with the leadership qualities of Billy, Pat, and Doug. In all honesty, I preferred to be with the leadership group but was unwilling to give up my gang because of their unqualified acceptance of me. If I were to focus all my attention on leadership, what would happen if I could not make the grade? This dilemma was unsolvable to me at the time. I did not realize that straddling the fence was the source of the saddle sore I was experiencing. My inability to recognize this situation was causing me considerable problems.

RESERVE OFFICER TRAINING CORPS

LSU is a land grant institution, and as such, male students were then required to complete two years of ROTC (Reserve Officer Training Corps) training as partial recompense for the land granted to the state of Louisiana by the federal government under provision of the Morrill Act of 1862 that required the University to offer courses in agriculture and the mechanical arts in addition to providing training for future officers of the Army and Air Force. For this reason, some universities choose to include the A&M designation to the university's name, although Louisiana State University does not.

As classes began, freshmen were assigned to either the Air Force or Army on some basis to which we were not privy. Once this assignment took place, it was virtually impossible to make a change, especially from Army to Air Force. The Army cadets were required to wear a tie and carry a rifle, while the Air Force cadets sported open collars and carried no weapons. The non-freshmen at Broussard Hall enjoyed watching freshmen return from ROTC headquarters after having been assigned to the Army as they communicated the information about the tie and rifle to them. They would then take the opportunity to instruct us on the benefit of checking with upperclassmen before making decisions regarding things about which we knew nothing. Their enjoyment heightened when a newly-assigned Army cadet vowed to return to ROTC headquarters for the purpose of changing to Air Force. I, in addition to three other freshmen ballplayers, provided this enjoyment for them. Upon arriving to the Army desk where I had previously signed up, I was directed to a room full of recently-assigned Army cadets who had just developed the same itch I had to become part of the U.S. Air Force ROTC program. After sitting in the lobby for about 45 minutes, an Army officer informed those of us who were attempting to be released from the Army that the issue was not being released from the Army, but that the Air Force had no open allocations and therefore our efforts could not bear fruit. With that information, all but about ten left in defeat. I requested to speak to the officer privately. I asked if he thought my chances would be enhanced if I were able to get someone in the Air Force to request my services, to which he responded, "Absolutely!" I then went to the Air Science building where the top brass of the Air Force were officed. After reviewing the chain of command in the lobby, I asked if I could speak with Captain William V. Rice, OIC (the AFROTC's top officer in Baton Rouge). I was granted an audience with Capt. Rice, and once he learned I was from Tampa, he mentioned that he had spent some of his career at Tampa's MacDill Air Force Base. I proceeded to tell him my ambition was to become an Air Force officer and (hopefully) be stationed at MacDill Air Force Base. He asked why I was interested in the military and the Air Force in particular. I explained that my older brother and my uncle were serious military men and I wanted to follow in their footsteps. As to why the Air Force, I said I wanted to be able to serve my country and possibly do some of my service in my hometown. He did not realize I was interested in opting to continue with ROTC for my junior and senior years, but I quickly assured him I was. He then summoned his administrative officer and gave him instructions to enroll me into the Air Force ROTC and make whatever arrangements were necessary to get me released from the Army ROTC.

With that victory under my belt, I proudly returned to Broussard and made sure the appropriate people knew what I had accomplished. I was happy to have made the switch from the Army to the Air Force, not so much because I did not want to wear a tie or carry a rifle, but because I was able to pull off something that demonstrated to my peers that my skills were not limited to football.

The Air Force ROTC signed up a good cadet in AFC (airman first-class) Armando Flores and some immediate benefits were just around the corner.

Part of the ROTC routine was (marching) drill time each Tuesday and Thursday afternoon from 1 to 3 PM. There were droves of cadets heading toward the drill fields each

Tuesday and Thursday and I could not help but notice a particular group that headed toward a building, and then, upon our return toward the dorms, they exited the building looking as fresh as daisies. I asked a couple of them what they did in the building and they said they were auditioning for the marching band. September and October weather in Louisiana is very similar to what I was used to in Florida and I thought it would be a great idea if I could somehow audition for the marching band and escape the torrid heat we marched in prior to football practice. The next time we headed to the drill field, I obtained permission from my commanding officer and joined the flock of band hopefuls headed toward the band shell. It was a rather casual atmosphere and most of the participants just took a seat and the band instructors spent the first couple of weeks organizing us into groups. I was assigned to the percussion group since I told the band instructor that I had played the cymbals in high school. What I meant to say was that I knew someone who played the cymbals in high school. Nonetheless, I found myself in the cool confines of the band building for several weeks until it was my turn to audition. The instructor asked me to take a seat at the drums and give him a "one-two" followed by a "one-two-four." I had no idea what he meant, so I just hit the drums the only way I knew which did not make a great impression on him. He asked again for a "one-two" followed by a "one-two-four," and I again gave him all I had. He said he thought I had played the drums in high school, to which I responded, "I played only the cymbals because we had a very large band." My thought was I would be able to bring the cymbals together at the same time the other cymbal players were doing so, but it just didn't work out that way. The instructor suggested I enroll in drum lessons within the music department if I wanted to once again audition for the Air Force ROTC marching band. I told him I thought that was a good idea, but that I was probably going to join the everyday cadets on the drill field.

I reported to my platoon leader, Lieutenant Eugene G. Coco. I explained to him I had not made the cut with the band and was reporting for duty. Lieutenant Coco was easy to get along with, but at the same time, extremely serious about his involvement with the ROTC and took the opportunity to re-communicate that fact to his platoon as he communicated it to me. He furthermore indicated his intentions were to win the marching competition later in the semester. During the five or six weeks that I was auditioning with the band, our platoon had become very adept in marching. Couple that with my "goof off" mentality, and I was a burr in Lieutenant Coco's saddle. He soon approached me with a deal that was hard to pass up. "Armando," he said "because you missed so much time, you're having a slowing effect on our group's progress. I don't know if you'll be able to catch up with the rest of the group and this could have a negative impact on our ability to win the marching competition. If you do not mind, I will allow you to miss marching drills until such time as I deem it appropriate for you to return. It may be a few weeks or a few months, but I will contact you when I'm ready for you to return." (I thought the *military angel* had just arrived in Baton Rouge and lighted upon me with this wonderful plan.). I told Lieutenant Coco I understood his position and I would do whatever I could to assist him and the platoon in winning the marching competition even if it meant staying away from the drill field. He said he appreciated my attitude and would not forget what I was doing. My buddies at the dorm could not believe the story except for Tuesdays and Thursdays when they headed to the drill fields and I headed for my bed.

After this arrangement had gone on for some time, David Poché asked if he could use my military shoes to play golf. He said the shoe repair shop just off campus did a nice job of converting regular shoes to golf shoes by adding cleats. I was happy to accommodate David in this regard and felt it was the least I could do to assist a fellow cadet.

Late in the second semester, I received a notice in my P.O. Box stating that if I missed another marching drill I would have to repeat the entire year of marching. I quickly retrieved my shoes from David and was reporting to my platoon when I noticed that each of the cadets wore medals on their shirts and a military item called a "rope" over their left shoulder indicating proficiency in a particular area, in this case, marching. I soon discovered the reason I received the note was because Lieutenant Coco had been promoted and I was now reporting to Second Lieutenant Richard Hebert. He asked me where I had been for the past four drill meetings, to which I responded, "I believe you should have this conversation with Captain Coco." He suggested we both do so after drill that day to which I agreed.

While marching it is not uncommon to cross sidewalks and sometimes streets or other paved areas. Every time we did so my cleats made a sound very familiar around golf courses, but not on drill fields. Second Lieutenant Hebert was trying to figure out what the noise was and pinned it down to a group of 4, which included me. He asked each of us to raise our shoes and when I raised mine, he asked, "What the hell is that about?" I told Hebert why my shoes had golf cleats and I could tell he was not very amused with my story. After drill, we met with Captain Coco (Hebert's superior) and Captain Coco kept his promise. He told Second Lieutenant Hebert I was on special assignment at his request and that he should consider me up-to-date in every respect. Second Lieutenant Hebert agreed, but he grimaced as he issued me the medals and "rope" to put over my left shoulder (which were earned by my fellow cadets). I soon got up to speed and was able to march with the best of them.

While my lighthearted experience with the military played out in Baton Rouge, there was a serious military confrontation developing in and around Cuba. In 1962, Cuban leaders became convinced that the United States was planning an attack on Cuba. They asked Russia for more military aid. Russia responded by sending missiles and materials to build launch sites. In October, the United States learned that Cuba had missile bases which could launch nuclear attacks on American cities. President Kennedy ordered a naval blockade to halt further shipment of arms and demanded that Russia remove all missiles and missile bases from the island. For several days, the world stood on the brink of nuclear war. Because MacDill Air Force Base is located in Tampa and because of Florida's proximity to Cuba, I was particularly concerned about the safety of my family and loved ones. Finally, Russia agreed to Kennedy's demands in return for a U.S. pledge not to attack Cuba. Russia removed the weapons under protest from Fidel Castro and my concerns subsided.

SAFE AT HOME

One dull Saturday evening in April of 1963, Joe Labruzzo and I were in the safe confines of Broussard Hall in compliance with Coach Mac's orders as a result of having missed a couple of curfews. We were innocently playing Boo-Ray (cards) around 9:45 PM in my room when we heard some unusual activity taking place outside the door. We went into the hallway and asked Mike Murphy and his basketball teammates who were responsible for all the commotion, "What's going on?" They were thrilled we asked. They had encountered a group of thugs who wanted to drag race for money and said the thugs would not leave them alone after they refused to pay up as a result of losing the drag race. So, they headed to Broussard Hall in hopes of finding some support.

Well they found it! Joe Labruzzo had a well-earned reputation for street fighting in Baton Rouge, which followed him from his hometown of Larose Cut Off (not to be confused with its neighboring community of Larose) situated deep in the bayou country southwest of New Orleans. We were bored, and Joe was up to settling this matter immediately. I had much less interest but had no choice other than to join him and thought we would make quick work of this matter.

Joe took the lead and quickly was in the face of the hoods in the lead vehicle. As Joe issued a series of ultimatums, one of the hoods' confederates from the second automobile let off a few rounds with a semi-automatic pistol to get our attention. Everyone ducked for cover, except for Joe who immediately assaulted the driver with whom he had been communicating and a melee broke out. The passenger from the second vehicle emerged to assist his associate who had been pulled from the car and was taking a beating from Joe, which served as an invitation for me to join the fracas. Additionally, a couple of our guys were engaged with a couple of their guys and the monotony of the evening had been broken. In a peculiar sort of way, it was fun.

The situation was progressing nicely until we noticed a significant bloodstain on Joe's shirt. One of the thugs took credit for stabbing Joe and displayed his knife while offering more to anyone willing to engage him.

Joe required no invitation and went to a friend's car for the purpose of retrieving his "fish gaff." This 10-inch fishing tool was turned into a weapon as Joe chased the hood, who had stabbed him, around the circular drive in front of Broussard until he successfully planted the gaff into this fellow's shoulder where the trapezium meets the clavicle.

Between Joe's blood and that of the gaff victim, it became obvious that this incident had escalated beyond the anticipated scuffle and law enforcement would soon be involved—a prospect no one relished.

Within seconds of Joe's retaliation, the thugs climbed into their vehicles and sped off. Joe thought I was in possession of the gun and told me to shoot them as they departed.

In short order, Campus Security and the Baton Rouge Police were on the scene. We answered a few questions and were taken to the campus infirmary to have Joe's wound checked.

Within thirty minutes of arriving at the infirmary, there must have been eight to twelve players who had heard of the incident and had come to check on us.

I don't recall how it happened, but I had a gash on my head that required six stitches and Joe's deep stab wound required five.

As we sat on beds at the infirmary, the physician was attempting to convince us to spend the evening. We respectfully declined his offer and were ready to head back to Broussard when a couple of players said that Coach Mac had just pulled into the parking area.

As he walked in, he could see we were fine and asked for our side of the story. After hearing our rendition, he asked with a disappointed expression, "Why didn't you let the basketball players take care of their own mess?" to which our reply, "We just wanted to help them," seemed very lame.

Even though further explanation was not required, Coach Mac explained that one of the main reasons we were confined to the dormitory was to keep us from *getting into* trouble but somehow we managed to *find* trouble nonetheless. It was hard to dispute the logic.

A couple of Baton Rouge police officers came into the infirmary and informed us that four of the suspected thugs had been apprehended and asked if we were willing and able to go to the police station for the purpose of identifying them. With Coach Mac's permission, we followed the officers to the police station and identified four individuals, including their ringleader, Jimmy Wade Singletary, who'd suffered an injury to his shoulder, and his right-hand man, Harold Courtney, who was a passenger in the second vehicle.

We later learned that Singletary and Courtney were not rookies to this sort of activity, and in fact, had a history of criminal encounters.

I did not realize it then, but God's Grace again protected me (and Joe).

It didn't register with me at the time, but Joe expressed to me later when discussing the incident, that I did not look sorry or humble when speaking to Coach Mac about the situation while at the infirmary. I responded that I didn't believe we had anything to be sorry about and that being humble was not appropriate for this particular situation. Joe disagreed with me, and it wasn't until years later that I understood what he was trying to communicate. Humility was not one of Joe's natural traits, but I do recall him seeming (or acting) sheepishly embarrassed in front of Coach Mac regarding the incident, which was contrary to how I felt having just rescued some of our fellow athletes.

The previously described accounts paint a blue picture and there were other instances that were equally blue; however, they only reflect a small part of my experience at LSU. There were many other experiences that were both pleasant and positive.

MORGAN CITY

After a practice session during the week before Thanksgiving of my freshman year, Coach Didier called us to a knee. After a little "talk" (which seemed a little nonsensical), he dismissed all the players that were not from either Mississippi or Louisiana. Charlie Moore and I were jogging off the field commenting about the peculiarity of the situation. That evening at dinner it became clear to us what the meeting was about when each of us received multiple invitations to join a player who was going home for the Thanksgiving holiday.

The invitation I accepted was from Willie Galloway of Morgan City, Louisiana.

Morgan City is a small fishing village situated on the banks of the Atchafalaya River about 120 miles due south of Baton Rouge, deep in "bayou country." You did not have to know much about economics to see that Morgan City was a poor area of what was generally considered a poor state.

Our ride let us off at the only diner in town, where Willie's mom worked. She offered us a meal, and even though we had eaten before leaving Baton Rouge, we took her up on her offer. She suggested we drive her car home and that she would catch a ride after her shift. After pulling away from the diner, we turned off the main highway onto a series of winding oyster shell roads, which led to Willie's mom's trailer home. There were three other trailer homes in this little area about 150 yards from a bayou, which I was told led to the Gulf of Mexico. The two-bedroom unit was old and in need of repair, but nonetheless, comfortable and Willie was very happy to be home.

Willie's mom was a very nice person, and it was quite apparent that she had her hands full trying to keep the family together. She, nonetheless, had a loving and positive personality, which had been passed along to her son. She reminded me of my mother from the standpoint of being a hard worker and having to keep the family together.

Willie and I sat around and chatted until someone dropped off his mother at about 10:30 PM. She brought home some potatoes and candied yams from the diner, and there was already a pumpkin and apple pie in the kitchen. We sat around and chatted for another couple of hours and then went to sleep. Willie slept on the couch in the living area, while I slept on an undersized twin bed in his cluttered room.

When Willie and I awoke on Thanksgiving Day, his mom was already at the diner. She told us to come by for breakfast and she would give us instructions on what to do before she returned with the Thanksgiving meal. Willie and I, without hesitation, headed to the diner to satisfy our hunger, which had awakened us. His mom got off work at 4 PM, and by 4:30 we were having Thanksgiving dinner.

Mrs. Galloway needed a carving knife and asked me to look for one in the trailer adjacent to hers while Willie was on the phone with his former girlfriend. I asked her if anyone was there and she said she didn't think so but to knock just to make sure. I certainly did knock, but I was still unsuccessful in finding the knife she was seeking when Willie came to my aid. Willie chuckled because he knew I was uncomfortable in someone else's home, but explained that we were in Morgan City and not Tampa.

The three of us, plus a lady friend of Mrs. Galloway's, had a wonderful Thanksgiving Dinner. I don't recall the particular wording, but I remember Willie's mom saying the sweetest prayer before we ate and thanking the Lord for all we had. You could feel the love between Willie and his mom and it caused me to long for my mother and Lemon Street.

We played cards and listened to the radio that evening followed by a couple of Pearl beers while playing pool at the local poolroom/gas station. In the morning, we fished the bayou with the local Justice of the Peace, who also owned the diner where Willie's mom worked. That afternoon, we met our ride at the diner and in a few hours were back in Baton Rouge. I thanked Willie several times for including me in his Thanksgiving plans, and I can honestly say, as I said to him then, that it was one of the nicest Thanksgivings I have ever experienced.

PLANNING AHEAD

During the football season, I had developed a nice relationship with Johnny Beck from Dallas, TX. Johnny was a nice guy with a friendly personality. A very small percentage of students had automobiles (or access to automobiles) in those days, but Johnny was one. Johnny was earning his way through college by working as one of the team (equipment) managers; consequently, we saw each other at least once a day. As I said, Johnny was a nice guy and having an automobile enhanced his personality dramatically. Somehow, in a conversation with Johnny, I understood him to say that he would be staying in Baton Rouge over the Christmas holidays, and if I wanted, I could use his car to drive home to Tampa. Concurrent with that understanding, Ray Loup, (halfback from Catholic High in Baton Rouge), and I had been fantasizing about going to Tampa over the Christmas break. Our main obstacles were lack of an automobile and funds. Ray understood Johnny to say the same thing I did, so we carefully laid plans to validate what we believed we had understood. We decided to ask Johnny directly, but we had to choose the right place and the right time. We decided the right place was the Bengal lounge and the right time was after Johnny had consumed a pitcher of beer we were going to purchase for him. The plan worked like a charm, and Johnny confirmed to us at the Bengal lounge, subsequent to downing a pitcher of beer that we could, indeed, use his vehicle to drive to Tampa over the Christmas Holidays. We were delighted and immediately began making plans.

Ray had never been out of Louisiana and was very excited about the prospect of us making this trip together. Ray and his family lived in Port Allen, just across the Mississippi River from Baton Rouge. The Loup family was 100 percent Cajun, or as they prefer to call themselves, "Coon asses." Cajun people are descendants from any combination of Acadians (French settlers who migrated from Canada), French, American Indian, Spanish, Afro-American, or any other nationality or ethnic group occupying southern Louisiana during its formative history. From the Loup home you could see the smokestacks billowing twenty-four hours a day, seven days a week at the Exxon refinery in Baton Rouge where Mr. Loup earned a modest living for himself and his family. Located on the eastern shore of the Mississippi River, the refinery was less than a mile from their home via ferry, or about seven miles if you drove over the Mississippi River Bridge connecting East Baton Rouge Parish to West Baton Rouge Parish. Ray's family consisted of his mother and dad, his attractive, slightly younger sister Bonnie, her twin brother, and of course, himself. They were an extremely close-knit family with high standards on a low budget. I know Ray's home did not occupy 1,000 square feet, but it could have been five times that size and still not contain the love of its residents.

No matter when we visited Ray's home, the topic of conversation would inevitably lead to the Florida trip. One thing I learned from our conversations was that no one was aware of how far it was between Baton Rouge and Tampa. The Loups were operating under the impression that after exiting Louisiana, one just crossed Mississippi, Alabama, and you were on Tampa's doorstep. The fact is when you enter Florida; the majority of the trip is still ahead. I wasn't about to enhance anyone's knowledge of Florida's geography at the risk of providing information that could moderate my traveling partner's interest in our trip, especially when the trip finances already assumed his participation. Mr. Loup's excitement about his son's trip to Florida expanded each time I visited. He began to have Johnny Beck's automobile "checked out" on weekends, and as a result purchased two spare tires (rims included), giving us a grand total of two. More about the Florida trip later.

HELPING A FRIEND

I had access to another automobile through a rather quirky circumstance that occurred the first couple of days of class. In mid-September I received a phone call from Geraldine Scolaro who had graduated from one of the all-girl Catholic high schools in Tampa. She explained that she was in somewhat of a dilemma and thought I could assist her. She went on to explain that she had not realized that freshmen were not allowed automobiles and had driven her car to LSU from Tampa. Being a freshman, she was unsuccessful at securing a parking permit. She then said that her friends told her that football players were able to get around this policy. I told her I knew nothing of what she spoke, but I would look into it and get back to her with an answer ASAP. After a little investigative work, I was able to secure a parking permit and called her with the news. "Geraldine," I said, "I have some good news and some bad news. I was able to get you a parking permit; however, the parking permit is for the lot adjacent to Broussard Hall" (3/4 mile away from her dormitory).

She cheerfully replied, "I have no intentions of using the car often and parking the car at Broussard poses no problem for me if it is not a problem for you. Furthermore," she added, "you are welcome to use the car when you need to."

She had no idea of the consequences of that statement. I told her I had no intentions of using her car and I was happy to be able to secure a parking permit for her. She picked me up later that afternoon to have the permit affixed to her windshield by the campus security personnel and I drove her back to her dormitory before heading back to Broussard in her red 1961 Chevrolet Impala Super Sport convertible.

During our outing she convinced me I should at least use her vehicle for important things such as picking up or leaving off friends at the airport. I agreed, and she left me a set of keys in the event I had to move the vehicle for one reason or another. You should have seen the look on the fellows who saw me pull into Broussard with Geraldine's vehicle, Florida license plate and all.

VISITORS FROM TAMPA

I received a phone call from Steve Malzone and he informed me that he, his brother Denis, and our friend Pete Dearolf were planning a trip to New Orleans and wanted to visit me in Baton Rouge. I was excited about having a visitor and it could be nothing but fun with these three characters. Many of my friends on the team already knew of Steve through stories I had told them and from the supply of "custom" jackets Steve had sent me. Steve's family business manufactured athletic wear and Steve had given me a Speedline (his company's trademark) catalog with a standing offer to select any jacket I wanted and he would have it made and sent to me at LSU (as had been the case throughout high school). Even when I did not select a jacket, Steve would manufacture and send a couple in LSU colors, naturally causing my friends to ask where I'd gotten the jackets.

I phoned Geraldine and asked her if I could pick up my friends at the airport with her vehicle. She said, "Thank you, but you don't have to call me when you need my car. I hope you all have a nice time." I told her they were arriving at the New Orleans airport, and she replied, "No problem." I could not make it to the airport when their plane arrived, so we agreed to meet at their hotel. When I arrived at the hotel, they had already been partying and were so rowdy they had been warned to calm down or be evicted. They were evicted within a half-hour of my arrival. We decided to go out on the town and then drive back to Baton Rouge for the weekend. We spent the evening on Bourbon Street and were asked to leave a couple of bars, including the Playboy Club. Indicative of the evening was our experience in a particular bar where we considered the service to be substandard. In recognition of the service, we left a tip of a few pennies. As we exited the establishment, the waitress threw the pennies at us exclaiming "Here, take these with you, you'll need them to get out of town."

Let's face it; your behavior has to be suspect to be evicted from a Bourbon Street hotel and two bars within a six-hour period.

We arrived in Baton Rouge in the early hours of the morning and retreated to the dorm beds I had secured for them prior to going to New Orleans. At breakfast the next morning, several of my friends came by our table to welcome and meet my friends from Tampa. Steve was providing a play-by-play account of what took place the evening before and had the guys holding their stomach while they laughed. They so enjoyed the story that they were making plans with Steve for that evening. The evening stretched to the entire weekend of partying capped off by a memorable occurrence.

The last evening, we were eating inside a restaurant that also provided curb service. Our group occupied several seats along an exterior wall of the restaurant where the curb service activity could be viewed. As we enjoyed our meal and each other's company, some of us noticed a vehicle approaching a parking space at what appeared to be an unusual rate of speed. Before we could warn the group with their back to the wall, the vehicle jumped the curb and crashed into the restaurant pinning three of our group, one of whom was Denis Malzone. Fortunately, no one was seriously injured, but the scare gave us something to poke fun and laugh about. Steve had the group in stitches when he assured everyone that *the automobile would have found his brother, Denis, (even) if he were in the men's room.*

THE DICHARRYS

Coach DiCharry's brother, Guy, lived in Baton Rouge. He was a successful insurance executive and entrepreneur. He and his wife, Cynthia, had a wonderful family and were so kind in every respect. Guy, Cynthia, and their four children, especially their adopted son Johnny, were avid Tiger fans as you might expect. Guy often took me fishing, and with the entire family, we would go camping in the bayous of south Louisiana where they maintained a nice trailer home for this purpose. Guy always told me to bring a friend, if I cared to, and when I did, they always wanted to join me again. The three I took occasionally were Ray Loup, David Poché, and Pat Screen. On Sundays, Cynthia would put out a spread that made it very difficult to say you had something else to do. My friends felt the same way and always enjoyed Sunday afternoon lunch and dinner at the DiCharrys'.

One particular outing in the bayou provided Ray Loup and me with an education far beyond anything we had experienced on campus. Guy had warned us to be very careful with fishnets throughout the bayou as they represented the fisherman's livelihood. Neither Ray nor I heeded Guy's advice as we explored the backwaters and bayous of Saint James Parish in Guy's 14' flat-bottom boat powered by a 40-horsepower Mercury engine that Saturday morning. We navigated our way deep into the backwater and avoided most of the fishnets we encountered, which had been marked by "homemade" buoys. As we continued, we approached a fishnet, which we considered to be poorly marked. We slowed down and discussed the merits of going around the net as contrasted to attempting to go over the net at full throttle. Our teenage logic prevailed, and over the net we went. After clearing the propeller of vegetation and fishnet, we proceeded on our adventure. We had been gone from camp about two hours and our appetites were telling us it was time to head back. We followed both the physical and mental markers we had laid down and were pretty proud of ourselves as we approached the area where we had jumped the fishnet.

We had already decided to circumvent the net when a Cajun fisherman, right out of the movie *Southern Comfort*, calmly rowed toward us. In a combination of broken English and Cajun dialect (indigenous to that part of the country), he questioned us regarding our knowledge about who had tampered with his fishnet. Ray, a Cajun himself, and I listened intently to the man who spoke to us with confidence and a double-barreled shotgun across his lap. We were very humble and assured him that we knew nothing of what he asked and found ourselves in effect asking permission to continue back to camp. He queried us a bit longer about what we were doing in the bayou and offered some advice before bidding us farewell. "Youse fellas," he instructed, "oughts to be reeeal careful whens youse outs tryings to have funs where a man is working to feeds his family. Somebodys who messes with anothers man's business can gets hurts reeeal bad if he's ain't careful, youse knows whats I'm tryings to said?" With that advice, he nodded approval for us to leave, knowing that he and his shotgun had clearly delivered his message. Ray and I realized we had narrowly escaped trouble and listened carefully to all Guy had to say thereafter.

THE ODD COUPLE

Across the hall and a couple of doors away roomed two fellas who turned out to be close friends of mine. David Strange and Doug Moreau were sons of LSU coaches. David's dad was LSU's chief recruiter and Doug's dad was LSU's Head Track Coach. They were both accomplished athletes in their day and had passed that tradition to their sons. David was a "pumped up" 220-lb. Guard/Linebacker and Doug, at six-foot, two inches and 180 pounds, played Tight End. I found it interesting that their room was located by the air-conditioning unit serving our wing of the dorm. In my estimation, it was the worst-located room (because of the A/C noise), and assigning David and Doug to this room stemmed off any conversation of favoritism amongst the troops. Doug had little to no experience in "wrongdoing," while David was a free spirit with a maverick personality tailor-made to my liking. David, unlike myself, as you might expect, knew how to interact with coaches, as did Doug.

I'm embarrassed to say that one of the activities in which David and I participated involved loading my .22 caliber pistol with blanks and causing havoc on and off campus. One afternoon, David and I had returned from such an outing and were shooting the pistol with live rounds behind Broussard Hall. Billy Truax stuck his head out of the second-floor window of his room and sternly, but politely, asked that we discontinue shooting the gun as he was about to nap. We disregarded his request, and a few minutes later, he made the request again with some ire in his voice. David and I were in a rebellious mood and decided to reload the gun with blanks and threaten Billy (in a kidding manner) when he would undoubtedly next emerge with heightened ire because we had not heeded his request. Sure enough, a few moments later, Billy stuck out his lathered face (he was shaving) and told us once again to discontinue shooting the pistol at which time either David or I (whoever was playing with the gun), pointed the pistol at Billy and ordered him to retreat or be shot. Billy, obviously annoyed, responded, "There're other guys studying or trying to nap and you guys are bothering them!" We fired a few rounds of blanks at him to make good on our promise, and he retreated with a disgusted look on his face.

David and I decided to end the day's mischief and turned toward the empty real estate behind the dorm to fire off the remaining blanks in the gun. To our surprise and shock, we learned that there was a live round in the gun when we saw the bullet hit a log at which we were aiming. There was not much discussion between us, but the look on our faces indicated that we knew we had just escaped a potentially serious tragedy.

COUNT ME IN

"Let's go to Opelousas!" someone said, and before they finished the sales pitch, I said, "Count me in!" as I wondered, where is Opelousas? "There are plenty of bars with women who like to have fun," the person continued, as if I needed enticement. We were soon on our way in a packed sedan owned by the University, proudly bearing an emblem indicating that the vehicle was assigned to the athletic department. David Strange was driving the vehicle I assumed was assigned to his dad as we raced west on Highway 190.

In addition to David and me, the other passengers included Ken Cormier, David Poché, Mike Duhon, and I believe the remaining passenger was Ray Loup. Twenty miles or so out of Baton Rouge we noticed police and ambulance lights just past a culvert that ran beneath a dirt road about 1,000 feet ahead of us. We slowed to see what happened and soon realized we had just come upon an automobile accident in which the driver was killed. We pulled past the scene, parked the vehicle, and proceeded to find some detail. Apparently, there was alcohol involved, and the driver could not keep the vehicle within the narrow confines of a culvert, careened off the road and hit a concrete embankment, the impact of which killed the driver. The remaining two passengers were being taken to a hospital and were in serious condition. That was a sobering scene and caused us to be careful as we proceeded toward Opelousas.

In the middle of nowhere, we came upon a bridge spanning a river just outside Krotz Springs (the capital of nowhere). Neither Highway 190 nor the bridge was lighted, and when we were about halfway across the bridge, David turned the vehicle lights off in an attempt to scare us. He was moderately successful aided by the absence of moonlight and following the accident scene we head just witnessed. He slowed the car to a crawl and continued to turn the lights on and off, contrasting the difference on that pitch-black Louisiana evening. As he pulled the light switch on, he inadvertently pulled the switch from its socket and was having difficulty reinserting it. The other fellas, especially David Poché, thought David was still playing around, but from my vantage point, I knew he was not.

As he continued attempting to reconnect the switch, we noticed a pair of headlights behind us at a distance, but closing the gap at an uncomfortable rate of speed. Everyone soon figured out that David was no longer playing, and the car became fearfully quiet as each of us watched David and the auto approaching the bridge. The bridge was quite narrow and consisted of only two lanes headed in opposite directions. There was no lane for disabled vehicles. Mild panic overcame a couple of guys as the vehicle behind us drew closer. (David Poché climbed over the side rail of the bridge in anticipation of being rear-ended by the approaching vehicle.) The rest of us were also out of the car keeping David informed as to when he should exit. I had already spotted the place to which I would climb at decision time, which was uncomfortably close.

Just as the approaching vehicle began to ramp up the bridge, David was able to reinsert the switch and turn on the lights. We all jumped back into the vehicle, waiting on David Poché, and once he was in, he accelerated off the bridge. We attempted to shed our fear by laughing and inserting humor to this close call, but we all recognized we had just "stared serious danger in the face." By the time we reached our destination we were emotionally drained, but nonetheless, gave it a yeoman effort to make the best of the evening. The women there were as advertised, and before the evening slipped away, the experiences we had encountered earlier were but faded memories.

Back on campus, I continued to benefit from my Jesuit education. Jesuit of Tampa has always enjoyed a reputation for superior academics. This was demonstrated to me as I attended classes, many of which were repeat material of what I had taken my junior and senior years in high school. In the case of algebra, English Literature, and English Grammar, not only was the material the same as what we covered in high school, but the textbooks were identical as well. This gave me an opportunity to get a sound foundation on my GPA while not spending too much time on the books. It also gave me an opportunity to help some of my teammates, specifically with algebra. My study habits had improved tremendously during my junior and senior years in high school, and thus, knowing how to study and allocate an appropriate amount of time to it, came naturally.

Another activity that came naturally was attending church on Sundays. Initially, I attended Sunday morning services, but as the first semester drew to a close, I became a regular at the Sunday evening service. This obviously gave me the opportunity to maximize Saturday nights. When I attended the morning services, I would walk to the church with any number of guys, which generally included Renè Viosca, Doug Moreau, Pat Screen, Ruffin Rodrigue, and Billy Truax. The evening group generally included Boo Levert, Ray Loup, Joe Labruzzo, and Don Schwab. Joe and I were becoming chronically late and thus were missing the group more than joining them. On top of that, we were leaving Mass as early as allowable to still qualify for credit. Here's where our theological depth kicked in. We said to each other, "If God knows everything, and we believe that He does, doesn't He know we are only going to get credit and we really don't feel like being at church. So, if He really knows our heart, do you suppose we are getting credit for attending?" We both agreed we were not getting credit under this circumstance, and therefore, decided to quit going until we wanted to attend with an appropriate motive.

CHRISTMAS IN TAMPA

Christmas was approaching and I was diligently crossing off the days on my calendar till our departure. Judy's parents were picking her up from college in Georgia and we would be arriving in Tampa close to the same time. Ray Loup and I were making final arrangements with regard to Johnny Beck's vehicle. The 1958 Ford Fairlane's appearance gave one reason to pause; nonetheless, we reasoned that if it had made it from Dallas to Baton Rouge, it could make it from Baton Rouge to Tampa and back. One of many concerns was the condition of the tires. Mr. Loup assisted us in this regard by appropriating two additional spare tires. When we attempted to place the tires into the trunk, we noticed the trunk was filled with "crinolines." (A crinoline is an article of women's clothing used in those days to make dresses protrude from the waist down). These items were actually stuffed into the trunk to such a degree that they expanded outside the trunk as the lid was raised. We called Johnny and asked if we could dispose of these items to which he responded, "No, don't throw them away, they belong to my sister and she wants them!" He then reiterated that the car also belonged to his sister, which explained why he would allow her to occupy the entire trunk of the car with crinolines. We removed enough of the crinolines to make room for the spare tires. As we did this, we noticed that the vehicle had no spare tire of its own.

The weather forecast called for bitter cold on our day of departure and that's exactly what we got. The temperature was in the high teens as we departed Baton Rouge and would drop as the day progressed. Our route took us east on Highway 190 through Hammond and Covington, Louisiana. We were having a great time talking, telling jokes, and listening to the radio when we noticed the fuel gauge read empty. We thought we had a faulty gauge, but decided to fill up anyhow. We then recognized we had a problem because we pumped eighteen gallons of gas when we should have used no more than five gallons at that point. That problem was compounded by the fact that we had limited funds if a repair was needed, and were traveling on a Saturday, which significantly limited the number of places that would work on automobiles.

With that in mind, we immediately began looking for a place where we could check out our problem. We were losing fuel rapidly when we pulled into a gas station with an outside work bay off the highway between the rural towns of Mandeville and Lacombe, Louisiana. This area is located proximate to the northeastern shore of Lake Pontchartrain and the effect of that body of water coupled with a severe wind made outside working conditions unbearable. It was now about 11 AM and the man with the Cajun accent who had put the car on the "lift" informed us that he was working until noon and his family was expecting him. We explained our dilemma, but received no sympathy. He asked if we would hold two, approximately five-by-six-foot sheets of metal on the side of the bay from where the wind was blowing so that he could concentrate on the task at hand. We of course obliged him in this regard and held what were formerly "Gulf Oil" signs with gloves he provided as the biting wind attempted to discourage our efforts. Ray and I had no thought other than to continue, but we wondered about the Cajun whose motivation seemed to waver with each blast of cold wind.

He discovered we had several leaks in the fuel line and told us we should call off the trip because no one would fix the problem today or tomorrow because of the weather and because no one around these parts was open on Saturday afternoons or Sundays. We retorted, "That's not an option because people are expecting us and we have no other means to get to Florida, not to mention we have to travel back to Baton Rouge in the vehicle." He said replacing the fuel line was not difficult, but he did not have any metal tubing in stock and the nearest place to purchase some was in Slidell, approximately sixteen miles away. To our surprise, he asked, "What do you want to do?" In unison we responded, "We have to get it fixed!" "Do you want to wait here or ride with me?

We opted to ride with him to ensure he would not change his mind and head home. We climbed into the cab of his old, beat up GMC truck as he locked up the filling station and fuel pumps. On the way to Slidell he asked if we played football for LSU. We said we did, and he explained that he was a long-time fan before the Billy Cannon and Chinese Bandits era.

We were only ten minutes away from the filling station when the radio station announced it was noon. Raymond and I glanced at each other, but neither of us mentioned it, nor did our Cajun friend. Thankfully, the heater in that beat-up GMC worked like a charm and, soon we were headed back after purchasing twelve feet of fuel line and some fittings. He never mentioned price and we never asked for fear of queering the deal. We figured after driving thirty-two miles and paying for the purchase, he was pretty committed to finishing the repair in order to collect from us. After removing the defective fuel line, he used it as a model from which to fashion the line he had just purchased as we resumed holding the metal shields.

The more he worked, the more we wondered how much the bill would be. After completing the task, he asked us to join him under the lift to view for ourselves that the line was no longer leaking. We did so and were now facing the time of reckoning.

"How much do we owe you?"

"How does eight dollars sound?"

I'm sure he could tell from the smile on my face, that I was very satisfied with the charge. But there was one additional hurdle to clear. In an effort to conserve cash, I asked if he would take an LSU laundry check as payment.

With a perplexed look on his face he asked, "What da hell you mean, laundry check?"

I explained that ballplayers received a check for $15 a month to cover laundry expenses and Ray and I had saved ours as a means of financing this trip. He didn't particularly care for the idea but agreed to it after I suggested he pump two dollars of gas to bring the total to $10 and then he would only have to give me 5 dollars in change. He shook his head and muttered something to the effect, "I don't know why da hell I'm giving this fella five dollars after working on his car for 2 ½ hours in this weather for this laundry check." I explained we really appreciated all that he had done and told him to call either Ray or me if he wanted to go to a football game next season. He nodded affirmatively and wished us a good trip.

We were pushing the vehicle to make up for lost time as we entered Mississippi when we heard a loud "bang." Ray was struggling to steer as the rearview mirror indicated we experienced a blowout separating the tire from the rim, which was now lying on busy Highway 90. We were just east of Bay St. Louis, and since there was no emergency lane, Ray eased over to the right-hand lane and drew to a stop. We proceeded to change the tire while having to jam some of the crinolines in the back seat while we retrieved one of our two spare tires. The wind was now whipping across the Gulf of Mexico as Ray guided traffic to the left lane as I secured the tire to the car.

People, unabashedly, displayed empathy and appreciation as they honked their horns and made unflattering hand gestures as they passed. We agreed we were happy the blowout occurred in the daytime as we would not want to be changing a tire in that weather without the benefit of sunlight.

We continued east on Highway 90 at a speed above the limit, but not fast enough to attract the attention of the police. Somewhere between Gulfport and Biloxi, I noticed the vehicle again became difficult to steer and slowed down to investigate. What we feared had happened. We were using our second and last spare tire and were yet not out of Mississippi. We again occupied the right-hand lane to change tires and again caused traffic to congest. This time I served as the flagman as Ray tended to the tires. We again experienced the warmth and southern hospitality of drivers who passed by us in our moment of need.

We were repacking crinolines when a sheriff's vehicle pulled up behind us with lights flashing. He asked why we were blocking traffic, and after we explained he asked us for ID. While examining our driver's licenses, he asked who owned the vehicle. I told him Johnny Beck owned it, and he asked, "Where is Johnny?" I told him he was in Baton Rouge and we were using his vehicle for our trip to Tampa. He asked to see the auto registration and Ray and I began to search for it to no avail. He explained that we would have to follow him to the police station if we were unable to produce the auto registration and we requested another chance to search for it. Our newfound motivation led us to find the auto registration clipped to the steering column in some sort of holder.

With pride I handed the registration to the deputy sheriff which prompted him to ask, "Who is Sheila Townsend?"

"I have no idea. Why do you ask?"

"Because the car is registered to Sheila Townsend of Dallas, Texas."

Ray and I looked at each other and I told the deputy "Sheila must be Johnny's sister who also owns the crinolines we just stuffed into the trunk."

After asking us many of the same questions a second and third time, he offered the following."Arrrr-main-dough Floorees; you have a Florida driver's license, you attend school in Louisiana, you borrowed this vehicle bearing a Texas tag from Johnny Beck, who also goes to school in Louisiana but does not own the vehicle he loaned you, which is registered to Sheila Townsend of Dallas, Texas, who you never met, but say you believe is Johnny Beck's sister, and you expect me to believe this story?"

With my most sincere look and tone of voice, I offered, "Officer, it does sound a little fishy when you say it the way you just did, but it's the absolute truth." "You boys git in this heah car and git on outta heah, you heah me?" "Yes sir," we replied as we did just as he asked.

Our trip was uneventful as we journeyed through Alabama and into Florida. Ray's question confirmed to me that he knew little of Florida's geography when he queried me as to how much farther Tampa was when we were only twenty minutes east of Pensacola. He smiled (as if I was jesting) when I told him the bulk of the trip was still ahead. We devoured the box lunches from Broussard and the sandwiches Ray's mom prepared for us before we were out of Mississippi and our appetites were again peaking. We agreed we would stop at the next place that "looked like" the food was good and did so at a diner in Marianna, Florida. Our choice was excellent! We both ordered the fried shrimp and were pleased with the generous portion of jumbo shrimp accompanied by French fries and coleslaw.

The temperature continued to drop and the wind continued to howl as we trekked east on Highway 90 toward Tallahassee. The generator light began to flicker as we left Marianna and by the time we reached Chattahoochee it stopped flickering—it remained on. We knew this meant trouble, but I knew if we could only make it to Tampa, Uncle Vince would fix the generator and anything else in need of repair. Such was not the case.

The electrical system of the car was failing because the generator was not charging the battery and the battery could not continue as the sole source of electrical power. We really noticed the problem as we climbed the hills in north Florida and the lights would dim and the engine would stall and restart itself down the hills due to the high-speeds at which we were traveling. We decided to turn off the lights and use the vehicle ahead of us as a guide. We did this for fifteen minutes or so, even though we realized it was scaring the automobile we were trailing.

Then the inevitable happened; the engine stalled and would not restart. We pulled off the highway onto the shoulder and discussed our options. We decided our best option was to backtrack the ten to fifteen miles to Chattahoochee as we were unsure how far it was to the next town in the direction we were headed.

It was approximately 10:30 PM as we began hitchhiking on Highway 90 West. Before long, a late-model Lincoln Continental applied its brakes as they passed us, which we correctly assumed was because they wanted to give us a ride. We entered the luxury sedan driven by a distinguished-looking lady accompanied by her husband who suffered disability to the lower extremities. The couple was very cordial, and the man asked us if the vehicle they saw parked headed east on Highway 90 was ours, to which we replied that it was. He affirmed our decision to head back to Chattahoochee since Tallahassee was quite away off. The regal appearing man who sat in the seat in front of me had a tartan blanket draped over his lap and was holding a tray adorned with hot coffee, an assortment of cookies, and playing cards. We both took them up on their offer for some coffee and cookies. They informed us that the weather bulletins had announced that record-setting low temperatures were expected that evening and it would've been quite dangerous to be out in the cold for any length of time. We communicated to them how appreciative we were of this gesture and once again thanked them as we exited their automobile in front of the only hotel/motel in Chattahoochee.

As we entered the lobby, one could sense the drastic change in temperature. No one was at the front desk and I made the mistake of ringing the bell to gain the attention of the desk clerk. We should have just spent the evening on the couches in the lobby, but that option was no longer available as the owner emerged from her room with her hair in rollers and outfitted in a thick terrycloth robe. "Can I help you?" she asked.

"Yes, ma'am. It's freezing outside, our car broke down east of town, and we have nowhere to stay and no money."

"I can let you have a room for $17 or you'll have to leave."

"We don't have $17 and we can't go out into the cold because we'll die."

"If you don't want to rent a room, you'll have to leave."

I was becoming agitated with her attitude and told her "We're not able to pay for a room and we're not leaving this lobby." As she ordered us to leave, I asked Ray "Which couch do you want?" and proceeded to make myself comfortable on the other one.

Within five minutes, two Chattahoochee policemen entered the lobby and asked the proprietor, "What seems to be the problem?" The woman, in a very ugly tone, explained the situation perfectly. The policemen told us we would have to leave the hotel and we could use the telephone at the police station to make whatever arrangements were needed. Both police officers were in their early twenties and as soon as we closed the door to the squad car and headed toward the police station, they commented to us, "Isn't she a bitch?"

Unsure of their motive, I replied, "I can understand her position, but it is too cold to spend the evening outside."

"Yeah, you're right," one of the officers replied, "but she doesn't have to act like such a bitch about it and especially at Christmas time." Again, we did not respond as we pulled into the police station.

The station consisted of four rooms, two of which were cells, a combination kitchen/game room, and the main room in which police business was conducted. On the kitchen table were doughnuts and coffee, checkers, and playing cards. The officers could not have been nicer and told us to make ourselves at home and spend the night if we so desired. We took them up on their offer and spent the evening in one of the cells, which had two "cot-sized" beds. But before turning in, I used their telephone and Ray played checkers and cards with them. I called Judy in Georgia to inform her of our dilemma. She immediately offered to pick us up on the way to Tampa if we could not get the car repaired in the morning.

We were up at daybreak and were greeted with a fresh supply of coffee and doughnuts. I asked the police officer if he could recommend someone to look at my vehicle, but he said things were pretty slow in Chattahoochee on Sunday. We sat around the police station playing cards and eating doughnuts until Judy called around 8:30 AM. She said they were ready to leave Douglas, Georgia and her dad estimated they would be in Chattahoochee by approximately 1 PM. I couldn't believe it would take that long until I had a chance to study a map during the Sunday morning void. We were far west of where they were and quite a distance out of the way. Judy told me that her parents did not mind the inconvenience and having spent a considerable amount of time with them over the previous year, I was not at all surprised.

Mr. Stallings pulled into Chattahoochee with his late-model dark blue Buick Roadmaster and pulled up to the police station as we had earlier agreed. The Stallings' skin tone was closer to that of the officers than that of Raymond and me, giving the officers comfort that they had done the right thing in extending us courtesies as they had. We thanked the police officers for their hospitality and climbed into the back seat of the Buick with Judy.

Mr. Stallings immediately asked about my plans for the distressed vehicle. When I responded that I yet did not have definitive plans, he suggested we have the Ford dealership in town take a look at the car while we were in Tampa and we could have them repair it at their convenience over the holidays. Additionally, he said he could deliver Raymond and me back to Chattahoochee when they transported Judy back to Georgia. That became our plan.

Dealing with an automobile dealership was foreign territory to me, but to Mr. Stallings it was like playing in his backyard. We drove to the Ford dealer and Mr. Stallings instructed the service manager what he wanted done with the vehicle stranded on Highway 90, approximately fifteen miles east of town. He asked me to hand the manager the keys and told him he would be contacting him within a few days. Ray and I knew we were in good hands. The rest of the trip to Tampa was nothing but fun for Ray and me as Ray answered many questions from Judy and her parents and I enjoyed watching the interaction.

Christmas vacation was a lot of fun. Ray and I visited my friends and family and hung out, mostly with Judy. Everyone enjoyed Ray because of the guy he is and because of his intriguing Cajun accent. This trip was a true holiday for Ray since he had an opportunity to see and visit many of the things that make Tampa a destination city. I was bored regarding visiting Busch Gardens, but Judy convinced me that Ray would enjoy the outing, so the three of us teamed up with the thousands of visitors and toured the brewery and animal attractions. It was a cool morning and Ray was wearing a nylon athletic jacket that tied at the bottom. By early afternoon it warmed up and Ray wore his jacket open with the white tie-down strings dangling. As we strolled through the Audubon section of the gardens, a 3 ½ foot exotic bird viewed the strings hanging from Ray's jacket as worms and went after them with a vengeance. It was hilarious to see this 210 lb. star halfback backpedaling and tripping over items and people as he attempted to avoid the bird's assault. My natural inclination was to assist Ray in this situation, so I attempted to shoo the bird away. When things calmed down, I noticed Judy was bent over laughing uncontrollably. She described to Ray and me what she witnessed, and we joined her in laughter. For the next month or so Ray brought up the bird assault every other day and it continued to provide laughs.

The situation at home was still tense even though Frances and Gene tried to convince me otherwise. They did not want me to worry while I was away and also did not want to expose our dirty laundry to our guest from Port Allen. My mother also tried to paint a rosy picture, but I knew better. I spoke with Gene privately and he confirmed what I had sensed, things were not better but worse. My hands were tied because Luis was calculating enough to be on his best behavior for the two weeks I was home and return to his normal self after I was gone. This, of course, would allow him to plead ignorance if I was to confront him with a concern in the future. I, nonetheless, knew he was a rat and, more importantly, he knew that I knew he was a rat.

Notwithstanding all the trouble at home, Frances was comfortable at the International Bank of Tampa, and more importantly, was enjoying the time she was spending with a young man named Joe Caranante. Gene was doing well in the classroom and on the football field at Jesuit and found solace with his girlfriend, Sylvia Jean Tinnaro.

As planned, Mr. Stallings was driving us to Chattahoochee to pick up Johnny Beck's sister's vehicle which we were told was running fine after replacing the generator with a rebuilt one. While in Tampa, I asked Mr. Stallings how much the repair bill at the Ford dealership was and he told me the service manager quoted the total price at $47. Accordingly, I managed my money during the Christmas holidays and added that amount to my budget for the return trip to Baton Rouge.

When we arrived in Chattahoochee, I again was experiencing that "missing Judy" feeling, which was awful. Nonetheless, there was nothing I could do about it and I marked it up to poor planning because Judy could have attended LSU had we made arrangements earlier. We said our goodbyes at the Ford dealership and Ray and I walked into the service department to claim the vehicle, one of us "teary eyed." We described the vehicle and the lady behind the cashier window indicated where to sign the invoice of which she gave me a copy. The bill was $47, and Ray and I were reaching into our pockets when the lady told us the bill had been taken care of by Mr. Stallings. Ray and I stared at each other and thought *Merry Christmas and thank you Mr. Stallings. What a guy*.

It was Sunday morning, and we were heading west on Highway 90 hoping for better luck than we had experienced two weeks earlier. We were west of Chipley, Florida when we heard an all-too-familiar "bang." We had another flat tire, but this time we had no spare. We came to a stop on the side of the road by a parking lot of what I assumed was a Baptist Church. I could hear the congregation singing hymns familiar to me from the times I had attended church with Judy. Ray and I discussed the situation and came up with a poor solution to our problem (even though it certainly looked right to us that day). One of the things David Poché was most proud of was his ability to pop open the trunk of any 1958 Ford by merely striking the trunk about four inches beneath its lock. David would not go by a 1958 Ford without thumping the trunk, thus causing the lid to open, which provided him amusement as he considered the driver's reaction upon his return. Neither Ray nor I had tried popping a trunk in Baton Rouge, but we were willing to give it a try that Sunday morning. We spotted a 1958 Ford in the church parking lot and walked toward it with larceny in our hearts. Ray gave the trunk a thump, but it would not open. He tried again with the same result. I then gave it a try, and the trunk sprung open. We removed the spare tire, quietly closed the trunk, and rolled the tire about sixty feet to our car on the road. We made the switch in what seemed like record time and placed the blown-out tire in the trunk with the crinolines. We continued west on Highway 90 and were nervous until we reached the Florida/Alabama state line.

(Sadly) we were proud for having maneuvered through our problem outside of Chipley and often included this caper when recounting our trip to our friends in Baton Rouge. The truth of the matter is that we had acted like uneducated and unloved hoodlums. Not only did we victimize an unsuspecting person worshipping in church, but we risked embarrassing our families, our friends, our school, and ourselves; and, to demonstrate our callousness, we did the deed having been the beneficiaries of Mr. Stallings' kindness earlier that morning.

I don't know why God allows some people to get caught and others not to in these circumstances, but I suspect it has something to do with showing us, when life is viewed retrospectively, how unworthy of God's love and grace we are.

We made it safely through Alabama and Mississippi and were nearing Baton Rouge when we experienced our fourth blowout in Denham Springs. We noticed a salvage yard on the opposite side of the highway about a block away and drove the car, flat tire and all, onto their property. A lean, crusty old fellow, wearing curled cowboy boots and a cigarette dangling from the corner of his mouth, walked up to the car and looked at the vehicle as if he was going to make us an offer. Even though Johnny Beck had nothing to do with all the trouble we experienced, Ray and I were growing increasingly disgruntled with him and may have considered an offer on his sister's vehicle. We didn't, but we managed to make another poor decision. We told the man at the salvage yard we needed a tire that would get us to Baton Rouge (about twenty miles) and we didn't want to spend any money for it. The man immediately told us we had come to the wrong place and that he could not help us. We told him we would trade the two rims we had for a tire and rim. He again told us he had no interest. We told him to look at the vehicle and take a part which would still leave the vehicle drivable and that he would take as trade for a used tire. He again said he had no interest in anything in our vehicle with the possible exception of the radio. We told him he had a deal.

We drove no faster than forty miles per hour for the remaining twenty miles into Baton Rouge fearing another blow out. We rehearsed how we would tell Johnny about having to trade the radio because we were broke and needed the tire. It sounded a lot better in rehearsal than it did when we actually told Johnny. To make matters worse, Johnny said he totally understood and was not at all upset. It was like taking a dagger to the heart. Ray and I felt so bad we offered to buy a radio to put back in the vehicle within a couple of months. Johnny told us not to worry about it, but within a month a friend of Guy DiCharry's sold us a stock radio for eleven bucks (including installation).

Things seemed different to me in Baton Rouge. I enjoyed the Christmas break, especially seeing Judy, friends, and family; but being home wasn't quite as I had anticipated. I continued to miss Judy and my family as much as ever, but my longing for Tampa had diminished significantly. I realized that the things I enjoyed in Tampa could be duplicated in Baton Rouge, and therefore, it was up to me to acclimate myself to my new home away from home. It had taken me approximately four months to rid myself of a severe case of homesickness, but I now felt perfectly comfortable in my new surroundings and was experiencing a feeling of freedom I had never experienced before.

DIVIDE AND CONQUER

Over the Christmas holidays, the coaching staff decided to split up Charlie Moore and me. There were a couple of other roommate changes due to academics, but ours was the only one that was behavior related—a dubious distinction indeed.

My new roommate was Lawrence "Boo" Levert (pronounced La-vair). Boo came from a well-heeled family in Thibodaux, Louisiana. For decades, his family had owned and operated Rienzi Plantation in Lafourche Parish whose main crop was sugar cane. This area of Louisiana has a reputation for spicy food and politics. Boo's family had been a key player in south Louisiana politics dating back to the days of Huey Long, and his father, Dee Dee, currently held the unofficial position of political boss in that region. Boo never flaunted his family's power or wealth, but it was evident in many ways. The year was 1962, and Boo, at a university that did not allow freshmen automobiles, drove a brand spanking new 1962 Ford LTD hard-top coupe with leather bucket seats and all the extras of the day, which included A/C, automatic transmission, power windows, power locks, power brakes, carpets, etc.

Through Boo, I was introduced, to the "three to a page" checkbook he used and whose checks were drawn on his family's business account. Most of the players on the team operated on a tight budget, but that would not include Lawrence "Boo" Levert. Boo did not abuse the privilege, but on the other hand, he was never short of funds. We would always kid him about never entering the check amount into the check register. We asked how he kept his account balanced utilizing this method, and to put this issue to bed, he finally broke clean with us.

"I'm just following my fadder's instructions." he told us, "He told me just to write checks when I need money, and his bookkeeper would take care of the rest."

You can imagine our reaction when we heard that explanation. With all these financial resources at his beck and call, Boo could have been quite a pain in the *you know where,* but to the contrary, he was a great guy in every respect. While it might sound like a contradiction in terms, Boo and his family were pure Cajun. From an outsider's viewpoint, being pure Cajun *generally* meant you were Catholic, loved music and dancing, sports, drinking and partying, hunting and fishing, telling stories, you lived in the southern region of the state, liked gambling (playing cards [Boo-Ray, in particular]), you were loyal, generous, proud, all-around fun loving, and chain-smoked cigarettes. Boo qualified in almost every category—he didn't chain smoke.

Boo invited a group of us spend a weekend with him at the family plantation in Thibodaux. About ten of us made the hour-and-a-half trip southeast of Baton Rouge, but the only ones I recall are David Poché, Ken Cormier, Ray Loup, George Rice, Doug Moreau, and of course, Boo. Driving to his plantation home on a winding road beneath the shade of one-hundred-plus-year-old oak trees rivaled scenes from *Gone with the Wind*. Off to the right of the main house was where we parked our vehicles as help from their plantation staff took our drink orders and relocated the autos to another parking area. After visiting with Mr. and Mrs. Levert on their front porch, which wrapped around three quarters of the plantation house, David began to whisper to each of us, individually.

His attempted subtleness was a complete failure as he whispered to me; "They're washing our vehicles and filling them with gasoline." I was equally impressed by this example of Southern graciousness, but I was able to maintain my composure, unlike my friend. There was much to do at "Rienzi Plantation," including swimming, horseback riding, ranching activities (branding cattle), and so on, but the activity that I preferred most was about to begin. This was not the first time that employees of "Rienzi" prepared for a Southern barbecue including steaks, pork ribs, chicken, sausage, plus all the sides and desserts one could hope for. The party moved indoors after sunset and turned into an ongoing social gathering until people tired and went to bed. However, before the evening was over, Boo's dad asked Boo to ask us if any of us had any interest in "running the dogs." With my impetuousness at a peak level, I quickly indicated I had interest. I pictured, as I had seen in movies, us on horseback tracking a fox with the assistance of dogs running alongside the horses. The other guests were not as quick as I was, but soon volunteered as well.

As one might expect, the plantation was well-stocked with food and beverages of every kind. Two of the kitchen walls consisted of commercial refrigerators and freezers, which we were told to use "as if you were home." Most of my friends enjoyed food and beer to their heart's content, but I spied an article of food in the refrigerator that garnered all of my attention. Earlier that evening, I noticed the stainless steel canisters used to fill the desert-serving dish with whipped cream. The cream was delicious and all of a sudden, I was face-to-face with two of the canisters I had seen earlier. I asked Boo if it was okay to have some, and with his approval, I kept a canister by my side most of the evening.

It was becoming late in the evening and because we had to rise early in the morning to "run the dogs." the sensible thing to do would have been to go to sleep. However, the testosterone was flowing freely and someone suggested we ride horses bareback. Several of us stripped down to our underwear and mounted horses under the light of a half moon. We remained in the large corral area and had fun showing off to each other and acting silly.

A couple of guys who had enough sense not to mount the horses were also in the corral attempting to liven the spirits of the horses in a variety of ways. Through their efforts, several of the horses began running, then stopping abruptly, throwing the rider. An area of the corral was muddy and had standing water, which provided a big laugh when Ken Cormier and David Poché were thrown from their horses into the mud.

Five-thirty in the morning came quickly and I was not so sure "running the dogs" was such a good idea after all. Nonetheless, we had committed to Boo's dad, who in turn had informed the Sheriff of Lafourche Parish that we would meet him at an appointed place at 6:30 AM. We were treated to a delicious breakfast before traveling a few miles into the backwoods of the parish. A jovial, pot-bellied sheriff resembling one of the correction officers in the movie *Cool Hand Luke* greeted us with smiles and hugs. While hugging us, he and his deputies were wiping our necks with handkerchiefs and face towels as they conversed among themselves and with Boo in a Cajun dialect. This seemed a bit peculiar, but I was beginning to get the picture as I realized there were no horses and a mobile kennel with at least a dozen bloodhounds. Sheriff Leander Boudreau asked us to gather around him as he gave us instructions. He pointed to the property across the road and said we would begin running there, staying on paths through the thick woods and underbrush until we reached a clearing of about 4,500 feet (fifteen football fields), the end of which had a pump house, where he would pick us up in about thirty to forty-five minutes. Just at the time I was about to ask him where the horses were, he gave us a signal to begin.

As is generally the case, the group broke up into two subgroups, wide receivers and backs in one, tight ends and linesmen in the other. I don't know what the skill group (football term) was discussing, but the linesmen were bemoaning the fact that, instead of being in bed at this uncivil hour of the morning, we were involved in a training exercise for the local sheriff's pack of bloodhounds, directed at honing their skills for tracking fugitives from justice, and to make matters worse, we were doing it for free. The longer we jogged, the fainter the voices of the skill group grew until we could no longer hear them. Even while running in the shade of the thick woods, we were sweating profusely. As was David's specialty, he had already anticipated the heat factor once we broke into the clearing and was communicating to all who would listen, details of the drudgery ahead. As we broke into the clearing, we saw the other group approximately 2,000 feet ahead and widening the gap. At the same time, we heard the faint sounds of barking dogs.

We obviously had to reach the pump house before the dogs reached us. We continued to negotiate the 4,500 feet of real estate as we gauged the sound of the bloodhounds. Before it was evident, David opined that we would never outrun the hounds to the pump house. Fear and familiarity caused us to yell at David to shut up, yet it was becoming apparent he might be correct.

Conversations ceased and all the "big men" were focused on reaching the pump house. As we looked over our shoulders we could see the hounds breaking into the clearing and gaining ground on us. They barked incessantly and the large flaps over their ears seemed to poetically add to their graceful strides. However, it was self-preservation and not poetry that interested us at that moment. We only had 1,000 feet to the house, but these canine creatures seemed to be gaining confidence that they would reach us before we reached the house, and their perceived confidence was adding to our grief.

One of David's steps on the uneven pasture twisted his ankle and caused him to simultaneously cry for help. "Flo don't leave me here! Flo, please don't leave me!" I yielded and allowed him to mount his 230-pound body upon mine, but I could do nothing but walk under that load.

The hounds did not slow down just because we had, so I told David I was taking him to the lone tree some thirty-five feet ahead. By this time, our conversation had deteriorated to a combination of yelling, crying, and panic. David told me he did not want to get into the tree, but I told him it was our only option. He was hysterically thanking me and wishing me well as I left him in the tree and began sprinting toward the pump house. All but two of us had reached the pump house, and the two who had not, were less than 200 feet away. The entire group was attempting to provide encouragement by cheering me down the stretch and it was working. I uncovered a spurt of energy I did not know I possessed as I ran toward the group of yelling cohorts. It was too close for me to look back, so I just relied on their assessment that I could make it. When I was forty feet away, I could hear the dogs so clearly that I thought each step would be the one at which they caught me. The guys, while continuing to encourage, began entering the pump house and kept the door open as I approached. As I leaped toward the front of the doorway and entered the house on all fours, a couple of guys assisted me in while another slammed the door shut behind me.

Within an instant, you could hear the dogs scratching the outside of the metal pump house as they continued to bark. Before long, the sheriff and a few of his deputies arrived to kennel the dogs and transport us back to our vehicles. I commented to Sheriff Boudreau how close a call I had just experienced, and he began to laugh until he realized that I did not consider it a laughing matter. He then said that, had we been perfectly still when the dogs reached us, we would have been safe because the hounds are trained to circle the object of the hunt and continue to bark until he and his men arrive.

He implied that he had communicated those instructions to us before the "run," but if he did, I certainly did not hear him.

We had another party that evening at "Rienzi" and the people who did not participate in the "run", and especially adult friends of the Levert's, enjoyed hearing the many renditions of the day's activities. That evening's party was also designed for us to meet Boo's belle, Linda Ledet (pronounced La-day). She was a refined and lovely young lady, of whom Boo was quite fond.

It was both an enjoyable and interesting weekend that provided many laughs and memories.

SPRING FOOTBALL

Even though I did not fully understand the importance of spring practice, I approached it with excitement for the opportunities that lay ahead. The twenty practices within a thirty-day period were grueling. Overall, I was satisfied with my performance, especially in the "Purple & Gold" spring game, even though I did not give 100 percent at all times, a habit I had brought from Jesuit. Why I didn't give 100 percent remains a mystery to me, though I somehow believe it to be related to my inability to completely trust coaches.

A comical recollection regarding spring practice has to do with David Poché. David would purpose himself each day to go by the locker room to view that day's practice schedule. Then, regardless of the schedule, he would report to us that day's workout schedule was the toughest he had ever seen and was replete with contact drills. In addition, he would assume the role of weatherman and insure us that day's conditions would be unbearably hot and humid. We kidded David about this (mostly when he was not around), but in his mind, he was giving us an accurate assessment of what was ahead. Of course, he would occasionally be correct, and then would proudly tell us "What did I tell you about today's work out?"

JACK'S

One particular spring day, Ray Loup and I stopped at "Jack's" in search of a relaxed game of pool and a cold longneck. Located in Bogalousa, Jack's is a Cajun version of a New York-style Italian social club where like-minded men meet to discuss what interests them: business, women, sports, and women, while playing pool or "boo-ray" (cards), eating ethnic food, and consuming beverages intended to aid in relaxation. Those with other agendas simply aren't welcome. That day at Jack's, Ray and I witnessed evidence of that fact.

Soon after arriving, we noticed a "Blondie" who was out of his element. Presumably, the poor manners he exhibited resulted from his advanced level of intoxication. Nonetheless, he was oblivious to the fact that his act was not playing well at Jack's.

"Blondie," the moniker assigned to strangers by the local Cajuns, was undoubtedly related to the fair complexion and light-colored hair of the alien.

The locals were confident that the cowboy-looking Blondie, dressed in jeans and wearing Texas-style boots and shirt, was not from this area of Washington Parish, and that alone made him suspect. He was considered a drifting cowboy looking to occupy his day.

The formidably-built Blondie engaged in consuming cold draughts between challenging men not near his equal. His efforts were met with no takers. Neither Ray nor I were fearful of Blondie, but we certainly were hoping we would not be given the same offer others had rejected.

Blondie's grating demeanor escalated when he was refused an additional beer coincidental with the depletion of his cash reserve.

A patron, either enjoying the spectacle or thinking it would aid in controlling Blondie, sponsored another beer for the out of control alien. A better example of contributing to the delinquency of an adult would be difficult to fathom except for the fact that afterwards another person bought yet another beer for Blondie.

Unenthusiastically, the bartender announced that Blondie would not be allowed to drink anymore regardless of who provided the financing—a pitifully obvious intervention way too late.

The announcement infuriated the staggering and slurring blond boozer, but added to the entertainment he unwittingly provided. He was now without distraction and free to focus his full attention on challenging Jack's faithful. It was just a matter of time before he would make his way to the pool-playing patrons.

As Blondie inched his way nearer, Ray and I assessed the practicality of using the cue sticks we held in our defense. Thoughtful people would have left the premises, and a few had. Ray and I, perhaps not wanting to give the appearance that we feared the circumstance Blondie caused, did not.

At about that time, proprietor Jack Saia made a call to someone who apparently gave him comfort that this unfortunate situation would soon be remedied. Armed with that news, Jack, in the local dialect, uttered to his concerned patrons, "Leon is on his way." In a strange sort of way, that information soothed the anxious, which piqued Ray's interest and mine.

Within moments, the front windows of the establishment displayed a Louisiana State vehicle engaged in the peculiar activity of backing in at the front entrance to Jack's. Exiting the state vehicle was Leon Boudreaux of the Boudreaux clan. In Washington Parish, the Boudreauxs were well-known for either using or ignoring the law as they saw fit in the execution of their duties as moonshiners, hunters, fishermen, dog catchers and the like. On this day, they would ignore the law in the spirit of expediting matters.

As Leon exited the state vehicle, I witnessed another peculiar move when he opened the trunk lid before entering.

I whispered to Ray, "He's done this before." Ray smiled and nodded affirmatively.

Leon methodically removed his sunglasses, carefully storing them in the breast pocket of the jacket he removed, then unbuckled and removed his gun and holster as he proceeded toward the bar, handing these articles to Jack for safekeeping, and listened, in local dialect, to Jack's briefing.

His every move confirmed that this was not Leon's first day at the rodeo. I knew very little Cajun, but I understood the plan precisely as did the remaining patrons, with the exception of Blondie.

Leon observed the inebriated Blondie and positioned himself to be the next target. When challenged, Leon, in a low and humble tone that was easily heard by everyone, calmly expressed to Blondie that it was a good time for him to leave.

Blondie was too drunk to understand the wisdom in Leon's suggestion; not to mention Leon's role in this matter. Blondie scoffed at Leon's idea and again challenged the composed newcomer.

Leon repeated the soft suggestion and improved the proposal by offering to provide transportation to the parish line. Again, unable to recognize the value in the offer, Blondie responded by taking a wild swing easily avoided by Leon.

Leon offered again, and again his offer was rejected.

In between Leon's bids, some of the onlookers jeered Blondie and encouraged Leon to teach Blondie a Cajun lesson. "He's earned it," they used as justification.

Leon did not require much prodding. Barely six feet tall, wiry, and rugged looking, Leon was experienced, confident, and calculating. A sober Blondie would have been a fair match: Blondie's youth and strength versus Leon's age and experience. The metal tips on his pointed cowboy boots advertised what was coming.

It was obvious to all; Blondie was not leaving without a fight. He was alone and in trouble.

Avoiding another feeble attempt by Blondie, Leon countered with a crisp shot to the jaw dropping Blondie to his knees. Disobeying Leon's casual order to stay down, Blondie got up swinging wildly without results. Leon folded Blondie over with a compact blow to his stomach, then temporarily straightened him with an experienced upper cut causing Blondie's legs to wobble before collapsing beneath him. Leon checked his fist for blood as Blondie's mouth bled. "He won't get up," some hoped, while others wondered. His youth and strength worked against him as he managed to stand and wipe his mouth.

Blood is a discouragement to some, an encouragement to others. What Blondie needed was discouragement, but as the "Toro" finds additional strength with the sense and smell of its own blood, so did Blondie find a surge of strength as he smelled, sensed, and tasted his.

Blondie charged Leon and was stopped by the bar as Leon changed positions, not unlike a matador. Blondie regrouped, took aim, and again went after the deft Boudreaux. This time, his charge was met with a thunderous strike to the side of Blondie's head, and blood was everywhere. Leon wiped the blood from his hands using the bar towel provided him by Jack and sternly ordered Blondie to stay down.

The locals and I were impressed with the stamina exhibited by this unwelcome visitor.

Defiantly, Blondie attempted to bring himself up to his knees when Leon introduced Blondie to his metal-tipped boots. He kicked the determined but defenseless drunk in the head, the ribs, and in the groin as he continued to order him to stay down. With each kick, Blondie grimaced, but he would not stop trying to get up, causing the composed, but somewhat astonished Boudreaux to step up his assault for fear of leaving the locals with the unwanted reputation of not being able to finish the task. Leon was not about to risk losing face amongst his own.

An ugly situation got uglier. Leon would have no more of Blondie's brashness. Stay down or get more. The slightest inkling of Blondie's defiance was met with a fierce blow of the metal-tipped boots. To our amazement, Blondie kept attempting a comeback, and each time, his attempt was thwarted by Leon.

Similar to Cool Hand Luke's futile attempt to overcome his foe in the classic movie, Blondie kept trying to hit Leon until he passed out in a fizzling fit of rage.

With that accomplished, Leon tidied himself, took a sip from a beer Jack designated as his, and recruited a couple of guys to place the unconscious body in the trunk of the state vehicle. He then removed his sunglasses from his coat, put them on, and adjusted his holster to his liking before donning his coat, shutting the trunk lid, and driving off.

Many of life's most important lessons are not taught in a classroom but are thrust upon you without warning. Such was the case that day in the sleepy town of Bogalusa.

A week later I ran across a small article on one of the back pages in the local newspaper stating that an unidentified body of a badly beaten husky white male was found in a ditch off Highway 11 outside of Bogalusa. The dead man who appeared to be in his late-twenties or early-thirties was wearing a western style shirt, blue jeans, and boots. I immediately took the article to Ray, and while we didn't discuss it much, I assumed he experienced the same gnawing sensation in the pit of his stomach.

(BAD) HABITS ARE HARD TO BREAK

Class work continued to be a breeze, but bad habits will track you down. Allow me to explain. As part of an English class, I was required to prepare and submit a term paper. I procrastinated and soon found myself in a bit of a dilemma. Did I want to give up a significant amount of my social time to meet this obligation, or was there another solution? Remi Prudhomme assisted in my decision by offering me a completed term paper on "The Arms and Ammunitions of The Hungarian Revolt" (one of six choices offered by the English professor). All I had to do was have the paper retyped since it had been previously submitted to another English professor. This was the purest form of plagiarism. Since there were a dozen or more English sections, I deduced that my chances of being found out were 1 in 12 or better.

Mickey Croix approached me the week the term paper was due and asked if it would be all right if he submitted the same term paper to yet another professor. I told him I did not see any problem and he proceeded with the plan. About a month later, the buzz around the dining hall was that Mickey was caught submitting someone else's work in a class, was given an F, and was facing suspension from the university.

I, without hesitation, went to Mickey's room to gain detail on this gossip. Mickey communicated to me that his professor considered the term paper inconsistent with other work submitted by him in the class and began to question him about the term paper's content. Mickey had not even read the term paper, thus, he could not answer any questions and was therefore left with no option but to admit that the paper was someone else's work. Of critical importance to me, he said he did not divulge where he obtained the paper. My mind kicked into overdrive as I pondered the possibilities. Do professors notify other professors in situations like this? Were there other copies of the term paper in circulation, and if so, would they all be scrutinized? And the only legitimate question, why didn't I write my own paper? The time I saved by not doing my own paper was now available to me to worry over whether my fate would be the same as Mickey's.

Each time our English class met, I looked closely at the professor for any irregularities. Then one day, the professor announced to the class, "One of the students in this class has done a particularly nice job with the structure of his term paper and I wish to recognize this person and ask him a few questions which I believe would benefit the rest of the class. So, Mr. Flores, at the end of today's class I would like you to explain to your fellow students how you structured your term paper and why you chose that particular method." Thoughts raced through my mind. Am I being set up? Had others besides Mickey and me turned in the same paper and were they attempting to bag us all? Nonetheless, I had no choice but to proceed as if I were, indeed, the proud author of the paper I submitted.

With five minutes remaining, the professor ceased teaching and asked me to stand. "Mr. Flores, would you share with the class how you structured your paper and why you chose that particular method?" Not knowing where further questions might lead, I humbly explained that I used the method I was taught in high school. Realizing I had less than five minutes, I gave a brief outline of the paper which I had read a dozen or so times since Mickey's incident.

"The paper," I explained, "was divided into three sections. The first section deals with the social conditions in Hungary at the time which caused turmoil and invited revolution, namely, anarchy, poverty, and governmental distrust. The second section describes the various competing factions attempting to garner power, their means, methods, successes, and failures. While this section gives a strong indication of which group ultimately prevails, the third and final section focuses on the new ruling regime and contrasts what life in Hungary was like after the revolution with the conditions promised by the new powers, comparing both to what it was like before the revolution."

Class ended, and people were exiting the classroom as I was explaining the reason I chose the structure. In addition to being familiar with this structure from high school, I believed it followed a logical sequence, which was easy to understand and reference. As I collected my books, the professor commented how impressed she was with the paper and said that were it not for a few grammatical errors, I would have received an A, however, I should be proud of the A minus I'd earned. I said I understood and tried to generate a smile concealing my true feelings.

I realized, again, that I had just dodged a bullet. The shallow decision I made caused me to be uneasy for the remainder of the semester. The ill-gained ten to twelve hours paled in comparison to the countless hours spent wondering when this deed would be uncovered.

If the quality of my future decisions did not improve, I was destined for nowhere but trouble. In financial terms, I was misusing assets and was headed for bankruptcy.

GEORGIA ON MY MIND

Automobiles were scarce among underclassmen, but my buddy David Egnarts sported a 1961 Volkswagen Beetle, nonetheless. David was a good friend, but I must admit, from the moment I saw his automobile I visualized he and I traveling to Georgia to visit Judy. What made this vision a strong possibility was that David did not have a steady girlfriend at the time and his keen interest in *if there were pretty girls* at the school Judy attended? I told him we should find out for ourselves, and he agreed. Judy began making arrangements on her end, and David and I were making plans for a weekend visit to South Georgia College in Douglas, Georgia.

The challenges with this trip were much different than the Christmas trip. The roadworthiness of David's Beetle was not an issue, his German-manufactured VW purred like a Singer sewing machine and had about the same horsepower. However, traveling from Baton Rouge to Douglas, Georgia on a Friday afternoon and returning by high noon on Sunday, posed more of a logistics problem, but one we were willing to manage. Another concern, held by David, was the travel constraint imposed upon him by his father. According to David, he was free to travel within the state of Louisiana but not outside its boundaries. The solution to us was simple. David would not use his fuel credit cards outside the state and he had to avoid any activity which would reveal his venture outside of Louisiana, like getting a traffic citation.

David was a very generous person evidenced by his suggestion that he would use his family's fuel card to fill his vehicle inside the state line, and he and I would split the fuel cost until we returned to Louisiana. You can't beat that deal.

After lunch on Friday, we retreated to our rooms, locked the doors, and invested in a 2½ hour nap in anticipation of a sleep-starved weekend. After participating in the voluntary workout (which we were not allowed to miss), we departed Baton Rouge traveling east through Hammond and into Bogalusa, Louisiana, just inside the state's eastern boundary. As planned, we filled David's car with fuel.

I was excited about the opportunity of seeing Judy, and David was excited about meeting Judy's friend, Ann. The trip proceeded without flaw, but neither David nor I anticipated the trip taking ten hours. We enjoyed ourselves, though, reminiscing about occurrences during the year, discussing our future, listening to the radio, singing our favorite songs, etc.

We arrived in Douglas, Georgia after traveling some 575 miles at 5:45 AM and to say things were quiet was an understatement. We drove to Judy's dormitory and were told by a security guard that the residents were not allowed to leave the dorm until 7 AM.

We sat in the car for a while until I came up with the idea of freshening up before we met the girls. We thought we would shower in one of the men's dorms, but we did not bring towels. We, however, did not let that stop us. We were the first in the shower and relaxed under the spray of hot water for about a half-hour before students began arriving one by one. As soon as there were four or five guys showering, we figured there were enough towels to cast a shadow of doubt that we may have picked up the wrong towels for drying. While drying, we noticed some of the students placed shaving gear by the sinks and mirrors while they showered so we took the opportunity to shave, as well. The towel shortage caused a bit of a problem between some students who were upset when other students were using their towels because we had used theirs. We offered the towels we used to any who needed one, but had no takers. David and I chuckled as we departed when we heard people in the shower complaining there was no hot water.

We called Judy and told her we were in town and would be picking them up at her dorm at 7 AM sharp, and at that time David and I were introduced to Judy's friend, Ann. I could tell by the look on David's face that he was very pleased with Judy's selection for him and Ann's face expressed the same.

We ate breakfast at a local diner, and while Judy and I caught up with things, David and Ann required no assistance in becoming acquainted. The girls took us on a tour of the campus and then the town of Douglas. We spent the balance of the day walking around, holding hands, and talking about the things we had written about in our letters. To see David and Ann, you would have thought they had known each other for years and were thrilled to see each other after a long separation. In fact, we commented on how well they were getting along. As for Judy and me, we were having a nice time, but something seemed a little strange and I could not put my finger on it. Her responses were not as crisp as they once were and her interest seemed to have shifted toward the worldly. On top of that, she was developing a cavalier attitude very unlike the girl who had captured my heart eighteen months earlier. I expressed these feelings to Judy, but she insisted that nothing was wrong and that I was tired from traveling all night. I know what I know, and I knew something was different, but without concrete examples, all I would do was cause a fuss if I continued with my concerns. If a concrete example is what I wanted, I received my wish even though I did not care for the circumstances. In a poor attempt to act nonchalant, Judy had the gall to reach into her purse and retrieve a pack of cigarettes and matches. As she placed the weed between her lips, I asked, "What's this about?"

"I have been smoking for a while, but not very much," she said in a faux-confident tone intended to demonstrate her independence and self-determination. I was disappointed but not surprised, and expressed these sentiments to her. She attempted to slough it off by saying, "It's no big deal. Don't let it worry you."

"I definitely don't like you smoking, but that's a minor issue in comparison to this new you, who I'm not sure I like very much. Furthermore, I don't think you should be smoking, and I certainly don't want you smoking around me."

She put the cigarette back into the pack and the pack back into her purse, and I could read her mind, "Yeah, but you won't be here tomorrow."

We had an enjoyable rest of the day and evening after the tobacco incident and recognized that we should make the most of what time we had left.

The girls had a midnight curfew, after which our plan was to travel back to Baton Rouge to arrive in time for our noon meeting on Sunday. Lapsed time from the naps we took on Friday afternoon till our time of arrival on Sunday was approximately eighteen hours. As the day drew on, we began to feel weary but decided we would be able to make up the sleep we missed on the trip back. Our plan was to take two-hour driving shifts allowing the person not driving to snooze.

As expected, time did fly by and we found ourselves delivering Judy and Ann to their dorm in time to make the midnight curfew. Saying goodbye this time was not as bad as the previous time because spring break was about six weeks away and I would see Judy then.

Judy and I chuckled because we couldn't get David and Ann untangled as we prepared to leave. We heard them tell each other they would stay in touch, which we both considered a longshot.

We were dog tired and David asked if I minded taking the first driving shift. I, of course, agreed and we were headed west on Georgia's winding, rural roads, me at the wheel and David stretched back as far as his seat would allow and snoring away. After driving for about thirty minutes, I realized that the two-hour shifts were not going to work. I seriously doubted if I would be able to complete one hour. During the next fifteen minutes, I conjured up a dirty trick to play on David. In addition to providing me with extra time to sleep, I was sure my plan would provide some good storytelling material in the locker room. The plan was to advance the clock in the car (neither of us wore watches), explain to David that one-hour shifts would make more sense, and then turn the driving to him. I was only shorting him fifteen minutes, but they were precious minutes. David said he could not believe he had been sleeping for an hour, but I assured him he had pointing to the clock on the dash of the car as he took the steering wheel out of a sense of duty. An hour later, he woke me and told me he could not drive another minute, agreeing that it was a good idea to abandon the two-hour shift strategy.

On my second shift, I intended to drive forty minutes, but at the 29-minute mark I again advanced the clock and informed David it was his turn to drive. "There's no way I slept for an hour!" exclaimed David. "Are you sure it's been an hour?"

"David, I felt the same way when you woke me, so I know how you feel." It bothered me when he uttered, "I don't know if I can stay awake for an hour," but I changed positions with him and was sleeping before we were a quarter-mile down the road. I was empathetic with how David felt when I woke him, because I was in disbelief when he woke me after a full hour. David was asleep by the time I shut the door after getting behind the wheel. I was weighing in my mind whether or not I should cut this shift short, but decided to do so.

"Flo, there ain't no way in hell I've been sleeping for an hour," said David in an agitated voice.

"What can I tell you, David, it's hell isn't it?" I said as I pulled the car to the shoulder of the road.

"Be ready for me to ask you to drive before my hour is up because I don't think I'm going to make it," said David as he began his shift. It didn't seem like ten minutes had passed before I felt the car, abruptly, pull off the road with David yelling every expletive he could muster. "You dirty son of a bitch! You rotten bastard! You been screwing me all night!" said this steaming Cajun amongst a bevy of other words I recognized as French curse words whose exact meaning I did not understand, but whose intent was abundantly clear.

"What are you talking about?" I answered, knowing all too well David had uncovered my scheme.

"You know what the hell I'm talking about," he retorted in his strong Cajun accent. "I heard the man on the radio give the jacking time the first time I drove, and I thought maybe I had an Alabama or Mississippi (Central Time) radio station, but now I know I didn't, because you been jacking with the clock because he just gave the time again, and it ain't nowhere near what this clock shows."

"Maybe this clock ain't working right," I said.

"Quit screwing with me, Flo," answered David in an increasingly angry tone. "You know you been jacking me around all night you dirty bastard."

I broke out laughing, but David didn't for a few seconds. He then joined me laughing, but asked me to take the wheel because he was too tired to drive. I, of course did, and David was sleeping like a baby again. I was paying for my joke because it had been an hour and 45 minutes and I was literally nodding at the wheel. "David, you gotta drive. I can't stay awake any longer," I said as I reached over and shook his shoulder.

"Don't talk to me about driving, you dirty bastard," he responded.

"If I fall asleep at the wheel and wrap this car around a tree, you're going to have a lot of explaining to do to your old man, assuming we're alive."

"Come on, Flo. Don't give me that crap. You know I need to sleep," pleaded David.

"David, I know you're sleepy, but I'm telling you, you need to relieve me at least for a half-hour," I said in a tone that delivered the message.

"All right, you son of a bitch," he said as he changed positions with me. "But I'll be waking you in thirty minutes, not thirty-one, you hear me?" he said angrily.

"I'll be ready in 35 to 45 minutes." I said knowing it would aggravate him.

"I'll be waking you up in thirty minutes! Count on it!" he said as we roared down the Mississippi highway.

SPRING "BREAK"

Geraldine Scolaro called to ask if I wanted a ride to Tampa for spring break. I, of course, told her I did and we made plans for the trip. Two other LSU students from Tampa were also riding with us, and we would be picking up two fellas who attended Loyola University in New Orleans and who had been schoolmates of mine at Jesuit.

A couple of days before we were leaving, Geraldine called again with a problem she wondered if I would be able to help with. It seemed like one of the passengers she gave a lift to school back in September had not paid his share of expenses which came up to eight dollars. Geraldine said if I were able to collect the amount from Jack Feiner, I would not have to share in the expenses to and from Tampa. I told Geraldine I would be happy to collect the eight dollars and equally happy to share in the expenses to Tampa and back.

I picked up Geraldine and we returned to the Broussard Hall parking area to meet Jack and Jeannie Feiner. I was shocked when I saw Jeannie because she was an absolute knockout and I wondered how I did not know her in Tampa, since she attended Jefferson High School, a school where I had known many students. Jack, on the other hand, looked like a neo-hippie. Geraldine informed me that the round-trip cost would be eight dollars because of the extra passengers in New Orleans.

After being introduced to the Feiners, I informed them that the first-order of business was to collect the round-trip amount as I was in charge of finances. Jeannie gave me her eight dollars and before I took Jack's money, I informed him that he owed an additional eight dollars from the trip in September. He acknowledged that he owed the September amount, but asked if he could pay that amount on the return trip. I said he could not; I needed the $16 before he entered the automobile. He said he didn't have enough money and could pay the September amount when we reached Tampa. I again told him he couldn't get into the vehicle without handing me $16. He kibitzed with Jeannie, and then paid me $16 with a disgruntled look on his face. I did not take it personally; I was just doing my job.

We pulled up to a spot close to Loyola University that was indicated on the makeshift map Geraldine had given me and without a hitch there stood Anthony Traviesa and Dennis Decidue. I don't mind telling you, six passengers in that Impala was tight. Depending on the seating arrangement, sometimes it was pleasant and other times it wasn't.

It was nice to be home for about seven days, but it sure went quickly. Judy was leaving Sunday afternoon and our group was heading back the next morning. I had been with her each of the seven days and was at her home that Sunday afternoon when her parents would be driving her back to Douglas, Georgia. Things between us weren't the same as they had been back in August. It was hard for me to put my finger on it, but it was that same strange feeling I had sensed when David and I visited Douglas six weeks earlier. I should have seen it coming, but I had not. Judy said there was something she wanted to tell me before they left for Georgia. "Since we're so far from each other, I think we ought to see other people. What do you think?" she asked as we sat on her front porch. A bomb could have gone off beside me and I would have not noticed because one just exploded in my heart. She attempted to soften the blow by saying she still loved me, and that it was better for both of us. I didn't buy one cent of that three-dollar bill she was trying to pawn off on me.

After a few seconds, I regained my ability to speak and answered, "We'll do whatever you want to do." She hugged me and told me everything was going to be fine. It was a one-way hug, because I had no desire to participate. We remained on the porch engaging in some small talk, and within minutes, she and her parents were headed north on Florida Avenue toward Douglas, Georgia. I was able to manage my emotions to that point, but when their automobile turned left from 26th Avenue and we were out of each other's sight, a flood of tears poured from my eyes. I was trying to piece together how this could happen, but couldn't come up with the first piece. The best person I had ever known, the girl I loved and thought I would marry, had just delivered news to me that I thought was impossible. I sat on the porch and cried for about a half hour when Mama Ed came out and offered me water. I took the water, thanked her, and told her I would be leaving in a few minutes.

I was headed south on Tampa Street toward my home but had to pull off of the street and onto the parking lot of the International Bank of Tampa because I could hardly see through the tears. After a few moments, I was on I-275 south approaching the Armenia exit.

I thought I was composed when I entered my home, but the first thing my mother asked was, "What happened?"

"What do you mean?"

"Did something happen between you and Judy?"

"I don't think so, but I want to lay down for a while." I stayed in bed until it was time to leave the next morning. I was hurt like never before.

The trip back occupied my mind, and while there was plenty of opportunity to get to know Jeannie Feiner better, my heart was just not in it. The heartache I felt was very similar to the homesickness I had endured the previous semester, but more intense and relentless. I was, indeed, injured. I had just experienced one of life's tough lessons. No matter how much you love someone, or how perfect someone seems, *every human has the capacity to disappoint.*

I may have made more over her comments than she intended because the tenor in her letters did not change much. I gathered from reading her letters that she felt we were still boyfriend and girlfriend, but that we were just able to see others. That thought was foreign to me as well as confusing. I've always been the "all or nothing" type, but even though I was somewhat confused, I continued to communicate with her as if I was okay with the new arrangement. As the weeks went by, this arrangement began to backfire on her. She seemed to be under-whelmed with the people she was meeting and I was sensing she wanted to return to our normal situation. Meanwhile, this newfound freedom was working out well for me. The prospects were plentiful, and the activity was nonstop if you allowed it to be.

HIGH YELLA

"Any of you guys ever heard of a high-yella," asked Jerry Stovall as he walked up to our group at the dining table. We all wondered the same thing. Why is this All-America senior, who was drafted by the St. Louis Cardinals and was a Heisman Trophy finalist, interested in what we know about a high-yella? We must have looked perplexed because he offered assistance by adding, "You know what I mean, someone who's mixed." I immediately took the lead and told Jerry I knew exactly what he was referring to and that we called them mulattoes in Florida. He responded, "That's it, Florees, you know exactly what I'm talking about!" I was beaming with pride when Jerry asked if any of us had interest in joining him and a couple of other guys to a party Friday night with some high-yella women.

Before Jerry could utter another word, I said, "I'm interested." One by one, the others at the table warmed up to the idea and within minutes we were planning where and when to meet for Friday night's rendezvous.

With eager anticipation, our group, which consisted of Pat Screen (yes, "the pope"), Joe Labruzzo, Donald Schwab, Ken Cormier, David Poché, Doug Moreau, and a few others, paced in front of Broussard Hall until a few vehicles arrived to transport us to our yet-unknown destination. The driver of the automobile into which I climbed was none other than my friend, Robbie Hucklebridge. In addition to me in the vehicle were David Poché and Ken Cormier in the back seat, and Mickey Cox up front. We headed south out of Baton Rouge and I asked the question we all wanted the answer to. "Robbie," I asked, "just where is this party we're going to?"

"It's quite a ways outside of town, but it'll be worth it."

"Do these women live out there or are they going to meet us?"

Robbie's response gave us reason to pause. "These women's husbands left today for a ten-day shift on an oil rig out in the Gulf of Mexico and they generally let us know when their husbands are leaving so we can party with them." Ken was sitting between David and me and we each gave the other a nudge with our legs as if to say *we didn't know anything about any husbands.* The silence cued Robbie to provide us assurance when he offered, "They have to be on the rig by 6 PM, which is why we're going out this late to make sure there are no hitches." None of us responded to Robbie, and about that same time, I noticed a vehicle passing us driven by teammate Butch Chaney. I mentioned it to Robbie, but he discounted it saying he also thought the guy looked like Butch, but it wasn't. I, however, was confident it was Butch and wondered why Robbie denied recognizing him.

We arrived at a dark and desolate location familiar to none of us. We cautiously and quietly exited the automobiles and met on the shell road and waited for instructions from our leaders. As background to the whispered instructions from Robbie and, guess who, Butch Chaney, were the sounds of crickets and tree frogs, complemented by the wind howling through the bramble and tall, southern pines. "Let's be really quiet as we climb this barbed wire fence," instructed Butch "because we want to make sure everything is okay."

"Flo, what does he mean *okay*?" inquired Pat Screen.

Keeping with the quiet theme, I shrugged my shoulders, nodded my head, and whispered, "Got me." As we approached a four-by-ten-foot galvanized metal gate, which provided easy access onto the property. Pat asked that I hold his crutches while he negotiated the gate. He had been injured during spring practice, missing the last two weeks with a severe ankle sprain and was continuing to nurse the injury under doctor's orders. Ken Cormier had experienced a similar injury to his knee and was also on crutches, but like Pat and the rest of us, he did not want to miss this opportunity to socialize with the team's elite. As we proceeded across the property toward a "shack," Butch and Robbie continued to signal us to be quiet.

After traveling about a quarter-mile we were about fifty feet from the shack, which had a fire going when Butch announced our arrival. "Leeann, we're here," said Butch in a higher than normal pitched voice in an attempt to sound cordial and friendly. We all listened intently, but there was no reply. Butch again announced our arrival and there was again no reply. I know the rest of the guys felt as I did, interpreting this as a signal to end this outing and return to Baton Rouge.

Butch gave it a third attempt and Leeann responded, "Butch, is that you?"

"Yes, sweet Leeann, it's me and I brought my friends like I told you." We were hanging on each word spoken by Butch and Leeann, and when Butch asked, "Is it alright if we come in?" we were terrified by a man kicking open the front door, yelling "Who's out there, Leeann?" and firing shotgun blasts in rapid succession. Simultaneously, shotgun blasts were heard and seen from both sides of the shack, and without thinking, I found myself sprinting toward the cars in an attempt to save my life while visually replaying in my mind, the blasts of fire coming out of the end of the shotguns.

As I raced toward the road, I was not surprised to be passed by speedster Joe Labruzzo, but was surprised when crutch-less Pat Screen and Ken Cormier passed me with the gait of an Olympian. We were all uttering unintelligible sounds of fear as we approached the fence which some of the guys were climbing while others simply leaped. Both Pat and Ken cleared the fence with ease. As I approached the gate, I made the decision to jump over it rather than climb over it. My decision was sound, but my execution was faulty, and as I planted my right foot to spring over the gate, I realized I had jumped too soon and landed on the metal gate, knees and thighs first. Unbeknownst to me, 230 lb. David Poché was right behind me and had made the same decision I had, used the same "spring off spot," and achieved similar success landing right next to me causing the gate to collapse. We immediately got back onto our feet and took off running down the oyster shell road.

As we distanced ourselves from the shack, we realized that the sounds of shotgun blasts had transitioned into sounds of laughter, and as we peeked over our shoulders to confirm what we heard, we saw a group of guys slapping each other on the back and holding their stomachs and laughing. It became apparent to us we had been the subject of a hoax. Our hearts were pounding at a rapid pace, we were perspiring profusely, our pants were ripped and dirty, and our knees and thighs were bruised, but we were alive. We were at first angry, but quickly realized being angry would accomplish nothing, so we turned back, walked toward the group and joined them in laughter.

Within twenty minutes most of the group had returned, but Joe Labruzzo was nowhere to be found. The last account of anyone seeing him had him sprinting into the woods across the road. We formed three search parties, each with a shotgun, which was to be fired when we found Joe, and set out in different directions calling Joe's name as we walked through the woods. An hour later, we met back at the road and were concerned that we were unable to find Joe. We went looking again, and about 45 minutes into the second search, we heard a shotgun blast indicating Joe had been located. When we got back to the road, everyone was laughing and getting details from Joe about where he had been for almost two hours.

Jerry Stovall, Fred Miller, Lynn Amedee, and the rest of the coordinators of the night's event invited us to join them at a local watering hole in Baton Rouge. We had a great time recounting the entire evening. Jerry Stovall commented, "I knew this was going to be a good group when Florees said they called high-yellas, mulattoes in Florida."

SUMMER OF '63

By summertime, Judy had abandoned her idea of seeing others, and, as I anticipated from reading her letters, was ready to reinstitute our previous arrangement. With cautious enthusiasm, I agreed but I was not able to flip the switch and make everything all right. It took time for me, and even though things eventually became "special" again, I had been taught never to let your guard completely down.

C.T.R.D. (City of Tampa Recreation Department) was my employer for the summer of 1963. I was going to be a playground director for two-and-a-half months before returning to camp in Baton Rouge on August 15th. I could have earned more money working road construction, like my buddy Ted, but I chose the cerebral route which allowed me to relax some while working the summer. Another plus working for the city was being able to work with Judy. She had every intention of not working that summer, but I convinced her that working would be fun.

We attended a workshop in Drew Park (a sort of tryout camp), and at the end of the week were assigned our playgrounds. The fact that Judy and I dated was no secret, and therefore, we were assigned to different playgrounds. I did not agree with the decision but understood the rationale.

Judy and her male counterpart were assigned to Ragan Park on Lake Avenue. I, on the other hand, was assigned to Jackson Heights playground without a female counterpart. Ream Wilson, my supervisor, informed me Jackson Heights was too dangerous an area for a female director.

In today's world, the City of Tampa would have been exposed to at least two lawsuits; one from a woman's group contesting the opinion the area was too rough for a female, and one from the individual being asked to manage a playground with half the manpower. But that was another day and things proceeded without a hitch.

During June, Judy and I came up with an ingenious idea, albeit a year late. She submitted an application to transfer to LSU, and in July she received confirmation of her acceptance. This was a day for celebration and provided both of us with a new outlook on school. We had never attended school together and we're looking forward to this opportunity.

The conditions on Lemon Street had continued to deteriorate, even though there was an attempt by my mother and Luis to convince me otherwise. Gene and Frances cautioned me of something regarding Luis, about which I was already aware. They indicated his behavior, when I was around, was totally different than it was otherwise. I knew what they were saying was accurate and was never deceived by his pseudo humbleness and transparent kindness. What I didn't know was how to correct the burgeoning problem which was concerning me more and more.

What inadvertently improved things around the house was the fact that Luis opened a sandwich shop on Howard Avenue, just south of Interstate 275, which occupied most of his time. The shop was open from 7 AM till 10:30 PM, and that represented an unintended blessing for Gene and Frances.

However, the situation was not all good; my mother would go directly to the sandwich shop from her full-time job at Sunstate Slacks and work there until closing. This meant that everyone was on their own regarding meals, which was only an inconvenience. Our real concern was the effect of that schedule on my mother's health. Discussing the matter with her, predictably, accomplished nothing.

As for my brother Bob, things were going well. He and his wonderful wife Rosie were filling their new home on Fig Street with babies at the rate of one a year until they were the proud parents of five girls. He was employed at Gulf Tile on Main Street in West Tampa in the accounting department and was enjoying both his work and his family.

Frances continued to spend the majority of her time between work as a teller with the International Bank of Tampa and being courted by Joe Caranante. She, of course, was a substitute mom to Gene and me when I was in town.

Gene was entering his junior year at Jesuit in the fall and continued dating the love of his life, Sylvia Tinnaro. He was becoming quite the academic scholar and was enjoying similar success on the football field. I planned on asking Coach Strange to include Gene on LSU's prospect list.

I continued working at the playground and enjoyed the advantage of engaging in unsanctioned, pre-camp conditioning drills prior to my departure.

I received from LSU a first-class airline ticket—Tampa to Baton Rouge. Out of curiosity and mild interest, I checked with the Greyhound bus line for their fare from Tampa to Baton Rouge. My interest swelled when I learned the difference was more than $100. I decided to make the switch, without realizing what a 720-mile bus trip was like. I had just made a big mistake.

My brother Gene waited with me at the Greyhound bus station until my bus departed at about 4:30 PM. For the first hour I actually enjoyed the ride, but after that it became boring, and in time, escalated to monotony. I had not realized that buses stop at every hint of a town. I was able to sleep on the bus but woke up each time we pulled into some *podunk* town. Many passengers were traveling between the smaller towns; therefore, each time we stopped there was quite a commotion with passengers getting off and on. When I arrived in Baton Rouge at 1:45 PM, I had been on the bus for twenty-one hours and was literally disoriented. I profited $105, or five dollars an hour. I was glad to have the extra cash, but I wouldn't do it again.

I was in tip-top shape when I reported to camp in Baton Rouge and was prepared, amongst other things, to run the obligatory mile in less than six and half minutes.

It was great seeing the guys again, but there was little time for socializing. The coaching staff was working diligently to prepare us for our opener against Texas A&M on Sept. 21st in the not so friendly (to our opponents) confines of Tiger Stadium. After several days of conditioning drills, we transitioned into our game plan versus the Aggies.

I learned, to my disappointment, I was targeted to be red-shirted for the season. "Red-shirt" is a term used in college sports describing a one-year deferment of game eligibility for the student athlete. The red-shirted player is allowed an additional year of eligibility in exchange for foregoing participation in actual games during the red-shirt season. My disappointment was not focused on being red-shirted, but that my services on the field were superior to several of the players targeted to play that season. In retrospect, I recognize two factors that contributed to this decision by the coaches: 1) my reputation and behavior off the field, and 2) my failure to recognize that the previous spring is when manpower decisions were formed. More than anything, my pride was hurt and I was embarrassed. I was learning that keeping my pride intact was my responsibility and not that of my coaches, teachers, or friends, and certainly not my girlfriend. The fact that a majority of LSU's top players, including many of my best friends, had been red-shirted and that Judy would be arriving in a few weeks soothed the pain.

A couple weeks before transporting Judy to Baton Rouge, Judy's parents purchased a 1963 Ford Thunderbird. This lemon-colored four-seater was Ford Motor Company's statement to the marketplace that it was serious about the sports/luxury market. It was truly a design marvel with all the amenities one could imagine.

They were motoring up the highway when Judy's dad noticed the oil indicator light on the dash flickering. It was a little concerning since they were now a couple of hours north of Tampa, but maybe it was just a loose connection, they hoped. The flickering persisted and they stopped at a service station in Lake City, Florida to have it checked. The mechanic was unsure as to the actual cause, but was, nonetheless, able to get the light to remain off by reseating the oil seals. They remained trouble-free for the remainder of the trip until they reached the outskirts of Baton Rouge and the oil indicator light began flickering again. Mr. Stallings was understandably perturbed and disappointed by the performance of this brand-new vehicle on its maiden voyage. Within walking distance of the midtown hotel in which they stayed was a service station with a qualified mechanic. Mr. Stallings left the vehicle there for an afternoon and the mechanic was successful in finding the cause and fixing it. Mr. Stallings was presented with a bill for less than $20, fuel top-off included.

It had been only a month since I had been with Judy and her family, but it was great to see them again, especially on my turf. I was proud to introduce them to my friends, especially Mr. Stallings, who represented to me the dad I had longed for since I was six years old.

We dined at Baton Rouge's premier restaurant, Bob and Jake's, which I had not been to since my first night in town a year earlier with Clifford Duke. Performing at Bob and Jake's that Saturday evening was national vocal recording group Frankie Vallie and The

Four Seasons, singing their classic hits including, "Big Girls Don't Cry" and "Can't Take My Eyes Off of You." Part of Vallie's routine included singing amongst the audience and seeking their participation. It was the best Baton Rouge had to offer, but not to be compared with the dining and entertainment available 75 miles away in Baton Rouge's big sister city, New Orleans. As was the case with Clifford that first evening a year ago, there were no ordering restrictions that evening or any time you ate with the Stallings. It was an enjoyable evening that capped off Judy's parents' short visit. Now that I have a daughter of my own, I realize the confidence her parents must have had with me because they were depositing their prize possession into my care. They had nothing to worry about. I was committed to and enjoyed taking care of Judy and she enjoyed being in my care.

That fall in Baton Rouge was nothing but fun for Judy and me. Judy quickly made friends with my friends and we enjoyed going on double dates with many of them. The couple we double dated with the most was Pat Screen and his girlfriend, Judy May Higgins. That's right, Judy Kay and Judy May. What made this arrangement special was that Judy Kay and Judy May became friends outside of our dating, so when Pat and I were not available, the two Judys would get together.

Judy May had a soft, but distinct southern drawl and I would always mimic her and Pat, who had a strong New Orleans accent. Pat was a jokester like me, but he couldn't find anything with which to needle Judy and me, that is, until one night when the four of us went out to dinner and movie. The movie was the classic horror film of the day, *Whatever Happened to Baby Jane?* starring Bette Davis and Joan Crawford. We were, indeed, scared by the movie and were recounting specific parts as we exited the theatre amongst the crowd when out of nowhere and for no apparent reason, Judy Kay fell to the sidewalk as if she had been struck by an assassin's bullet. I immediately came to her assistance, but because we were both laughing so hard, she had difficulty regaining her balance. As I attempted to help her back on her feet, she somehow lost her balance again, and through some awkward fumbling and grabbing, we were able to avert a second fall. Pat and Judy May were "holding their stomach" laughing about the mishap and it was soon apparent that Pat finally got what he was seeking. As expected, he would describe, with animation and detail, Judy's fall and my lame attempt to assist her to anyone who would listen.

Even though we went out with other couples, we felt most comfortable with Pat and Judy May. So comfortable was the relationship that Judy May (sorority sister of Tri Delta's local chapter) and Pat asked us to be their guest at Tri Delta's gala event of the year. Neither Judy nor I enjoyed formal events, but nonetheless, felt obliged to join them to what turned out to be a very enjoyable evening.

Another notable dating experience was with David Strange and his girlfriend(s). If you recall, David's father was LSU's chief recruiter, and as such, David and I (through our association), would have first crack at entertaining high school prospects on weekends. We were issued $100 per prospect for expenses such as eating, entertainment, etc. We became adept at determining which prospects required our undivided attention (high maintenance) from those who required very little of our attention (low maintenance). We, of course, preferred the latter and it often worked out that way. When we assessed a prospect as low maintenance, we would arrange a date for him and transport him and his date to the Bengal lounge, leaving instructions with the manager to keep an eye on our prospect and serve him and his date whatever they ordered and David and I would square up with him when we returned around midnight. Meanwhile, David and I would take our girlfriends out on the town and make a profit after expenses. Some of those prospects could drink a lot of beer, but at 25 cents/draft and one dollar/pitcher, we were assured of making a profit. Occasionally, Coach Strange would communicate to us the importance of signing a particular prospect and would remind us to focus on the mission at hand if we wanted to continue entertaining prospects. I don't recall ever losing a prospect David's father described as a must.

JFK

The date was November 22nd, 1963. The clock on my radio read 12:25 PM as I was leaving my dorm room to attend our regular Friday meeting at 12:30, when I heard a news bulletin on the radio reporting an assassination attempt on the life of President John F. Kennedy. I raised the volume on the radio and was joined by Mike Vincent who was also on his way to the meeting when he heard the news through my open door. The details were sketchy, but we listened to gain what information we could regarding this tragic event. A few minutes later we left for the meeting, which was already in progress as we entered the room. "Where in the hell have you all been?" asked Coach Mac.

I, obviously, had an air-tight response when I answered, "Coach, I would have been at the meeting in plenty of time, but I heard a news bulletin indicating President Kennedy had been shot." Normally, **any** kind of response would have been met with snickering from the team, but that was not the case this day.

Coach Mac was visibly shaken by my response when he called for a moment of silence out of respect for the tragedy regarding our President. He then limped back into our meeting by uttering, "Let's try to focus our attention on Tulane."

He proceeded with the meeting agenda, and within minutes, was interrupted by someone communicating to him the news I provided earlier. He told the team that President Kennedy was in serious condition in a Dallas hospital following an assassination attempt and some of tomorrow's football games were being cancelled. Shortly thereafter it was reported that the President had died. Coach Mac said, even though it would be difficult, we would continue to prepare as previously planned until if and when the status of our game changed. It did not, and we continued preparations amidst a very somber atmosphere.

We met the Tulane Green Wave the following evening in Tiger Stadium before 55,000 mourning fans who witnessed a 20 to 0 Tiger victory while many listened to radio accounts of the President's assassination. It was the first time in many years Tiger Stadium was not filled to capacity for an LSU game.

After the game, Pat Screen and Judy May Higgins, Walter Johnson and his girlfriend, and Judy and I, traveled to New Orleans for the weekend as planned prior to the President's assassination. Pat's parents were out of town and we had the use of their comfortable home in the heart of New Orleans. Pat, keenly aware of my interest in food, had been raving about a delicacy I had never tried: artichoke hearts. Pat's parents had thoughtfully prepared a generous supply of delicious and "meaty" artichokes with an olive oil-based sauce as accompaniment. As hors d'oeuvres to our late-night snack, Pat, Walter, and I went through the supply with zeal, not disappointed at all that the girls displayed little interest in the artichokes.

Walter was already watching the news coverage of the assassination when I woke up and joined him in the TV room. Before long, Judy joined us and said that Judy May and Walter's girlfriend were still in deep sleep. The three of us witnessed what was an unbelievable sight as we saw Jack Ruby pull a pistol from his pocket and shoot Lee Harvey Oswald on nationwide TV. TV coverage in that day was not near as sophisticated as it later became; even so, they continued to show the tape over and over from every angle available to determine how security had been breached. Almost immediately, there was supposition that Jack Ruby had ties to, and was acting at the direction of, the mob. Our nation had been rocked by the assassination attempt on President Kennedy, and the murder of Lee Harvey

Oswald added to the nation's shock. Even though the mood was somber, we enjoyed the balance of the weekend before returning to Baton Rouge.

Two weeks later, Pat and I were in New Orleans again, this time for the Southeastern regional meeting of the Fellowship of Christian Athletes (FCA). From my viewpoint, Pat was a logical choice, but I still can't believe Pat was given approval to select me as the co-representative for our team. Pat told me it indicated that the coaches had recognized that I was making a turnaround, but I said they just couldn't find anyone else. Nonetheless, we had a nice time meeting and interacting with representatives from other teams even though we were in a different spiritual world. These FCA people openly spoke of Christ as if He was in the room with us. Others gave their testimony of their encounter with Christ and how their life was changed subsequent to the encounter. When asked at our table when we met Christ, Pat and I both responded in grade school from our parents and the nuns who taught us religion. This response initiated a peculiar look on the faces of our tablemates. Having attended church with Judy provided me an insight into what was going on, but Pat was experiencing the culture shock I had experienced a couple of years earlier. On the way back to Baton Rouge, I explained to Pat that these people were okay but could not answer his question as to why we didn't know any of these kinds of Christians on our team.

YULETIDE SEASON

Geraldine again asked if I would be in charge of finances for the Christmas trip home and I gladly accommodated her. With the addition of Judy, one of the regulars had to be eliminated. I suggested Jack Feiner and Geraldine agreed, asking me to inform Jack.

Jack was now certain that I didn't like him, which was not accurate; we simply didn't have room for everyone.

Geraldine, Jeanie Feiner, Judy and I, drove to New Orleans to pick up Dennis Decidue and Anthony Traviesa before heading to Tampa.

Because Judy was with me in Baton Rouge, trips home did not have the same appeal they once did. Of course, I always enjoyed seeing my family and friends, but I was ready to head back to Baton Rouge before the Christmas holiday was over.

Living conditions on Lemon Street were no better, and probably worse. Situations like ours seldom improve on their own and generally deteriorate. Luis continued to smile when I was around, but it was clear to me it was contrived.

I had been yearning for my own transportation for some time and was considering taking Vince Russo's offer to take his pickup truck to Baton Rouge. But before I approached Uncle Vince with my plan, I visited a couple of car lots to see what my $650 would buy. I felt very uncomfortable dealing with used car salesmen and asked Mr. Stallings to join me in my search. Our first visit was to Bill Currie Ford on Florida Avenue about two blocks north of 26th Avenue.

Amongst other vehicles, the salesman pointed out a low-mileage 1963 Ford Falcon coupe. It was a standard shift, stripped-down model and the asking price was $699. I liked the vehicle and was trying to figure out where I could get the additional amount required. Mr. Stallings suggested we visit a couple of other dealers before deciding on a vehicle, but

I told him I had already done so and had not seen a vehicle I liked as much as this one. Then, Mr. Stallings took me to school on buying a car. "I'll tell you what we'll do," he told the salesmen, "if you will replace the two rear tires and add a heater, we will write you a check for $600, all taxes and other expenses included."

The salesman provided the standard line, "I don't know if the boss will accept that offer, but let me go talk with him about it."

"Take your time, we'll be at my house just two blocks from here and you can call us at 229–2263."

"Can you just wait here a moment, Mr. Stallings?" asked the salesman, not wanting to commit the cardinal sin of allowing the prospect to leave the lot.

"We'll wait here a couple of minutes, but then were leaving."

Within a couple minutes, the salesman returned and said, "You've got a deal if you'll pay for the license tag and transfer of title." Mr. Stallings' facial expression and body language made me think he was ready to say, "No deal," when I asked if I could speak to him a moment. I told him I was planning on getting a license tag in Louisiana because their fee was $6 for two years versus $14 a year in Florida. He queried me about requiring a permanent address to register an automobile, but I told him I had all that worked out.

He then told the salesman, "Replace those two bad tires with good ones and have a heater installed and we'll come back with a check for $600 even." The salesman asked for a deposit and Mr. Stallings told him to get the car ready and we'll come back with the whole amount when he calls. The salesman said he would need his manager's approval. I told Mr. Stallings to go home and I would wait for the manager's answer because I wanted to stay behind to get a closer look at my car anyhow.

I was excited about owning my first vehicle, and even though my Falcon was as plain as they come, I was as proud as if I owned a Ferrari. I showed the car to my friends and family and was excited about showing it to my buddies in Louisiana. My brother Gene was also excited about my car and used it a couple of nights before I left.

BACK TO BATON ROUGE

What an adventure it was for Judy and me to take a trip from Tampa to Baton Rouge on our own. About an hour south of Tallahassee, I told Judy I was tired and wanted to sleep in the back seat. She told me she clearly understood the directions I gave her regarding where to turn in Tallahassee but that if she had any questions she should wake me for clarification. "If you don't take U.S. Highway 90 West in Tallahassee, we'll be heading to Georgia, which we don't want to do," I said, as I tried to position my six-foot two, 240-lb. body in the back seat of that Falcon. She told me to sleep well as everything was under control. Every few minutes, I would awaken and ask about our position. The last time I asked, she responded, "I'm not exactly sure, but I think we're very close to the Georgia state line." With that bit of information, I popped up in the back seat and tried to figure out where we were. She was correct. We were less than three miles from Georgia. I took the wheel from there and maneuvered through some back roads before meeting Highway 90 about seventy miles west of Tallahassee.

My friends in Baton Rouge were impressed with my new vehicle. Since less than 20 percent of team members had a vehicle, having my own was extra special.

I contacted Guy DiCharry since he previously offered me the use of his home address as my own if I wanted to register a vehicle. I was calling mostly out of courtesy, because if it was a problem with him I had several options including Ray Loup, David Poché, Doug Moreau, and David Strange.

Guy said it would be no inconvenience whatsoever and he would be pleased if I would use his address. Additionally, he informed me, as an investment, he recently purchased a service station just off the LSU campus on Nicholson Drive. He said that he was renaming the station "Tiger Texaco," had just hired an experienced mechanic, and would appreciate it if I would trade there myself and also tell my friends. I told him I would trade only at "Tiger Texaco" and would be happy to tell my friends. He then said something I considered peculiar. "Mondy, I'd like you to charge your purchases because it would give me an idea of how my manager operates." I didn't quite understand what he meant and did not like charging purchases, but nonetheless, I agreed to accommodate his request. The reason I did not like charging purchases was because my money management system was not sophisticated enough to include credit. My system was basically this: if I had money in my pocket, I could do whatever that money afforded. If I had little or no money, I had to apply the brakes on spending until I could get some. I managed to stay out of financial trouble with that system and was reluctant to change, but decided to charge my purchases to accommodate Guy.

A few weeks went by and I charged an oil change and a fill up at Tiger Texaco, saw a couple of my friends there, and knew Boo was doing his business there. Every time I made a charge purchase, I would place that amount of cash in an envelope in my desk drawer in my room. I didn't like keeping cash in my room, so the next time I needed gas I paid cash. The following day I received a call from Guy and he asked me how things were going. I told him everything was fine and that I had been to his station a few times and was impressed with his manager Emile. That's when I realized that they were running a tight ship at Tiger Texaco. Guy informed me Emile told him I had paid cash for my last fill-up and that he would appreciate it if I would charge *all* my purchases. I told him the reason I paid cash was because I already had a couple of charges and didn't want the charges to get too far ahead of me. He said he understood, but to please charge future purchases and not to worry about them getting too far ahead of me. I thought that was rather presumptuous on his part, but didn't think too much of it.

While Judy and I were at the DiCharry home for dinner one evening, I brought my envelope with the cash and my list of what I had purchased at Tiger Texaco. That's when Guy informed me that he had no intentions of sending me a bill, and he and Cynthia wanted to do this to help out because they realized that finances during college years could be tight. Now everything he had told me regarding charging purchases at Tiger Texaco made sense. I told him I felt uncomfortable with this arrangement and did not want to abuse our relationship. He explained that he had no concern about me abusing the relationship and knowing the kind of person I was gave him comfort in making the offer in the first place. I was both flattered and humbled by Guy and Cynthia's graciousness and felt as I had witnessed another example of human kindness.

THE BIG EASY

Early in the school year, Pat Screen, Judy May, Judy, and I had planned a trip to New Orleans for Mardi Gras. When the time came, Coach Mac strongly suggested that the team as a whole should stay away from New Orleans during Mardi Gras and annunciated several reasons in support of his request, all of which were correct and sound. Nonetheless, sound reasoning is not what 19-year-olds base decisions on, and off to New Orleans we went in my powder blue Ford Falcon.

"There are 2 million people in the city of New Orleans today, twice our normal population," said the radio announcer as we drove toward the French quarter. We kicked off "Fat Tuesday" with chicory coffee and beignets at Café du Monde in the heart of New Orleans' French quarter before a sightseeing tour led by Pat. Pat was the third generation in his family to be raised in New Orleans and he was very proud of his city. Likewise, New Orleans was very proud of their native son, who was a celebrity throughout Louisiana, but especially in New Orleans. Pat's dad, a partner in a prestigious law firm in the Big Easy, arranged for us to view the parade from atop a building in the Vieux Carre. It was a terrific spot from which to watch the parade, but it was a bit confining, so we chose to walk the streets with the maddening crowd.

As evening drew near, the effects of alcohol combined with Mardi Gras' atmosphere of conviviality, began to manifest itself in various ways. Women were not only baring their breasts to gain favor with those throwing beads and doubloons but it was uncommon to travel a short distance in the French Quarter without witnessing an altercation or at least the threat of one. As we turned a corner, I noticed the New Orleans police dealing with a reveler out of control. As I studied the situation further, I noticed that the reveler was none other than my former Jesuit classmate, Jack Gonzalez. The more he resisted their efforts to cuff and place him in the paddy wagon, the more they used their nightsticks on his shins, head, and back. His nose and one ear were bloodied as he sat cuffed to the metal bench in the paddy wagon until they accumulated a full load before going to the police station. I learned later that he attended Mississippi State University, and like us, was in New Orleans for the festivities. That evening we visited several nightclubs on Bourbon Street, which featured talented jazz musicians including Al Hirt and Pete Fountain. We then closed the evening as we began it with coffee and beignets at Café du Monde.

Springtime in Baton Rouge was great. On Sundays, Judy and I would go to church and then we would picnic at the University Lakes on boxed lunches prepared by the cafeteria staff at Broussard. It was Judy's idea to go to church and occasionally I would test her resolve by saying I wanted to go to the Catholic Church, also. She never complained about going to both services, so I dropped the tactic and we generally attended First Baptist of Baton Rouge. After our picnics, we allocated time to study. We took an American history course together and Judy would take copious notes while I attempted to distract her throughout the lecture. Consequently, I heard very little of the lecture and she would tutor me. What made her task difficult was keeping me awake, and when I was awake, keeping me focused on the subject matter. Whether we were at the Lakes or in the lobby of her dormitory, I would attempt to interject fun into the tutoring. I was the poster child for Attention Deficit Disorder before it was tagged as ADD.

Tony and Janet unknowingly provided us endless entertainment. We did not know the couple's names but we named them Tony and Janet after the Hollywood couple Tony Curtis and Janet Leigh, a hot item in 1963. Before we sat down to study, we would browse the lobby for a seat with a view of them. Like us, they must have been on a tight budget because they were in the lobby almost every evening. If they were not there when we began studying, we would sit in an area that allowed us a view of all who entered the lobby and then would relocate to an area where we could watch them. It is hard to describe in words the entertainment value this couple provided but I'll give it a try. While attempting to study they would distract each other constantly (It would be like me dating me). Their method of distraction was the essence of their attraction. First of all, they were oblivious to the fact they were entertaining other couples and that's what made them unique. One would initiate changing positions so they would be facing each other and then proceed with a series of "sweet nothings". These "sweet nothings" were communicated in a light whisper with no more than eight to ten inches between their faces which were engaged in an intense focus on each other that tuned out the rest of the world. The light whisper would then fade into mouthing the message with exaggerated facial expressions and often complemented with a theatrical "pawing motion" mimicking a tiger or lion pursuing his mate. The receiving member of this duo would then reciprocate in like fashion. Believe me, it was a riot, and Judy and I can't help but laugh when we reminisce many years later.

TAMPA VISITORS

I was pleased to receive a call from Aunt Louisa informing me that she and Tanya would be visiting Loyola University in New Orleans as Tanya gathered facts regarding colleges she was considering after graduating from Plant High School. She asked if Judy and I would be able to visit with them during this trip. I wanted to see them and I did not want to disappoint her with the news that New Orleans was currently "off-limits" because of a recent incident involving three of our players, so I noted the particulars of the trip, and at the appointed time, Judy and I met them at their French quarter hotel.

We had a delightful time with them sightseeing and walking the streets of New Orleans and catching up with old times. We ate raw oysters on the half shell at Felix's Oyster Bar and then enjoyed an excellent meal at the Commander's Palace. Later, we visited several jazz spots and made the obligatory stop at the French quarter's most famous nightspot, Pat O'Brien's. We, of course, capped off the evening with chicory coffee and beignets at Café du Monde.

Aunt Louisa planned to rent me a room and have Judy spend the evening in their room. I did not want her to go through the extra expense, but she insisted.

The following day we were looking forward to brunch at Brennan's. After waiting the typical 45 minutes, we were seated and were soon partaking of their extensive and exquisite menu. We were enjoying the meal and each other's company when I felt a hand on my shoulder accompanied by the salutation, "Hello Florees, isn't the food here delicious?" I looked up to see who belonged to the hand on my shoulder and returned a smile to LSU's athletic director, "Gentleman Jim" Corbett (The moniker "Gentleman Jim" was befitting this man who was a true southern gentleman). I immediately stood up, shook his hand, and introduced him to Aunt Louisa, Tanya, and Judy, clearly stating that my purpose for being in New Orleans was to facilitate the trip for our guests from Tampa. I recognized there was a chance that Coach Mac could learn of my whereabouts through this encounter, so I wanted to make sure "Gentleman Jim" would articulate "why" I was in New Orleans in the event the conversation ever took place. We concluded pleasantries and Mr. Corbett made his way to his table. Out of the corner of my eye, I followed him to an alcove off the next room where he joined three other men, one of which I immediately recognized as Coach Mac. I knew my goose was cooked and was now trying to figure how to keep it from being overdone. I thought about saying I was with Pat Screen, since residents of New Orleans were allowed to visit home with prior approval, but I didn't know if Pat was in Baton Rouge or elsewhere and was in no position to take the risk. I then thought about saying my aunt and cousin were in town because of an unexpected death in the family, but remembered I had just told "Gentleman Jim" that they were in town visiting colleges. It was beginning to look like the truth was my best route. About then, Coach Mac looked over his left shoulder and waved which I took as acknowledgment that "Gentleman Jim" had communicated my presence to him. We were through with our meal and Aunt Louisa was reviewing the bill before paying, so I decided to show my respect by going to their table to say goodbye.

"Hello Coach," I said, "Did Mr. Corbett tell you I'm in town to show my aunt and cousin around Loyola University."

"He did," said Coach Mac as he turned toward the guests at the table and said, "I'd like you to meet one of our players, Armando Florees, from Tampa, Florida." With that introduction, I reached to shake the hands of two men who were introduced to me as Mr. Pat Screen and a representative of the New Orleans Tiger Club.

"I'm pleased to meet you Florees, I've heard a lot about you from (his son) Pat," said Mr. Screen in his combination New Orleans/Irish accent.

"Yes sir, Mr. Screen. Pat and I are good friends. We Jesuit guys have to stick together," I responded, remembering that Pat had told me his dad was a big Jesuit of New Orleans booster, while at the same time thanking God I didn't tell Coach Mac I was in town with Pat visiting his family.

"He tells me you'll be visiting with him when he comes home after spring practice," said barrister Screen.

"Yes, sir. That's the plan," I responded, never having discussed going home with Pat.

"We are expecting big things from Florees," said Coach Mac, which was news to me but nice to hear causing me to wonder if he meant the comment or was just providing me with *ear candy*.

Nonetheless, I excused myself after telling Mr. Screen and the other gentlemen how much I enjoyed meeting them and told Mr. Screen I would make sure I told Pat that I finally had the chance to meet his dad.

With that accomplished, I shook both the hand of "Gentleman Jim" and Coach Mac while indicating I would see them in Baton Rouge, to which Coach Mac replied, "Yes, you will."

As we exited Brennan's, I was confident the matter was handled as well as possible.

We spent the balance of the day sightseeing and reminiscing before Judy and I headed back to Baton Rouge. We exchanged hugs and kisses with the Russos. They expressed how much they enjoyed our visit, and Judy and I returned the sentiment.

FRIENDS

One reason I had a propensity to sleep while Judy tutored me was because I was trying to do too many things. In addition to carrying sixteen semester hours and trying to entertain my girlfriend, I was engaged in off-season "voluntary" workouts. These rigorous workouts were, of course, mandatory. They included activities such as isometric training, weightlifting, agility and conditioning drills, wrestling, etc. These activities took place in the bowels of Tiger Stadium, secluded from any outsider's view or knowledge.

One day while engaged in a weightlifting session with my teammates, someone mentioned that Billy Cannon and Jim Taylor were coming to work out at our facility. Billy Cannon and Jim Taylor were marquee names in the NFL and were legends to the LSU faithful because of their heroics as members of LSU's great teams in the '50s that culminated with Billy Cannon leading the 1958 team to becoming National Champions. When David Poche' nudged me on the shoulder to tell me he just saw Jim Taylor, I began looking around for a glimpse myself and neglected my duty as "spotter" for the individual who was bench pressing at the time. While I continued to gaze, I heard someone gasping and looked down to see it was the person for whom I was "spotting." I quickly lifted the weights off his neck, and though he was never in grave danger, he was embarrassed by our teammates laughing. That, coupled with an environment overflowing with testosterone, motivated him to lash out a couple of expletives my way. I had already apologized but accepted his reaction because of the embarrassment he had just experienced. However, Dough (short for "dough belly") Smith, encouraged by his good friend Jacque Jones, pushed the issue farther than called for forcing me to tell Dough "enough is enough." When he continued with his tirade, I approached him intending to put my fist at the source of his yelling. At that time, in an effort to keep me from getting into further trouble with Coach Mac (I was currently a member of the 600 (disciplinary) club), David Strange and David Poché attempted to restrain me by each grabbing an arm, creating for Dough the cowardly opportunity to punch me square in the mouth, which he did. I was able to land a couple of solid punches to his head before players and coaches separated us, but I clearly received the worst end of a contest, which, under normal circumstances, would have been no contest. My two front teeth were knocked back toward the roof of my mouth, held from falling by a few strands of flesh. My top lip was split open to beneath my nose and was bleeding profusely. I was handed a towel by assistant trainers, Tracy Ladd and Herman Lang, and was escorted to Doc (Marty) Broussard, our team's head trainer.

Doc performed what I consider a minor miracle. He placed the teeth in their correct position after giving me a shot for pain in both my upper gum and lip. He then fashioned a piece of sponge rubber into a crude mouthpiece which he told me to bite on with mild pressure for about 30 minutes. He then proceeded to stitch my split lip to which he later applied an icepack to minimize swelling. He told me I had a slim chance of keeping my natural teeth but that if I were to lose them, he knew of a dentist who did a wonderful job with permanent false teeth. He said I would know within a month if my gum tissue would accept my natural teeth. He also said that those two teeth would be extremely sensitive for the next couple of weeks and provided me with pain pills for that eventuality. I didn't like the way all this sounded, but I recognized that I didn't have much choice in the matter.

I didn't feel much like studying that evening, but I had plans with Judy to meet at her dorm at 6 PM for a tutoring session. I decided not to tell her in advance about my injury and called her from the lobby phone when I arrived. I had a bandage across my entire upper lip, which was now severely swollen. I waited by the elevators for her descent. When the elevator doors opened and we looked at each other face-to-face, I attempted to produce a smile hoping to alleviate any concern she might have after viewing my condition. As I smiled, she returned a "courtesy smile" and walked past me into the lobby. I called her name and recognizing my voice she turned around looking past me and then at me saying, "Mondy, is that you?" As I responded, "Yes", she realized it was me and automatically changed gears from girlfriend to mother. In a very loving and compassionate manner, she wanted to know what happened. We decided to go out for ice cream in place of our tutoring session as I told her the story.

I was happy to return to Broussard because I was tired and wanted to get to sleep early for a change.

MISSED OPPORTUNITY

"Flo, wake up. Flo, wake up," urged Boo.

"What time is it?" I responded to his hurried attempt to wake me.

"It's ten to 5 and I'm going to Thibodaux to get married. I'd like you to be my best man."
"Boo, we've only been sleeping 2½ hours and we got a meeting at noon."

"I know and we'll be back by noon."

"Boo, can we go next week?" I asked half sleeping, half awake.

"No Flo, it's all set up and I've got to go now," said Boo while shaving. "C'mon Flo, I promise you we'll be back by noon."

Thinking I was having a bad dream or that Boo was kidding, I responded "Count me in next week," as I wrapped the pillow around my ears to muffle the sound of Boo's electric shaver. Things quieted down and I returned to the deep sleep I was enjoying before the incident.

My alarm was set for 11:15 so I could grab lunch before our noon meeting. I met Joe Labruzzo in the cafeteria line and he asked rhetorically, "You know Boo is in Thibodaux getting married this morning?"

"I thought he was kidding or I was having a nightmare when he woke me up this morning saying something about getting married but he must have been serious. How do you know about it?"

"Because he came to our room at about 5:15 AM and got Don (Schwab) to go with him."

I started to feel bad because I knew I had disappointed Boo, and to make matters worse, I knew Boo would have joined me if the roles were reversed. It was simply a case where I failed to gauge the seriousness of Boo's request.

Shortly thereafter, Boo and Don Schwab arrived at Broussard with a tired but happy look on their faces. They came to our table and provided detail of the morning's event, during which he told Joe and me that Don acted as his best man. This news made me feel even worse since Don was beaming with pride at being selected for this honor by our good friend, Boo.

On the way to the meeting, we discussed the importance of keeping the news of Boo and Linda's nuptial quiet since it was in violation of one of Coach Mac's ordinances. Specifically, Coach Mac strongly suggested (required) players considering marriage to gain his approval before the blessed event. This should have been achievable since Linda would remain in Thibodaux until Boo returned for the fall practice.

Before we entered the meeting room, I congratulated Boo again and expressed to him how bad I felt because I hadn't recognized the seriousness of his request seven hours earlier. In typical fashion for Boo, he put his arm around me as we walked into the meeting room and graciously said, "Don't worry about it. I understand. The only thing I had to explain to Linda was why Don was there when I told her earlier in the week you would be with me." He didn't intend it that way, but that comment made me feel even worse. I almost told him I wish he would have told me earlier in the week, but I knew it would have sounded like an excuse.

SPRING TRAINING

March 15th arrived and I was in tip-top shape and determined to make a good showing at spring practice. With Judy at LSU, I was getting into far less trouble with the exception of missing curfews. However, I had achieved only negligible improvement with regard to communicating and relating with the coaching staff, particularly Coach Mac.

Nonetheless, I enjoyed a very productive spring, grading well in Saturday scrimmages, and I was looking forward to the spring game. We practiced from 3:30 to about 6:15 every Tuesday, Wednesday, and Thursday afternoon and scrimmaged every Saturday from 10 AM till Coach Mac decided (usually 1 PM or thereabouts). On Mondays, Wednesdays, and Fridays, I had a class that met from 2:00 to 2:55 PM. Judy and I both had free time before 2:00, thus, we would meet during that time as love birds do. On a particular Wednesday, Judy and I walked to Tiger Stadium so I could get a look at the day's practice schedule. As we walked toward the Student Union Building for a cup of coffee before my 2 PM class, I noticed Coach Mac driving his car. He saw Judy and me walking on the sidewalk and smiled, nodding his head in acknowledgment. I kidded Judy telling her I was glad he saw us because it probably improved my image with him figuring he probably assumed I would be dating a "high-yella" instead of the Southern Belle.

After class, I hustled over to the stadium and was hurriedly getting dressed for practice with a couple of other guys who also had 2 PM classes. We gave it our best effort and arrived on the practice field about 30 seconds after the beginning whistle which caused you to stand out because the other hundred guys have a 30-second lead on you for the opening 440-yard run. After the run, we lined up for calisthenics and those of us who were late were questioned aloud to make a point to the rest of the team. When Coach Mac asked me why I was late, I told him it was because of my 2 PM class. He rudely discounted my response and said in a public manner, "Don't try to BS me Florees, I saw you walkin round campus holding hands with your blond girlfriend after 2 PM."

In typical fashion I quipped back, "That's an easy one to check out Coach, my professor will tell you I was in class from 2:00 to 2:50 PM."

"I don't need to speak to your professor, Florees. I know what I saw," answered Coach Mac in his *don't argue with me* tone. I knew from experience not to argue with him, but my mouth continued to run ahead of my brain. I was deflated by our exchange and began to wonder if my efforts were being recognized.

Judy's parents came to Baton Rouge for a visit during spring practice and I was excited about the possibility of Mr. Stallings attending our Saturday scrimmage. Practices were closed to the public, but when Mr. Stallings indicated he was interested in seeing our scrimmage, I made arrangements for his entrance into the stadium. I had an outstanding scrimmage that day (supported by the coaches' grade of my performance), sparking Ray Loup's comment to me, "You oughta see about Judy getting her parents to stay a little longer." It really does make a difference when you're doing something for someone who's important to you.

After the scrimmage, we traveled to New Orleans for dinner and a night out on the town even though New Orleans was off-limits for players during the season and during spring practice. I didn't bother asking permission because I didn't think Coach Mac would grant me permission and because I thought the chance of getting into trouble with Mr. and Mrs. Stallings was nil.

Mr. and Mrs. Stallings were in their 40s, even though Judy and I thought they were old.

They enjoyed music and expressed interest in hearing Pete Fountain and his jazz ensemble. We had dinner at the Elmwood Plantation, a first-class restaurant with a reputation of being controlled by local mafia boss, Carlos Marcello. The ambience was exquisite, the Caesar salad was excellent, and the prime rib melted in your mouth. We then visited a couple of jazz joints in the French quarter before ending the evening at Pete Fountain's club on Bourbon Street.

The next morning, we enjoyed brunching at Brennan's (where weeks earlier I had experienced the unplanned encounter with Coach Mac) and did some sightseeing, including Jackson Square and some of the nation's oldest cemeteries. Because New Orleans is below sea level, burial plots are above ground, and some are quite elaborate and interesting with regard to epitaphs and dates. We then traveled back to Baton Rouge in plenty of time for my 6 PM meeting.

Mr. and Mrs. Stallings stayed a couple of additional days before returning to Tampa via the Smokey Mountains.

The remaining week of spring practice went very well, and I was pumped about the Purple and Gold game because Judy would be in the stands. My performance that Saturday evening was at a high level and I was looking forward to our campaign for the fall of '64.

NO INSURANCE

A peculiar occurrence regarding a new coach provided an interesting incident during spring training.

The news about a coach from the University of Alabama transferring to LSU was buzzing around the locker room, but I didn't give it too much attention knowing I would get the "inside scoop" from David Strange.

Rumor had it that Coach (Pete) Johnson's illicit relationship in the small town of Tuscaloosa, Alabama had been exposed and the incident was casting unwelcome attention and pressure on the University of Alabama's highly-regarded football program and on Alabama's most revered citizen and dean of college coaches, Paul "Bear" Bryant.

Apparently, Coach Bryant's solution to the problem was to export Coach Johnson. Coach Mac was a disciple of Coach Bryant, having played for him at the University of Kentucky, and agreed to add Coach Johnson to the LSU staff hoping to lower the pressure in Tuscaloosa.

David confirmed the rumor along with some inside information. Additionally, because I had an automobile, David passed along the warning Coach Strange had given him not to loan Coach Johnson his vehicle under any circumstances. Associated with Coach Johnson's troubles in Tuscaloosa were DWI (driving while intoxicated) arrests, a couple of which involved auto accidents. I thanked David for the tip, even though I could not imagine Coach Johnson, or any coach for that matter, asking to borrow a player's car.

I actually liked Coach Johnson, though his behavior was a bit peculiar. He was intense on the field and gave the impression he was interested in "performance only." I welcomed that attitude and got along fine with him. There was, however, a tactic of Coach Johnson I loathed: he was a "yeller." We already had a "yeller," (Coach Peavey), and I anticipated that the addition of another "yeller" would add misery to our workouts. I was not disappointed. Sometimes, they yelled at the same time and it was difficult determining which one to tune out. They sounded like mating cockatoos on steroids. In addition to his intensity and yelling, the fact Coach Johnson wore a wool Alabama "letter jacket" with a towel rolled up under the collar during practice each day (regardless of the high humidity and hot temperature not atypical in south Louisiana during the spring), and you have a situation that could cause a person to vomit, which is exactly what he did after each practice session. We would look over our shoulders as we headed for the locker room to witness this strange occurrence each day.

One Friday evening, David Strange and a couple of guys were visiting in my room when we heard a knock on the door. As the door opened, there stood Coach Johnson with a look on his face that motivated two of my visitors to depart leaving David and me in the room with the uninvited and unexpected coach.

"Floorees, I need to borrow your car," uttered Coach Johnson, in an authoritative tone, misusing the authority associated with his position. David looked at me in such a way as to require no words to transmit his thoughts.

David excused himself from the room as I responded, "Coach, I was planning on using my car this evening, but I'll be happy to drive you anywhere you want to go and pick you up when you're ready to return."

You would have thought I'd questioned his mother's virtue as his face turned red, the veins in his neck expanded, and in a controlled yell, he said, "I'm not looking for a damn cab, Floorees. I need a car and I want to use yours. I'm sure you can hook up with one of your friends for tonight."

I was developing responses as I listened and came up with the following response, which seemed reasonable to me but lame to him. "Coach," I said, "there's another problem I didn't want to bore you with. My mother told me I am the only one covered on the automobile's insurance policy, and therefore, no one else is allowed to drive my car. But coach, I'll still be happy to drive you wherever you need to go."

"Bull sh*t, Floorees, to hell with you and your car" he said as he abruptly left my room.

Coach Johnson lived in Broussard Hall, so I waited a few minutes before walking to David's room where he was waiting to hear how things went. David congratulated me on how I handled the situation but laughed and commented on how he would have loved seeing Coach Johnson' face when I gave him the story about the insurance coverage.

"I didn't even know you had insurance, Flo."

"I don't."

David laughed harder.

The next morning, the breakfast line was so long that it led into the foyer of Broussard Hall. That was not uncommon for Saturday morning because the entire squad, less some non-returning seniors, were all eating breakfast at the same time in preparation for Saturday's scrimmage.

The grapevine had some "late news" as information was passed from person to small group to person until it finally reached us. Remi Prudhomme turned to us with a telling smile and said, "Coach Johnson borrowed Danny LeBlanc's car last night and wrapped it around a tree by the Lakes early this morning."

I glanced toward David and received his *what did I tell you* look before passing the information to those behind me in line. Throughout breakfast, I had several friends pat me on the back and utter, "Nice decision last night," with a smile on their face.

I later learned that Coach Johnson had continued to ask for the use of a car until he finally gained approval from Danny. Danny's late-model and sporty Pontiac LeMans was totaled, as Coach Johnson, who was also totaled, walked away with a few minor bumps and bruises and a DWI citation.

Coach Johnson attended practice that Saturday and participated with his duties as if nothing had happened the preceding evening. He even vomited after practice.

Coach Johnson was a likable individual despite the fact that he had some serious issues.

CONGRATULATIONS

On one of the last weekends before summer break, a group of us organized a levee party (Louisiana's version of a beach party). The news of this event spread around and we had a group of sixty to seventy people at this gathering on the banks of the Mississippi River. It was an enjoyable time because of the people attending, but the Gulf beaches of Florida, it was not.

As the day wore on, the sun acted as a catalyst to decisions already influenced by Bud, Jax, and Pearl, and guys began to contemplate swimming across the mighty Mississippi. I didn't require the influence of beer to make a stupid decision; I could do it naturally. After several attempted the feat without success, I decided the time was right to demonstrate my skills at negotiating the currents of the famous river. I estimated the distance across the river to be about 4/10ths mile, which is no problem for the average swimmer; the challenge was dealing with the fierce currents. Judy attempted to convince me that this was not a good idea, but emotion prevailed.

I jumped into the muddy water and swam the African crawl for about fifty yards before transitioning to the sidestroke. Changing from side to side with the sidestroke was the most efficient way to navigate myself to the other side. The mighty flow of the current altered the directness of my anticipated route. Nonetheless, I persisted. I was becoming tired but not concerned because I felt I could dog paddle with the current and eventually be able to reach shore at a bend in the river. On shore, some were cheering and some were laughing, but all were having a good time with the exception of Judy. As I reached the midpoint of the river, I was very tired but maintained my determination to make it across. As I continued down river, my friends looked smaller and smaller and I lost sight of Judy in the crowd. I alternated swim strokes until I was about twenty yards from shore when I adopted the backstroke to emote laughter from the loyal few who followed my progress. I was exhausted when I reached the other side and did not look forward to seeing Judy, because I correctly anticipated that she was upset with my childish decision to swim across the river. She joined Ray Loup and David Poché as they drove across the bridge to retrieve me. She attempted to muffle her voice, but Ray and David knew she was upset by this reckless act and was communicating her feelings.

When we returned to the party, René Patterson made an announcement to a few of us that he and his girlfriend, Marcely LeNette, had been married since February and that she was with child. People began doing the math and privately questioned the February date, but let me again emphasize, privately. We congratulated 6 ft. 7, 265-lb. René and his wife, Marcely LeNette, when someone asked the magic question, "Rene', does Coach Mac know about this?"

"No, he doesn't, and I was just going to ask your opinion on how I should handle this with him." Many opinions were offered, and he later asked mine when we were alone. I told him I was certain Coach Mac would not impose the normal sentence for this infraction (dismissal from the squad) and the worse situation he would face, in my opinion, would be to be re-enrolled into the 600 club.

René told a few of us that he was meeting with Coach Mac on a particular afternoon and we were waiting at the dining hall to hear Coach Mac's reaction. René had been named to the all-SEC team the previous season and the coaches were expecting great things from him in the fall. This made for an interesting scenario, since previous offenders were kicked off the team. René walked into the dining hall and joined us to share the results of his meeting.

"René, I wish you would have told Dorothy Fay (Coach's wife) and me earlier because we would have and will give you and Marcely a wedding gift," René quoted Coach Mac as saying. That generated a tremendous roar of laughter from our group as several of us repeated the quote mimicking Coach Mac.

"René, were you invited to the 600 club?" I asked.

"He didn't say anything about it."

That response generated much laughter.

Rather than learning a lesson, this was merely confirmation of a lesson I learned earlier in my life: Special people get special treatment. I believe that's the way it should be, and I would not want it any different.

The 1963/64 school year was great, due in large part to Judy's company. It was time to depart to Tampa for the summer.

Judy and I had accumulated so much "stuff," that I had to purchase a "roof rack" for my Falcon to transport everything back. We thoroughly enjoyed the trip back, listening to music and reminiscing, but mostly being together.

SUMMER of '64

Judy had been so busy at LSU that she opted not to work this summer. This option was not available to me, so once again, I spent the summer as a playground director. This summer, however, I lobbied for and was assigned to West Pines playground, 1½ blocks from my home on Lemon Street. The proximity to my home allowed me some advantages not available elsewhere. For example, I was able to leave my most valuable asset, my Ford Falcon, in my garage shielded from the summer sun's scorching effect and I was able to lunch and take a power nap within the flexible one-hour allotted.

The biggest news around the Flores household was my sister's engagement to Joseph Paul Caranante and their upcoming wedding scheduled for August 9, 1964.

Joe sold advertising time for a local radio station and my sister continued in the banking business with the International Bank of Tampa.

We were all excited about the upcoming marriage, but no one more than Aunt Louisa who began assisting my sister in the planning process. Aunt Louisa was attentive to every detail, but the area to which she gave special attention was making my sister feel special. Each week until the wedding, she provided Frances with a gift and an update on the plans. I was happy for my sister as she was showered with the same attention I received as I prepared to leave home for college. My sister was deserving of the special attention and Aunt Louisa enjoyed providing it.

This was the third summer I interacted with the Iavarone family via their restaurant on the corner of Buffalo and Highland Avenues and named for the patriarch of the family, Carmine Iavarone, who I never had the privilege of knowing since he had passed away in August of 1956.

The twins, Carmine and Malio, were about to enter the seventh grade at Sacred Heart Academy on Florida Avenue when cancer claimed the life of their beloved father. Following his passing, the responsibility for the Iavarone family was placed squarely on the shoulders of their mother, Frances, with the aid of the oldest sibling, Eugene (Gene). Gene was a senior at Jesuit High where he played baseball and had garnered the interest of several major league teams, including the Cleveland Indians. He chose to drop baseball and school to assist his mom at the restaurant. The remaining member of their immediate family, Theresa, was entering the fifth grade at the same school her twin brothers attended, Sacred Heart.

Times were tough for the Iavarone family for several years. Their home was a two room structure located behind the restaurant which accommodated Frances and her dad, Pops, in one room, and the four children in the other. The home had no kitchen or hallway. Mrs. Iavarone, however, was of the breed that knew how to stretch a dollar, and that skill, combined with a growing and loyal clientele at the restaurant, contributed to improve finances for the Iavarone family to such an extent that they were able to build a comfortable custom home on the Hillsborough River, a short distance from the restaurant.

Theresa also contributed to running the restaurant which became a textbook example of a "family affair."

Carmine and Malio were stellar athletes on Hillsborough High School's 1960, #1 state ranked football team that compiled a 10 and 0 record. Recognition for their play was noted on the all-City and all-County teams.

After graduating from Hillsborough High School, Malio decided to continue his football endeavor at Garden City Junior College in Garden City, Kansas, while Carmine joined his brother Gene and their mother on a full-time basis.

However, the situation at Garden City took its toll on Malio's enthusiasm. In addition to schoolwork and football practice, Malio and his teammates were asked to "bus" tables at Garden City's Wheaton Inn (combination motel and restaurant) to earn money for room and board. Even though Malio enjoyed the work, especially when he was asked to become the Inn's cook, he longed for his family and friends, especially his girlfriend, Shirley Valdes, who was beginning her freshman year at Florida State University. Add 1,700 miles distance from Tampa to the mix, and Malio decided to attend the University of Tampa, instead.

He enjoyed his experience at UT but began contemplating where he would be when his college days were over and decided that the best use of his time was with his family at their restaurant.

Malio's addition to the staff at Carmine's Restaurant allowed his brother Carmine to meet his military obligation with the National Guard by completing basic training in Fort Jackson, South Carolina, followed by a six-month boot camp in San Antonio, Texas. Upon returning from San Antonio, Carmine joined Gene, Malio, and their mom as the permanent management staff of their family business.

As was the case in previous summers, my exposure to the Iavarones came about when I dined at their popular restaurant with Judy and her parents. All of the Iavarones were gregarious, but Carmine and Malio were especially attentive to us, and before long a friendship began developing.

The twins worked separate shifts and each would invite me to return to the restaurant after leaving Judy off for the evening. It was in that setting that I began to meet many of their friends and acquaintances, some of whom would become lifelong friends. Amongst that group I met JC Valenti Jr, better known as "Baby Joe".

Baby Joe was a fun-loving guy with an exuberant personality. In fact, it was his love of fun which contributed to him becoming "academically ineligible" to return to FSU. He was undaunted with that news and returned with his fun-loving ways to his hometown of Tampa.

Through Baby Joe and the Twins, I was introduced to Joe Lumia and Bennie Lazzara. Joe Lumia, Bennie, and I share an uninvited and unwanted distinction. They had also lost their fathers to the deeds of an assassin during their youth.

Before long, the four of us became good friends and our various escapades ultimately ended at Carmine's. Concurrently, I began to introduce my group of friends to the group at Carmine's and without any planning, Carmine's restaurant became our base of operations. My group, of course, included Steve Malzone and Ted Cannella who did not know that life existed north of Columbus Drive.

Overall, the summer of 1964 was enjoyable. In addition to meeting new friends, things were going generally well and we were all excited about my sister's upcoming marriage.

Judy and I had fun double dating with some of our new friends, our old friends, and just hanging out with our families. Work was boring, but it provided the funds to finance the fun. In addition to eating at Carmine's, we enjoyed going with groups of anywhere from six to twelve (and sometimes, eighteen) people to eat at various restaurants on both sides of Tampa Bay. Some of the restaurants that come to mind include Steve's Rustic Lodge in Thonotosassa, Branch Ranch in east Hillsborough County, Seeley's Holiday Ranch at the apex of Dale Mabry and Florida Avenue, the Beachcomber at Clearwater Beach, and Wolfie's Delicatessen at Del Webb's Sun City in St. Petersburg.

Christ the King Catholic Church in south Tampa was the venue of the wedding between Joseph Paul Caranante and Frances Flores on that warm Saturday, August 9, 1964. My sister looked beautiful in her long flowing gown and it was difficult to hold back the tears as my brother Bob escorted her down the aisle. My mother was proud of her only daughter, as were her brothers.

The reception at the Davis Islands' Garden Club capped off what was a beautiful day celebrating this important day in our lives.

Matters on Lemon Street worsened for my brother Gene. It seemed the grief Luis had spread between Frances and Gene was now totally focused on Gene. Arguments over petty matters not only persisted but intensified.

An example of how Luis was received by others is typified by an incident that happened at his place of employment. While he and my mother continued to operate the sandwich shop on Howard Avenue, he took employment at Redwing Carriers as a mechanic's helper. From time to time, he would receive threatening telephone calls at our home. Gene and I got a chuckle from hearing his explanations to my mother of these calls. Even though we knew no details, we were certain there was some basis for the threats.

One day, an officer of the Tampa Police Department delivered Luis home. The story relayed to us by the police officer was that Luis lost all braking capability of his vehicle and was yet skillful enough to downshift and guide the car off Adamo Drive and into a ditch on the side of the road. Upon inspection of his vehicle by the towing company and police, it became obvious the brake lines on his car had been purposely cut allowing the release of brake fluid, thus, incapacitating the auto's braking system. As we already surmised, the police officer explained to us that whoever was responsible for this act was trying to seriously injure or kill Luis. When he asked if we knew who might be responsible, we responded we had no idea except for the threatening calls. Luis told the police he did not know who was behind the threatening calls—a bold-faced lie. The policeman later told us that they were unable to get any solid information at Redwing Carriers but that Luis was not well liked by his fellow workers; information that was no surprise to us.

The heat was sweltering in Tampa on that August 12th evening when Judy and I were enjoying the comfort of her air-conditioned home. Judy answered the telephone and handed it to me with a startled look on her face. "It's Gene," she said as I took the phone from her. In a very serious tone, Gene asked me to come home immediately because Luis was threatening him with a gun and he was defending himself with a butcher's knife. I told him I was on my way and to try to keep the situation status quo until I arrived. Judy asked me to call her later as I sped away.

Within ten minutes, I was pulling into my driveway not remembering the route I took or stopping for any traffic signals. As I exited my car, Irene Fernandez, my next-door neighbor was standing in our front lawn and told me it was a good thing I showed up because there was some serious trouble going on. I entered the house and found Luis and Gene on opposite sides of the kitchen table jawing at each other and my mother pleading with both of them to put down the weapons. On my first request, Gene handed me the knife, which I placed on the table before asking Luis to hand me the .45 automatic he was wielding. He was attempting to communicate to me in Spanish gibberish that Gene did not respect him and that he no longer felt comfortable in our home. I told him the only way we could settle this matter intelligently was to put down his gun. He said, if he did, we would both jump him and therefore that was his only defense. After a couple of minutes (which, of course, seemed a lot longer), I, with my mother's help, convinced him to hand me the pistol. I removed the ammo clip and dislodged the bullet in the chamber before throwing the gun into my bedroom.

Gene wanted to dismember Luis and I felt the same way. As I grabbed his shirt and threw him against the wall, my mother anticipated our intentions, stepped between us and, with a crying plea, begged us to quit fighting. As an accommodation to her, I once again grabbed him by his shirt, escorted him out the front door throwing him off the front porch onto the lawn with instructions I did not want to see him back in our house for any reason. As preposterous as it seems, my mother began begging me to allow him another chance, to which I adamantly responded, "No way in hell." She was so focused on "not losing her husband" that she had abandoned all common sense and was unable to gauge the peril of the matter. My mother handed him some clothes and he departed. I could hear her crying in her bedroom as Gene and I discussed the nightmare we had just experienced. It was obvious to me that I could not leave Gene on Lemon Street alone.

Uncle Vince called to make sure that I was planning to go by their home before departing for Baton Rouge. While visiting, I told him and Aunt Louisa about the prior night's incident. Vince became furious, went to his bedroom for his .38 caliber pistol and suggested we go to the sandwich shop on Howard Avenue and "teach Luis a lesson he would not soon forget." I explained to Uncle Vince I was appreciative of what he wanted to do, but I did not think that was the right approach. I further explained that I believed Luis got the message and that we had seen the last of him. He told me I was wrong and that as soon as I left town, Luis would move back into our house. I thought he might be correct and that pretty much sealed it for me; I was not leaving Gene alone in this circumstance.

I called Coach Mac in Baton Rouge and explained the situation to him. He said he understood my dilemma and that I was doing the right thing to concentrate on these family matters. He asked me to call back when I decided exactly what I was going to do. I was pleasantly surprised with his compassion.

It turned out that Uncle Vince was correct. Luis was temporarily staying at a friend's house until I left town. My mother coyly asked me when I was leaving for school and was shocked when I told her I wasn't returning until this matter was under control. She urged me not to jeopardize my scholarship and that everything would be fine. I told her as long as she maintained a relationship with Luis it was impossible for everything to be fine. After a few weeks, she realized I was not bluffing about remaining in Tampa and moved into a duplex Luis had rented leaving Gene and me alone on Lemon Street. While our preference was to have her home, we were fine with this arrangement.

Things were day-to-day. Gene began his senior year at Jesuit and I reenlisted as a temporary full-time playground director at West Pines—1½ blocks from home.

The weeks were slipping by and it soon became evident to me I would miss the 1964 season (and fall semester). I was quite upset about not being able to go back to Baton Rouge, but it was not about me; it was about Gene.

As instructed by Coach Mac, I called to give him an update on my situation. He seemed empathetic, and again, told me that I was doing the right thing, wished me luck and said he was expecting me back for the spring semester.

KILLING TIME

My new friends Baby Joe Valenti, Bennie Lazzara, and Joe Lumia were all enrolled at the University of South Florida for the fall semester. They suggested, since I was just killing time, that I join them. Having nothing better to do, I did.

Joe Lumia was serious about becoming a CPA with one of the Big Ten firms and was diligently focusing his attention on his schoolwork to that end.

Bennie, however, was coasting this semester and intended to return to the University of Florida to complete his undergraduate work before entering their law school.

Then there was Baby Joe. His attention to fun at FSU had temporarily revoked his privileges there and he was seeking to "shore up" his GPA in hopes of returning. He, however, had no intentions of giving up fun to accomplish this goal.

Baby Joe, Bennie, and Joe Lumia were also disappointed I was not returning to Baton Rouge.

We had developed a close friendship over the summer, and even though Bennie and Joe Lumia were diehard Gators, the three of them had much respect for LSU and were planning a trip to Baton Rouge for the Florida game. Baby Joe, on the other hand, was an avid FSU fan and wanted to make the trip to witness LSU deliver Florida an old-fashioned "wupping," a common occurrence during that era.

Nonetheless, it was not to be in the fall of 1964, and the four of us decided to make the best of our situation in Tampa.

Joe Lumia (Lammy) was planning on meeting Baby Joe, Bennie, and me at the coffee shop in the Student Union building on this particular morning. As previously mentioned, he was always very serious about his schoolwork, a sentiment not shared by the rest of us, especially Baby Joe and me.

Baby Joe and Bennie were aware of my exploits at LSU regarding my 22-caliber pistol.

The three of us agreed that our meeting was a perfect opportunity for me to scare Lammy since the night before we were involved in a disagreement/argument.

I retrieved my pistol from my automobile, loaded it with blanks, and tucked it in my waistband at the small of my back.

There were hundreds of students changing classes as I stood at the steps of the Student Union building awaiting Joe's arrival. Baby Joe and Bennie assisted me as lookouts for Joe's arrival as well as campus security.

As was typical for Joe, his shirt pockets were replete with pencils, pens, and miscellaneous items common to CPAs-in-waiting. As he approached with arms full of thick accounting books, wearing prescription sunglasses he had just exchanged for his reading glasses, he noticed the faces of Bennie and Baby Joe and returned their smile with one of his own. As he rotated his gaze toward me, he noticed I was not smiling and adjusted the look on his face to match mine.

He was 20 to 25 feet from me when I lashed out at him, "I'm tired of you being a baby about everything and arguing about minutiae!"

His face indicated confusion as to why I would cast such a public reprimand upon him about a private issue, at which time I pulled the revolver from my waistband, pointed it directly at him and fired two shots followed by four rapid shots.

Joe looked like he exploded as he covered the areas on his chest and abdomen where he believed he had been shot sending books, papers, pens, pencils, and two pair of glasses into flight. So believable was his reaction that other students scattered for safety while others screamed with fear.

Everyone, including Joe, realized it was a prank within moments and their assumption was supported by the laughter from Baby Joe, Bennie, and me.

I could read the emotions on Joe's face as those I experienced when engaged in the "High yella" incident and knew his immediate anger would soon transition to laughter, and it did.

We assisted him in picking up his books and paraphernalia, all the time laughing and slapping each other on the back and enjoying the moment.

Lammy said he thought he was dead when he saw the fire coming out of the barrel of my gun.

The majority of students who witnessed the hoax seemed to enjoy it, but in an abundance of caution, I returned the gun to my automobile and was prepared to tell campus security I caught a ride to school with Baby Joe in the event I was fingered by some malcontent as the shooter and they wanted to search my vehicle.

Because Joe was so serious about his academics, we were able to pull off another prank at his expense.

Baby Joe and I would alternate disrupting Joe's classes posing as a representative of the administration seeking a student named Joe Lumia for the purpose of delivering an urgent message to call a (bogus) phone number. What made the joke effective was Lammy's reaction.

As soon as we entered the classroom, you could see Joe becoming nervous as one of us whispered the concocted message to the professor.

Joe often threatened to expose us, but we never believed he had the heart to do so. Consequently, he would approach the professor and the representative from the administration office (Baby Joe or me) in a very serious mode until we were a safe distance from the class. Then he would alternate laughing and chastising us but mostly pleading with us not to do it again.

GENE'S SENIOR YEAR

One advantage of staying home was being able to see Gene play football for Jesuit. His sophomore and junior years were the same years I was in Baton Rouge, and therefore I had never seen him play at the varsity level.

Coach DiCharry was now Jesuit's head coach and Gene and Coach DiCharry's son, Ray Jr, were team leaders and top performers. However, they had a situation to overcome.

The previous spring, Gene, Ray, and their close friend, Danny Someillan were apprehended by the Tampa police for "shooting out" windows with BB guns in the Palma Ceia area. Each participant directs credit for the idea to the other two but all admit to being willing participants otherwise.

After discovering that the three perpetrators had clean records, the police escorted each of them home, beginning with Ray Jr. Gene and Danny recall the look of fury in Coach DiCharry's eyes when the Tampa police delivered his son, Ray, to him that evening. They also recount Coach administering a beating to Ray, which they witnessed through the sheer window treatment of the DiCharry home as the police cruiser headed to Lemon Street for the second stop.

My sister and mother answered the door when the police delivered Gene and expressed personal disappointment but gratitude to the police officers for doing their job and electing to escort the boys to their homes instead of the police station.

Danny's reception was similar to Gene's.

Their perception of Ray's penance was validated when Gene (Danny attended Plant high school) saw a bruised Ray at school the following day.

Even though we make light of it today, it was a concerning behavioral event that, if not stemmed, could have escalated into serious problems. It amounted to a case of having too much time on their hands. As the nuns at St. Joseph's used to tell us, "Idle hands and minds are the Devil's workshops."

Nonetheless, Coach DiCharry overlooked this breach of behavior and agreed to put it behind them if they were committed to acting as model citizens.

The 1964 football campaign at Jesuit was moderately successful as the Tigers instituted the Single Wing offense featuring Ray DiCharry Jr. supported by a staunch defense led by Gene Flores.

The contest with Robinson High School was particularly interesting. I was invited by Coach DiCharry to view the game from the sidelines and witnessed a hard-hitting game in which Jesuit valiantly stymied the offensive threats of a powerful and deep Robinson Knight squad.

Larry Smith, Robinson's all-state running back, returned the opening kickoff for a touchdown and Robinson converted the extra point making it 7–0 with less than 15 seconds expired. It remained 7–0 going into the second half when Jesuit scored on a well-executed sweep around right end for 12 yards. Jesuit then faked a pass off the same sweep formation but was stopped on the six-inch line by a host of Knight Defenders that had not bitten on the fake. Both teams threatened in the fourth quarter, but neither was able to score and the game ended 7–6.

Even though the Tigers were unable to chalk up the victory, their impressive showing against one of the state's better teams proved to them that they could compete with anyone on their schedule.

It was a genuine thrill for me to watch my younger brother play and watching him served to soothe the disappointment of not participating, myself.

FUNNY HOW THINGS HAPPEN

During this time, the relationship between Judy and me was on-again, off-again. We argued about things so unimportant I cannot recall them. She took a sabbatical from college during the fall semester and resumed a light class load in the spring.

The gang from Carmine's restaurant and I would participate in "touch" football on the weekends as a means of getting our "football fix."

The participants generally consisted of former students from both Jesuit and Hillsborough High Schools. The skill level of the participants covered a wide range, but the competition level was fierce.

A friend and former standout defensive back and punter at the University of Tampa, Ron Perez, attended several of these games for the fellowship value. He had not heard of my decision to remain in Tampa and was therefore surprised to see me participating.

As any good alumnus would do, he immediately asked if I was interested in speaking with the coaches at the University of Tampa about playing football.

I expressed my gratitude for his sentiments but explained that I would be returning to LSU when my family matter was resolved.

When I communicated to him that I was unsure as to when that would be, he took it upon himself to bring a University of Tampa coach (and former teammate of his) to one of our pickup games. After the game, he introduced me to Charlie Bailey, UT Defensive Coach. After chatting a while, Charlie Bailey suggested I meet with UT's D-line Coach, Charlie Livingston.

Charlie Livingston had been a very successful and accomplished player at the University of Miami and his reputation was well known to many, including me. I had no intention of playing for the University of Tampa, but I was intrigued by the opportunity to meet Charlie Livingston and I did.

Coach Livingston convinced me to consider UT by *soft selling* the idea of attending school during this uncertain time with an open door to transfer back to LSU whenever I wished to do so. He also explained that the University of Tampa was very interested in my brother Gene and it would be a great experience for us to play together.

Mentioning Gene pressed a hot button with me, and I agreed to continue the conversation with head coach Sam Bailey. Regardless of how my meeting with Coach Bailey would turn out, I was impressed with Charlie Livingston and was drawn toward his confident demeanor and flattered by his willingness to invest time and effort with me without any commitment from me that I would be around for his payday.

Meeting Coach Bailey (Seaweed Sam) was quite an experience. His persona was a cross between John Wayne and Clint Eastwood. His tall, lean, muscular physique was accentuated by a deep tan expected on a man whose craft was executed under the hot Florida sun.

Coach Bailey had been a stellar athlete on the University of Georgia's championship football teams, which featured Heisman Trophy recipient Frank Sinkwich. His Humphrey Bogart-like annunciation was a perfect complement to his tough man demeanor, which I later learned masked a truly sensitive and compassionate individual.

While discussing the opportunities at UT with Coaches Livingston and Bailey, I was shocked when Coach Livingston said he received a good report from the LSU coaches regarding my play. I never considered that he might call LSU and I thought he might have been bluffing until he said, "They didn't give me much detail, but said that even though your behavior had improved, there was still room for (further) improvement."

That statement concerned me because I didn't want the UT coaches prejudging my behavior. However, after further discussing expectations on both sides, I began to get the impression that they were expecting me to be a leader on the team...a prospect to which I looked forward.

The three of us agreed I would begin class in the spring semester (to commence in about three weeks), which would allow me to participate in spring football, and my brother Gene, would begin in the fall of 1965, also on full scholarship. Coach Bailey indicated that Gene's grades were so good that he was eligible for an academic scholarship as well, which would in effect, allow UT an additional athletic scholarship. When I inquired as to why he was sharing that information with me, he said it was for informational purposes only and that I should be proud of Gene's academic prowess. I believe that's called a *win-win*.

Coach Bailey also agreed to provide me $55 monthly because I had chosen to live at home.

Both coaches indicated that they were very pleased to have the Flores brothers join the Spartan family and then Charlie Livingston added, as he chuckled, "Ask Gene to leave his BB gun at home." Coach Livingston then took me around the athletic department and introduced me to various coaches and other people.

Before leaving that afternoon, I asked Coach Livingston what the proper thing was to do with regard to contacting Coach Mac at LSU and he suggested that I let him or Coach Bailey handle it from their end.

With that accomplished, I was happy about the opportunity to get back into football even though I was unsure as to what to expect at the University of Tampa.

As I traveled the sub-two-mile journey home, I remember thinking, *Isn't it funny how things happen?*

THE UNIVERSITY OF TAMPA

The spring semester at UT commenced in late January. It was a short and easy drive from my home to the bustling campus. On my first day of class, while walking from Plant Hall to the parking lot, I was approached by a burly and gruff individual who asked if my name was Amando Florees.

I responded, "You're close, but my name is Armando Flores," which generated a scowl on the face of the individual who introduced himself to me as Greg Bonfe.

"I understand you came from LSU."

"You've done your homework."

Somewhat agitated that I did not ask him anything about himself, he offered, "I just came from Southeast Louisiana, in Hammond. Have you heard of Southeast Louisiana?"

"Yes, I have, but why are you at UT now?"

In a sort of "duh" fashion, he responded, "Why do you think I'm here? I flunked out. Same reason you're not at LSU, right?"

"No," I said, "I didn't flunk out. I had other reasons."

"Whatever you say," Greg responded, fishing for detail.

"How does a Louisiana guy end up at the University of Tampa?"

"I'm not a Louisiana guy. I'm from Syracuse, New York."

"Well, how does a guy from Syracuse, New York end up at Southeast Louisiana?" I queried.

"I don't know how other people do it, but I got in trouble at Syracuse, grades and other things, and somebody gave my name to the coaches at Southeastern. You know, you ask a lot of questions for somebody who doesn't give much information."

"I've got to get somewhere; we'll talk again later," I said, and then added, "Nice to have met you, Greg Bonafee."

"The name is Bonfe, not Bonafee, and it was nice to meet you, too. See you around."

One of the first differences I encountered at UT was the dress code. On my third visit to campus, I was approached by a member of the SES (student enforcement squad) and advised that I was in violation of the dress code on two counts, wearing jeans and not wearing socks. I advised the young lady that I was unaware of such dress requirements but that I would adjust my attire accordingly. She handed me a copy of the dress code, which was intended to prevent future violations. To my surprise, shorts and shirts without a collar were prohibited.

CHOOSING A MAJOR MADE EASY

I was party to an interesting occurrence with my academic advisor. At LSU, I had taken a course taught by an instructor reputed to be friendly with the athletic department, which was intended to give those considering physical education as a major an introduction to various sports and athletic activities. As such, the 18-week course included two weeks with each of the following activities: gymnastics, wrestling, boxing, tumbling, baseball, basketball, football, archery, and golf. The credit for this course was three semester hours.

As my advisor enumerated the courses that were transferring from LSU, she counted each of the activities in the introduction course as individual three-hour courses giving me credit for 27 hours versus 3. I allowed her to continue, thinking she would catch her error but she never did. She concluded by saying, "Mr. Flores, with the exception of tennis and swimming, you have completed the practical portion of your physical education major and need, in addition to completing the core curriculum, the following classroom courses," as she handed me the list she had just compiled—and that's how I decided on a PE major. It was thrown on my lap.

I didn't feel I was shortcutting the university or my future students because I felt I knew enough about sports to teach it right then. As a matter of fact, I was trying to figure out a way of not taking the tennis and swimming courses prescribed to me by my advisor.

THE GOLDEN GREEK

Before class one day, an individual introduced himself to me as Deno Kutrumbos from Asbury Park, on the Jersey Shore. The Greek with the golden tan assumed I knew the location of the Jersey Shore and I did not inform him otherwise. "With a school of 2,500 students, it's easy to spot a new student, especially when he's 6ft 2 and weighs 250 lbs.," he continued as we headed toward class. "I understand you transferred here from LSU, and given the course we're going to, you must be a PE major."

"Yep, you're right twice; make it three times if you count my height and weight," I responded as we entered the classroom. Deno then introduced me to a couple of his friends who suggested he invite me to a party that evening on *the island* (New Jersey for Davis Islands).

I told him I appreciated the invitation, but I worked evenings.

When I responded, "9:00 PM" to his question about how late I worked, he said, "That's no problem, the party will just be getting started around 9 or 9:30."

"Getting started around 9 or 9:30 on Wednesday night; what time is this baby over?" I inquired.

"Whenever," he answered as class began.

I mused over this conversation for about ten minutes before tuning into the subject matter orated by Dr. Miller K. Adams.

I arrived at the home on Davis Island, which Deno had given me the address to, and sure enough, the party was going strong. I thought, *Lucky neighbors,* as I entered the home with music blaring and people enjoying themselves and communicating above the music.

"Whose house is this?" I asked as Deno greeted me at the door with a handshake. He pointed to a couple of U T students on the other side of the room and offered me a drink. They had an array of choices that rivaled any lounge in town, but I opted for a longneck beer. While walking around the room with Deno, I noticed several people referred to him as the *Golden Greek*. I asked Deno if he preferred *Golden Greek* to Deno, and he said it did not make any difference to him but that most people called him Deno, which was also a nickname. His legal name was Charles.

After being introduced to and conversing with several people at the gathering, I decided to leave because I considered the possibility of a neighbor calling the police and I did not want to be holding a beer at age twenty in that eventuality. So, I told Deno I enjoyed myself and that I would see him on-campus. It was evident to me that this was a different college crowd than I was used to. It was the middle of the week and they were engaged in a full-blown party. Additionally, beer, with this group, took a secondary position to alcohol and my olfactory senses were introduced to new smells. I was unwittingly being introduced to a segment of our society that previously I had only seen on TV.

BECOMING COMFORTABLE AS A SPARTAN

Before spring practice began, I was engaged in voluntary workouts that were, unlike LSU, indeed voluntary. As a practical matter, everyone attended even though there was no attendance recorded or required. Even though I met the players at a meeting earlier, this was a great opportunity to get to know the guys in a somewhat relaxed setting. The activities we engaged in were similar to those I was used to, namely running, blocking dummies and sleds, wrestling, agility drills, and optional weight training.

I was reacquainted with a friend I had known for many years who transferred in from FSU. His name was Vernon Korhn and while he was a quarterback and defensive back at Plant High School and at FSU, he was strictly a defensive back (DB) at UT.

Vernon's parents had both died while Vernon was a youngster. His mom died of pneumonia when he was seven and his dad died of a heart attack when Vernon was fourteen years old. His uncle's family, the Zacchinis, who made their living being shot out of cannons at circuses, raised him. Edmondo Zacchini was the first to develop the "human cannonball" act circa 1918, and he, along with his family, performed this daredevil event in their native Italy and throughout Europe.

John Ringling, of Ringling Brothers Barnum & Bailey Circus, made it a point to catch the act in Europe. So impressed was John Ringling by "IL Palla di Cannone Umano" (The Human Cannonballs), that he negotiated a deal with the family's patriarch, Edmondo, bringing the Zacchinis to the United States in 1920. Their relocation brought them to the winter headquarters for circuses and carnivals in the U.S., Tampa Florida.

Vernon's mom, Amelia Fargnoli, was sister to Josephine Zacchini, Edmondo's wife. Through her association with the circus business, Amelia was introduced to and courted by a young German man by the name of Vernon Korhn who was employed in the carnival business. Their courtship resulted in marriage and the fruit of their union was my friend, Vernon Korhn Jr.

Vernon was a terrific fella as well as a talented athlete and scholar. He was rehabbing from an injury sustained while at FSU, and this, coupled with some family matters of his own, made staying close to home a good fit for him.

Upon my transfer to the University of Tampa, I was introduced to the term "tramp athlete." The term did not necessarily carry a negative connotation, though a couple of the transfers could cause one to take that view. Approximately 40% of the players had attended other schools and transferred to UT for a myriad of reasons, the most common of which was academic performance, or lack thereof. The entrance requirements at UT were comparable to, and in some cases higher, than those of other universities in the state but the university had a provision for probationary acceptance for "special-needs" cases, which generally meant athletes with academic complexities at prior institutions or students whose families had the capacity to be significant donors.

Some of the schools previously attended by members of the UT squad during my era include Alabama, Florida, FSU, Georgia, Hardin Simmons, Kentucky, Southeast Louisiana, Syracuse, Wisconsin, and of course, LSU. This made for an interesting mix on our team. Several of the transfer students had families of their own, children included. One particular individual was involved with a couple of girls while separated from his second wife and had children with both wives. During the off-season he was a bartender at a gay bar not far from campus.

Another interesting characteristic of the UT team was its propensity for tattoos. In the mid-1960s having a tattoo was not the common practice it is today. Of the sixty guys on the team, about fifteen of them had tattoos (some had multiple tattoos) ranging from a girl's name, to the yellow rose of Texas, to a dagger adorned with a serpent, to a fox chasing a rabbit running to a hole particularly located on one's anatomy. Additionally, two of the tattooed players rode motorcycles, Ron Boone from Texas and Bill McCoy from Kentucky. While the end product differed, the circumstance leading to being tattooed was almost always the same, alcohol and sometimes alcohol and drugs. I don't recall a single instance when a player in the bright light of day and sober, made a decision to get a tattoo. The decision was always made under the cover of night and under the influence of alcohol and/or drugs.

There was plenty of alcohol consumed at LSU, mostly beer, but to the best of my knowledge, there was very little drug activity. Other than this little pink pill (amphetamine) which was touted as an energy enhancer, I was unaware of any drug use whatsoever amongst the football team. This was not the case at UT. That same little pink pill was used by a handful of players for practice sessions causing that handful to require higher doses and stronger drugs for games. An interesting side note is that most of the players who consumed drugs were not starters. Consequently, after games they still had this inventory of synthetic energy and would inevitably spend the balance of the weekend wreaking havoc on the community.

I always attributed the accelerated use of drugs at UT with the fact the student body had, and still does have, a very large component from the Northeast, specifically, New York and New Jersey. While the football team had very few northeasterners, access to that aspect of life was prevalent because the football team and student body were totally inter-socialized. Add to the scenario the fact many of the students from the northeast lived off campus and were funded by families with financial means, and you have the basis for my reasoning.

RED MGB

Bennie Lazzara infected me with the *sports car fever* he cured for himself with the purchase of an MGB roadster. Prior to that time, I was perfectly satisfied with my trusty Ford Falcon and no car payments.

I asked my sister to ask her boss, Melvin Smith (Mr. Smith to me), Loan Officer and Vice President of the International Bank, if I could discuss a loan from the bank for this purchase. She arranged the meeting and I arrived at the bank at the appointed time.

Mr. Smith was engaged with a client but acknowledged my presence and informed me that he would be with me shortly. Meanwhile, my sister was tending to other bank customers in her capacity as Head Teller. To entertain myself as I waited, I walked over to the *Forms* area in the lobby and proceeded to prepare a counter check payable to myself in the amount of $150. I forged the check with the name "Sam Bailey" and joined in queue for my sister.

She was wearing her business face as I approached her window and did not respond favorably to my request for samples. I told her that since she was not in the mood for jokes to just cash my check and I would wait for Mr. Smith in the lobby. She professionally perused the check astutely indicating that it required my endorsement on the back. I cheerfully endorsed the check and she began counting out bills totaling $150. I held the $150 in my hand and asked if she noticed any similarities between Sam Bailey's signature and my own. She glanced at the signatures on the check, and in a state of controlled panic, immediately removed the $150 from my hand and replaced it with the check I had originally given her. She informed me that people were watching and that I should not be playing around like that. I told her that if she did not cash the check, I would have no choice but to take my business elsewhere. She said she thought that was an excellent idea and about that time Mr. Smith signaled that he was ready for me.

Mr. Smith was an established and well-respected executive. I had known him for years through my sister but we had never discussed business. Utilizing southern charm that came natural to him, he put me at ease by indicating Frances had told him I was interested in purchasing an automobile. I indicated I was, indeed, interested and began showing him details regarding the auto. After discussing the matter for a few minutes, Mr. Smith showed me the numbers. Using the proceeds from the sale of my Falcon as a down payment, my payments would be $49 per month. I told Mr. Smith I liked the deal and where I should sign.

Then he asked me an important question. "How are you going to make the payments?" Then, in a demonstration of financial prowess, I responded I hadn't considered how I was intending to pay for the automobile but that I was willing to work an additional shift at a playground to finance the purchase. In a very cordial manner, he suggested I work that out before we went any further. The prudent thing to do was to forget purchasing the MGB and enjoy the financial freedom associated with driving my trouble-free Falcon. But few twenty-year-olds are prudent, and that included me.

I was willing to work an additional shift at Rey Park to finance my purchase, but I didn't realize this would conflict with spring practice. Coach Bailey scheduled a night workout each week to allow us to escape the heat and acclimate our vision to night conditions, which is when most of our games were played. I decided to discuss my dilemma with Coach Bailey and that turned out to be a good decision. After listening to me explain that I was short on cash and was planning on working part-time to meet my financial commitments, he had a suggestion. "You're going to have plenty to do between practice and the classroom, and if you add work to the mix, the other two might suffer. So, I'm going to have Leila (his secretary and Mrs. Ellis to me) prepare an additional $55 check for you each month. Would that make things work out for you?" he asked. I thought he was poking fun with me but the fatherly smile on his face indicated otherwise.

"Coach, you don't have to do this. You've already been great to me," I said.

He interrupted "Mondy, I'm happy to do it and I feel comfortable it's the right decision. So, get over to the bank before Melvin changes his mind."

I can't tell you how *accepted* his gesture made me feel. The $55 provision was nice, but what really impressed me was Coach Bailey's concern for me spreading myself too thin. I got the impression that he was genuinely concerned for me and I was simultaneously pumped up and flattered.

I returned to the bank for a prearranged meeting with Mr. Smith. "Well, did you decide how you were going to make the auto payments?" He asked.

"Yes sir," I naively responded, "Coach Bailey is providing the money." I was quickly interrupted by a "flushed-looking" Mr. Smith, as he peered around the bank to see who may have heard my comments.

"Mondy, I didn't hear what you just said and I believe you ought to keep that information to yourself." His message was clear, his intentions were gracious, and his delivery was both caring and professional.

"Yes sir." I replied. "I shouldn't have provided so much detail."

He ended the conversation by saying, "Everything is fine, but athletic departments are under increased scrutiny these days, even though I'm sure Coach Bailey has everything worked out properly. Enough said?"

We completed the paperwork, and I was soon the proud owner of a red 1965 MGB Roadster.

Bennie, his girlfriend, Judy, and I in short order became sports car enthusiasts. We drove all over Tampa Bay in our *two seaters* and a trip to the East Coast on the weekends was not uncommon. We even engaged in rally competitions with the girls functioning as engineers, which at times was challenging and required patience. When Bennie and I were not with the girls, we spent time cleaning and tinkering with our favorite toys. With a not-so-subtle suggestion, Judy procured for me an extremely nice wooden steering wheel to replace the stock model that came with the car. His girlfriend did the same for Bennie and we invested many hours changing out the wheels ourselves at Bennie's home on River Drive. It was a carefree and enjoyable time in my life and provided some relief from reality.

During voluntary workouts, I perceived a healthy cockiness among several of the players. I was unable to discern whether the cockiness was earned or whether it masked a shortcoming or two. Nonetheless, spring practice was upon us and I would soon find out *who was who* talent-wise and I'm sure my new teammates were interested in seeing if my bite matched my bark.

I soon learned that we had a very talented pool of players and the coaches' challenge was to mold us into a cohesive unit.

It was obvious why John Perry was regarded as a preseason All-American. John was a talented wide receiver with the toughness and tenacity of a linebacker coupled with the grace and speed of a gazelle. He was a diligent worker and natural team leader. He was the same size and stature as Joe Labruzzo and possessed the same fearless attitude. Little wonder why John and I immediately became close friends. He was from *party central* Miami where I'm sure he developed his playful attitude, and play he did, both on and off the field.

Another player from the south Florida area was Jim Underhill (nickname Spud). Spud was a big, powerfully built, speedy fullback out of Hollywood, Florida. From a pure talent standpoint, he was among the top three or four on the squad but his performance didn't always measure up to his talent. The issue with Jim was his moods. One day he would come to practice and perform at the level of a NFL player but other times he would perform at a level that would not impress the coaches at Jesuit. Regardless of his performance level, he always wore a look on his face that communicated discontent and negativity. When he was good, he was great but when he was bad, he was awful. The question with Spud was always, which spud would show up today, the baked potato too hot to handle, or the bowl of vichyssoise usually served cold.

Then there was my newfound friend from Syracuse New York, Syracuse University, and most recently Southeast Louisiana, Greg Bonfe. Greg was one of the fastest players on the team, one of the strongest, one of the hardest hitters, and certainly, one of the toughest. This tough Italian took no guff from anyone and was prepared to settle matters with his fist at all times. He didn't realize it at the time, but he often had a scowl on his face. Whether things went right or wrong on the field, the look on Greg's face was the same. He actually had the Italian version of Jim Underhill's countenance. Beyond that look, however, was as fine a person as you could ever hope to meet, and as I would learn later, as good a friend as there is.

Greg and I became friends without trying, but had not that been the case, I believe I would have made an effort to be his friend because I sure didn't want him as an enemy. As was the case with Underhill, Greg was long on talent but short on leadership. The ironic part of this leadership deficiency was that neither Jim nor Greg recognized the situation and therefore made no effort to correct it.

Greg contrasted a player on the team named Dan Sykes who played the same defensive position (middle linebacker) as did Greg but always had a combination of a determined look and a positive smile and was always upbeat. Greg would match or outperform Dan in drills and in scrimmages but remained behind him on the depth chart. Why? It was the intangibles that made the difference. Don't misunderstand me, Dan was a fine player and deserved the accolades showered on him by the coaches. Although quiet, he was well respected by his teammates who voted him co-captain. He was coachable, dependable, predictable, amiable, and quite capable. Greg, in the eyes of the coaches, was only capable. In my opinion, Greg was everything Dan was and more but tapping into Greg's potential required a different tack than was in use at UT at the time. Nonetheless, that was only my opinion and, even though no one asked for my input, I recognized Greg was becoming increasingly frustrated with the coaches, and the coaches with him. I offered him a couple of suggestions, but he responded that he was not interested in politics. I knew exactly what he meant.

I was extra sensitive to players' perceptions by their peers and by the coaches and was committed to using my experience at Jesuit and LSU as a steppingstone rather than a millstone. I was also willing to provide help to anyone who sought help but unwilling to be drawn into a negative attitude.

I knew I had the ability to be a leader but the question remained, was I willing and able to break the habit I had fostered of challenging authority and was I willing to allow the coaches to channel my abilities as they saw fit. It required an element of my personality I had not previously developed, namely trust. I was, however, certain that the maverick role I had previously embraced had not worked for me and I was interested in seeing how the other half lived. Something that concerned me was that, since I am not a conformist by nature, I anticipated that being a "yes man" would be very uncomfortable for me.

I worked hard at practice and kept an upbeat attitude at all times (within my personality). I performed well and looked for opportunities to be a leader. To my pleasant surprise, there were many. After the second week of practice, co-captains John Perry and Dan Sykes asked me to join them at leading the team in warm-ups before practice. I never figured out if they did this on their own or if it was suggested to them by Coach Bailey, but nonetheless, I was pleased with the invitation and count that as the day I was *officially* regarded as a leader amongst my Spartan teammates.

By the end of spring practice, I was very impressed with our squad. We had quality players at every position including special teams. Our only shortcoming was depth. The number 2 man at most positions was also a quality player, but after that the quality dropped off significantly.

UT had a rich tradition of playing their spring game against UT football alumni and friends. I include friends because many of the alumni would bring friends who played at colleges other than UT but just wanted the opportunity to strap on a helmet. Most of the alumni who participated were in the central Florida area but some came from as far as West Virginia, Texas, Pennsylvania, and Georgia. This made for a "rock-em soc-em" ballgame that had much fan appeal.

It was exciting for me to line up against former UT stars I had followed as a youngster. Included in the group were Billy Turner, Don Herndon, Tom Spack, Bill Minahan, Tom Mahin, Tony Yelovich, Mike Skorulis, and crowd favorite, Fred Cason. The current Spartans were attempting to execute offensive plays and defensive schemes against a high-quality opponent and the former Spartans were attempting to exact a pound of flesh just because they could. It was generally an enjoyable evening in which both parties achieved their objectives.

A lesson I learned during the spring of '65 was that a leader does not have to be a "yes man." You can say "no;" it's how you say it that matters.

In addition to learning to disagree without being combative, I experienced a couple of additional situations that reinforced an earlier learned lesson, *Special People Get Special Treatment* (SPGST). Obviously, a prime example of SPGST was the method in which Coach Bailey handled my situation as it related to my employment interests. However, I learned there was some SPGST of which I was unaware.

Let me explain.

I frequently met with ballplayers for breakfast at Ayre's Diner just off the UT campus, and I noticed that when settling the bill, Jim Underhill would add a tip to his ticket and merely sign the ticket in lieu of paying cash.

While leaving the diner one morning, I asked Spud about his arrangement with the diner and he explained that he and a couple of other players were able to eat meals at the diner through some arrangement between the diner and the UT athletic department. I asked who his contact was, and with a slight hesitation, he responded, "Sandspur Sam."

As soon as class concluded that day, I paid Coach Bailey a visit for the purpose of determining whether I was *special* enough to enjoy the Ayre's perk. "What can I do for you, Mondy?" asked Coach Bailey as I took a seat in his office. "You had a helluva nice spring," he commented before I could respond.

"Thanks, Coach. I'm counting on us having a good year this fall,"

"I am, too," he said. "Your professors indicate you are doing a nice job in the classroom, as well. If you stay out of trouble, you'll be the total package."

I was honored by his comments and wondered if I should proceed with my request and decided the time could not be better. "Coach, I understand Ayre's allows selected players to eat at the diner without paying and I was wondering if I could somehow qualify for the privilege."

"You qualify, Mondy, and I want you to know we are thrilled to have you on our team. You have exceeded our expectations and we're expecting big things from you on the field and in the area of leadership. You can begin signing tickets at Ayre's in the morning. Hey Mondy, don't forget," he said with a smile, "one of those $55 checks you receive every month is because you don't eat on campus."

I was more pleased with Coach Bailey's spirit than the outcome of the meeting and I do not think I would have been disappointed if he had told me he was unable to put me on the Ayre's perk. Notwithstanding those sentiments, I was pleased to be on the Ayre's training table.

During exams for the spring semester, John Perry suggested we have lunch at Valencia Gardens, a popular Spanish restaurant also just off campus. I was impressed with his restaurant selection and with his familiarity with the maître d' and several of the waiters. I thought John was somewhat cavalier when he ordered Garbanzo Bean soup, Angel's Salad, and Arroz con Pollo, followed by a Flan de Leche café solo. We discussed the team and he communicated to me how pleased he was personally to have me as a Spartan. I returned the compliment and added I never thought I would be as comfortable as I was so soon. As I reached into my pocket for funds to pay for my half of the bill, John nodded and said, "This one's on the university." You know I had to ask how, and I did. John and I had developed into good friends and I in no way considered my question an infringement on our relationship. "Coach Sam made this arrangement for me because sometimes that cafeteria food gets 'old.' I'm sure he would do it for you if you asked," John said, realizing the idea was already swirling in my mind.

As I traveled to Coach Bailey's office in the George B. Howell gymnasium adjacent to Phillips Field, I struggled with the fine line of taking improper advantage of a good situation vs. not taking advantage of an opportunity targeted for people in my situation. Even though I felt there was nothing wrong with approaching Coach Bailey regarding the Valencia perk, I decided against it.

The next week I got a call from Coach Bailey advising me that film from the spring game and on our first opponent next season, McNeese State, was available for viewing if I was interested. I showed up around 9:30 AM on Saturday morning with my brother Gene to view the film. I figured it was a good opportunity to get Gene involved prior to fall practice. Around 11 AM Coach Bailey stuck his head into the film room and asked that I see him before I left. Upon doing so, he advised me that he had arranged for me to eat meals at Valencia Gardens on the same basis I had with Ayre's diner. I asked how this came about and he said he thought it would be of help to me. He was correct. I thanked him for his consideration and generosity and exited that day appreciating the fact that I had not broached the subject with him as I had previously considered.

FIFTH AMENDMENT TO THE US CONSTITUTION

Judy and I continued dating throughout the summer of '65 and we both enjoyed the company of our new friends. We double-dated and attended parties, but most of the time we just enjoyed each other's company. Judy loved the beach, so I took her there often, and we both enjoyed our other major activity, dining out. I continued with my "cush" job as playground director at West Pines. I would then visit and/or go out with Judy and generally end the evening at Carmine's visiting with my friends, Carmine, Malio, BJ (Baby Joe), Bennie, and Lammy.

Eight months earlier, on October 18th, 1964, Carmine had married his grade school sweetheart, Barbara Borrego, and the big event this summer was the nuptial of Malio and his grade school sweetheart, Shirley Valdes. The event was scheduled for June 27th.

The Iavarone twins and I continued to get to know each other and a strong friendship was in the making. Family was (and is) very important to us and we shared several familial similarities of which we had no input. We are both half-Sicilian, we lost our dads at an early age, and were raised by dedicated and caring mothers, each of us had a sister and two brothers with one of the brothers named Gene. Their mother's name is Frances and my sister's name is Frances, our K-12 experience was a combination of private and public schools, and we were blessed with quality family members. This common background, in my opinion, contributed to the foundation of our friendship, which today remains rock solid.

Shirley Valdes had just completed her teaching internship at Roosevelt Elementary School in Tampa as her final requirement before graduating from FSU and was preparing for the upcoming wedding. She was content driving her Plymouth Fury, which had been her brother Richard's before being reassigned to her by her parents, Eddie and Alice, but Malio had other plans.

Malio had shown interest in my MGB roadster, but I had no idea that he intended to buy one. Earlier one afternoon, he mentioned to me that he was going to trade in Shirley's Plymouth shortly after they were married and buy a MGB. Later that afternoon, he said he didn't want to wait three weeks until the marriage before acquiring the MGB, and within the hour, he asked me to join him as he rode over to the Valdes home to ask Shirley's dad for the title and automobile so he could make the purchase that very evening. I chuckled at his suggestion until I discerned he was not jesting. I had met Mr. Valdes casually and was not keen on the idea of furthering our acquaintance under these circumstances. Nonetheless, Malio eased my concerns and I joined him on the ride to the Valdes home located on the south side of Robles Park on east Adalee.

Malio extended to Mr. Valdes the courtesy of a phone call before arriving, so he was aware of Malio's intentions. I studied the interaction between them as Malio confidently explained his plan and I wondered if Mr. Valdes intended to give Shirley the vehicle in the first place. Mr. Valdes conversed with Malio in his typical cordial and jovial manner. Within five minutes, Malio had accomplished his mission. Malio drove the Fury and I followed in his Lincoln Continental as we backtracked to the restaurant. I had to leave because Judy was expecting me, and the next time I saw Malio he was sporting a red MGB roadster identical to mine.

We played with Malio's new toy for a few days and within that period of time his enthusiasm for the car began to wane. At the same time, the attractive roadster had caught the eye of Malio's friend and former schoolmate, Reggie Sedita. Before you could say "transferable warranty" a deal was struck, and Reggie was the proud owner of a "nearly new" MGB.

Shortly thereafter, Reggie proudly drove his European auto to Gainesville and during the trip experienced engine difficulty. The car was towed to David Hines Auto Imports, the Tampa dealership from where it was originally purchased by Malio. What was anticipated to be only an inconvenience for Reggie turned out to be much more. With the automobile's odometer reading less than 2,000 miles, the assumption was that any and all repairs would be covered under the manufacturer's warranty. Warranty coverage in this particular instance was crucial because repair of the MGB included replacing the engine at a cost of $1,000, a huge sum in 1965. However, there was a caveat in the warranty's "small print" voiding the twelve-month/12,000-mile warranty beyond the original owner. This classic case of "consumer abuse" was ultimately shouldered by Reggie after he and Malio did everything they could, including attempting to retract the sale. This experience taught each of us a harsh lesson with Reggie being the prize pupil at no small expense.

As was the case with Carmine and Barbara, Malio and Shirley's wedding ceremony at Our Lady of Perpetual Help Catholic Church was a beautiful event. While Carmine and

Barbara's reception was held at the Davis Islands' Garden Club, Malio and Shirley chose the Gasparilla Room at the Curtis Hixon convention center for their celebration. Both receptions were festive events celebrating the union of four wonderful people who happened to be amongst my closest friends.

In addition to the enjoyable time Judy and I had at both functions, we both remember (especially Judy) engaging in heated arguments following each reception. So heated were the arguments that they resulted in us "breaking up" both times. I'm assured by Judy that I was to blame for both arguments which were caused by me not paying enough attention to her, leaving her for long periods of time and socializing (paying attention) with others, especially girls. Under the Fifth Amendment to the Constitution of the United States of America, I exercise my right as a citizen and have no comment.

If the humidity is unbearable, you can cut the air with a knife, and the "real" temperature hovers between the high 90s and low 100s, then it must be mid-August in Florida and time for *two a day* practices in preparation for the fall season. Several players, including my brother Gene, Bobby Fernandez, Verlin Williams, and I engaged in preseason conditioning drills and touch football games at West Pines playground where I was employed. But now it was time for business.

Eighty to a hundred of us checked into Lykes Hall, our home for the next two and a half weeks. Amongst the group checking into Lykes Hall were the coaching staff, trainers, and team managers that included Gene's good friend and mine, Danny Someillan.

I roomed with Vernon Korhn, and seventeen-year-old Gene roomed with Greg Bonfe who was six years his senior. We ate our meals at the cafeteria in the Student Union building next to Lykes Hall and practiced at Plant Field, which today is Pepin-Rood stadium and Sam Bailey baseball complex.

I asked Gene how he liked his roommate and he responded that he liked him fine but was concerned because several players, including Jim Underhill, were visiting their room for the purpose of smoking cigarettes. He said he was going to hang around our room until it was time to go to sleep because he didn't want to get caught with the smokers and it was hot in their room because they opened the windows in an attempt to rid the room of the cigarette smoke and smell.

Bobby Weeks was a talented player and a fragile personality. George Carter, who had been a year behind me at Jesuit, was also a talented player as well as a strong personality, and for some reason was bent on making Bobby's first experience at UT a memorable one. George, a defensive end, was six-foot-three and a muscular 225 pounds in contrast to wide receiver Bobby Weeks whose 170 pounds was evenly distributed over his small but wiry frame. There seems to always be a freshman or two selected to be taunted and Bobby had somehow been tagged with this dubious distinction. In addition to being the butt of jokes, Bobby was threatened by several players, led by George, to be wary of "things" that might happen while he slept. Bobby begged for dispensation from anything that would detract from his much-needed sleep but his request fell on deaf ears.

While everyone slept, someone slipped into Bobby's room and lit a cherry bomb beneath his bed which, when exploded, achieved its purpose of rattling Bobby. Bobby understandably was quite upset and in directing his anger at a laughing George Carter, he accelerated the brutal assault. Within fifteen minutes, everyone was back in their rooms hoping to get some rest before morning.

At approximately 4 AM, someone entered Bobby's room as he slept and lifted the foot of his bed and slammed it into the wall (again) causing sheer terror for Bobby and disruption throughout the dorm. The old-timers were laughing but the freshmen observed with trepidation, wondering if they were next.

Coach Prinzi, serving dorm duty, approached John Perry and me with the following advice, "We have a full and challenging day tomorrow. I suggest you put a stop to this so we can all get some sleep." I was impressed with coach Prinzi's calm and sensible approach to the matter. I told John I thought it would be better if I approached George Carter by myself and he agreed.

Using some testosterone/ego psychology, I explained to George that Bobby couldn't take much more and asked George if he could assist me in quelling the attack on Bobby. He recognized we had experienced enough excitement for one evening and gave me his word that Bobby was safe for the balance of the night.

Coach Prinzi woke everyone at 5:45 AM; time to have breakfast and be on the field at 7:30. It was a typical first day practice with many of the players moaning about the heat, while a few attempted to raise spirits with positive comments and leadership during drills. What was not typical was that I was part of the latter group.

That evening, John Perry visited my room with a pair of electric shears in his hand and informed me of the tradition of shaving the heads of the freshman ballplayers for the bargain price of two dollars (the cost of a regular haircut) per head. I liked the idea and joined John as we went door-to-door shaving heads and collecting dollars.

As we entered Gene's room, I explained the situation and slipped him two dollars. When finished, John told Gene he was exempt from the two-dollar tariff because he was my brother. I explained to John I was appreciative of his sentiment but that Gene should pay like the rest of the freshman. He agreed and I could detect a faint smile on Gene's face as he handed me his two dollars.

While most did not care for the traditional freshman haircut, all but one understood it was inevitable and cooperated. However, a young Ron Brown, from Sayre, Pennsylvania, explained to John, Spud, and me that he would not mind paying the two dollars but he could not let us cut his hair because it would not sit well with his girlfriend back in Pennsylvania. I thought he was engaged in a poor attempt at humor as I plugged the shears into the wall socket. He handed Spud the two dollars and pointed to his girlfriend's picture on the desk as he moved his head when John approached with the shears. I explained we could cut his Fabian-style hair the easy way or the hard way but we were going to cut his hair; the choice was his.

He boldly attempted to convince us otherwise, and at that juncture I realized he was serious. John and Jim Underhill (Spud) felt the same as I did but looked to me to communicate this since Ron was a lineman. As I began explaining that we had no choice but to cut his hair, he again attempted to convince me otherwise with the same lame excuse. I explained to Ron we had already spent too much time at this stop and the price of the haircut would soon be five dollars. He offered five dollars if we would not cut his hair. I then communicated to Ron he was going to have a difficult time at UT if he was unable to understand situations as he was doing with this one. He decided not to wage what would have been a futile fight when I explained to him that I was now considering shaving the hair from another area of his anatomy if he persisted. While John shaved his head, he wore a scowl on his face that I guessed was intended to communicate to us we had made him angry. This young fellow had a lot to learn.

An unexpected pleasure during two-a-day practices was the attendance of my brother Bob and Uncle Vince. Uncle Vince would generally attend the morning workouts while he ran errands for his employer, the Coca-Cola Bottling Company, while Bob would attend the afternoon workouts on his way home from work. With temperatures in the mid to high 90s accompanied with humidity that causes drivers to use their windshield wipers in the morning even though it has not rained and wearing thirty pounds of equipment while charging through rigorous conditioning and contact drills, seeing Uncle Vince and my brother Bob represented the cool drink of water drastically needed because water was deemed to be counterproductive and thus not allowed in that era. Gene and I often commented on what a lift it was to see Bob and Uncle Vince enduring the torrid temperatures and enjoying themselves as they watched their loved ones labor.

As we prepared for our opener vs. McNeese State in Lake Charles, Louisiana, a couple of interesting developments began to take on a life of their own. Being the *only game in town* in 1965, the local sports community began to *manufacture news* by expanding a comment made by Coach Bailey regarding the importance of tackle play in the outcome of a football game. He went on to say that UT was stronger than it had been in many years with my addition to an already seasoned and talented group of athletes at the tackle position.

Tampa Times sportswriter, Chico Genovese, learned that my former roommate at LSU was now McNeese State's top tackle and a story was born. He queried me as to how I would handle a situation in which my opponent had the benefit of knowing my strengths and weaknesses having practiced together for two years. I simply responded that I had also practiced with him for two years and that I was well aware of his strengths and weaknesses. David Poché was, indeed, a talented player and I had no intention of adding to his built-in motivation with a slip of the tongue.

Concurrent with this storyline was a lesser known but no less important development regarding my Uncle Vince. Uncle Vince often expressed to me his desire to make the trip to Lake Charles. I didn't give it much thought until one evening a week before the game at a workout at Philips field, home of the University of Tampa Spartans (forerunner to Tampa Stadium [the Big Sombrero], which was sent to its demise to give birth to Raymond James Stadium).

As we tuned up for McNeese State under the lights, I noticed a crew installing a new scoreboard donated by the local Coca-Cola bottling company and that circumstance somehow motivated me to ask Coach Bailey whether Uncle Vince could travel with us to Lake Charles. Uncle Vince was employed by Coca-Cola, and even though it was a stretch, I know he did what he could to get Coca-Cola's management to support UT. Coach Bailey accepted my request with his usual businesslike demeanor and told me he would give my idea consideration. On Monday of the following week, the traveling squad was posted in our locker room and to my pleasant surprise Vincent Russo of Coca-Cola was listed among other para-Spartans including Tom McEwen of the Tampa Tribune, Andy Hardy of WTVT Channel 13, and Doctors Leonard Annis, Buck Younger, and John Tyner.

I couldn't wait to communicate the news to him, and after I convinced him I was not teasing he became more joyful than I.

We drove to Tampa International Airport together that Friday not yet knowing that it was to become a ritual we would enjoy during my entire stay at UT.

Vernon Korhn was my roommate on the road and that was a match made in heaven. Vernon was a calm individual and a student of the game, qualities I could ascribe to few others on the team, especially as it relates to calmness. I cherished peacefulness then as I do now, and Vernon fit the bill in every regard.

As bedtime approached, we experienced normal hunger but realized it would be better to manage this desire considering the purpose of our trip. Nonetheless, Vernon and I yielded to Uncle Vince's offer to bring us a couple of cheeseburgers before he and his traveling companions explored the nightlife of Lake Charles. The next morning at breakfast, I heard others commenting on what Uncle Vince brought them to eat the evening before and was hoping this news would not reach Coach Bailey.

McNeese State was dedicating their new stadium with our game and the full house was, indeed, raucous.

The local paper in Lake Charles had hitchhiked onto Chico Genovese's discovery regarding David Poché and me so we decided not to speak to each other until after the contest.

The game was a hotly-contested battle in which UT prevailed by a small margin preserved by a fourth-quarter blocked field goal credited to none other than me, and of which I had no knowledge (the ball hit my helmet), until I was congratulated by players and coaches on the sideline.

After the game, it was good to visit with former LSU teammates David Poché and Paul Guidry. They gave us credit for having a good team, and as the season progressed, I saw the wisdom of their opinion. We won all of our games except for two and a tie against favored University of Buffalo. Amongst our victories was a 2-0 victory over the number 1-ranked small college in America, the University of Maine.

The season provided ample excitement, but there was some drama off the field worth mentioning. As we prepared to play the University of Buffalo, in Buffalo, New York an opportunity became a disappointment (putting it mildly) for my friend and teammate Greg Bonfe.

As a show of support, his large family in Syracuse planned a trip to Buffalo. As was often the case, Greg was crossways with the coaches and his planned participation in Saturday's contest was tentative. It was a bitterly cold November day that Saturday in Buffalo, but from the point of view of Greg and others, including Uncle Vince and me, the real coldness was in the hearts of some UT coaches.

Greg was undoubtedly one of the finest players and persons I have ever met, but he had yet to develop the skill of *getting along*. My experience gave me empathy for Greg's situation, even though there was little I could do except try to encourage him to cooperate with the coaching staff. He was well liked by players, students, and the entire football staff, with the exception of the only ones who counted—the coaches. Much of this *disconnect* could be attributed to the times. There was little debate between coaches and players, teachers and students, bosses and workers, etc. This *attitude of the time* squandered talent and Greg's situation was a perfect example.

At halftime, the score was 7-7. Only a few of the players (those with brains) chose to wear long-sleeved shirts and leggings under our uniforms as did the Buffalo players. Consequently, those of us who went without the undergarments spent most of the intermission trying to stop the bleeding on our arms and calves, which had been exposed to intermittent frozen turf amidst a bone chilling 14-degree temperature. Greg was amongst the group without brains but was not bleeding because he had not set foot on the field. While he visited with me, he mumbled his disappointment with the coaches about not getting playing time and as I cautioned him to keep his comments in check, Uncle Vince was agreeing with everything he said which was fueling what was becoming a raging fire. I felt Greg was going to see plenty of action during the second half and told him so and that he didn't want to risk spoiling that opportunity with comments about coaches. He told me he thought I was wrong but that he would yield to my suggestion.

During the third quarter, UB completed several short passes in the linebackers' zone, which contributed to a scoring drive that put them ahead 13-7. I thought this would initiate Greg's insertion into the game, but I was wrong.

Everyone on the bench wore parkas stuffed with towels to keep them warm, but Greg's parka remained unsnapped and open as to release the steam he was generating.

As the game progressed, Greg's family, led by his brothers and uncles, along with sympathetic fans began to chant, "We want Bonfe." This had the effect of raising Greg's temperature and galvanizing the coaches' resolve, neither of which needed help. Additionally, a few players on the sideline were snickering and focusing more on the tension between Greg and the coaches than on the game. I decided to voice my opinion to Coach Bailey. "Coach," I said, "I think Greg can help us shut them out for the rest of the game." to which he responded, "Mondy, do your job and let me do mine." He wasn't angry with me but the message was clear; he did not want to discuss the matter further.

Midway through the fourth quarter we scored a touchdown to tie the game 13–13. We lined up to kick the extra point and UB called a timeout in an effort to freeze our place kicker, figuratively and literally. We lined up again, but our ace place kicker, Ernie Casares, never had the opportunity to score the decisive 14th point as our long snapper mishandled the snap which never made it to the holder.

It was a disappointing game because of the blown opportunity against a favored team on their turf in weather that was tailor made for them. Additionally, a few of us were emotionally spent due to the gut-wrenching drama between Greg and the coaching staff that unfolded throughout the game.

The itinerary called for us to eat a post-game meal before our return trip to Tampa. Uncle Vince sat with Greg and me on the bus trip from the stadium to the restaurant as I attempted to soothe Greg whose anger continued to build. He said he wanted to slug the defensive coordinator and return to Syracuse with his family. I told him to forget the idea and we would work matters out back in Tampa. He gave me no response but continued to steam.

We were at the beginning of the group as we entered the restaurant and Uncle Vince and I sat down at a table while Greg went to the men's room. As soon as we sat down, a nervous

Uncle Vince told me that Greg was not going to the men's room but was waiting just inside the entrance with the intention of confronting the coach and hoping the incident would escalate into fisticuffs between them. I leaped from my chair and made my way to where Greg was. By this time, many had figured out what was about to happen and were lingering for an eyewitness account. Uncle Vince joined me in trying to convince Greg to abort his plans, but Greg decided he was on the correct course of action. As I saw coaches getting off the buses, I simply grabbed Greg in a *bear hug* and ushered him to the most remote table in the restaurant. "Greg," I said, "if you feel you still want to hit him when we get back to Tampa, then do it. But now is not the right time. You'll end up accomplishing nothing except embarrassing yourself, your family, our team, and the university."

He mumbled something unintelligible in response but seemed to yield to my suggestion. Before the food arrived, he said he was not hungry and was going for a walk. Uncle Vince accompanied him and assisted me as a sentry during the return trip.

Greg was still angry when we arrived in Tampa, but assured Uncle Vince and me that he would not do anything stupid. I stayed in touch with Greg over the weekend and the next time I saw him he thanked me for keeping him from making a grave error and shared the same sentiments with Uncle Vince over the telephone.

I knew exactly how Greg felt but could not convince him of that fact. I had pleaded with him and Gene, and while they occasionally threw *ear candy* my way, neither backed up their conversation with action. Neither of them could see how their attitude was affecting their relationship with the coaches, and therefore, saw no need to change things.

When a person doesn't recognize the problem, it's almost impossible to get them to do something about it. I know that to be the case because two years earlier I walked in the very shoes I was attempting to get them to walk out of.

MY COUISN JOE

"You're assured of a B and can possibly end up with an A if you take Mr. Nosti for art," I was told by John Perry and Dan Cogin, which sealed the decision for me as I scheduled classes for the fall semester. "He likes football and football players who show him respect," they added to assure me I was making the correct decision.

Later that day, I met Baby Joe for lunch and we reviewed each other's class schedules. "I didn't know you were going to take art or I would have told you to take it with my cousin, Joe Testasecca," commented Baby Joe.

"Are you telling me your cousin teaches art at UT?" I responded.

"Oh, yeah. He's an accomplished artist in his own right and teaches art as an avocation."

"Well, it's just as well because a couple guys put me onto a professor who will deliver a sure B, and if I play my cards right, possibly an A."

"I can do better than that," Joe said, "I can get my cousin to give you an A and you won't have to show up for class very often."

"Wait a minute, Baby Joe. Two minutes ago, I didn't even know you had a cousin who taught art and now you're telling me I can get an A and don't have to show up very often?" "That's what I'm saying," cajoled Baby Joe.

"Can you give him a call and see if he's up for this program?"

"There's no need to call him, Mondy, I see him all the time and I can assure you there is no problem," he responded in a tone intended to allay my concern.

"BJ, I've got a great deal already with Mr. Nosti, but if you're certain about this deal, I'm heading back to make this change immediately."

"It's a sure thing," said Baby Joe. "And I'll go with you to make the change."

At the first meeting of class, Mr. Testasecca introduced us to a project termed *a color wheel* whereby we were to segment a 30-inch circle into many (I don't recall the exact number) equal pie-shaped parts beginning with a totally white segment and adding more dots to each segment until the final segment was totally black. The idea was to demonstrate that many figures we see are merely a collection of dots at different degrees of concentration. He concluded his remarks by saying that the project was not necessarily difficult as much as it was tedious, time-consuming, and required discipline to distribute the 36 hours he estimated it would take over the course of the semester.

I took Mr. Testasecca at his word regarding the time required to complete this assignment and was thrilled that I was exempt because of my friendship with Baby Joe.

The class met three times a week and my plan was to attend once per week.

The routine was generally the same. He would spend the first 15 or 20 minutes making points about our reading assignment, and then give us the rest of the class to either begin reading the next assignment or work on *the color wheel*.

About the third week, which was about my third visit to the class, Mr. Testasecca began observing the students' progress with *the wheel* and toward the end of the class he asked to view mine. I proudly opened my three-foot by three-foot art pad and showed him the blank sheet accompanied with my exaggerated smile.

He asked why I had not begun the project and, while maintaining my smile, I whispered to him that I was Baby Joe's friend. With a perplexed look on his face, he invited me to join him in the hallway to complete this conversation. "And what's the connection between Baby Joe and the color wheel?" he asked.

Not wanting to share the portion of my conversation with Baby Joe I considered privileged, I said, "Baby Joe said he would talk to you and explain that I was not very gifted in art and that he thought you would be understanding of my situation."

"How can we assess your giftedness if you don't make any effort?"

"Are you saying you would like me to do *a wheel*?" I asked, realizing how stupid the question sounded.

"That would be my recommendation," he responded as we headed back into the classroom. "And Mr. Flores, I would also recommend you attend all the remaining classes."

As I walked away from the class, I was unsure whether Mr. Testasecca was joining Baby Joe in this charade as a practical joke, or if I had, in fact, made a terrible decision in changing art professors.

The next time I saw Baby Joe I carefully studied his reaction as I explained to him my encounter with his cousin, Joe Testasecca. I couldn't detect a flaw in the quizzical look on his face and began to develop an awful feeling in my stomach. Reacting to the look on my face, Baby Joe said he would speak to his cousin and see what was going on.

I'm an optimist by nature, but I didn't have much confidence things were going to improve. Baby Joe's report to me confirmed my feelings.

"He said just do your best and you'll be okay," Baby Joe timidly offered with an apologetic look on his face.

In an effort to protect Baby Joe's feelings, I explained to him if everyone else in the class could do the work, I was sure I could, also. While that statement was certainly accurate, I asked myself, *why couldn't I have been satisfied with my sure B by attending class and being respectful to Mr. Nosti?*

It was pure greed. I had been bitten by my own greediness.

That pretty much ended our conversation regarding art and I spent the entire semester sweating a course that could have been a piece of cake.

My former exaggerated smiles and boldness toward Mr. Testasecca transitioned into humble glances crying for mercy. As it worked out, I was **given** a C in the course.

JUST HAVING FUN

Notwithstanding the art class debacle, Joe and I developed a close friendship in college. His friends became my friends, and my friends became his. He liked my family and I liked his. Baby Joe especially liked my brother Gene. We all shared a common interest in humor, which manifested itself in many ways, but none better than a routine that developed between Baby Joe and Gene.

Gene was experiencing little to no playing time, and in an effort to relieve frustration, he began to warm up at field goal situations during games as if he was the kicker. He was doing this for the benefit of his friends, led by Baby Joe, who would chant and cheer for him throughout the game. When Gene began his warmup antics, Baby Joe and company would ratchet up their cheering and this, of course, motivated Gene to exaggerate his act. To add fuel to the fire, our friend and team manager, Danny Someillan issued Gene a pair of square toed kicking shoes which emboldened Gene to warm up next to the actual kicker who did not care for Gene's act. Nonetheless, Gene would continue his charade as long as Baby Joe egged him on and Gene would even kick a couple of balls into the kickers net. All this was carefully orchestrated behind the bench and without the knowledge of the coaching staff.

I got a kick out of it also, but shuddered to think what would have happened had Coach Bailey had gotten wind of Gene's self-conceived and directed production.

Another friendly interaction between Gene and Baby Joe was their version of *bumping cars*. Gene drove a 1954 Chevrolet Bel-Air which was virtually indestructible and which he purchased from our next-door neighbor, Irene Fernandez, for the sum of $60 cash. Gene and I painted his car with left over interior house paint we found in our garage. Baby Joe, on the other hand, drove a loaded, navy blue 1965 Chevy Super-Sport. The third participant was Vernon Korhn. Whenever any two of the three saw each other in their vehicle, bumping their vehicles ensued. Vernon's car was much closer to Gene's class than Baby Joe's. Nonetheless, Baby Joe, often resulting in damage to his vehicle (which concerned him not), delivered the most aggressive attacks. Damage to Gene's and Vernon's vehicles generally blended in.

SWIMMING, ANYONE?

One of the many benefits of attending school in Florida is, of course, the weather. There are limited locales throughout the country where water activities can be enjoyed practically year-round.

My buddy, Deno, and I enrolled in a required swimming/lifeguard course for physical education majors. The 1PM class met twice a week for an hour-and-a-half at the Davis Islands swimming pool. Both Deno and I had classes that ended at 12:30 PM, so there was no time for lunch until after class. To thwart the effects of hunger, I picked up a "submarine" type sandwich on the way to the swimming pool and ate it while changing clothes. I would've preferred a sandwich and a half but only purchased one for budgetary reasons.

Without exception, Deno would ask if he could have a bite of my sub while we changed into our swim trunks, and as the class progressed, the number of bites he requested also progressed. Deno was a dear friend and I was happy to share my provisions with him except for the fact that one sub was just plain inadequate for me.

Meanwhile, during the semester I continued to frequent Carmine's Restaurant and one evening I had an interesting experience. While relieving myself, I was engaged in conversation with my friend and former Spartan basketball standout, John Pellegrino, who was using the adjacent urinal. I couldn't help but notice the bright blood-red color John was generating, and recognizing that I had recognized this peculiarity, John began to joke about his ability to urinate in different colors. He then explained that he had injured his kidney while playing basketball and was on a medication called *Pyridium,* which caused his urine to turn bright red. My immediate thought was to get some of these tablets and place them into my sandwich so that Deno would ingest them prior to swim class knowing that sometime during class, if he was like me, his secret act would be exposed and would provide levity to a class that could use a laugh. "How many pills does it take and how long after you to take these pills does your urine turn red?" I inquired of John.

"One tablet and about one hour."

I enthusiastically told John of my plan and he eagerly went to his automobile and retrieved a half-dozen *Pyridium* tablets as his contribution to my scheme.

I was enthusiastic about the next swim class and had selected a sub I knew to be one of Deno's favorites.

As I changed into my swim trunks, I flaunted my *Pyridium*-loaded sandwich at Deno, but for the first time he didn't ask for a bite. I took unusual care in hanging my clothes and placed the sandwich next to Deno. He glanced at it but continued changing clothes as if he had made a decision to refrain from his previous practice of assisting me with my sandwich. Time was running short and I had to interest him in the sandwich. "I had a hamburger on the way," I said to Deno "so you're welcome to half this sub if you're interested." That did the trick. With five or six hurried bites he gobbled his half of the sandwich, which included hot pastrami, melted Swiss cheese, sauerkraut, and three *Pyridium* tablets. The show was on.

As a courtesy to the instructor, Alice Rodriguez, and as a means of covering for myself, I informed her of my plan and told her that with her permission, I intended to make a commotion of the event if and when it happened.

She asked if Deno could take such a prank and I assured her there would be no problem in that regard. She smiled and I accepted that as tacit approval realizing that she did not want to be officially linked with the hoax.

I kept my eye on Deno throughout the class and was beginning to wonder if this medicine reacted differently with different people. For the last twenty minutes of the class, Ms. Rodriguez asked us to come to the edge of the pool (on the deep end) as she gave us some final instructions. Deno was positioned by other students and I had to wedge my way into position (next to him) if this thing was going to work as conceived.

A couple of our water mates looked at me strangely as I positioned myself next to Deno causing others to move. I was certain they would later understand that I was on a mission.

My eyes were on Ms. Rodriguez, but my sight was focused on Deno. Approximately five minutes into her comments a cloud of red water emanated from Deno's swim trunks at which time I forcefully pushed myself away from the side of the pool yelling "Shark! Shark! Shark!" Everyone but Ms. Rodriguez was initially befuddled but quickly recognized what was happening and joined in the laughter, no one laughing harder than Deno. Ms. Rodriguez was laughing so hard that she dismissed the class and walked away from the pool.

Deno wanted to know the particulars of how I pulled off this stunt and we laughed as I shared the story with him while we treaded water in the pool. Only a confident person can take such a joke and Deno fit the bill.

THE JERSEY SHORE

Stunts such as the one pulled on Deno added a little flavor to college life. Deno was typical of the UT student from the northeast in that they had chosen UT because of the weather, sports, parties, and amongst these activities they were committed to somehow squeezing in a degree (not to be confused with getting an education).

Deno lead the charge in the categories of sports and parties amongst the group from New Jersey and promoted New Jersey at every opportunity.

Asbury Park, on the Jersey Shore, was nothing short of Mecca according to Deno. The winter's snow was pristine and plentiful and Asbury Park's proximity to New York City made his hometown the nation's winter wonderland. Additionally, and according to Deno, Asbury Park produced a plethora of talent that operated the *boardrooms and Broadways* across this nation.

Deno was understandably proud of his hometown where his mother, Anita, raised him and his younger brother, Teddy, in their home above her popular restaurant named *Little Campus*. So avid was his constant portrayal of this bedroom community to New York City that one got the idea he was making an extreme sacrifice to be away from this jewel of the northeast known as Asbury Park.

We became such close friends that Deno invited me to Asbury Park for the Christmas holidays. I had been to New York once before as a 12-year-old and was excited about revisiting the Big Apple. We motored from Tampa to New York in Deno's late-model, yellow Plymouth convertible with two other students who were also from the Jersey Shore. The three of them asked if it would be all right if they fine-tuned their tans on the way and I agreed to the benign request.

As we negotiated the highway out of Tampa, my three traveling companions utilized a tanning aid known as a *reflector*. They placed the foil covered cardboard on their shoulders and around their neck to achieve a balanced tan on their neck and beneath their chin. With the top down, the radio blaring, and three of the four passengers donning *reflectors*, we had New Jersey written all over us as we drove through Ocala.

It was fun for a while, but a problem was beginning to develop. I enjoyed the loud music but the bright sun and wind generated by traveling 70 mph was becoming a nuisance. I did not want to impede the tanning process but I knew that traveling all day like this would be miserable, at least for me. I reluctantly informed them of my problem and they negotiated an additional hour before the top would go up and the AC turned on.

As we arrived in Asbury Park, the ground was covered with snow and the homes and businesses gaily expressed the Christmas season with their decorations.

Meeting Deno's family substantiated every impression I had of him. This warm Greek family reminded me of mine. His mother, Anita, was a hard-working and dedicated single mom, and his aunts and uncles could have been doubles from mine. Additionally, it was very obvious from the first time I met his younger brother Teddy that they were very close. We engaged in the traditional hugging and eating well into the evening before retiring upstairs above the *Little Campus*.

There was a party or social event each of the nights we were in New Jersey, and during these gatherings I noticed an interesting occurrence. Deno, who as I previously mentioned had acted as a goodwill ambassador for Asbury Park in Tampa, was now actively promoting Tampa to all his friends on the Jersey Shore. He explained to them that he lived in a land of enchantment amongst the Palm trees and sandy shores which neighbored the breathtaking and therapeutic bay waters of the Gulf of Mexico. Additionally, he described his residence as a waterfront bungalow on an island close to Tampa. "I never have to deal with snow and I left my coats, hats and earmuffs in Jersey. I can fish from my front lawn and can go boating or sailing between classes." He continued about all the advantages of living in Florida as his audience listened intently and covetously. What really got my attention was when he finished his pitch with "I don't know if I'll ever be able to come back."

It soon dawned on me that he was describing his life on Davis Islands. I couldn't wait to speak with him alone so I could query him as to which story was true since he told both in such a convincing manner. He chuckled as I broached the subject of his double life knowing I had now seen his *hold card*. He agreed to never again tout the Jersey Shore to me.

We had a delightful trip to New Jersey, which of course, included a couple of visits to New York City, but we were all ready to return to Deno's true love, and mine as well, Tampa, Florida.

ART IN STEAKS

How would you like to sink your teeth into a mouthwatering, prime Chateaubriand, accompanied with a fully-loaded, velvet-soft, baked potato and a five-star Caesar salad? Would you enjoy following that up with a piece of banana cream pie or Key lime pie (or both)? Well, Gene and I certainly did.

Bern's Steak House of Tampa, Florida has a reputation far beyond the city in which it has been operating since the 1950s. Bernard (Bern) Laxer and his wife Gert moved to Tampa from New York City, and in 1953, bought a diner on Cass Street for $1,500 and called it Bern and Gert's Little Midway. Three years later, they bought a place called the Beer Haven on South Howard where they established Bern's Steak House and, as they say, the rest is history. Their focus was quality and service—a winning combination every time.

Bern and his wife Gert toiled in their new enterprise, which—in time—developed into a five-star restaurant earning a reputation as one of the country's top steakhouses. Bern's extensive and quality wine selection expanded his steakhouse's notoriety beyond the U.S. and into Western Europe. From the onset, the restaurant catered to the businessperson with an expense account and the well-to-do.

Featured at Bern's, where the phrase *Art in Steaks* was born, was and still is aged beef in a variety of cuts and thicknesses, incomparable Caesar Salad and onion soup, homegrown vegetables (led by their fabulous French-fried zucchini, onion rings, and a melt in your mouth baked potato dressed at the table), scrumptious desserts (including Brazilian Snow and unmatched banana cream pie) and, as previously mentioned, a wine inventory without peer.

Becoming a waiter at Bern's required a year's apprenticeship before Bern would allow a waiter to serve his loyal clientele. Being a waiter at Bern's became a prestigious position in the restaurant industry, carrying with it a handsome income based solely on tips. Most of the waiters were professionals who raised families with their income, but sprinkled amongst them were a few UT students trying to earn a few bucks while going to school. Two such students were friends and fellow football players John Perry from Miami and Verlin Williams from Bluefield, West Virginia.

Verlin and his wife Sally (who was in nursing school) were parents to two lovely girls and Verlin used his position at Bern's to finance his household and Sally's schooling.

Gene and I were good friends with Verlin and prior to getting married he often ate at our home. He was well aware of our interest in what was served within the hallowed walls of his employer.

One evening, an impromptu visit by Verlin began what became a welcome ritual at our home. Apparently, it was the practice of some of the waiters to *trim* the leftovers of the dining guests and take home what could only be termed a *super doggie bag.*

One evening, without advance notice, Verlin decided to share his *super doggie bag* with Gene and me. At approximately 12:30 AM, a light tap on our bedroom window awakened Gene and me. When we pulled back the thick drapes and saw a hand maneuvering a large bag to and fro, we didn't know what to think. We got out of bed and cranked open the window to view the person to whom this hand belonged. We discovered Verlin was attached to the hand as he crouched in the flowerbed next to our home.

With his typical large smile, he asked, "Are you guys interested in some Chateaubriand, baked potato, Caesar's salad, and oh, I almost forgot, some banana cream pie?"

Without uttering a word, we returned the smile and Verlin instinctively knew to meet us at the kitchen door. He entered the house with a mild grin and his grin grew as he witnessed the interest with which Gene and I treated his unannounced visit. We quickly set the table and brought out six Cokes from my mom's well stocked inventory providing the signal for the banquet to begin.

Verlin recognized how much we enjoyed his visit, and thus, frequently visited us, thereafter, sometimes just leaving a *super doggie bag* when he was unable to stay. Verlin was a fun-loving guy and he enjoyed the fellowship even though it delayed his bedtime by an hour or so.

Tragically, a few years later, when Verlin was a football coach at Leto High school, he lost his life in an automobile vs. train accident on his way to Leto High School for a game one Friday evening. Gene and I were shocked at the news and could identify with the plight of his two young daughters left in the capable care of their shocked but committed mother, Sally.

PALM BEACH

Judy and I dated through the spring and summer. We double-dated with friends, ate at restaurants, went to movies and to the beach, so on and so forth.

In June of 1966, we planned a trip with our friends Bennie Lazzara and his girlfriend to Palm Beach, primarily to gaze at the mansions that make up that community. Judy's dad was kind enough to offer us his comfortable and luxurious Buick Roadmaster for the trip. We took our time as we headed east on Highway 60 toward Yeehaw Junction where we took the Sunshine Parkway south to Palm Beach.

We engaged in the usual activities such as shopping, dining and we even took in a movie, but our primary purpose was to check out the winter homes of the rich and famous. I recall being impressed by mansions of people whose names we did not recognize and being underwhelmed by mansions belonging to people whose names were recognized in this country and around the world.

One such case was the Kennedy compound. The home of assassinated President John F. Kennedy's parents (the one that was regularly seen on television depicting the Kennedys as America's family, usually engaged in a game of football amongst the brothers, uncles, nephews, etcetera), located on the north end of Palm Beach was situated on a gorgeous oceanfront setting; however, the structure itself was quite common, in need of renovation and repair, and simply not up to par with their neighbors.

We were driving around this opulent setting when Bennie thought he heard the name of a couple of our friends on the radio. The station was not coming in clear so we changed from station to station listening for any news that might confirm Bennie's claim.

Within a few minutes, we heard the news from a central Florida radio station that our friends, Nelson Valenti and Mac Farrington, were killed in an auto accident returning to Tampa from a baseball game in which they had participated. Bennie called Tampa to gain clarification of what we hoped was not true, but our wish was not granted. We learned that Mac was driving Nelson's Corvette at a high rate is speed, lost control, and careened into a tree once he lost control of the vehicle.

We immediately headed back to Tampa and arrived at a dismal gathering at the home of Nelson Valenti. It was a harsh example of this life's frailty. One moment you're engaged in the American pastime and the next you have abruptly checked out of this life leaving your family and friends to mourn and question why.

Nelson was a close friend of Bennie's and mine and was cousin to our good friend Baby Joe. Mac and Bennie were teammates at Hillsborough High School and I had developed a fondness for Mac over the previous two years.

Mac detailed automobiles at a car lot across the alley from Judy's home on 26th Avenue and I would visit with Mac each time I called on Judy and he was at work.

Mac was a playful, yet focused individual and our common interests fostered our friendship.

The loss of my two friends hit home again when I picked up Judy to attend Mac's funeral. I went over to the detail area of the car lot and someone had placed a bunch of flowers in front of a picture of Mac in his Hillsborough High football uniform. Hanging on the wall was a baseball jersey with the sleeves cut off which Mac had been wearing the last time I had seen him.

It was difficult to enjoy the balance of the summer in the wake of such a tragedy, but life goes on.

GENE, DOUG, & THE DOLPHINS

Doug Moreau completed a stellar career at LSU and was drafted by the Miami Dolphins, who in 1966, held preseason camp on St. Petersburg Beach. Doug called and said that he would like to come by and visit on his way to St. Pete. I was pleased at the prospect of seeing Doug again.

He arrived at our home on Lemon Street during the Fourth of July holiday and brought a bag of tomatoes grown by his dad in Baton Rouge. I did not eat tomatoes at the time, but I had heard comments about them while in Baton Rouge touting them as simply *the best tomatoes one can eat*.

Shortly after Doug arrived, my brother Gene returned home from the beach with a serious split in his scalp of which no one in our house was aware. I thought he looked peculiar as he shook hands with Doug, chitchatted for a minute or two, and then signaled me to come into the bedroom because he wanted to discuss something with me privately.

He relayed the story that he was at one of the beach resorts the previous evening/early morning and a couple of intoxicated students from Jefferson High School were harassing the sister of his good friend, Joe Ficarrotta. He did what any self-respecting friend would do and came to her aid. A fight ensued and a beach chair was used on his head resulting in the gash to which he pointed.

His point was simple. He knew who the individual who had hit him with the chair was and wanted revenge. His question to me was, "Are you coming with me?" I assured him I was, but suggested he get a little sleep before we headed back to St. Petersburg Beach.

He agreed that napping was a good idea because he spent the entire night and morning searching for this individual who, after perpetrating this deed on Gene, realized he had bitten off more than he could chew, and immediately went into hiding.

I poured some hydrogen peroxide over the wound before Gene took his nap. Meanwhile, Doug was putting together bits and pieces and probably thought not much had changed around the Flores household. I explained to Doug what was going on and I could tell by the look on his face I was confirming what he was thinking.

We visited for a while before Gene woke up. The first words out of his mouth were,

"Are you ready to go? Because I am. Doug, you're welcome to come with us if you want to."

I was sure this was not exactly what Doug had envisioned when he decided to visit, and even though he nodded affirmatively, I told Gene that I would ride to the beach with Doug but we would leave him at his hotel. Then, he and I would handle this matter. A relieved Doug responded, "Whatever you guys want to do."

After leaving Doug at the Dolphin Inn on St. Pete Beach, Gene and I proceeded to follow every lead we could come up with in search of TP.

Finally, I ran into my good friend, Peter Lopez, from my days at West Tampa Jr. High who also attended Jefferson and he provided me with the following information. "Armando," he said. "You and your brother are looking for TP, is that true?" I told him we were, indeed.

"Well, let me tell you what happened," he continued, "TP has been moving from friend's room to friend's room and he came to my room late last night for a while until I found out about the fight and I told him he could not stay here because you are my friend. He left, but he asked me not to say anything if I saw you. I told him I would not say anything unless you asked. So, do you have any questions?"

Peter was my best friend at West Tampa Jr. High, and even though we had not seen each other in several years, I appreciated the spirit in which he communicated.

"Yeah, Peter," I said. "Have you seen TP, and do you know where he is?"

"I'm only telling you this because you asked," he said, "TP was here very early this morning, but I heard he headed back to Tampa and is hiding at his grandmother's on Lake Avenue."

I thanked Peter as Gene and I discussed the matter. Gene wanted TP and wanted him now but did not want to drag him out of his grandmother's home. Gene commented, "How about this football star hiding at his grandmother's."

The summer progressed and TP was nowhere to be found. Mutual friends told me that he completely gave up going out. He would alternate weekends between his home and that of his grandmother and one of his aunt's.

EVERY DOG HAS ITS DAY

Gene and Ted Cannella weight-trained in our garage, which we referred to as the Lemon Street Gym. On a hot, steamy August evening, I took a phone call for Gene who was lifting weights with Ted. He was dirty and sweaty and asked who was calling. I was becoming a little agitated acting as the go-between for Gene and his caller, so Gene, grudgingly, came into the house to take the call after I told him that the person on the line said it was important.

Gene said to the caller, "Are you sure it's him? Keep an eye on him and I'll be there in twenty minutes."

"Great news," he said to Ted and me, "TP is at the Islands Club and this guy I know is going to keep his eye on him until we arrive."

Ted, in typical fashion, responded, "That's great news; I've been waiting a long time to smash TP's face" (notwithstanding the fact that he had never met TP). With that exchange of Christian love, Gene and Ted were cleaning up and getting dressed for our showdown with TP.

We arrived at the Islands Club on Davis Islands and Gene's contact was at the door.

Without Gene asking, he described TP's location in the crowded lounge. Ted suggested I stay at the front door because they were going to convince TP that his best option was to take this matter outside the club. "Now, if you see all hell breaking loose in there, come help us," Ted told me as he and Gene moved people aside as they approached TP.

TP was visibly panicking as Gene ordered him outside. He told Gene that he didn't want to fight, that he was sorry for what happened at the beach and that he had been drinking heavily, but Gene would hear none of it.

Gene and Ted told TP in unison, "We're going to take care of this in here or outside—it's your choice," with Ted adding, "And you can bring any of your 'chicken sh*t friends.'"

Recognizing that he was not going to talk Gene out of this confrontation, he followed Gene and Ted out the front door.

He and his two friends were shocked to see me.

The six of us, followed by a crowd of thrill seekers, went around the side of the building as Ted commented, "I'm sorry there're no chairs for you."

TP immediately begged for mercy, to which Ted responded, "Just kick his ass, Gene, so we can get out of here."

On Ted's cue, Gene knocked TP to the ground with a ferocious left to the head splitting the skin beneath TP's right eye and rendering him helpless.

While saying, "What the hell are you looking at?" Ted punched TP's friend—who had a cigarette in his mouth—sending him to the ground at TP's feet.

He then said to the remaining member of TP's trio, "Why don't you help your chicken sh*t friends, you chicken sh*t?," causing the guy to walk away. "I'm not surprised, because that's the way chicken sh*ts are," were Ted's parting comments.

As we exited Davis Islands, we saw a police car heading the opposite way and we assumed they were called about the fracas.

WE NEEDED MORE THAN "TURF" SHOES

The balance of the summer was normal. Gene, Verlin, and a few other UT players came to West Pines playground every afternoon to participate in conditioning drills as we prepared ourselves for the upcoming season.

(For some reason or another, Judy and I would part company during football season and 1966 was no exception. I cannot recall the reason for this particular split and neither can she).

The entire team was excited about our prospects this season having just come off a very successful 1965 campaign and a spring practice where many players demonstrated a high skill level as they competed for starting positions.

I knew I was liked and respected by my teammates but I was nonetheless flattered when I was voted by the players as team captain along with Dan Cogan and Dan Sykes.

We had a typically tough schedule and a unique travel opportunity. We were playing the University of Houston in the *eighth wonder of the world*, the Houston Astrodome. (The Astrodome had opened the previous season with a natural turf playing field, but apparently, no one checked with the botany department at the university because the natural turf did not survive *indoors* which necessitated the development of the new synthetic turf called *Astroturf*—the turf on which we would play.)

We experienced a bombshell during our final week of two-a-days when Coach Bailey asked us to huddle before our morning practice and broke the news to us that our top receiver and tri-captain, Dan Cogan, had been declared ineligible.

It was reported to NCAA that he had played a year at another university and had not disclosed that information. The source of this information was not communicated to the University of Tampa, but it was rumored that the information was leaked from a school on our schedule.

In addition to being our top receiver, Dan was a positive influence on the team and would be sorely missed. His departure resulted in Dan Sykes and me becoming co-captains and charged with the responsibility of picking up the slack created by Cogan's departure.

As we prepared for our opener, Uncle Vince asked if he was traveling with the team this year and I responded that I had heard nothing to the contrary. Sure enough, his name was posted on the travel list gratifying both of us.

Our season had progressed nicely as we prepared to meet the Cougars of the University of Houston. Houston was a powerhouse in those days led by All-American candidates, fullback, Hoyle Grangier and wide receiver, Dickie Post.

We arrived in Houston on Friday and were bused directly to the Astrodome to give us an opportunity to familiarize ourselves with the new playing surface called *Astroturf*. We donned our uniforms (without pads) in the plush, state-of-the-art facility and headed to the field where everyone started commenting on the traction (or lack thereof) of the *Astroturf*. (*Astroturf* was essentially a high-grade indoor/outdoor carpet made of extended plastic fibers, which were "zipped" together in sections approximately twenty yards square.) We, of course, wore standard metal-tipped cleats which allowed for no traction whatsoever on the *Astroturf*.

Coach Bailey immediately contacted the facility manager who said he was planning on providing us with alternative shoes if we desired. The choices offered were essentially soccer shoes (short rubber cleats) or basketball shoes known as *chucks*, short for the *Charles Taylor* brand. We were bewildered by this set of events, because everything in football starts with the feet. The players were pretty much split on which shoes to wear. I chose the soccer shoes but took a pair of *chucks* in case I changed my mind. I asked our equipment manager to find out what the University of Houston wore and the misinformation provided to him was that they were pretty well split between soccer shoes and *chucks*. Wearing soccer shoes was a tremendous improvement over football cleats, but still a far cry from the traction on a natural grass field.

Game day for us was *Band Day* for some 500 high school bands in Texas. We were told that they had been at the Astrodome since early morning going through their final preparations for the pre-game and halftime festivities. Both teams were delayed beginning our pre-game warm-ups as the PA announcer ordered and pleaded with the bands to leave the field. The straggling 80 to 100 band members picked up the tempo as both teams were allowed on the field for warm-ups.

Upon hitting the field, I sent a tired and unusually slow-paced Uncle Vince (he and his cohorts, Doctors Buck Younger and John Tyner, along with Andy Hardy from WTVT, were out-on-the town the night before) on a reconnaissance mission to determine what kind of shoes the University of Houston players were wearing. He reported that their players' shoes were different from ours. Theirs, he reported, were like coaching shoes with leather uppers and ridged rubber bottoms. I made mention of this to Coach Bailey and he immediately offered me his shoes. I appreciated the offer, but wasn't interested in stuffing my size 13 feet into his size 12 shoes. As I declined his offer, for some reason I said to Coach Bailey, "What will you wear if I wear your shoes, Coach?" to which he replied, "Hell, I'll just walk around in my socks. I feel like I'm in someone's living room anyway."

Our defense kept the potent Cougar offense in check through late into the third quarter, but their systematic substitution scheme took its toll and we dropped a hard fought battle to a very good Houston team. Our footwear was definitely a disadvantage, but not enough to change the outcome of the game.

THE 1966 WORLD SERIES

Back in Tampa, I had become quite friendly with Carmine and Malio. I frequented their restaurant every weekend and enjoyed their company. Part of the tradition of Carmine's restaurant was the annual betting pool on the World Series.

Basically, 100 possibilities for the outcome of the World Series were posted on a chart and any interested party could purchase one or more squares for $10 each for a chance to win the grand prize of $1,000. The only caveat was that the winner agreed to leave $100 at the bar to cover the cost of libations for the participants and their friends.

Each time I visited the restaurant, one of the Twins would encourage me to buy a square since they were a hot item and would not last long. Not being a gambler and having high regard and specific need for the $10 entry fee, I shrugged off their sales pitches and never gave the betting pool much consideration.

One particular Friday evening, Malio was adamant (as he can be) about me buying a square and advised me not to take too much time thinking about it because there was only one square remaining.

I again told him that I appreciated the offer but had no interest.

He then offered to split the square with me, but once more I rejected the offer thinking I could find better use for the five dollars than in that betting pool.

Malio wouldn't take no for an answer and made me the classic *offer I couldn't refuse.*

He said, "I'll loan you the five dollars and you'll only have to pay me if we win."

I chuckled and told Malio that was a generous but ridiculous offer and that he should purchase the remaining square by himself.

He countered with, "No, I want to split the square with you because I think you'll bring good luck."

I informed him that I had never won anything of any consequence before and he responded, "It doesn't matter."

I embarrassingly shook hands with him on the deal and never thought about it again.

A FEW DAYS HENCE...

As I was dressing for practice, I received a note from the football office to call Malio before practice and the note was marked urgent. Because the note was marked urgent, I proceeded to the football office fully dressed with the exception of shoulder pads and helmet and placed the call.

In an exciting and inquisitive tone, Malio asked, "How do you like the Series so far?"

I responded, "I haven't been staying up with it, how are we doing?"

"How are we doing?" he said, "I'll tell you how we're doing! If the Orioles win today by one run, 1-0, 4-3, 10-9, any score by one run, we win the $1,000."

His enthusiasm ignited me, and I must have had a smile on my face from ear to ear because everyone in the locker room was asking me, "What's up?"

I told Gene and Greg and before we hit the practice field the conversation about me possibly winning $1,000 (even though my share was $500) was buzzing amongst the players and coaches.

Coach Prinzi approached me during calisthenics and asked if the rumor was true.

One of the managers had a pocket transistor radio and the entire team was keeping up with the score.

To provide some perspective on what $1,000 meant in 1966, I had purchased my 1965 MGB roadster the previous year for $1,875.

Coach Bailey was understandably irritated with all this interest in the World Series and blew his whistle to gather the team to communicate the following message, "We've got a damn game to prepare for and who wins the World Series ain't got a damn thing to do with it! Now, whoever has that radio, turn the damn thing off before I crush it!"

I felt as if his comments were directed toward me even though I was making a point not to seem interested in anything but practice.

Things got worse when someone put out the news that the Orioles were leading 1–0 after 4 innings.

A light buzz hovered over the team and I distanced myself from any conversation regarding the Series. My sole source of information was from my friend and team manager, Danny Someillan.

Then, a forceful strike of lightning emanated from the ominous clouds and the accompanying thunder was followed by Coach Bailey's announcement that practice would resume on the basketball courts inside the George B. Howell gymnasium.

The previous summer, Coaches Charlie Bailey and Vic Prinzi were struck by lightning as they played golf, and before Coach Bailey could finish his announcement, they were off the field.

By the time we had changed into shorts and court shoes, Coach Bailey had someone set up a couple of TVs at opposite ends of the gymnasium with the World Series game on and the volume off.

Everyone considered that a nice gesture by Coach Bailey and I am sure he thought it would contribute to the quality of our practice, but it backfired on him. By the seventh inning, Baltimore was nursing its one-run lead with Dave McNally on the mound.

Each time McNally retired a batter, a muted but audible response could be heard from the players causing Coach Bailey to end practice and allow us to watch the balance of the game in the gym.

Just about the entire team stayed as we witnessed Dave McNally, in a truly remarkable performance, keep the Los Angeles Dodgers scoreless for the rest of the game resulting in Malio and me winning the grand prize of $1,000.

I jumped in and out of the shower so fast I was leaving the locker room while people were still entering from the gym.

It was pouring rain as I headed north on Boulevard and turned right on Buffalo Avenue leaving the short distance to Highland Avenue left to negotiate. The parking lot was jammed and I parked behind Malio knowing I would be leaving before him.

As I entered the bar I was greeted with cheers and chants from the group as if I had somehow contributed to Dave McNally's effort. Malio directed me to stand on top of the bar as he began the ceremonial payoff.

He counted out ten $100 bills in synchronization with the counting bar patrons. He then took back the last $100 bill, flashed it to the crowd and announced, "Drinks are on Mondy!" to a roaring and appreciative crowd.

After a half-hour or so, I was getting ready to leave and asked Malio to join me in his office.

I handed him five $100 bills and a five-dollar bill according to our earlier agreement.

To my surprise, he told me that the whole $900 was mine.

I told him, "No way. If the $900 belongs to anyone it belongs to you!" and placed the entire amount on his desk.

He immediately grabbed the stack of bills and forced them in my shirt pocket. We discussed the matter for a few minutes and I pleaded with Malio to at least take the $500, but he would hear nothing of it.

I reminded him that I didn't even put up my $5 for the square and he responded, "Yeah, that's right. Give me the $5 you owe me."

As I handed him the $5, we hugged and he told me, "Congratulations!"

On the drive home, I thought to myself what a generous man is Malio. Splitting the prize would have been over generous considering I had put up no money in the first place.

But causing me to walk away with the $900 was a gesture of generosity I will never forget.

When I reached home, I peeled the nine $100 bills in front of my mother and tried to explain to her how I won the money, but she never did understand.

I told her that because I won, she won, and that she could pick out the refrigerator she was saving for and that it would be a gift from Malio and me. She communicated the obvious when she told me I had a good friend in Malio. I gave Gene $200 and that was one happy trio living at 2112 Lemon Street.

WHY NOT SHOW OFF?

The next morning, I was in class but could not pay attention because I was thinking of the seven $100 bills in my pocket. My buddy Deno was sitting two seats up one row away and I continued throwing little pieces of paper at him until I gained his attention.

As he watched and the professor lectured, I peeled seven $100 bills onto my desk and the puzzled look on his face transformed into a wide smile as he mouthed to me, "Where did you get that?"

I just grinned and mouthed back to him, "I'll tell you after class."

He looked back about every five minutes and smiled until the class was over.

THE MONSTER MECHANIC

As mentioned earlier, I had become good friends with Carmine and Malio, and one day while visiting with Carmine, he began to tell me about his friend who ran an auto repair shop. His friend, according to Carmine, was only about 5 ft. 9 in. and weighed approximately 165 pounds but possessed the strength of the Bible's Samson. He explained that because his friend worked primarily on generators and starters he had developed strength in his right arm beyond comprehension.

As proof of this individual's strength, Carmine said he had witnessed him defeat any and all comers in the contest of arm wrestling. He went on to say that the size of the opponent mattered not; his friend was undefeated. I thought he was attempting to interest me in arm-wrestling this fella, and if so, he was successful.

I told Carmine that I could not imagine losing to an auto mechanic who weighed 165 pounds regardless of how many generators and starters he repaired, and with a grin on his face, he asked if he could set up the contest. Carmine reminded me his friend arm-wrestled right-handed which was a disadvantage to me since I am left-handed. I returned his grin and told him I was ready anytime.

When I finally met this individual, I thought Carmine was playing a practical joke or smoking some weed of which I was unaware. I shook hands with this muscular but diminutive individual and thought to myself that either Carmine has an inflated opinion of these bar room strongmen or I was about to learn that drinking BUD not only made you WEISER but made you STRONGER.

Several of this individual's friends were present for the contest, which placed me in a peculiar predicament. If I defeated this auto mechanic, what had I accomplished considering the fellow weighed 165 pounds? On the other hand, in the unlikely event I lost to this Buffalo Avenue micro-hero, I could expect the same reception Goliath received after the shepherd David took him down with one stone in the first round of their unscheduled winner-take-all event. Nonetheless, everyone was there to see us arm wrestle and I was ready to get this matter behind us.

I must admit, this fella's pre-contest antics were impressive including rolling up his sleeve and exposing this weapon that was honed daily by loosening and tightening generators and starters. He stared me in the face as if *ABC's Wide World of Sports* was covering this event while the promoter (Carmine) went over the rules and prepared to start the event.

The contest was over before Carmine's hand came down to rest position after giving us the "Get ready... Get set... Go!" cue. If my eyes had been shut, I would have thought Carmine had replaced his friend with one of the eighth-grade girls from Sacred Heart Academy just down the street. Carmine and I controlled our reaction at that moment but later shared a good laugh about the whole event.

CARMINE'S TURN

Some months later, Carmine proposed another challenge to me. He admitted that within a restricted area he would not be able to elude me carrying a football but in a space the size of a football field, I would be unable to contain him. I again checked his pockets to make sure he wasn't smoking anything that would cause him to hallucinate. After being satisfied that he was sober and serious, I offered to take him up on this challenge at Phillips Field, then home of the University of Tampa Spartans. He again provided me with that smile I was beginning to become accustomed to and we agreed to meet on the field at 11 AM Saturday.

We were both in our very early twenties and each had a healthy opinion of our abilities. After a few pleasantries as we stretched and warmed up, Carmine suggested I line up on the 50-yard line and he would begin on his own 20-yard line and attempt to cross the goal line behind me. I was really beginning to wonder if working in his smoke-filled environment, eating rich food, and listening to bar stories was affecting his thinking. I felt extremely comfortable on Philips Field, having thwarted many an individual who had attempted what Carmine was planning. Nonetheless, what are friends for if we cannot allow someone to indulge in a fantasy now and then?

With both of us in position, Carmine began his fantasy trip to the goal line slowly, step-by-step, creating a path from approximately 10 yards inside the south sideline heading obliquely toward the North sideline inviting me to take an angle on my approach toward him. While he continued to advance beyond his 35-yard line, I could only think of how I would take him down with enough force to make a statement, yet not hurt my good buddy. As he crossed the 45-yard line, I was about eight yards from him and closing. As he approached midfield, he picked up the tempo and made a full speed move toward the south sideline. I had him in my crosshairs, and when I altered my trajectory to meet him on about the 47-yard line, he applied the brakes and redirected himself toward the opposite sideline. I immediately changed direction, but was only able to grasp the air inches behind him and with a roar of laughter he led me to the goal line.

We laughed and discussed what happened, and in my mind, I had placed too much emphasis on how I would take him down, thus placing the proverbial cart before the horse. I asked if we could make it the best two out of three. Carmine obliged, but the outcome was the same.

Carmine and I laughed as we sat on the field. We then retreated for a spot we frequented on Saturdays...Bexley's Fried Chicken on Main Street in the heart of West Tampa.

A SELF-INFLICTED WOUND

During my last semester on-campus, I took *The History of the Seminole Indians*, taught by Dr. James W. Covington, a renowned authority on Indians in general and Florida Indians in particular who had also authored the textbook used in the class. I needed three semester hours of history to complete my Bachelor of Science degree and chose this class because I had previously taken a course with Dr. Covington and enjoyed his method of teaching. I was cruising through the course with a solid B as finals approached and I was excited about ending my classroom requirements after this semester, leaving a semester of internship before graduating.

During the final examination a dear friend of mine slipped me a note requesting answers 14 through 30 of the multiple-choice exam. Obviously, I was concerned about getting caught but considered the risk low because Dr. Covington was both laid-back and would walk out of the classroom during exams from time to time.

I quickly rationalized my decision by convincing myself that the individual requesting the answers would have provided the same to me if the situation were reversed.

I jotted down my responses to questions 14 through 30, folded them into a very small package, and pitched the package perfectly at the side of my buddy. He nodded appreciatively and began to transfer the information to his answer sheet. Within seconds, Dr. Covington tapped me and my friend on the shoulder and asked us to join him in the hallway. I knew I had stepped in it, but I did not know how messy *it* would be.

Dr. Covington explained to us that his office had been broken into over the weekend and the exam had been stolen. There were three sections of this class and he was carefully observing each to determine who was responsible for the deed. He asked what was on the paper I pitched to my friend, and my friend, in an attempt to excuse my participation, responded that he initiated the request for the information I provided.

I admitted to Dr. Covington that what I had done was wrong, but wondered what the connection was between that and the break-in to which he referred.

In his kind and gentle manner, he said that he saw no reason to discuss the matter further since he had already discussed the situation regarding the break-in with university officials and they would be handling the matter from this juncture.

You could have knocked me over with a feather. Thoughts immediately ran through my mind including embarrassment to my family, friends, and coaches, and the affect this would have on my scholarship. I contemplated the possibility of expulsion, failure to graduate, and the effect on my career. Then my mind invited thoughts of newspaper coverage and the public embarrassment I would bring to my family, the university, to Jesuit, to my friends, and on and on. Despair joined my pity party and I became angry with myself for using such poor judgment. What should have been my last day of class became nothing short of *Black Tuesday* for me. Nonetheless, I had purchased my ticket to this dance and I had to work myself out of the mess I created. I wanted to be comforted by Judy, but this was during a period in which we were not dating.

After being interrogated by the dean assigned to these matters, we were told to be available for a meeting (code for trial) with the Student/Administration Academic Council within the next few days.

I was dejected as I made my way to my car when a girl I dated occasionally asked how I was feeling because she'd heard what happened, which answered another question for me: Who would know about this incident? The answer was, everyone. She asked where I was going and when I told her I was just going to drive around she asked if she could join me. I told her I appreciated the thought but I wanted to be alone.

I headed home but did not want to see anyone, so I drove to the Courtney Campbell Causeway, parked, and pondered my situation. I felt so bad that I did not want to discuss this matter with anyone but realized I had to get my act together and face the music.

Upon returning home, my mother asked what was wrong with me because I looked sick. I felt sick, so that made sense. She informed me that a couple of my friends had called but I didn't feel like speaking with anyone on the phone or otherwise. At just about that time, Gene called and told me to call Verlin Williams at work because he knew something about who had broken into Dr. Covington's office.

Verlin (our friend who brought the steaks) was one of the calls my mother had communicated to me, so I called him at Bern's Steak House but the person I spoke with said it was too busy for him to take a call. I explained to her that it was an emergency, and when she asked me if I was sure, I became a little testy and responded, "Do I have to explain all the particulars to prove to you it's an emergency or are you going to put Verlin on the damn phone?"

When Verlin came on the line, he told me that he'd heard from a friend of his that a couple of guys in his friend's fraternity had broken into Dr. Covington's office and stolen the final exam.

"Who are these guys and where can I find them?" I asked.

He said he didn't know but that I could call a friend of his who could give me the number of the alleged perpetrator.

I called Verlin's friend and he admitted to telling Verlin about the break-in, but he said he did not want to get involved. I told him that I appreciated his position but I simply had to find out who these guys were.

He hemmed and hawed but would not name the individuals. I asked where he lived because I wanted to discuss the matter with him face-to-face, and he, without hesitation, gave me the names of the two individuals and the name of their apartment complex on Davis Island.

I traveled to the apartment complex and found the name of one of the individuals on the mail slot. I knocked on the door, but no one answered. I continued to knock because I heard music and I thought he might be in the shower or possibly not wanting to see anyone. Still, no one answered. I walked around to the back of the apartment and noticed the barbecue grill going but no one around.

As I peered through the sliding glass doors, a heavy northeastern-accented voice from the pool area asked if I needed any help. I said I was looking for the persons who lived in this apartment, and he said that he lived there.

I introduced myself and he told me his name was Marc. I was perturbed he told me his name was Marc when I had introduced myself using both names.

"Well, is that Mr. Marc or Mr. and Mrs. Marc?"

He responded, "Just Marc. How can I help you?"

I told him I was there regarding some University of Tampa business and wanted to know if he was a student at UT. He said he was.

I then asked him if he had just completed the Seminole Indian history course. He begrudgingly gave me his one-word answer, "Yes." The golden-tanned northeasterner was hesitant to say anything more, so I decided to get right to the point.

"I learned from a reliable person that you and another person stole the final exam from Dr. Covington's office and I'm here to talk with you about that."

His demeanor became somewhat more agreeable and he asked if I could return around 9:30 PM because his roommate would be back by then and he thought his roommate should be included in the conversation. I asked if his roommate was the other person who stole the exam, but he said just come back at 9:30 and we can discuss it then. I told him I would be back at 9:30 PM sharp. As I drove back to Lemon Street, I wondered about the 9:30 meeting and what this scoundrel had in mind.

Gene was home when I arrived, and he told me that Coach Bailey had called and wanted me to call him in the morning. He asked what Verlin's contact knew and I told him about my visit with Marc. Without hesitation, he told me that he wanted to go to the 9:30 meeting with me.

At 9:30 PM on the button, I knocked on the same door I had knocked on earlier that evening, but this time the door was opened by Marc. I introduced Gene to Marc and Marc introduced us to his roommate Alan.

Alan looked familiar to me. I thought I recognized him from school. He seemed like a nice fellow because of his friendly smile, which I also recognized from school. In fact, I thought I remembered being cordial with him during some discussion we had with a mutual friend earlier in the year.

Nonetheless, I said, "What's with the Marc and Alan when we gave you guys our full names?"

Alan immediately responded, "My last name is Silverman and Marc's is Cohen."

I told them why we were there, and after discussing the matter for about twenty minutes, they reluctantly admitted to the theft. Marc offered to come up with some money if we kept the information amongst ourselves. I told him there was not a chance of that, and that if it weren't for me being blamed for this theft, we wouldn't even be having the conversation.

They muttered something about the trouble they could be in and I simply responded, "I don't know of another way to handle it."

As we were exiting the apartment, I offered the following, "Why don't one of you guys take the rap for the whole thing?"

As we exited Davis Islands, Gene asked, "Why do you care if one or both of those guys take the rap?"

I responded, "I don't."

I didn't know if being able to identify the actual thieves would help my situation, but I knew it could not hurt. I was uncomfortable feeding Alan and Marc (Alan anyway) to the wolves, but I wasn't about to unduly damage my reputation (further) to save their skins.

The next morning, I called Coach Bailey and explained my version. He encouraged me by saying that I was doing the correct thing, and before he heard my explanation he knew I had no part in breaking into the professor's office. He also said he was preparing to call both the president of the university and the dean in charge of this matter on my behalf. I thanked him and headed to the university with the information I gathered the previous evening.

Dean DeCarlo was both professional and sensitive regarding this matter as he sensed I was seriously wounded by it and was, without doubt, remorseful about my actions. However, he explained, "If your account regarding Alan Silverman and Marc Cohen holds up, you still have to deal with providing answers to your friend, or cheating, whichever you prefer."

I was somewhat taken aback when he used the term *cheating*, but I also didn't know what else you could call it, except maybe, *providing answers to my friend*, which he said as well. It's one of those situations when someone else does it, it's *cheating*, but when you do it, it's *providing answers*.

I was keeping my friend (co-conspirator) advised of the progress I was making but I had a lot more work to do and did not want to delegate any of it. A couple of items were encouraging but I was still extremely concerned for my future.

My teammate and co-captain Dan Sykes' girlfriend was one of three student representatives on this council, and even though I did not know her very well, we were always friendly. Dan, I was confident, would do everything he could on my behalf. Also, one of the administration representatives on the council was related to my and Gene's good friend and team manager, Danny Someillan. As a matter-of-fact, Danny had already told Gene that his cousin had contacted him regarding this matter and was going to help every way he could. I was appreciative of these contacts, but I was still leery of the upcoming meeting. Danny's cousin, Roberto Fernandez, Registrar of the university, asked to see me in his office and provided some comfort, but of course, could not promise anything.

The ensuing days were miserable, and I was relieved, though anxious when the meeting day finally arrived. I wore a shirt and tie to the meeting in an effort to project the genuine humility and remorse I was feeling. To my surprise, I was asked to sit in another room while the meeting took place and told that I would be asked to join the meeting only if clarification on a topic was required. (I later learned that the reason for this was to minimize the possibility of hard feelings by the accused toward any of the panel members.) I was not asked into the meeting, and within twenty minutes, I was informed of the results by Dean DeCarlo.

He advised me that the panel unanimously found that I was in no way involved with the greater charge of breaking into Dr. Covington's office and/or stealing the final exam, but that I was found culpable with regard to the lesser charge of providing answers, and for that reason, I was to receive an academic "withdrawal failing" (WF) and would be eligible to retake the course and complete graduation. He asked if I had any questions, and when I responded I did not, he said I was free to leave.

I thought that I had been treated fairly, but I didn't realize how fairly until Danny's cousin, Roberto Fernandez, later explained that an "academic" WF simply means I withdrew from the course while failing. The reason for the withdrawal is not recorded and therefore my record has no mention of the *incident*. He further explained that it was not uncommon for a student to receive a WF when they withdrew from a class for a myriad of reasons, including health, financial, personal, etc. He said that he had lobbied for me to be given a WP (withdraw passing) but because the council was resolute to issue a WF to the other involved party, it would be inappropriate to issue different outcomes for the same offense. I was pleased with the outcome even though I was still disappointed in myself for exercising poor judgment.

I informed Coach Bailey of the result and he was also pleased to learn the incident would not be a part of my permanent record. I then went to see Dr. Covington to apologize for my actions and asked for his forgiveness. He said that he had no hard feelings, and that in his opinion, I had gotten caught up in circumstances that hopefully would provide a lesson I could benefit from in the future. He was right and I could not have said it better.

I explained to him that I would be interning the spring semester, and if he did not object, I would take another history course from him during the summer to complete my requirements for graduation. (It would have been expedient to take the class while I was interning but it was not allowed by the university. The policy was intended to eliminate the possibility the interning student diluting focus from the internship by taking additional courses, which is precisely what I would have done.)

I felt vindicated when Dr. Covington said he would be happy to have me in his class. I spent the spring semester as a PE intern at Robinson High School under the tutelage of my friend John Pellegrino.

John was Robinson's Head Basketball Coach and one of their Physical Education instructors. He was also single and as carefree as they come. John was a few years older than me. I had followed his athletic career at Hillsborough High School and the University of Tampa where he was a standout basketball player. Working with John was the closest thing to playing all day and getting paid for it (at least John got paid).

The kids at Robinson loved John. From each PE class John would select two sets of players (one for him and one for me) and we would compete all-day at the sport in season. We alternated between softball, volleyball, football, and the kid's politically incorrect favorite, *Smear the Queer* (STQ) – a variation of rugby. STQ was sort of a reward for the students and we only engaged in this game about once a month. Class size ranged from 100 to 300 kids and we had half of them remove their shirts designating the teams as shirts and skins. We then tipped the ball off at the 50-yard line of the football field and the rest was unrestrained havoc as each side attempted to advance the football across the other side's goal. John and I also participated. The kids loved it when John wore a vintage 1940s leather football helmet and told the kids it was the World War II aviation headgear he used when he shot down Japs during an air raid on Iwo Jima.

Frequently, there were injuries during the game, generally bruises and sprained wrists, knees or ankles. Occasionally, we would experience a broken leg, arm, or dislocated shoulder. This was a fine example of your tax dollars at work.

It was not mandatory, but the majority of kids participated. John and I often sent our torn jerseys and shorts to the home economics instructor who was kind enough to have the class repair the garments for class credit. None of the aforementioned would be possible in today's delicate political climate and that's probably a good thing.

When it rained, we gathered the entire class in the gymnasium and ran the same film each time—the 1958 Chicago Bears highlight film featuring Tampa's Rick Casares.

In a childish sort of way, my experience at Robinson High School was a great time. John and I would frequent Carmine's lounge and sometimes close up the place with Carmine or Malio at 3 AM, then head to the Pancake House and enjoy breakfast before turning in around 4:15 AM. John would occasionally go straight from the Pancake House to the Robinson gym and sleep in the coaches' office until the first coach arrived for work. Then we would begin the process all over again.

DECISIONS, DECISIONS, DECISIONS

During the spring, Joe Thomas, Director of Player Personnel for the Miami Dolphins, convinced me that I should attend pre-season camp the first week in July at St. Andrews Academy in Boca Raton, Florida. The Washington Redskins and New York Giants also contacted me in this regard, but I had little interest in relocating to either venue. First-year linemen in those days earned $9,500 plus a $500 signing bonus, I was told by Joe Thomas.

I was living at home and had no rent, electricity, or phone to pay from the $6,600 salary I would receive as a first-year coach/teacher. Having no burning desire to play professional football plus not being lured by an attractive compensation package represented two strikes against this decision. The third strike I had pitched, myself. Also, there was the matter of the Vietnam War. The selective service draft in 1967 utilized the lottery system. With 366 days (leap year included) in the pool, my birthday equated to a draft number of 109. At the time, people were drafted with numbers in the 80s and depending on the escalation or de-escalation of the war in Vietnam that number could go up or down. Full-time, degree-seeking students were deferred, as were teachers and other specified professions.

The Vietnam War had taken on a very political tone and it seemed to many, myself included, to have no real purpose except for the U.S. not to lose face in the arena of global politics. This was not a high-tech war. Our soldiers were in and amongst the enemy day and night. Many of the enemy didn't wear uniforms. Some of the people with whom our troops came into contact during the day, tending to their crops and caring for their children, became the enemy under the cover of night. Many of our soldiers were losing their lives in what appeared to be an unending war, and many of those not returning in body bags had sustained serious physical and mental wounds. I heard war stories from friends returning from Vietnam and the picture they painted was frightening. Thus, I was committed to maintaining my deferment as a degree-seeking student until I could make the decision on whether or not to become a coach.

Now for the third strike. The poor judgment I had demonstrated in history class was about to distribute consequences. To maintain my deferment, I had to complete a history course by the end of the summer because I was a fifth-year senior (you were allowed five years to complete a four-year degree).

I met with and shared my dilemma with Dr. Covington. A class he taught met on Monday and Wednesday evenings from 6 to 9 PM. I was brazen enough to ask if I could cease attending classes once camp began (July 6th) but continue to take tests and the final exam by mail. He did not accept my proposal, but agreed to allow me to miss one class per week after camp started. I took him up on the offer and contacted Joe Thomas regarding my situation. To my surprise, he said he did not think it would be a problem, but that if it were, he would get back to me. Joe called a week later and advised me that he had discussed the matter with George Wilson (head coach) and Coach Wilson agreed to allow me to miss the Wednesday evening practice until I completed the class. As a matter of fact, he had an arrangement with a couple of players to whom he issued permission to miss a practice now and again to wrestle. One such player was linebacker "Wahoo" McDaniel, who earned more wrestling than he did playing football. Joe said to make sure to revisit the matter with Coach Wilson upon arrival at camp.

I was surprised and somewhat disappointed because I thought this issue might represent a graceful exit from my football career. As previously mentioned, my interest level in pro football (at the compensation level in those days) was not very high and I felt I was pursuing the profession to satisfy the expectations of others. Nonetheless, I was soon preparing for camp to be held at St. Andrews Boys' Academy in Boca Raton, Florida.

Knowing my last day of work would be July 2nd, my supervisor at the recreation department, Ream Wilson, assigned me the task of guarding the Sulfur Springs swimming hole, which had been shut down due to contamination of the springs. Even though the facility was fenced and locked, kids were climbing the fence and swimming in the springs, disregarding the sign warning danger, and more importantly, presenting a potential liability to the city.

Twelve years earlier, this popular north Tampa swimming hole proudly displayed a sign that read, *No Dogs, Latins, Niggers, or Jews*, but in the summer of '67, a *Latin* named Armando Flores was asked to secure the facility from the descendants of those very people. Ignorance has always flourished.

So, with my portable radio, sunglasses, newspaper, and Cuban coffee, I would trek north on Florida Avenue, past Judy's home, in my red MGB and perform my boring guard duty from 9:30 AM to 6:30 PM, five days a week.

I traveled through the typical summer rains to and from work. My automobile was beginning to lose favor with me for several reasons led by the normal heat generated by the transmission in this non air-conditioned sports car and by the inherent and incessant dripping from the convertible top each time it rained.

North Florida Avenue was replete with auto dealers and I began to entertain the idea of trading my sports car for an air-conditioned, American-made hardtop vehicle before my trip to Boca Raton. An acquaintance I knew from Carmine's restaurant owned one of the Florida Avenue car lots and always expressed to me that I should see him if I was interested in trading automobiles. He had a half-dozen low-mileage Ford Fairlanes on his lot and I began investigating their values versus my MGB's in anticipation of a trade. Finally, I calculated what I thought was a good deal for me and I went to his lot with my automobile, title, and a check for $650.

My strategy was to place the title and the check in front of him and propose trading for one of those Fairlanes. I caught him by surprise one morning, and before he could say *hot coffee*, I delivered my pitch to him. He looked at my check, paused, and to my surprise, said, "You've got a deal; pick out any of those Fords you like and I'll get you the keys." I was expecting a haggle from him, and because I didn't get one, I began to question the deal in my mind. I didn't display any emotion but I felt like I had just been had, and all of it, of my own doing. What made the situation worse was the accommodation he provided regarding the tires. I told him I liked a particular vehicle but preferred the tires of one of the other cars. He smiled and said, "No problem, I'll have one of the guys switch the tires for you." I was unable to determine then and have yet to figure out whether this person was demonstrating an act of kindness or whether I had botched my calculations so badly that he was thrilled with my offer. Nonetheless, I was the proud owner of 1967 Ford Fairlane with AC (albeit, aftermarket AC). I spent the bulk of the next three days at work cleaning and polishing my automobile while occasionally "shooing" kids who were attempting to climb the fence to go swimming.

July was upon us and I was headed for Boca Raton.

I reminded Dr. Covington that I would only be attending the Monday class from this point on. He nodded affirmatively and wished me well at camp.

Upon arriving in Boca Raton, I was greeted by the sports anchor from the local TV station in West Palm Beach, Jim Gallagher. Jim was a Jesuit graduate and brother to one of my Jesuit classmates as well as an acquaintance of my brother-in-law, Joe. Jim taped an interview with me chronicling rookies arriving at camp, which aired during the sports segment of the evening news.

Others took notice, and I'm certain, wondered how I rated this attention especially when this rookie class included All-America quarterback Bob Griese of Purdue University and his All-America teammate, Larry Czonka from Syracuse University.

Jack Harper, running back from University of Florida and resident of Lakeland, Florida was my roommate during camp. Jack was small in stature but offset this limitation with a burning desire to compete.

A few players whose company I enjoyed included Howard Twilley, receiver from Tulsa University, Jim Riley, a high draft choice defensive end from the University of Oklahoma, and of course, Doug Moreau. Joe Thomas' responsibility was to sign all unsigned players ASAP.

At lunch one day, he handed me a piece of paper indicating my appointment time with him. When I arrived at his office, I met an offensive lineman named Alfonse Dotson. Alfonse was a big, strong, black tackle from a small Texas college. He asked, "How much you going to work for?" as we waited for Joe to call us into his office.

"I don't know," I replied, causing a quizzical look on his face.

"Well, you better figure it out quick," he offered just before Joe opened the door and invited both of us into his office. We were both surprised by the move, but I later surmised that it was Joe's way of communicating that he was treating us the same. Nonetheless, after about 45 seconds of chitchat, Joe placed a contract in front of each of us for $9,500. As we read the contract, Joe explained that we were fortunate to be offered a $9,500 contract because several linemen had already signed contracts for $8,500. I doubted the veracity of his statement but decided to keep my thoughts to myself.

Alfonse said, in a careful manner, "A friend of mine who works for the San Diego Chargers got himself a $10,000 contract." tossing the ball back to Joe.

"It costs more to live in California than Florida." Joe quickly responded in a manner indicating he had dealt with Alfonse's comment before.

Having heard about signing bonuses from Doug, Howard Twilley, and Jim Riley and not knowing what else to do, I chimed in with, "How much is the signing bonus?"

Joe paused, looked me square in the eyes, and said, "I can write you a check right now for $500 if you both sign your contracts."

Alfonse was ready to sign his contract, but put down the ballpoint pen when he heard me ask, "Can you make the signing bonus $1,000?"

Joe said nothing as he peered into our eyes as I scratched my arm where there was no itch and Alfonse moved his empty mouth in a chewing motion. Joe got up from his chair and said, "Let me check something and I'll be right back."

While alone in the room, Alfonse smiled and said, "That was a smooth move, my man. You a salesman in your spare time?"

I smiled and placed my index finger over my lips as I pointed to the phone and whispered, "Shush, there might be a mic in the room."

Alfonse looked at me as if he thought I had seen too many James Bond movies and we sat there for a few minutes before Joe Thomas returned.

"I can do $750," Joe said in what was quickly turning into a used car conversation.

Alfonse, again, grabbed his pen as I told Joe Thomas, "$900 and you've got a deal."

"I can't go a nickel higher than $750," Joe said in a convincing tone and Alfonse and I signed our contracts and waited for Joe to write our $750 signing bonuses from his "three to a page" checkbook.

We shook hands with Joe and headed back to the dormitory to rest before the afternoon session.

As we split, Alfonse shook my hand and said, "I owe you a Pearl (beer); hell, I owe you a six-pack of Pearls."

Everything was going fine, except those Wednesday afternoon trips were killing me. The cafeteria staff would fix me a boxed lunch, which I ate as I raced up the Sunshine State Parkway to Yeehaw Junction where I connected with Highway 60 West into Tampa.

There was no one home on Lemon Street when I generally arrived at 3 PM, which allowed me a couple hours of sleep before heading to class. My mother would fix me a meal and a snack for the return trip and I would chat with her and Gene till 5:40 PM allowing me plenty of time for the seven-minute trip to UT.

Each time I left, my mother made the same comment, "You must really want to play football for that team to go back and forth every week. If you're not careful, you're going to get hurt driving back so late. Why don't you get a job here? You graduated from college."

There wasn't much I could say since I was less than enthusiastic about this endeavor, so I would tell her I knew what I was doing, even though the statement was a stretch.

I took No-Doze to stay awake in class and again for the trip back to Boca.

We played an exhibition game (preseason game) against the Washington Redskins at the Fort Lauderdale High School field. The game was essentially a scrimmage between the teams without runbacks of either punts or kickoffs. Also, defenses were not allowed to stunt or blitz. Admission to the game was either 75 cents or $1.25 and there was no charge for parking. I think we lost.

RULE CHANGE

Posted on the bulletin board in the dining hall and in the locker room was a notice that all previous approvals to miss practice were canceled and anyone having to miss practice for any reason must (re)obtain permission from head coach George Wilson.

I was not completely surprised by this notice because some discontent was breeding amongst the troops due to a few players who were allowed to miss practice so that they could wrestle professionally throughout Florida. The most notable of the group was "Wahoo" McDaniel, our first-team middle linebacker who would sometimes miss three practices a week to meet wrestling dates in Fort Lauderdale, Jacksonville, and just down the street in West Palm Beach. Players began to complain and Coach Wilson had to do something to remedy the situation.

However, Coach Wilson was part of the problem. He fraternized with players, including those who wrestled. A couple of times, I witnessed him with players in a bar overindulging in social activities during which the players he fraternized with addressed him as "George" rather than Coach Wilson. That seemed rather odd to me even though I later learned it was not uncommon, especially amongst veteran players.

Nonetheless, I went to see Coach Wilson to reinstate my approved absence from the Wednesday afternoon practice session.

"Florezz," he said. "We've got a problem. You've got yourself a legitimate reason for missing practice, but I don't have any choice in the matter. I'm not letting anyone miss practice, including Wahoo, so I can't have any exceptions. You think about what you have to do, and I'll respect your decision."

"Coach," I said. "I don't have much choice in the matter, either. If I drop out of class, I have a real good chance of being drafted within 45 days, and to be perfectly honest, I don't have much interest in going to Vietnam."

"I understand," he said. "George Jr. is in the same predicament," referring to his son who was vying to be the quarterback for the Dolphins.

He offered to speak to someone in the National Guard in Miami as he had done for George Jr. and Frank Emmanuel (linebacker from University of Tennessee) if I had interest, but I told him I didn't want to chance it and possibly end up in Vietnam.

With that, he again said he understood and wished me well in whatever I did. We shook hands and I told him I wished him and the Dolphins a successful season as he saw me to the door.

I went to my room and began packing my belongings. Jack told me he thought I was doing the right thing even though he hated to see me leave. He may have just been being nice, but I appreciated his comments, nonetheless. I visited with Jim Riley and my buddy Doug Moreau before departing and they shared similar sentiments.

Before leaving, I decided to take a shot at getting a pro rata share of the weekly expense stipend and it worked. The cashier had me sign a receipt for the $96 I was given and I was once again traveling up the Sunshine State Parkway headed for Tampa City.

WHO IS MONDY FLORES?

On the trip to Tampa I had a lot of time to replay my conversation with Coach Wilson. I never doubted my decision, but I wondered what kind of impression I had left with him. Did I leave him the impression I was adept in using the freedom offered by our country but was unwilling to fight to preserve this freedom for those who would follow? And more importantly, what was I willing to do or not do for this country that offered a better way of life for my ancestors and for countless others? Forget Coach Wilson and the Miami Dolphins, the more important question was, *Who is Mondy Flores?*

The sound of the road beneath my car as I traveled 70 miles per hour provided the perfect background for considering these questions. I reflected back to my transfer to the University of Tampa in the spring of 1965, which was the first time I remember anyone discussing the Vietnam War. Previous to that time, news of the war was carried periodically on the national news, and rarely, if ever, on the local news. In 1965, the Vietnam War made the transition from the end of the national news to its nightly lead story.

The Vietnam War had begun in 1957 when Communist guerrillas (Viet Cong) began attacking villages in South Vietnam in response to South Vietnam's President Diem signing a new constitution into law in 1956 declaring that South Vietnam was a republic (even though he and his family continued to control the government). Even though the U.S. provided military advisers to South Vietnam in the 1950s, it wasn't until 1965 that we began sending our military troops, which became the catalyst for our country's interest in what was happening there.

From the onset, our (U. S.) resolve regarding this war was weak. We seemed to have no definitive plan for winning the war and returning our troops. This lack of focus was not lost on our troops in Vietnam who began questioning our purpose, which in turn fueled the fire of war dissidents who developed into antiwar activists. All these dynamics were playing out at a time when our culture was questioning anything and everything. My generation was given much more than any generation before it, and while some were using this newfound freedom and opportunity, some were abusing it.

With that scenario playing in my mind, I had a choice to make. Do I join the revolution, or do I try to be part of the solution?

The decision was clear for me.

Most of this counterculture activity was carried out in an environment of heavy drug use. The reality I encountered at UT (regarding drugs) was mild by comparison to what was happening in the culture at large.

The TV and print media provided their view as to what was happening in Vietnam and it was not pretty. Our troops in Vietnam were portrayed as alcohol abusing, pot smoking dissidents who were unfocused, poorly-led, and who mistreated Vietnamese children and women at will. While undoubtedly some of that activity did take place, I am certain it did not occur with the frequency suggested by the media, who after all, measure their success by market share and number of papers sold.

The music of the time supported the culture. Most of the popular music groups not only made no attempt to hide their use of drugs, illicit sex, and contempt for the government, but openly promoted these practices in their music and performances.

The reason the decision was clear for me was because I may be what I am, but what I am not is a hypocrite. I was not about to fake or conceal my position on any of these matters. While I was certainly no angel, I had then, as I have now, a tremendous respect and high esteem for women instilled in me by those women who were most important to me at the time, specifically, my on-again, off-again girlfriend, my sister, and of course, my mother. This respect from me was available to all women desiring such respect.

As for drugs and alcohol, I had over the years developed both a philosophical and practical position which served me well then as it does now. Simply put, from a philosophical perspective, I have <u>never</u> seen a case where illicit drugs or alcohol assisted anyone in accomplishing anything of value apart from escaping the reality of the moment. While I recognize the appeal of *self-medication* for coping with tough times, I believe meeting problems *head-on* is not only the superior method but the only effective one in dealing with difficult issues. The obvious reason for its superiority is because it is the only opportunity to permanently address issues, while the use of alcohol and/or illicit drugs is, at best, temporary, only masking the problem and carries with it serious and negative side effects; relationally, emotionally, and physically.

From a practical standpoint, illicit drugs and alcohol are expensive, and in effect, they aggravate one's problems instead of mitigating them.

Finally, I believe the most effective way to change our government's direction is to change those who represent us in government. While the process of doing so is ugly, the alternative used in the 1960s was uglier. The *bottom line* is if I had been called to war, I would have proudly served.

As I approached Tampa, I was comfortable with the answers to those questions I posed to myself and I was prepared to join the workforce upon the successful completion of my history course at UT and play whatever Viet Nam cards I would be dealt.

I loathed the prospect of having to explain the situation as to why I wasn't playing football to everyone who asked, but I was, nonetheless, relieved to be out of football. The first words out of Uncle Vince's mouth were, "Maybe you can go out again next year." I had no response.

I completed my history class with Dr. Covington, thus validating my graduation, and was now qualified, or should I say certified, to teach Physical Education.

COACH, DO YOU HAVE ANY OPENINGS?

School was about to begin and whatever good jobs were available were filled. Nonetheless, I prioritized the schools in which I had interest and began calling the head coaches to determine if there were openings and interest.

My first choice was H.B. Plant High School.

I was interested in Plant for several reasons, not the least of which was the fact that it was the closest one to my home on Lemon Street. To my surprise, Coach John Burgess suggested I come to Plant to discuss what possibilities existed. I explained to Coach Burgess over the telephone that I was in need of a job for the upcoming school year (which began in a couple of weeks). He indicated that he understood and I quickly made my way to the Plant gymnasium, which he supervised during the summer. When I arrived, I found Coach Burgess to be a very nice man with a keen, albeit dry, sense of humor. Within fifteen minutes of our conversation (conducted while he observed the kids in the gym), Coach Burgess offered me the position of Assistant Junior Varsity Coach.

I was shocked when he offered to go into the classroom to make room for me as a PE instructor. I had little interest in going into the classroom, but would have considered doing so to land a job. As if it were an answer to prayer, Coach Burgess communicated to me that he was bored with PE and saw the opportunity of hiring me as an omen (a term I would learn later he used often) for him to return to the classroom and teach history.

I made no attempt to discourage his thought process and asked, "When do I report?"

He indicated that he would have to gain approval from the school principal, Charles Vacher, but said he anticipated there would be no issue in that regard and would call me to confirm before the workday ended. I expressed my appreciation for the offer and told him I would be waiting for his call. He then asked what I had planned for the balance of the morning, to which I replied, "Nothing, if I'm positive I have this job."

Knowing that I was going to continue to seek employment, he suggested I watch the kids for a few moments while he called Mr. Vacher. I agreed, and within a few minutes, he returned from the coach's office with a disappointing look on his face, yet communicated to me that I was hired. I asked about the look on his face to which he replied, "I'm not sure I want to teach history." I thought, "What's up with this guy?" as he continued. "But that's my problem." I was confused, but soon realized that this was merely a sample of Coach Burgess' dry wit. "With that out of the way, do you want to play badminton?" he queried.

"Sure." I responded, thinking he just wanted to get to know me better.

When he found out I had athletic gear in my car, he, in a light cynical tone, said, "You must be a serious athlete if you carry athletic gear in your car. To make this fair," he continued, "we'll play to 15 and I'll spot you 14 points and the serve."

I smiled as I thought, "I know they're smoking pot at UT, but I didn't think it had reached high school coaches."

"Would that be okay?" he asked with a serious look through his thick horn-rimmed glasses.

"Surely, you jest." I responded, prompting coach to say, "I can't give you 15 points or the game would be over."

We made our way to one of the four badminton courts set up in the gymnasium giving me the first impression that he spent a lot of time with this activity (I never considered it a sport). In a military tone, he proceeded to inform me of the ground rules and advised me to begin serving when I was ready.

My first serve gave me an early indication I was in trouble when he spiked it to the opposite side of the court within four inches of the line.

"You only score when you serve," he said, "so the score is *love all*." He then began to pick me apart. By the time the score was 8–14 (I was given 14 points), I realized I was way over my head. When I stood at the back of the court, his serve would barely clear the net causing me to rush the net (to no avail). When I lined up near the net, he would send the serve far over my head inviting me to believe the serve would be out, yet each time, the serve would "die", falling just inside the back line. When I adjusted my position between the back and front positions, he served the shuttlecock to my forehand or backhand with the same precision and result. I was a good racket sport athlete in excellent condition, yet I could not score a point on this thirty-something-year-old coach. He uttered throughout the match, "Youth and speed versus age and experience." I had no response to his opinion. I learned yet another important life lesson. Presumption is dangerous.

On the morning I headed to Plant High School to complete paperwork and meet Mr. Vacher, I read an article in the Tampa Tribune chronicling an impending teacher strike. After our meeting, I asked his thoughts regarding the strike. He calmly chose his words carefully as he responded making it clear to me that he was on the management side of the issues. I then walked over to the coach's office where spirits were high and the conversation was unguarded. Coach Burgess gained everyone's agreement that we should act as a group, and even though a couple of the coaches were not in favor of striking, we should participate as a unit. I had not officially begun work but, nonetheless, agreed with the group.

"If you don't hear from me by Sunday evening, no one shows up for work on Monday, right?" asked coach Burgess.

Each of us, either audibly or with an agreeing nod, gave assent.

Bob Quierolo, Assistant Principal, had instructed me to call him at home if I was ever going to be absent from school. Not knowing if those instructions included a strike situation, I phoned Bob on what would have been my first day of school and advised him of my planned absence. His response was both curious and thought-provoking. He seemed like a nice man but I was still surprised by his comments.

"Armando," he said, "are you telling me you are participating in the strike or are you telling me you are not feeling well and therefore will miss school today? Because if you're telling me you're not feeling well, I will code your absence as a "sick day" and you'll get paid as if you worked."

The option he presented started my mind racing with the idea of getting paid while on strike, a strategy I was prepared to share with Coach Burgess as one that would financially strap the school system, thus improving our (the teachers) ability to negotiate. I didn't know anything about the art of negotiating, but common sense told me that the county would be in a much weaker position if they had to pay all the teachers sick pay while they participated in contract negotiations. Coach Burgess indicated that he liked the idea but didn't think we should make it an official strategy. I agreed and indicated its *unofficialness* is what would add pressure on the county. We discussed the idea a bit further, but Coach Burgess decided he would not personally employ the strategy, even though he gave me comfort if I desired to do so. I pondered the situation for about 30 seconds and called Bob Quierolo back and advised him I was not feeling well. He told me he remembered when we met a few days earlier I was coughing and he was sorry to hear I was not feeling well. He suggested if I was not better the next morning, I should call him again. I called him the next morning and each morning of the strike until he told me I had depleted my sick days.

I was bored sitting around the house with nothing to do, so I visited my friend Carmine at his restaurant. Carmine was in the planning stage of some light renovation in his restaurant's kitchen and welcomed my assistance. I'm fairly handy, but next to Carmine, I was considered by him as a master carpenter.

Together, we disconnected some unused exhaust fans and made plans to cover the openings. We merely measured the size of the openings and bought sheet metal in precut sizes leaving us with the simple task of fastening the sheet metal over the openings in the walls. We spent the entire week on this and a couple of other minor projects. Even though Carmine was happy to accomplish this task, the best part of the week was spending time together, laughing, telling stories, and eating as we labored. The only restriction we had on eating was our imagination. To this day, we still comment on the fantastic hamburgers we concocted. We took the absolutely delicious dinner loafs baked by Bill (their in-house baker) and formed hamburger patties to the size of the loaf (about six inches) from meat to be used for meatballs, then cut a generous slice of sweet onion, placing all of them on a very hot flat grill, adding a thick slice of Parmesan cheese during the final 30 seconds. We added salt and pepper to taste, a few slices of dill pickle and we enjoyed the best hamburgers we've ever tasted before or since.

The strike was settled and school began, albeit a few days late. I joined Dave Davenport and Dan Riveiro as the boys' physical education staff. We had so many boys (150 to 250/class) that all we were expected to do (I was told) was monitor attendance, participation, and cooperation (no fighting). I was told that establishing and maintaining discipline in PE was a difficult task at some schools but it was a walk in the park for Dave, Dan, and me. As a matter of fact, it was not uncommon for one of us to watch the entire group while the other two tended to other matters.

The last period of the day, which began at 2:20 p.m., was limited to athletes who participated in their sports in lieu of PE. It was an efficient setup, allowing us to begin practice an hour earlier.

The football aspect of the job was fun and challenging, but the bulk of my assignment, teaching PE, was indescribably boring. If it were not for participatory visits by Carmine and Malio, I would've gone stir crazy.

Carmine and Malio visited so frequently that I was authorized by Coach John Burgess to provide them with lockers in the coaches' dressing room. All the coaches loved visits from the twins, which generally generated interesting conversation, many laughs, and often food.

Carmine, especially, enjoyed his trips to Plant. He would arrive around second period and would play all day. We would draft "All-Star" players from the pool of students as they arrived and then we would compete in the seasonal sport throughout the day. (Who can say I didn't learn anything from John Pellegrino at Robinson High?)

Carmine or Malio would visit me during the day, and more often than not, I would visit them at their restaurant in the evenings. Our friendship grew from the huge investment in time and conversation. On the weekends, it was not uncommon for me and a group of friends, including Baby Joe, Joe Lumia, John Pellegrino, Dana Kirk, and others to visit with them until they closed the lounge (3 A.M.) and then join them for breakfast, putting us home in the neighborhood of 4:30 A.M. Sometimes, in lieu of breakfast, we would relocate to the Plant High School gymnasium and play 4-on-4 or 5-on-5 full-court basketball. News of the basketball games began to spread amongst our friends and the group grew allowing us the luxury of reserve players.

Interestingly, professionals, including lawyers and dentists, participated in these games causing concern of injury for those who used their hands to earn their living. Dentists, Nick Colmeneres and Richard Valdes (Malio's brother-in-law) often voiced this concern but it never deterred their participation. This nocturnal activity generally concluded around 5:30 A.M., allowing the participants time to cool down, shower, eat breakfast, and dress for work.

We generally ate breakfast at the Pancake House, but one particular morning Malio invited me to have breakfast with him at his home. I gladly accepted, but as we approached his neat and manicured home in Wellswood in the quiet of the morning, I began to wonder how Shirley would take to the idea of making us breakfast without forewarning while she prepared herself and her two babies for nursery before beginning her day of teaching elementary school children. I voiced this concern to Malio, but he assured me that there was no problem.

We sat at the kitchen table and shared the newspaper as Malio boldly rattled off the breakfast fare he (we) desired. Through the corner of my eye I could see Shirley frantically managing her morning as these two overgrown brats read the newspaper and sipped on coffee and juice. Shirley was as gracious as always, but I felt uncomfortable, nonetheless, as I attempted, unsuccessfully, to make my 275-pound body invisible, or at least, less visible. I earlier sensed from comments Malio made regarding Shirley that there was no one on earth he loved, respected, or revered more than her, but I wondered if he was putting her mild and even temper to the test. I thanked her for each item she brought to the table and attempted to communicate my appreciation for her effort, but was nonetheless relieved when she finally loaded the kids into her station wagon and bid us farewell. Malio, like me, was (and is) a high-maintenance individual, but fortunately, he was (and is) married to a special person who understood and catered to his special needs. I received a glimpse of how important it is to marry the right person.

Breakfast was much simpler and safer when we merely drove to the Pancake House and ate breakfast amongst the population who was either transitioning to or from work. After breakfast, I returned to Plant and went to sleep on the cot in the coach's office until the first coach arriving for work served as my wake-up call.

In addition to PE, I was assigned two Study Halls. Study Hall was, and I suspect still is, a euphemism for inventorying students. The school auditorium was used for this class and the primary objective was to establish and maintain order amongst 200 to 400 students with raging hormones who were interested in almost anything but studying. In addition, it was not uncommon for a teacher who was experiencing a discipline problem to ask if the problem could be exported to the Study Hall under the pretense that the teacher would be more effective with the remaining students. I did not require such sophisticated reasoning for inclusion into my Study Halls and even received students from my fellow PE instructors who wanted to rid themselves of disruptive students not interested in dressing out for PE.

My strategy in managing this herd of students was simple and effective. I assigned students seats in rows that neighbored two empty rows, thereby minimizing the temptation to communicate. Then I assigned a captain to each row with the dual duty of checking attendance and managing compliance with our *no talking* requirement. These captains were individuals who demonstrated leadership capabilities and enjoyed carrying out the responsibilities of the position. The demand for these captain positions was so great that I often had to utilize co-captains in order not to disappoint a qualified student.

The *carrot* for the class was a weekly talent show dubbed by the kids *Plant High School Presents* or the outdoor *Study Hall Escapade*. If the class behaved from Monday through Thursday, I would allow the students to conduct a student talent show. The kids would perform various talents ranging from singing and/or playing a musical instrument to reading poetry to magic tricks, juggling, etc. The kids really enjoyed the talent shows and therefore exercised peer pressure on anyone who jeopardized their weekly treat. When the weather was nice (and the kids met the behavior criteria), we would relocate to the covered football stands where the students could socialize as they observed their fellow students engaged in PE. Students having PE prior to or after Study Hall were allowed to "double up" on PE in lieu of Study Hall or vice versa. It was a fun time for the students and many of the teachers who had free periods would attend the talent shows for their own enjoyment and occasional participation.

We actually had no *bad* students. We had some who were *tagged* as serious discipline problems but that was related to problems they were experiencing away from school and were using school as the *stage* to act out their frustrations. Some of the most satisfying experiences I had during my two years coaching were those associated with assisting troubled individuals to work out their problems.

GENE & SYLVIA

My brother Gene made the difficult but correct decision to quit football and invest that time into earning money. He maintained his full academic scholarship and eliminated the aggravation he had experienced for two years. I'm certain that had I not been on the team he would have quit sooner. What I didn't know at the time was that he was planning on marrying his high school girlfriend and love of his life, Sylvia Jean Tinnaro, and that his plan was to get his finances beefed up in anticipation of that event.

He took an afternoon/night job with United States Post Office at $5.50 an hour and he loved earning the $8.25/hour overtime rate which he often received. On the weekends, he worked with his best friend, Danny Someillan, at Danny's father's Citgo service station on the corner of North Boulevard and Columbus Drive. He considered the time he worked with Danny as leisure time and he often told me he would prefer to be with Danny at the service station than sitting around the house. He took his books with him and studied during lulls. Gene was a master at managing his money, and in the fall of 1968, he and Sylvia announced that they would be married on December 21st of that year.

It was a simple and sweet event at Christ the King Catholic Church attended only by their families and very closest friends. The afternoon reception was held at our home on Lemon Street. They honeymooned at the Coral Reef on St. Pete Beach.

Gene and Sylvia moved into a neat duplex on Lemon Street, two blocks west of the home Gene grew up in. Sylvia worked at Lerner's Dress shop and Gene continued his schedule of two jobs while a full-time student.

Carmine and Barbara Iavarone had outgrown their Davis Island home and Carmine asked if I thought Gene had interest in the home they were vacating on Como next to Berkeley Preparatory High School. I told Carmine I was sure Gene had interest but his budget was tight. Carmine said he was flexible and that I should have Gene call him or come by the restaurant.

After meeting with Carmine, Gene came by the house with a grin on his face from ear to ear. He told Mama and me that he had just bought Carmine's Davis Island home. We were both as thrilled as he but wondered how he could manage the payments. Without asking, he offered, "And the best part is my payments don't change. Carmine asked how much I was currently paying at the duplex, and when I told him, he said he would sell it to me for the same monthly payment."

"What about the down payment?" I asked.

"Carmine said he did not want a down payment; and he's leaving their washer and dryer." Gene answered with a humble and appreciative smile on his face.

"You've got good friends in Carmine and Malio," said Mama knowing that we were well aware of that fact.

"I can't wait until Sylvia gets home from work; she'll be so happy to hear this news," Gene said as he hugged us on the way out.

Sylvia was, indeed, happy and they both enjoyed their new home where they would later start their family.

Over the years, Gene reminded me many times of something he knew I knew. "Mondy," he would say, "you know I could have never purchased Carmine's home if it were not for Carmine and Barbara." After the first three times, he never expected a response from me; he just wanted to say it.

I have come to realize that when someone does something for your loved ones, it is a nicer feeling than if they did it for you directly.

JUDY?

Judy and I continued to date, off and on. It seemed like getting married was becoming less probable than more.

Judy was occupying her time by carrying a light load at the University of South Florida toward her degree in education and working in the record department at the Britton Plaza J C Penney store. As time passed, we began seeing less and less of each other and more and more of others.

I dated several young women and had a nice time but it just wasn't the same. Several of them were eager to become serious, but I had no interest in that idea. I had been exposed to *something special,* and as a result, was very picky about with whom I wanted to spend the rest of my life with.

MY CAREER

Throughout my coaching experience, Carmine and Malio spoke to me regarding my interest in working outside the school system, namely in business. As I indicated to them, I never gave the subject much thought because the business world was completely foreign to me. I explained that other than visiting Steve (Malzone) at Speedline Athletic and going into the bank to pay our Lemon Street mortgage, the only exposure I had to business was spending a lot of time in their restaurant and lounge. Carmine, however, continued to talk to me about business and encouraged me with his belief that I could be successful in that arena.

"But what can I do?" I asked.

"I don't know," Carmine responded, "but you're much more capable than many of the businesspeople who come into my restaurant, so I'm sure you can do something. What do you think about sales?"

"Sales?" I exclaimed. "You've got to be kidding. I've never sold anything in my life."

"Well, I don't know how it works," Carmine said, "but I know plenty of salesmen who spend the afternoon in my lounge and are still able to make a decent living. Some of them went to Hillsborough (high school) with me and I can tell you they're not as sharp as you and they don't work near as hard as you would."

I couldn't figure out if Carmine was trying to make me feel good or if he was imbibing too much of the products he served in his lounge. Nonetheless, he continued to encourage me to consider business as an alternative to my current profession. I was flattered with his opinion of my capabilities and was appreciative of his concern for my welfare; however, I was well aware of my inexperience and lack of business knowledge, and consequently, I had no vision of how I could contribute to a business enterprise.

"Can you come to the restaurant Thursday night at 8:30 to meet a friend of mine?" asked Carmine while visiting with me at Plant High School.

"Who's your friend?" I responded.

"A guy I went to high school with who played football at FSU and was with the San Diego Chargers. I'd like you to come by for a *cup of coffee*; his name is Jack Edwards," he said hoping to impress me with the football credentials.

"Yeah, sure," I answered, "but why do you want me to meet him?"

"He's got this good job with Zee-rox and he said they're looking for sharp guys to hire," explained Carmine.

"So, what does he want to talk with me about?" I said thinking ahead of this meeting and not wanting to embarrass Carmine.

"Don't worry about it," Carmine said. "The worst thing that can happen is that we eat a big steak."

I wasn't very interested in this meeting Carmine had set up, but my mouth was watering thinking about that big steak as we approached lunchtime.

"What kind of products does Zee-rox sell?" I queried.

"I'm not sure," Carmine answered. "I think they've got something to do with antifreeze or something."

That sounded right to me.

"Zee-rox is pronounced Zear-rox and is spelled X-e-r-o-x. The name Xerox comes from the word xerography, which is a combination of two Greek words meaning 'dry writing.' Xeros means 'dry' and 'graphy' means writing. Xerox is the only dry copier on the market," explained Jack Edwards as I dressed my salad with more Roquefort than needed. As he continued explaining the process, it became abundantly clear that "talking" was Jack's strength. He artfully explained to two people who had never used a copier the superior features and benefits associated with the Xerox product line. He seemed to possess the knowledge of a professor and the communication skills and smile of a politician. His smile, while charming, was short of genuine.

Jack excused himself to take a phone call and Carmine seized the opportunity to tell me, with a smile on his face, to forget the antifreeze and asked if I understood what Jack was talking about. I explained to Carmine that I understood the concept but I would not want to be tested on the subject. Carmine laughed and suggested I listen to Jack's entire pitch before I determined whether or not I had interest. I agreed as I began to help myself to the broiled shrimp in garlic butter sauce just placed on our table by Carmine's working manager and confidant, Stephanie Baucom.

Jack returned to the table and continued his exposition on the Xerox Corporation. Jack was a raconteur of the highest degree and he entertained us throughout the evening. The high point of the evening (for me) was when he made the statement, "Mondy, we're a Fortune 500 company and within five years we intend to become a Fortune 100 company. Our plan to accomplish this goal is to hire people with exceptional capability and potential such as you." I glanced at Carmine whose hand over his mouth was concealing a smile as I wondered if Jack had been consuming the snake oil he was selling.

"Exactly which capabilities and potential that I possess are you referring to?" I asked this individual to whom I had been introduced all of 2 ½ hours earlier.

"Your accomplishments playing football at UT, your ability to communicate, and your work ethic," he responded without a smile on his face.

I glanced around the dining room as I wondered who else might have heard this audacious statement while at the same time trying to detect any Candid Camera(s). I recall thinking to myself, "Did this guy just equate playing football to business?" I knew one of us was way off and I didn't think it was me. I would later find out I was wrong.

Jack concluded the evening by advising me that he would be at Plant High School next week to demonstrate some Xerox equipment he was proposing to the Hillsborough County School Board for selected schools throughout the county. He went on to say that we could continue our conversation after the demonstration if I had interest.

At my suggestion, Jack arrived at the coach's office prior to the meeting for a cup of coffee with the coaching staff. He knew a couple of the coaches, but they all knew him and his accomplishments at FSU, and to a lesser degree, San Diego.

Jack pulled up in his late-model Cadillac El Dorado. A tan vinyl top that matched the interior accented the white exterior. Jack donned the jacket to his tailor-made brown suit and his signature smile as he followed me into the coach's office. I introduced him to coaches and within thirty seconds the backslapping and storytelling indicated everyone's comfort level with each other.

Jack sat in the general vicinity of the coaches but not close enough to give any of the faculty or administration the idea he had a connection with anyone. I watched him as he listened attentively to the boring minutiae being communicated to us by our principal, Charles Vacher. At the conclusion of the meeting, Mr. Vacher communicated to the group that we were part of a trial to determine if there was a better way to reproduce instructional and test material than the current method of mimeograph. He went on to say that Mr. Edwards from the Xerox Corp. was in attendance at our meeting for the purpose of explaining the trial and to train key operators within each department to assist casual operators within their respective departments. With that introduction, Jack addressed the podium and delivered his signature smile as he was greeted with customary applause.

Jack skillfully and professionally explained the shortcomings of our current system and introduced the Xerox 2400 as a solution to improved productivity and professionalism to our group. Jack went on to explain that the time freed up by not having to spend hours preparing masters for the mimeograph equipment could be converted into spending more quality time preparing course outlines and material. Being a PE Instructor and coach, I saw no use for the Xerox equipment with the exception of an occasional update to our football playbook. Since Coach Burgess' wife, Moe, prepared the playbook and took care of changes out of her house, I never gave much thought to what was involved in its preparation. Nonetheless, Coach Burgess clearly understood what was involved and led a team of eager faculty members in volunteering to be trained as key operators.

Since I wanted to learn more about the equipment myself, I asked Coach Burgess if it was okay for me to be trained also, to which he responded, "If it's okay with Jack, it's okay with me."

Jack was pleased with the level of interest and anticipated a successful trial.

ATMOSPHERE OF BOREDOM

One of the applications (uses) and uniqueness of the Xerox equipment in 1969 was its ability to copy onto plain paper. This, of course, allowed for the use of colored paper stock.

Our county paychecks were printed on light green paper, very close to the stock we had on hand at the school. Traditionally, the coaches made an unauthorized run to the bank on paydays in conjunction with leaving the campus for lunch.

Dave Davenport and I, in an atmosphere of boredom, decided to reproduce Coach Dan Riviero's paycheck on the school's green paper stock and present the authentic check to him at the teller's window when the teller questioned the copy he was attempting to deposit. When John Burgess heard of the prank, he asked that we wait till he concluded the history class he taught prior to lunch so he could enjoy Dan's reaction.

We drove to the Atlantic Bank in Coach Burgess' assigned (even though he did not teach) Drivers Ed station wagon. We later learned from Dan that he considered it peculiar that all the coaches in the station wagon went into the bank that day, even though a couple of coaches (myself included) banked elsewhere. The rest of us milled around the lobby on that busy Friday afternoon as Coaches Davenport, Riviero, and Burgess prepared their deposit slips. To the casual observer, it must have seemed like we were preparing to rob the institution. We were all surprised when the teller accepted Dan's deposit of the phony check and each of us muffled our laughter as we exited the bank.

As we traveled to South Tampa's fried chicken landmark, Palios Brothers, Dan continued to inquire as to what was considered so funny to our group. During lunch, Dave Davenport told Dan that Mr. Vacher was unable to attend our luncheon but that he authorized Dave to make a presentation on his behalf to Dan Riviero for his outstanding achievement during the preceding month. Dan grinned as Dave attempted to communicate this charade with a straight face but could not contain himself as Dan studied the award (his real paycheck) Dave handed him as a token of appreciation for his accomplishment.

With an increasingly serious tone to his voice, the muscular and hot-tempered former tight end for the Universities of Kentucky and Tampa demanded an explanation. Dave explained between laughs as he held his stomach that Mr. Vacher had gained approval for an additional paycheck for Dan in recognition of his superior performance. Dan had not yet figured out why he was holding an additional paycheck, but he was certain something was not *kosher in the deli* because he knew the school system did not operate in this fashion. We finally explained to Dan why we were laughing but were unable to transfer the comedic value fueling the good time we were having (at his expense).

Dan immediately began to lambaste us with (obvious) reasons we shouldn't have duplicated his paycheck along with the attendant perils of our actions. His seriousness further fueled our laughter and our laughter further fueled his seriousness.

Dan got everyone's attention when he suggested that the bank manager may have already detected the phony deposit and was in contact with Mr. Vacher in that regard. Furthermore, he said that Mr. Vacher, if contacted, probably went to the coach's office looking for him and learned that we were all off-campus without permission.

The tone of our group immediately transitioned from silliness and laughter to seriousness and concern. After checking with the office, we traveled back to the bank *to make things right.*

Dave Davenport was the lead apologist for our group, and even though the bank manager understood that the prank went further than initially intended, he suggested we eliminate bank transactions from our pool of jokes and distractions. We assured him that we would and we transitioned back *into our joke mode*, this time joined by Dan Riviero.

As it related to Xerox, I definitely liked what Jack Edwards was doing better than what I was doing, but I didn't know if I was qualified. However, the more I conversed with Jack the more comfortable I became about my ability to do his job. So, I developed a strategy.

It was May, and Jack wanted to set up an interview with Xerox's big boss in Florida, branch manager Ed Muse, whose office was in Orlando. My strategy was, in the unlikely event that I would receive a job offer, to schedule my start date the first day after my commitment to Plant High School. This would allow me almost three full months to determine if I was suited to and liked the Xerox environment.

When Jack informed me that Mr. Muse was coming to Tampa from Orlando for the single purpose of meeting with me, I commented, "You've got to be kidding. Shouldn't I be speaking with a manager in Tampa rather than this heavyweight from Orlando?"

Jack indicated Xerox had just entered a "hiring freeze" and Ed Muse wanted to determine for himself if I was worth all the fuss Jack was making over me.

I told Jack that I did not realize he was making a fuss over me and that in the event this opportunity did not work out I did not want him to look bad. He smiled and indicated to me that I was in the driver's seat. "Driver's seat," I thought to myself, "How can I be in the driver's seat when I don't even have a (business) driver's license".

My conversation with Mr. Muse was spent mostly talking about football. What I didn't realize then was that many of the questions he asked regarding football were, in fact, interview questions. When he asked what the characteristics of a winner were, he was, in fact, asking what I thought the characteristics of a successful businessperson would be. When he asked about the importance of leadership on the team, he was asking about business leadership, and when he asked about game preparation, he was, in fact, asking about the preparation required before meeting with a customer. I did not realize he was gaining all the information he wanted as he interpreted my responses. He was a smooth operator getting his answers without me even knowing he was asking questions.

He must have been impressed, because he offered me the position and asked if I could begin in two weeks. When I explained to him that I could not leave Plant High School or my coaching staff (we were in spring practice), he interpreted my intentions in the noblest fashion.

I was pleased, surprised, but mostly flattered with the offer. Apparently, this captain of industry thought I could be successful in his company.

LOOKING FOR CONFIRMATION

I casually informed my mother of my impending career change and got a curious response.

"I hope you know what you are doing, because you're giving up a good job you went to college for. What are you going to do when everyone buys one of these machines you're selling? You better think about that before you quit."

I knew there was an appropriate response to her question; I just didn't know what it was.

That Saturday, I took Judy to dinner and a movie and was nonplused by her reaction to my plans for a career change. She seemed to treat the matter as if I was changing automobiles and I was becoming irritated. What really perturbed me was when she asked the same question my mother did. I, again, felt kind of stupid not having a response. I was hoping Mr. Stallings would be awake when I took her home because I was looking for some confirmation from a businessman regarding my decision.

He was reading his Bible, sitting in his easy chair as we walked up the steps to his home. I told him of my plans and he asked several questions about our product line, benefits, and other questions I was ill-equipped to answer. I saw no enthusiasm from him regarding our conversation, which prompted me to ask, "So what do you think about the decision I made?"

"Well Mondy," he said, as he scratched his forehead and squinted a bit, "I believe you'll do well because you're a smart fella and I know you'll work hard; but I'm just wondering what you'll do once everybody who needs one of those machines buys one."

I couldn't believe he asked that question. Furthermore, I couldn't believe I was still unable to answer the question that had dogged me three times in as many days indicating how naïve I was about the career I was considering. I was looking for confirmation and it was nowhere to be found.

On a Saturday late in May, Malio asked me to join him for some shopping at one of Tampa's premier men's clothiers, Jack Pendola's. While Malio asked the salesman questions and opinions, I casually looked over the store merchandise. Then Malio said, "Let's pick three out of these five," as he pointed to the suits strewn over the clothes racks. I gave him my opinion as to the three I liked best, and he agreed, saying to the salesman, "He'll take these three."

That was the first time I realized he was helping me, not the other way around. We went from neck to toe, buying ties, shirts, socks and shoes. I didn't know how good I was going to be my first day of work, but I was certain to look good.

To be truthful, I had not considered wardrobe with regard to my new job and would have gotten off to the wrong start had it not been for my caring friend.

EARLY YEARS 1945-1969

Me - 1945

My mother

My father

My father and mother - 1947

Uncle Vincent & Aunt Cici, Tio Joe & Tia Maria, my father and mother

My maternal grandmother Mamagrande (Giuseppina Greco Ficarrotta DeLaRoca DiDio)

My paternal grandmother Abuela Juana Camarero & my sister

My Aunt Mary (Tia Maria)

My Uncle Joe DiDio-US Marine Corp-WWII

My Aunt Frances(Cici)

Me and my Papa

Me, my father and Tanya Russo

Me, age 3

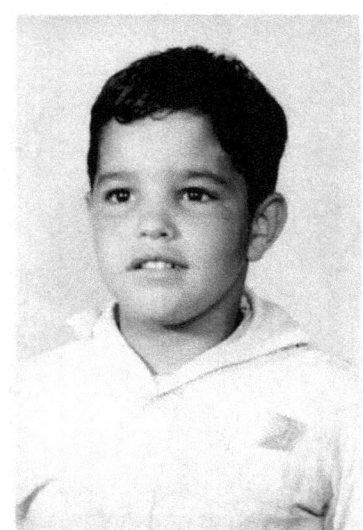
Me in 1st grade

1st Communion 1950 class (6th row, 3rd from right)

Me, my brother Gene & Tanya Russo

Me, School days

My brother Gene, School days

Me and Gene

My brother Bob's gradution from Spring Hill and our mother

My brother Bob & Rose's wedding

Me, 17 year old Jesuit High Senior

Me at Jesuit 1960

My buddies-Ted, Steve, me and Denis, Christmas 1962

Judy and me Clearwater Beach

Me, LSU 1963

1963 LSU Fighting Tigers (#70 1st row, 2nd from left)

Me at LSU 1963

Judith and me LSU 1963

Me, Judy, Tanya & Aunt Louisa-New Orleans 1964

Court date for the thug who threatened LSU basketball players

Malio, Joe, Me, Bennie, Carmine, Baby Joe

UT fightin' Spartans (#77 2nd row, 6th from left)

Hall of Fame - Class of 1986

UT Spartan 1965

University of Tampa

Gene-defensive tacke UT Spartans 1965

My buddy Danny Someillan, Head mgr UT Football (on ladder)

Judy and me in my red MGB on Bayshore Blvd

Part Two

*MIDDLE YEARS
THE BIG LEAGUES (1969-1998)*

XEROX

Thirty days earlier, I hadn't known what "Fortune 500" meant, and on June 7th, 1969, I was employed by one of the blue-chip companies comprising the list.

My friend and former schoolmate, Lou Piniella, had made it to the big leagues. He was enjoying a fine rookie season with the Kansas City Royals. He enjoyed living in the Midwest and was pleased with the opportunity presented to him by this expansion club.

His level of play was stellar, earning him the distinction of being voted American League Rookie of the Year.

I considered my opportunity with Xerox as *a chance at the big leagues* and was determined to give it all I had.

My first day at work was somewhat of a culture shock. It was strange to see everyone dressed at 8 AM as if they were going to a wedding or funeral. The women in the office had their hair coiffured and the smell of perfume was a stark contrast to the aroma I had become accustomed to from the coaches' office at Plant High School.

Every industry has its own language, and the office products industry is no exception. Everyone was communicating with each other using terms that only a "Xeroid" (an inside term for Xerox employees) could comprehend.

Nancy, the secretary/receptionist, offered me a cup of coffee as she advised me that Charles Johnson, the Sales Manager, would be with me in about thirty minutes. I read some material on the company while I waited for Charles, and during the wait, just about every employee in this friendly office introduced themselves to me. I was impressed with what seemed like a positive attitude of the employees.

Charlie, as he asked to be called, escorted me into his office and provided me an overview of my training. Xerox employed a state-of-the-art training program that featured its highly-acclaimed Professional Selling Skills module, referred to in the industry as PSS. The expensive PSS module was sold separately to many major corporations for training of their sales forces. In addition to PSS, the self-administered training program included the history of the company, an overview of the product line and the various product applications, and a module on *effective listening*. Charlie explained that I should be finished with the in-house training within forty-five days, during which time I would be scheduled for a two-week sales school at Xerox's National Training Facility in Fort Lauderdale, Florida. With that information, I carried my box of training material into an empty office which would be my home for the next six weeks.

Later that morning, Charlie came into the office to ask if I had any questions. He then advised me of a prospect who insisted on having me come out to his business to discuss what model Xerox copier he needed. Charlie explained to the prospect that I was on my first day at work and was probably (certainly) not qualified to make a recommendation. He said the customer insisted on seeing me and suggested I take the territory salesman with me to assist (carry) on the call. I thought he was kidding until he handed me the message that indicated the prospect was Baby Joe Valenti of JC Valenti, Inc. Charlie saw me smile as I read the message prompting him to ask, "Do you know this guy?"

"Oh yeah," I said, "I know him."

I thought Baby Joe was kidding when I returned his call, but he insisted he was interested in a copier.

The salesman in whose territory Baby Joe's company was geographically located, George Knutsson, was pleased when I asked him to join me on the call (referred to in the industry as a "bluebird.")

We ate lunch and met with the decision makers at J. C. Valenti namely, "Blue Eyes" (Baby Joe's dad), Uncle Nelson (Valenti), and of course, Baby Joe. We laughed at the stories Baby Joe and I told, but especially Baby Joe's account of my brother Gene warming up for field goal and extra point attempts during UT football games.

Baby Joe asked me which copier was right for his operation and I told Joe I should turn this part of the meeting over to George since I had not yet learned how to turn the machine on.

George went over the product line and pricing with Baby Joe and asked if he had any questions. Baby Joe said, "Just one. Will Mondy get credit if I buy a machine?"

Recognizing this was important to Baby Joe, George said, "Normally, he would not be eligible for commissions until he returned from sales school, but I think we'll be able to work something out between us."

"If you can, then I'll take this one," he said.

That scenario sums up Baby Joe as well as any. Helping people, especially those he loved, was what he was all about.

On the way back to the office, George commented, "Baby Joe must like you a lot because he needs that copier as much as I need a third ear."

I was developing the feeling that Xerox was the right place for me. The training was comprehensive and I was gaining an understanding of what was expected of a professional salesperson. It was all about results... *productivity* as contrasted to *activity*.

As in all organizations, Xerox had its leaders, followers, and those that weren't smart enough to do either.

The Village Inn Pancake House around the corner from our location at 3710 West Kennedy Boulevard was the unofficial meeting place for Xerox salesmen. There you could get a flavor for what these guys were really thinking. At first, I was surprised to hear the negativity demonstrated by these so-called professionals. I soon realized that it comes down to the same common denominator, people are people. Whether they are on a football team, a school faculty, or employed by a Fortune 500 company, people are people. As I heard many of these individuals complain about a myriad of topics including compensation, pricing, territories, etc., it became abundantly clear that anyone who would apply themselves to the task at hand and resist taking part in these bitch sessions, would soon be a top performer. That's exactly what I intended to do.

Approximately 150 sales trainees from all over the country arrived in Fort Lauderdale for the two-week sales school in July of 1969. As a matter of fact, one of the sales trainees on the team to which I was assigned was from England. Her name was Stella Wilson and she hailed from one of the New York City branches. She was a tall, attractive brunette in her late-twenties or early-thirties who knew how to use her good looks and British accent to her advantage. This was a time when Xerox was attempting to establish itself as a leader in the hiring of minorities, specifically, blacks and women. She was a *premium hire*, which meant she had meaningful sales experience prior to Xerox and was compensated accordingly.

During the *get to know each other* portion of our first meeting she described herself as *assertive*, but she was, in fact, nothing short of *aggressive*. She had the chutzpah to express to the group that, in addition to honing her sales skills, her main objective in attending this sales school was to win the Most Valuable Participant (MVP) award.

In retrospect, I am certain the pressure to succeed in a man's world contributed to her overzealous persona.

Stella and I were on a collision course as I was committed to becoming the best salesperson I could and was not about to let this transplanted *Brit* take the *big award* unless she earned it. I am certain others on our team of approximately fourteen felt the same way and were challenged by their managers, as I was, to bring home the MVP award.

Four days into the first week things were very competitive. You could feel the tension as individuals stumbled while participating in role-playing the techniques we were learning.

As a means of retaliation (and totally uncalled for), Stella *accidentally* poured a half-carafe of hot coffee over the lap of a sales trainee from Pittsburgh who used poor judgment by showing her up in front of her peer group. She was taking this MVP thing much too seriously.

There was some leisure time figured into the two-week schedule, but primarily, this was an intense training session intended to equip *green* (no experience) and *brown* (wrong experience) sales reps with the ability to conduct a professional sales presentation to any level management and selling any product.

The location of the training school could not have been better (or worse, depending on your perspective and objective). Xerox occupied a substantial portion of the Sheraton Lauderdale Hotel located in the hub of Fort Lauderdale's tanned and hard body social scene. In an unplanned sort of way, this environment served to weed out those who would not be able to discipline themselves in the loosely-supervised fashion of Xerox in those days. An added temptation to some were the four bars and lounges located throughout the hotel, and to others the three hotel restaurants, one of which boasted a five-star gourmet rating and the one I chose each evening. Expenses were not an issue for the high rolling Xerox Corporation, and everyone enjoyed the advantages (or disadvantages) in their own way.

Xerox had this training down to a science. About the middle of the second week, they had us chomping at the bit to try our skills in front of real customers.

The last half of the second Friday was dedicated to giving out awards and socializing with the group before everyone departed. Many of the trainees, especially those from the northeast, made their travel arrangements on Sunday so they could squeeze in a couple more days of Florida before returning to their concrete jungle. As for me, my bags were packed and loaded into my powder blue Cadillac Eldorado in an effort to get a jumpstart on the four-hour drive back to Tampa.

Training school was perfect for me. I was a sponge soaking up all the information I could in anticipation of storming the City of Tampa with my recently acquired skills.

I found it interesting that in two short weeks friendships/associations that last a career (and beyond) can be developed. I even felt a little sorry that Stella didn't take the MVP award to New York, but I was pleased for the fella who took it to Tampa.

My positive experience at the training school sealed my decision to resign my coaching position at H. B. Plant High School. I was preparing to call John Burgess to tell him of my decision, but he called me first.

"I didn't appreciate reading about your decision to change careers in the Tampa Tribune." John said to me over the telephone. "It's been embarrassing to field calls from (school principal) Charlie Vacher and others regarding the article when you and I haven't discussed your decision to leave."

I apologized to John for any embarrassment I might have caused him and explained that I had no communication with the Tribune regarding the subject and was planning to call him the next day or so to inform him of my decision. He accepted my apology and wished me well in my new endeavor.

During my discussion with John Burgess, he informed me that the article in question was built around a conversation between Carmine and a sportswriter for the paper who frequented Carmine's. When I asked Carmine why he let the cat out of the bag, he calmly responded, "I didn't realize it was a secret and I knew you weren't going back to Plant anyhow."

How could one quarrel with that response?

While at sales school in Fort Lauderdale, a management change took place in the Tampa office. Charles Johnson was relieved of his duties and was replaced by C.R. "Bud" Reed.

The company line on Charlie's dismissal (firing) was that headquarters in Orlando was not satisfied with the production of the Tampa office. Some were saddened by Charlie's departure; others gladdened. As for me, I was ambivalent. He was a nice enough fellow, but he did not appear to have the management skills required to handle the rogue group in Tampa.

Bud was the antithesis of Charlie. His style consisted of a nice blend of toughness and fairness under the umbrella of *results* and his word was his bond. If Bud said it, you could count on it.

You'd think everyone would rally around a manager with these traits, but such was not the case. He represented a threat to those who were used to not being managed and they instinctively attempted to undermine his efforts. However, this tough-talking Texan was up to the challenge.

After being assigned to work with other sales reps in their territories for couple of months, Bud offered me a territory of my own, South St. Petersburg. A couple of self-appointed mentors counseled me not to take the territory because, according to them, it had no potential. I explained to Bud my only hesitation about working in south St. Petersburg was the commute. He comforted me with his assurance that the territory assignment was temporary and that he would relocate me to Tampa when the opportunity presented itself. He was pleased with my willingness to cooperate and on October 1st, 1969, I was a commissioned sales rep for Wall Street darling, Xerox Corp.

Not to minimize the importance of the sales techniques learned in Xerox's PSS course, *selling* comes down to knowing your product, knowing your competition, and *beating the bushes* (making sales calls). Of the three, the component with the highest rate of return is clearly beating the bushes.

I was distraction free. I had no wife, no children, no bad habits, no hobbies, or competing (with work) interests. Judy and I continued to see each other on an on again/off again basis and were currently in the *off* mode.

The main potential distraction for me came from within the company. I was constantly invited/encouraged to attend *unofficial* meetings (bitch sessions) at the Village Inn Pancake House. I had attended these meetings with sales reps to which I was assigned during my training, but now that I was responsible for my own territory, I saw no purpose or value in attending.

Essentially, the basis for that decision was the same as it had been in high school and college. The big difference for me was that, unlike high school and part of college, I was able to assess the situation, anticipate the probable consequences of each, and make a decision consistent with the outcome I was seeking. With that perspective, I turned over every rock I came across in my territory and was among the top three salesmen in the Orlando branch for the fourth quarter of 1969.

By design, sales rep salaries were intended to be a small portion of total compensation with the largest portion coming from *incentive* (commission and bonus).

It was customary for sales managers to inform sales reps of their annual salary increases for the upcoming year around the middle of December. I considered it quite an awkward situation sitting in a bullpen with thirty or so sales reps waiting to be called by the sales manager for this purpose. What made the situation awkward was that the sales reps second-guessed every move the sales managers made and the requested confidentiality was routinely breached as sales reps freely communicated with their friends upon the conclusion of their meetings.

As I waited my turn to meet with Bud Reed and new manager, Lee Snow, I was subject to unsolicited and unwanted coaching by several sales reps who considered themselves my mentors. The main coaching point they wanted me to remember during my meeting was to be gracious in accepting any criticism but to insist on and negotiate a $40/month raise from the $25/month they anticipated I would be offered. I explained to these well-intended but misguided coaches, that I felt uncomfortable negotiating anything with the sales managers since I had been in my territory for less than ninety days. They said that my performance had earned me the right to negotiate, and that if I did not do so, I would cost myself the difference between $25 and $40 a month. My salary was $415 a month and a $40 increase would've been almost a 10 percent hike in less than ninety days or an annualized pay increase of forty percent. I considered it disrespectful to challenge the sales manager's decision this early in my career and decided before entering their office to accept whatever they had planned for me.

After engaging in small talk for a couple of minutes, Bud asked me what kind of increase I thought I deserved. I had not anticipated such a question and was not prepared to respond, but nonetheless, told him that I had not given the situation much thought and would be satisfied with whatever they had decided. Bud said he appreciated my attitude but he wanted a number from me. I thought this was a perfect time to the use the $40/month number my mentors had suggested but at the same time I did not want to appear greedy or brash. I said I could understand a zero increase since I was made a sales rep less than ninety days previously, but I could fathom $40 a month if they were very pleased with my performance thus far but that I would be perfectly contented with anything in between.

Bud smiled and said, "Mondy, Lee and I are very pleased with the job you have done, and furthermore, we're just as pleased with the leadership you have demonstrated. Even though you're the least tenured salesman in this office, many of the veteran sales reps look up to you and they're studying how you conduct yourself. I even heard attendance at the pancake house is down since you don't go to the meetings. Lee and I feel like we can count on you to keep this information confidential... Your increase, effective January 1st, is $150/month."

When I told them how much I appreciated their confidence in me, they both smiled and Bud said, "I feel I'm making one of the best investments I've ever made."

As I exited Bud's office my (self-appointed) mentors were looking to me for information. When I offered none, as I gathered my belongings, they asked using the international sign language of *thumb up* or *thumb down*. I gave them the *thumb up* with a smile as I left the building. It wasn't the money, since my expenses were considerably below my income, but I really felt appreciated and I was committed to showing them that they had made the correct decision in placing confidence in me.

As promised, Bud changed my territory to one in East Tampa which included a declining Ybor City. Bud had restructured all of the Tampa territories and gave the existing sales reps their choice of territories in an effort to turn up the heat on what he considered an underperforming bunch. By allowing them to participate in the restructuring and choosing of their territories, he felt he would achieve an improvement in the sales reps' attitude, and thus, their performance. What I didn't know was that I was his ace in the hole. He anticipated that I would perform well in the un-chosen territory, thereby raising the bar for the sales reps who had the privilege of restructuring and choosing their own territories.

After a few weeks, it became evident why the territory to which I was assigned was not chosen by anyone. My territory consisted primarily of mom and pop businesses in a blighted area of Tampa which included College Hill and Belmont Heights. The desirability of my territory was best described by one of the partners in a two-man, black operated legal office when the lawyer greeted me with the following comment, "Ah-mahn-dough, what did you do wrong to deserve this territory?" Within my first thirty days, that lawyer was my customer. The upside to my territory was no one ever called on the businesses, including the competition.

My experience told me that the necessary ingredient in this recipe was persistence. I had seen persistence prevail time and time again in football, in academics, and in my brief business experience in south St. Petersburg. I recalled the paraphrase of a former President of the United States when he said, "Nothing in this world can take the place of persistence. Talent will not; nothing is more common than unsuccessful people with talent. Genius will not; unrewarded genius is almost a proverb. Education will not; the world is full of educated derelicts. In this world, persistence and determination are keystones to success. Throughout time, *pressing on* has resulted in success that was otherwise unthinkable for people, organizations, teams, and businesses." I was prepared to implement this *call to action* to the best of my ability.

One must develop the skill of dealing with rejection to be successful in life, but nowhere is the necessity of developing that skill more important than in sales. The ratio of *noes* to *yeses* is staggering in the sales profession and if a person is unable to deal with that basic premise, they would better be served in another profession.

Each profession has its hurdles which serve to limit the number of people attempting to earn a living in that particular manner. In medicine and law, the hurdles include schooling, the time and financial investment of schooling, and the startup cost associated with establishing a practice. In athletics, the overriding hurdle is the tremendous investment in preparation and training. In law enforcement and the military, one must deal with the possibility, though remote, of losing one's life in the line of duty. The entrepreneur's hurdle is capital. Some hurdles are more obvious than others; for example, consider the hurdle of the trapeze artist, but be assured, all professions have hurdles.

Rejection, in some form or fashion and to different degrees, is present in all professions, but in no profession is it more of a factor in *making it* than in sales and in Hollywood. If you can't deal with rejection, don't be an actor or a salesperson.

For the first quarter of 1970, I was the top salesperson in the Orlando Branch, the number two salesperson in the Southern Region, and number seven in the U.S. Stack rankings which were issued quarterly within Xerox to stimulate peer pressure by recognizing everyone's comparative performance. (This technique was used by the Jesuits during my high school years very effectively). I am not noting these rankings as confirmation of my sales skills or ability but to demonstrate the importance of persistence and effort. I gave my all each day and learned early *never accept a no from someone who can't give a yes.*

My friend Malio said it best, "Mondy went about his business like he was in the Marines." Salespeople typically don't schedule calls before 9 AM or after 4 PM. I viewed the first and last hours of the day as times when I would have less competition for decision makers' attention. This approach didn't always work as some customers set aside those times to organize or wind down, but generally, entrepreneurs/business owners appreciate dealing with vendors at times other than 9 to 4 because that is time they could be dealing with their own customers. This would be especially true of professionals such as lawyers and doctors.

As I reflect on those days, I realize that I was providing an intangible that was very important to my clients but was simply second nature to me... honesty and dependability. I never promised more than I could deliver and I always delivered what I promised. A prime example of this was the communication of delivery times. A constant issue between Xerox sales reps and their customers was Xerox's perceived inability to meet quoted delivery dates. Delivery dates changed weekly due to sales in relationship to inventory. A particular product could have a quoted delivery time of two weeks and a week later, the same product delivery time could be five weeks. In an effort to impress the customer, sales reps generally gave the quoted time and then indicated they would attempt to deliver the product sooner than the quoted time (if possible). Like all people, customers lock on to what they want to hear and expect delivery sooner than the quoted time. My approach was quite different. Realizing that the customer was getting along fine before I sold him a particular product, I felt like he could live a few more weeks or months without enjoying the benefits the new product would bring. Therefore, I always doubled the delivery quote. When the equipment arrived sooner than quoted, I was inevitably viewed in a favorable light by the anxious customer. It was that simple. Do you recall the saying, "People cause 85% of their problems?" Well, some are able to get that percentage to 95 without much effort.

I was pleased with my performance and even more pleased with the fact that I enjoyed what I was doing.

In March of 1969, while overseeing PE classes and coaching, the days seemed like they would never end. More often than not, it was not the students who were watching the clock, it was me. Twelve months later, the days flew by... a pretty good indication I was enjoying what I was doing.

IT CAN'T BE ALL HONEY WITH NO BEES

A friend of mine often reminds me, "It can't be all honey with no bees."

I felt the sting of a bee when my manager, Bud Reed, asked me to consider taking a territory in Sarasota. Furthermore, he said if I decided to take the territory he wanted me to relocate to Sarasota rather than commute. This request really gave me pause because I hadn't considered working anywhere other than Tampa (Bay), and since I lived with my mother (who now lived alone), I had minimal expenses which did not include rent. Additionally, my on-and-off relationship with Judy was on the *on* mode and this move would obviously curtail my ability to see her.

Even though I gave Bud the impression I was open to his idea, I didn't see much merit in it. I decided to run the idea by my counselors.

My "Latin" counselors Vince Russo and Malio Iavarone offered the following: Uncle Vince asked if I was going to be paid more for working in Sarasota. I told him I had just received a healthy increase 90 days prior and I did not think this move would result in another increase. I remember adding, "It's not like they're asking me to work in Fangoulo, Georgia; people actually like Sarasota."

Malio's response caused me to sit up in my chair and listen more intently.

"Would you repeat that?" I asked, not believing what I just heard.

"You gotta go. You gotta do it," he repeated. "Bud wouldn't be asking you to do this if it wasn't important to him. You do this for him and he won't forget it."

I couldn't believe my ears. I was seeking confirmation for my thinking about not moving, and I received just the opposite. I later approached my Anglo counselor with the same question and was also shocked by his response.

"If you want to advance in a company, you have to be willing to go where they ask you to go," was the sage advice I received from Judy's dad.

Buford T. Stallings moved to Tampa from Georgia when he was not yet ten years old and lived all his life within ten miles of where he grew up, yet he was counseling me to move if I wanted to advance my career. I thought he was either joking or he preferred that I not see his daughter so often. Upon closer examination, I detected no smile on his face. I shared with Judy what her dad told me and asked her opinion.

"He's probably right," she said.

I was becoming increasingly confused and was convincing myself there was a conspiracy to get me out of Tampa.

I pondered the idea over the weekend and met Bud in his office early Monday morning with my decision. "I'm looking forward to working in Sarasota, Bud, but I have one question. Why?"

Working his Texas drawl somewhere between James Dean and John Wayne, he said, "Mondy, I'm not going to bullshit you, but I need your confidence on this one. I've got a big problem in Sarasota and I'm using you to fix it. The sales rep down there has been bitching to me since I took this job and I'm tired of it. He's convinced that sales reps in the outlying areas don't get any recognition or attention and that almost all the promotions go to sales reps in Tampa/St. Petersburg due to the superior territories and exposure to management. Last month he mentioned you as an example.

"Flores has had a territory for only a few months and he leads the branch, Bud. What does that tell you?" asked the sales rep in Sarasota.

Bud told the Sarasota rep that he didn't think I would have any interest, but asked if he would he want to flip-flop territories with me if he could talk me into the idea.

"In a minute!" the sales rep responded. "But you're not going to talk Flores into switching territories with me. He knows he has a sweet patch in Tampa."

"Mondy," Bud continued, "Norman Michael is about to get himself on a bull he can't ride. He thinks he's switching the worst territory in the branch for the best. He'd better hold on tight."

Later in the week, Bud and I drove to Sarasota so that Norman could show me the territory.

I had met Norman before at sales meetings and he seemed to be a very nice person. His niceness was confirmed during our visit. However, I learned in a few short hours that he was not a sales rep; he was order taker. He was making a (meager) living off existing customers and cold calling for new business was a low priority for him. His territory consisted of all of Manatee and Sarasota counties. As we traveled the territory, he suggested that I not waste time on certain areas as he was sure they presented no opportunity. He spent 90% of the day showing us where prospects did not exist and the remaining 10% was dedicated to showing us where his favorite customers were located. It was sad and comical at the same time. He was totally unaware he was giving up the Garden of Eden in exchange for an unnamed desert.

Malio was more excited than me as we traveled one weekend to Sarasota for the purpose of finding me an apartment. We visited a couple of places before settling on a unit above the Columbia Restaurant on St. Armand's Circle in the heart of Sarasota's chic tourist area. I'm happy Malio offered his assistance because without his input I may not have settled on this particular location which turned out to be a great place to live.

On my last Thursday in Tampa, fellow sales rep Wayne Underwood insisted that I have lunch with him. I often met Wayne for lunch so I was a little puzzled when he kept leaving me reminder messages. I drove into the parking lot at Carmine's restaurant and noticed Wayne's long, navy blue Cadillac as I parked mine. As I made my way into the main dining room I noticed several other Xerox reps, which was not uncommon, but then I began noticing clerical personnel. I realized something was up when I saw Bud Reed and Lee Snow standing with smiles on their faces. It seemed to me as if there was an office meeting scheduled that I had known nothing about. I was right because I wasn't supposed to know anything... it was a going away luncheon hosted by my pals, Carmine and Malio. It was a very nice affair and everyone enjoyed the gathering. I've never been the surprise party type, but I was touched by the fact my pals would go to the trouble and expense of organizing this send-off.

In addition to me, 1969 was a year of career changes for two friends, Ted Cannella and Malio Iavarone.

The Iavarone brothers, Carmine, Gene, and Malio came to the realization that to maintain the lifestyle to which they had become accustomed, they would have to split up... Carmine's restaurant simply could not support the rapidly-growing Iavarone clan. It was agreed that Carmine would maintain the restaurant and buy out his brothers, his sister, and his mother.

Gene purchased a bar/lounge on south Dale Mabry and Malio purchased the Tropics Steakhouse from Mary LaBarbera, also located on south Dale Mabry. Malio and Shirley were betting the farm on this venture, selling their Wellswood home and Shirley returning to work as a teacher.

As for Ted Cannella, he viewed his initial employer, General Telephone, as a dead-end street and was uncertain of his then-current career with the Computer Complex, a computer time-sharing company owned and operated by our friend and former schoolmate, John Oliva. He was aware of the success I was experiencing and wanted to try his luck with Xerox Corp. He figured that if a PE major with coaching experience could succeed, he should be able to, as well.

The week before Thanksgiving of 1969 I introduced Ted to Xerox management, and before Christmas he was onboard. Ted was perfectly suited for Xerox. He was intelligent, articulate, assertive (called aggressive in those days), and prone to spend more than he earned (providing, from the company's standpoint, additional incentive to earn commissions).

To my surprise and pleasure, Ted was assigned the territory contiguous with mine beginning at Bee Ridge Road in Sarasota and continuing south to the Lee County (Fort Myers) line.

Ted proposed a temporary living situation where he was to move in with me until he could get on his feet. I was happy to accommodate him, but emphasized the temporary aspect of our arrangement citing the cramped one-bedroom apartment as the reason. Ted agreed and guaranteed the arrangement would last for no longer than ninety days.

Ted did not make good on his guarantee, but nonetheless, sharing my apartment with Ted and working together with him for nine months turned out to be an enjoyable and fruitful time and a cherished memory.

Business-wise, we benefited from the arrangement. In the evenings, we would discuss our successes and failures, focusing on the *whys* of both outcomes. It was like iron sharpening iron. When we had a particular account that was difficult to crack, we arranged a double-team, which generally ended in a favorable outcome.

Our social lives were put on hold until the weekends. Our (my) black and white TV was used only for watching the news. The rest of the time we focused on business, even while we played Gin Rummy, and our performance reflected our commitment. We were consistently top performers in the Orlando branch, Southern region, and nationally. Our work was recognized by our managers, our peers, by Xerox, and last but not least, in our paychecks. What had been known as the sleepy burg of Sarasota (and south) was being transformed into a Xerox Mecca within the Orlando branch. Ted and I outperformed any two territories within the state of Florida and beyond. This, of course, included the well-heeled territories near Orlando which serviced the construction of a family theme park which would open a year later known as Walt Disney World.

What was the reason for our success? Was it that Ted and I were smarter than our peers? Did we possess superior sales skills or abilities? Were our territories superior to those in Tampa/St. Petersburg, Orlando, Jacksonville, or Miami (ask Norman Michael)? Or, did we just work harder than everyone else? There is no single answer, but my opinion on the matter has to do with our persistence and work ethic. As unromantic as it sounds, success is 90% perspiration and 10% inspiration; and never, never, never quitting.

As an additional reward for our success, Ted suggested one afternoon that we go to the movies to take in a new release starring Joe Namath and Peter Fonda as rebel leaders of a motorcycle gang. I did not mind taking in the movie, but viewing it on a weekday afternoon gave me a problem. My thoughts turned to my mother leaving for work each morning at 7:10 AM and returning at 4:20 PM. How could I justify going to the movies in the afternoon on a weekday while my mother was laboring at her job as a *trimmer* for Sunstate Slacks some seventy miles north of the proposed movie theatre? I visualized her perspiring over a bundle of slacks while I ate popcorn and viewed a movie in the cool confines of Sarasota's Bijou Theater.

Ted convinced me we were well within our prerogatives with such an outing and on this particular summer afternoon I found myself with my buddy, skipping work to take in a movie.

We were in the theatre before 12:30 PM in order to qualify for matinee purchases of discounted tickets. We had our choice of seats and were the only patrons I noticed wearing coats and ties. We each purchased a cold drink, a hot dog, and a tub of popcorn before taking our seats. The rest of the moviegoers consisted of housewives with children and teenagers trying to escape Florida's summer heat.

As we viewed future attractions, the Pathe News, and the cartoon, I couldn't relax. If I wasn't thinking about my mother laboring at the non-air-conditioned pants factory, I was looking over my shoulder to see if Bud Reed or Lee Snow, our managers, were entering the theatre. Then I would glance at Ted smugly enjoying the on-screen offerings as well as his popcorn. I thought to myself, Ted's dad is wearing a coat and tie himself as he fits his business clientele with expensive clothing at Wolf Brothers of Tampa and his mom was probably cleaning the kitchen in her air-conditioned home off Tampa's Bayshore Boulevard as she prepared to watch an afternoon soap opera.

Ted occasionally looked over and told me to relax. Easier said than done. All in all, it was a miserable afternoon for me as I was unable to come to grips with taking off the afternoon (without permission) even though I was the leading sales representative in the Southern region and third nationally.

ATTA BOY

The most effective way to reward someone for a job well done is with compensation and/or promotion. "Atta Boys" are nice, but they only have a short-term affect.

After a sales meeting in November, Bud Reed, my manager, told me to call his boss, Roy Webster, the Branch Sales Manager in Orlando, to schedule an appointment to interview for a newly-created position intended to increase duplicator sales (the future of the company) throughout the branch. The High-Volume Product Specialist (HVPS) position would report to Roy in Orlando.

During the interview, I was pleased and surprised to learn from Roy that I had sold more duplicators (high-volume products) than anyone in the state of Florida and more than the next two highest sales reps within the Orlando branch. His face communicated disappointment when I responded to his question that I didn't have any magic formula for my success. I was fully aware that I was trying to convince (sell) Roy that I was the best person for the job and sensing his disappointment with my response, I grasped for something else to say.

By his reaction, I could tell I had redeemed myself when I told him I was lucky and gave him my definition of luck. Roy raised his eyebrows and smiled broadly when he heard me say, "Luck is when preparation meets opportunity."

For years I had heard coaches repeat that statement, but little did I know I would be using it myself that day.

"Where did you come up with that?" Roy inquired.

"Well it's true, isn't it?" I responded, evading his question because I was not sure an athletic slogan was appropriate in this business setting, and at the same time, allowing him to consider whether or not I was the author.

"You bet it's true!" He exclaimed. "Do you mind if I use it?"

"Be my guest," I responded while trying to contain the smile building up within me.

"Look, Mondy. it's obvious you can sell duplicators," Roy commented. "But can you get others to do it?

"Why can't I?" I responded, and with that the interview was over.

I had previously received many "atta boys" for my performance, but now I was being considered for promotion, not only as recognition for the job I had done, but more importantly, in anticipation of the job I *would* do.

Effective January 1, 1971, I was slated to be the Orlando branch's first High-Volume Product Specialist.

AN OFFER I COULDN'T REFUSE

My brother Gene followed my footsteps and was coaching at Tampa's Leto High School when he invited me to watch the game from the sidelines with the other coaches for their intra-city rivalry with King High School. We planned to celebrate the anticipated victory at the recently-opened Malio's Steak House so we left my automobile there and traveled to Leto High School in Gene's county-assigned driver's education vehicle.

After Leto's hard-fought victory, we headed to Carmine's restaurant before going to Malio's to meet the other coaches. As we entered the jammed parking lot, we noticed Stephanie Baucom, Carmine's manager, pacing the parking lot with a serious look on her face. Before we could disengage the motor, Stephanie was at our vehicle advising me in her heavy Spanish accent that Judy was looking for me and that it was important. This was a few weeks after we had agreed to break things off permanently because we (she) could not resolve the religion issue. (It was no issue for me, since I was religiously inactive, but to her, being *unevenly yoked* was causing her consternation.) I immediately went into the restaurant and dialed 229-2263. I had to gain an understanding of what was so important considering I hadn't spoken to her since then.

"I understand you're looking for me," I said as she answered the call.

"I want to speak with you, if you have time," she responded in the soft and humble tone that was naturally her.

"Now? Tonight?" I asked, seeking clarification. "I'm with my brother Gene and my car is at Malio's," I added.

"I would like to speak with you tonight, but you can eat first or you can you eat something here if you like," she offered.

"Is everything okay?" I asked, attempting to gauge the urgency on this awkward request.

"Everything is fine. I just want to discuss our situation."

Without further probing, I told her to allow me around an hour to bid farewell to the group I was meeting and for Gene to drive me to my car at Malio's. In an unconvincing voice, she told me not to change my plans, followed closely by thanking me for doing so.

As we traveled I-275 south to Malio's, Gene asked the question I was also pondering.

"What do you think she wants to discuss?" he asked. He made me feel as though he had an opinion and that he hoped his opinion was correct.

I told him that I figured we would discuss our relationship again but that I didn't know what was new that would change anything.

Judy and I were both twenty-five years old and had been dating *on and off* for nine years. During our *off* times we had both dated other people, but neither of us was willing to *go the distance* with any of these substitutes. I had no qualms about marrying Judy, and to my knowledge, Judy's only reservation about marrying me was what she considered would be an uncertain spiritual atmosphere in which to raise our children in light of what she interpreted as my dull interest in spiritual matters. I understood her position, but was unwilling to act interested in something which did not interest me at her level.

As Gene entered the jammed-to-capacity parking lot at Malio's, we were greeted by Malio waving his arms amidst the vehicles attempting to get our attention.

"Judy's looking for you," is all Malio said with a somewhat serious look on his face.

"I know. I got the same message at Carmine's," I responded as I transitioned from Gene's automobile to mine.

I tested the speed limit as I traveled north on Interstate 275 toward the Florida Avenue exit, and in less time than was normally required, I exited my vehicle which I parked in front of Judy's home.

I was greeted by Judy as I walked up the steps of her front porch who exhibited a serious but friendly look as we engaged in a hug.

As we entered the house, she informed me that her mother was asleep and that her dad was reading in the bedroom. With no one in the living room or kitchen, I found it peculiar that she suggested we have our conversation in my car.

"Do you still want to get married?" was the first question she asked after I closed the car door.

So much for small talk, I thought. "Do I still want to get married?" I muttered beneath my breath allowing me time to deal with the question to which I already knew the answer. Knowing what her response would be, I nonetheless asked, "Is this the reason you wanted to meet with me tonight?"

"Yes," she responded in her soft and innocent manner.

"Well, yes," I replied, wanting to communicate that my feelings for her remained unchanged.

"If you do, there's something I want to make sure we both understand. I want you to agree to give me complete control in raising our children (to come) with regard to religion and all other spiritual matters."

It sounded to me like an offer I couldn't (and didn't want to) refuse. At the time, I had little interest in spiritual matters and remember thinking "What's she going to ask for next, permission to mow the lawn?"

"Yeah, I've got no problem with that." I responded trying to contain myself.

"Then let's go inside and tell my parents," she suggested, as if they were expecting us.

It was 11:30 PM, or so, and Mr. Stallings was now reading in the living room as we entered the house. We began catching up with each other as Judy went into her mother's bedroom to summon Mrs. Stallings to what I later figured out was a prearranged marriage summit meeting.

Mrs. Stallings emerged with Judy, both hinting a faint smile.

Judy announced to her parents that we were going to get married and sought their blessing.

They, of course, were very pleased with the news and told us as much as we hugged each other as they wished us well. After minimal small talk, Judy and her mom began planning the event, and within an hour, everything was set. Either Judy and my future mother-in-law were natural event planners, or this was not the first time they had given consideration to this topic. Nonetheless, I never witnessed such efficiency by them before or after.

While the wedding planners discussed particulars, Judy's dad came up with a gracious and thoughtful idea.

"Judy," he said, "I think I'll get you (and Mondy) a new automobile as your wedding gift because the one you have is about worn out."

Without hesitation, and certainly before I was able to construct an appropriate *thank you*, Judy responded, "Daddy, I don't need a new car but you can get me some new tires for the one that I have."

I was astounded at her response and asked if I could speak with her privately in the kitchen.

Judy adored her father, and coupled with an appeal to common sense, I remarked in a whisper, "I don't think you want to deprive your dad of the joy he will receive in giving you (us) a new automobile. He's a businessman, and I'm sure he thought through his offer. Anyway, what are we going to tell people ten years from now when they ask what your parents gave us as a wedding present… a set of tires?"

Judy correctly assessed that it was *my* joy I was concerned with above that of her father's and repeated that all she wanted was a new set of tires. I was engaged for less than an hour and could not believe that I was already at the doorstep of a dispute.

She finally succumbed to the idea of a new vehicle when her father and I (mostly her father) reasoned with her that this would probably be the vehicle she would have when she had her first baby and she needed the safety of a new vehicle in addition to the fact that her current vehicle was not air-conditioned.

A COVENANT, NOT A CONTRACT

A contract describes what you *have* to do; a covenant describes what you *desire* to do.

December 19, 1970 was a memorable day in my life as Judy and I entered into a marriage covenant in front of our families and friends at her childhood church, uptown

Tampa's Palm Avenue Baptist, in a ceremony presided over by her brother, The Reverend Buford Trent Stallings.

My mother often told me, "When you associate with good people you can expect good things and when you associate with troubled people you can (and should) expect trouble." On that Saturday in 1970, I exchanged covenants with the finest person I have ever known and I was enthusiastic about the future.

ABBREVIATED HONEYMOON

On the first night of our honeymoon at the swank Eden Roc Resort on Miami Beach, we held 9 P.M. dinner reservations at the popular "Pub" restaurant on the ground floor. As I perused the menu, I was already set on ordering their acclaimed house specialty... prime rib. They offered three different cuts, the Prince/Princess, the (medium-sized) Queen, and the one that garnered my attention, the King (Arthur) cut. The experienced waiter warned me about ordering the King cut because of its size and strongly discouraged me as I attempted to get Judy to quantum upgrade her order from the Princess to the King. He articulated the fact that seldom does anyone finish the King cut and he was certain Judy would be unable to do so. I advised him to relax and assured him Judy had help (from me) if she faltered in her attempt to conquer the King. He rolled his eyes as he informed us he would be back shortly with our salads.

Judy and I did a poor job of pacing ourselves with the hors d'oeuvres, salad, and bread considering we knew we would soon be visited by the King (cut).

At the right time, the waiter ushered in the King(s) who represented every bit of the formidable challenge about which we had been forewarned. Judy immediately and accurately commented on the fact that she would not be able to finish her serving and I would be lying if I did not say I was pleased to witness her admission.

Even though I was more than comfortable three-quarters of the way through my King cut, I continued as if on a mission to accomplish some perverse objective.

As I unbuttoned the top button to my trousers as an accommodation to King Arthur's presence in my stomach, I inexplicably pondered whether or not I should assist Judy in her failed conquest over her King cut. She made her opinion known when she suggested we ask the waiter for a *to go* bag as a compromise position to what she accurately assessed I was considering.

Sleep and romance were not in the cards on the first night of our honeymoon as I sheepishly accepted the tender care Judy rendered for my acute case of *gastro-overload*. She administered undeserved sympathy and Pepto-Bismol as she kept me company while I moaned the night away. I learned a lesson and a character trait of Judy's that night. The lesson was that undeserved sympathy is sweeter than sympathy, and that I was married to a woman who was committed to me when I wasn't at my best.

As I continue to learn more of this world in which we live, my appreciation of this trait of Judy's continues to grow.

We decided to cut our honeymoon short because we wanted to take advantage of the holidays to do a few things to our Orlando apartment before I began work in 1971 in my new position.

OUR WEDDING

Judith and me sealing our wedding vows with a kiss

Judith feeding me cake at our wedding

Malio, Steve, Gene, me, Ted, & Carmine at my wedding 1970

Off to Miami Beach

Our Honeymoon 1970

MERRY CHRISTMAS

After spending Christmas Eve in Tampa, we were traveling to our first home (together) in Orlando at the La Costa Brava apartments.

As I fueled my 1969 Pontiac Grand Prix at a station at the 22nd Street exit off I-4, I accommodated Judy on a request I would have never done on my own. On that bitterly cold Christmas Day, as I cleaned my car's windshield while the automatic dispenser pumped gas into the tank, a man our age asked if I would give him a ride. The fact that his appearance was that of the stereotypical street wino and the smell he emitted gave confirmation to his appearance had no effect on my decision because I had no intention of giving him a ride. I asked where he was headed so I could graciously tell him I was headed in a different direction. When he responded, "Anywhere," I was certain I didn't want to get involved with this man. I told him it would not work out because my automobile was full, so I wished him *good luck* as I locked my car to pay my fuel bill.

"Can we give that man a ride?" I was greeted with as I entered the car. "It's cold and it's Christmas."

"He doesn't have anywhere to go," I responded, "So what's the difference if he's cold here, in Lakeland, or in Orlando?"

"Can we help him get somewhere?" Judy continued, as if she did not hear what I just told her.

"Judy, he doesn't have a *where*, is what I'm trying to tell you," I said in a typical *Men are from Mars* fashion.

"Could you just tell him we're going to Orlando and we would be happy to leave him anywhere between here and Orlando?" She asked in her sincere and feminine manner.

"If I do," I said, "I guarantee you he'll want to ride to Orlando."

"Please?" she asked. "Look how fortunate we are to have a nice automobile and a comfortable place waiting for us in Orlando."

As I rearranged the backseat to accommodate our new friend, he informed me he would be right back with his duffel bag. That bit of information alerted me to the fact I should also begin rearranging the cargo in the already-full trunk.

We engaged in small talk with our guest as we approached Lakeland and Judy was feeling sorry for him as we listened to a tale of the previous night's events which culminated in a brawl in which he was knifed in the abdomen. I glanced over my right shoulder to see the wound he was showing as proof of his story and I was exposed to yet another confirmation of why I should not have offered this man a ride. The inside of his olive military issue parka and his shirt were drenched with blood; fresh, dried, and in between. He refused our offer to drive him to the nearest hospital and said everything would be okay. He produced a pint of whiskey from a pocket in his parka when, before he could remove the top, I told him there was no drinking in my automobile. He gave me a strange look as he put the bottle away and soon was passed out.

I accelerated east on I-4 while I delivered a few facial expressions to Judy intended to communicate my displeasure with the entire matter. She continued to feel sorry for our guest, as I did, but I was additionally concerned about my leather seats.

He continued to groan as he slept and, within a few moments, he placed his nasty boot on the console between our seats. I was enraged by this move and was ready to end his portion of trip when Judy, while masking her urge to laugh, pleaded with me to overlook the incident. I yielded to her desire but was becoming increasingly uncomfortable with the situation.

My discomfort with the entire matter peaked when he flatulated (I hoped). I told Judy I had enough and I was leaving him on the side of the road. She pleaded with me to transport him all the way to Orlando as if he had an actual destination. I reluctantly agreed and again increased my speed.

As we approached Orlando, we finalized our plan of action. It was simple. I handed Judy a pistol I retrieved from the center console (having to lift his boot) and we agreed she was to use it only in the event he produced a gun when I communicated to him that the trip was over. Our slow roll came to a stop in a Dunkin' Donuts parking lot on Orange Avenue about two blocks south of the Orange County Medical Center. Before waking him, I placed his duffel bag against the outside wall of the building and was prepared to do whatever it took to end this association.

Fortunately for all concerned, our Christmas experience ended without incident. We, however, spent the next 48 hours feeling sorry for the fella while fighting off the guilt we experienced for not doing more.

GROWING UP

Twelve months earlier, I was living in my mother's home and was responsible for no one but myself. I did anything I wanted to do, when I wanted to do it, and answered to no one. I appreciated that measure of freedom, but was ready and willing to give it up for the companionship of my best friend. Even though I did not realize it then (because I had nothing to compare), Judy was, and continues to be, a *low maintenance* individual (what a blessing). Largely due to her well-developed sense of self and her understanding of how and why she fits into this world, she never bought into the propaganda issued by the elitist leftist organizations in this country ostensibly led by the National Organization of Women (NOW).

While many of these organizations operated under the noble and needed prima facie banner of equal pay and opportunity for women, their actual agenda was sinister and counterproductive. Many of the women leading these organizations had experienced ugly and traumatic relationships with male figures in their lives, and as a consequence, were hell bent on making everyone pay for their unfortunate circumstances. Their theme, while terribly flawed, was simple and attractive to the uninformed. *Men will continue to do anything to control the power and money in society* was woven into everything they said and did.

History's standard for measuring quality of life, namely, wealth and longevity, was completely disregarded. The fact that the majority of wealth in this country belongs to women and that women, on average, outlive men by more than six years was never voluntarily discussed by these organizations. When confronted, their militant response to these facts was, "Tell that to the woman working on the assembly line in Michigan who is exposed to chemical carcinogens and, statistically, will die in her early fifties." While that red herring comment is accurate as well as dismal, that doesn't change the fact that the math to support the statistics requires a man somewhere to die six years earlier (in his forties). As the saying goes, *figures don't lie, liars figure.*

While Judy clearly recognized there are many atrocities perpetrated on young girls and women each and every day by ruthless and deranged men, common sense, as uncommon as it is, told her that painting all men with the same brush is not the cure. On the contrary, Judy's experience with male figures in her life (like that of millions of other women in this country) was nurturing and pleasant, and it was her objective to propagate this legacy within her own family. Her faith and upbringing contributed to her being comfortable with the circumstances of her life and she needed no title, position, nor career to boost her sense of worth. Quite the contrary, supporting my career efforts and preparing to expand our family was a most noble vocation from her perspective (and mine) and she was committed to those ends.

Throughout my life, I would benefit, time and time again, from her selfless attitude and commitment to me and our family. As a great comfort to me, she possessed a tremendous (even greater than mine) appreciation for what it took for me to be successful with my career and was flawlessly supportive of my efforts.

I know she got this trait from her mother who occasionally made the comment, "You get tired working with your back all day, but it's much more tiring working with your mind." I never before understood that remark having always worked with my back.

I considered myself quite accomplished at age twenty-five, but that sentiment alone indicates that I had a lot of growing up to do.

ON THE ROAD

Geographically, the Orlando branch consisted of the territory bordered on the north by the communities along the I-4 corridor (Tampa to Daytona Beach), and on the south by a line from the Jupiter Inlet on the east coast to Naples on the west coast. The Atlantic Ocean and the Gulf of Mexico were the east and west boundaries. This sales territory was covered by three sales teams, one each in Tampa and St. Petersburg, and one in Orlando. Each team consisted of ten to fourteen sales reps.

The largest single concentration of business was in the Tampa/St. Petersburg area, followed by Cape Canaveral, and then Orlando, which was preparing to open a theme park southwest of town on the order of, but much larger and improved, than the charter park in Anaheim, California, called Disneyland.

Consequently, the majority of my time was spent away from Orlando. The Tampa office would have been a much more efficient location for my position (and for the branch, for that matter), but as a newlywed, being away from Tampa was, indeed, a benefit. The only reason it made sense to be located in Orlando was that I was accessible to my boss, Roy Webster.

There existed no job description; my orders were simply to increase duplicator sales. The High-Volume Product Budget for the Orlando branch was my budget.

Given this set of circumstances, my plan was simply to provide training to the sales reps in groups and work individually with those who wanted my assistance on a request basis. Minus the professional naysayers, the demand for my services steadily increased as the news traveled around the branch that working with the duplicator specialist led to increased sales, which of course, translated to increased commissions. It was an example of the capitalist system at work.

Judy and I made new friends in Orlando, entertained old ones (plus family) from Tampa, and enjoyed living on our own (even though the proximity to Tampa was nice). When we socialized in Orlando, it was mostly with my boss, Roy and his girlfriend, Jenny (his and my administrative assistant), and with the Orlando Sales Manager, Ron Shamlaty, and his wife, Janet. We mostly went out to dinner and occasionally visited each other's homes for special events like a Super Bowl party or a trip to Cape Canaveral to witness a space shuttle launch. It was, indeed, a fun time for Judy and me.

Judy dedicated herself to being an outstanding wife and was extremely successful. I hardly ever saw her during the day, because, when I was in Orlando, Roy and Ron wanted me to have lunch with them to discuss what and how I was doing, and in retrospect, engage in some old-fashioned male bonding and team building. Nonetheless, my bride never complained about my work schedule and always supported my efforts.

The evenings, however, were ours. We would either go out to eat or Judy would prepare a tremendous meal utilizing a variety of cuisines. In either case, we generally topped off the evening with a visit to the nearby Carvel ice cream shoppe.

A SWEET ENDING

On a particular evening, Judy prepared a pineapple upside-down cake to follow one of my favorite dishes she had prepared, linguine with white clam sauce.

The timing of dessert was different for Judy and me. Traditionally, she had learned to place an interlude between the meal and dessert, while my upbringing suggested dessert simply followed the main course without interruption.

In keeping with her tradition, Judy suggested I read the day's mail while she showered and we would have desert in a half-hour or so. It sounded like a good idea, but I continued to glance at the cake on the counter as I reviewed the mail. Before I knew it, I cut myself a piece of the small cake (about four generous servings) and was cutting my second when I decided to check to see how much longer she would be. When she told me it would be a while because she was washing her hair, I ate the second piece and was doing some *trim work* on what was left.

Twenty-five minutes later, the sound of the water from the shower continued to roar and I convinced myself Judy would not be offended if I had another piece. What remained of the cake was very unappetizing, and in my opinion, could have been offensive... especially to the person who baked it in the first place. That twisted logic motivated me to get rid of (eat) the evidence and offer to take Judy to Carvel's. As she exited the bathroom, I proposed my plan to her and she snickered, knowing that I loved pineapple upside-down cake. When I told her I had eaten the entire cake, she thought I was joking and continued to laugh. When I convinced her I was not joking, she laughed the hardest and we laughed all the way to Carvel's.

What would have been World War III in the home I had grown up in, was merely a comical occurrence to Judy and she taught me yet another lesson, namely, don't make something out of nothing (pick your battles).

UNANTICIPATED PERIL

Our office in north Cocoa Beach was five miles south of Cape Canaveral and provided an unobstructed and truly spectacular view of the shuttle launches from the rooftop of the eight-story building.

On July 26, 1971, the Apollo 15 space mission was scheduled to launch the Saturn V (reusable space vehicle) from Kennedy Space Center Launch Complex 39A.

Judy and I were invited by Roy to witness the launch from atop the roof of our Cocoa Beach office. We had planned to go to the launch alone but felt uncomfortable declining Roy's invitation since he was going by himself, in addition to his being my boss.

Roy picked us up at our La Costa Brava apartment with the top down on his convertible and we traveled east on the Bee Line Expressway amongst the thick, though moving, traffic.

Roy Webster was a large bear-like, gregarious man with a balding head and a baritone voice which had become raspy over the years as a result of his overindulgence in drinking and smoking. The permanent flushed look on his face and the absence of an index finger on his right hand, which he said he lost grinding meat while working in a butcher shop as a youngster, were perfect complements to his persona. He was a committed chain-smoker who alternated between Kool and unfiltered Chesterfield cigarettes. He said that while he preferred the Chesterfields, they were too hot and smoking the Kools in between Chesterfields allowed him to light one cigarette in the morning and continue smoking all day, lighting his next cigarette with the one he was just finishing. He jokingly, and prophetically, announced that this technique would hasten the achievement of his ultimate purpose in life: death. Further assistance in hastening the accomplishment of his self-proclaimed ultimate objective was provided by his allegiance to Canadian Club and Wild Turkey. Roy also loved to eat thick steaks, onion rings, and baked potato with sour cream, melted butter, chives, and bacon chips, a fare we often ate together. Roy would occasionally miss a meal; however, he never took a vacation from cigarettes or whiskey.

On the roof of our office building were about fifty people, twelve of whom were Xeroids while the rest were guests of the other major tenants in the building. The event was well-organized evidenced by the spread of quality heavy hors d'oeuvres, extensive refreshments, and that access to the roof was by invitation only and required wearing ID tags.

The successful Apollo 15 manned lunar landing mission was the first in a series of three advanced missions planned for the Apollo program. Its primary scientific objectives were to observe the lunar surface, survey and sample material and surface features in a pre-selected area of the Hadley-Apennine region, setup and activate surface experiments, and conduct inflight experiments and photographic tasks from lunar orbit.

The space vehicle with a crew of David R. Scott, commander; Alfred J. Worden, command module (CM) pilot; and James B. Irwin, lunar module (LM) pilot, was launched as scheduled on that clear July morning at 9:34 AM. It was breathtaking to witness the ascent of that huge structure and mind-boggling to ponder the fact that it would land precisely on the Hadley-Apennine region of the moon, the crew would disembark, conduct several experiments and collection exercises, re-embark and 295 hours, 11 minutes, and 53 seconds after liftoff from Cape Canaveral would splashdown precisely at 26 degrees 7' N, 18 degrees 8' W in the Pacific Ocean on planet Earth.

I contrasted this feat to the inability of the A/C technician at the Pontiac dealership in Orlando who had been attempting to regulate the air conditioner in my Grand Prix so that it would not freeze up during peak demand times for the past six months without success. Go figure.

The trip back to Orlando became unnecessarily hazardous. The bumper-to-bumper traffic in the sweltering heat incited aggressive driving and flaring of tempers. Roy was as aggressive as any and his temper was anything but under control. He had imbibed a considerable amount of alcohol at the shuttle launch and seemed to be preparing for a launch of his own. He traded comments and obscene gestures with the raucous group returning from the launch and he fueled his frustration, as did many others, with a steady swig on the bottle. The times we stopped were perilous because of his interaction with the others feeling no pain, and when we were fortunate enough to travel at 40 to 50 mph, the peril shifted to the danger associated with a crash. I offered several times to take the wheel, but Roy would hear nothing of it. Doing so would acknowledge that he had overindulged; a situation to which he simply would never agree. The entire trip continued in this fashion making what should have been a pleasant experience into a borderline nightmare.

I was disappointed with myself for not insisting that Roy allow me to drive, especially when I recognized that my motivation for not doing so was, clearly, the enhancement of my career. Everything turned out fine, but *not doing the right thing* could have been a memory that plagued Judy and me throughout our lives.

Lesson learned: I promised Judy (and myself) on July 26, 1971, that I would never again fail to take appropriate action if she or I (and later, our children) were in a similar situation.

TAMPA

Things were going well for me in Orlando, yet I yearned to be a sales manager even though I had only been in my position for seven months.

The sales manager in Tampa, Lee Snow, surprised everyone when he resigned to begin his own sales training organization. He and his family enjoyed Tampa (having moved from Oklahoma City) and he accurately assessed that advancement with Xerox would require additional relocations and that the sales manager position was not a career position with Xerox (at the time, Xerox used the sales manager position as a pass-through position to bigger and better opportunities for their fast trackers).

In an attempt to head off the possibility of problems with me, Roy immediately communicated (to me) that I was not a candidate for the job because I had only been in my position for seven months, and more importantly, that Xerox had an unwritten policy of not promoting sales managers to manage the team on which they had previously worked.

This policy was intended to avoid placing a new sales manager in a situation where he had to overcome the issue of leading people to operate in a prescribed manner when the very people he was assigned to lead were aware that when he was in their position, he did not operate in the manner he was now prescribing. It was, indeed, a valid position for Xerox because asking someone to do something you are not (or were not) willing to do, does not go over very well and presents an immediate credibility issue.

I wholeheartedly agreed with what they were trying to accomplish, but this policy simply did not pertain to me. On the contrary, my work habits as a sales rep only enhanced my position to lead sales reps to operate diligently in every aspect of their job.

Armed with the knowledge and conviction that this situation did not pertain to me, I set out to convince Roy that I was the right person for the job. The task was formidable because Roy did not like his positions challenged and he had already told the Branch Manager, Bob Windham, that I was not being considered.

RIGHT IS RIGHT

Right is right and wrong is wrong, and I was not about to allow Roy (or anyone else for that matter) to deny me this opportunity based on an invalid reason. Even though I thought I was the most qualified candidate, I did not make that claim, nor did I feel Roy was obligated to promote me to this position; I just wanted to be considered based on my merits.

I respectfully discussed the matter with Roy and he was empathetic to my viewpoint but told me that he was going to import someone from another branch. While communicating to him that I respected his right to select whomever he thought was best for the position, I asked if he would give me the opportunity to make a pitch for the person who I thought was the best candidate before he made his final decision. He granted my request, and even though he knew the answer, he asked me who I considered to be the best candidate.

When I responded, "Your High-Volume Product Specialist," he feigned exasperation and said, "You just don't quit, do you?"

"I thought we were trying to rid this branch of quitters. Am I wrong?" I retorted quickly.

"No, you're not wrong," he said with a chuckle in his voice. "Go sell something."

DOWN TO THREE CANDIDATES

Even though it seemed like two months, Roy honored my request two weeks later, telling me that he had narrowed the decision down to two candidates.

"Am I one of the candidates?" I asked.

"No," he responded.

"Then you're down to three candidates, correct?"

"Yeah, I'm down to three," he responded, as he attempted to mask a grin.

At that moment, as if I had requested someone from Central Casting at Disney World, into my cubbyhole of an office walked Barney Williams (Sales Rep in Orlando who daily earned his reputation of being a slacker, a whiner, and a quitter [even though he was a nice guy]) to ask me a question. Before he could do so, Roy congratulated him on selling a high-volume product to one of his prospects who for years simply would not do business with Xerox. Only because I had literally forced Barney into preparing a proposal for this customer and bringing him into our office for a demonstration and assisted him in both (while he continuously tried to convince me that this customer would never do business with Xerox), he felt compelled (in my presence) to tell (admit) to Roy that he would have quit on this customer had I not kept pushing him until he got the order (or a legitimate reason why they did not want to do business with us).

After Barney's departure, Roy commented. "Hell, did you set me up for that?"

"Set you up for what?" I said, "I didn't even know Barney was in the building and I didn't congratulate him, you did. Can we discuss me versus the other two candidates over lunch? I've got a couple of other guys trying to quit on some deals and I want to make sure they don't."

"Yeah, we'll have lunch. But I have to make a decision in the next few days." "I hope you'll feel comfortable in making a decision after lunch," I said.

YOU CAN'T GO WRONG BY DOING RIGHT

"One of the guys is a High-Volume Product Specialist like you in Atlanta and the other a sales manager in South Carolina who I know and previously worked with. Both are well tenured, over two years in their positions, and are respected for what they do," Roy said in an effort to defuse what he correctly assessed could become a contested discussion.

As we both ordered the beef barley soup and a Reuben sandwich, I asked "Didn't they just hire a sales manager in Atlanta?"

"Yes, they did, and he was considered for the job but probably didn't get it because it was for the same team he had previously worked on."

"So, Xerox's unwritten policy is applicable to this fellow, correct?" I asked.

"Apparently so," Roy said.

Roy and I had become pretty good friends over the past seven months, good enough that I felt comfortable responding, "So, your counterpart in Atlanta was reluctant to place this individual with over two years' experience, during which time all the people he worked with, including his former team members, would have been able to get first-hand knowledge of his work habits, to manage his former teammates. Is this a correct assumption?"

"I guess it could be," Roy answered knowing exactly where I was going with this line of thinking.

"Doesn't Atlanta have eight or ten sales teams?"

"I believe you're correct. Maybe you'd like to go there."

"Not a bad idea, but I'm confused; with the need for sales managers in Atlanta, how could they let this qualified candidate slip away?"

"You know we're all part of the same company, don't you, Mondy?" responded Roy sharply.

"Why certainly, but isn't it human nature to keep your best and export your second-best?"

"Not in theory," retorted Roy.

"Are we talking theory here or the real deal?"

"Anything you want it to be," responded Roy looking like he was becoming a little irritated because the conversation was not going as he planned.

"I'd like it to be real world because we've never sold anything on theory even though Rochester (Xerox's U. S. headquarters) believes everything we sell is because of their theory," I responded (giving him back the comment about Rochester he often used). "Let me ask you, Roy, would you let me interview with Atlanta or another branch when opportunities arise?"

"You're motivating me to do just that," he said as we both laughed.

"Roy," I said. "What it boils down to is that you're considering someone who was not the top choice in Atlanta to get the job done for you in Tampa." "Eat your soup," he said.

After a pause, he added, "Mondy, you're going to be a sales manager. It's just a question of when."

"That's exactly my point, Roy, I have this opportunity to be sales manager in Tampa, and if I don't get it, by the time another opportunity arises in Tampa I'll be somewhere else managing a team because management here was hesitant to promote someone from within because of their past work habits, which we both agree does not pertain to me. Am I crazy, or are we allowing unwritten rules to take precedence over common sense?"

"I'm going to catch hell from Dallas (Southern Region headquarters) and Bob Windham (his boss) if I promote you over seasoned candidates when you've only been in your position seven months," he lamented (revealing to me his true concern).

"Just think of the hell you'll catch if the Tampa team doesn't do well," I respectfully offered.

"Let me think about it overnight," Roy responded, as he considered my points.

"What about the sales manager in Carolina?" I inquired.

"The more I think about our situation, the less interest I have in him," Roy responded.

My non-response affirmed Roy's comment, even though he neither sought nor seemed interested in my affirmation.

I paid the tab and we returned to the office. Before parting, I offered (in a light manner) the following comment, "You know, Roy, you can't go wrong by doing right".

A TWO-FER

Ted had made it abundantly clear to me that he wanted a shot at my position when I was promoted, and he, of course, expected my full backing. That represented no problem whatsoever, because Ted was, in my opinion, the best choice in the Orlando branch.

Ted and I had discussed the Tampa Sales Manager opening over the previous two weeks, and even though he was in Sarasota, he said that the rumor mill had me in Tampa. He also said the rumor mill had a few on the team happy, and a few not so happy.

The next morning, I was summoned into Roy's office where a business discussion ensued. Roy did a masterful job of concealing the true purpose of the meeting until he asked the question, "Who, in your estimation, is the best candidate for the High-Volume Specialist job in the event it becomes open?"

"Ted Cannella or Barney Williams," I responded.

"Barney couldn't sell a high-volume product if his kid's life depended on it," responded Roy to the bogus name I had provided along with Ted's.

"I guess that leaves Ted," I said. "But are we talking about this because I'm getting fired or promoted?"

It made me feel good to see Roy's unbridled enthusiasm when he told me I was the new Sales Manager in Tampa.

With pride he added, "I guess you know this decision puts me under the spotlight and my ass on the line."

"I know it does Roy, and I want you to know I appreciate your confidence in me. I'm sure you left room on the line for my ass as well."

"You betcha, I did," he responded with a grin on his face that did not detract from the seriousness of the response.

We discussed the matter of my replacement and Roy suggested that we relocate the High-Volume Product Specialist position to Tampa because two-thirds of the business was in the Tampa/St. Petersburg area, thus the move would increase my successor's efficiency. He also suggested that my successor report to me even though he would continue to work throughout the entire Branch.

Roy granted approval to promote Ted as my replacement but he suggested I interview other people to give the appearance that I was considering all qualified applicants and to minimize the inevitable shop talk about me promoting Ted because he was my friend.

I told Roy that I would actually consider other candidates and we both smiled as we realized I had already made up my mind regarding Ted.

I later learned that Roy had discussed the Tampa Sales Manager opening with Ron Shamlaty, the Orlando Sales Manager, who enthusiastically endorsed my candidacy. In fact, Ron suggested to Roy he could not go wrong by allowing me to hire Ted as my replacement, a double promotion which Ron referred to as a *two-fer*.

Ron was never fearful of competition and was always a team player.

WELCOME HOME

Judy and I were happy to relocate back to our hometown even though we had some reservation about disturbing the peaceful existence we enjoyed in Orlando.

We were the second family to move into the newly-constructed Carrollbrook Condominiums and we enjoyed the company of our family and friends even though the activity schedule occasionally became frantic.

We socialized primarily with Carmine and Barbara Iavarone, Malio and Shirley Iavarone, and Baby Joe and Betty Valenti in addition to some Xeroids, and of course, our families. Activities generally included going to the movies, eating (in large groups) at popular restaurants such as Steve's Rustic Lodge, Branch Ranch, Bern's Steak House, the Pizza Parlor, the Columbia, and of course, everyone's favorites, Carmine's and Malio's. We also enjoyed eating at each other's homes as we unwittingly experienced the end of an era—preparing meals at home. Additionally, we and the Valenti's occasionally visited the increasingly-popular theme park east on I-4, Walt Disney World.

Living in Tampa gave Judy the opportunity to visit with her family, mainly her mother, and I was able to spend time with my family as well, mostly with my brother Gene.

Gene had made the bold move of resigning from the low-risk environment as a coach and Drivers' Education instructor at Leto High School to become a sales rep with a leading pharmaceutical company. The move was both bold and necessary because Gene's modest school system salary was being stretched by the responsibilities he took on as head of his household. He and his wife, Sylvia, decided that she would stay at home to care for their first child, Kriste, while Gene would manage the task of providing finances to cover their uncomplicated lifestyle, which included a mortgage on their Davis Islands home, car payments, and a couple of life insurance premiums. Simple math demonstrated the need for him to seek a career that provided upside potential for him and the obvious field he examined was sales.

Gene welcomed the challenge of a sales position, hoping he was investing in a career that would not only meet his and his family's financial needs and wants but would provide him the work fulfillment he was not experiencing at Leto. He would not be disappointed as he began what would develop into a stellar career in more ways than met the eye.

REUNION

I anticipated that some of the Tampa team members would not embrace my reunion as their sales manager for no other reason than I was aware of their lax work habits and their constant whining. My presumption turned out to be correct.

Their apprehension was understandable. Some of the sales reps had been there seven or eight years, a few more than ten. After all, when I was hired from a coaching position 25½ months previously, I couldn't spell Xerox and now I was their manager. A few sales reps were pleased with my return, but there were as many who were not and a couple opting to wait and see.

One of the sales reps upset with my return was an individual named Carl Fields. Carl communicated to me that he was going to support me even though he thought he should have been appointed sales manager based on his seven-year tenure and his close relationship with Xerox's Vice President and Southern Region General Manager, Jack O'Callaghan.

I responded to Carl that I was pleased to have his support and I understood his disappointment in not being selected. (What I didn't tell him was that I was unimpressed with his 84% of plan and the negative attitude he had displayed during the time we were both sales reps on the Tampa team.) During the first sales meeting, I gained a first-hand appreciation of the support I could expect from Carl.

We met in the bullpen (the area designated for sales reps to make phone calls and do paperwork) where Carl sat in his chair cocked back with his feet on the counter wearing sunglasses, eating pizza, and washing it down with a longneck Budweiser.

I walked into the bullpen promptly at 7 PM, and when I saw Carl's demeanor, I fabricated an excuse that I needed an additional five minutes to organize data for the sales meeting. I gestured to Carl to join me in my office (separated from the bullpen by a common wall) and I gently closed the door behind him as we entered the office.

"Carl, is this the kind of support I can expect from you?" I asked somewhat rhetorically.

"What's the big deal? Are we going to run things like a football team?" He inquired with a sarcastic tone.

"I don't think so. If this was a football team, a couple of leaders would have called you out before I got there. Furthermore, I expect each team member to work diligently to overachieve their individual goal so that the team can overachieve its goal. At 84% of plan, you have a ways to go and you can count on me to assist you in any way I can. Now free your area of any food and alcoholic beverages and I'll join you in the meeting in a couple of minutes."

Carl's facial expression and body language indicated he was perturbed by our meeting. He did not positively participate in the meeting and cocked his sunglasses on his head demonstrating to me he had no intention of kowtowing.

One of the points I made during the sales meeting was that I intended to work with each sales rep as often as I could, and when I did, I expected them to have a complete day scheduled to close deals or move deals closer to closing as opposed to just meeting their contacts.

I pondered our confrontation and attempted to heal what could become a serious situation if not handled properly. I, however, could not remedy this situation on my own; I needed Carl's help. I could not understand why he wanted to battle me in a situation he could not win. Nonetheless, he did.

I scheduled to work last with Carl for two reasons. First, I wanted to give him ample time to consider the futility of his approach in dealing with me, and secondly, I needed time to assess how the other team members were taking to my style.

I met Carl at the office on the Monday of the week I was going to work with him and shortly after eight o'clock we were on our way to downtown Tampa to secure business from one of Carl's major accounts—or so I thought.

As we traveled east on Kennedy Boulevard in Carl's black Corvette, I asked him to brief me on who we were going to see and what kind of business we were attempting to close.

"I'm going to introduce you to my key contacts so we can break the ice and then on future calls we can talk business with them," Carl apprised me.

"Surely you jest, right?"

"No, I'm serious. I thought this would be the most effective way to approach my accounts," Carl retorted.

"Take me back to the office, Carl. I don't have time for this, and to be honest, I lack confidence in your opinion of what's effective based solely on your year-to-date performance," I communicated to him in a serious tone.

He then had the unmitigated gall to tell me he was close friends and played tennis with Jack O'Callaghan, the Xerox boss of bosses in Dallas.

I asked if there was a message to that comment I was missing and told him he should feel free to contact Jack O'Callaghan and anyone else he desired to contact at his pleasure.

As we sat in his sports car in the Xerox parking lot, I told him something that I'm sure he already knew, that I did not intend to tolerate his unprofessional approach to his assignment which was yielding sub-par performance. I did, however, restate to him that I would do anything and everything I could to assist him in improving his performance but that offer was only valid if he wanted my help. I also told him I was contemplating putting him on probation if I did not see improvement in his performance, or at the very least, his attitude. True to his character, he made no comment as I exited his automobile.

BLITZ OR BE BLITZED

A month later, we conducted a team blitz. Under the blitz arrangement, I paired a top-performing sales rep with an underperforming sales rep to double-team prospects in an effort to close business that was teetering and hopefully would close with a different approach.

Twenty minutes after the sales reps left the office, my secretary informed me that she had overheard bits of conversations indicating that Carl had organized a Poker game at his house for those not interested in participating in the blitz.

I could not determine whether someone purposely allowed that information to be heard by her so I would be enticed to follow up on it, or whether Carl's desire to derail my efforts had reached this level. Nonetheless, I had to check it out.

I made a couple of phone calls before leaving the office and stopped by the Fourth of July Café to pick up a large *café con leche*, Cuban toast, and a copy of the *Tampa Tribune* before proceeding to Carl's home on Davis Islands. As I approached the U-shaped driveway of his home overlooking Tampa Bay, I began identifying vehicles parked on his driveway and on the street. Including Carl's Corvette, there were six cars, five of which I knew belonged to my sales reps. The sixth one, I assumed belonged to Carl's wife. It was interesting that all the sales reps at Carl's home were under budget. Birds of a feather do indeed flock together.

I parked my Coupe DeVille in plain view on the street beneath the shade of a fully-matured oak tree which nurtured the mild sea breeze hoping one of the sales reps would see my vehicle before lunch.

Sure enough, at approximately 10:35 AM, after enjoying my coffee and toast and while reading the newspaper, a sales rep approached his vehicle as I spied him. He either did not recognize me or acted like he didn't, prompting me to toot my car horn to get his attention.

Forcing a smile on his shocked face, Warren Sims walked toward my vehicle as I had gestured him to do.

"What are you doing here?" inquired Warren in a timid tone.

"The important question is what are *you* doing here?" I responded in a tone not unlike that of the Jesuit priests when they had caught me "red-handed."

Utilizing quick response skills which are generally part of a sales rep's repertoire, Warren responded, "We're fine-tuning our blitz plans," attempting to defuse the apparent tension.

"Wouldn't you include the sales reps I paired you with this morning to fine-tune your plans?" I asked. He had no response. "Warren," I continued. "Tell the fellas to finish the hand they're playing and that I want to see the five of you in my office at high noon, not to be confused with 12:01. Okay?"

"Okay," Warren uttered as I started my automobile and slowly drove away.

In a weird sort of way, I was reliving my high school experience with Coach O'Connell, except this time, I was the coach. In 1959, he executed a cleansing of our football team after particular members had refused to abide by his warning and here I was in 1971 about to do the same thing for the same reason. Coincidentally, Davis Islands was again the venue.

I did not want to drive off talented individuals who, if handled properly, could make a contribution to the team, but I could ill afford to allow a few malcontents to negatively influence the other team members. Furthermore, if I did not deal with the likes of Carlton at this juncture, the problem would only intensify. I'm confident Coach O'Connell experienced the exact sentiments.

DECISION TIME

"It's decision time for you fellas," I told the card playing group. "You've got to make the decision whether you want to work as a Sales Rep for Xerox on this team in Tampa or whether you want to work somewhere else. My commitment to you is that I will assist you to the best of my ability whichever choice you make.

I'm placing each of you on PIP (Performance Improvement Plan), sometimes referred to as Probation. I'm told those who successfully complete the plan refer to it as *Performance Improvement* and those who do not call it *Probation*. So, whether you're on Probation or Performance Improvement is up to you. If we understand each other and, if there are no questions, let's try to maximize the afternoon."

CHEZ LOUIE

All but Carl took the PIP seriously and were working diligently at their respective assignments. Carl continued to complain that his territory was inferior to that of others and his budget was too high, exactly opposite of what the case was in reality. These complaints are typical of a sales rep who is under-skilled, under-committed, or contemplating quitting. Carl was not under-skilled.

One afternoon, I returned from a meeting in Orlando and my secretary informed me that Malio was looking for me. This could have meant that he wanted me to taste a new menu item he was considering at his restaurant, interested in looking at new automobiles, or he may have wanted to stop by the Blue Flame for some barbecue on the way to watch the University of Tampa football team practice, all activities that normally interested me, but I was too busy that particular afternoon.

"Uh, that salesman that you're, um, having trouble with is here at the, um, the Chez Louie. I've been calling you since 1 o'clock because I thought you would want to know. I, uh, gotta get out of here," Malio uttered clandestinely.

"Thanks, Malio. I'll take it from here," I responded appreciatively.

As I traveled the short distance from the Xerox Office to the Chez Louie, I recognized that Malio did not provide this information without consternation. As is common in the bar business, they must live by the Las Vegas code..."What goes on here, stays here." However, Malio was willing to risk tarnishing his reputation to help out a friend. Nonetheless, I had to seize the moment if I wanted to rid my sales team and myself of this cancer.

As I entered the Chez Louie about 3:30 PM, and before my eyes made the adjustment to the dimly lit lounge, I was welcomed by a familiar voice accompanied by hand gestures to join him at his table for a drink. As I walked toward his table, I recognized my host as long-time acquaintance, Caesar Rodriguez, joined by a man whose face I recognized and what appeared to be an attractive woman, considering the low light.

As we engaged in small talk, I spotted Carl at the opposite end of the lounge in the company of two women. More importantly, he spotted me as well. I thanked Caesar for the drink, and before leaving, I paid the waitress to serve Carl and his guests another round on me and to deliver a note I had written on a napkin.

Once I saw Carl acknowledge the note, I retreated to the office.

The note simply read, "Meet me at my office at 5:30 PM," serving the primary purpose of confirming to Carl that I had witnessed him at the Chez in the middle of the work afternoon.

Before meeting with Carl, I cleared the matter with the appropriate people in Orlando and Dallas and gained approval to terminate Carl's employment on the spot.

Not unexpected, Carl attempted to explain away why he spent the afternoon at the Chez Louie. I appreciated the creativity with which he delivered his plea and wondered why he had not applied the same creativity toward his assignment. Nonetheless, after his delivery, I gave him the opportunity to add anything he wanted. When he communicated he had nothing more to add, I summarily and gently terminated his employment.

Terminating an individual is a very unpleasant experience, though some individuals make the experience less unpleasant. Such was the case with Carl.

The news of Carl's termination spread through the branch like a wildfire, and as expected, those who were working diligently fully understood and accepted (some welcomed) the decision, while those who were not diligent whined about my decision to everyone except me.

DOG BITES TWICE

The Tampa team's performance steadily improved, and by the end of 1971 we were at a monthly rate that placed us number one for the fourth quarter and poised for a very good—if not great—1972. Our success did not go unnoticed, nor was it without incident.

My counterpart managing the St. Petersburg team was a very aggressive competitor who let his zeal get away from him.

A couple of consecutive months of the Tampa team having an order backlog greater than that of the St. Pete Team yet getting less equipment installed prompted me to call the administrative manager in Orlando to gain an understanding of the matter.

I was in disbelief when the admin manager told me that Nolan (my St. Pete counterpart) had been calling Orlando each month and changing scheduled installations from my team to his. I immediately summoned Nolan to the phone and asked the admin manager to repeat what he had told me. Nolan, in his shifty and pseudo-humble manner, had the gall to say that I had given him permission to make the changes. Since Nolan used a bold lie in an attempt to explain away his unprofessional tactic, I called him a bold-faced liar with Tony (the admin manager) on the line and advised Tony to advise all with the authority to make such changes that no such change involving the Tampa team was to be made without my prior written approval.

Immediately after the phone conversation, I went into Nolan's office to confront him face to face. The fear in his face and demeanor was obvious as I leaned over his desk and rhetorically asked why he did what he did and why he concocted the totally untrue excuse when he knew I gave no such permission. He looked down to the floor and to his left and right rather than make eye contact. When I broke the silence with an angry "Why, Nolan?" he said he was sorry and that it would not happen again.

"You can bet your ass it won't," were my parting words.

Nolan correctly felt he got off easy with this offense. I later found out from one of my sales reps that Nolan thought I was going to physically assault him. He had read my emotions correctly, but I was not going to jeopardize my future with an unprofessional act in retaliation to his desperate act. However, I was twenty-six years old and Nolan was unsure of whether or not I had graduated from the manner that some twenty-six-year-olds might have employed—a sentiment I was pleased he had pondered.

Call me naïve and gullible, but I allowed myself to be bitten by that dog again.

Nolan often came by my office for small talk and we rode to the frequent meetings in Orlando together. I perceived him as trying to put the past behind us and re-establish our relationship, and even though I was (and continue to be) very reluctant to trust someone who has violated my trust, I was willing to do so in this case.

Occasionally, our Branch Manager in Orlando, Bob Windham, would make a comment about my reports being received late. He was a standoffish type with a fake smile on his face at all times. I took his comments lightly and assumed he was attempting a stab at humor for the simple reason that all my administrative requirements were being mailed with more than ample time to arrive in Orlando by their due dates—or so I thought.

On the drive home, I asked Nolan if Bob had made any comments to him regarding late reports and he gave me an ambiguous response emphasizing what we all knew, that Bob was a poor communicator.

The Monthly Forecast was the most important sales report in the branch because *forecasts* at every level were derived from it culminating in the national forecast at headquarters in Rochester, New York.

On this particular afternoon, Nolan came by my office to inquire if my forecast was ready so he could place it in the same envelope and drop it in the mailbox outside our office in time for the final pick-up at 6 PM. I was dealing with other matters and told him it would be very close to 6:00 before mine was ready but that he could leave the envelope with his forecast and I would mail both or he could just drop his in the box now and I would mail mine later, but before 6:00. He said he had things to do and he would do them until 5:55 or when mine was ready. Minutes before 6:00, Nolan came by my office and I handed him my forecast and reminded him to make a copy for me before placing it in the mail.

Mid-Monday morning was interrupted by a phone call from an upset Bob Windham bending my ear over not receiving my forecast and thus causing him problems in compiling his own. I apologized for the infraction and was hesitant to tell him that there must be a problem with the mail between Tampa and Orlando but did so anyhow.

"The mail's working fine for Nolan," he barked in a sarcastic tone.

"You're not telling me you have Nolan's forecast and not mine, are you?"

"I have everyone's except yours is what I'm telling you, Mondy, and I'm tired of it."

"It must still be in the envelope," I told Bob. "Nolan made a point of placing them in the same envelope before mailing them."

"Carol, check the envelope Nolan's forecast came in. Mondy says his was in the same envelope as Nolan's," he barked to his secretary.

I overheard her say it was empty in the background followed by Bob impatiently telling me "Nice try, but no cigar."

I asked Bob to allow me ten minutes and I would get back to him with an explanation that would exonerate me. He reluctantly agreed and I immediately busted into Nolan's office where he was conducting a meeting with one of his sales reps.

"Come back in ten minutes," I told the rep as I held the door for him.

As I locked the door, Nolan asked, "What's up?"

"Explain exactly how you mailed our forecasts the other day," I asked causing a fearful look on the face atop his 180-pound frame.

"I inadvertently sealed the envelope with my forecast, so I addressed another one for yours and placed both of them in the mailbox before 6:00," he said.

"So, you placed both envelopes in the box at the same time? Am I understanding you correctly?"

"I don't remember if I placed them in the box at the same time or different times, but I know yours was put in the box right at 6 PM after making the copy you asked for," Nolan responded as he fiddled with the pencil on his desk.

"So, you're saying you're not positive that my forecast was in the box before 6:00, but yours possibly was, right?

"Possibly," He said with the look of a rat on his face.

"Nolan, you're an a##hole, a polished a##hole but an a##hole, nonetheless. An a##hole delivers sh*t and that's your specialty." I told him, hoping to provoke anger.

But this veteran rat remained cool as he calculatingly and faux humbly said "I'm sorry; I thought I was helping you."

"Save that horsesh!t for somebody else. I'm getting Windham on the phone and you're going to repeat your bullsh!t story to him so he can know what a classy rat ba$tard I work with."

As I dialed Windham's number from the guest phone in Nolan's office, I was furious with myself for allowing this worm to sabotage my efforts a second time. I could not conceive of a 33-year-old professional sales manager engaging in such unprofessional antics aimed at attempting to look good by making his competition look bad.

Windham's reaction to Nolan's repetition of why my forecast arrived late was not what I expected as he ended the phone call by saying, "I trust you'll be mailing your own from here on out, and give your info to Carol so I can get some work done."

In my opinion, he not only discounted the point for which I had Nolan on the call but he also sounded agitated that we (I) had wasted his time.

In retrospect, he was correct on both points. He wasn't interested in the labor pains; he only wanted to know the size of the baby.

A GIFT FROM OUR NATION'S CAPITAL

Warren Black was introduced at a subsequent branch meeting as the replacement for Nolan who was being promoted to the branch sales manager position in Jacksonville. Warren had been a branch sales manager in the Washington, D.C. Commercial Branch and was taking this demotion to accommodate his wife's medical condition that required a warm climate. Before that day, I hadn't known that D.C. had both a commercial and a government branch, but it certainly made sense.

Everyone congratulated Nolan on his promotion but there was not a sincere sentiment directed toward him that day except those he didn't hear. Warren smiled a couple of times during the meeting giving indications that he was timid and reserved.

I was asked to give Warren a ride to Tampa that evening so he could meet with the St. Pete Team in the morning. It was on that trip to Tampa that I was exposed to what would end up in serious trouble if not nipped in the bud.

Before we ramped on to I-4 toward Tampa, the chain-smoking Warren Black, who had refrained from smoking thus far, suggested we stop for a "pop" on the way. When I rejected his suggestion, he asked if I would stop at a convenience store to pick up a carton of cigarettes and a couple of 6-packs. I told him that Tampa was only an hour and a half away and I didn't want any beer so he should make his purchases accordingly. I gassed up while Warren made his purchase and squeezed in a smoke. I detested the smell of cigarettes in my car which prompted me to hang a PLEASE DO NOT SMOKE placard I kept in my glove compartment for situations such as this (an idea I borrowed from Mr. Malzone). I decided against hanging it on this occasion because I didn't want our new sales manager to get the impression I was against everything he did or wanted to do. Warren displayed sensitivity and a manipulative tendency when he asked if I would mind if he smoked with the windows down so not to smell up my car.

As we motored west on I-4, Warren alternated drags on his unfiltered cigarettes to swigs on his longnecks two-to-one. He began feeling me out on various topics as he formulated his strategy on dealing with me. Each question he posed provided me insight on the Warren Black he wanted me to know.

"What kind of guy is Windham?" Warren began.

"I know it's impossible to do, but if you could construct a perfect boss, Windham would be that guy." I responded in a quasi-serious tone. "Anyway, we don't work for Bob; we work for Roy."

Warren smiled at my response as he learned that there must be people outside the D.C. beltway who've been around the block a couple of times.

In an attempt to show me his vulnerability, he explained that being around the Orlando office for a couple of days he had gotten the impression that Windham was pretty much a jackass. I asked whether that was a personal observation or did someone offer him their opinion. He said it was just a vibe he'd gotten watching him operate and from comments he'd overheard around the office. Even though he was right on target, I told him that such a vibe had not reached Tampa (just in case he was a double agent of Bob's).

"Is Roy Bob's go-fer or does he actually run sales for the branch?" he continued.

"Since you had his position in D.C, I'd be interested in your opinion in a few weeks," I answered causing him to smile again as he tossed another nubbed cigarette out the window.

"Can we trust him?"

"Before we determine that, shouldn't we determine whether we can trust each other?"

He laughed hoarsely as he said, "I don't know why I'm asking you these questions, I guess I just feel like I know you well enough, though we just met. If someone I just met was asking me these questions, I'd let them out on the side of the highway."

He laughed and coughed simultaneously as I took my foot off the accelerator.

"What's your team quota for the month?" he asked after regaining his composure.

When I responded, he immediately asked if my budget was higher or lower than other teams in the Branch.

"I don't know," I replied.

"Well, it seems to me it should be lower than the Orlando team's budget," he said knowing he had piqued my interest.

"Why's that?" I asked.

"Well, for openers, Tampa doesn't have a Disney World in their backyard, does it?" he said with authority, which brought up a question I had pondered.

"No, we don't, but how do you convince the Orlando sales manager that he should have a higher budget?" I asked, masking my lack of experience in these matters but expecting Warren to have an answer that would interest if not benefit me. I was not disappointed.

"It's not your job to convince him; that's Roy's job. You don't give a sales rep with the tallest and best office buildings the same quota as the rep who handles a mostly rural, or even worse, a blighted area," he said, stating the obvious.

This fundamental concept Warren brought up demonstrated to me, and perhaps to him, how green I was. (I was making it on effort, energy, and enthusiasm without an important component: brains.).

Though I presumed the answer to be no, I asked the question, nonetheless. "Is that how it's done in D.C.?"

"Yes," he responded, tossing another cigarette butt out the window.

"What's your team's expense budget?" Warren queried.

"What do you mean?" I asked.

"How much are you allowed to spend to promote sales amongst your team?" replied Warren with his rephrased question between drags on the recently-lit cigarette dangling on his lip.

"Warren, I understand the question, but I can't respond because to the best of my knowledge we don't have specific team budgets for promoting sales."

Taking an exaggerated drag on his cigarette as he exchanged the empty six-pack for the full one, Warren asked "Well, how do you get reimbursed for your team expenses?"

"Simple." I replied. "I just submit an expense report to Orlando for whatever I spend, and in a couple of weeks I receive my reimbursement check."

"Wow!" he exclaimed. "We just hit a Bonanza."

"How's that?"

"Having a budget limits the spending amount. No budget means no limit," he answered with a huge smile on his ruddy face.

I understood what he said but I thought his logic was a stretch.

As it worked out, he was correct, and I would learn many things from Warren—as many *not* to do as *to* do.

"I'm sorry your wife's ailment is what brings you to Florida."

"There's nothing wrong with my wife. Ali's her name. We just wanted to move to Clearwater Beach and get out of that congested mess in D.C."

"Didn't you need a doctor's order to pull that off?"

"Yep. I actually got two (doctor) friends of mine to provide letters," Warren said, beaming with pride.

"Welcome to Florida," I responded as we entered Hillsborough County thinking the sleepy Orlando branch was about to undergo a radical change.

"You ever heard of Bern's Steakhouse?" Warren asked trying to find something that garnered my interest.

"Oh, yeah."

"Do they have big, nasty porterhouses, lobster tails, Caesar salad, and imported beer?' he continued, knowing by the expression on my face that he had, indeed, found an area of interest to me.

"That would be the place if you don't mind finishing the meal with made-on-the-premises banana cream pie."

After a great meal, I delivered Warren to his hotel and told him I'd see him in the morning at the meeting Nolan had called to introduce him as their new manager.

SWEET (UNINTENDED) REVENGE

I've always been amazed at how someone who has wronged a person can act like nothing ever happened. I'm no psychologist, but you have to have a screw or two loose to pull that off.

Nolan acted as though we'd never experienced the unauthorized changing out of my team's deliveries with his team's deliveries or the mailing our forecast reports together incidents and wanted to socialize both at and away from the office. I put him off every chance I could, but it was difficult denying him when he suggested we jog together before work since we lived a couple of blocks apart in Carrollwood.

He even aggravated me jogging when he allowed his high-strung Chihuahua to run along with us in the dark of the morning. We accidentally made contact with the animal now and again while jogging when the dog ran too slow ahead of us or decided to go a direction other than the way we were heading. Nolan assured me that Pepito was a survivor and was learning to stay clear of us each time we made contact.

One particular morning, Pepito was briskly running ahead of us, beside us, and behind us causing me to repeatedly look down in an effort to avoid stepping on the canine. A patch of rough terrain caused the little fella to alter his gait when I felt something unusual under my left shoe followed by a screeching sound. We immediately stopped and Nolan attempted to reconstruct Pepito's torso as I observed the situation which was beginning to transmit a queasy feeling to my empty stomach. Nolan correctly assessed the need for a vet and gathered the distressed animal in his hands for this purpose. I wished he would not need my assistance and my wish was granted as he told me that his wife, Marilynn, would drive them to the nearby animal clinic.

Judy provided the concern for our family as she checked with the clinic and Marilynn on Pepito's condition. I showered, dressed, and downed an abbreviated breakfast before heading to the office.

Nolan arrived at the office about mid-morning with a look of loss on his conniving face. Pepito was gone.

D.C. MEETS TAMPA

Bold is an understatement when describing Warren's approach to his career.

Warren would arrive at the office between 9:30 & 10:00 sucking on a cigarette with his tie untied wearing a suit that had earned him the moniker 'Mr. McWrinkle' in D.C. (it followed him to Tampa), displaying a big smile on his ruddy face ready to conquer the world. His first order of business was to suggest that we discuss strategy at his (and my) favorite coffee shop, El Cuatro Julio (the 4th of July) in the heart of West Tampa. From there, he would suggest lunch at one of his two favorite restaurants, Carmine's or Malio's. He would always recommend topping off lunch with a "Banana Barge" from Carvel, an idea which always gained my attention but which we only executed once or twice a week. He would use the balance of the afternoon to conduct business and was ready to continue conducting business (including monkey business) over supper followed by visiting a nightclub or two before calling it an evening. Could it surprise anyone that he looked tired when he strolled into the office around 10:00 the next morning?

FORT WHERE?

Bold antics abounded in Warren's repertoire, but none in my opinion topped his Phantom Field Trip.

It's true that one man's pleasure is another man's pain and such was the case for Warren and me. I considered it a meaningful advantage that my sales team's geography never required me to travel overnight to work with a sales rep, while Warren considered it a huge advantage that his sales team's geography required considerable overnight travel. We were both comfortable with our situations.

Warren maintained close communication with his D.C. cohorts, especially the top man and his close friend at the commercial branch, Barry Mandelbaum.

All Xerox training took place at the Sheraton on Fort Lauderdale Beach, and his friend Barry was scheduled for a two-week training session in February of 1971. Barry, without hesitation, invited Warren to join him in Lauderdale, and Warren, without hesitation, eagerly accepted.

With a straight face, Warren asked me to cover for him while he visited with Barry for two weeks.

"You're going to use two weeks' vacation to visit Barry. He, indeed, must be a good friend."

"It'll be a blast being with Barry in Fort Lauderdale, but I'm not using any vacation. This is a business trip. Barry knows all the latest info and we can benefit from my trip."

Warren's business face cracked into a smile, then a laugh, when I told him to save that horsesh!t for someone in the "sod" business.

He went on to describe his plan and what he hoped my participation would be. "If they ask, I'm telling Roy and Bob that I'm working with Jerry (the Fort Myers sales rep)." "What if they call Jerry?" I asked.

"It's highly unlikely, but if they do, I'll just call Jerry and tell him to pick me up at the airport. That would really screw up my plans, but I don't believe it will happen, do you?"

"Like you say, it's unlikely, but it is possible. I'd be more concerned with the Xeroids in Fort Lauderdale talking to the point where it gets to the wrong person—or right person, depending on your perspective."

"Not a problem. Barry's the only one who'll know and he's certainly not going to say anything. I'm going to the airline office to purchase my ticket to Fort Myers today so I can go back in a couple of days and have it reissued to Fort Lauderdale. Can you believe it's $12 cheaper to fly to Lauderdale than to Fort Myers?"

Warren spent half of February in Ft. Lauderdale partying. He returned tanned and refreshed informing me that he planned a similar trip for later in the year when another friend was scheduled for training in Ft. Lauderdale. If he experienced any guilt whatsoever, he did a masterful job of disguising it.

TED FINDS A PLAYMATE

It didn't take long for Ted to become friends and running mates with the charismatic and fun-loving Warren. They were, indeed, birds of a feather.

Even though Ted reported to me, his service and responsibility was to the entire Orlando branch. Ted was effective in his assignment causing heavy demand on his time. He attempted to satisfy the needs of all three sales teams, but his efforts were inordinately skewed toward my team because of our friendship (and because he reported to me), but mostly to Warren's team because of the extracurricular activities.

One of the strategies imported from the District of Colombia by Warren was hiring "extra" sales trainees which would allow more on-the-job training and general assistance to sales reps who earned the privilege. Since we were never given a budget, he assumed we could not be accountable for the associated cost, and as it worked out, Warren was right again. We were embarking on hiring female sales reps at this time, and as a matter of fact, I had just hired the first female sales rep in the state. We were always conscious of sales reps' appearance, but appearance would take on an increased position amongst hiring criteria with the advent of Warren Black.

Simply stated, Warren's hiring philosophy regarding women was, "You can teach an attractive woman to become an effective sales rep, but you can't teach an effective sales rep to become an attractive woman." Though obviously flawed, no one argued with his philosophy, me included, even though I'm certain the various women's groups emerging at the time would have welcomed the opportunity.

As previously noted, one of the common and effective methods of drumming up business was the territory blitz. Warren would often seize the opportunity to employ this technique in the Fort Myers/Naples area importing every resource he could muster from the entire branch but hoping no one would accept his offer because of the possible interference with the anticipated after-hours activities. Again, he was right; no one accepted his offer except those who had little or no choice which included the growing number of sales trainees out of the Tampa office, a demographic becoming more and more skewed toward (attractive) women. It was difficult to argue with the success of the blitzes, especially since the cost was a non-issue since it was not a budgeted item. Warren was a master at working the system.

One morning, while going through a mountain of paperwork, I ran across an expense report from Ted requiring my signature. I had previously approved his expense reports even though his time and expenses were spent with sales teams in addition to mine. This one, however, was relatively large (over $1,700) and included two week-at-a-time visits to the Ft. Myers area and associated costs such as hotel, food, and entertainment. Since the lion's share of the expenses were for activities connected with Warren's team, I simply returned the report to Ted with the note indicating to have the report approved by Warren. Within fifteen minutes, a distraught-looking Ted knocked on my door and asked if he could talk to me (a courtesy I was not accustomed to, nor expected from Ted). When he proceeded to ask if he could close the door, I knew a dose of his wrath was headed my way. "You can lock it if you wish," was my common response to that question.

A cigarette dangling from his lip, his left foot on the coffee table and his facial expression indicating he was fighting off gas pains, he cocked his head to one side as if he was ready to jump into a rendition of Heartbreak Hotel and boldly uttered, "What the hell is wrong with you?" lightly tossing his expense report onto my desk.

Though his inquiry was perfectly clear to me, I countered his bravado with, "Could you be a bit more specific?"

"I've got tons of things to do and one of my closest friends hassles me about an expense report," he whined.

"Poor baby, everyone's picking on her and she has so much work to do on top of everything," I countered communicating I had no intention of allowing his drama to alter my position. "If you have a bona fide reason I've overlooked, tell me. Otherwise, take your expense report to Warren for approval. I assume one of the hotel rooms and some of the meals on your report were for his benefit."

"You're unbelievable. Warren was right," he muttered, leaving my office no less distraught than when he had entered.

He knew he was pushing the envelope on this one, and I figured from his parting comment that Warren knew, as well. Ted and I were quite familiar with each other and why he allowed Warren to convince him to attempt to persuade me to join in on their shenanigans (without any of the benefits, I might add) was somewhat of a mystery to me. There would be other mysteries in our future.

LA COSTA DEL SOL

Xerox was known for showering its top performers with extravagant "award trips" and 1971 was no exception. Top performers and their spouses from around the U. S. gathered in the south of Spain, a region referred to as La Costa del Sol (The Sun Coast) to celebrate the previous year's accomplishments.

Ted, his wife, Sandra, Judy, and I met our chartered jet to Málaga, Spain in Atlanta and that's where the fun began. The flight crew included several French stewards who were very difficult to understand and who seemed excessively controlling in the exercise of their duties. Add to the scenario, a plane load of demanding, self-centered overachievers able to lubricate themselves with an open and unlimited bar, and it was easy to understand why the French refer to Americans as "Ugly Americans." Our group made strides in confirming the moniker.

The thickly-accented stewards finished their words with a "vizzee vizzee" sound as they attempted to get the raucous crowd to take their seats for a final count before takeoff but met with considerable resistance from a crowd intent on visiting with friends from other parts of the country they hadn't seen in a while, probably since their last award trip. As they worked their way through the smoke-filled cabin, two of the stewards made the mistake of trying to get Ted and Sandra back to their seats. The Cannellas, especially Ted, were oblivious to the stewards' requests. As they raised the volume of their *vizzee vizzee*-ending commands, Ted would occasionally direct his attention in their general direction and respond with a sequence of "vizzee vizzees" that frustrated the stewards and initiated an eruption of laughter from the Xerox crowd adding to the stewards' frustration. They increased their tone and Ted increased his as he was fueled by the group's laughter. With a cocktail in one hand and a cigarette in the other, Ted mimicked the foreign flight attendants laughing back to his roaring audience and the confrontation gained temperature. Anyone knowing Ted knew he meant no disrespect toward his verbal combatants, the problem was that not many knew Ted well enough to make that assessment. Certainly, the recipients of his antics did not.

As I glanced over the engaging crowd, I came across the stern look on the face of the Orlando branch's boss of bosses, Bob Windham. I needed no interpreter to understand the message that look and his body language was sending me: fix that problem and fix it now. Transitioning from hearty laughter to a forced smile, I approached Ted with an appeal to go back to his seat and was met with the same "vizzee vizzee" response that the uniformed attendants faced, proving my point that his antics were not necessarily directed at our foreign crew, though I doubted they saw it the same way. Nonetheless, amongst hugs and laughter, I whispered to him that Windham was observing the entire situation and wanted it to end now. He gave me additional "vizzee vizzees" while he spied Bob Windham and then proceeded to take his seat as if it was his idea, and while doing so, delivering another series of muted "vizzees vizzees."

The crew completed their required checklist and we embarked on our flight across the Atlantic toward España, the land of my paternal ancestors.

OLÉ, BRAVO

Our trip to Spain was replete with optional activities, including side trips, sightseeing, shopping, and the like. Each day's activity was capped by an exquisite banquet accented with live entertainment preceded by a two-hour cocktail session where everything flowed freely.

Judy and I selected much of what we did with Ted and Sandra including our day trip to Torremolinos, southern Spain's headquarters for bullfighting.

The morning of shopping and sightseeing in Torremolinos was followed by lunch in the quaint town before the bloodless bullfighting exhibition scheduled for the afternoon.

We, excluding Judy, imbibed *Sangria* throughout the extended lunch, so much so that individuals with Spanish-sounding names, (Ted [though Cannella is Italian] and I), joined the musical accompaniment singing Spanish songs, not impeded at all by not knowing the lyrics and doing our best to add to the good time everyone was enjoying. Not wanting to yield the spotlight to her husband (and his friend), Sandra, from Villa Rica, Georgia, joined Ted and me singing Spanish songs interspersed with classic American tunes allowing the entire U. S. contingency to participate. Judy enjoyed our performance and laughed with friends as we led the energetic crowd with song and dance aided by a steady flow of Sangria.

We relocated to the bullfighting arena and continued our boisterous conversation and singing while a professional matador (bullfighter) instructor explained bullfighting fundamentals to an unappreciative audience. His instruction was followed by a brief exhibition with a retired 2000-pound *toro* (bull) whose guile was, in my opinion, managed with saltpeter or its equivalent.

Our proximity to the arena provided a unique perspective to the massive and dangerous beast. The animal's tremendously-developed front quarters, erect stature, and formidable set of horns, perfectly complemented the powerful aura it exuded.

As professionals in all walks of life are often capable of doing, this instructor made maneuvering around the bull seem so simple that a spectator might muse about being able to accomplish what this small and not particularly athletic-looking man was touting as one of the world's most perilous sports.

Ted and I chuckled at the instructor's insistence that this was not a sport for the common man. The Sangria component in our blood coupled with our penchant for showing off was not enough to motivate us to accept the (bogus) offer the instructor made to enter the arena with this flare-nostriled behemoth until he evened the playing field by introducing a *torito* (little bull) as the full-grown model was enticed out of the arena.

How could one pass up this offer made in front of our newly-formed friends and associates to demonstrate our athletic prowess? The 400-pound torito stood barely waist-high to a six-foot man and the torito's horns were only five inches long and blunted.

Judy pleaded for me not to go while Sandra encouraged Ted's interest. I was second in line with Ted behind me as we paid little attention to the final coaching points offered by the instructor to our group, dubbed by one of us as the Fearless Five.

The first matador was from Oklahoma and proudly indicated he was familiar with cattle having been raised on a ranch eight miles west of Broken Arrow. He must have spent a lot of time around the chuck wagon because after avoiding the torito's unimpressive initial move, he found himself in the bull's crosshairs for five consecutive charges knocking him around the clay like a stuffed rodeo dummy. Showing no empathy, Ted and I laughed at the Okie's performance while the audience was mixed with laughter and concern.

Judy caught my attention and was signaling me to leave the line and rejoin her in the stands. I didn't want to cause her concern, but I couldn't retreat to the stands and face the tongue-lashing I would get from the very people who heard my pitch about how my Spanish heritage gave me a natural affinity toward the art of "tauromaquia" (bullfighting).

Having fun with the crowd, I approached the section in which Judy sat with a flower gently clenched between my teeth and tossed the flower to her causing the already-engaged group to voice their approval with enthusiastic cheers while she only acknowledged my gesture with a suppressed smile.

MY TURN

It was not a good sign that the medical staff was still attending to our friend from Oklahoma as I was handed the matador's principal tool: the cape. The last instruction I recall from the instructor was not to approach the bull when it was close to the wall, but to retreat to the center of the arena causing it to approach me, the matador.

As I cautiously approached the torito, it cocked itself into a rearward leaning position. Eyes fixed on the unusually large matador, it continually gauged the distance between us determining the optimum moment required to maximize the effect of its lunge. Then, simultaneously with a full-body twitch, it charged me not attempting to mask its intent.

My instinct for self-preservation more than athleticism was my ally for Round One as I fluttered the cape positioned to my right, while taking small quick steps to my left. I felt more fortunate than skillful at this point and would have been satisfied to end the match but became prey to the "Bravo! Olé! Bravo!" chants of my associates. Hence, I positioned myself for the animal's next attempted assault. With every deliberate step toward the animal, I resisted the negative image of my Okie predecessor kicking up clay dust with his torito-propelled body.

Round Two provided details I had not previously seen. The resolve in the bull's eyes coupled with the mucus dripping from its flared nostril's made me realize that I had misjudged this voluntary activity and was staring peril in the face. Nevertheless, my best choice was dealing with the challenge at hand. For the second time, the bull twitched as it lunged and I again eluded its charge. I was, indeed, playing with house money and was looking for the cashier's window.

Amongst the urging of the supportive crowd (Judy excluded) to give it one more try, I began my retreat intending to pass the cape to Ted, the next matador-for-the-day, when I developed this urge to tempt fate...just one more time. I felt somewhat confident having eluded the torito's charges and decided to, once more, test my Spanish ancestral skills.

This time I shifted some concentration from my foe to my friends—not a good idea when your foe weighs four-hundred pounds and drips mucus from its nostrils. As I approached the bovine, it retreated. I advanced, it retreated. A third time I stepped forward, it stepped backward. Each retreat elicited a roar from the partisan crowd which intensified when I hand-gestured for quiet.

I recollected the instructor's last words and coincidental with that moment, I recognized the bull was backed to the wall. Without a twitch, the animal suddenly thrust itself toward me, but I was prepared. With improved grace, I separated myself from the cape and maneuvered away from the anticipated trajectory of my combatant. My strategy was flawless; however, the cooperation from the animal was seriously flawed. Instead of following the lure of the cape, the animal charged to its right, synchronized perfectly with my move to my left, making solid contact with my thighs and propelling me high into the air.

After the collision, I have no recollection of subsequent events until seeing Judy's concerned look as I was being tended to by the medical staff and noticing the concerned look on Ted's face as he entered the arena. I was bleeding from my mouth and nose and my arms and hands were tingling and had reduced feeling.

Later, Judy told me I had asked those attending to me, "Did anyone get the license tag number of the Greyhound bus that ran over me?"

I would later receive, from around the country, photos taken by eyewitness associates and friends of my Toreador experience inquiring if the feeling in my hands had been restored. It would be nine months before the tingling was gone and the feeling in my hands would return to normal.

From the photographs received, however, I was able to construct a complete sequence of the incident, including my approach to the bull, the bull's retreat, the actual collision, various positions of me in mid-air, and my reentry into the arena showing that the first part of my body to make contact with mother earth was my face.

I never gave it much thought then, but now I clearly recognize how fortunate I am not to have sustained serious and permanent injury.

WHY DIDN'T I THINK OF THAT?

I sat where I could see Ted's matador adventure while the medical attendant cleaned blood from me and asked questions to determine whether I was cognizant.

Ted achieved the same outcome as me, albeit by a different path. He was knocked down by the confident bull on his first attempt at an "Olé!" and continued to be knocked down each time he attempted to regroup. The torito (Mr. Torito to us) repositioned Ted all over one side of the arena with Ted never being able to rid himself of this pesky bovine. Ted was bleeding from his thigh, side, and arm; his clothes were ripped, and in some places, torn off.

As Ted approached me, after being rescued by a trio of Spaniards suppressing their urge to laugh, he rhetorically asked in his typical Elvis style, "Got any more ideas?" as if participating in this *clown fest* was my doing.

We went to the office to sign papers, release documents I'm certain, and were told the remaining participants opted out causing me to wonder… *Why didn't I think of that?*

AFRICA

We boarded a well-worn propeller-powered plane for a day trip to northern Africa and landed in Morocco where we were greeted by a ten-man band made up of primitive stringed and percussion instruments intended to add to the authenticity of the implied mysteriousness of the culture. The green and gold native costumes and heavy face paint contributed to the ambiance until Ted pointed out three musicians wearing winged-tip dress shoes unintentionally exposed from beneath their full-length garments.

"Hell," Ted said, "I think one of the guys with winged tips is wearing a Rolex. He probably has an IBM meeting to attend when he's done here."

We all chuckled as Ted's observations were passed along to other members of our group.

We spent the morning sightseeing and shopping in a negotiator's paradise where prices were negotiated on the spot and haggling was the norm. We, however, abused the culture, negotiating on items we had no intention of purchasing but were just trying to out-negotiate each other. Ted and I (mostly me) infuriated a merchant to the point that he removed the item from the counter and told us he didn't want to sell it to us at any price.

We, of course, then started upping the offer (solely as a means of getting the merchant to retreat from his position) and once he agreed to our offer, we lowered it, causing him to ask us to leave his store.

We laughed as we exited adding to the *Ugly American* image we were promoting. Our immaturity and ignorance of other cultures was no excuse for our behavior. We were just trying to have fun, but the merchant was trying to earn a living. Later that morning, Judy made purchases from the same merchant as partial atonement for my actions.

We were unable to satisfy the appetites developed from our rigorous sightseeing and shopping even though we lunched at Morocco's premier eating establishment. Raw oysters, followed by bone-in rib eyes with baked potatoes and onion rings accompanied with Caesar salad (heavy on the anchovies), and followed by New York cheesecake was not on the menu nor understood in this lean—and, perhaps, healthy—culture. Consequently, we unsuccessfully attempted to fool our western taste buds with a bowl of unrecognizable vegetable soup, camel meat (we were told) and gravy, and rock-solid bread. No one ate much and I wondered if the family of the merchant I abused that morning operated this restaurant and was exacting retribution. If so, it was deserved by me and the merchant won.

That afternoon, we were exposed to the nomadic group known as Berbers. These nomads live in the southern part of Morocco, in and around the high Atlas Mountains. Berbers are frequently found in small, make-shift tents plopped in the middle of the desert or in the mountains near an oasis or river. They raise farm animals to use not only as a food source, but as currency for their barter system. Berbers are comprised of various ethnic groups, each with different languages, customs, lifestyles, and even skin tones, suggesting that there was hanky-panky going on with some of the sub-Saharan peoples at some point in the past. Other than the hanky-panky, you could not help but contrast their culture from ours: wake up with the sunrise versus alarm clocks, slaughtering an animal versus the Publix meat department, hot desert climate to climate-controlled A/C, and one very similar—cooking on an open fire compared to grilling on the barbeque. It seemed then that they were so far behind us, but when you include drugs, crime, the constant pressure of western culture to achieve and amass, they may not be as far behind as a National Geographic article might suggest. Nonetheless, it is a different thing to read about other cultures versus experiencing it firsthand, albeit only for a single day. It sometimes seems to me that the further we advance, the closer we are to where we began.

By nine o'clock that evening, I had disassociated myself from the plight of the Berbers as I enjoyed Western delights which were not available to us just nine hours earlier. It is the seduction of comfort, pleasure, and abundance that, in my opinion, distracts us from the important things in life. Long after the campfire light was out in the Berber camp we visited that day, lights were burning in many offices and homes so people could try to figure a way to advance themselves, not realizing that they were actually losing ground where it counts most: with their families. If children spell love T-I-M-E, and I believe they do, many people were demonstrating their love to something other than their families. Oh, the price of success.

The balance of the trip was equally enjoyable and Judy and I were able to relax (even though my insecurity caused me to wonder if my team was performing adequately in my absence) and enjoy a great time as Xerox management planted seeds of what next year's trip would be like for the company's Top Performers.

SPAIN AND MOROCCO

Judith and me leaving for Spain 1972

Me and my Moroccan friends

Judith taking a Moroccan taxi

Me underestimating the bull

GENE & IBM

Returning to Tampa was welcomed after spending a couple of weeks in one of Europe's most popular playgrounds. I'd had my fill of traveling, sightseeing, hotels, and, believe it or not, feasting.

My brother Gene met Warren and me for coffee at the 4th of July one morning, and in between drags on his cigarettes, Warren was asking Gene all sorts of questions as if they were interviewing for a position. When Gene left, Warren commented, "Why isn't Gene working for Xerox?"

"Because we don't hire relatives."

"He's not related to me," Warren countered. "And I damn sure could use him on my team. He's head and shoulders above the potential of anyone on my team and I'm going to convince him to come with us before IBM convinces him to go with them. How would you like to be competing against him every day? I sure as hell wouldn't."

"What about the hiring freeze?"

"That doesn't bother me. I'll fire a couple of reps if I have to, but I'm not letting him get away and I damn sure don't want to see him pitching IBM products." (IBM had just entered the reprographic business and Xerox was committed to making their entry difficult and costly.)

I was thrilled with Warren's enthusiasm and shared his assessment of Gene's capabilities, but it would have been counterproductive for me to be championing Gene's cause. If Warren wasn't blowing smoke, it could not be a better situation to have my counterpart so interested in Gene's services.

"Come with me to my office while I call Windham to get permission to hire Gene, in case he asks any questions about Gene I can't answer. You think we can convince him to join us, don't you?"

"He's married; he has a child, a mortgage, and a company car. I don't think he can make it on a trainee's salary to be truthful."

"That's exactly the kind of info I need to know. I'm going to tell Windham that Gene will have to be a $2,500/month premium hire (a provision that allowed more money during training for experienced salesmen who couldn't make the switch to Xerox on the $1,000/month new hire training salary) if we're going to convince Gene to change his mind from IBM to Xerox."

"I think Gene makes $1,800/month," (an amount I knowingly inflated).

"Keep that to yourself, because I'm telling Bob it's going to take $2,500 or we'll be facing him in the streets everyday pitching Big Blue."

"You're convinced he's going to work for IBM, are you?"

"I'm not willing to give them the chance."

Warren had the gall to get Bob Windham out of a meeting to take his "urgent" call. "What's so important, Warren?" Bob asked, prepared to chastise Warren if the reason didn't meet his standard.

"Bob, I've got a chance, a slim one I might add, to kick IBM in the teeth by hiring their top recruit and I need you to get "Region" to make an exception to the freeze today because I've asked this guy to hold off accepting IBM's offer till noon tomorrow. Can you help?" I had to do all I could to keep my jaw from dropping.

"Bob, as you probably figured out already, this guy is a premium hire for them and we'll need approval for $2,500/month to pull this off."

"Warren, Region will never go more than $2,000/month, I can assure you of that."

"Bob," Warren interrupted. "You've got to convince them that we have to beat IBM's $2,300/month offer or we'll pay dearly in the marketplace if we have to face this guy every day."

"Will he take $2,000?"

"Not a chance. He's holding a $2,300/month offer in his hand as we speak and I'm using the additional $200/month as a carrot."

"One last question; why are you so convinced this guy is a potential superstar?"

"I was hoping you'd ask. As you know, IBM takes pride in their selection process and they are chomping at the bit to engage his services; and, more important, his last name is

Flores and he's just like his brother. It's scary, Bob."

"Why didn't Mondy bring him to our attention?"

"Same question I asked. You ready for this? Mondy said he thought it was in conflict with Xerox's Nepotism Policy. I couldn't believe he said that, he must have played without a helmet," Warren responded as he covered the phone mouthpiece and muted his laugh for my benefit.

"I'll get right back to you, and tell Mondy I said, 'I would be very disappointed in him if he could not hold off his brother's decision till I get an answer from Dallas.'"

"You got it Bob, but please convince them to approve this hire ASAP. Tell Ogletree (Region's boss of bosses) what if Gene, that's his name by the way, took this offer from IBM and convinced Mondy to go with them?" Warren said while, again, covering the phone mouthpiece and trying to mute his laugh emanating from his ear to ear grin as he sucked every bit of smoke from his filter-less cigarette.

"Warren, you are a scary guy," I said as a backhanded compliment, which he fully appreciated.

What a masterful (though misleading) job Warren did of convincing Bob that hiring IBM's premium recruit was a tactical coup of utmost importance. I couldn't help but wonder what shenanigans Warren and his cohorts had pulled in D.C.

That afternoon, Bob called Warren and proudly communicated that he was successful in gaining approval to hire Gene Flores at $2,500/month.

Warren relayed Bob's enthusiasm over gaining the approval to hire Gene and was kind in allowing me to communicate the offer to Gene that evening. For the first time, Warren asked, "Gene does want to work with us, doesn't he?"

"It's either us or IBM."

ON THE ROAD AGAIN

The Tampa team consistently performed among the top teams in the nation, and at the beginning of the summer of 1973, I was asked to consider promotional opportunities in both Region Headquarters in Dallas, Texas and National Headquarters in Rochester, New York. True to form, my selfless and supportive wife told me that she had no preference between Dallas and Rochester, and to the surprise of both the staff in Dallas and the staff in Rochester, I (we) chose a newly-created position on the National Sales Staff in Rochester as liaison to the Northeast Region headquartered in White Plains, New York.

My thought process was simple. I had traveled to Dallas for meetings often and I never developed an attraction to the "cowboy" lifestyle. More important, it was clear to me that if I was going to make it to the top, getting the Rochester experience could do nothing but help.

During my final interview in Rochester, I was able to negotiate a perk that became the envy of my counterparts and a tremendous comfort to me. I was the only southerner in our group, and during previous interviews I had been told that parking in Xerox Tower was only available to employees who were on what was referred to as *confidential payroll* (at least three levels above my position) leaving me to seek outside parking at one of the nearby lots for the going rate of $70 per month. The $70 bothered me, but was only second to fighting the frigid winter weather Rochester is known for. As Jack Crilley and I discussed the requirements of the position, I occasionally interjected a question about Rochester winters such as, "How much snow does Rochester get?" or, "Is it true your blood actually thickens in this kind of weather?" Also, knowing the answer, I asked Jack "Why wasn't the Northeast Region chosen by the other four region liaisons?"

"They gave different reasons for choosing their particular regions, but, in my opinion, I believe their decisions were influenced by the well-deserved *difficult reputation* of the Northeast region."

"Because you said, 'well deserved,' am I to infer that you agree with their reputation?"

"Without a doubt. They complain about everything and fight any and all change. In their closed minds, New York City and Boston (and I'm from Boston), are different from the rest of the world," he responded without pause. Then, after a pregnant pause, he stated and added, "You're a hard guy to read. You seem to be comfortable with the PQ (position requirements) and bothered by the Rochester weather. Am I way off on this one?"
"Actually, I hadn't realized it, but you're pretty much on target; people are people in my estimation, so I don't anticipate any unmanageable problems in that regard, but managing that Rochester winter gives me concern."

"Didn't Jim Higgins tell me you played football?" he asked rhetorically in an attempt to get me to put the tough winters into perspective.

"Yes, I did; and playing in Buffalo in November is fresh on my mind."

"Look, Mondy. I've been instructed not to let you get away, so tell me, what's it going to take to seal the deal?"

"Assuming the dollars are in order, I think we're right down to inside parking."

"There's a year wait for Tower parking for those who qualify, and as I already told you, you have to be on confidential payroll to qualify. I'm not on confidential payroll either, and therefore, I have to park outside; it's really not that bad," he responded with a hint of attitude beginning to surface.

"I'm just responding to your question," I reminded him as the interview time drew to a close and a secretary waited outside Jack's office to escort me to another interview with a competing department.

"I don't think this is going to work, but if I'm able to pull this off, would we be your number one choice?

"I think so, assuming the dollars are right."

"Then promise me you won't commit to another group until I get back with you later in the day."

"What if another group puts pressure on me for a decision?"

"I'm confident you can handle the matter," he responded with a suppressed smile.

Covered parking was not a deal-breaking issue for me, but I was not about to show all my cards at this juncture. Also, my choice of regions, if I had been first to choose, would have been the Northeast region, another card I didn't want him to see.

Before my last interview, Jack informed me he had gotten me the inside parking and would provide the details over dinner that evening. He then sought my confirmation that, if the money was right, we indeed had a deal, to which I responded affirmatively.

JOE REGISTER

Judy and I were given a glimpse of what was in store for us when Jack informed me that he would take care of the expenses if Judy and I wanted to visit New York City on the way to Rochester for our house hunting trip, and Boston on the way back. I inquired as to what he meant by *expenses,* to which he responded, "Have the time of your life and send me the bill." I found I was capable of taking orders; we did just that.

After the second day of house hunting, my patience was wearing thin, but Judy and the sales agent, Joe Register, were developing an interesting friendship. Probably in his fifties, we considered Joe an old man. He was short, somewhat hunched back, unassuming, understood the Rochester housing market, and had the patience of Job.

Joe had maintained a healthy and lucrative relationship with Xerox employees for some time and as we traveled up and down the streets, he pointed out homes of Xeroids we either knew or knew of.

While he and Judy *walked* home after home after home, I remained in the automobile reading material pertaining to my new assignment.

In Tampa, we enjoyed our comfortable three-bedroom, two-and-a-half-bath, 1,800 square foot, condominium and were now considering a much larger, five-bedroom home with a full basement atop a mountain in Fairport, New York, a bedroom community to Rochester. Was I missing something?

Joe convinced us that a larger home was the one we wanted because of two reasons. First, we should consider the home purchase as an investment because Xerox Corporation was paying all the closing costs on both ends and would pick up the closing costs again when we sold it in a couple of years providing us a handsome profit (assuming the continuance of the steadily-rising market) and secondly, a larger home was always more desirable because of the clientèle coming into the area, namely Kodak employees and other Xeroids. We bought Joe's pitch and moved to our new home at 42 Mountain Rise in Fairport, New York in the summer of 1973.

BON VOYAGE

The Iavarone families were thoughtful and gracious in hosting a *bon voyage* party. We were able to receive and return well wishes from family and friends alike, giving everyone the obligatory, "Come see us, if you can." To our pleasant surprise, more than we anticipated took us up on our offer (more on that later).

We booked a *double sleeper* on the AutoTrain, and with our 1972 Cadillac Coupe DeVille loaded on a train car behind us, we enjoyed a delightful time watching the scenic countryside between Orlando and Washington D.C. The leisurely drive from D.C. to Rochester was equally enjoyable as we saw a part of the country that was new to us.

What a special time it was to take a few days traveling with the person I love most in the world and without the burden of a *performance budget*, a respite I would not enjoy again for many years. It was like dating again. Without a worry in the world, we discussed everything and anything, laughing mostly, and recognizing the blessed lifestyle we had been afforded. We planned places and things we wanted to see and do and vowed to make the most of this opportunity. We lived for eight months away from home when we first married and enjoyed it very much, but this was going to be a totally different experience because we recognized that in all probability we would not be returning to Tampa. If my career continued to advance, there would be no positions at the appropriate levels available in Tampa (with Xerox). We were not concerned in the least; we viewed our future as an adventure and were excited about what it would hold.

WHY KODAK IS IN ROCHESTER

August is the nicest month of the year in Rochester, New York and we enjoyed the mild days and cool evenings that were destined to give way to what Rochester was famous for. We often barbecued in the backyard and elicited a smile from our neighbors, Verlin and Betty Rasmussen, when we commented on the delightful weather. Mild mannered Verlin, would occasionally utter, "Tell me about it in November."

Judy and I took advantage of our childless state as we visited the sights upstate New York had to offer and became acquainted with many of the quality eating establishments.

Not realizing that everyone who visited us would want to see Niagara Falls, we visited the awesome sights and sounds associated with this legitimate wonder of the world several times. In those days, Judy was enthusiastic about preparing evening meals, but we often dined out at the likes of Gepetto's for Italian, The Rail Station for steaks, and the Fairfield Inn for the best deep-fried, beer-battered Halibut available anywhere if you could stand the hour to hour-and-a-half wait one had to endure (until we became friendly with owners Mark and Sarah Troxley). Occasionally, Judy would join me on business trips, which made those trips a true delight for me.

On a typical Tuesday morning in November as I drove to the office, I recalled contrasting the dark ominous clouds to what the weatherman was predicting for Florida. All vehicles traveled with headlights beaming as if it were 10 PM. "Plan on seeing a sunny day sometime late in May," said my boss, Jack Crilly, "And now you know the reason Kodak is located in Rochester, New York—the world's largest natural darkroom."

THE MARKETPLACE OF IDEAS

The environment at Xerox Square was the polar-opposite of my experience in the field.

In the field, (over) achieving budget is and will always be king, but in a setting where budgets belong to other people, *ideas* are the *coin of the realm*. However, one's ability to portray serious concern for budget achievement can be quite useful, a talent possessed by many at headquarters, myself included. Writing also is a valuable talent, since many ideas were communicated on paper or summarized on paper after being communicated verbally.

Within sixty days, Bob Reiser, boss of bosses, and Dave Kearns, Bob's boss and President of Xerox, were using my (writing) services providing me great exposure to top management. I was invited to lunch with them a few times as we discussed issues they wanted to understand from a field perspective, something field personnel were reluctant to provide fearful of coming across as less than positive. Bob and Dave particularly liked my response to their question regarding how headquarters staff was perceived in the field.

"In short," I said. "Staff spelled backwards is FFATS." They roared at the response and subsequently used it on occasion.

I'll always remember a comment Dave Kearns made to Bob in my presence. "Bob, we'll always be able to attract the country's best and brightest, but our success will be tied to our ability to keep them." Though I didn't know exactly what he meant, it sounded prophetic in the raised paneled executive suite as Bob nodded affirmatively and transitioned from his normal in-charge look to one of solace in support of Dave's opinion.

I recall thinking, *Is this what top execs talk about?*

EXCUSES VS. SOLUTIONS

During a session to uncover the reasons why certain branches were unresponsive to mandatory (Rochester) programs, some of my counterparts were giving what I considered to be lame excuses.

"Are these guys stupid? They sound like a bunch of excuse merchants." I thought as I listened to them recite the same excuses I'd heard from the managers in the branches in my region.

After responding to the grilling about why the Northeast region and the six Manhattan branches in particular resisted implementing programs, the usually quiet Bob Reiser made a comment that altered the room temperature.

"I hope you fellas learned something this afternoon. Mondy, the newest member of the team, has provided solutions among a sea of excuses. I'm not particularly interested in why the branches are not cooperative unless they have a better idea, in which case we'll evaluate it. Their choice is to use our plan or submit a better one for our approval. Doing neither is unacceptable. If you anticipate further problems, you might ask Mondy to join you as you figure out how you're going to get cooperation from the regions on these matters and on matters to come. We'll meet again to discuss your progress," he said as he exited the room.

I was pleasantly embarrassed by his remarks, though I totally understood from whence he was coming. My approach with the Northeast managers was simple. "Unless I'm misunderstanding Reiser and Kearns, and I don't believe I am, your choice is to do what we've asked (and I'm here to help in any way you would like) or give me a better way to accomplish the task at hand, which I'm relatively sure they will adopt if you're way is deemed superior. So, which one do you want to work on?"

OUR NATION'S CAPITAL

My counterpart responsible for the Mid-Atlantic region, Andy Parks, asked if I would accompany him as he was willing to try my approach with some of the branches in and around Baltimore. I told him I would be happy to join him, but only after we made our pitch to the region's VP & General Manager in Washington, D.C., Richard Fuchs. Without inquiring, he told me that Fuchs would not have time to see us, and with that statement, I understood precisely why he had been unsuccessful and why he responded the way he did during the meeting with Reiser. My associate was lacking in vision, perspective, and perhaps, chutzpah.

When he again attempted to get me to join him at the branch level, I simply said that going to a branch without the blessing of the "region brass" was a recipe for failure, not to mention a waste of time. To lighten the mood, I added that I had some relatives in Baltimore I would like to see and that I loved Maryland crab cakes—not necessarily in that order.

Unbelievable to me, my counterpart had never met Fuchs and was apprehensive to do so now fearing that Fuchs would think we were wasting his time.

Fuchs had been in his position for only the previous nine months. Before that, he had worked in Rochester for—you guessed it—Reiser. He admired Bob, as did most who knew him, and simply could not have been more accommodating.

After telling us that he was going to communicate his desire to implement the programs we discussed you could see the confidence in Andy swell. "I'll provide updates, Richard," said the reborn Andy Parks.

"Don't bother," said Fuchs. "Just send me an exception report on those who are resisting and I'll provide whatever support is needed. Bottom line, you can tell Bob that the Mid-Atlantic region will not be a problem."

Andy was bursting with pride as we got into the rental and headed to Baltimore. His presentation to the managers at the branch was made with confidence and authority knowing he had the backing of the region's big dog.

That evening, I enjoyed visiting with my Aunt Ci Ci and three cousins followed by a great meal at the famous Housener's in old Baltimore, which included crab cakes and Blue Point Oysters.

SICILIAN SISTERS VISIT UPSTATE NEW YORK

My mother and Aunt (Tia) Mary were among many visitors whose company we enjoyed while living in New York, and without trying (and in some cases without even knowing), they would provide unmatched comedy.

My mom spoke Italian, Spanish, and English fluently but could only read and write English commensurate with her 8th grade education. Tia spoke Italian and Spanish well, but murdered English in an entertaining manner. Her reading and writing was limited to English at an elementary level but proved not to be a hindrance to her in her world. Neither had the slightest difficulty in communicating a point in English, even though Tia's communication sometimes required questioning by the listener. They spoke to each other interspersing Italian and Spanish without realizing they were doing so. Unless the subject matter was very serious, their conversations almost always contained laughter. They were not strangers to sorrow, but generally saw the bright side of life.

Judy and I planned on taking them to Niagara Falls and then Toronto over the weekend, but until then, Judy was in charge of entertaining them while I was at work.

LIGHTS OUT

A few days into the visit, the Sicilian Sisters (SS) told me they wanted to talk with me after Judy had turned in for the evening. Without Judy hearing, I asked why they wanted to wait till Judy retired and they quickly communicated their displeasure with my question by the looks on their Sicilian faces.

Judy had bid us goodnight about ten minutes earlier when they decided the time was right. "Look, Honey. We don't want to cause any problems between you and Judy; you know we love Judy. But, while you're at work, all the lights in the house are on. We turn them off, but later they're on again," reported the SS spokesperson, my mother with a concerned look on her face which she shared with her SS comrade and sympathizer, Tia Mary DiDio Mortellaro.

Their concern stemmed from their upbringing and their experience of the Great Depression and was indeed heartfelt, but I couldn't resist the opportunity to rib them. "You scared me. I thought you were going to tell me she was seeing a man while I was at work. I'm pleased to hear she's only turning on lights and not some man," I said in jest. This was not appreciated by the SS who were thinking I was making light of the issue. As I roared with laughter, their scowls turned into smiles and then they joined me as we laughed at the non-issue as I turned off the kitchen lights.

At breakfast the next morning, Judy and I had to suppress our laughter as I told her of the prior evening's revelation. They, of course, would not have wanted Judy to know they told on her.

LA CUCARACHA

We crossed into Canada from outside of Buffalo, New York to see the superior view of Niagara Falls, a breathtaking experience regardless of how many times you see them. We did all the touristy things, including taking photos before heading to our final destination, Toronto, Canada's gem.

We had reservations at the plush Four Seasons Hotel in the heart of downtown and we discovered we were not alone. As we approached the hotel, the traffic thickened and then slowed to a crawl with a heavy presence of military personnel and Canada's finest, the Royal Canadian Mounted Police (RCMP). As we made our way closer, I asked a Mounty about the commotion and he explained that the Canadian Prime Minister, Pierre Trudeau, was arriving.

This information triggered a thought, and as I gained distance from the accommodating Mounty, I failed to manage the urge I had to blow the air horn installed in my car which played the not-so-subtle but widely-familiar stanza of the Mexican favorite, *La Cucaracha*. I did not anticipate the effect of this ill-conceived idea when all activity in the area came to a halt as people sought to identify the source. My passengers donned a look of guilt as I pretended to join in the search for the prankster. While it was difficult to positively identify the exact source of the sound, I am confident the 1974 Gold Cadillac with the white Cabriolet vinyl top driven by the large dark-skinned man was a prime suspect.

There was no conversation in the car as we wondered if we (I) had violated some ordinance, or worse yet, committed a crime of which we were unaware. Slowly we continued up the boulevard as it seemed we were being targeted by officials communicating via walkie-talkie-type devices. I thought we were safe as we entered the below ground parking facility of the hotel, and as it worked out, I was correct.

Having loved ones around during tough times can be an asset. Not long after it was apparent that playing *La Cucaracha* to welcome the Canadian Prime Minister to Toronto was not a good idea, members of my caring and sensitive family took turns expressing their feelings about my poor decision, not remembering that they were thoroughly enjoying the prank until we became the focus of what we thought was a concerted effort to apprehend the perpetrator. Only at that point did they see the error in my attempt at humor. Love has no bounds.

WEST TAMPA

After an enjoyable time of sightseeing, relaxing and dining, we took an alternate route back to Niagara Falls for one last view before crossing the border to the U. S. of A. The border patrol asked the usual questions as he examined my New York State Drivers' License, including the purpose and length of our trip into Canada. During the examination, I noticed the serious looks on the faces of my mother and aunt in the rear view mirror. Being of immigrant parents and experiencing an up close and personal perspective on the bolita industry's relationship with the police years earlier left the Sicilian Sisters somewhat suspect of law enforcement, thus, the serious looks. After determining that Judy was my wife, the officer asked, "Who are the passengers in the back seat?" With that inquiry, the SS locked their eyes straight ahead as if we were illegally transporting Jews across the German border during the Nazi reign of WWII.

"My mother behind me and that's our aunt behind my wife," I offered.

"What's your name?" asked the officer of my mother through my opened window.

"Katie Flores," responded my mother unenthusiastically as she continued to gaze straight. I lowered her window in an effort to enhance communications.

"May I see some identification?" followed the officer.

"What does he want?" she asked.

"Mama, he wants to see something you might have in your pocketbook that has your name so he can tell who you are."

"I already told him my name," she told me as she rustled through her purse and handed him her Social Security card.

"Ma'am, this card is not valid for identification, and anyhow, it belongs to Katie DiDio and you said your name was Katie Flores."

Judy and I were no longer able to suppress laughing and started doing so noticing we were alone in finding comedic value in the circumstance.

"That was my name before I got married," offered my mother in defense of the inconsistency with her Social Security card.

"When were you married?"

"I first married in 1936."

"That's almost forty years ago. Do you have any other form of ID, maybe a drivers' license?" asked the officer as he motioned the vehicles behind us to take another lane.

"She doesn't drive," I said as my mother handed him a plastic card which he examined. Then, with a perplexed look, he asked, "What is Maas Brothers?"

Judy busted out laughing followed closely by me and again we were laughing alone. As I gained my composure, I explained that Maas Brothers was the Florida version of Saks, but on a lower scale. Judy and I continued to laugh without company. Then he asked her the simple question, "Where were you born?" seeming like he wanted to wrap up this investigation, and she, without hesitation, replied "West Tampa, at the Centro Español." Judy held her stomach as we busted up laughing.

I quickly explained that (West) Tampa was on the Gulf coast of Florida, from which all of us hailed.

He returned her card, and even though I had previously explained that Tia was our aunt, he asked who she was and asked if she had any ID. I told him her name was Mary DiDio Mortellaro, that she was also born in West Tampa and she was Katie DiDio Flores' sister and my guess was that her ID was probably inferior to that of her sister's.

He motioned us along, and within moments, we were back in the States.

Judy and I laughed some more as we recounted the experience. As the SS realized that they were safe, they joined in our laughter.

"Mama, why did you tell the man you were born in West Tampa?" I asked.

"Where did you want me to tell him I was born? I wasn't born in Ybor City or Sicily, I was born in West Tampa at the Centro Español."

TOWELS AND ARTIFICIAL FLOWERS

Included in my mother's and aunt's itinerary was a trip to midtown Rochester for sightseeing, shopping, and an opportunity for me to join them and their guide, Judy, for lunch.

The Midtown Mall was connected to Xerox Square by two elevated, climate-controlled pedestrian walkways which were a luxury during the summer but an absolute necessity during the notorious winters. Their plan was to call me at around 11:20 AM so I could show them around my office before escorting them to lunch at the Executive Dining Club atop the Midtown Plaza Hotel located in the mall across one of the walkways. The office tour went without a hitch except for my inability to answer my mother's (private) question, "What do all these people do?"

We shared a couple of orders of the club's specialty, prime rib, and two orders of walleye pike accompanied by their classic Caesar salad. Someone had told Xerox President, David Kearns, that I had family visiting from Tampa and he was gracious in stopping by our table on his way out to welcome our guests.

"Welcome to Rochester, I'm Dave Kearns," he said, smiling, as he extended his hand to my aunt and then to my mother. "You certainly picked the right time of year to visit Mondy and Judy," he continued. "It will get quite cold in a couple of months and you'll be glad to be in Florida. I've got to go, but Mrs. Flores, I want to thank you for loaning us your son and daughter-in-law. Mondy does a terrific job for us and we'll miss him when that time comes."

A simple "thank you" would have sufficed but not for my mother. She had no clue who Dave Kearns was (not that it would have changed anything), and without hesitation, said, "Mondy is very smart and he is a very hard worker."

I broke out laughing and the smile on Dave's face grew into a controlled laugh as he conveyed his appreciation for the comment without risking offending my mother. "I couldn't agree more," said the polished executive as he excused himself. "I hope you enjoy the rest of your visit."

Those comments were the embodiment of my mother's feelings for her children. If it would have been any of her other children, her comments would have been the same.

For some inexplicable reason, my aunt and mother were chronically compelled to buy towels (without need) and my aunt's compulsion included artificial flowers. Visiting another region of the country proved to feed their impulses.

As we traversed across the mall, my aunt spied a towel display and asked if we could get a closer look. As she and my mother communicated in Italian about the towels, Judy and I correctly sensed a purchase in the making. The salesclerk, who seemed just as interested in towels as the Sicilian sisters, answered any and all questions with authority. As the sales lady rang up the sale, my aunt searched her well-stocked pocketbook for her change purse where she kept her bills as well as a ridiculous amount of change. As she separated the paper currency into denominations, she dropped her change purse casting change outward in a three-foot radius from where the purse met the floor. Without hesitation, my portly aunt dropped to her knees to collect the change, which I estimated to be in excess of what was in the department store cash register.

Judy and my mother continued to consummate the sale with the salesclerk, leaving me the obvious choice of assisting my aunt in reclaiming her wayward coins. While on my knees with a fistful of nickels, dimes, and quarters, a couple of my contemporaries asked, tongue in cheek, if I needed some cash. I refused, but thanked them for their offer and continued to pick up change as I viewed shoes, pant legs, and hem lines. As we collected almost all the silver, I suggested we leave the pennies, which I estimated to be worth around a dollar. With a look of contempt, my aunt clearly communicated what she thought of my suggestion and we continued our efforts until every coin was retrieved. If there was an additional coin to those dropped by my aunt, we made a profit.

Judy and my mother laughed as we joined them in an upright position. I then asked my aunt if she wanted to pay for some of her towel bill with the oversupply of coins we just retrieved and I received a look identical to the one I'd received when I suggested she abandon her uncollected pennies, again clearly communicating her opinion of my suggestion.

Judy was thoughtful, not to mention merciful, in suggesting that I go back to my office and that she would take Tia and my mother to the department where they could buy artificial flowers.

After their visit, we were visited by friends and family alike, and with the exception of developing niagaraphobia (the fear of seeing Niagara Falls again), we enjoyed every visit.

Things were going well for our family of two and Judy and I made the most of our situation by exploring beautiful upstate New York and southeastern Canada on extended weekends.

TURN THE HOSE

The underpinning of why Xerox was considered a darling on Wall Street was Xerox's ability to consistently grow annual earnings at the rate of 15% or better. Thus, those who orchestrated such performance at Xerox Square in Rochester and Stamford, Connecticut were dubbed by Wall Street as America's best and brightest. This assessment allows one to appreciate the saying, *A rising tide lifts all vessels.*

Nonetheless, performing well amongst corporate America's best and brightest confirmed to me that business is not as mysterious and difficult as those who benefit from such descriptions would have you believe. Yes, it certainly takes dedication, fortitude, hard (smart) work, and a measure of intelligence; but doesn't everything worthwhile? To the chagrin of some business executives, business, in my opinion, is not brain surgery.

Meanwhile, in Tampa, my brother Gene was doing very well as a sales rep and would soon be promoted to Product Specialist, relocating and reporting to the Branch Sales Manager in Orlando, and then promoted again to Sales Manager in Atlanta.

Gene had coined the phrase, "turn the hose," to describe the process Xerox employed when deciding to implement a new strategy and the hoses were being positioned. In June, the financial gurus predicted the possibility of falling short of the self-imposed 15% hurdle for 1974, and a mild panic erupted. All hiring across the country was frozen and all non-essential staff (ffats spelled backwards) positions were targeted for elimination. To set the tone, Rochester began reassigning staff personnel to line positions (positions with budgets), and those without line positions to fill (or replace a lesser performer) were given notice—commonly referred to as being fired. Xerox Square was buzzing. Phone calls were being placed across the country in hopes of lining up positions within and without Xerox.

Our immediate boss, Jack Crilly, confirmed the rumors at a meeting and simultaneously informed us that he and his boss, Jim Higgins, were attempting to find us (me and my counterparts) positions across the country. He then said that he would be taking the position of Branch Manager in Boston, causing some to wonder if he had taken care of himself before concerning himself with us. What was there to wonder about, I thought.

After the meeting, Jack told me (off the record) not to be concerned because the Southern and Northeast regions said they wanted and had positions for me. When I asked if he could be a bit more specific, he said that he could not.

I immediately called Judy and she responded in character: "The Lord's in charge. He keeps an eye on (the needs of) the sparrow, so He will most certainly take care of His children." I appreciated her long view on life, but my focus was somewhat shorter: eating and mortgage payments, to be specific. As I gazed out my window, I noticed no sparrows in distress and I assumed (hoped) that I was God's child (I was certain Judy was), so I was able to appear unconcerned. As generally was the case, she would be correct.

Higgins, the consummate politician, called and told me not to worry, that he was in contact with our friends, John Ogletree and Terry Bigham, Vice Presidents of the Southern and Northeastern regions, respectively, and that I was safe. When asked if he could be more specific, he cryptically reported to me that he could not. He then directed me to inform the secretary to take messages and for me not to communicate with anyone about any opportunities until he got back with me. He loved the drama. I did not.

Then an interesting opportunity presented itself. Wayland Hicks, protégé of Xerox President, David Kearns, stopped by my office ostensibly to chat. He possessed the fine business quality of intensity without intimidation and in that manner informed me that Kearns was dissatisfied with the performance and management at Rank Xerox (England) and had asked him to handle the matter. Even though I was not exactly sure what "handle the matter" meant in this case, I was sure that upon the successful completion of this tour, Wayland would be able to write his own ticket within Xerox.

"I need someone capable and trustworthy to make this work. Are you interested?" he inquired as he locked onto my eyes attempting to see into my brain and read my thoughts. "When do you start?" I asked, buying time to understand the implications of his offer.

"I'm leaving tonight," he said, attempting to make that sound normal. "And my family will follow in a month or so. Mondy, I think this is a wonderful opportunity and we can have some fun with the Brits. Think about it and call me before you leave."

Considering I had no firm offers, I was somewhat interested, yet puzzled as to how this would play out long term. I had no interest in working my way up to become President of Xerox Germany or to live in Europe more than a couple of years. Wayland, in my opinion, would go anywhere he was needed or wanted—a modern-day Lawrence of Arabia, if you will.

I ran the idea by Judy and was amazed when she indicated it might be fun. When I reminded her about our plans to increase our family, she pointed out that babies are born in England every day. Her closing sentiment was that she was fine with whatever I decided as long as I sought God's direction in the matter. "Pray for a clear answer," she suggested.

"And I will do the same."

Judy's suggestion was difficult to argue with as it had no downside of which I was aware, and if God was, indeed, paying attention to the interests of the sparrow, He perhaps had an interest in my situation.

ANOTHER OFFER I COULDN'T REFUSE

Into my office walked "Gentleman Jim" Higgins, puffing on his Cuban cigar and not trying too hard to conceal the smile on his Irish face. In his patented understated manner, he asked, "How would you and Judy like to move to New York City?" "Can you put a little meat on that bone?" I asked.

"Call Terry Bigham (Jim's close friend and NE Region Vice President of Sales and Marketing) and he'll explain the offer. If you decide not to take it, I will." Jim said, cracking a smile.

Terry, indeed, made me an offer I couldn't refuse. He was my primary contact in the NE Region during my Rochester tour, and we interacted flawlessly. Terry was a straight shooter, not inclined to embellishment, so I listened intently.

"Mondy, you know better than most that Frank Mann (Region Sales Operation Manager reporting to Terry) is a fine guy, but he is out of his element. His staff likes him, but he can't get them to implement programs or processes effectively. Branch managers don't respect him professionally, so it's a vicious cycle. I'd like you to take his place for six months to a year and help me get our branches marching to our drumbeat. The experience will look great on your resume' and I'll make it financially very attractive by paying all your personal living expenses during your tour, and at its conclusion, I'll recommend you for a special duty bonus. Jim Higgins has agreed to continue to pay your salary and bonus during this assignment, and when you're done, you can choose any branch that comes open in the region if you decide not to go back to the Southern region. What do you think?" "I'm flattered, but I have a couple of questions."

"Shoot."

"What do you mean by, 'if I decide not to go back to the Southern Region,' and tell me a little more about the financial attractiveness."

"I spoke with John Ogletree (Southern Region VP & GM) and he made it exceedingly clear to me and Jim Higgins that we could not even discuss a branch manager's position, or any other position with you, until you turned down what the Southern region offered you at the conclusion of this temporary assignment, which would last no longer than one year. You see, Mondy, when you go to Rochester, the region you came from has first claim on you, and John made it clear that he'll make something you find attractive available to you when this assignment is over; in fact, he'll do it now if you want. By the way, he wants you to call him before it's official if you decide to take this assignment. As for the financial end, you'll be able to bank all your salary and bonus because the region will pay for everything you spend."

"Terry, help me understand '*everything*.'"

"Everything is everything."

"Are my home mortgage, lawn care, and utility expenses in Rochester part of everything?"

"Certainly; as are taxes, insurance, repairs, upkeep, snow removal, auto maintenance and repair, groceries, medicine, and so on. Mondy, simply put, you deposit your paychecks into one account and open another account for all expenses and we'll pay for them; that's the deal."

"Terry, why are you doing this?"

"I'm sure you're the right guy for this position and I realize you have other options; so, I thought the opportunity for you and your wife to live in New York City with all expenses paid plus being able to bank your paychecks would get your attention."

"Let me run this by my wife, but unless there's a major flaw I don't see, count me in."

"If she comes up with a flaw, give me a chance to correct it."

"You got it. I'll call you before noon tomorrow. What's the starting date?"

"Yesterday."

Judy was excited with the opportunity and we opted for New York City over London.

GREAT NEWS

I stretched the simple relocation to three weeks giving Judy and me a little R & R culminating with a going-away bash at the Higgins' home. It was at this gathering that I broke my promise to Judy and announced to the group of around forty associates and friends that Judy and I (mostly Judy) were pregnant.

Judy was unimpressively disappointed that I would reveal our 36-hour secret without her knowledge, but I just couldn't conceal my true excitement any longer as friends asked if we were excited about the prospect of living in NYC. Judy had educated me on the propriety of waiting a month or so before announcing her pregnancy, but I knew that in a month's time our only contact with this group would be by telephone—a prospect that posed little interest to me. By the end of the evening, she was basking in the conversation that surrounded the news of our first child.

The target due date was April of 1975. The target venue was unknown with Westchester County, New York; somewhere in Florida; and the long shot, London, as logical possibilities. We had truly enjoyed our first five years of marriage, especially given the circumstance of being away from our families and friends, a circumstance that allowed us to bond in a very special way which we continue to cherish till this day, but having children was always atop our agenda. We were ecstatic with the prospect of enlarging our family by 50% and discussed every detail over and over again. Good times lay ahead.

The long-awaited news in Tampa was well received, especially by our families led by Judy's and my mom. Even though Judy's parents had recently visited us in Rochester, Meme and Pa were planning a trip to NYC to spend time with their childbearing daughter and son-in-law in celebration of the upcoming blessed event.

THE CITY SO NICE, THEY NAMED IT TWICE

After deciding that it would be much easier for me and safer for Judy, we opted to take a mid-rise, three-bedroom, three-bath condo with parking in the building a half block from the Northeast region headquarters in White Plains. The bedroom community of White Plains in chic Westchester County had all the amenities Judy and I sought. I could—and did—walk to work, I was accessible to my childbearing wife, we were within walking distance of a plethora of fine restaurants, and not least of all, we could be in NYC in no time at all.

Typically, I would enjoy breakfast with Judy (who continued to prepare breakfast for me even though I tried to persuade her to sleep in now that she was sleeping for two), then leave the condo on foot at 8:20 AM, weaving my way through the gridlocked streets, sometimes waving to co-workers traveling at a rate beneath mine, and arriving at my office before 8:30. My very competent secretary loved using the covered parking space assigned to me. The uncommon business lunches I had were scheduled around my lunches with Judy. We either dined at a nearby restaurant or ate at the condominium, followed by a walk among the many shops in the area. Sometimes, we would drive to Manhattan for lunch, walk around the city, and have dinner at Seafare of the Aegean, my all-time favorite seafood restaurant, before going to Shea Stadium (Yankee Stadium was under renovation) to watch the Yankees. Other times, we'd employ the same routine substituting a Broadway play or sightseeing for the trip to Shea. We were carefree in those days and enjoyed every aspect of our circumstance. Banking 100% of my paychecks was icing on the cake.

Judy and I were twenty-nine when what we considered to be her aging parents (Meme was sixty-one, Pa was fifty-nine) visited us in November of 1974. They were in good health and were enthusiastic about visiting Manhattan. We gave them the royal tour, including carving out time for shopping. I forewarned them that this wasn't Tampa and that the price of most things was negotiable. Pa and I were looking at many things while Judy and Meme spent time with delicate items. Before long, Meme identified an Edna Hibel collector's plate depicting a Japanese mother and child which was part of a series by the same name. She had negotiated a price of $78 and wanted my assurance that she was not falling prey to the merchants of Gotham City. Prior to touching that plate, I had no knowledge of Edna Hibel or collector plates, and consequently, their value. What I did know was that my ability to deal with a Jewish merchant was superior to that of my WASP mother-in-law's. For one thing, this was our turf, and we were skilled in navigating the sometimes-murky waters of this densely-populated island.

Examining the plate, I smiled at the man beneath the yarmulke and said we'd give him $50, tax included. He politely declined, stating that $78 was a good price. I told Meme (while my Hebrew friend listened) that what he meant was that $78 was a good price for him. He responded by saying that if I checked with other merchants in the area, I would be satisfied with his price, opening an opportunity to close the deal while demonstrating to my in-laws how it's done in the big city. I massaged the truth and told the merchant that my in-laws were boarding a plane that evening and that if he didn't take my improved offer of $55, that plate would never see Tampa, Florida. This veteran salesman said he could do no better than $78 and that he doubted we could do better elsewhere, attempting to gain my interest by offering no tax if paid for in cash. Meme was happy to pay the $78, but I told her we would do better elsewhere. She yielded to my suggestion and we (I) began bargaining with other merchants only to find that the original deal negotiated by my mother-in-law was better than anything I could do by $20. By this time, the stores were closing so I convinced Meme to allow Judy and me to give her the plate for Christmas, a mere month away. She agreed, probably to save face for me, and before Judy and I left for Christmas in Florida I gave a mid-eastern merchant on renowned Fifth Avenue, $98 for my mother-in-law's Christmas present. She (we) laughed about that experience till she was promoted to heaven.

THEY DON'T LOVE ME, THEY LOVE MY NUMBERS

If our deal in New York wasn't already enough, my good friend Lou Piniella was playing for the New York Yankees attracting Judy and me to become instant Yankee fans.

We went to many home games and often went to dinner with Lou and Anita after games. Additionally, I scheduled many of my trips to coincide with Yankee games on the road and it was fun carousing with Lou and some of his teammates after games even though I could not hoot with the owls too late into the night if I wanted to soar with the eagles the following morning.

Lou was visiting my office this particular day, and it didn't take long before the news reached the region's boss of bosses, Irwin Engleman. My immediate boss, Terry Bigham, phoned to ask if Lou would be kind enough to stop by Irwin's office on his way out. Lou has always been very accommodating in this regard, so before leaving for lunch, off to Irwin's office we went. Irwin and Terry engaged Lou in light conversation before moving on to baseball. They asked all the typical questions, plus asking Lou for tips they could pass on to their children regarding the art of hitting a round ball with a round bat that can approach the hitter with considerable movement. Lou responded gracefully and posed a few business questions to Irwin and Terry which they found interesting. I noticed Irwin examining Lou's two-day beard and attire, a golf shirt, casual slacks, and Italian slip-ons without socks, prompting him to comment, "Lou, it must be nice to play baseball for a living. You're able to get up at your leisure, visit friends and take care of personal matters before going to the ballpark to play a game you love in front of fans who love you."

After a slight pause, Lou, in his unique manner, responded. "Heh, love me; the fans, and management for that matter, are fickle. It all depends on how I perform. If I go 3 for 4 with a couple of RBIs, they love me; if I go 1 for 4 and leave two men on base, I'm a bum. They don't love me; they love the numbers."

With an understanding grin on his face and pointing to a nine-inch stack of computer printouts, Irwin said, "Lou, see that stack of paper? We're measured in every conceivable way possible. If the numbers are good, they love us. If the numbers are short of expectations, we're bums. They don't love us either, they love the numbers."

"Yeah." Lou responded quickly. "But if my numbers aren't where they're expected to be, I'm gone."

"What do you think happens here?" asked Irwin rhetorically. "Ask Mondy."

We all got a chuckle from the friendly exchange which reminded me that every person thinks their situation is unique.

HOW LONG COULD THIS POSSIBLY LAST?

This was the first time in my adult life I was able to be completely at ease. When I walked out of the office I could only see in front of me—what a sense of freedom. There is something to be said for occupations that don't require one's attention away from the job. They're generally less paying and less prestigious, but for good reason.

What a strange and wonderful feeling it was to meet my best friend and pregnant wife for dinner at a fine restaurant, then walk down the street for cheesecake and cappuccino, followed by a leisurely stroll till we decided we wanted to call it an evening—all without a care in the world. I had no family concerns, no relationship concerns, no health concerns, no financial concerns, no business concerns, no concerns about the past, the present, or the future. I asked myself how long this could possibly last.

THE SUNSHINE STATE

During my assignment in the NE Region, I developed a close relationship with my boss, Terry Bigham. In December of 1974, Terry asked if I was satisfied with the decision that I'd made last summer and what I wanted to do next.

I told him that I was, indeed, satisfied and what I wanted to do next depended on what options were available to me, but running a branch seemed like the next logical step. He agreed and said I could pretty much pick my branch in the NE Region, but realized that the Southern Region had first crack at my services.

"Mondy, I know you and Judy want to get back to Florida, but that means you'll be waiting on Orlando or Miami. Assuming other Southern Region locations like Albuquerque, Nashville, and Houston don't draw the same interest for you guys, you're welcome to stay in your current position with your current arrangement until a branch you like becomes available. How does that sound?"

"Terry, saying you guys have been great to me is an understatement, and you are correct in that many of the Southern Region locations outside of Florida don't have particular appeal to Judy or me. Let me discuss this with her and I'll get back to you in a couple of days. Should I call John Ogletree (Southern Region VP & GM) first?"

"Yes, definitely do that. But let me understand your preferences. How would you rank Boston, Houston, and New York City?

"Boston and New York are a tossup, and Houston is a distant third."

"That's what I thought. Other than for a barbeque, I can't see you in boots and a cowboy hat." He was correct.

NEW YORK

Judith catching me doing something

Judith & me 1972

Judith Kay & me 1971

Me, my mother, and Tia Maria at the Four Seasons Hotel in Toronto

Tia Maria and mama trying to re-enter the USA without identification

Me cranking up my "Egg" for some barbecue in Rochester NY

Xerox Square My office in Rochester NY

Me shoveling snow

Terry Russo clearing my drive

JK Icicles

Me playing in the snow

JK playing in the snow

Me Fireplace

JK Fireplace

Uncle Vince, Aunt Louise and me in Rochester, NY

Uncle Vince and me

Pa, Judy, Meme, me taking the train to NYC

Me, Judy, Meme, Pa Niagra Falls

Xerox VP recognizing Miami branch as top class 1 branch in the USA

WEST PALM BEACH

John Ogletree was a tough old ex-Auburn football player who I also liked a lot. He had called when I first was promoted to Rochester to congratulate me and to make sure I realized I was on loan to headquarters and that I should have full expectations of returning to the Southern Region upon completion of my tour. Additionally, when in Rochester (which was often), he would come by my office to say hello, or if I was out, leave his business card. I was flattered by both gestures.

He incorrectly assumed that I was dying to escape the northeast, but said he had approval to spin off the West Palm Beach/Fort Lauderdale area into a branch in July of 1975 and was planning to ask me to be the Area Manager (a branch manager in every respect except for the service responsibility) in April and then the Branch Manager in July. I recall his facetious albeit comical comment, "I know it's not Newark, New Jersey, but what do you think?"

Judy and I were pleased with the location, but Judy said she had little interest in relocating from New York to Florida so close to her delivery date in April, so consequently, we agreed to relocate at our convenience in January, but I would be responsible for the budget commencing January 1st, 1975—another way of saying that the party was over.

SPECIAL TIME WITH MY BROTHER

My brother Gene and his family were living in Orlando where Gene's Xerox career was advancing very nicely. With a wife and two children, he had shed the anti-authority creed he followed in college, and was indeed, becoming more and more part of the authority base within Xerox.

During December of '74, Gene and I decided to go to New York to take care of details on our Rochester home and spend a few days in Manhattan as I ostensibly buttoned things up in White Plains. Judy had planned on making the trip, but at six months pregnant, was thrilled to have Gene join me for my farewell visit to the Empire State.

Gene had not previously been to New York and we were excited about making the trip together. We stayed at The Plaza Hotel in Manhattan and went to Rochester only to meet the movers before returning to the Big Apple.

You name it and we did it: The Empire State Building, The World Trade Center,

Chinatown, Little Italy, the diamond district, the Statue of Liberty, Wall Street, Broadway, Carnegie Hall, we even ice skated at Rockefeller Center (not exactly a thing of beauty). We engaged in all these activities, making certain we dined at our list of restaurants, which included the Seafare of the Aegean (a couple of times), Spark's Steak House, Gallagher's, and Pier 52.

Throughout the trip, we commented on how fortunate we were to visit our maternal great grandparents' place of entry into the United States in a manner they could have never envisioned as they struggled to improve their lot so that those who followed would enjoy the fruit of their foresight and effort. We were, indeed, doing just that.

Additionally, I thought, *How often are adult siblings able to carve time out from their families and busy careers to engage in unfettered time such as we were doing?*

Both Gene and I were blessed with good friends, but clearly we were each other's best friend making the trip extra special.

THE GOLD COAST

The east coast of Florida from Miami to Palm Beach is referred to as the Gold Coast, and for good reason. Some use the reference to describe the golden tans sought by the beach crowd, but those in the business world refer to the gold (wealth) of many of the area's inhabitants, many home-grown but more transplanted. Both references are accurate.

We could not find a home immediately, so we decided to rent until we were able to find something we liked, thinking this assignment would last for five years or so. We found a nice three-bedroom apartment overlooking beautiful Lake Worth onto prestigious Palm Beach—winter quarters for the Kennedys, the Rockefellers, and the like.

The Xerox office was conveniently located two blocks away in a newly-constructed office building with all the amenities, including my favorite, covered parking. The furniture, artwork, and layout attested to plans on making this office a branch soon—its appointments were nicer than any Xerox office I had ever seen, and I had seen many.

The sales manager was the veteran Larry Carter, a likable fella who I remembered from meetings when I was a sales manager. His numbers indicated that he was quite productive, and that's what was of interest to me.

The first time I went to the facility on Palm Beach Boulevard, Larry was in the process of moving out of his (Branch Manager's) office in deference to me, but I told him to stay put for the time being as we had an oversupply of prime office space. He insisted on moving, citing that it would be easier now than later.

I asked him to arrange a meeting for us with the two Ft. Lauderdale sales managers for lunch that day. I wanted him to go with me and give me an overview of his plans and personnel while we traveled. Within twenty minutes, he reported to me that neither of the sales managers was available to meet that day, one because of a prearranged lunch and the other because he was in Miami doing something—some things just don't change. I told Larry to tell the one with lunch plans to break those plans unless they were with a significant (in terms of size) customer, in which case Larry and I would join him; and to tell the one in Miami that I was planning on either meeting him in Ft. Lauderdale for lunch or at my office in West Palm at 5:30 PM, his choice. If any of them had an issue, I wanted to talk with them on the phone. Larry made no effort to conceal his smile and said his guess was that the four of us were going to have lunch together.

On the way to Ft. Lauderdale, Larry asked permission to speak candidly and confidentially. I told him that this was the kind of conversation I preferred. It was almost noon, and I had known him professionally since 8:30 that morning if you dismiss our previous encounter in Orlando.

"Tom" (one of the sales managers), "is a conniving and scheming individual who cannot be trusted."

To lighten the seriousness of his comments, I said "Doesn't conniving and scheming mean the same thing?"

"I suppose you're right; but if they don't, he's both."

"Next, you're going to tell me Jerry (the other manager) is worse than Tom, right?"

"I don't know the other guy very well, but he seems to be a whiner and he's good friends with John Woods (the Miami Branch Manager)."

"If you're correct on both, I'll probably get along better with Tom; I don't do well with whiners."

The perplexed look on his face indicated that either he hadn't gotten the answer he wanted or he was confused with my reaction.

"Larry, I'm not going to ask them, and I'm pretty confident, even though you can never tell, that they're not going to offer, but how do you think they would describe you?" "They'd probably say I'm a scatterbrain," he responded unabashedly.

"Would they be correct?"

"Partially."

THE PARTY'S JUST BEGINNING

Valet parking at the "Bunny Club" on the intracoastal waterway was backed up as Larry pulled right behind the vehicle in front of us taking a ticket from the golden-tanned, very attractive and totally white-clad attendant as if this wasn't his first time.

As Tom and Jerry stood to shake hands, my mind drifted to the cartoon characters of the same names. I noticed that the spread of the bell bottoms on their white pants exceeded Larry's and the rest of their mustached appearance spelled South Florida. The Gold Coast would be, as I suspected, totally different from the Florida I knew.

The Bunnies were quite successful in causing their intended distraction as they served such South Florida favorites as conch and ceviche, with mango salsa, of course.

I had little expectation of accomplishing anything more than meeting each other face-to-face and was not disappointed. Their response to me asking what could be improved to assist them in accomplishing their goals (code for sales budgets) was revealing and gave me an insight into them that I sought.

As Jerry used the facilities and Larry went to get his car, Tom seized the opportunity to ask if it would be okay to share something with me in confidence. As I gave my okay, I anticipated what my good friend of ninety minutes might tell me, and I was not disappointed. He said he thought it would be helpful to me if I knew that Larry was a scatterbrain.

The term dysfunctional entered my mind.

KICKING-OFF THE NEW YEAR

I was to be in New York on a particular day to attend an appreciation dinner in my honor with the NE Region staff arranged by my former bosses, Terry Bigham, Jim Higgins from Rochester, and Irwin Engleman, Terry's boss.

I was surprised that John hadn't asked me to rearrange my schedule in order to attend the 1975 Miami Branch Kick-Off, the most important meeting of the year. I didn't like the message it would send if I were in New York, at essentially a party, when over 500 Miami Branch employees (a number of whom would be West Palm Beach Branch employees in six months) were being charged-up to accomplish the Operating Plan for the year, so I asked Terry to reschedule and he gladly did.

"It's freezing up here, maybe we'll have it in Palm Beach," Terry jested.

I had not yet met John Woods in person and had only spoken to him on the phone twice before driving to Miami a day in advance to familiarize myself with whatever role John had selected for me as part of the Kick-Off meeting.

When discussing the plans for West Palm Beach with John Ogletree back in December, he had instructed me to call John Woods to discuss the position which he said he had discussed with Woods and to which Woods was in full agreement.

When I called Woods, he said it was not necessary for me to fly to Miami just to meet him since there was no need for an interview given that John Ogletree had already selected me for the new branch. I understood his logic but offered to come anyway, expressing to him that I was reasonably sure Ogletree would allow him to select another person if he decided I was not the right guy for the position. He told me that he had already recommended someone else for the position, but was told that the position was going to be filled by Mondy Flores. I asked him if that gave him heartburn, and he responded, "Not at all."

Though he looked old to me at the time, John Woods was probably in his late-forties or early fifties on that January day in 1975. He asked how I liked the facility in West Palm, explaining that he hadn't visited there since moving into the new digs (some eighteen months earlier). We small talked, and I learned that John was from New York and was the branch manager at a Long Island branch prior to relocating to Miami fulfilling his lifelong ambition of living in South Florida. He said he spoke to a couple of his NE Region friends about me and received good reports, except that they said I paid too much attention to corporate matters (whatever that meant).

He took me from office to office, introducing me to the various department heads and other key people. During the tour, I noticed the branch sales manager's (BSM's) office was located on a separate floor occupied by the Miami sales managers and sales reps and the office that normally would have been occupied by the BSM was occupied by a flirtatious strawberry blonde who held the position of Personnel Clerk, a position that in most branches did not warrant an office at all, much less one amongst the senior staff. To head off any questions, I suppose, John explained to me that the BSM (also from New York) requested to be located close to the action.

Since he had yet to mention it, I asked if there was any role that he wanted me to play in the next day's meeting and his response was, "It's not necessary."

My previous assignment had afforded me the opportunity to visit many branches, and through that experience I developed a sense of how branches operated by observing people's activities and their conversations. When I was talking with John, a service technician asked to see him who then proceeded to ask him for permission to attach a trailer hitch to his company vehicle. Later, a sales rep came into John's office to tell him they were out of a particular form and that the sprinkler downstairs was wetting people walking on the sidewalk. Curiously, John attended to each matter.

Pier 66 in Ft. Lauderdale was the venue for the Kick-Off meeting which was followed by a raucous and rowdy party lasting into the night where the alcohol flowed freely and much good food was consumed amongst the salsa dancing and storytelling. Miami-fashionable bell-bottomed suits and revealing, form-fitting dresses for the women accented this South Florida celebration ending a poor 1974 and hopes for a successful 1975.

PALM BEACH STORY

Judy's pregnancy blossomed by the week and we were waiting for our firstborn with great anticipation. The topic of conversation as we dined at our favorite restaurants, always centered on the baby to come, followed by, if it was a girl, we would name her this or that or maybe even the other, but if it were a boy, Armando would be his name.

I couldn't get comfortable with idea of holding my first son in my arms and calling him Charlie, Fernando, Bill or any other name but Armando.

My choice of names if our firstborn was a girl was Amanda. Perhaps, that sounds selfish.

We continued to look for houses without success and it became depressing to spend a couple of days looking at homes and not be able to feel good about any of them. Judy had set the end of February as the deadline for moving into a home. Otherwise, we would stay in our apartment until after the baby was born.

We became experts at identifying the homes of the rich and famous along Palm Beach, and even tried to identify individuals when dining at Palm Beach hot spots like the Petite Marmite. When family and friends visited, they always wanted to see the Palm Beach mansions. It was becoming Niagara Falls all over again.

On my birthday in 1975, I received a call from John Ogletree at my home (it was a Saturday) informing me that Rochester, as a result of missing their fourth quarter projection to Wall Street, had issued another round of cost cutting that included freezing all new branch openings, and consequently, my position of Area Manager was eliminated, as well. "If you haven't bought a home yet, don't," he said, "because we'd like you to move to Miami as BSM."

"John, they already have a Branch Sales Manager in Miami and my wife is seven months pregnant. She has little interest in changing doctors again, or in moving to Miami at this time."

"I'm totally sensitive to the situation with your wife and we'll do whatever it takes to accommodate her situation. As for the BSM in Miami, the position will be open by the end of the day. I'm going to call John now, but I wanted to make sure you were okay with going to Miami before I tell him you'll be taking the BSM job. Do I call him?"

"What are my choices?"

"A branch in Texas will open this week, one in Atlanta in a month or so, or you can work as my assistant here in Dallas until a branch you like opens. I'm confident Terry Bigham would have a branch for you in the northeast, but I'm hoping you'll stay with us."

I had no stomach for suggesting to Judy that we move to Texas, Georgia, back to New York, or anywhere else for that matter, so Miami was looking like the best alternative at the present. "I'll take the job in Miami, but I can tell you John's not going to like the idea."

"I know Harvey Neumann's his friend and that he brought him in from New York, but he'll just have to deal with it," he said.

WELCOME TO MIAMI

Judy was fine with the decision, but asked if I would solely take on the responsibility of selecting our home in Miami and if it would be okay to stay in West Palm for ninety days or so after the arrival of the baby before moving. Neither was a problem, except that, through this experience I would realize, I was somewhat susceptible to separation anxiety.

"I'm not going to tell him; you tell him," was Woods' charge to me when I called to discuss the matter. "And the people around here aren't going to like your decision; Harvey is well liked."

Two thoughts sprang to mind: The first was, shouldn't John have said, "Welcome to Miami," somewhere in our conversation? And second was, how did this become my decision?

I would learn that this approach to situations that were not to his liking was not atypical. Additional things I would learn included that John was a nice person, intelligent, a bit of a schemer, utilized selective amnesia when convenient, openly treated his friends favorably at the expense of others, and avoided conflict at all cost—the latter being a huge shortcoming for a Xerox Branch Manager in a market such as South Florida.

I could not determine if John had been inadequate as a Long Island branch manager, and had thus been unloaded by the Northeast region, or if the Miami Branch, one of the largest in the country, was too much for him to handle. Whatever the reason, the way he was managing was tantamount to rearranging the deck chairs on the Titanic. Unbeknownst to this lucky Irishman, much-needed assistance (from a motivated Spaniard) in identifying the icebergs and redirecting the ship toward safe waters was on its way.

Harvey Neumann was not only in over his head as BSM, but he had a negative outlook on the world, and to compound matters, had serious health issues which may have contributed to the aforementioned traits.

It was, indeed, awkward telling Harvey that I was taking his place and that he would be on temporary assignment, reporting to me at reduced compensation until I could identify a position that matched his abilities.

"What the hell does that mean?" he queried.

I gave it to him straight as I responded, "Dunno; what do you think you'd be successful at?"

With a semi-scowl (and bad judgment), he answered, "The job I've been doing. The job you're taking from me."

His response didn't surprise me.

In thirty days, I transitioned from the plum of plum assignments in Westchester County, New York to a snake pit assignment in Miami, Florida. I had spent one and a half years telling people how it should be done and now I had the opportunity to do it myself. I was ready for the challenge.

CHEZ VENDOME

The only thing I didn't like was that Judy and our to-be-born child were in West Palm and I would be spending most of my time in Miami. However, I had a plan.

I rented a suite at the boutique David William Hotel a half-mile from the office and the popular Miracle Mile shopping area of Coral Gables. Typically, I would spend Monday mornings and Friday afternoons at the West Palm Beach office for obvious reasons. I scheduled individual plan and/or review meetings with one of the local seven managers every Monday, Tuesday, and Wednesday over dinner at the exquisite Chez Vendome located in the David William Hotel. The posh ambience contributed to the relaxed mood I was trying to create for the managers. Some were uncomfortable with the arrangement, but before long they seemed to appreciate the fact that I was trying to gain an understanding of the obstacles they faced in their assignments. In fact, I communicated to them that my role was simply to remove or mitigate any and all impediments to them accomplishing their goals and budgets.

"Since my budget is the sum of your budgets, easy math tells you I cannot achieve my budget, if you don't achieve yours. We're all wearing the same color jerseys."

As is generally the case, some bought into the program sooner than others and a couple would be unable to make the grade.

The first to convert was a middle-of-the-pack performer named Gil Aleman.

Gil was born in Santiago, Cuba and completed his high school and post-high school education in the Washington, DC area and in Puerto Rico. He was hired by Xerox in Puerto Rico and later promoted to sales manager in Miami—*Mecca* to Cubans. My *prima facie* opinion of Gil was lacking because of his soft-spoken demeanor and his attention to fashion. Upon meeting him and noticing his bone-colored suit with full-belled pants, I considered him a pretty boy. However, in short order I was impressed with his talk about how he was going to do things, fully recognizing that talk is a plentiful commodity when compared to its scarce companion: walk. With that in mind and as we dined on Caesar salad, prime rib, and lyonnaise potatoes, I asked Gil why he hadn't previously implemented the concepts we agreed were essential to effectively managing a sales team and his response was textbook accurate.

"Because there's no support from the top. If you try to demand anything from the sales reps, they run to John or Harvey for help and generally get it."

His Cuban accent was no impediment to communicating his point, but I wondered if the wine was acting as a catalyst or whether he was, indeed, fed up with the frustration of carrying a gun loaded with blanks.

"Aren't you taking a risk, telling me that your bosses are not supportive of your efforts to get the job accomplished?"

"I don't think so, because if things don't get turned around soon, there's going to be many changes and I'm already at risk." An astute observation I thought.

Over Cherries Jubilee and Cuban coffee, I posed the question, "What makes you think I won't be part of the problem?"

"They would have let John continue as is if they were happy with our performance, but since John had no choice but to take you, I've got to believe Region wants changes and wants them now."

Another astute observation I thought.

"Gil, may I ask how you came to the conclusion that John had no choice but to take me?"

"It's common knowledge. John told his inner circle, and they told the people they trust and someone they trust told me."

"How do you know this isn't all a fabrication?"

"Like I said, Region can't be happy with our performance the last couple of years and it's obvious that John's not comfortable with you around. He didn't even like it when Region put you in West Palm, how do you think he likes it with you in Miami?"

"Finish your cherries," I responded. After a brief pause, I continued, "Gil, you can count on me supporting any effort that is moral, legal, and ethical and will improve performance." "I'm counting on it," he said with a sense of appreciation in his voice.

As we wrapped up the evening, I was pleased with Gil's understanding of what it took to be a top performer in the Xerox culture, but I was not yet convinced he could pull it off even though I was pulling for him as I needed a leader to emerge from among the sales managers in the most serious way. I would not be disappointed.

As Gil departed, he informed me, partially in jest, that he was available anytime I wanted someone to eat with at the "Chez." I would learn later that the lean and suave Cuban loved to eat good food. I knew then that no matter how things turned out, he wasn't all bad.

My evening meetings at the Chez Vendome proved to be very productive as I was able to engage in meaningful discussions without the barrage of distractions and interruptions so commonplace at the office.

JUDY KAY

Judy has always been comfortable being alone. I've always considered it a tribute to her self-esteem and character not to require the company of others even though she takes much pleasure in the company of our families and good friends. While we lived in Baton Rouge, Orlando, Tampa, Rochester, and White Plains, she never required others to keep her busy; she's always felt comfortable in her own skin. West Palm was no exception. I attribute that to her close relationship to Christ.

Judy fully appreciates the importance of one in a position of authority to focus on their job and never called me at the office to pass the time or to fill a gap in her day. I always called to check on her and I could sense the pleasure and great anticipation she was experiencing throughout her pregnancy. It became obvious to her that the arrival of our first child would, for the foreseeable future, eliminate any gap in her day or need to pass time and she was enjoying the balance of her free time as we marched toward the expected delivery date of April 18, 1975.

Our weekends were special as we enjoyed each other's uninterrupted company, knowing things would soon change forever—a highly-valued sentiment for both of us. We dined at Mannero's, often enjoying their great prime rib and their famous Gorgonzola salad. Not once did we eat there or anywhere else that we did not project that soon we would have a little guest with us. Isn't life great?

I invited her to come to Miami for a few days to walk through the three or four homes I had narrowed it down to, but her interest was elsewhere. "I know you'll choose the correct one," followed by, "If you really want me to, I will, but I know you'll pick the right one."

HARVEY, HARVEY, HARVEY

As a goodwill gesture, I delegated the assignment of distributing the branch budget among the sales teams to my predecessor, Harvey Neuman. I hadn't found a suitable position for him and thought the task would preserve some measure of his self-esteem during a time that I'm sure was tough for him.

Harvey, to my chagrin, was not only late in completing the task, he was unable to distribute the entire budget, citing that the sales managers thought the budget was too high as the reason.

"Harvey, I'm trying to find a position for you, but you're making it tough for me. I didn't ask you to gain the sales managers' opinions of what their budgets should be; I simply asked you to distribute the branch budget that has been assigned to us by Region. Do you believe the budget is too high?"

"My opinion shouldn't matter. The sales reps and sales managers should have the best feel for what they can sell, not you or me." He offered as a teacher speaking to a pupil.

Even though this scenario was perfect for him and the sales managers to be pulling a prank on me as the new BSM, I discounted the possibility. Frankly, I thought he didn't possess the creativity.

"Have you ever met a sales rep or sales manager that complained that their budget was too low?"

"Can't say that I have."

"Have you ever met one that complained that their budget was too high?"

"All the time."

"Harvey, Harvey, Harvey." I said before asking him to call a meeting of the sales managers to accomplish what he was unable to.

LIFELONG FRIENDS

After arguing with me about my wanting to occupy the BSM's office that was adjacent to his and occupied by the personnel clerk and his close friend, John finally relented. He wasn't pleased with the outcome of the argument having told his close friend she would not be moved. He could, of course, have played hardball and refused to make the obviously appropriate move, but that was precisely the point. It was obvious to all that the personnel clerk had no business, other than monkey business, occupying the office she occupied. Said another way, if the clerk would have been a male, he would have operated in obscurity, occupying space in some cubicle on another floor. The personnel clerk was not a fan of mine and joined a growing list.

Normally, Harvey's secretary would have transitioned into being my secretary. Harvey highly recommended her which was tantamount to the "kiss of death." Therefore, I was now looking for a secretary. I wanted to hire from within because I thought bringing someone in from the outside would send the wrong message and I was already sending too many of those.

I was interested in trust and character ahead of anything else, and upon interviewing Mari Venezia, I knew I had found the right person. Sprinkled throughout the interview, the young newlywed made several edifying references regarding her husband while responding favorably to my questions. The fact that she was a relative newcomer gave me an additional reason to select her over the more qualified (on paper) candidates—I assumed she had not yet been negatively affected by the bad apples in the branch. My hunch was correct, and Mari turned out to be a valuable asset as I led a campaign to change the hearts and souls of a dysfunctional but talented sales organization.

The high-octane Mari Venezia went about her assignment with the zeal and commitment that are familiar to those who know her. It was difficult not to notice her promotion of her husband, Frank, who was an associate in the meat department at Publix. She would say Frank was this and Frank was that as she communicated while she carried out her duties. Knowing my wife was in West Palm and aware of what nights I scheduled meetings at the Chez Vendome, gave her the perfect opportunity to get me to meet the love of her life, Frank. She craftily set up a steaks-on-the-grill dinner at her and Frank's apartment luring me with the idea that Frank would personally select and cut the steaks for the affair.

Meeting the somewhat-nervous Frank was, indeed, a treat. His energy and zest for life mirrored Mari's, leading me to wonder if they made time to sleep. When I posed that question, they concurrently related the fact that they often slept on the balcony outside of their second-story apartment. I was not surprised.

I identified with the admiration they had for each other, but I had never witnessed any two people that enthusiastic about verbalizing their feelings for each other. It was truly a breath of fresh air.

After that evening, Mari probed for my opinion of Frank. I told her he seemed to be all she advertised, but that wasn't what she was looking for. "You've interviewed many people. What do you think he'd be good at?" she asked.

"According to those steaks we ate the other night, he's pretty good at that."

That, again, was not what she was looking for, so she tried again. "Can you think of anything around here he'd be good at?"

Frank seemed to have the initiative and desire to be successful in sales, but I wasn't prepared to form an opinion base on a delicious steak dinner. So, I delivered to Mari exactly what she was looking for when I suggested that she ask Frank to take the battery of tests for sales applicants, and if the test warranted, we could arrange for a couple of sales managers to talk with him. She coordinated what is generally a four-month process into less than two, and before you could say filet mignon, Frank was a Xerox sales trainee.

Mari and Frank were happy as could be, but Frank's hiring into our sales organization put Mari (and thus, me) in an awkward position. As my secretary, Mari had access to and knowledge of all confidential information regarding every sales rep and sales manager in the branch, including compensation. Though her scruples and character were without question, keeping her in her position wasn't fair to her or the sales group. As we considered what opportunities existed in the branch outside of sales, the idea of having Mari take the sales test surfaced, and before you could say Pittsburg rare, Mari was also a sales trainee.

I did not relish the idea of searching for a secretary again, but the Miami Branch sales ranks had been bolstered with the addition of Frank and Mari Venezia. Mari and Frank would end up stellar sales executives and tremendous positive influences on a branch in desperate need of positive influences.

Much more importantly, the seed for two **lifelong friends** had been planted.

ARMANDO FLORES III

Judy and I were happy when Meme and Pa offered to come a couple of weeks early to tend to Judy's needs as we zeroed in on the baby's April 18 due date. I know Judy appreciated the help, and their coming took the pressure off me of trying to stay in the West Palm area until the baby arrived.

Around 1 PM on Wednesday, April 2, 1975, I received a call from Judy advising me she had visited the doctor because she was experiencing contractions and the doctor said she should proceed to the hospital because she would be delivering the baby in about ten to twelve hours. She told me to finish what I was doing before heading to the hospital because she was in good hands with her parents and there was no need for me to rush.

I, however, could not get my mind off what was happening in West Palm and decided to excuse myself from the meeting I was attending and leisurely go by the David William to gather some clothes to leave for the dry cleaners and pick up my toothbrush before heading to the hospital. Why I decided to go by the hotel at all has always puzzled me and was something Meme brought to my attention now and again over the years as a source of amusement. Meme interpreted it as an automatic reaction of a nervous first-time father. Other than killing time, since Judy emphatically told me the birth would be no sooner than ten hours, I have no better explanation.

I bought a double Cuban coffee espresso before heading north on I-95 and thought about the event that was unfolding. I was hoping and praying that things would go smoothly and that both Judy and the baby would be healthy. Cell phone technology had not yet reached the marketplace, thus allowing one to think while driving—I thought of the way things would be with a baby.

The clock in my Coupe de Ville read 5:23 PM as I entered the Palm Beach Gardens Hospital parking area. A man resembling Pa was pacing the lot and started toward my vehicle as I turned down a lane in search of a parking space. The only unoccupied spaces were designated with a stork carrying a newborn sign. As I slowed to contemplate stretching my qualifications to use such spaces, the man I thought was Pa came up to my car barking directions at me. Sure enough, it was him and he was trying to get my attention to tell me that the baby was due any minute.

I left the parking of my car to him and ran in the direction he was pointing through the various checkpoints to the delivery room where I was to assist Judy through the delivery as her duly qualified Lamaze coach, but to my surprise, Armando III was being washed by the nurse and the smiling mother was watching my reaction.

The 6-pound, 11-ounce, 23-inch long Baby Mondy was born at 5:28 PM and the clock in the delivery room displayed 5:32.

I was able to hold Judy's hand and congratulate her on a job well done as we shared our time of bliss, and it was difficult to hold back the tears of joy. Meme and Pa came into the room smiling from ear to ear with Pa asking if I arrived in time.

What a wonderful day April 2, 1975 was for Judy and me.

On Friday, we brought Baby Mondy to our home with the care you would afford the Crowne Jewels.

HE'S MARRYING MY SISTER

Back in Miami, things were in turmoil. People who had been allowed to operate with a large measure of freedom were now asked to provide information about how they spent their workday. Sales managers were required to spend one full day per week in front of customers with sales reps who were under budget in an attempt to determine if the sales rep's problem was skill- or activity-related—or both.

Good sales managers were already doing this. These requirements were met with great resistance from many sales reps and some sales managers. Harvey and John chimed in with their opinions, as well. They, of course sided with the sales reps and managers. John asked (told) me to back off from the close scrutiny because it was causing serious consternation amongst the rank and file. I explained to John that our performance of two back-to-back negative months warranted this action in my opinion, and that I was certain Region management was gnashing their teeth over the dismal performance of their largest branch. What were we to say when they came a-calling? That we hoped things would get better? I think they would expect more from us (me). John knew where I was going with this, so he withdrew his request, but he insisted I was doing the wrong thing by applying pressure.

As a compromise, I made the reporting requirements optional for sales reps over budget. How could one argue with your supervisor wanting to review your activity if you were not achieving your budget?

Gil Aleman suggested that we step up our hiring to have trained sales reps ready to take territories from those who would not make the grade. The additional reps would also serve indirectly to send a message to those slacking that their positions were not safe. My only addition to Gil's suggestion was that we make a concerted effort to hire blacks, Latinos, and females in every possible instance, because we were, in my opinion, under-represented within these groups. Having worked in Rochester, I was quite aware of what was coming, and I thought it prudent to get a head start.

As I had anticipated, "Does a black, Latin female count for three?" was the first question.

This pressure was too much for one of the sales managers and he tendered his resignation.

I decided to fill that opening with a black candidate to set the example of doing what I was asking people to do.

Unfortunately, we had no such candidates within the branch in large part due to the fact that we had no black sales reps. Fortunately, in my opinion, we had no white candidates, either. John Woods vehemently disagreed and ordered me to fill the vacancy with Harvey explaining to me that black managers don't do well in Miami. How he knew that was a mystery to me since we'd never had a black manager in the branch.

I tried to change John's mind by explaining that Harvey's style was not compatible with what I was requiring sales managers to do, and without hesitation, he responded "Bull Sh#t! You just tell him what he has to do, and he'll do it."

Harvey, unwittingly, helped my case when he told me during an interview (out of stupidity or brilliance), that the budget for the team was too high and that he would only consider the job if the budget was adjusted downward 25%. I indicated to him that I understood his concern, but since I didn't see it the same way, I suggested he ask John to override my decision and lower the team's budget.

He bit and made my case.

I arranged for a black sales rep out of Dallas to come to Miami to interview for the job. I picked up A. J. Moore at the Miami airport and suggested we do some of our talking while I accomplished a few errands around town, the most important of which was to meet with the woman whose house Judy and I were set to purchase. I explained that he would be able to see some of Miami and that we'd visit the branch later in the day. The suave and articulate A. J. was okay with the plan.

The dark blue suit, rep tie, and lace-up shoes indicated the style in Dallas was closer to that of New York's than to Miami's.

Mrs. Dryden was fine with my request of bringing someone with me as she relayed the particulars of the house to me. The well-preserved and genteel Mrs. Dryden painstakingly took us through the house, providing considerably more information than I wanted or could remember. Most of the info was categorized in an impressive binder for me to keep.

While going over the particulars regarding the lawn, she asked A. J. an awkward question. "Duke Ancrum has taken care of our lawn and landscaping for a very long time and my husband and I would strongly recommend him to you if you don't already have someone. He's a black man and he's very reliable." She then glanced at A. J. and asked, "Do you know Duke Ancrum, Mr. Moore?"

I was ready to bail him out of this awkward spot when he responded with impeccable courtesy, "No, Mrs. Dryden, I don't; but I'm sure I'll meet him if I move to Miami. I now live in Dallas, Texas."

She gracefully accepted the response of the well-dressed professional gentleman never considering the insensitivity of her question.

She bade us farewell and walked us to the door after concluding the tour, and as we walked toward my auto, she asked me if Mr. Moore was considering moving to Miami to work for me, to which I responded, "No ma'am. He's marrying my sister."

A. J. was several paces ahead of us, but I thought he could hear us without much effort. When he heard my response, he took a full breath of air in an effort to control his desire to laugh. Mrs. Dryden controlled herself as well as she waved goodbye to the Latin man buying her home and his black brother-in-law to be. She couldn't wait to share this with her soon-to-be-retired stockbroker husband.

As soon as we were out of earshot, A. J. and I unleashed the laughter we were suppressing. That experience jump-started a relationship between me and Xerox's first black sales manager in the state of Florida that would flourish and flourish.

Within a week of announcing A. J.'s promotion to Miami, I received several unsigned notes and letters telling me I had made a mistake in hiring a Negro for the position and two people gave me a book that chronicled the failures of blacks during WWII. One of the books was given to me by John Woods.

A black female from our administrative group told me in the elevator that I had done a courageous thing. I then realized many eyes would be focused on A. J.

TAIL WAGGING THE DOG

As previously mentioned, I began my work week in either West Palm or Ft. Lauderdale and ended it the same way. I was not advertising nor trying to hide the fact that I was scheduling my time this way to maximize my time with my wife and newborn son.

On a particular Friday afternoon, my capable and loyal secretary, Marla Curley, left a message at the West Palm office and with Judy for me to call. I was walking baby Mondy in a stroller around the West Palm Sports arena as I often did. Upon retrieving the message, Marla informed me that a sales rep was making a big deal of the fact that I was unavailable on Friday afternoons and he had a buzz going in the branch about it.

Without asking, Marla had already gathered the information on this sales rep I wanted. I was not surprised to learn that Mike Malar was 77% of budget for the 1st quarter and finished the previous year at 71%. I wondered if the 6% improvement contributed to his boldness. He worked for Steve Cowan on the GEM (government, education, and medical) team and was a key member of John Woods' inner circle. I had met Mike but didn't know much about him. We had so many performance issues that his being 77% of plan put him on the back burner; however, he had just placed himself on the griddle.

I told Marla to have Mike and Steve by the phone at 4:30 because I wanted to talk with them jointly. I dressed and traveled the half-mile to the office at 4 PM where I learned Mike had called for me several times but had chosen not to leave a message. Additionally, I had the opportunity to visit with Larry Carter for a few minutes before placing my call. Larry provided useful insight into both Mike and Steve. Before calling Miami, I called Lauderdale and learned Mike had done the same thing there.

Putting the pieces together prepared me to play hardball when I made the call. "Mike, what can I do for you?" I asked.

"Nothing."

"Nothing? Didn't you ask Marla where you could find me, and didn't you call Lauderdale and West Palm looking for me?"

"Yes, but I got it worked out."

"What was it that you got worked out that you needed me for?"

"Did you call Lauderdale and West Palm looking for Mondy?" inquired a puzzled Steve Cowan.

"Yes, but it wasn't important," Mike responded hesitantly.

Taking the words from my lips, Steve asked. "Why didn't you call me?"

"I couldn't find you, so I called Mondy," Mike said, digging himself deeper with each response.

"Well," I said. "You've got us both now. What was the issue you needed us for?"

"It was nothing big; it had to do with a presentation I am going to make to a customer and I wanted your opinion."

"Look, Mike. I'm sure your intentions are good, but you have to understand we have over a hundred sales reps in the branch and if we don't take an organized approach to their management, we'll never be able to give them the individual attention they seek and deserve. As for me, I'm willing to help every way I can, but I've got to focus my attention on the ten sales managers reporting to me. Don't misunderstand me; I want you to come to me anytime that Steve, for whatever reason, can't handle your situation. Don't you agree, Steve?"

"Absolutely. But I'm still trying to figure out why Mike needed you in the first place," Steve said, communicating clearly where he stood on the matter. "When are you going to make this presentation, anyway?"

"Wednesday morning."

"Then why did you have to find us this afternoon?" asked an annoyed Steve Cowan.

"Look," I said. "Whatever the reason was, I'm sure the presentation on Wednesday is very important and I'd like to go with you."

"Thanks, but I think it would be too much, maybe another time," offered an increasingly meek Mike Malar.

"Steve, let me make this suggestion. I don't want to tell you how to manage your team, but you may want to consider moving Mike up on the list of sales reps we are trying to help since he has demonstrated his desire to do what's right; but that's strictly your call.

Whenever you do work with Mike, I'd like to be involved or at the very least kept abreast." After a little bit of small talk we concluded the conversation.

This incident was indicative of the lack of discipline and order in the Miami branch. We would never experience success if we continued to allow the tail to wag the dog.

REUNITED

We planned the move from West Palm to Miami during the 4th of July holiday. I rented a two-bedroom suite for Judy, Mondito, and myself and kept my suite for Meme and Pa who were coming to help out with the move.

Security was high at the David William because Nicaraguan President Anastasio Somoza and his family were in Miami for one of their frequent shopping trips. Armed bodyguards in dark suits were everywhere: posted atop the hotel, at all entrances, and alongside the Somozas at all times. They communicated with one another via radio wearing ear pieces and mics, and appeared to be very serious about their responsibility.

Pop asked if I thought all the security was necessary and I told him that Caribbean dictatorships were pretty volatile, even though I knew little about the situation in Nicaragua. (Four years later, in 1979, rebel forces would cause Somoza to resign from office and leave the country. Apparently, he was a bit too light on security when he was assassinated the following year while living in Paraguay.) It felt great to be under the same roof again.

We lived in a very nice neighborhood in south Miami just off Old Cutler and King's Bay. What made the neighborhood nice were the nice neighbors, the lush vegetation, and the extensive bike paths. The area was conducive to walking and we did plenty of that. A short walk across Old Cutler put us on the Charles Deering Estate, a historic site situated on the southern part of the Biscayne Bay Aquatic Preserve and a short bike ride put us in Matheson Hammock, a wonderful park. On weekends, I would bike, with Mondito riding in a forward-mounted baby seat, to Parrott Jungle (north of our house), then pass our home on the way back to our second destination, Monkey Jungle (south of our home). The approximately twenty-five-mile trek gave Judy some time to herself, allowed Mondito to nap on the fly, and provided me with time I sought with Mondito alone. When I returned in the afternoon, the three of us would fire up the barbeque and play in the pool.

Neither Judy nor I liked being jerked away from West Palm to Miami, but as we settled in Miami it became clear to us that we were better off. For us, the cosmopolitan flair of Miami trumped the quaintness of West Palm. The only drawback was that I wasn't running the entire show in Miami as I would have been in West Palm, even though running the sales organization for such a large branch was quite challenging. Overall, things were great in south Florida.

EX-JOCK MEETS EX-ASTRONAUT

Judy's brother, Elbert, and his wife, Thelma, were visiting at the time of the Eastern Airlines Doral Open and I did the proper brother-in-law thing by offering to take him to the golf tournament. He was an avid golfer and was thrilled with the prospect of attending one of golf's premier events.

Xerox was a lead sponsor, and as such, was allotted eight VIP passes to the event. When my secretary asked John's secretary for two of the passes, we were summarily turned down citing that major account salesman, Ross Mattingly, was using them in connection with key

Dade County customers. I asked Ross and his sales manager to meet with me regarding this topic and to bring the eight passes to the meeting.

After the expected dancing (lying) it was determined that Ross (Woods' good friend) was taking his father-in-law and a few friends to the tournament. As an act of benevolence, I allocated two passes to Ross, gave three to top performing sales reps, one to a service manager and kept two for Elbert and myself.

At one of the VIP functions, former astronaut and then current Eastern Airlines Chairman and CEO Colonel Frank Borman, publicly thanked the two lead sponsors and graciously offered to return the favor if the opportunity ever presented itself. The other lead sponsor, Ryder Corp, was already doing big business with Eastern Airlines as were we, but, as is always the case in business, we both wanted more. With that in mind, I suggested lunch to Colonel Borman and he trumped my offer by asking me and Elbert to be his guest for lunch at his office followed by a tour of Eastern Airlines' facility. I explained that Elbert was visiting but that I was enthusiastic about his offer. I asked John Woods to join me and was somewhat perplexed when he declined to meet with one of our largest customers, particularly when they still presented opportunity for tremendous growth.

I expected a nice executive dining facility, but my expectations were exceeded when a first-class meal of shrimp cocktail, hearts of palm salad, sautéed black grouper, capped off with fresh berries and Cuban coffee was presented by formally-attired personnel. It was, indeed, a delightful afternoon, which included a tour led by the colonel, himself. I thanked Colonel Borman for his business and for the lunch and tour, and he assured me that Xerox had earned our position with Eastern Airlines. Colonel Borman wrote his direct phone number on the business card he handed me, and I recall being curious as to why his card only indicated his name and Eastern Airlines. The very pleasant and considerate Colonel Borman concluded our meeting by telling me to use the direct number if I ever needed his help.

As I drove the short distance to our Coral Gables office, I thought that if Elbert hadn't wanted to go to the tournament, I wouldn't have had the opportunity to meet Colonel Borman in this unique fashion.

I relayed to John how the lunch went, and curiously, he told me that I shouldn't have taken the passes from Ross. John was becoming increasingly frustrated with my approach to the business and mumbled at least once that his contacts in the Northeast Region were correct when they told him I paid too much attention to corporate matters. What that amounted to was that I was disturbing John's party in the name of business.

ORIOLES PITCHER TURNS CHARTER CAPTAIN

I was stirring up problems for those satisfied with mediocrity, and one of our poster children for mediocrity was former Baltimore Orioles right-hander, Rich Hartnett.

As is often the case with baseball players, Rich fell in love with Florida while spring training in Ft. Lauderdale as an Oriole. He loved sport fishing and found himself in the Mecca for his love. Rich became so proficient at sport fishing that at the conclusion of his

MLB career, he seamlessly transitioned into a career as a charter boat captain. Apparently, the drop in compensation from baseball to boat captain caused him to seek part-time work, thus he took a part-time sales position with Xerox. The major flaw with this scenario was that Xerox offered no part-time positions.

As we (me and the sales managers) focused on sub-performing sales reps, we eventually got to the bronze-tanned Rich Hartnett. As I tried to decipher the sales manager's explanation as to why Rich was woefully under budget, I learned that the sales manager was suffering from misplaced and unwarranted empathy. The only accurate message he provided was that Rich was well-liked. I expressed to the manager that since we did not have a *congeniality* category, we should concentrate on Rich's other qualities if he was going to improve to the level necessary to remain a Xerox employee.

"Okay, how do you want to approach this?" he inquired. The sales manager ignited my ire with the question.

"Charlie," I calmly explained. "I hope I'm wrong, but I'm getting the feeling you think Rich is my problem and you're willing to do whatever I ask to help me solve this issue." As he looked at me with a *deer in the headlights* look, I continued, "The way I see it is that any problem on your team is primarily your problem and you can look to me for assistance when you get *stuck in the mud*. It only becomes my problem when you're unable or unwilling to handle the issue. At that point, my problem is actually with you, not with the sales rep who may be faltering from a lack of management support. With that said, how do you want to proceed?" My frankness with Charlie elicited an interesting response.

"Mondy, I believe Rich is conducting his *charter fishing* business during working hours."

I must have looked dumbfounded when I asked, "Would you repeat that?" "You heard me correctly," said the embarrassed sales manager.

"I gotta be truthful with you, Charlie. I'm having a hard time focusing on what to do about Rich because I'm consumed with trying to figure out how you would allow this to happen and wondering if some form of this is happening with other sales reps on your team?"

"John (Woods) knows about this and he's apparently okay with this arrangement." "Forget John for the moment; how do you feel about the situation?" I inquired.

Responding the only way, he could, Charlie said "If I have your backing, I would confront Rich about this situation, but I can tell you as soon as he feels some heat, he'll run to John."

Charlie was correct. Within a couple of weeks, John made it a point to tell me that Rich was a skilled charter captain and if I, or any of my friends, wanted to go deep sea fishing, we couldn't do any better than with Rich.

When I asked John if he thought Rich might be doing any of fishing during working hours, he immediately responded, "No way. Why would you ask that?"

"Well, because he wears the tan of a professional golfer and he's 68% of budget?" As was often the case, John didn't like my response.

"He only fishes on the weekends and holidays," John retorted.

I was attempting to instill some discipline and accountability in this *country club atmosphere* and I was meeting with resistance at every turn. My only choices were to continue my campaign of confrontation or to allow them to crumble my resolve, even though I recognized that I was introducing anxiety into many people's lives. I was doing this without the support of my boss and fully recognized the danger in doing so if I did not have the support of region management in Dallas. I continued to press on.

SAFE HAVEN

To contend with the pressures of work—and there were many—I required a *safe haven* and that is exactly what my wife (and son) provided me at home.

To provide a *safe haven*, the provider must feel safe. Judy has always possessed a clear understanding of who she is and what is important in life. She is quite fulfilled in her family and her faith, and that fulfillment is manifested in how she lives her life. Judy learned early in life that making her husband feel important and providing a supportive home environment go a long way in contributing to a successful marriage. She is excellent at both. In addition, she is, and has always been, a selfless person doing for others. These are the traits that initially attracted me to her and which I continue to enjoy. In a nutshell, I had hit the spousal jackpot, which allowed me to concentrate on the issues at work with the utmost confidence that everything at home was being handled as it should be. Thus, I considered my home to be my *safe haven*. While my associates ran to various watering holes after work to seek comfort and relieve tensions, I simply headed home.

As I commuted home each evening, I disciplined myself to leave my business concerns in Coral Gables and transition my focus to my family where solace and comfort awaited me. As I traveled south on Le Jeune, I forced myself to discontinue any thoughts of work by the time I crossed Dixie Highway. I considered the area from Dixie Highway to Cutler Circle as the DMZ (demilitarized zone) and beyond the circle to my home as friendly territory. My personal challenge was to transition my thoughts to those of my family by the time I was leaving the DMZ, which I became very proficient at doing.

The closer I got to our home in the quietness of south Miami, the happier I got. I was always met by a loving and supportive wife and a loving son. Judy has always had the ability to place matters in their proper perspective, and as we discussed the happenings of the day, I was able to recognize that regardless of the issues with which I was dealing, the sun would again rise the following day. Her long view perspectives, coupled with her motherly instincts, provided the perfect demeanor for creating an atmosphere of peace. Judy loves to *mother* and I love to be *mothered*.

I can't emphasize enough the importance that the *safe haven* Judy provided meant to me in accomplishing my business objectives while maintaining my sanity. Throughout my career, I witnessed many of my associates dealing with family (mostly spouse) problems while at the office highlighting the blessing Judy provided me each and every day.

DOCTOR JOAQUIN DE POSADA

Just as life in New York City is different from in the rest of New York, so is life in Miami different from in the rest of Florida. A metaphor for that difference is Dr. Joaquin De Posada.

For a while, I had noticed a crowd would gather two or three days a week around lunchtime for a visiting self-help guru who was ostensibly demonstrating to the attendees how they could manage "concern areas" of their lives; things such as smoking, losing weight, sleep issues, etc. were addressed at these meetings. Private sessions could be scheduled for advanced cases or situations requiring privacy, such as issues regarding spousal relationships, boss/employee relationships, depression, anxiety, and a host of other concerns.

Dr. Joaquin utilized positive thinking as the cure for most ailments, but the Cuban immigrant doctor hypnotized his "hard to cure" clients to wellness. In lieu of an entrance fee, he accepted contributions from his group clients but had developed a fee schedule for the one-on one "hard to cure" clientele.

Dr. Joaquin was the Cuban forerunner to Dr. Phil.

"Who arranged these meetings and what do we know about this doctor?" I inquired.

No one would openly divulge who had organized these meetings, but everyone knew the doctor. He was one of our sales reps—a poor performing sales rep at that.

"You got to be bullsh*##ing me," responded Gil Aleman, the hypnotist's sales manager, to my inquiry regarding our guest self-help moderator. "That's it. I've been telling that sonuvabitch he's been spending too much time around the office and he has the 'gran huevos' to do this—he'll be on probation before he leaves the building."

It was always a prudent move to have another person present during meetings when individuals were placed on probation and I volunteered to be that person because I wanted to hear first-hand how the *doctor* would justify his position. Upon hearing of Gil's plans, several of the other sales managers offered to take my place only because they shared my motive, but I wasn't about to miss this one.

I observed the smooth operating Gil, himself a Cuban refugee, begin the process and step by step, he explained exactly what was expected of the good doctor, how his performance would be measured and, of course, the seriousness of the matter...if Joaquin could not achieve the specified goals, he would be terminated.

Dr. J (as he preferred to be called) lamely explained that his *healing* sessions at the office did not detract from his performance as a sales rep, instead, he provided the number one sales rep excuse: *a weak territory*. Gil made no attempt to resist the urge to reply, "Weak territory, you say? You'd better start hypnotizing some of your prospects or you're gonna be in the hypnosis business full-time."

"Look, Gil. Don't try to threaten me. In a couple of hours, I could have two-hundred Cubans protesting and picketing this building."

"That's it. Get the hell out of here. You're fired, and bring all the damn Cubans you want."

"I didn't say I *would* bring protesters, I said I *could* bring them."

"I heard exactly what you said, and in case you didn't hear exactly what I said, I'll say it again. Get the hell out of here. You're fired."

Among rising emotions, Dr. J cast his pre-hypnotic gaze upon me hoping I would be the voice of reason, but instead, I just gave him my best *there's nothing I can do* look.

It was well worth the time. I not only got to see the *fire in the belly* of the normally calm and collected Gil Aleman, but I was also afforded the rare opportunity to coach Gil on the benefits of never losing your cool with a subordinate.

"You're right," Gil said. "But if I had it to do over, I'd still fire the bastard."

"I'd probably do the same," I said. "Let's go to Joe's and celebrate over stone crabs." The smiling Aleman grabbed his coat and off to South Beach we went.

TURNING THE TIDE

Changing attitudes is never an easy task, but between weeding out the incorrigible and diligently working with those desiring to improve and adapt we were beginning to turn the tide. The main obstacle remained my boss. John Woods embraced the improved performance but was against our effort to instill discipline into the workforce. It was a classic case of *enjoying the music but feeling no responsibility to pay the fiddler.*

The only time it bothered me was when visitors from Dallas or Rochester commented on the distinct improvement of our sales organization and John, all of a sudden, morphed into an apologist for discipline among the workforce. He even occasionally uttered our creed, "*inspect* what you *expect*," causing eyes to roll among those who were engaged in a full-blown battle and were seeking his support when visitors were not present.

Nonetheless, life is not perfect, and you've got to work with what you have and we did, experiencing steady, though sometimes slower than expected, performance.

WHEN E. F. HUTTON SPEAKS, PEOPLE LISTEN

A few months after Charlie and I discussed the poor performance of his sales rep, former Orioles pitcher Rich Hartnett, Charlie was at his wits' end and wanted to fire Rich. He explained that Rich's performance had continued to slide, and he was certain that it was directly related to the amount of time Rich was allocating to his true love, charter fishing.

Considering that it takes nine months to a year for a sales rep to carry their own weight, it's always a professional as well as personal loss to have to fire someone who has the capability of doing the job; however, sometimes there is no alternative.

Charlie looked at me as if I was smoking dope when I asked him if he was confident that he had given Rich every opportunity to succeed. "I thought you wanted me to fire him," Charlie uttered feebly.

"Charlie, firing someone should always be the last resort and should only be used when it is determined that the individual *cannot* or *will not* do the job. I don't want anyone fired who's doing, or can be coached into doing, the job: why do you think I would want to fire Rich?"

"I just thought you did," said a confused-looking Charlie "I'll think about it some more and get back to you."

That misreading, on Charlie's part, of my attitude towards firing someone caused me to recall some counsel I had received earlier in my career and that I would receive again in days to come.

In one fashion or another, I had been told by my bosses in Tampa, in Orlando, and in New York that I should be aware that the combination of my voice (tone) and physical stature made for an intimidating communication style, especially for some who didn't know me well. One person likened it to the then-popular Wall Street firm, E. F. Hutton's TV commercial where a gathering of business executives are talking among themselves when the focus of the camera pans over to a particular businessman and all the talking at the meeting ceases and everyone turns toward this particular businessman who continues to convey his thoughts and the voice on the commercial says convincingly, "When E. F. Hutton speaks, people listen."

I was never sure if these communications were intended as a compliment or as correction, but the more I thought about it, I became convinced that it was both.

Had I unintentionally mis-communicated with others? Were some of the unpleasant *discussions* with my wife caused by this E. F. Hutton style? Surely not, I told myself; we had known each other since we were sixteen. How could she not know my true intentions, I rationalized. What about my boss? Had I contributed to the professional wedge that was developing between us? Was I a *divider*, or one who *united* people? And the people who reported to me, where they just going along with what I was preaching out of intimidation or were they buying into my philosophy?

All these questions and self-doubt came as a result of Charlie's (mis) interpretation of my attitude on firing. If I wasn't communicating effectively on something as critical as someone's career, what else was I misfiring on?

This is precisely why one has to act according to what is *right* as opposed to what is *popular*. A person should not be offended if their boss requires them to do what is *right* over what is *popular,* but requiring someone to do what is *popular* over what is *right* can be quite offensive. The key, obviously, is being <u>certain</u> about what you believe to be *right* and to communicate your point with compassion and respect.

A KINDER & GENTLER MONDY

A couple of weeks after Charlie and I had discussed Rich Hartnett, a smiling Charlie showed me a copy of a sports magazine featuring Major League Baseball Spring Training and, lo and behold, included with the article was a half-page photo of three Yankee players bone fishing off the coast of Ft. Lauderdale with none other than "former Oriole pitcher and current fishing guide and captain," Rich Hartnett. The three Yankee players were Thurman Munson, "Catfish" Hunter, and "Sweet Lou" Piniella.

"Do you think Lou will tell you on what day of the week this photo was taken?"

"I'm confident I can gain that information," I said to a smiling Charlie. "I'll get back to you."

I was surprised Lou kept a calendar, but after checking it he advised me that the fishing trip had taken place on a Thursday. All day, Thursday.

Lou explained that this captain had a *state of the art* boat and was a master at catching big fish using outriggers and kites. "We caught some animals that day. If they're out there, Captain Rich will put you on them."

"I'm looking at a schedule and I see you guys had a game that day in Vero Beach, how does that work?"

"Billy (Martin) gives us (veteran players) a day off now and then for something important like fishing or golf. It gives him an opportunity to evaluate the rookies. We use this guy a lot, Mondy. If you want to catch some nice fish, you can't do any better than using

Captain Rich. He used to pitch for the Orioles."

"Yeah, I know. When he's not fishing, I'm told he's a sales rep for Xerox."

"No kidding. How does he do for you?"

"Not as well as you described his fishing prowess, but maybe he doesn't have the time he needs to do our job."

"Uh, oh. What are you going to do?"

"I'm not sure, but my thoughts are to give him the opportunity to choose the career he thinks is better for him on a full-time basis."

With that information, Charlie decided he wanted to get someone to schedule a workday charter with Rich, then show up at the marina with the person to confront Rich and use that incident to establish cause for terminating Rich for violating the terms of the probation under which he was currently operating.

It sounded fine to me, but as a general practice, I asked Charlie to get his plan blessed by *personnel* and *legal* prior to enacting it. Again, and more importantly, I didn't want to miscommunicate with Charlie as I had before, so I asked if he was sure he had given Rich every opportunity to succeed and if Rich understood the consequences of not meeting the objectives of his probation.

"You have a copy of his probation package; are you going soft on me?"

"Not at all. I just want you to afford him (and anyone else in that situation) the same courtesy and compassion you would like if you were in the same position."

"Did you get *saved* or something? You seem to be morphing into a kinder and gentler Mondy."

Later that day, Charlie asked me to call our legal people because they said, "We were exposing the company to a lawsuit by utilizing this *entrapment* tactic as a means for catching Rich in violation his probation."

I, too, had no success with legal on this issue, but I had a viable alternative.

Over the phone, I told Charlie to scrap his plans to schedule a charter with Rich, but if he wanted to accomplish the same thing he could simply work with him on an unannounced (surprise) basis forcing Rich to either cancel a conflicting scheduled charter (for which he would have had already collected a deposit). This approach would force Rich to expose where his commitment lay.

"I love it! That's exactly what I'm going to do. I wonder why I didn't think of that."

"I was wondering the same thing."

"Forget that kinder and gentler Mondy I mentioned this morning. I like this one better anyway."

"Slow down, Charlie. Be firm, fair, and compassionate with him." "Yes, Monsignor," is how Charlie ended the conversation.

In a couple of weeks, Rich resigned from Xerox and was somewhat bitter that he could not continue on what was essentially a part-time basis.

He asked to speak to me before leaving the building at which time he told me he could only think I was the driving force in his having to leave because prior to my arrival no one was placing that much emphasis on performance.

I'm certain he did not intend his comments to be complimentary, but that's how I received them.

John Woods told me we lost a good man in losing Rich Hartnett.

NEW FRONTIER

Everyone makes mistakes. The key in dealing with mistakes is recognition and correction, ASAP. Waiting while hoping the problem will fix itself or go away causes the problem to fester and grow.

Such was the case as I embarked on crossing a new frontier within Xerox by hiring the first female sales manager in the state of Florida. A few years earlier, as sales manager in Tampa, I had hired the first female sales rep in Florida—a move that turned out to be quite successful, and I was bent on taking this idea to the next level.

Our branch population of female sales reps continued to increase, and I thought that hiring a female sales manager would bolster their effort. I've always believed that having a management team that reflected the make-up of the work force was not only the right thing, but a positive thing, as well. The concept was flawless; the execution was not.

Joan Hurley has the dubious distinction of being the first female Xerox sales manager in the state of Florida. Even though I ignored Xerox's unwritten policy of not promoting a person to manage the team they came from, I was sure that, with my help, she could overcome that obstacle. She was a top-performing sales rep and former school teacher who seemed to have it all. She was intelligent, articulate, energetic, and as a bonus, quite attractive. How could she not be successful?

Her pre-announcement to my staff and to my boss brought some suggestions of caution which I discounted as ultra-conservative from the staff and just more of the same from my boss. In retrospect, I should have heeded their caution.

Her formal announcement didn't generate the enthusiasm I had expected from our female employees, but it did generate the expected whining by those who felt they were more qualified and second guessing from the second guessers. I discounted the feedback again.

I immediately began receiving anonymous notes and memos complaining about the methods Joan employed, citing locking the door at the start of meetings (sending the message not to be late) and requiring attendees to have paper and pencil for note taking. Those complaints in and of themselves didn't bother me too much, but I was concerned when some indicated permission had to be granted prior to speaking.

My trusted and capable assistant, Marla Curley, was able to match a few of the notes with handwriting samples from our files, thus identifying a couple of the writers, one of whom was female.

I discussed these matters with Joan, and she assured me that they were a result of the team (ten men and two women) going through the process of digesting the fact that their boss was a woman. To help me better understand the situation, she suggested I visualize having a woman boss. Her suggestion did help make her point.

The complaints persisted and I was being forced to investigate the source of the smoke that was thickening. I didn't want to attend her meetings because I didn't want to give any indication that I thought there was a problem; but I had to do something. Off the record, a couple of the other sales managers gave me feedback they were hearing and it was becoming clear to me that there was a problem.

I separately summoned the two writers (including one female) identified by Marla and they were anything but shy about describing Joan's management style. They independently used the terms caustic, demeaning, and counterproductive in characterizing her management approach.

"Is there anything she's doing well?" I asked.

"It's well-known that you don't like sales reps hanging around the office. She's been able to accomplish that with little or no effort," one answered.

There was a rebellion brewing and Joan was clueless. Each time I brought up an issue, she had what she thought was an explanation.

"I'm sure it's inaccurate, but there's a rumor that permission has to be granted prior to speaking in your meetings."

"I thought we didn't manage to rumors," she responded, much as a teacher would to a third grader who was breaking a class rule. Her peering eyes and haughty tone provided an unintended example of what people were complaining about.

"That's sort of true. But we have to determine if the rumor is accurate or not. If it is, the rumor becomes an issue and we definitely manage to issues."

I was taken aback by her explanation that requiring the reps to gain permission resulted in meeting efficiency. Her experience as a third-grade teacher had trumped whatever common sense she possessed.

"Joan, if you had my job would you conduct meetings in that same manner?"

"*Probably* not. The sales managers are more sophisticated than that group of babies I have."

That response brought everything into focus. She lacked empathy and respect. That's equivalent to competing in the 100-meter dash with ski boots.

"Joan, do you know that two of your sales reps have children who are older than you?"

"No. And what's that got to do with the price of coffee in Little Havana?" she snapped.

She was actually utilizing my *rapid-fire technique* (and a line I sometimes used) to demonstrate her ability to deal with the strong-minded members of her team. After all, she had witnessed them professionally confound her predecessor contributing to why the sales manager position was open in the first place. She wasn't about to let that happen to her. Her motive was understandable—her method was not.

"A major component of the price of coffee in Little Havana has to do with the way the coffee-drinking clientele is treated. If they're not valued and respected, they'll go elsewhere for their coffee. Do you understand where I'm going with this?"

"I feel trapped. If I don't discipline them, they'll run over me like they did Oscar, (previous manager) and if I do, I'm considered the wicked witch."

"Joan, there's middle ground between those two extremes, and that's your challenge, to find the spot where mutual respect and productivity can coexist and then flourish. Let's work on coexisting first."

Joan tried and tried, but at the end of the day she couldn't make the leap. When pushed, instead of using finesse, she pushed back harder using the *velvet hammer* to crush her adversary. The power of the velvet hammer is in never using it. Your subordinate knows you have it and never knows how or when you might use it, but the moment you do use it, it mysteriously turns to Jell-O.

The whole ordeal lasted nine months, and for the last five of them I knew it wasn't going to work even though I wanted it to. In that, I allowed my heart to manage my brain; not a good idea in business. My failure to take appropriate action caused unnecessary grief for all concerned.

Joan was reassigned to a sales rep position but was unable to restore her self-image and subsequently left the company. If I had done a better job of vetting Joan, I would have discovered her propensity to over control situations and engage in unwarranted conflict which would have motivated me to go another direction.

Lesson learned. New Frontiers can be treacherous; chances for treachery increase when preparation is incomplete.

GENTLE BREEZES OF SOUTH MIAMI

Back at the homestead, things were great with the exception that Friday evenings took too long to arrive and Mondays arrived too soon. We either cooked out or went to a number of great restaurants in South Miami, including my favorite that served *pargo ala Russa* (snapper Russian style). Either way, the evenings were centered on Mondito. He behaved reasonably well but preferred cooking out because that included pool time, which he loved. Additionally, it often included Frank and Mari, who he also loved.

Saturday mornings were generally occupied by bike trips to Parrot Jungle (eight miles one way) by way of Matheson Hammock, or to Monkey Jungle (twelve miles one way) the opposite way, and sometimes both. After napping, Mondito generally arose smiling in search of his bathing suit.

Frank prided himself on being a good cook and I generally assisted his efforts in preparing pork legs and ribs, Italian sausage, and big, thick Porterhouse steaks. As an alternative to grilling, we would prepare tasty Italian dishes indoors. When in season, we capped-off our meals with fresh strawberry shakes and/or shortcakes from a stand not far from the house. Within short order, the Venezias bought a home near ours and the frequency of the get-togethers increased.

We hosted a steady stream of family and friends headed by repeat (and always welcome) visits from Uncle Vince and Aunt Louisa, Nana and Grandpa, and Meme and Pa.

As previously mentioned, Judy had developed (in my opinion, by observing her mother) a genuine desire to make things at home extremely pleasant for me, resulting in a refreshed soldier reporting for duty on Monday mornings and a soldier always eager to return to base camp. The key components Judy utilizes in accomplishing her mission are respect, listening, and edification, all under the umbrella of love. An environment in which you are respected, where your concerns are attentively listened to and where you are edified, all accomplished in an atmosphere of love makes for a place you will yearn for.

Since we were wed in 1970, I've always loved going home and being home, and I thoroughly enjoy being home today. I don't take that blessing for granted and I continually remind myself that it wasn't always the case. Just as importantly, I realize that I play an equally important role in providing that same safe haven I revere for Judy and our children.

My job required occasional overnight travel and I was always raring to return to the gentle breezes of South Miami. I often wondered what must have been going on in some of my contemporaries' homes to warrant them getting to out of town meetings a day early, stay an additional day, or both. I could only surmise that *gentle breezes* didn't flow in their homes.

As an example, because the Miami Branch led the region in sales for the 3rd Quarter of 1975, I was awarded a weekend trip to Dallas for fun and frolic that included a Cowboys football game as the guest of Southern Region Vice President and General Manager, John Ogletree.

I liked John very much and he knew it, but as soon as it was evident that Miami was going to win the contest, I began trying to figure out how I was going to decline the trip without offending John. Judy thought it was *politically correct* for me to go. She was right, but I didn't want to go without her and Mondito. With that in mind, I asked John Ogletree if it would be okay if John Woods (my boss) went in my place because I didn't want to leave Judy with our six-month old with colic (the colic had been gone for a couple of months, but it sounded good). Ogletree offered to fly Judy's parents in from Tampa to help with Mondito, but I told him I wanted to be around for my sleep-deprived wife.

John Woods appreciated me suggesting to John Ogletree that he go in my stead and he loved the weekend. He left a day early and stayed an extra day. The Sunday afternoon of the Cowboys game, I was at the Orange Bowl with Gil Aleman and his wife's uncle, Alberto, watching the Dolphins beat the Raiders. When I got home, Judy told me that Mondito had slept like a baby. The Venezias came over; we fired up the grill and played with Mondito in the pool as we witnessed the Porterhouses go Pittsburg.

The next time I spoke with John Ogletree, he told me that his wife said to tell me that giving up a chance to see the Cowboys play to stay home and help Judy with the new baby suffering with colic was simply the sweetest thing she'd ever heard. Now, ain't I sweet.

LEARNING TO WIN

We not only won the 3rd Quarter, but we won the 2nd Half of 1975 and we were developing momentum to carry us into 1976.

We had suffered several casualties, some of which were previously noted, but you don't get better by ridding yourself of sub-performers if you don't replace them with better performers, and hopefully much better ones.

Such was the case for us. In sales, it is not uncommon for current salespeople to recommend candidates for hire. After all, who knows better what the job entails? We even offered a finder's fee if we hired someone they recommended. We had to be cautious, because some were recommending multiple candidates to increase their odds of getting a finder's fee. If there is a weak spot in your plan, a salesman will find (exploit) it.

Nonetheless, good performers were recommending good candidates and it became evident that those who were not at or above budget were vulnerable. Many of those who were struggling began to seek help while others resigned before being asked to. The credit for this rebirth has to be put on the sales managers. They were learning to win, and they liked the feeling.

The once mild-mannered Cuban-born Gil Aleman was emerging as the leader of the group. He was becoming adept at anticipating what to do and he was committed to doing what was right at all times. A. J. Moore, Xerox's first black sales manager in Florida, was improving at a rapid pace. He was just like Gil, except he asked more questions before taking action, the correct thing to do until you're absolutely sure of what it is you're doing. It wouldn't be long before A. J. was able to fly solo. I was hoping more of the managers would improve at the pace of Gil and A. J., but at least they were headed in the correct direction. There was one exception, Tom Mangano in Ft. Lauderdale.

Tom was the sales manager who, on the first day I met him, warned me about trusting Larry Carter, the sales manager in Palm Beach, who later that day issued the same warning about Tom. Larry was right. Tom was a conniver, a liar, and a divider but until those traits were exposed, he was quite charming and border-line charismatic. I, however, was on to him early in the relationship.

One of the benefits of growing up in West Tampa was being exposed to many characters like Tom; so many that I was able to spot them almost immediately and I still can. In West Tampa, this type of phony was referred to as a *raton-suco*, translated as *sweet-rat*. Tom always vocalized a positive and team-oriented approach, but his deeds did not follow. He'd been brought to Ft. Lauderdale from Long Island by John Woods, and because of that, he considered himself untouchable. He always blamed the mail when late with reports or claimed that a communication had not reached him when he was not prepared to discuss an item. I had Marla keep track of items sent to him in two categories: with his paycheck or expense reimbursement check and without. 100% of the time he received mail overnight when a check accompanied the mail, compared to under 40% when there was no check. There are coincidences, and then there are facts.

WHAT HAVE YOU DONE FOR ME LATELY?

In 1974, the Miami Branch was tied with Houston for dead-last among the twenty-four branches of the Southern Region. A new branch manager was placed in Houston and I was placed in Palm Beach, then Miami. Region management was serious about turning around the performances of two of their largest branches.

If Class 1 branches like Dallas, Atlanta, Miami, and Houston didn't make plan, the region couldn't make plan. Smaller Class 2 and 3 branches like Albuquerque, Knoxville, Orlando, and Jackson simply couldn't make up the shortfall of the Class 1 branches. As was often said in region meetings, Class 1 branches steer the region ship.

In 1975, after a poor start, we managed to scratch out an 11th place standing and 2nd among Class 1 branches behind Atlanta, which was 5th overall. (I was very proud of my brother Gene who managed the top sales team in Atlanta.) The important aspect of our performance was that we were at an *on-plan* rate for the last five months of the year.

Theoretically, we would make plan in 1976 **if** we could maintain that rate. (And, if pigs had wings, they might fly).

During 1976, corporate management decided to split Class 1 branches, when feasible, in an attempt to reduce these behemoths to a more manageable size. It was an expensive enterprise considering the additional manpower required.

The logical split for Miami was at the Dade/Broward County Line. I assumed I would be given the Ft. Lauderdale/Palm Beach Branch and John Woods would keep Miami. It didn't make any difference to me except that I was not looking forward to moving again and I was certain Judy would not cherish the idea either.

Dallas, a chronic under-performer, was the first to be split, then its cousin to the south, Houston, the then-current Class 1 problem child since Miami had extricated itself from that dubious distinction. Later that year, Atlanta was split and I was confident that Miami was next.

Class 1 splitting was going on all over the country, leaving Washington D.C. Commercial (The Federal Branch was recognized as a different animal and was always a separate branch) and Miami as the two largest branches in the country and the obvious choices for the next splits; but it never happened.

I was disappointed and made my feelings known to region management when they inquired. John Ogletree assured me that he was working on something for me that I would like—whatever that meant. I was only disappointed because the sales managers and I were doing the heavy lifting and we were sharing the benefits with someone who not only didn't help but was a hindrance. I had recognized long before that having a supporting and capable boss was a bonus, and if I was going to be successful, I would have to do so with or without my boss's assistance.

In spite of remaining a low-performing behemoth, the Miami Branch was improving month-by-month without looking back. The sales managers accepted the fact that past performance, good or bad, was of no consequence to the job at hand, it was all about **now**, or as we referred to it, *What have you done for me lately*? Our people got caught up in winning and it was contagious. The competition between the sales teams was healthy and contributed to our success. It was nice to see that a considerable number of our top performers were old hands who hadn't performed particularly well before but were now flourishing in the new environment. We finished the year 5th overall and 1st among Class 1 branches which were being measured on a *pre- and post-split* basis for 1976. Gene was again the top sales manager in Atlanta.

FINE-TUNING

The only flaw in our 1976 performance was that the Ft. Lauderdale team was lagging and should not have been.

Ft. Lauderdale was as fertile a business climate as existed in the whole country and sales manager, Tom Mangano, was consistently the bottom sales manager and was unable to break above 85% on a year-to-date basis. In the *bitch and moan* category, however, he led the branch.

At a sales managers meeting to discuss plans and budgets for 1977, I stated the obvious when I said that in order for 1977 to be a success, all teams would have to be 100% or better and that I expected each sales manager to communicate that message to their team requiring each sales rep to be at 100% or better for their team to consider the year a success. Furthermore, I promised to spend most of my time with the lower performing teams in an effort to accomplish this goal. The managers of the top performing teams immediately began clapping and cheering. Tom's body language indicated his disdain for the plan.

I began sporadically visiting Ft. Lauderdale unannounced, which is generally an indicator of a trust gap. As expected, Tom was unappreciative of my visits and asked if I was trying to catch him doing something wrong.

"Quite the contrary," I responded. "If you'll let me, I'm trying to catch you doing something right."

In character, John Woods questioned me as to why I was working with Tom so often. I wondered if he thought I had an additional reason for wanting to be in Ft. Lauderdale and in order to quell any such thoughts, I invited him to join me when his schedule permitted. I was confident he would not take me up on my offer and I was correct.

Tom knew what had to be done and he knew how to do it; he had to humble himself, dine on some crow, and adopt a positive and disciplined approach, all of which were difficult for him in my absence. These are the toughest of cases because they are not skill- or activity-related; they are attitude- (DNA-) related. As the saying goes: A leopard cannot change his spots nor a tiger his stripes.

My other fine-tuning project was a totally different issue. Steve Collins' team's sales performance was always at or near the top, but administratively they were atrocious. By definition, this should be an easy situation to remedy. The branch administrative manager, Tony LaRocca, was constantly complaining to me about Steve's team's lack of concern regarding the administrative aspect of the job, and rightfully so. He presented example after example of documents that were incomplete, illegible, contained errors, or some combination thereof in support of his case.

He was correct, but I couldn't focus on that issue at the time because there was, simply, a bigger fish to fry. I explained to him that he couldn't expect me to walk away from the open heart surgery with which I was involved to deal with the hangnail he was bringing to my attention. It was understandable that Tony took no solace in my response, but I had no choice. I offered to pay for any overtime related to this issue until I could get to it. He reluctantly agreed and I jumped on it at the first opportunity.

Steve was Type A and as hyper as they come. As he arrived five minutes early for our 6 PM meeting, I told him to sit and that I would be with him in a moment. Seconds later, he asked if he could make a call while I finished reading. I told him to wait; it wouldn't be much longer. Sixty seconds later, he said his call would only take a few minutes. Again, I told him to keep his seat. He adjusted himself in his seat, wrote something in his planner, checked his wallet, and again adjusted himself, all the time staring at me while I was reading. After a few minutes, I asked, "Do you know why we're meeting?" "Should I?" he retorted.

I explained how pleased I was with his team's sales performance and the contribution they continued to make towards the branch's marked improvement. I went on to say that his team was accomplishing the difficult part of their assignment but was falling short on the easy part, namely their paperwork.

"Your team's administrative ineptitude is causing havoc for the branch administrators and is negatively impacting their performance."

"You've got to be kidding me. You called me here because my guys send in orders with the wrong zip code? Come on, Mondy, don't we have more important things to do?"

I was astonished that he had no concern for the administrators and that he felt as if I was wasting his time discussing the matter.

"Did you feel like I was wasting your time when you first got here?" I asked.

"I think I could have been more productive than watching you read," he responded, continuing to wonder why I was focusing on this minutia.

"I agree, and the admin people feel the same way. They feel their time is not valued when they're required to look up zip codes and correct other errors just because the sales reps don't take the time to provide the correct info in the first place, kind of how you felt watching me read."

"Isn't that what admin is here for, to process our paperwork?"

"*Process* is accurate, but they are not here to clean up after us. Think about it. What could they accomplish if all 111 sales reps burdened them with unnecessary clerical errors? Steve, let's keep this in perspective; 98% of the job is selling and you guys are doing a fine job. We're talking about *crossing t's* and *dotting i's*. I think you'll agree that sales reps on other teams aren't necessarily brighter than yours, so it becomes a matter of management emphasis. Your team is not giving this matter much attention because they don't see it as a priority, and they don't see it as a priority because, as you expressed earlier, you don't. I've apparently done a poor job of communicating to you why it's important, and that is why we're meeting. I want you to make administrative performance an important part of how you evaluate your people, as I will be doing in your evaluation. We all have things we consider more important than paperwork, so management attention is how I see this situation improving. I'm going to give it attention and I'm counting on you doing the same. Do we understand each other?"

"Yeah, but let me ask a question. You seem to function fine administratively. What's your secret?"

In response, I reached into my desk drawer and pulled out my Norelco mini-cassette recorder, encased in its black leather pouch, and showed it to Steve who simultaneously jumped out of his seat and frantically backed away from me as if I had pointed a .44 magnum at his face.

"Don't start telling me I've got to receive Jesus," said a startled and confused Steve Collins.

I unzipped the case and slowly pulled the recorder out with my thumb and index finger and I could see Steve begin to regain his composure as he recognized what I had intended to show him.

"Whoa, I thought that was a Bible and that you we're going to tell me I had to be saved. A couple of friends are using the Bible on me and I guess I'm a little rattled; I thought your recorder was a Bible. They're telling me that if I don't receive Jesus as my personal savior, I'm doomed to eternal damnation; they use John 3:16-17 to make their case."

"Let me summarize my case. If you don't get your team to pay attention administratively, I'm going to provide you a preview of what eternal damnation will be like. Are we clear on this matter?"

"We're clear, but I can't believe I'm telling you something that has eternal implications and you're still focused on administration," Steve uttered as he exited.

JOKE TO JEWEL

1976 was an outstanding year for our branch and our success transformed what used to be drudgery into fun. The Southern Region Boss of Bosses, John Ogletree, told the senior management team over dinner one evening that what used to be referred to as *The Joke in the Caribbean* was now referred to as *the Jewel of the Caribbean*.

However, not everyone was contributing to the sheen of this newly-named jewel.

CONFLICT OF INTEREST

Vito Cagnina relocated from New York to Miami—not exactly an uncommon occurrence. He opened a copy shop and ordered two high-volume Xerox duplicators and four mid-range copiers and our salesman and sales manager were ecstatic. Their bliss was curtailed when Vito's equipment order failed Xerox's credit check. Vito didn't have bad credit, he suffered from insufficient credit. Then things got interesting.

After a couple of weeks of wrangling, Mr. Cagnina's company, Biscayne Copy Center, purchased a $25,000 surety bond guaranteeing payment to Xerox up to that amount. The plan was that after six months of on-time payments, Biscayne's surety bond would no longer be required. The bond barely made Biscayne Copy Center a reasonable credit risk, thus, our administrative manager placed Biscayne on our watch list, which included accounts that were considered suspect for a variety of reasons.

Tony, our admin manager, was a cross between Attila the Hun and Sherlock Holmes when it came to late payments. He was in my office with Biscayne's file when they were two days late recommending that we disable their Xerox equipment until payment was received. That was a pretty harsh recommendation considering that Biscayne was in the retail copy business. "Can you visualize what that would do to them if we disabled their equipment?" I posed to Tony.

"Yeah, reaching for their checkbook and writing us a check," Tony responded.

"Have someone call Vito and tell him we'll have to disable his equipment if his bill isn't paid in full by Friday."

"I'll do it, but we're just giving this clown three more days of free service. He's not intending to pay us; he's a scam artist."

"Why did we credit approve him if you felt that way?"

"Because the boss ordered me to."

I learned at that moment that loyalty was not one of Tony's attributes. This knowledge would be critical in dealing with future events.

"Why would John do that?"

"In my opinion, Vito is more than one of our customers to him. For one thing, when Biscayne calls for service, John somehow knows about it and he directs our service dispatcher to send the service tech to them before customers who are already scheduled."

"Whatta you make of that?"

"Everything in the kitchen isn't kosher."

Concurrent with that bit of info, the account rep for Eastern Air Lines (EAL) was bemoaning the fact that his customer informed him that they would soon be cancelling a couple of duplicators because the volume of reproductions previously done on the equipment would now be done by none other than Biscayne Copy Center. A week later, the number of duplicators EAL was cancelling was up to four.

My first thought was, how did Vito, who had been in business for just over five months, convince one of our major accounts to make such a drastic decision?

I told the sales manager to visit with the decision maker(s) and to give me a written report on how this could happen without his and the account rep's knowledge.

"If it turns out Vito's that persuasive," I told him, "I'm going to offer him a position."

Then things got *very* interesting. The sales manager told me that his visit at EAL revealed some critical information but that it wasn't the kind of information he thought should be put it in writing. I told him I would help him with that decision after hearing what he learned.

It was clear why Steve didn't want to memorialize his visit at EAL, but I didn't give him another option. I trusted Steve, but general consensus was that he was less than stable and I wasn't about to risk him later developing amnesia or another version of what he told me that day, so I told him to dictate the entire account of what he had just told me to my secretary and to come back the next day to review the typed copy for accuracy and for his signature. Recognizing that he was without a choice, he reluctantly did so. Because of the seriousness of the information contained in his report, I explained to him that I would allow him to choose two persons in our office in addition to my secretary to witness his voluntary signature (but not the content) affixed to the document.

If what Steve reported was accurate, John Woods had made a career-changing decision when he introduced Vito Cagnina of Biscayne Copy Center to several executives within EAL for the expressed purpose of suggesting that the executives allow Vito the opportunity to study their current reprographic methods and make recommendations to improve the management of EAL's reprographic requirements. What John brought Vito into EAL to do was, of course, the job description of the Xerox account rep.

Meanwhile, Colonel Frank Borman, EAL's Chairman and CEO, had written me a letter asking me to speak to the student body of an inner-city school his company had adopted for the purpose of exposing kids to American industry who'd had limited exposure.

I called the colonel and suggested we have lunch somewhere on Calle Ocho, but as I anticipated, he turned the offer around and asked me to join him at EAL's executive dining room. I was beginning to think he was uncomfortable with the "Little Havana" area of Miami.

After agreeing to speak to EAL's adopted school, I told Colonel Borman that a Xerox employee had uncovered an internal situation that appeared to be less than kosher, and because the situation involved EAL, I wanted to bring the matter to his attention and perhaps gain his opinion without displaying either company's dirty laundry. Unbeknownst to me, he was dealing with some serious suspicions of fraud involving employees at EAL's Miami, Newark, and Philadelphia airports as it turned out, and thus, he was quite interested in the matter to which I referred. I presented him with a redacted copy of Steve's report as I explained why I could not leave a copy as it was an internal document, and more importantly, that I had no way of knowing if the references to EAL executives were accurate.

He took some notes and said he would call in a week or so. When Colonel Borman called back, he suggested we meet in his office.

At our meeting, he introduced me to a private investigator whose services he had engaged on the matter I'd brought to his attention eight days earlier. The former Ft. Lauderdale detective started his report by saying that John Woods, Vito Cagnina, and Gary Brownstein (an EAL executive) were members of the same south Miami tennis club. (I found the information interesting, but was surprised that the Colonel hadn't shared that with me over the phone.)

Then I learned why he'd called the meeting. The P. I. then said that Vito Cagnina was married to John Woods' sister and that John Woods and Gary Brownstein were silent partners in Biscayne Partners, a Delaware-incorporated company licensed to conduct business in the State of Florida under the name of Biscayne Copy Centers and whose president was Vito Cagnina.

When asked how this information could be verified, the P. I. provided a package of information containing documents related to the alleged business connections.

Colonel Borman suggested that we coordinate our meetings with John Woods and Gary Brownstein so that they would be unable to develop a strategy. I was impressed with the Colonel's swift reaction to this matter and to his suggestion of a coordinated effort. I told him I had to discuss this matter with my boss in Dallas and that I was certain our legal department would be involved in some way.

Colonel Borman said he wouldn't do anything until I called him.

DIFFICULT CIRCUMSTANCES

Reporting this matter to Southern Region Headquarters in Dallas was clearly the correct thing to do and not doing it would have been an abdication of my professional responsibility, however, actually doing it was more difficult than I anticipated. What made the situation particularly uncomfortable for me was that I was (very) interested in the position that I assumed would become available as a result of the information I was reporting. Regardless, I had no choice in the matter. I had been exposed to similar scenarios while in Rochester and knew that once this info was verified, John Woods' days with Xerox in Miami would be few, and I was correct.

John Ogletree and henchman Dave Holland immediately boarded a plane for Miami and asked me to bring the affected sales manager and sales rep to a meeting away from our office to discuss the matter. They brought the region's top lawyer with them and the six of us met at the Royal Sonesta Hotel on Key Biscayne.

As good as John Ogletree was at putting a good face on almost any situation, he fell short on doing so for this one. The sales manager and sales rep were extremely tense as we were called up to John Ogletree's suite. As we rode the elevator, I attempted to put them at ease by telling them that the only thing they were required to do was to relay the truth. They nodded affirmatively, but that did not put them at ease.

John Ogletree shook everyone's hand, acknowledged that this was a difficult situation for all involved and proceeded to explain the agenda. "Sometimes things are different from how they appear, so we want to make certain we understand this situation so we can be in the best position to rectify what needs rectifying. To make sure we get it right, we've engaged the services of a (court) stenographer."

That comment brought a look of surprise to the faces of the sales manager and sales rep as they looked toward me as if saying, "You didn't say anything about a stenographer." I was somewhat surprised as well, but I actually thought it was a good idea to get everyone's comments on paper. I had already run the sales manager through a similar exercise when I had him dictate his account to my secretary and sign it in front of two witnesses of his choosing. That fact gave me comfort that at least his story wouldn't vary from what he told me earlier. His account was part of the package I sent to Dallas and I was confident that he knew that.

After interrogating each of them alone for about forty-five minutes, they were dismissed, leaving me to answer questions posed by the *"Dallas Mafia."* My session was short and painless.

Dave Holland suggested we have dinner alone while John Ogletree and the lawyer fine-tuned their strategy.

Over dinner, Dave did a poor job of disguising his attempt to gauge my interest in a branch manager's position in Albuquerque or Jackson. I, on the other hand, made no attempt to disguise my disinterest in relocating to either New Mexico or Mississippi.

"Are you telling me you're not interested in any branch outside of Florida?" asked Dave, disgruntled.

"I don't want to put it that way but that's about what it comes down to, and while we're placing all of our cards on the table, I'm not very interested in Jacksonville. Dave, this may sound weird to you, but I would prefer to manage a branch in New York City or Boston than anywhere in the Southern Region other than Miami or Tampa, in that order. Remember, I was considering managing the Mid-town Manhattan Branch when John Ogletree convinced me to take the West Palm job anticipating it would become a branch in 1975."

"Yeah, yeah, yeah, I remember all that, but circumstances change and we have to be flexible. We don't like to put people in Class 1 branches without previous branch manager's experience and the Tampa branch manager just got the job."

"When you say *we*, are you referring to yourself and John Ogletree, because I think John O would consider making an exception in this case."

"That's pretty damn presumptuous of you, and even if you're correct, you're aware that Rochester is very much against the idea based on history."

"If by Rochester you mean Higgins, Reiser, and-or Kearns, I believe they would be okay with it, as well."

"Presumptuous is an understatement; you're downright arrogant."

"I'm not arrogant; I just understand what this branch needs, and I know I'm the guy for the job. You recall that in 1974, Miami was tied with Houston for dead last and in 1976 we were the top Class One branch and 5th overall. We don't believe in coincidences, and our performance this year supports our belief. Dave, it has been my observation that branches that are able to do well in sales get into trouble when management allows salespeople to run roughshod over service and administrative personnel. I don't allow that to happen now, nor would I as branch manager."

"You're pushing hard for something that could be your undoing. What happens if things turn south in Miami?"

"The same that would happen in Albuquerque, Jackson, or Manhattan."

ASTUTE MOVE

When a credible person wants to convince me of something, I listen to what they have to say, and depending on the facts and how well they articulate their position, I form my decision. I don't respond well to people putting or attempting to put pressure on me. Doing so actually works against their cause. Conversely, I generally don't intend to pressure others for the same reasons, though I recognize my natural demeanor can sometimes be perceived as pressure. There is obviously a fine line between convincing and pressure.

With that said, I purposely did not mention my desires to John O during his visit, though I was confident that Dave would and I was sure Ogletree would not be surprised in the least.

One week later, I was summoned to meet with Dave Holland and John O in Dallas. I was pleased to be appointed Miami Branch Manager even though my appointment meant John Woods' unceremonious departure.

During my thirty-hour round-trip to Texas, Tom Mangano, the underperforming sales manager in Ft. Lauderdale, submitted his request for physical and emotional disability. John Woods, who was still technically in charge, approved the bogus request, thus saving Tom's bacon.

Before boarding my return flight, my confidant and yet-to-be-named replacement, Gil Aleman, advised me of Tom's disability request, adding, "You've got to admit, it is a pretty astute move."

He was correct.

CAN'T GET NO SATISFACTION

Things couldn't be better for me. If you would have told me when I was a student at Jesuit High school in Tampa, Florida that at age thirty-two I would be married to the finest person I've ever known, would be the father of a wonderful two-year-old son and expecting our second child, would be the top dog at one of the largest field operations of a Fortune 100 company and living large in South Florida, I would have had no alternative but to have you committed to a treatment facility under the Federal Baker Act statute. How could this be, and what did I do to deserve this wonderful life?

The home front was flawless. My caring and thoughtful wife had graduated to wife, mother, and expectant mother and was handling this challenging task like the champion she is. She was made for her situation. She always wanted to be a loving and caring wife and mother, and she was a perennial MVP at both. Judy was happy for me that I had a position that challenged my ambition and satisfied my ego, and I was happy for her because she was in the exact position she desired. We've always cherished each other's company, and having a child with another on the way made our time together more precious. I often had to pinch myself to ensure that I wasn't dreaming.

In 1977, Judy and I had been married six-plus years, and as indication of my localized naïveté, I was just beginning to realize what a special person I had for a spouse. It was not that I hadn't realized she was special (that's what attracted me in the first place); it was that I was operating under the false assumption that most men enjoyed a similar situation. I was naïve, indeed. People frequently took the liberty of making me aware of their spousal problems and I was beginning to realize that my situation was, indeed, special. That realization added to my marital euphoria.

I was learning that a major obstacle for many people wasn't competition in the marketplace, but discord in the home. To state that not having to deal with discord at home was a distinct advantage would be a gross understatement. However, I recognized that some became adept in dealing with the problem by simply shutting it out (compartmentalizing the issue) while on the job. The problem with that tactic is that the issue is waiting for you when you get home and probably has festered, thus lending happy hour the faux attractiveness it enjoys. Interestingly, the main complaint I received (directly and indirectly) from employees was that I never joined them for drinks at happy hour.

My personal life continued to be great, and my already good professional life improved significantly with the promotion of Gilberto Aleman to Branch Sales Manager (my previous position). The move was welcomed by all, and I'm confident that some—if not all—of the sales managers preferred working for Gil. Over the previous two years, Gil managed to maintain a healthy level of empathy and developed the required professional toughness his previous management did not support. His ability to deal with the non-stop issues of the sales organization gave me great latitude in focusing my attention on the service and administrative components of the business. For the first time since arriving in Miami, I enjoyed the luxury of some free time.

Over the next few months, I was able to enjoy the finer aspects of management. I was able to transition into a benevolent executive bestowing congratulations and platitudes when warranted, leaving the heavy lifting to my capable staff. Additionally, I was occasionally able to leave home a little later and leave the office a little earlier, as well. Those prerogatives allowed me to work a sensible schedule as opposed to what I had been working.

With things in my life going so well, I wondered why I didn't feel satisfied. I had everything I wanted and nothing to complain about. I was happy, yet I wasn't peaceful; I couldn't *get no satisfaction*. Did Mick Jagger know something I didn't? I found the situation puzzling, if not strange.

AN OFFER I WAS REFUSED

Then, out of the blue, I received a call from Malio who made me an offer worth considering. Essentially, his restaurant, Malio's Steak House, was growing leaps and bounds and he needed help in managing the enterprise. He said that if I would provide that help, he would compensate me with a 50% ownership stake and we would split everything going forward evenly. Could this opportunity provide the *satisfaction* I was seeking?

The *prima facie* attraction was moving back to Tampa and ending the moving carousel that had become a part of our life. Though moving had heretofore been exciting and educational, with one child on the ground and one on its way, Judy and I correctly assumed that the excitement and education would transition to chaos and increased challenges in raising a family. Additionally, having my own business was a very attractive idea to me as I had often dreamed of not answering to a boss, and having a 50/50 partner would be a step in that direction. A negative I had to consider was the restaurant hours and the bar/lounge component that was a large piece of Malio's business. I have always felt more comfortable at home, and with two children and a wife who was my favorite person to be with, the thought of spending late hours away from them was unattractive.

Judy was always supportive of my career aspirations, and though she wasn't thrilled with the idea, she supported my choice to make this significant change as she, I later discovered, had taken the matter to the Lord in prayer. So, off to Tampa I went to consummate the deal while she remained in Miami, pregnant and caring for Mondy III and praying that this business trip would be unsuccessful.

Much of my business career had exposed me to fine restaurants across the country and I was eager to inject some of my ideas into the premier restaurant scene in my hometown. Malio shared my excitement. He was his normal ebullient self, and by the time we reached the lawyer's office to close the deal I was stoked and ready to help take this very successful soon-to-be two-family restaurant to the next level and beyond.

As we entered the conference room of one of Tampa's most prestigious law firms; Gibbons, Tucker, Miller, et al; we were greeted by the shy, but able, Brad Miller who had been Malio's lawyer for a long time. Brad informed me that until this deal was consummated, he was representing Malio's Inc. and Malio personally, and asked me to sign a document memorializing that I was informed of that fact and that I agreed to proceed without representation. I signed the document and listened to Brad outline the deal as he believed Malio explained it to him. I responded that I agreed to what he said in principle, but that a couple of items required further explanation. Most of the table was covered with documents Brad intended to explain to us and that we were to sign indicating our agreement.

I had both practical and legal questions for the first three sets of documents. Malio had none. I noticed Malio turning serious from his usual jovial self and attributed it to the seriousness of the matter. I had additional questions for the subsequent two sets, again Malio had none. Things got really quiet and I figured that either Malio's questions were the same as mine or that Brad had previously explained the items to him in greater detail.

On my next question, Malio asked Brad if they could leave the room to speak which I found awkward. Upon returning, Brad—not Malio—informed me, with Malio present, that Malio did not want to proceed; translated, the deal was off. Needless to say, I was shocked and asked the obvious question, "Why"? Brad and I both looked to Malio, and he responded, "I kept listening to the questions you were asking Brad and I pictured you being my boss in a few years, and I can't work with a boss so I can't do the deal. I'm sorry I put you through this, but I just can't have a boss and I know in time you'll be my boss."

I had no response except to ask Malio if he was sure, and if I'd asked anything in particular that gave him concern. He said I had asked the right questions and that's what made him feel I would be his future boss. With that, Brad left the room and Malio repeated what he had just said a couple of minutes earlier, adding that he loved me and that he hated for this to turn out this way but he had no choice. We tearfully embraced and headed for the restaurant to eat before he took me to the airport. I'm sure the food was good, but it was a weird evening. As I look back, Malio's decision was one of the greatest blessings I have experienced, and I've had many—he may feel the same way.

Off to Miami I went to my loving and praying wife and family, back to managing the Miami Branch, one of the most coveted positions within Xerox Corporation.

DON JUAN TO DON BOSCO

Barry Nickerson had it all. The West Point graduate and former football player's career was advancing at a rapid pace and his future was limitless. He was married to his high school sweetheart and beauty queen and they were parents to three healthy children. The Nickersons lived in one of Dallas' upscale suburbs and were involved in the social and arts scenes in the Dallas/Ft. Worth Metroplex. Their life was a story waiting to be written.

The 6-foot 2-inch Barry knew his good looks and articulate manner made him attractive in and out of the business arena and he took full advantage of the fact. Unlike other staff (ffats spelled backwards) personnel, he was always welcome to visit the Miami Branch. Miami was his hometown, and he loved returning and joining us for dinners at the various Cuban restaurants, and of course, Joe's Stone Crab. He could always justify visiting our branch because of its sheer size and importance to the Southern Region and we made it easier for him by requesting his assistance. Gil Aleman loved playing competitive tennis with Barry and relished utilizing Barry's talents with his sales managers. Because Barry's methods produced results, his services were always in demand. It was a match made in Xerox heaven.

The virile and energetic dynamo we called Barry was also a *Don Juan*. After tennis and/or dinning with us, his night was just beginning. He would change into his disco attire and into the hearty Miami nightlife he would charge. I would gauge his previous night's success by whether or not he would have my assistant send roses to his newly-made acquaintance. I kidded the bloodshot (eyes) and sleep-deprived *Casanova* by mentioning that his nocturnal prowess could become expensive. He retorted by explaining, "You guys take me to dinner and I use my meal money on flowers. It's your basic win-win." That bold retort demonstrated that Barry felt as if our relationship had developed beyond business, and he was correct. Barry had become a friend.

On a subsequent visit, Barry asked if he could spend thirty minutes or so with me to discuss something of importance to him that he thought I would find important, as well. I told him we could discuss the matter presently, but he indicated he preferred to be away from the office. My experience told me to proceed with caution.

That evening, while changing into tennis gear, Barry asked where I expected to spend eternity. I told him my choice was heaven and asked if I would see him there. He said, with a sheepish grin, I would *definitely* see him there.

"Definitely?" I repeated. "Did you get your assurance from God?"

"As a matter of fact, I did," he responded with a gentle and humble spirit. "That's what I wanted to discuss with you. Can I show you where I found God's assurance?"

"Sure, go ahead, but don't forget that Gil and Tony are holding a court for us."

With a tender spirit, Barry began to direct me to several Bible passages that supported his position. I smiled as he proceeded because Judy had previously exposed me to the same verses.

"Barry, this won't take thirty minutes because I'm familiar with these verses and I believe them for the most part."

"You do? Why didn't you ever tell me?"

"I guessed that you weren't interested in Bible passages and I didn't want to interfere with your nightlife."

"You're probably correct, but it's obvious to me (now) I was traveling at a high rate of speed on a dead-end highway."

"No argument here."

As we walked to the tennis courts, Barry asked me how long I had been *born again* and I responded as I had to Judy many times, "I'm not exactly sure, and I think *born again* is a Protestant term and I ain't one."

Barry, Gil, and Tony were better players than me with Barry being slightly the best, so Barry and I were partners.

As we took a drink before the match, Gil whispered to me to be careful because he thought Barry had *found Jesus*.

"He's not going to try to baptize me?" I jokingly whispered back.

Gil grinned as we took our positions for the two-out-of-three competition.

After a closely matched first set, Barry dominated and the match only required two sets.

After I announced the score, "Nickerson/Flores: 2; Aleman/LaRocca: love," Tony and Gil suggested another two-of-three match.

Barry was okay with the idea, but yielded to me. I considered it an opportune time to exert *executive privilege*.

"Another match, in my opinion, would only add to your frustration and delay our encounter with the jumbo stone crabs waiting for us at Joe's. However, if Barry is willing, we will agree to provide another lesson during his next visit."

We chuckled as we separated to get ready to go to Joe's. As Barry and I returned to his hotel room to shower and get dressed for dinner, Barry commented, "I'm curious as to why you think *born again* is a Protestant term, because in the book of John, the Pharisee, Nicodemus asked Jesus, 'What must I do to be saved?' and Jesus replied, 'You must be *born again*.'"

"I guess because I've never heard the term from anyone but a Protestant. I guess I could be guilty of a *hasty generalization*. Do you consider yourself a Protestant?"

"Yes."

"You're supporting my position. Barry, as a youngster, I went to St. Joseph's Catholic School and one of the saints we learned about was Don Bosco, the educator saint. The last time you were here, I referred to you as *Don Juan*. Six weeks later, I'm inclined to drop the *Juan* and replace it with *Bosco*."

"This *is* an important topic and I'm moved to share this information initially with those who are special to me."

"I'm flattered that you consider me with such high regard; I feel the same way toward you, Barry, but can we defer this conversation till we help Joe move some crabs out of his inventory?"

"Yes, that's fine; and I want you to know I'm much happier that you think of me as Don Bosco and I am committed to trying to live a saint's life."

"Barry, are you going to be as effective as you have been with your new outlook on life?"

"I'll be more effective now that my motives are higher. If nothing else, I'll be much better rested. And I thought you wanted to defer this conversation..."

WINTER WONDERLAND

That was how the Xerox staff (f fats spelled backward) in Rochester viewed Miami, and that was why, when practical, they would schedule their visits in the dead of winter. Thus, in January of 1977, I received a call from a staff person wanting to schedule an operations audit for the branch.

These audits were intended to flush out any issues that could be impeding the branch's performance and that, if not dealt with, could result in legal exposure for Xerox. The locations for these *audits* were generally selected on a random basis with consideration given to climate. If you can recall ever viewing a national weather report during this time of year, the reason Miami was selected by people living in Rochester would be abundantly clear.

My Rochester experience caused me to realize that putting these people off would send up a red flag, thus my response to the person calling to schedule the audit was, "Bring your suntan lotion and leave your earmuffs at home."

A week or so later, I received a call from Dave Kearns, Xerox President, inviting me to join him and the heads of the various international operations who were conferencing in Miami. He said that if I didn't want to attend the entire conference, he would like me to join the group for the final day's summary to be followed by dinner. I told him I was flattered by the invitation and that I looked forward to seeing him. The conference could have been held in the frigid climes of Rochester or 125 miles from Dave Kearns' home in Manalapan (south of Palm Beach). Everyone was in agreement with Dave's choice.

The Rochester staff was delighted when I introduced them to our management team as a group that was well-qualified in rendering a service to us by providing a third-party view of our operations with the intention of helping us uncover anything that may be impeding our effort to maximize performance. The manager of the group expressed his appreciation for my introduction, though he said he noticed a couple of skeptical looks among the group. I assured him there were more than a couple of skeptics.

They interviewed employees from Palm Beach to Key West, and three weeks later were prepared to present to me their preliminary assessment, which would morph into their final report after I was given an opportunity to respond, which would then be presented to the Rochester executives upon their return.

The day they wanted to meet with me conflicted with the International Conference's summary, so I gave them the choice of either the preceding Wednesday or the following Friday. I was certain the staff member in charge would choose Wednesday, thus allowing him and his staff the opportunity to blow out of town a day early and give me the opportunity to take Friday off with Judy and Mondy, but no such luck; he immediately chose Friday and indicated that some of them were having their families come down to Florida as a result of the delay. I hadn't recognized how attractive the seventy-five-degree temperature was to these snowbirds. Nonetheless, I was able to adjust my extended weekend to include Monday instead of Friday.

Dave Kearns was his usual charming and motivating self as he facilitated the final day's agenda, sprinkling points representing the consensus of the group among the (non-negotiable) points that he wanted the group to understand as being essential for success. As I listened, I recognized he was doing the same thing I was doing, but on a much larger scale—much, much larger.

One of the traits that most accomplished people exhibit is making everyone feel special. Dave Kearns is quite accomplished and great at making people feel special. He introduced me to the group as having worked *with* him in Rochester before turning a tired organization in Miami into a showcase for Class 1 branches. I was obviously flattered by his comments and wondered how they would stack up against the preliminary assessment I would be hearing twenty-four hours later and that Dave Kearns would be seeing in a couple of weeks.

As dinner broke up, I made it a point to express my gratitude to Dave for including me in the conference and his response was memorable.

"Mondy," he said, "don't think for one moment I don't know how difficult your job is. I get to interface with top-tier individuals such as you and those here today to get my points delivered, but you face the gamut—from the motivated to the insurgent—and have to deal with a management culture that's only interested in results. Few are able to manage in that environment. Keep up the good work and stay in touch."

Those seventy-five words were among the most encouraging (professional) comments ever said to me. Having a difficult and stressful assignment became much easier to deal with knowing that Xerox's top executive was aware of the degree of difficulty. On the drive home, I pledged to myself to do a better job of communicating with those with tough assignments within my sphere of influence.

The first person I was able to practice my pledge with was waiting for me when I arrived home. In addition to being a tremendously challenging assignment, being a wife and mother is relentless. In my view, time-off for a wife and mother is not as refreshing as time-off for a husband and father—the responsibility of children is always present.

I was still floating the next morning as I prepared to meet with the audit team. They were ready to proceed when I asked if I could take a moment to express my appreciation for the time and effort they'd spent in our branch over the past three weeks and to recognize how difficult it must have been to only see their families on the weekends.

They then began their presentation, which was broken down by function, to be followed by their overall summary and suggested action plan for correction. There were always a couple of former branch managers on the audit team to lend credibility to their findings and to their suggested action plan. The others were understandably poised but cautious as they were seeking field assignments after their tours in Rochester. After ninety grueling minutes of listening to what could only be described as *minutiae*, they finally informed me that they were prepared to summarize and suggest a plan of action.

"Before we do that," I interjected, "can I summarize what I think I've heard thus far? At our West Palm Office, someone is storing boat supplies in one of the unused offices, and from time to time, the landlord complains of a boat on a trailer being left in the parking garage. In Ft. Lauderdale, they would like better furniture which they feel should be comparable with the furniture in the West Palm and Miami offices and they feel as if they have a parking problem. Also, in Ft. Lauderdale, two technicians want permission to attach trailer hitches to their company vehicles. In Miami, the employees feel there is a parking problem and both technicians and sales reps feel they are not welcomed in the office by management. And finally, in the Keys there is no parking problem, but they feel isolated and they don't get many (company) visitors."

"That's pretty much it," came the reply. "Except that the employees in the Miami office want free Cuban coffee like they have in Ft. Lauderdale."

"Okay, I've got it." I said, as I thought to myself, *Is this all these people have after three weeks? Hotels on Miami Beach, stone crabs at Joe's, rental cars and they discover Miami employees want free Cuban coffee? Maybe I should be happy.*

The assessment continued, "We are terming the aforementioned items as *minor; to be cured by branch personnel* (where applicable), leaving two remaining items that pertain specifically to you. First, I don't know how you're going to react to this, but generally speaking, the employees feel as if you don't have much interest in socializing with them and they cite you not going to happy hour as the prime example. Do you have any comment?"

"Let me hear the second item before I comment."

(Under these circumstances, I considered maintaining my composure to be a tremendous accomplishment, though I began to fume internally realizing that these people had no idea what it took to manage a branch and recalling my previous day's conversation with none other than Dave Kearns as he expressed his appreciation for the fine job that was being done under difficult circumstances in Miami. To say the least, Kearns would have been shocked listening to this bureaucratic concoction of pseudo-issues. Nonetheless, I mustered more control than I thought I possessed and continued to listen to this charade.)

"The second item may seem somewhat trivial (how could it be more trivial than what I'd just heard, I thought), but we view it is an opportunity to improve morale with minimal effort on your part. Generally speaking, the employees feel that you dress too conservatively and cite the smaller size of the bell bottoms of your pants and the dark color of your suits as examples. There are a couple of other small items not worth your time. We would now like to hear your thoughts on our findings."

Cognizant of maintaining my composure, I addressed the group, "As I mentioned earlier, thanks for your time and effort in providing a third-party view on how our branch is being managed. As you know, we had to reschedule this meeting so I could attend the Xerox International Conference yesterday. As I listened to issues discussed by the presidents of the various Xerox entities outside the United States, it became abundantly clear to me that the major challenges faced outside this country are, for the most part, similar to those faced in the U. S. and the same as those faced here in South Florida. The major challenges can be summarized as follows: First, the success of our company centers on management's ability to identify, hire, and keep the *brightest and best* employees the marketplace has to offer. *Keeping* the brightest and best is the most challenging objective we face because, generally speaking, the brightest and best don't have much of an appetite for being micromanaged. It is viewed by them as stifling and as an assault on their capability.

"Secondly, we must develop aggressive but achievable objectives and clearly communicate these objectives along with an agreed-upon way to measure success. Once this is accomplished, it is management's foremost responsibility to shield their people from any and all obstacles which may impede their ability to accomplish their company objectives—in other words, to protect them from counter-productive activities which inevitably appear.

"And thirdly, management's responsibility is to assist and train our employees to be better equipped to accomplish their position requirements.

"With that in mind, I will not respond to the points which have been brought to my attention today other than to say that I'm pleased you did not find any substantive issues, and again, I appreciate your efforts."

There was a noticeable hush as everyone gathered their belongings.

Three weeks later, my friend and former boss in Rochester, Jim Higgins, called to congratulate me, saying that he couldn't recall ever having seen an audit report as positive as ours. The Miami branch was now recognized as a model Xerox operation.

ALISHA MARIE FLORES

The expectation of our second child in mid-December was to be the crown of a wonderful 1977. It was before the time when baby gender was known prior to birth, so we had been hoping for a girl but would've been happy just as long as the baby was healthy.

Mid-December meandered into late December and I was wondering if I was going to qualify for our second child tax credit in 1977. December 30th started as a lazy Friday for us as we visited with Frank and Mari Venezia at our home. The "Chamber of Commerce" day invited us to sit on the front lawn as we doted over Mondito and waited for our new arrival. Judy was two weeks past her due date, and to say the least, she was "ready." Without fanfare, Judy advised me that it was time to go to the hospital and asked Mari and Frank to watch over Mondito.

We calmly entered Baptist Hospital in South Miami, and while I completed the paperwork, Judy was ushered to the delivery area. I was Judy's Lamaze delivery coach, and when I joined the delivery team ten minutes later, I was informed by the doctor that things were ready to happen. Within twenty minutes, we were the proud parents of our baby girl, Alisha Marie Flores.

Unbeknownst to us and without any knowledge of what was happening, Meme and Pa were on their way to Miami for the big event. Upon arrival at our home, Frank and Mari updated them, and without hesitation, they scurried to the hospital to share in the excitement of the new arrival.

It was a great help to us to have Judy's parents stay for a couple of weeks while we (mainly Judy) became acclimated to the double duty we'd gladly invited. Our lives had changed forever thirty-three months earlier with Mondito's arrival, and we recognized that it would change again, this time exponentially, with Alisha Marie completing our family.

I'm quick to admit that it was easier on me. As Judy and Meme dealt with the demands of a newborn and her adjusting big brother, I was responsible for making sure we maintained an adequate supply of food and the like and entertaining Pop, who was not only my father-in-law but my special friend. We took Mondito on various outings and I showed Pop around Miami; we even went to the 1978 Orange Bowl game where the highly-favored and 2nd-ranked Oklahoma Sooners were soundly beaten by the 6th-ranked Arkansas Razorbacks before a sellout crowd.

DALLAS CAB DRIVER

My New York experience had left me somewhat cynical toward cab drivers, but this cab driver was different. The thirty-something-year-old black man wore a peaceful smile as he asked, "Where to, suh?"

When I gave him the address, he confidently said, "You must be a *Zee-rox executuv*."
"Nice guess," I said.

"Wasn't much of a guess; that Lemmon Street address is the Suhdern Region Headquartahs fo Zee-rox and by the looks of yo tan, you's comin from Mississippi o Flowreedah," he proudly stated.

"Another nice guess. I'm from Miami, but don't judge where a man's from by the color of his skin because I'm this color year 'round and I try to stay out of the sun as much as I can."

"You right, boss. I's hope I's din't oh-fend you by noticin' you's got color; I's got quite som natral color myself that the Lawd gave me."

"I'm not offended at all, and I got my color the same place you got yours."

"Awl right!" he responded, "Dah Lawd don't make no mistakes; you's da shade you is and I's da shade I's is becuzz dats da ways He wants it; no Jesus don't make no mistakes. Ain't no mistake I's carryin you to yo meetin' this moh-ning eedah; it's why da Lawd has me in dis heah bitness of cabbin. You sees, I's carries lots of executuvs back ans fohth to Love Field ans dats where da Lord's 'spects me to do His work. Be awlright ifin I's telya whats dah Lawd tolds mees ta telya?"

"Are you sure the Lord wants you to tell *me* or anyone you pick up?"

"Good questin, suh. I sees hows you's a executuv; truth be, suh, Jesus take care of who's gits in mah cab; I's ain't dat qualified, but He is. Cans I git started?"

"Go ahead, but give me the short version."

"Yeh, suh," he cheerfully said. "You's gots a willin' heart an da Lawd loves a willin' heart."

Using verses from his Bible (while driving his cab), he proceeded to explain man's problem (sin), God's solution (Jesus' sacrifice on the cross), and man's choice (to accept or reject Jesus' sacrifice offer) as clear and succinctly as I've ever heard the gospel message presented before or since. His heretofore language shortcoming dissipated with the sincerity and Bible acumen he exhibited in giving me the message he was certain God had for me.

As I exited his taxi, I couldn't help but notice how satisfied this man seemed by simply carrying out what he termed as "what God wanted him to do." In stark contrast to the serene spirit of this mobile minister of the Gospel of Jesus Christ, I was going into a meeting with very unsatisfied and edgy men focused on the mundane objective of placing a Xerox machine in every location in the southern United States that was capable of paying for such a service. While our objective *seemed* more urgent than his, his—if true—was without a doubt, more important. As is generally the case in our culture, *the urgent takes precedent over the important,* and within thirty minutes—make that fifteen—I had managed, with the help of my boss, to store this man's compelling message into the recesses of my mind.

Today, decades later, I cannot tell you who was present, or what, specifically, was covered at that meeting in Dallas, but I recall with great specificity what that black minister, posing as a cab driver, told me and I can still picture his warm smile as he asked for permission to tell me.

There is, indeed, a huge difference between the urgent and the important.

COMFORT ZONE MORPHS INTO JWC

Back in Miami, things were smooth—or, as smooth as one could reasonably expect in a home with a newborn daughter and her big brother reaching for his third birthday. The main thing is that they were healthy, even if we (especially their mother) were physically taxed by tending to their every want. I could—and would—recover at the office; Judy had no such respite.

Over the previous three years, the Miami branch transitioned from an underachieving country club operation to a professionally-managed, high-achieving entity that was regarded as a model for Xerox Class 1 branches. This metamorphosis was not without its casualties, but nonetheless, everyone contributing to the current effort was much better off and the former *politicos* were either gone or defanged—and in either case, no longer an impediment to those seeking to advance their careers on a level playing field.

As for me, I was just beginning to reap the benefits from succeeding in the gruesome struggle of leading the charge to change the culture from politics to performance. One of the benefits was my somewhat more relaxed work schedule made possible by the fact that my senior staff had become quite adept in managing their own function and they were in the process of developing a spirit of collegiality among themselves. This cohesiveness allowed me to delegate much of what I was previously doing administratively, resulting in the dual benefit of developing my management team and freeing my time to observe, evaluate, coach, and be absent—the aspects of my position I had been hoping would come. One could say I had achieved my *comfort zone*.

One Friday afternoon in January, I had taken the day off to be with the people I loved most—my family. That afternoon I attempted to give Judy some free time by taking Mondy for an extended bicycle excursion on a trail that included stops at Matheson Hammock, Parrot Jungle, and Monkey Jungle. After the nearly four-hour trek, we transitioned to the pool before lighting the coals for our evening barbeque. It was while I was in the pool and periodically tending to the grill that I received an interesting call from my buddy Malio in Tampa.

"What are you doing?" he inquired in his patented type-A fashion, "Can you have dinner with Jim Walter and me tonight?" "Are you and Jim in Miami?" I asked.

"No, but we can be there in forty-five minutes on Jim's plane," he responded, giving me the feeling he was expecting nothing less than a *yes*.

I was mouthing my predicament to Judy when Malio suggested I make dinner reservations for eight o'clock and he would call me in thirty minutes with the details on where to pick them up.

Malio called back and explained that upon calling home, Jim learned his wife was experiencing a "low moment" related to her bout with cancer and asked if I could visit with him in Tampa in the next week or so.

Even though I wasn't exactly certain of the reason for the visit, I assumed it was related to a career opportunity. My assumption was later confirmed by Malio when he called and further explained matters.

Judy and I discussed what we considered a slim possibility of returning to Tampa with caution. We enjoyed living in Miami and had become accustomed to living away from our hometown; nonetheless, we were aware that Miami would not be permanent unless I was comfortable ceasing to advance my career, a prospect which did not interest me. My Xerox future seemed limitless and I had an appetite for advancement to match. Why would I alter the course I was on that was pointed exactly to what I sought—more money and power. Judy, on the other hand, had zero interest in either money or power, but returning to Tampa offered stability in which to raise our children and would put us close to our parents, who were in their early sixties (which we then considered elderly).

Our next Xerox choices of interest included London (Rank Xerox); Stamford,

Connecticut (World Headquarters); and, as a distant third, back to U. S. Headquarters in Rochester, New York. In a perfect world (prior to Malio's call), we were leaning toward London because we considered it a unique experience we could accomplish while the children were young and then return stateside, probably in Connecticut.

Jim Walter Corporation (JWC) was best known throughout the south for its homebuilding division, Jim Walter Homes, which began selling and building *partially-built homes on your lot* to returning soldiers after WWII. But by the time I met Jim Walter, he was Chairman and CEO of a conglomerate, which was Tampa's first and only Fortune 200 company with interests in coal mining, cast iron pipe, paper, banking, bolts and nuts, machine tools, plastic, window components, doors, plumbing products, roofing, drywall, insurance, real estate, and strangely enough, retail and wholesale jewelry, in addition to its well-known homebuilding and financing division.

I found Jim Walter to be a charming and interesting person interested in making his already comfortable life more comfortable by heeding the advice of Wall Street in addressing their major concern regarding JWC: its lack of successor management talent. According to Wall Street investment bankers, that shortcoming was already negatively affecting the company's stock price, and the negative effect would only increase as Jim and the company's President and Chief Operating Officer, Joe B. Cordell, approached retirement age. Jim was 58 years of age and Joe was 50. Wall Street's assessment that successor management within the company was deficient mirrored Jim and Joe's opinions, thus, their top priority was to remedy the situation.

On April 1, 1978 Joe Imhoff, a seasoned former high-level executive with W. R. Grace in New York City, began his career with JWC, followed thirty days later by Vincent J. Naimoli, a distinguished Notre Dame MBA with extensive high-level managerial experience, most recently in Baltimore, and Armando Flores, former Xerox Branch Manager from Miami. Both Imhoff and Naimoli were products of an international executive search firm, and I was the product of local restaurant entrepreneur, Malio J. Iavarone.

Let it suffice to say that my chances to succeed Jim and Joe as top executive did not look good on paper. However, like most competitions, this one would not be contested on paper. Another thing, my *comfort zone* remained in Miami. I not only had to contend with a new career and company with a totally different approach to business, but I had to do it without the safe haven of my family who remained in Miami for a few months until I arranged for temporary living arrangements while our home was constructed in Carrollwood Village.

On the plus side, our moving days were over and Mondy and Alisha would be able to experience the stability of being raised in what would become their hometown. As for Judy and me, we were able to reunite with family and close friends and enjoy our hometown's comforts. While we were happy to move back to Tampa, we both had cherished and benefited from our experiences living in New York and South Florida.

CULTURE SHOCK

My first day at work with JWC was both interesting and tragic. My boss, Joe Cordell, had arranged for me to meet the presidents of the three divisions which had been assigned to me. The president of Jim Walter Plastics (JWP), Chuck Adams, traveled from JWP headquarters in Baltimore, and the president of our jewelry division, Wedlo, Inc., Pete Petro, made the trek from Birmingham while the president of Jim Walter Window Components (JWWC), Marty Levine, was on standby as JWWC was located at our corporate headquarters at 1511 N. Dale Mabry Hwy.

After a cordial meeting with Pete Petro, I went by my office only to find a distraught Chuck Adams weeping uncontrollably and murmuring some unintelligible words, I assumed, directed at me. I soon understood he had just learned that his two-year-old granddaughter had died in her sleep while in the care of his wife, the girl's grandmother. He could not compose himself and I asked for his airline tickets so I could have someone get him on the next flight to Baltimore. While doing so, my mind shifted to Miami and my young ones. The person handling the flight changes advised me that one of our corporate aircraft would be ready in thirty minutes to fly Mr. Adams to Baltimore. That was a nice touch by someone, I thought, as I transported Chuck to the JWC hangar. As Chuck boarded, I told him to tend to his family matters and we would reschedule our meeting for another time.

My meeting with Marty contained an interesting component. While engaging in small talk, Marty asked if I would like to have dinner with him and his wife at their home on Culbreath Isles. I respectfully declined his offer citing, intentionally incorrectly, that I had plans. He said he understood, but that he wanted to spend some time with me alone. I asked *how alone* he wanted to get since we were the only two in my office. He explained he wanted to meet away from the office so we would not be disturbed. I then offered to instruct the person outside my office not to allow anyone but Jim or Joe to interrupt our conversation, to which he responded, "That's exactly who I don't want to see while we're talking."

"Look Marty, I don't know what you want to tell me, but I'm not about to tell Jim or Joe after five hours on the job that they can't interrupt a business conversation that they, I'm certain, know more about than I do."

"That's the problem; they think they know more about an issue within JWWC than they actually do."

"Why don't we just fire them?" I said in a manner intended to communicate the preposterous nature of his request. "Just tell me what you want to tell me and let's gamble that we won't be interrupted."

"You don't have enough time to listen to what I want to tell you this afternoon. which is why I wanted to have you join me and Rhoda, my wife, for dinner. Would it work better if we had dinner at Bern's?"

"Can't do it tonight, Marty, but tell me how long you need and we can schedule it for another day in or away from the office—your choice."

"I'll need a half-day of your undivided attention. Do you play golf?"

"I don't play golf, and do you realize we could watch *Gone with the Wind* in half a day?"

"My story is more complicated than *Gone with the Wind*. Okay, I'll schedule some time with your secretary for next week if I'm still here."

And that's how my first day at Jim Walter Corporation went, except it wasn't quite over because Joe Cordell asked if I wanted to join him and his wife, Joyce, for cocktails at his house after work and then get a big juicy steak at Malio's or anywhere I wanted.

GUERRILLA WARFARE

Malio's Steakhouse was the hottest place in Tampa Bay and the primary reason centered around the flamboyant owner, part-time executive recruiter, and my good friend, Malio.

I generally take off my suit coat while eating, and that evening I did just that, draping it over an unoccupied chair upon being seated for supper at Malio's. At the first opportune moment, Malio informed me that neither Joe nor Jim removed their coats while eating to which I jokingly replied, "I won't hold that against them."

He laughed, then removed my coat from the chair, folded it in half (length way) and placed it on the chair back, informing me the reason for his action was that my coat was too big in the "open position" and would scare my new bosses. I laughed and was reminded of Malio's innate and keen sensitivity to nuances as to people's preferences. It was, in fact, his attention to such detail that gave the patrons of his restaurant the feeling that they were special.

Unbeknownst to me, Jim joined us for dinner, and with one exception, not a word of business was discussed. After several martinis, Joe asked what I thought of the division presidents reporting to me and offering stern advice casting doubt regarding the JWWC president's veracity and capability. I told him I would keep his advice in mind as I completed my assessment of him, but I asked if the executive was that flawed, why he was still working for us? Joe offered, "The answer to that question is part of the reason you're here. I don't want to bury this guy, but in my book, he's a no-good lying bastard and I'd keep my eye on his ass if I were you."

To pierce the veil of seriousness that had overtaken the moment, I attempted to inject some humor by saying, "I guess a bonus for him is out of the question."

Neither laughed, prompting me to say, "That was a joke." I gained weak acknowledgement but still no laugh.

Shortly thereafter, Malio escorted longtime friend and local sports icon, Rick Casares, to our table to say hello and offer tribute to Tampa's captains of industry. Rick, his usual charming self, made small talk including congratulating the three of us on joining forces and then offered the following concern to Joe and Jim. "You know," Rick said in his imitable style, "ever since I heard Mondy was coming back to Tampa to work with you guys, I've had mixed feelings. I'm thrilled to have my buddy back in town and I'm certain both he and Jim Walter Corp. will benefit greatly from this association, but me and a couple of my friends have had to change our plans. You see, we were planning on sticking-up your joint."

Rick laughed, emphasizing the fact that he was joking with his remarks but he only elicited a slight grin from Jim and Joe, who were unconvinced that Rick was kidding. I controlled my laugh to conform to the reaction of my new bosses, and to bridge matters, I stood up and hugged Rick, acknowledging our friendship and my understanding of his comments.

Inside of ten minutes, two attempts at humor had failed, leading me to think I was entering a world that was foreign to me. Malio's take on the matter was to the point. "You know Mondy, I always told you that working with Xerox was like being in the Marines. Well, working with these guys is like guerrilla warfare, you never know where the bullets are coming from and it's not always obvious who's the enemy."

I understood exactly what he meant, and in the years to come, I would experience the wisdom in his analogy.

GENTLE BREEZES WELCOMED

The value of the gentle breezes generated by my family in Miami increased with my temporary long-distance arrangement and I looked forward to weekends at home with greater anticipation than ever. Normal interruptions by our baby daughter were a small price to pay for the love, joy, and comfort that only a family can provide. It worked out well that JWWC's principal manufacturing facility was in Hialeah because I was able to conduct my meetings with Marty at the facility which he visited often. The meetings were scheduled on Fridays and Mondays, thus facilitating my desire to spend additional nights at my home until my family relocated to Tampa. Even the expanded weekends seemed short which motivated me to accelerate their move. The plant manager in Hialeah offered to manage what care was needed for my home once the family left, a gesture which left me wondering whether it was bona fide or if it was an effort to restore matters back to their original state B. F. (Before Flores). It would be the latter.

Marty's tale was indeed complicated, but he was attempting to use the complexity to conceal his participation in a conspiracy that led to the seven-million-dollar inventory discrepancy (accounting term for loss) JWWC would ultimately book. That write-off (loss) was a huge number considering the company's total inventory which included four other plants (which constituted the other half of the division's inventory) totaled thirty-five million actual dollars ($42mm less the $7mm write-off). What all this amounted to was that for several years prior, several layers of management, including senior management of the division and possibly my predecessor, were cooking the books for the purpose of reporting greater profits than they'd actually achieved, thereby creating larger bonuses and raises for themselves and even leading to promotions for some of the co-conspirators.

Dealing with this kind of flagrant mismanagement was easy for me. I detested having to re-assign or terminate people who for some reason or other found themselves in a position in which they were skill challenged or where the requirements of their position had passed them by but dealing with greedy individuals who purposely fudged the numbers for their personal gain was like shooting fish in a barrel to me. The only tricky part was to determine who was telling the truth when the telling became abundant (which always happens when it becomes obvious that some are going to take the hit for this immoral and illegal enterprise and those who attempt to assist in a cover-up will be included in that group). Yes, greedy people have families and bills to pay just like those who find themselves in over their heads, but the differentiating factor in my mind is *intent*.

Conducting this investigation in Hialeah presented obvious benefits for me, but it was also beneficial to be present at the scene where the bulk of the sins were committed. I told Marty that I wanted him to conduct the investigation as it should normally be conducted given the egregious accounting acts committed but under my supervision so it would not appear as if corporate (me) was acting heavy-handed in the matter.

He agreed.

At my direction, Marty began at the lowest management level and asked individuals to explain how inaccuracies of this magnitude could have occurred without their knowledge. Their responses were all over the board, from outright confession to outright lying and every position in between. As we progressed, I noticed two things about Marty: 1) he exhibited no qualms about throwing his own people under the bus and, 2) he was, indeed, the lying bastard described by Joe Cordell.

Incidentally, I invited Joe to attend some of these interrogations, but he communicated that he had zero interest in that, though he did say he was interested in eating stone crabs (without Marty) at Joe's Stone Crabs on Miami Beach if I was interested. I, of course, indicated that I was, and we did. I was able to impress Joe by converting the standard hour-and-a-half wait to less than ten minutes with my connection to Matr'd, Roy. Over dinner, I expressed my regret about not being able to introduce him to Judy because of the kids' schedule. He comforted me by saying that he understood and that there would be plenty of time for that once my family moved to Tampa.

I attempted to give Joe an overview of what had been uncovered in the investigation, but he thwarted me by saying he was more interested in talking about fishing, football, and girls. By our conversation, you would have thought we were in a fraternity rather than managing a multi-faceted industrial conglomerate. I found Joe's disinterest in talking business both peculiar and refreshing. An interesting bit of trivial information presented itself that evening when, during our conversation, Joe and I discovered we were patients of the same Coral Gables dentist. He suggested I keep this dentist and we could set our appointments back to back and incorporate stone crabs with our visits—an attractive offer to be sure.

As I transported Joe to the corporate jet awaiting him, I told him that even though there were many items connected to this conspiracy that required further clarification, Marty's veracity was not one of them; from all that I could glean at this point, Marty was a nice guy, but nonetheless, a lying bastard.

"What did I tell you about that Jew?" he responded rhetorically, followed by, "I can't figure how you consider that bastard a nice guy."

As I headed home, I calculated Joe would be in Tampa about fifteen minutes after I got home, assuming I encountered no traffic problems. As I attempted to interpret the evening, I kept remembering Malio describing JWC as guerrilla warfare.

A DIFFERENT APPROACH

With Xerox, I had become accustomed to a structured approach to business where published comprehensive and specific *policies and procedures* ruled the day. At the other end of the spectrum, JWC operated with a set of *guidelines,* which were intentionally vague and flexible, thus subject to different interpretations depending on the desired outcome and the nuances of a particular situation. Frankly, it represented a breath of fresh air to me, but it could be extremely perilous as well.

A tiny example of the corporate culture shift was *documentation*. At Xerox, it was common to document any and all business arrangements and/or agreements as a way of ensuring understanding and developing a course of action with timetables agreeable to the originator of the document and their boss. After a couple of weeks on the job, I had not been asked a single business question, so I thought it was a good idea to discuss the course of action I was considering with Joe. He listened and chained-smoked cigarettes without commenting.

When I was done, I asked what he thought and was stunned when he said he had no comment. I then offered to summarize our meeting in writing for him which caused him to

ask me to explain my purpose for doing so. When I said it was so we would remember what was said in our meeting, he retorted, "I'll remember all I want to remember without a letter, won't you?"

Without much choice, I responded affirmatively but recall thinking I was in a foreign land speaking a foreign language to a foreigner. While sitting in my office trying figure out what was expected of me, in came Joe asking if I was interested in going fishing. I asked when, and he, looking at the weather through my window, said, "Can you be ready in thirty minutes?" It was 9:30 AM.

"Whatever," Joe responded, indicating he was unimpressed when I said I had a lot to do but I could do it at night or on the weekends if we were going fishing. He called his boat captain (Blue Chip) from my office and told him to meet us at the Tarpon Springs marina in an hour. As I headed from my office to my condo to change into fishing gear, Joe Imhoff and Vince Naimoli asked if I wanted to do lunch at Malio's. I asked for a raincheck and explained I had a meeting away from the office that I couldn't break. Joe and I spent the entire day catching kingfish in the Gulf of Mexico.

I did a lot of listening my first few months trying to understand the culture of JWC and who actually made up the *corporate power structure* as compared to those listed on the organization chart. Additionally, I had to alter my corporate language from *sales* (supported by financial and legal terms) to *finance* (supported by sales, legal, and manufacturing terms). *Everything* was viewed through a financial lens. When asked questions like, "Are you going to suggest the division change its accounting method from FIFO to LIFO?" or, "Do you think the division's *bad debt reserve* is adequate?" I typically responded, "What's your recommendation, and why?" and, "I'm going to have to think about that," until I could ask my personal accountant and high school friend, Pete Dearolf, or look up terms foreign to me at the John Germany Library at night. Pete was always gracious in schooling me on these matters, but I wouldn't be surprised if he questioned whether or not I would be able to function at my level with my financial inexperience. If he doubted my ability, he never mentioned it to me.

I was already a disciple of the management principle *never allow a subordinate to pass the responsibility of making decisions on to their boss,* so I wasn't about to let these guerilla fighters trap me verbally. Throughout my Xerox management career, I'd been schooled on the management process irrespective of function or products, and now, my schooling would be put to the test. I knew that *less was more,* so I attempted, against my nature, to listen much and speak little.

SETTLED

It was a great day when the four of us made the short flight from Miami to Tampa.

Judy and I had decided to custom-build our house on the property we purchased at 4015 Carrollwood Village Drive, so we moved into a four-bedroom apartment a mile or so south of our property so we could easily observe the construction. A toddler, an infant, a new career, a new company, temporary housing, construction of a home, and resettlement (family & friends) into your hometown should be a recipe for stress, and it was, especially for Judy who, while I was in the controlled and predictable environment of a plush office, managed our biggest responsibilities—Mondito and Alisha.

As always, Judy was able to send me off to work without a care at home. I always operated my business life with that huge advantage. Year by year, I observed my associates' home situations and recognized what a huge advantage I enjoyed. A person can manage but a certain amount of pressure, and when you're getting pressure from home, something has to give at work, an event I often observed but never experienced. Thank you, Judy.

Our first year back in Tampa was, indeed, a zoo. I was flying around the country meeting people and familiarizing myself with JWC and with the components that made it tick. With the use of the company aircraft, the nights away from home were fewer even though the days were long. The weekends were generally spent with family and friends and I needed the work week to recover. Judy had no such luxury.

We moved into our new and comfortable home on Carrollwood Village Drive during May of 1979 and today, May 24, 2008, I am writing this portion of *My Memoirs* in that same home and the only home Mondy III and Alisha ever knew growing up.

Between our marriage in December of 1970 and May of 1979, Judy and I moved eight times. The sight of moving vans used to bring on *agita,* but we have since overcome that knee-jerk reaction. Living in the same home, even though we lived through an extensive two-year renovation/disruption from 1998 through 2000, has been a delight and a source of many wonderful memories.

Sometime in mid-1980, I estimate, Judy and I considered ourselves settled.

WE AIN'T RUNNING NO DEMOCRACY

Joe B. Cordell went out of his way to make me feel comfortable at JWC. Sometimes it became a bit awkward and embarrassing. Often, someone would suggest having lunch together and Joe would beg-off citing previous plans; later, he and I would be seen having lunch together—awkward at the very least, I thought. Joe's take was different. He said he was around these people all day and considered lunchtime as an earned break.

I was wearing an *I Voted* sticker on my shirt this election day when Joe entered my office and asked if I wanted to go with him to vote. I pointed to the sticker on my shirt which did not impress him; he wanted me to join him. We left the office at 9:30 and were done voting at 9:50. Joe suggested we go to *Blanco's* for a cup of Cuban coffee. While at the coffee shop, Joe asked if I would join him in checking on a couple of shotguns he was having blued at Minardi's Gun Shop. I, of course, obliged and by 11:15, we were headed to Malio's for lunch. We were peering into Malio's through the locked main entrance trying to get someone's attention who would let us settle into a booth until they opened at 11:30. Joe was banging on the door and complaining that people were ignoring his attempt to get their attention when Malio pulled up in his showy Gold Porsche 928.

"What's the problem?" Malio asked with a smile on his face to counter the scowl on Joe's.

"We can't get anyone's attention to let us in," bemoaned Joe.

Without hesitation, Malio exited his auto, freed the key to the front door of the restaurant from his bulky key ring and handed it to Joe.

"Here, this is for you if you ever want to enter when we're closed; all I ask is that you lock up when you leave."

Joe was beaming with pride as we entered with Malio as he joined the key with the others on his key ring. We sat at our normal booth and were treated to hors d'oeuvres while we waited. Joe loved it when Malio told his help, "They'll just have to wait till we open," when they asked what to do about the people knocking at the (same) door.

Our extended lunch was extended even more when we were asked to join JWC Vice Chairman, J. O. "Bud" Alston and his brother-in-law visiting from Italy. Cocktails, wine, and stories flowed, and by the time we made the five-minute drive to the office, it was 4:35.

As the doors to the elevator opened, a vice president was exiting with briefcase in hand. He was understandably startled when Joe, indignantly, asked where he was heading at 4:35 in the afternoon. The VP's response fell on deaf ears as Joe gave him his patented *whatever* look after discounting the VP saying he wanted to vote. "Vote on your own time," grumbled Joe as we entered the elevator. I was embarrassed by the exchange and decided to express my sentiments.

"Why did you bust Bob's chops when we left the building at 9:30 this morning?"

"We ain't running no democracy here, and the sooner you figure that out, the better off you'll be. This ain't Xerox."

"Forget democracy, what about common courtesy to this corporate officer?" I respectively responded.

"There's corporate officers and then there's corporate officers, and that's as courteous as I'm going to get with that son of a bitch. That's the way I handled it. Someday, you may have a chance to handle it differently."

I've always felt you can learn something regardless of how something was handled. Learning what *not* to do is as important as learning what *to* do. Though this was an obvious example of what not to do, I would learn many valuable lessons from Joe.

ISAY STEMP

My eye caught an ad in the Wall Street Journal pitching a two-week course titled *Finance for non-financial Executives.* The ad featured the credentials of M. I. T. alumnus Isay Stemp, *master professor* at the American Management Association (AMA), who taught the course at the AMA's midtown Manhattan facility. It looked to me like something that I could benefit from, but I didn't want to give anyone, especially Joe or Jim, the impression that I thought I was deficient in the finance area even though I clearly recognized the deficiency. I phoned Isay Stemp, and after discussing my situation at JWC, I was convinced the course would be a good investment of my time.

I stayed at JWC's apartment on East 59th Street and 1st Avenue, a short taxi ride to the course venue at Avenue of The Americas and West 48th Street.

Dr. Stemp had the twenty or so participants describe their current positions and state what they hoped to accomplish by completing the course. That drill served me well as my first item of business was to assess whether or not I belonged in this group. I was surprised at the number of participants who were finance majors and were there to *brush up* due to a position change requiring a step up in their finance acumen. One of the participants was a priest from upstate New York who was a Notre Dame MBA and was relocating to Boston to handle the finances of that diocese. Another was a Northwestern University finance major who was changing disciplines from manufacturing to finance within his employer, Reynolds Aluminum. A third was a CCNY grad who was taking over responsibility for a charitable foundation located in Manhattan. She mentioned she had taken finance under Dr. Stemp eighteen years earlier when she completed her MBA. My classmates respectfully chuckled when I disclosed that I was a University of Tampa physical education major and I hoped to learn a bunch of finance during the upcoming two weeks.

On Wednesday of the first week, I managed to secure dinner with Dr. Stemp after reminding him that he offered to carve out some time for me to discuss my JWC position and offer an opinion as to what follow up measures, if any, might be beneficial to me. Over a cholesterol-rich dinner at Seafare of the Aegean, the Russian-born, Cuban-raised, Sy (the name he asked me to call him) discussed and went over executive summaries of the divisions under my responsibility that I had brought for this specific purpose. I noticed the confused look on his face as he asked me to describe the responsibilities of my last two positions at Xerox. After I concluded my brief response, he began to craft his assessment, which I gleaned was causing the fifty-something-year old some consternation.

"Mr. Flores," he began, before I interrupted to ask him to call me "Mondy." It seemed that my reciprocal offer only made Sy more uncomfortable. Nonetheless, he professionally proceeded by buffering the distasteful news by telling me how respected Xerox was for developing top-notch managers followed by his opinion that, while my managerial experience at Xerox was the best American business provided, my educational experience was not up to the challenges of my current position.

In an attempt to lighten matters, I told him that it was apparent to me that he had not been exposed to a first-class physical education program. He forced a smile and cautiously told me that he believed I was in over my head. I again tried to ease him by telling him I was neither offended nor surprised by his assessment, but that he was missing a couple of pieces to the puzzle, namely that JWC had a very competent financial support staff and that I considered myself very adept at utilizing staff, but more importantly, in my opinion, I had a wonderful wife and two wonderful children who were quite confident in my abilities.

His synthetic smile indicated to me that my comments had confirmed to him that his assessment of me was on target. Whatever he thought was of little consequence to me; the fact of the matter was that JWC indeed had competent finance staffers and my family was mightily confident in my abilities and letting them down was not an option. Over cherries jubilee, Sy told me to keep in touch with him and to call if I thought he could help.

The following Monday morning, while eating a snack from a street vendor, a man tapped me on the shoulder and asked if I was Mondy Flores. My affirmative response resulted in this man identifying himself as Alan Silverman, fellow U. T. alum and co-conspirator in the 1966 theft of a history exam. The golden-tanned Hebrew never alluded to the *exam caper* which had brought our lives together years earlier and neither did I. After catching up with each other, he explained that he represented clothing manufacturers and importers in NYC's garment district and offered me the ability to purchase top-of-the-line suits at retailer's cost: fifty percent of retail and no sales tax. Before I left the city, he introduced me to four contacts who would facilitate my orders. All I had to do was identify the suits and sizes I wanted at any fine men's store and my contact would have the suits delivered to a store in Miami (he offered to deliver the suits to Wolf Brothers in Tampa (where my good friend's dad sold men's suits), but I opted for Miami because of the problems I anticipated with Tampa deliveries). Alan lived in Miami Beach so that made it all the easier. As an opportunity for me to reciprocate Alan's suit offer, he suggested he might call me as he commenced renovations to his Miami Beach domicile confirming the business adage, there's no such thing as a free lunch.

Overall, the two-week class was quite productive for me, not to mention I'd made a terrific contact for buying suits. I was glad to be out of the lab and back into the real world where one's performance trumps one's résumé.

JUDGEMENT DAY

At the top of the most distasteful responsibilities of an executive is the termination of a subordinate. The decision has the potential to affect the individual's future, self-esteem, status among family and friends, as well as the family itself. Factors such as character, capability, personality, reputation, et cetera, contribute to the difficulty or make it easier. In the case of Marty Levine, those factors made the distasteful deed considerably easier. With the possible exception of capability, Marty scored very low in all categories. His reputation was that of a schemer and he was considered untruthful (a liar) and not trustworthy. If those characteristics weren't damning enough, Marty was a seasoned whiner.

I didn't realize the amount of attention within the company that was focused on my handling of this situation. It had become the custom within JWC to reassign "problem executives" rather than terminate them. That practice resulted in a "kinder and gentler" feeling among the executive corps, but the practice carries with it an expensive price tag, not only in terms of dollars but the insidious cost of the negative effect these "relocated problems" have on productivity. Nonetheless, I was a thirty-three-year-old executive on a mission, and while I considered myself sensitive to the plight of others, I was able to keep my feelings subordinate to my responsibilities. And so, I explained to Marty Levine that the facts as I understood them led me to the decision to terminate his services. He said that he expected to be removed from his position but thought he deserved to be reassigned rather than released. I told him I disagreed.

When advising Joe Cordell of my plans regarding Marty's release, he—true to his character—gave me no indication of his thoughts, but while briefing him after the actual termination, he said he thought I had made the correct decision and that the general consensus was that I would reassign Marty.

I offered, "If Marty's behavior doesn't warrant termination, we should consider removing termination from our personnel manual as an extinct practice."

"New broom sweeps clean," Joe said. "I'd like you to assist me in tidying up some additional bad actors."

"Are you telling me Marty was considered a bad actor?"

"Let's celebrate over a big steak," he said. "Where do you want to go?"

A NEW ARENA

Selecting Marty's replacement was an eye-opener for me. My first choice for the job was my friend in Miami, Gil Aleman. Gil was a top-notch executive and I was confident that switching industries would be no problem for him. His only deficiency was his inexperience in finance, as had been the case with me. Our mutual deficiency eliminated him as a candidate because hiring him could have been viewed as a case of the blind leading the blind. So, I went to Plan B: Hire someone with finance experience and *guide* that person to hire Gil as the VP of Sales.

I was determined to hire someone from within the JWC family of companies as a means of improving morale and demonstrating my minority belief that a professional manager could cross industries and manage effectively; after all, I was betting my future on that premise.

While studying the résumés of the various applicants, I noticed their ages were considerably higher than what I had become accustomed to at Xerox. As an illustration of that fact, four of the five people interviewing for the position began their careers before I was born and the fifth applicant had begun his career with Celotex Corporation on February 1, 1945—my birthday. That information led me to be more sensitive to a situation I had never personally experienced, nor would I ever experience: working for someone younger. In these cases, at least thirty-three years younger.

What I noticed about these candidates was their candor. One asked if I was just going through the motions but was going to hire one of my Xerox cronies. Another asked if I thought I was the one (of the three hired at the same time) that was going to stick. And yet another commented that he was perplexed as to why I was going outside the window industry to fill the position. I hired the Celotex executive, and within sixty days, he hired a Cuban-born Xerox executive from Miami named Gil Aleman.

Concurrent with these and other personnel moves was the arrival of very difficult business conditions brought on by a normal business cycle amplified by failing fiscal policies at the federal level of government. Difficult market conditions cause indecision in some and opportunity for others. My group of companies, not unlike the rest of JWC, experienced both, but the good decisions far outweighed the paralysis of indecision, and the tough times allowed me a clearer view of who the quality executives were. Prosperous times are desired by all, especially stockholders, but they don't afford the opportunity to distinguish the *talkers* from the *players.*

Joe provided wise counsel when he cautioned me to observe rather than join others' plans and decisions.

As he put it, "You're going to get credit for how your companies perform whether you observe them or join them; but how will you offer meaningful corrections if they (division management) consider you part of them? They're paid by the company they work for and you're paid by JWC. Don't allow that clear distinction to become cloudy."

As days became weeks and weeks became months, I recognized the wisdom of Joe's comments. I learned a lot by that tip, and it served as another illustration that I was, indeed, in *a new arena*.

IT CAN'T BE THIS EASY

While reflecting on my first two years with JWC, I often thought to myself, *It can't be this easy*. I was thirty-five years old and my life was better than I could have ever wished. My ever-changing priorities were being realized almost as quickly as I could recreate them and the future seemed bright as the noonday sun. I had the best job a person could hope for, and for the first time in my career, I had the opportunity to accomplish my (self-serving) professional and personal goals without the prospect of relocation. More importantly, though I didn't fully appreciate it at the time, I was and am married to a wonderful lady who knows me implicitly and who selflessly supports my every effort, strives always to make me happy, and—as if this cake needed icing—is dedicated to doing the heavy lifting as it relates to raising our children. As an added bonus, our family was the beneficiary of perfect health, something I took for granted and for which I considered myself rightfully deserving. Why? No particular reason. Just because.

Nonetheless, with all these wonderful things going on in my life, I continued to lack the peace I assumed these things would bring. The only way I could describe my situation was one of unmet fulfillment. I had more than I ever dreamed I would have, yet something was missing.

I've always been an optimist, but my optimism has always been rooted in realism. I had experienced emotional trauma as a six-year-old and again as a teenager, but was unaware of its effect on me. I'd had encounters with really bad people and with really good people, and I had become adept in distinguishing them. As is the case with everyone, these experiences contributed to my perspective on life. Indeed, my optimism was not Pollyanna-ish, but practical. I firmly believe that no one gains when pessimism is regarded as an acceptable method of dealing with issues. On the contrary, the prospect of a favorable outcome is greatly enhanced when (realistic) optimism is employed.

However it came about, I developed a keen awareness of the strife and dysfunction that exists in this world, which had the effect of showcasing the good fortune to which I was becoming accustomed, and which was becoming part of my expectation. I continued to think to myself, *It can't be this easy*.

ST. PATTY'S DAY, 1980

It was 1980, and we were in our tenth year of our marriage. Judy maintained her relationship with God by faithfully studying the Bible and attending—with our children—churches that used the Bible as the cornerstone of their ministry. As for me, I remained faithful, as well, but to my personal advancement. Without intending to do so, I had adopted the implied creed of most of the significant male role models in my life: focus on financial success and leave spiritual matters to the wife (if she were so inclined).

During our marriage, Judy occasionally brought me a taped sermon that she thought I would find interesting. I rarely did.

The sermon she heard on Sunday, March 16, 1980 met her criteria and she brought me a copy. I hastily agreed to listen to the sermon after our guests departed, but later asked for a twenty-four-hour deferral due to my fatigue. It was, reluctantly, granted.

Upon arriving home on Monday, I noticed that things were moving along ahead of schedule. Mondito and Alisha were bathed and in their pj's and the kitchen was completely in order, dinner plates and accompaniments excepted. Within minutes, I was kissing the kids goodnight, and shortly thereafter, Judy and I were enjoying a quiet dinner, together and alone—a rarity indeed.

After small talk, the reason for the heightened efficiency became apparent when Judy set up a tape player so we (I) could listen to the taped sermon to which my twenty-four-hour reprieve had expired. I became increasingly fatigued and negotiated an agreement to listen to the tape from our bed, a prospect Judy considered risky due to my propensity to sleep during sermons. Nonetheless, she conceded and, by eight-thirty, we began listening to roving evangelist Fred Brown's interpretation of *The Parable of the Pharisee and the Tax Collector* (Luke 18:10-14).

My receptors had been dampened by the preceding gospel hymns, which I considered *backwoods,* and I knew the prospect of me making it through the entire message was thin.

It was no surprise, then, when Dr. Brown's accent was tantamount to a native son of the Deep South, a connection he no doubt relished. I recall laying in bed with my arm over my eyes thinking, *God, why are You making me listen to this country bumpkin? What have I done to deserve this?*

Dr. Brown began his remarks by describing the attitudes of the hearts of these two men, the Pharisee and the tax collector.

I'll provide the actual text to serve as reference to his remarks.

Two men went up to the temple to pray, one a Pharisee and the other a tax collector. The Pharisee stood up and prayed about himself: "God, I thank you that I am not like other men—robbers, evildoers, adulterers—or even like this tax collector. I fast twice a week and give a tenth of all I get."

But the tax collector stood at a distance. He would not even look up to heaven, but beat his breast and said, "God, have mercy on me, a sinner."

I tell you that this man, rather than the other, went home justified before God. For everyone who exalts himself will be humbled, and he who humbles himself will be exalted (Luke 18: 10-14).

As Preacher Brown put it, one went to *pray* and one went to *brag*. He proceeded to describe how the culture of the day revered the Pharisee and despised the tax collector. It didn't get any better than it was for a Pharisee at the time of Christ, and it didn't get any worse than it did for a tax collector who was also known as a publican. The Pharisees were bent on doing right and had instituted over six-hundred laws and prohibitions to demonstrate their moral superiority. On the other hand, the publican was known to be morally bankrupt for he had previously sold himself out to the Roman oppressors to qualify to collect excess taxes from his Jewish brethren.

I immediately drew sides with the Pharisee, as I considered my sins to be far less grievous than most, and as an executive, I was convinced that my actions would never cause me embarrassment or ill will.

"Both were in the temple to pray to God, but their attitudes were different. You see," the evangelist explained in his Southern twang, "the Pharisee was impressed with himself.

After all, he was a man of accomplishment and stature in the culture and was looked up to." Fred Brown was attracting my attention as he continued to contrast attitudes.

"The Pharisee," he continued, "as he prayed, named sin after sin that others committed, setting himself apart from them, especially from the lowly tax collector. The Pharisee did not want to be lumped with such a depraved group."

I identified with many of his examples. In fact, he was describing my heart. I empathized with the Pharisee who did not want to be grouped with common sinners.

My chances of drifting off or falling asleep reduced to zero and I no longer noticed the preacher's *hayseed* dialect. *Where is this guy headed with this narrative,* was all I could think of. I was transfixed on each word he spoke.

"You see," Brown continued, "this Pharisee was well pleased with himself and he let God know how he felt when he bragged in verse 4: 'God, I thank you that I am not like other men—robbers, evildoers, adulterers—or even like this tax collector. I fast twice a week and give a tenth of all I get.' He wanted to ensure that God had it right."

Apart from fasting and giving a tenth, that prayer reflected my exact, though inflated, sentiments, so I was eager to hear the punch line.

Brown continued, "But the tax collector (the culture's most despised individual) stood at a distance. He would not even look up to heaven, but beat his breast and said, 'God, have mercy on me, a sinner.' I tell you that this man, rather than the other, went home justified before God. For everyone who exalts himself will be humbled, and he who humbles himself will be exalted."

At that moment, everything I had ever heard about God that was unclear became clear. Things I had read, things Judy had tried to explain, things I'd heard preachers say, even what that Dallas cab driver tried to convey to me in the seventies, suddenly were simple and easily understood. The tax collector went as a humble sinner before God pleading for *mercy,* while the Pharisee went trusting in himself, asking God for *justice* in recognizing him for the righteous person that he considered himself to be. I recognized then that the comparative *justice* I sought was the world's way of evaluating individuals, not God's. God compares us to Jesus and that's where I, the Pharisee, and everyone else come up short.

I realized for the first time, that my idea of what was required to get to heaven was just that, my idea and nothing more. If I was as *good* as I thought I was—and I wasn't—that wouldn't qualify me for heaven because *perfection,* not *goodness,* is what God requires, regardless of what I, the Pharisee, or anyone else thinks. God provides that *perfection* through His Son for me, the Pharisee, and anyone else; yes, even a tax collector. It was the culture's most despised person, not the most revered person who was justified according to Jesus.

I turned to Judy and said, "I understand what you've been trying to tell me for nineteen years."

She looked at me, quizzically, and asked, "You do?"

"Yes," I said, "I want to ask God to forgive me for my sins and ask Him to save me." I did just that, and my life was changed forever.

I immediately felt fulfilled as that hidden, lingering, and difficult to describe emptiness departed. I felt unshackled from the expectations of the world. My purpose in being successful changed without my giving the matter any thought or consideration. I now viewed success as a means of telling others of the miracle of transformation that had taken place in my life instead of wanting to be successful so I would be considered important, not unlike the Pharisee who was used as a mirror for me.

I thanked Judy for not giving up on me and I told her I was going to tell Meme and Pa the same thing. The three of them, along with Judy's brothers, had been praying for me since we'd met in 1961, and it was now 1980. I thought, *How does someone pray for something or someone else for nineteen years?* Later I learned that they were not the only ones who were praying for my salvation. I am forever humbled and grateful for their love and concern.

I also told Judy that I wanted to tell Malio of my experience, and within moments I was doing so. He was happy for me and said a lot of the right things, including his prediction that I would be much happier. He was correct, although, it would be *joy* instead of *happiness* that would enter my life, a distinction I did not understand at the time.

Malio is always thinking, and this evening was no exception. Out of the blue, he told me that he wanted Judy and me to meet Dr. Ron Seeley and his wife Mary who were also believers; he said we would like each other. He said their twin sons, Mark and Todd, played soccer with his son Derek, and he restated his opinion that we would like each other. I agreed to meet the Seeleys, though I recall thinking that the timing of his suggestion was rather peculiar. Some months later, Malio arranged the meeting, and as he generally is regarding these types of matters, we met two of our (to be) dearest friends through Malio's matchmaking service. In the years to follow, we would partner with them on ministry opportunities, be introduced to the church we still attend, enjoy their company for dinner and other social functions, and continue to consider them among our closest friends.

How did my life become altered instantaneously and without my input? I didn't know then, nor did I give it much thought, but as I began studying God's Word, I realized that *the absence of my input* was required. After all, I had done it *my way* for thirty-five years and was unable to see what had become clear at an instant. God does not need our help in our saving, but He does require our belief, which I was privileged to provide.

My salvation took place at 9:20 PM on Monday, March 17, 1980. It was St. Patty's day to many, but to me, it was the most important day of my life, my spiritual birthday.

And He also told this parable to certain ones who trusted in themselves that they were righteous and viewed others with contempt:

Two men went up into the temple to pray, one a Pharisee, and the other a taxgatherer. The Pharisee stood and was praying thus to himself, "God, I thank Thee that I am not like other people: swindlers, unjust, adulterers, or even like this taxgatherer. I fast twice a week, I pay tithes of all that I get."

But the taxgatherer, standing some distance away, was unwilling even to lift his eyes to heaven, but was beating his breast, saying, "God, be merciful to me, the sinner!"

I tell you, this man went down to his house justified rather than the other;

For everyone who exalts himself shall be humbled, but he who humbles himself shall be exalted.

Luke xviii; 9-14

Armando Flores

March 17, 1980

YOU MIGHT WANT TO WAIT SIX MONTHS OR SO BEFORE SHARING THIS WITH JOE OR JIM

It may read as an oxymoron to some, but I was *calmly enthusiastic* about sharing my salvation. So, as soon as I arrived at the office on Tuesday morning, I went to see Joe Cordell.

"I was just going to call you. Shake hands with Amanda Blake," Joe said, beaming. "Amanda played 'Miss Kitty' on Gunsmoke; Marshall Dillon's girlfriend."

"I remember. I was one of those guys who wanted to be Marshall Dillon," I said, as I wondered how many times Amanda had to smile as she endured Joe's trite intro and my lame response.

Whatever her actual thoughts were, she was understandably gracious as she was in Tampa to raise funds for Brenau University of Gainesville, Georgia, where Lauren Cordell, Joe's daughter, was a student.

After chit-chatting for a while, I excused myself and asked Joe to carve out fifteen minutes for me before I headed for Baltimore later in the day. I rearranged my travel plans so I could share my experience with my brother Gene in Atlanta en-route to Baltimore.

Joe and I took "Miss Kitty" to lunch at Malio's, and it was 2:45 before we returned. Time was becoming an issue, so I asked Joe's secretary to tell him I was leaving in thirty minutes and wanted to see him before I left.

"What's so important?" Joe asked as he closed the door to my office behind him.

I told him exactly what transpired the evening before and he responded with what was, to me, a most confusing statement.

"I probably never told you, but I was an RA as a kid and received many medals for memorizing Bible verses."

I was somewhat sidetracked by his response and time was working against me as I did not want to miss my appointment with Gene, so I simply told him I wanted him to know about my salvation before I left, but that I wanted to discuss the matter more and learn more about his RA experience when I returned.

"Perfect," he said. "But I do have a question. Can I expect the same kind of effectiveness from you? What I mean is, most Christians I know are soft; you're not going to go soft on me, are you?"

"I'm glad you asked. I believe I'll be a more effective manager because, heretofore, I've always run my decisions through my *personal filter*, checking to see how a decision would affect my career before considering the effect on the company. Now the company's good will not be clouded by my personal ambition, so as a result, I should be more effective."

"If the truth were told, everyone considers their own careers when making decisions and that includes Christians, so I'm counting on you not going soft on me."

"Like I said; I believe I'll be a better executive, and going soft is something I don't even understand. That is the kind of thing I want to discuss with you and I want you to do me a favor; if you think I'm soft on something, I want you to tell me."

"You've got it. Have a good trip. By the way, are you planning on sharing your experience with Jim?"

"Yes. As a matter of fact, I was going to tell him after I told you, but "Miss Kitty" sabotaged that idea. I'll catch him when I return."

Hartsfield International was, as usual, bustling when Gene picked me up for a delightful meal at Pitty Pat's Porch, Atlanta's landmark for *Southern dining*. It was great to see him and I promised myself I would do this more often.

We discussed many things, but mostly caught each other up regarding our families. Uncommonly, we had ample time, which allowed me to give Gene the detailed version of my conversion. His attentiveness was without blemish. He asked no questions and his interest seemed to increase as my account progressed. As I concluded, we arrived at the Delta departure area, where he parked his Mercedes Benz for the few minutes remaining before it was time for me to leave. "Mondy," he said in a caring tone. "To say the least, that is a very interesting story and one I intend to ponder. You know, I've looked up to you all of my life and I couldn't ask for a better brother than you've been to me. What makes your story particularly interesting to me is that if there's one thing I know about you, it's that you are not easily fooled, which is why I want to understand this situation better. If you don't mind, though, I would like to suggest *you might want to wait six months or so before sharing this with Joe or Jim*, to see if you still feel the same then.

In the past six hours, I'd been asked if *I was going to go soft* and had received a suggestion *to wait six months before going public* to test the validity of my experience. I understood and was appreciative of both sentiments, though it caused me to consider the possible consequences of my decision.

In Gene's case, I knew he was looking out for me with his suggestion. He knew, like most executives, that I had fixed costs including a mortgage, private schools, and other expenses to consider, and he wouldn't want me to jeopardize my earning power.

With that in mind, I responded, "Gene, I appreciate your concern for me, but I already told Joe and I'm going to tell Jim when I return. I know this sounds crazy to you, but if my becoming a Christian negatively affects my career, then so be it, because doing what the Lord wants me to do is more important to me than my career."

He looked at me somewhat bewildered and was comforted some when I said, "However, I don't envision a conflict."

"I hope you're right," he said.

I asked him to read some Bible verses in the Book of John so we could discuss them when we spoke next.

THANKS FOR STICKING WITH ME ON THIS ONE

Gene not only began reading the Bible, but he was soon attending a weekly Bible Study in downtown Atlanta on Wednesdays before work. We chatted on the phone often and shared things we learned and questions we had. At the conclusion of our calls, Gene often lamented that he had not *caught on* as I had. I reminded him that his only responsibility was to *seek* and the rest would be the work of the Holy Spirit. He accepted my counsel, but was eager for the peace he said he noticed in me.

On Saturday, December 6, 1980 I was, of all things, hunting with Joe Cordell and Jim Walter at *La Hacienda del Cazador*, Joe's ranch in Manatee County. Interestingly, I enjoy firing guns but loathe hunting. However, doing things one doesn't like doing is a part of life, business life included.

We were bundled up to counter the cold and Joe was warming his innards with periodic swigs from the bottle of Sloe Gin he carried as part of his required hunting gear, regardless of the weather. As Joe traversed through the thick brush and palmetto bushes in his hunting truck, we were jolted and jostled by the rough terrain. Joe seemed to make little attempt to avoid obvious obstacles as Jim and I were jerked to and fro. I couldn't determine if it was his age or the effect of the Sloe Gin, but Jim asked Joe to slow down as he was feeling *motion sickness* coming on. Joe accommodated the request relishing the idea that the ride was too rough for some.

Joking and storytelling is a common antidote to the boredom that is part of hunting. With that in mind, Joe inquired, "Mondy, does the Bible prohibit killing, and if so, is that prohibition extended to animals as well?"

"Joe, I'm confused. If you're asking if we should be repentant about all that bacon we ate a couple of hours ago, that's one thing, but if you're trying to introduce the idea that you are changing tonight's dinner to a vegetable plate instead of the Porterhouse steaks you advertised earlier, we're going to have a serious problem.

"By the way, and since I have both of you together, don't worry about that $750, 000 Sam Jacobson owes us; it will be collected by month's end."

Joe and Jim sprayed the entire cab of the truck with a fine mist of Sloe Gin as they attempted to contain their mouthfuls of the elixir while laughing.

As we returned to the *main house*, Louis, Joe's valet, handed me a note asking me to call my brother in Atlanta <u>immediately</u>. I controlled my emotions but was somewhat startled by the news, knowing that Gene had to have called Judy to get Joe's number and recall thinking what was so important it couldn't wait till I returned? Sizing up the situation, Joe suggested I return the call in the privacy afforded by the master bedroom.

Upon answering, Gene apologized for calling twice but said he wanted me to be among the first to learn that he had received Jesus as his Lord and Savior earlier that day. His voice crackled as he said, "Thanks for sticking with me on this one," and mine did also as I told him it was nothing more than he would have done for me.

"Your eyes don't agree with your smile; is everything okay with Gene?" asked Joe as I entered the media room where he and Jim watched pro golf on TV over cocktails. I explained my tears were *tears of joy* having just learned of Gene's conversion and they both offered the socially-proper congratulations.

My Pittsburgh-rare Porterhouse never tasted better as I considered the news I'd just heard from Atlanta.

"We didn't have this conversation, but if you don't mind me asking, why are you so confident Sam is going to pay us all of the 750 in the next three weeks when he's been using us as a bank for years?" Jim asked in his typical low-profile manner.

"Sam has a four-and-a-half-million-dollar window job with the Broward County School System that has to be completed by December 31, 1980, or his company has to pay a $500,000 penalty plus an additional five-thousand dollars a day until completion. By contract, the final step in achieving *completion* is the installation of the screens, which have been manufactured and are currently warehoused in our plant in Hialeah.

"Erskine (the president of our window-component company) has told me that on December 15th, Sam's company is going to receive a FedEx letter advising them that no product will be released from our company until all outstanding balances are paid in full. I'm going to be vacationing in New York with my family that week and I'm not sure when I'll be able to return the phone call I'm anticipating I'll get from Sam when Erskine tells him he's got to pay up to get the product (screens). By the way, I told Erskine that if he budges one nickel with Sam, he should negotiate an employment contract with him because he won't be working for us."

"Damn, I'm getting the hell out of town that week too, or people are going to think I'm out of town," Jim said as he grinned while pondering the firestorm that was developing.

"Joe, that leaves you," I said. "Assuming you don't go soft on us, I'm confident we will have collected all our money before December 31st. You won't be going soft on us, will you?"

"Are you sure you're not Jewish?" was all Joe could muster as we continued eating and having fun with what was inevitable.

RECESSION OR DEPRESSION

If it's happening to someone else, it's a *recession,* but if it's happening to you, it's a *depression*. As is always the case, tough times are the crucible of life separating the real from the fake, the genuine from the counterfeit, and specific to business, executives from pseudo-executives. Most business execs can preach the value of inventory turnover, customer satisfaction, quality products and the like, but ashamedly few are able to deliver. Why? Because they are either unwilling to make tough decisions or are unaware of what decisions are required to be made. The result is the same. When sales and profits are plentiful, focus on business principles wander for many execs adverse to bringing up matters such as unpaid bills (like Sam Jacobson's) or substandard product quality when things are going well? It is said that profit covers a multitude of sins and there had been a lot of profit and a lot of sinning and covering of sins at JWC. Few of my counterparts were willing to rock the boat, some in fear that they, themselves, would be a casualty of their doing. As for me, I simply viewed it as the reason I was hired.

My three companies were steadily improving and soon I was asked to take on additional companies, such as Jim Walter International, Briggs Plumbing, Southeastern Bolt and Screw, Jim Walter Paper, Southern Precision, and Miami-Carey. I was flattered by the confidence placed in me by Joe, Jim, and the Board of Directors, and I was bent on proving them correct. My time away from home increased as my responsibility increased, and I found myself globetrotting to places like Japan, China, South Korea, Europe, and South America. Judy joined me a few times, but her focus remained on the two little ones who resided in our home and shared our last name.

While enjoying one of my frequent lunches at Malios with Baby Joe Valenti, BJ asked many questions about my upcoming trip to Japan and China, leading up to the question that was foremost on his mind.

"What kind of an inconvenience would it be if Malio and I met you in Tokyo and Hong Kong and we did a little sightseeing?"

"Inconvenience is the wrong word; enhancement is how I view it."

The next time Malio visited our table, Baby Joe posed the question to him and the trip was on.

Gil Aleman, who had done a professional job of managing JWWC back to health, organized the trip to see if we could negotiate better prices, and perhaps, additional products for Southeastern Bolt & Screw, which I had asked him to manage in hopes of improving its business health as well. As usual, he was up to the challenge and within a year-and-a-half, was able to raise SBS's profitability to such a level that we were able to sell the company for a tidy gain.

Baby Joe and Malio arrived in Hong Kong a couple of days ahead of Gil and me, who had stops in Pusan, South Korea, and Taiwan, Republic of China.

It was a laugh a minute after meeting Baby Joe and Malio, beginning with our first trip from Kowloon to Hong Kong which are separated by a small bay. While Gil was checking with the *concierge* regarding the best way to get to Hong Kong, Malio was suggesting that we spend the whole day in Hong Kong because it took over an hour to get there, not to mention the hefty limo charge. Before Baby Joe asked for a limo (the way they'd gone the first two days), Gil said there was an MTR (Mass Transit Railway) station beneath where we were standing that offered around the clock service to and from Hong Kong. As we got off the de-escalator, we boarded the modern, clean, quiet, air-conditioned train that was loading and in less than five minutes, we were in mid-town Hong Kong. The cost for the four of us combined was five dollars. We laughed heartily and Malio offered, tongue in cheek, his and Baby Joe's services in handling negotiations for the rest of the trip, causing another eruption of laughter. We did all the tourist things, and in a couple of days were in the capital of *the land of the rising sun*…Tokyo.

We again engaged in sightseeing, fine dining, and shopping as we attempted to complete our crash course in Asian culture. During a visit to an ancient Shinto shrine in Osaka, we couldn't contain our laughter when Baby Joe would constantly attempt to *out bow* our Asian hosts when returning the customary bow (at the waist) with a deeper bow causing our Asian hosts to bow deeper which caused him to bow deeper and so on and so forth. You would have had to have been there to fully appreciate the comedic value. As we exited the shrine, I noticed the locals sipping water from ladles attached to large ancient-looking metal containers causing me to question the sanitary standards of this custom. Lo and behold, some fifty feet in front of me was Malio, third in line to sip behind a woman who looked as if she had just been released from—or was being committed to—a leper colony. Raising my voice would have been offensive to the culture, but I felt compelled to save my friend from being *caught in an Asian moment*, so I triple-stepped my gait and caught up with him just as he was about to put a germ-laden ladle to his lips and, coupled with friendly admonishment, I skillfully knocked the ladle away before it made contact with his lips. He thanked me and acknowledged that he did not know why he'd gotten in line. We laughed and added this event to our bank of fond memories.

The trip was enjoyable, but it doesn't take me long to miss my family and I couldn't wait to return to the comfort of Carrollwood.

FAR EAST TRIP

Malio, Baby Joe, and me in Hong Kong

Malio, Gil, Baby Joe and me in Japan

Japanese pay homage leaving Buddhist temple

Malio, me, Yoshi (guide), Baby Joe, Gil and Mariko (guide)

THE STROLL

While strolling the neighborhood with my cardiologist friend and neighbor, Dr. Eric Harrison, I posed a couple of medical questions regarding some mild irregularities I was experiencing that I had not considered important enough to mention to my wife. His reaction to my questions was exactly what I didn't want to hear. Eric was quite skillful in his response, but left no doubt regarding his recommendation that I visit him *post haste* at his Tampa General Hospital office for some tests to pinpoint the cause of what he termed as *activity-induced angina*.

Judy made no attempt to disguise her concern as I communicated Eric's recommendation.

On Friday of that week, based on an angiogram that indicated I had three severely blocked arteries, I was the recipient of a joint recommendation from cardiologist, Eric Harrison and cardiac surgeon, Dennis Pupello, that bypass surgery was the course of action required to deal with my atherosclerotic condition (blocked arteries). The good news was that, in spite of the obstructed blood flow to my heart, my heart function was unimpeded and showed no damage.

My mother had undergone bypass surgery several years earlier, so I was familiar with the procedure, but I was still stunned that, at age thirty-seven, I was to undergo a surgery I assumed was for older people.

Dr. Pupello was prepared to perform the surgery immediately, but I opted to think about it over the weekend and tentatively scheduled the surgery for the upcoming Tuesday. In retrospect, I should have followed Pupello's suggestion because all I accomplished by the delay was allowing myself extra time to think and worry. I recall thinking about the possibility of not surviving the surgery and whether my friends and family were coming by to see me because they might not see me again. The mind allows unwarranted notions if left unchecked.

Judy spent Monday night prior to the surgery comforting me at the hospital. We read Bible verses and discussed fear-induced recovery plans, including diet and exercise.

Early the next morning, I received an unexpected visit from Meme and Pa's pastor, Tim Wilson. It was nice when he asked if he could pray for my family and me and for the surgery, and during his prayer, I was especially comforted when he mentioned that *before I was born, God knew I would be in this hospital at this moment for this purpose with Judy by my side and that the outcome of this surgery was known by this same God.* I remember feeling comfortable that who really mattered was present and was in charge.

They've come a long way with bypass surgery since 1982, but back then, the recovery was compared to recovering from a combat wound resulting from *covering a hand-grenade,* a prospect I wouldn't wish on anyone.

However, there is a plus side to most events and this medical wake-up call caused me to view my life in such a way that was otherwise improbable. During most of the four days prior to and for several months after the surgery, I directed much of my thinking toward reassessing my priorities. My self-published hierarchy of career, family, and faith no longer worked. Had I not survived the surgery, of what value was my career and family (to me)? So, by default, my (compartmentalized) faith suddenly stood unchallenged in its proper preeminent position.

Because few things repulse me more than hypocrisy, I could not help feeling hypocritical about desiring to change my life's priorities because of circumstance rather than conviction. I fought off the urge to recognize this medical event for all that it was. Yes, from a physical standpoint, the all-important flow of blood to and from my heart was restored, but from a spiritual and eternal perspective, my heart was now connected to my Lord and Savior, Jesus Christ who created, saved, and (temporarily) slowed me down enough to see what is so obvious to me now, that eternal matters trump temporal matters regardless of how the culture treats them, and that my life should reflect that understanding.

To set matters straight, my salvation had taken place on St. Patty's Day in 1980 and I was definitely a changed person, but I had been unable to recognize how the pull of the world was impeding my walk with the Lord. It was subtle, but I was trying to be a businessman who was a Christian rather than being a Christian who happened to be a businessman. It was a matter of self-definition, and as I meditated at home and at work and while I walked the many miles of recovery, I asked God to reveal to me who He wanted me to be and what He wanted me to do, and though I fall short of the standard, I am certain I am focusing on the correct goal—His glory (and not mine), Him first (and second doesn't matter) and Him always (not just when it's convenient or when I feel like it).

That's the way I returned to the mahogany lair that was Jim Walter Corporation.

GOOD IDEAS

My ability to perform my duties was at its highest because my focus was clear—His glory, not mine. I no longer had to ponder how my well-being fit in with God's plan because following God's plan became my plan. An immediate benefit of yielding to God's plan was the mitigation of the pressure of my pressure-packed position. And it wasn't difficult. I wasn't trying to operate as if I were Moses, I simply (continuously) asked myself how God would mentor me regarding this or that, and I do not recall being confused on what route to take. Success abounded, and as a result, I was assigned additional companies, including responsibility of the Celotex Corporation, JWC's largest and most challenging entity with sales over a billion dollars and an overseas presence. Joe Cordell and Jim Walter either had significant confidence in my ability or they were trying to kill me. (I, of course, knew it was the former, if for no other reason, that JWC could not succeed if I did not).

The decision to move Celotex Corporation under my responsibility was met with mixed reactions. Those who sought to work in an environment where *performance trumps personality* were excited, while the *establishment* and those who thought that they should have been awarded the assignment were murmuring and complaining to anyone who would listen. *All* previous management of Celotex had always come from within, fostering the company's unfounded belief that they could not be adequately managed by someone who did not understand the nuances particular to their industry generally, and Celotex specifically, a sentiment not unlike I had encountered in the window, plumbing, home accessories, fastener, plastics, machine tool, international sales, and jewelry industries. Said differently, every industry believes theirs is unique and that outsiders are at the distinct disadvantage of not understanding their uniqueness. My perspective was just the opposite: a person from outside the industry should have the capability of viewing their methods with a fresh and unbiased view, and should be able to suggest ideas that work in other industries for their consideration, precisely what people who are set in their ways and resistant to change fear.

The president of Celotex, twenty-six years my senior and a forty-five year Celotex employee, made the five-floor trip up to my office to congratulate me and wish me success. I thanked him and told him I looked forward to working with him to improve his company's performance, which apparently hit a nerve, causing him to ask, "What kind of improvement are you thinking about?"

"I don't have specifics, but I'm assuming there are areas of opportunity for improving productivity somewhere within the organization; don't you agree?" I communicated in my most gentle manner.

"Well, of course," he said in an uneasy tone. "Maybe now is a good time to tell you what the scuttlebutt is about."

"Scuttlebutt?"

"There's a lot of uneasiness about the change. People think Bill (my predecessor) was ousted to make room for you and they are concerned that you don't have much experience in our industry and may want to make wholesale changes."

"Who's concerned, Frank?"

"Well that's not important. I just want you to know there's a certain amount of concern and I thought you should know."

"I'm a little confused. If it's not important, why are you telling me, and more importantly, what was your response to those who brought this to you?"

"I didn't have an answer for them. I told them the best thing they could do was do the best job they're capable of, but I got to thinking and I thought it would be a good idea if Joe and/or Jim met with our management team to respond to any questions they might have. What do you think?"

"I think a meeting is a good idea, but I don't think the meeting should be with Joe and/or Jim. I think it should be with me. After all, according to you, I'm the cause of their concern. If they're concerned about wholesale change that I might bring, don't you think I should be the one to respond? As a matter of fact, we are going to have our first point of contention if a meeting takes place with Joe and/or Jim without me being there, the reason being that I don't want someone else speculating as to what I might do in a certain circumstance when I can respond specifically. More importantly, I have no intention of being on trial for a crime that has *not* been committed. You do realize that this move has the full backing of the Board of Directors, do you not?"

"I understand, but as a compromise, can I ask that Joe or Jim join in the meeting?"

"I'm okay with that, but you'll have to ask them since you're the one that needs them there. I personally think it's a waste of their time and would not reflect well on you."

To understand what I would be facing and why there was turmoil with the decision to place Celotex under my responsibility, it is helpful to understand a bit more of the history of the Celotex Corporation.

The Celotex Corporation was established in the early 1920s. Their subsidiary, Celotex Company of Great Britain, started trading in 1925 from offices located in Australia House in The Strand, London and soon established itself as an importer of bagasse fiberboard insulation from the original Celotex manufacturing plant in Marrero, Louisiana. Over time, Celotex Corporation, headquartered in Chicago, Illinois, systematically added industrial product lines, and when the post-World War II surge in construction arrived in the US, Celotex benefited handsomely.

In the early 1960s, Jim Walter Corporation, which benefited from the same surge, began buying Celotex stock in a diversification effort, and by 1964, bought all of the outstanding shares making Celotex Corporation a wholly-owned subsidiary of JWC. This transaction had the dual effect of launching JWC and Tampa, Florida onto the national business map and introducing Celotex executives to a lesson in humility.

By 1964, Celotex was a nationally-known brand and its stock traded vigorously on the New York Stock Exchange. Twice as large as JWC and conducting business internationally, it was no wonder Celotex's top executives considered the JWC purchase of Celotex a case of *the tail wagging the dog*. The fact that Chicago was the nation's second-largest business center, rich in the arts, home to major medical and educational institutions in addition to professional teams in all sports and a major transportation hub added to their bewilderment. Jim and Joe conveyed to me on more than one occasion that the sophisticated, internationally-experienced top executives at Celotex never accepted the fact that they had to answer to *crackers* in that *baseball spring training Florida town called Tampa*.

The relocation of Celotex's headquarters to Tampa in the late sixties was met with major resistance, and in fact, had never been accepted by some transplanted Chicagoans. Then, in 1978, the arrival on the JWC scene of three (including me at the tender age of thirty-three) *outside* executives caused a stir among some of the company's senior executives. Now, some five years later, the announcement that Celotex (along with other companies) was added to my group, triggered the stir to re-boil. This time, my capabilities were not questioned, it was the same lingering internal belief that only a Celotexer could effectively manage Celotex.

Frank decided not to invite Jim but asked Joe to attend, to which Joe replied, "Only if Mondy wants me there."

I told Joe, who was my good friend in addition to my boss, that I was ambivalent on the matter and would leave the decision to his discretion. He thought the meeting would prove to be interesting and decided to attend. I was pleased because I wanted his feedback.

So, I met with approximately twenty Celotex executives so that they could "vent" and gain an understanding of "my plans." I responded to their questions for about thirty minutes, during which time no one voiced *any* concern. Either they were not as concerned as advertised or the person who brought the matter to my attention misread their concern or manufactured it for some reason unknown to me. I intended to uncover the answer.

To keep this *much ado about nothing* meeting from being a total waste of time, I decided to express my expectations and my *modus operandi* to the group. It was a repackaged message I had given many times before to various company management, and before that, to the Xerox crowd. In essence, I explained that I was employed by JWC and that I had no interest in working *for* Celotex; my interest was to work *with* them as a consultant and board member. I intended to utilize *their* performance to evaluate *their* management effectiveness and if I could offer a helpful idea or two, I would, but not to count on much of that because I expected the **good ideas** to come from within Celotex—after all, they are the experts in their field.

JIM WALTER CORPORATION

JWC board and spouses meeting in Madrid

Connie Walter, Joe Cordell, Jim Walter

Pondering strategic moves at Jim Walter Corp

Me recognizing Gil Aleman as the top executive among Jim Walter Corp Companies

UNDER OATH

As they say, *life was good*. My family was healthy, something I did not fully appreciate at the time because, with the exception of my bypass surgery five years earlier, it had always been that way. Mondy enjoyed a successful freshman year at Jesuit, making the honor roll and impressing the school's administration. The school administration was sufficiently impressed to select him to address (sell) the (potential) incoming freshmen and their parents on the benefits of the Jesuit experience. Judy proudly witnessed his eloquent presentation in front of a packed audience in Jesuit's chapel while I was out of town. Things looked bright at Jesuit as he decided to add football to his list of extracurricular activities as a sophomore.

Alisha was cheerleading, playing softball and volleyball, and winning all the speed events at Seminole Presbyterian's intramural track competitions while knocking out straight A's in the classroom, something she would do throughout her education culminating with a *cum laude* honor at her graduation from the University of Central Florida years later. Judy and I attended every function or event that involved Mondy and/or Alisha and we enjoyed family vacations all over the country during school breaks.

Joe Cordell had been CEO for a couple of years and JWC's portfolio of companies, with few exceptions, were performing nicely. Wall Street, however, always discounted our stock price because of the uncertainty of the potential asbestos litigation which loomed beneath the Celotex umbrella. (During the 1940s, Celotex acquired a company that used asbestos in some of its products and it was determined years later that ingestion of asbestos in sufficient quantities could cause cancer. When JWC acquired Celotex in 1964, JWC unknowingly acquired this and all future liabilities. By 1964, Celotex had ceased using asbestos, but that fact had no effect on the potential litigation value in the eyes of the plaintiff lawyers lining up for their pound of flesh.)

I had the benefit of being Joe's friend and Joe was the master, along with Jim, of *keeping it simple*. The *keeping it simple* principle has as its core belief that if you know *how*, you'll always have a job, but if you know *why*, you'll always be that person's boss. Therefore, as boss, don't get bogged down in the details of what those who work for you do (<u>how</u>), but keep your focus on *why* you have them in that position. Following this principle requires *effective delegation skills* (among the rarest of business skills; and notice I used the term delegation, **not** abdication). By definition, utilizing *keeping it simple* allows the boss much available time because you never allow yourself to get bogged down in something that someone who knows *how* can do, you simply allow them to study the issue and bring their suggestions on how to best deal with the issue to you for your blessing, the outcome of which should yield acceptable results (consistent inferior results require changes among the *how* personnel.) In theory, the time made available to the *why* manager should be used to think forward as to where the organization is or should be heading, and with imagination, could be done in an enjoyable manner, an idea not lost on us.

Some of the ways we melded enjoyable times with forward thinking, included eating, fishing, golf, etc. Most of the fishing and golf events were in Florida, but the eating endeavors knew no boundaries. Joe's Stone Crab in Miami or Spark's Steakhouse in Manhattan were not uncommon venues for us, and when a baseball game figured into our plans, I occasionally brought Mondy who needed no coaxing to miss school to attend a Yankee game in the Bronx or the World Series in California.

An abundance of "one-on-one" time was available to Joe and me and we discussed anything and everything. Joe frequently asked how my "Christianity was going," which I took more as an act of cordiality than genuine interest. Nonetheless, one night with the aid of several Rob Roys and a bottle of wine over dinner at Smith & Wollensky's in midtown Manhattan, Joe displayed an uncommon interest in how my "Christianity" would play out in some hypothetical situations with special attention to how I would respond to business questions that could be detrimental to the company while I was under oath. My response was simple; I had no such knowledge, and my desire was to keep it that way.

"You didn't answer my question," Joe snapped. "How would you respond if you *did* have such knowledge?"

"If I don't have such knowledge now and I'm requesting to keep it that way, doesn't that make your question moot?"

"Is that your answer?" Joe pressed as he sipped wine.

"Yes, that's my answer. Were you figuring on telling me something sinister about JWC?"

"No, just curious on how serious you're taking your Christianity."

"Did I satisfy your curiosity?"

"Indeed, you did."

It would be years later that I would learn the significance of my response that evening.

BARBARIANS AT THE GATE

Corporate takeovers, friendly or otherwise, were in vogue in the eighties. Companies with low stock prices compared to their net asset value were particularly attractive. With the exception of the unquantifiable legal exposure related to Celotex's asbestos problem, JWC was a perfect candidate. That's equivalent to saying, *if that horse didn't have a broken leg, he would win the Kentucky Derby*. However, that didn't stop the Wall Street barbarians.

Jim Walter was flirting with retirement age and he possessed a keen appreciation of *timing*. Though officially we were not for sale, some chum was carefully tossed into the Wall Street waters, and as is generally the case, sharks began circling. Kohlberg Kravis Roberts & Co. (KKR) the most well-known leveraged buyout (LBO) firm in the nation was the lead shark accompanied by sharks from Citicorp, PaineWebber, WesRay, Prudential, Gobain, Pacific Holdings, Drummond, and others looking for gourmet meals at fast-food prices. Our stock price was in the $20 range in the early 1980s, but by 1987 was trading in the low $40s. As the sharks focused on their prey, the price rose to the mid $40s with several of the sharks offering $50 to $55, *unofficially*. Dangling JWC in front of one shark and then another resulted in the Great White Shark, dba KKR, swallowing its Tampa meal at the gourmet price of $60/share or 3.3 billion dollars.

CONFUSION ABOUNDS

During the previous eighteen months, a few peculiar incidences occurred that were puzzling to me and a couple more were on their way.

Joe Cordell was taking considerably more interest in my time out of town than he had previously. While I vacationed out west with the family for two weeks, he informed me that he, Jim Walter, and some of our legal staff wanted to meet with certain Celotex management representatives to attempt to quantify the financial exposure related to Celotex's asbestos issues. The situation seemed quirky because our legal department was consistently monitoring their financial estimate of Celotex's asbestos exposure and because I was available for such a meeting the other fifty weeks of the year. He also mentioned he would like to have our legal people review my Celotex files, in addition to his and Jim's, in this endeavor. Another time, I was in the DC/Baltimore area for four days and every day Joe inquired of my secretary as to the time of my return. A couple of times he asked her to transfer my call to his office, at which time he would make small talk (not uncommon) interjected with some lame comments aimed at validating my return time such as *will you be here tomorrow in time to go to Malios for lunch? How about dinner?*

Meanwhile, a couple of my sources were advising me that meetings with certain Celotex executives were being conducted in the boardroom in my absence. A few days later, an executive involved in the secret meetings asked to speak with me in confidence and away from the office. He began our conversation by telling me that the group meeting without me had been required to sign *confidentiality agreements* and he was concerned about having this conversation with me because of my close association with Joe Cordell, who possibly was briefing me on the side. I told him I was not being briefed and he, nervously, went on to say he was certain he would be fired if it were known that he was sharing the confidential info with me. I expressed to him that I was sensitive to his concern.

After giving him an opportunity to change his mind, he gave me a summary of the meetings from a written outline he held in his hand. While he offered no opinion, the essence of his report indicated to me that JWC management was meeting to develop a plan on how to contain *all* of the asbestos litigation exposure within Celotex in preparation of spinning off (selling) the company, thereby leaving the remaining JWC asbestos free. Heretofore, JWC had relied on the *corporate veil* concept, which proffers the notion that corporations are shielded from the liabilities of their subsidiary companies by a veil of separation referred to as the *corporate veil,* but apparently, greater assurance than that offered by the *corporate veil* was sought. I thanked him for apprising me and assured him that his trust would be honored.

This air of clandestine activity was beginning to make sense, but I remained confused and somewhat upset as to how and why I had become an outsider. Then the confusion increased.

Joe was canvassing the executives regarding the amount they wanted to invest in the new company to be known as Hillsborough Holdings, LLC. When I asked what amount was expected of someone in my position, he indicated there was no such expectation or guideline. I didn't believe him and asked what amounts some of the other executives were investing, to which he replied, "I have been asked by the KKR people to keep that information confidential."

"It didn't take you long to change jerseys," I retorted (communicating to him that I wasn't buying that bull snot). "Would you mind if I contact Henry Kravis (KKR's lead dog) about this?"

"Yes, I would. Don't you think it would make the top guy look a little weak?"

"It might. I guess I was hoping the top guy could provide a little more direction on this investment question."

"Mondy, you're overthinking this. Just come up with a number you're comfortable with and let me know by Friday."

"Joe, if I'm thinking of a range from five-thousand to five-hundred-thousand, would you think a person in my position should focus on the lower end or the higher end of that range?"

"Mondy, I'm not going to tell you what you should invest and that's that. Let me know by Friday."

Joe was clearly uncomfortable in dealing with me in this manner and I didn't care for it either, but such is life in the corporate world.

COMFORT AT HOME

Judy's *long view on life* has given her the capacity to put things in their proper perspective and, as I asked her to help me dissect this matter, she once again came through.

She reminded me that, months earlier, during our summer vacation at Sand Key, I'd informed her that I had no intention of spending the next twenty-three years (I was forty-two years old at the time) working for JWC or any company for that matter. And if that was so, why was I stressing on what was happening at the office, especially when the KKR buyout was providing a financially-enhanced platform on which to exit? Our future, she continued, is in the hands of a sovereign God and that Joe, Jim, Henry Kravis, and everyone else were simply going to be used by God to accomplish His will. I'd known that, but I hadn't taken the *long view,* which caused me to stress over something I could not control. As a Christian, I am required to do my best and leave the outcome to God; in the heat of the battle, however, I had slipped into focusing on my glory, not His—a sure-fire recipe for stress and anxiety.

Now properly focused, I was looking to God for *specific* direction on my KKR investment amount. In our prayers, Judy and I asked for a clear sign or message as to specifically how much we should invest.

I decided to ask my longtime friend and confidant Gil Aleman how much he was going to invest and what guidance, if any, he had received from Joe Cordell. Gil was now president of the Celotex Roofing Division, and as such, he reported to the president of Celotex Corporation, Frank Burgen, who reported to me. If I could learn how much Joe had suggested Gil invest, I could figure out what his boss should invest, and then deduce what his boss' boss should invest.

As an expression of his loyalty and of his appreciation of our relationship over the years, Gil told me that Joe had suggested that he invest $100,000 and to keep that amount confidential. I was not surprised by Gil's cooperation and I was now in a position to take my next step.

I decided to tell Joe that I was thinking of investing $50,000 but that I didn't want the KKR boys to think I was not confident in the future of the company or was averse to having more *skin in the game.* If he suggested that I increase my investment, I would interpret that as a sign that he wanted the KKR group to think well of me (money, in one way or another, was a key factor in *every* decision KKR made) and that I figured into their future; if he accepted that amount, I would interpret that as a sign that he did not necessarily want me to be well perceived by KKR, nor did I figure prominently in their future plans, in which case I would, respectfully, not invest. This scenario would provide the *specific* answer I sought from God.

Joe entered my office sucking on his cigarette and fidgeting with his list as he greeted me with, "Well, did you decide on a figure?"

"I'm close, but I have one more question. How much are you and Jim investing?"

With a semi-scowl, he said, "Jim's in for a million dollars and I'm in for five-hundred-thousand. Does that satisfy you?"

"Not really, but I've made my decision. Put me down for five-hundred-thousand, as well."

"I can't give you five-hundred-thousand. That's way too much," Joe responded.

"Why? Is it too close to your number?"

"Mondy, I'm trying to help you and you're beginning to piss me off."

"Well, I've been peeved for a while with this cat and mouse game we've been playing. If you're trying to help me, why can't you answer my questions?"

"I can't say any more than I've said," he offered as he lit another cigarette from the one he'd been smoking.

"Well, is fifty-thousand satisfactory, Mr. Kra(vis), I mean Cordell?"

"Fifty-thousand is fine if you can stand to lose all of it."

That was the clear signal I'd been looking for. Fifty-thousand told me that I was not in their future plans, and his *if you can stand to lose all of it* comment told me that Joe was signaling me to invest less, so I immediately reneged by saying, "I'd feel more comfortable investing less and perfectly comfortable investing nothing.

"Mondy, off the record, I think you're making the right decision. If I could, I wouldn't invest a nickel, but I have to and I think you know why. So I'm putting you down for zero, correct?"

This comment further confirmed my decision, though I remained confused as to why Joe had become and remained uncharacteristically evasive with me.

"No problem, and if the KKR boys ask, I'll tell them you did good," I said, trying to inject some levity into what had become a touchy discussion.

"Whatever," Joe responded as he made his patented *whatever* hand gesture.

ANOTHER DAY OF BUSINESS IN THE BIG APPLE

A group of JWC executives were invited to New York for a meeting organized by KKR with prospective lenders (sharks in their own right) to *put a face* on and ask questions of the management team that would be protecting their 3.3 billion-dollar investment. The grand ballroom of the InterContinental Hotel was teeming with lenders from across the United States and Canada, as well as a few from Europe and Asia. As chance would have it, Henry Kravis and I were engaged in small talk when Joe Cordell joined in. Kravis was smoke-averse, and I must admit, I was delighted when he boldly asked Joe to put out his cigarette. Joe, of course, obliged, but I knew what was going on in his mind. A couple of minutes later, Henry excused himself and Joe shared his opinion on Kravis' request, followed by light interrogation regarding my conversation with Kravis prior to his arrival.

"Am I under oath?" I asked Joe, who was, at the time, uncharacteristically not interested in humor.

"I'd like to tell you, but your boss asked me to keep our conversation confidential."

"Screw you," he retorted.

"If I can convince myself you're not wearing a wire, I'll take the chance and tell you over a big nasty steak waiting for us at Spark's (Steakhouse) as soon as this circus concludes."

"I can't have dinner with you. Jim and I are eating with Henry Kravis at his home."

"Well, excuuuse me. I'm sure he'll be able to tell you about our conversation over Russian caviar and champagne. Would you like me to hold your cigarettes so you won't be tempted?"

Joe's scowl sufficiently answered my rhetorical question. I was fully aware that my comments were irritating him but you would have had to have been there to appreciate that my needling Joe was appropriate, at least in my opinion.

Everyone was asked to take their seats and the show began. The dais was comprised of a few KKR people and the eight of us from Tampa. Henry Kravis took the podium, and after a brief intro of the people on the platform, he directed the lending contingency to the last tab in their personalized binders provided by KKR, and unabashedly communicated to them that if they wanted more than the amount allocated to them they should make their request known to KKR by noon the following day with no guarantee that their request could be met, and that if anyone was unable to take the full amount allocated by KKR, they would not be included in future buyout transactions. I'd had eighteen years of experience in business at that point and had never seen anything quite like what KKR pulled off that afternoon in midtown Manhattan. Henry Kravis' mandate was accepted by the lenders as normal and professional, and it was neither. Without consideration of the lenders' financial positions or risk tolerance, they were told how much they were required to lend if they wanted to be included in future deals—a case of *my way or the highway* if there ever was one.

Before we left for Tampa the following day, we were told the entire amount for the buyout was in place. Just another day of business in the Big Apple.

BOMB ATTACK

To put it mildly, the atmosphere around the office was uncomfortable, especially for me. There was more whispering going on than at a church picnic.

The buyout plan called for approximately thirty-two executives to be signed to a two-year contract that would provide KKR comfort with management continuity and would provide management comfort that they would receive a paycheck for at least the next two years. Two days before we were to have the contracts signed, I had not yet discussed the matter with Joe. Joe entered my office about 9 AM sucking on a cigarette while chomping on Nicorette gum and asked permission to shut my door. To lighten up matters, I told him I would help him push my couch in front of the door if he so desired. He smiled, but didn't respond and popped another Nicorette.

"Mondy, I'm making some organizational changes and I want you to know about them before they're announced." He was as uncomfortable as I had ever seen him.

"I'm listening."

"I'm continuing as president and CEO, but I'm relinquishing my COO position to Kenny Hyatt and you'll report to Kenny."

We stared at each other and then he continued, "I know this is not what you wanted to hear but I didn't want you to hear it from someone else or read it for the first time in the announcement. I'd like you to know I still consider you one of my closest friends," he said, lighting a cigarette with one that was only one-third smoked.

I made no comment and Joe exited.

I was crushed. I was stunned. I felt as if I had been sucker-punched in my stomach and jaw simultaneously. I felt betrayed and cheated, embarrassed, and belittled. Overriding all those emotions was the feeling of confusion. My eternal perspective and my family were far more important to me than my career, but at that moment, my temporal perspective inappropriately reigned over my emotions. My pride was severely wounded. I was bombed by surprise.

I later congratulated Kenny. It was friendly, but awkward.

A week later, I still was without a contract and I began wondering. My wonders were soon put to rest.

Joe and Kenny entered my office and asked if they could shut the door. I'd been in several situations like this before with Joe and was not surprised when Kenny did all the talking as Joe worked the cigarettes.

"Mondy," Kenny said, "the Company has to sell off subsidiaries to reduce debt, which will result in an extensive reorganization, and when that's completed, there won't be enough left for you to manage."

You needed a chainsaw to cut the air in my office. I clearly understood the *you're fired* message, though my confusion grew.

"When's this effective?" I asked. "Does a year from now work for you?" I did not answer, and they exited.

A second surprise bomb in seven days.

Except for when I'd been fired while working on the construction crew building Tampa Stadium while at UT, I had never been on the receiving end of a termination event. As I suspected, it was not fun. Nonetheless, I was not going to let circumstances control my life or my future. I had some praying and some thinking to do, and I had the perfect wife for the situation.

Shortly thereafter, a third bomb was deployed. Celotex was sold to Drummond Company out of Jasper, Alabama and Kenny Hyatt went with the deal as Celotex's President & CEO.

The remaining company, renamed Hillsborough Holdings LLC, was asbestos-free and things began to come into focus for me. Joe later told me that he knew from my earlier comments about answering questions under oath that the spin-off of Celotex couldn't have worked with me. The clandestine meetings with Celotex executives in my absence, the copying of my Celotex files, the reorganization with me and Celotex reporting to Kenny Hyatt now made sense from the corporate perspective.

CAN YOU HELP?

I decided I had no interest in working for another company, so I was focusing my efforts on purchasing one of the JWC subsidiaries. The obvious choice was Jim Walter Window Components, but that idea vanished when the KKR price was forty-two million dollars and the most I was willing to pay was twelve million. I liked Southern Precision in Birmingham, Alabama, but again KKR was looking for fifteen million and my calculation indicated five million dollars was top dollar for me.

Because JWC was realizing top dollar from sales of the subsidiary companies during the early going, the prospect of my buying one of the JWC companies was beginning to look bleak. I was shepherding the disposition of our jewelry division, our fastener division, and our paper division when I witnessed another example of how the Lord works.

Butler Paper, the Denver-based paper distributor which had purchased Jim Walter Paper, scheduled a celebration at The River Club atop one of Jacksonville's bank buildings and invited me to attend. I considered every excuse I could think of, but none seemed appropriate, so I decided to go if the company plane was available. It was, so I went.

I sat next to Butler's president & CEO, and over the course of dinner, he asked for my help with a problem for which he had no solution. One of the thirty-three branches of Jim Walter Paper did not fit Butler's business model and he asked my opinion on how would be the best way to dispose of this branch in Birmingham, Alabama that distributed industrial supplies to the coal mining industry in Alabama. (I was very familiar with the operation because it did not fit the Jim Walter Paper business model either but I had approved its purchase three years earlier because it was such a moneymaker, generally referred to as a cash cow.) He went on to say it was too small to be handled by a business broker but that it was too big to shut down and take the expected loss.

"Can you help?" he asked.

"I can," I said, and in December 1988, I purchased Jim Walter Supply from Butler Paper Company of Denver, Colorado for one-million fifty-thousand dollars.

Things went so well with the renamed Supply Inc. that my weekly visits became quarterly visits by the end of 1989 and biannual in 1990. Traveling to Birmingham was comfortable and convenient since I was given an open invitation to fly on the JWC jet anytime I wanted, which traveled same-day, round-trip to Birmingham every week and sometimes twice a week.

It quickly became apparent that the bombs that had landed in my office a year earlier were more than offset by the blessing God had provided with Supply, Inc.

NATURAL MAN

As I grew in my faith, it became clear to me that my termination from JWC was a *natural consequence* of dealing with *natural man,* and if I were faced with the very same decision (as a *natural man*), I would have taken the very same actions because a *natural man* can only do what a *natural man* can do. It is (only) the regenerate man who has a choice. This understanding took away any hard feelings I might have otherwise entertained or harbored.

TEENAGE AND BEYOND YEARS

Life continued to be good, even though Judy and I were about to experience what teenage years for parents are all about.

Mondy made a series of bad choices in his later high school and college years. He knew I would have helped him *to my last nickel,* but conversely, if he continued with his dedication to self-destruction, it would be almost impossible to extract another nickel from me. Though he had seen and heard (at home) the opposite approach to life, he had chosen to seek immature pleasure and the approval of some of his like-minded acquaintances who, as a group, selected the nighttime scene at Ybor City as their venue of choice. Considering their goal, they would have been hard-pressed to have made a better choice. It was a rough and challenging time for my wife and me. Alisha was generally supportive of whatever Mondy did, but naïve or foolish she is not, and for his own good, she would not sanction the path to self-destruction he was on.

Alisha claimed boredom at Seminole Presbyterian, and contrary to my wishes, attended Chamberlain for high school, where she continued producing A's while taking several college courses. Though a couple of her friends at Chamberlain gave Judy and me *agita*, her overall experience there was fairly benign. Surprising no one, she qualified to attend any college she desired. After much consternation, she selected one of the gems of the south, Samford University in Birmingham, Alabama.

Before Alisha would leave for college, she conceived and orchestrated one of the most meaningful experiences I have ever been part of or that a parent could ever wish for. Without hint or suggestion, she requested a going-away dinner with her family and closest friends, at which time she would vow to remain sexually pure until she met and married the man God would choose to be her husband. At the dinner, she asked that I provide her with a ring she would proudly wear as an outward sign of her commitment to God, her family, her closest friends, and to her husband to be, and to remain pure until she married.

God was, indeed, honored by this demonstration of Alisha's willingness and dedication to obey His ordinance in a world that scoffs at the notion of sexual purity and incessantly promotes in-your-face promiscuity. I cannot express the joy and fulfillment this occasion provided her mother and me. It will always remain, unequivocally, one of Judy's and my most cherished memories.

Samford permitted freshmen to have vehicles, but at the same time, warned parents that, statistically, students with vehicles earned lower grades, implying that an automobile could be a distraction. From the onset, Alisha made her case on why she should be allowed to have a car from day one to Judy, but Judy bought the distraction argument, and after much discussion and deliberation, compromised to allow Alisha to take her car after posting an honor roll first semester. Alisha was adamant on the issue and countered with a twist to her mother's compromise position and suggested allowing her to take her "trooper," and if she was unable to achieve the honor roll, she would give up the auto privilege until she met the honor roll status.

They could not reach an agreement and agreed to come to me for binding arbitration. I soon learned one of the reasons why arbitrators recuse themselves from matters where they know the parties involved in disputes. Both sides gave convincing arguments and were on solid ground with respect to their positions. It was, indeed, a case of *prudencia historia,* allowing history in the matter to guide me to a prudent decision. That, coupled with the wrath I sensed I would get if I decided against Alisha, drove me to rule in her favor. I was aware that the mild look of disdain I received from Judy would soon dissipate and that I avoided a lingering ration of wrath from Alisha with my decision, but in actuality, I was independently in favor of Alisha taking her car simply because I felt she had earned the privilege and was willing to forfeit it if she could not achieve the honor roll in her first semester.

Malio and Shirley joined us on the trip to deliver Alisha at Samford. It was a fun trip as we took the scenic route through south Alabama, ending at the Embassy Suites Hotel in Birmingham, which by no coincidence, housed Ruth's Chris Steakhouse. We did all the activities geared for parents highlighted by Step Sing, Samford's most time-honored tradition where every campus organization participates in a talent competition hoping to win the coveted Sweepstakes Trophy. The entire spectacle is developed, written, choreographed, rehearsed, and performed by Samford students leaving the audience stunned by the quality of the performances. I still recall the performance of a country & western singer who I thought was wasting his time in college. Judy and I were sad leaving our prized possession so far away, but we were aware that this was part of the process of raising young ones.

We were in no rush to return, so we backtracked the scenic route we had taken three days earlier. Malio was driving south on US 231 when we simultaneously spied a blinking Krispy Kreme doughnut sign on the opposite side of the highway while passing through Dothan, Alabama. Malio risked life and limb as he frantically crossed two lanes of traffic to reach the place where he could make a U-turn that would allow us access to Krispy Kreme's drive-thru window. I supported the maneuver, though Shirley and Judy thought it was a bit impetuous—they obviously did not assign proper credence to the meaning of the blinking sign.

Malio and I were not going to be left short of hot glazed doughnuts due to traffic. Our excitement contributed to the poor decision we made in ordering two dozen doughnuts, justifying our decision on the second dozen by the fact that it cost only a dollar. Shirley and Judy went overboard eating three each, leaving the daunting task of managing eighteen to Malio and me. I do not recall if we managed to eat all eighteen, but I know it was not a pretty scene. As we traveled route 231 for about fifteen minutes or so, I mentioned to Malio that things looked familiar and I questioned whether or not we were headed south. Malio assured me that we had turned right out of Krispy Kreme and that would have put us back in the direction we were heading before the doughnut ambush. I needed a road sign to convince me, and sure enough, the next sign read 231 N. We were so immersed in gobbling doughnuts that we had forgotten we'd made a U-turn. I was glad we discovered the error before seeing Samford University on the horizon.

As we arrived home, I was missing Alisha more but resisted calling her, though that's exactly what I wanted to do. With my aid, she had won the battle of having an auto on campus her freshman year and Judy had accepted the decision. The matter soon became moot as she began, then continued, her "A" production at Samford.

Judy and I had mixed emotions. Though we missed her, we were happy Alisha was in a good college environment but we remained perplexed regarding Mondy. He is every bit as bright as his sister, yet he had chosen a different path. We asked the unanswerable, *How did this happen?* as we sought to do whatever we could to help. While we could not determine what had caused Mondy's lapse, we prayed it would be temporary and that he would soon discern that the tug of this world leads to destruction and does not line up with what we thought he wanted for his future. We were aware of teenage issues far more serious than what we were experiencing and could have comforted ourselves by accepting his behavior as a sign of the times, but we love Mondy too much to quit on him. We prayed about it, did everything we thought would be profitable, and left the rest in the sovereign hands of God.

Mondy was not satisfied either with how things were going for him and decided that in order to get himself back on track, he would try to make his way in a location other than Tampa. His mother and I were supportive of his decision and viewed this moment as a turning point in his maturation and an answer to prayer.

He narrowed his selection to Birmingham, Tallahassee or Colorado Springs. Judy and I prayed that God would guide him in his decision. We were hoping he would choose either Tallahassee or Colorado Springs because we had good friends in both venues (Ken and Amy Connor in Tallahassee and Jim and Carole Bowers in Colorado Springs) giving us a measure of comfort. He chose Colorado and as we anticipated, Jim and Carole were wonderful in making Mondy's transition seamless. We will always be grateful for their love and support of Mondy.

God opened many doors as Mondy began his journey to become what he himself knew he could and wanted to be. Though he was far away and we missed him dearly, we could not have been happier.

On a warm and sunny day in March of 1997, he began the trip we prayed would open his eyes to what God had in store for him. I vividly recall the heightened emotions that day as he pulled out of our driveway and headed toward Colorado. He spent the first night with his sister in Birmingham, then made it to Columbia, Missouri before arriving in Manitou Springs, a suburb of Colorado Springs where he had arranged lodging in one of Summit Ministries' spartan cabins.

Colorado was the right choice. The distance freed him from his friends who were also struggling to find their way. He met people who understood the connection between eating and working and functioned accordingly, and most importantly, he met and fell in love with the lovely Sarah Kate Honken. We knew things were getting serious between Mondy and Sarah when he invited Judy and me to catch a Mariners/Rockies game (our good friend Lou Piniella was the Mariner skipper) in Colorado and to meet Sarah and her family. We gladly accepted and enjoyed meeting Sarah and her parents, though time did not allow us the opportunity to meet her seven siblings. Spending time with Sarah and Mondy displayed some of the many attributes Sarah possessed that attracted him to her, including her sweetness and character.

Curtis Bowers, Jim and Carole's son, was a successful entrepreneur in that area of Colorado, and before long, he and Mondy became good friends. One of Curtis' endeavors was the popular Mona Lisa restaurant in downtown Manitou Springs where Mondy was offered an opportunity in the restaurant business as a kitchen cleaning engineer, which is sometimes referred to as a dishwasher. As is often the case, opportunity, hard work, and positive attitude soon make friends, and within a few months, Mondy found himself waiting tables mostly and eventually managing the restaurant. As their friendship developed, Curtis enlightened Mondy to the fact that, while he possessed the capability to do a variety of things, he was overlooking a most attractive opportunity—his own father's business in Alabama. Concurrently, Mondy was considering marrying Sarah and asked what I thought about him working for the company. In January 1998, he relocated to Birmingham and began working for Supply Inc., our industrial supply distribution company.

It took no convincing for Alisha to leave her Samford dorm and live with her brother in an apartment where they could cut up as they had in Tampa but now without parental interruption. Ten months earlier it was a bad idea, but now the time was right. It was an ideal choice.

Separation and long distance confirmed that Mondy and Sarah's love for each other was not one of convenience but genuinely of the heart. During Sarah's visit to Birmingham, Mondy proposed to her on Samford University's scenic campus, and as they say, the rest is history.

Judy and I benefitted from Sarah being available to come to Tampa early to participate in the wedding and reception plans, and we really got to experience that sweetness and character that we had first seen in Colorado. All parents desire that their children will meet and marry that "special person," and during that two-week time period, Judy and I were pleased to witness that Sarah was indeed that "special person." That two-week period, doing all those things mothers-in-law-to-be and daughters-in-law-to-be enjoy doing, began a bonding period between Sarah and us that flourishes to this day.

Mondy and Sarah were married on Redington Beach, Florida with Mondy's uncle, Rev. B. Trent Stallings, officiating a sunset service in front of family and close friends August 29, 1998, before heading to Sarasota for their honeymoon. A week later, Judy and I hosted a wedding reception for the newlyweds at Tampa's Palma Ceia Country Club before they returned to Birmingham.

Meanwhile, Alisha and some friends transferred to the University of Central Florida for the noblest of reasons—access to Disney World. They rented a very nice four-bedroom house as their headquarters and enjoyed activities galore, including a trip to Alabama where UCF's football team lost a nail-biter to highly-ranked Auburn in the game's final seconds. Their most frequent and popular activity, however, was far and away the Disney scene.

I was pleased to see her carefree enjoyment during her last two years of college, knowing the real world awaited her and that these days would provide fond memories in the years to come. Alisha always managed her school work effectively, that is to say, she knew which classes required her attention and which did not and scheduled herself accordingly. One particular semester, all her classes were scheduled on Tuesday, Wednesday, and Thursday, and if you were to miss a class or two because of a conflicting social activity, you could watch the class on closed-circuit TV in the comfort of your home—a nice deal if you can get it. Notwithstanding, Alisha always carried a full load of classes and always delivered a full load of exemplary grades, culminating with a *cum laude* designation upon graduation following a very short family tradition established by her uncle Gene at the University of Tampa.

ARMANDO III's PHOTO GALLERY

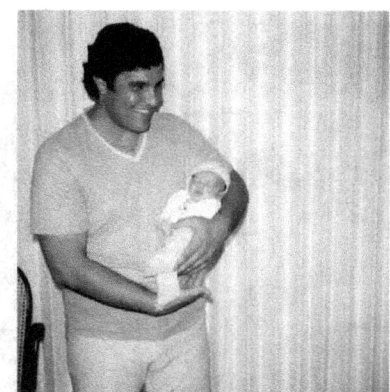
Me holding my son at 3 weeks old

Taking Mondito sightseeing in South Miami

Mondito, age 2

Frank and Mari Venezia with Mondito at our home in Miami

Mondito hitting clean-up for the Pirates

Mondito in a UT uniform

Mondito doing his soccer thing

Mondito, Judith, me and Alisha

7 yr old Mondito, and me

Mondito, Seminole Presbyterian School

Mondito getting an arm wrestling lesson

Mondy starts at Jesuit High School

Mondy, wide receiver at Jesuit

Mondy welcoming freshman to JHS

Mondy and me at his Manitou Springs cabin

Mondy and Sarah on the roof of his cabin

Mondy and Sarah dating

Mondy and Sarah dating some more

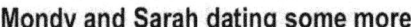

Mondy & Sarah's beach wedding

Sarah & Alisha at Sarah & Mondy's Wedding

Mondy & Sarah feeding each other at beach ceremony

Mondy & Sarah cutting cake at Palma Ceia reception

Judith, Mondy & Sarah at Palma Ceia wedding reception

ALISHA'S PHOTO GALLERY

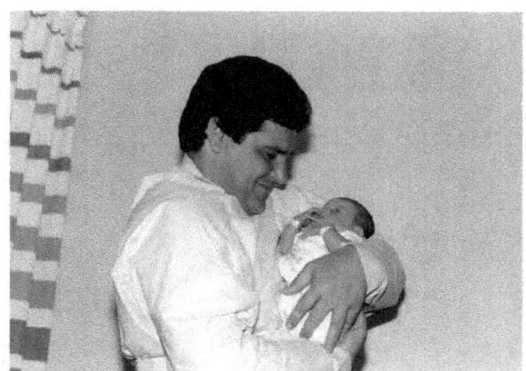

My Alisha just born at Miami Baptist Hospital

Alisha in the arms of her brother

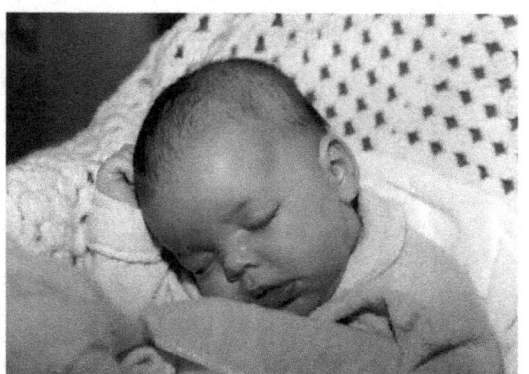

Alisha at 4 weeks

Alisha just being cute

Alisha, Bowman Center parade

Alisha in Tampa at 9 months

Alisha and her big brother

Alisha at her 2nd birthday party

Mondito recruiting Alisha to be a Gator

Alisha our little Geisha

Mondito, Papa Claus and Alisha

Family dinner at the Seabreeze

Grandparents day at SPS with Alisha 1985

Halloween

Alisha catches a ride on big brother

My favorite gal and me

Alisha at Seminoe Presbyterian School

My all time favorite volleyball player

Cheering when not playing

Sister and Brother time

Alisha Cum Laude from Chamberlain

Malio And Shirley helping at Samford

Me helping Alisha move to UCF

Alisha Cum Laude from UCF

Alisha & John

Sarah assisting Alisha 2002

John with parents Glenda & Al

Alisha & John's wedding 2002

Father-daughter dance at Alisha & John's wedding

Mondy with Alisha at Alisha & John's wedding

John and Alisha cutting the cake

FAMILY VACATIONS

Me and the kids enjoying the surf

Mondy and Alisha riding the horse at Disney

Me and Mondito in Daytona

Fishing with the kids in John's Pass

Mondy enjoying the view atop the World Trade Center

Our family taking a horse & carriage through Central Park

Mondy and Alisha Empire State

Mondy & Alisha at Yellowstone

Me & Alisha indian caves in Utah

Alisha & Mondy at Bal Rock, CO 1988

Our family on the rim of the Grand Canyon

Mondy & Alisha Manitou Springs CO

Our family - 90 miles from Cuba

Mondy in Oakland at the Reds-A's World Series

Mondito practicing with his firearm

Mondy & Alisha skiing in Winter Park, CO

Snowmobiling in Colorado

Alisha & Mondy at Clearwater beach

Alisha & Mondy at Graceland

Deno and our family

FAMILY AND FRIENDS

Sylvia and Gene at our home

Mama celebrating her birthday with her children at Malio's

Grandpa and Nana

My brother and sister enjoying lunch at Malio's

Judith with her parents

Judith's brother Elbert & his wife Thelma

Judith flanked by brothers Elbert and Trent

Judith's brother Trent & his wife Ana

My brother Bob & his wife Rose

My brother Bob & sister Frances

My sweetheart Alisha & me

Armando III & Armando Flores JR

John Cordova & Mondy Flores III

Alisha & John Cordova

Sarah & Mondy Dec 2000

Sally & Terry Russo

Terry Russo & Sister Tanya

Family enjoying dinner at Iavarone's

Carmine, me & Malio

John Oliva and me talking it over in our youth

Lydia & John Oliva

Gigi & Ted Cannella

Malio & Shirley Iavarone

Anita & Lou Piniella

My Pastor Ken Witten with wife Ginny

Janice & Barry Banther

Carmine & Barbara Iavarone

Ron & Mary Seeley

Richard & Shirley Martinez

Al Cordova and me

Pat & Theresa Burley

Lori and Steve Malzone

Betty & Baby Joe Valenti

Tommy & Glenda Depolis

Mari & Frank Venezia

Tony & Ann Gonzalez

John, Lou and Me

John & Me working on Mis Memorias

Mondy IV, John Oliva, Mondy and me
JHS Alumni Luncheon

TRIPS

Me and Judith at the Colosseum

Judith admiring the architecture at a basilica in Italy

Judith and me at the Roman Colosseum

Judith in El Yunque, Puerto Rico

Catching a big fish with Baby Joe

Chicago 2007

Judith with back to Toledo (Spain)

Key West, FL   Nov 2009

Me & Sweet Lou travel to Key West in his ocean vessel
EXTRA INNINGS

Part Three

LATER YEARS - FINISH STRONG (1999-THE APPOINTED TIME)

THE BEST THINGS IN LIFE AREN'T THINGS

We were experiencing smooth sailing early in 1999 and the forecast appeared to be more of the same. Alisha was closing in on graduation at UCF, and Mondy and Sarah were doing well in Birmingham, having worked through the disappointment of Sarah's miscarriage on the first day of the year. Employing the notion, "You are doing as well as your least happy child" as a barometer, we were doing fine.

On February 16, 1999, Judy and I were preparing to eat the Thai dinner we'd brought in when the phone rang. I wasn't going to answer, then I noticed the caller ID indicated UAB and the Birmingham area code—205. When I answered, the nurse went through the protocol of relationship identification, then proceeded to explain that Mondy had been severely burned and was being tended to in the UAB (University of Alabama Birmingham) Burn Center along with Sarah, who'd suffered minor burns on her foot. She medically described Mondy's condition, but the more I heard, the more confused I became, so I asked the question that was foremost on my mind, "Is his condition life-threatening?" to which she replied, "We are in the midst of assessing him and if he has to go on a ventilator, most certainly."

I (along with Judy, who had heard my part of the conversation) was numb. I asked the nurse to tell Mondy and Sarah that we would be there as quickly as possible and to please provide updates as they became available. We dropped to our knees and asked for the Lord's mercy. I mentioned to Judy that this situation had shed a new light on what God had done when He sent His only Son to die for our sin. Somberly, she concurred.

Among others, we called our good friend Barry Banther, and he prayed with us over the phone before the long night ahead until boarding a 7 AM flight to Birmingham.

We were touched by the considerate, warm, and loving gesture we experienced when we saw Barry at the airport the following morning. To get up before the crack of dawn to provide a well-needed hug for us was very much appreciated, but we had misread the situation. Barry was traveling to Birmingham with us and would be by our side throughout that frightful first day. Judy and I will never forget Barry's act of kindness and concern.

We went to Sarah's room upon arriving at the hospital and she gave us an update. She was receiving treatment for burns she suffered on her foot. A hospital rep escorted us toward Mondy in the ICU (Intensive Care Unit). We were very thankful Sarah had escaped serious burns but were taken aback when we witnessed Mondy's swollen and bandaged upper body and shaved head. He was supported with tubes and equipment everywhere. Judy and I were shaken to the core but were temporarily lifted when we recognized his attempt to smile when he first saw us. We held back the tears and attempted to act confident as we listened to the first of many briefings. What stuck in our minds was that his condition remained critical and he would continue to be monitored closely to determine the appropriate course of action. Barry led us in prayer as we asked for Mondy's breathing to continue without the need of a ventilator and that he would be assigned to a private room, hoping for his release from the ICU. Amidst the trauma, we thanked God for allowing Mondy to have access to one of the country's premier burn centers, a situation we would appreciate more in the weeks and months to come.

Barry left that evening as Uncle Frank and Aunt Mari arrived to comfort and support Sarah and us. The next day, Alisha arrived to be by her brother's side and gain a first-hand assessment of Mondy's status. She did not like what she saw and did not want to return to Orlando until matters stabilized, but I convinced her it was in everyone's best interest if she returned to UCF to complete her midterm exams with the understanding that she could utilize the one-hour nonstop flight back and forth to Orlando at will. She agreed and did just that. She placed her life in "park," and as often as she could put a couple of days together, she came to visit. I observed the positive affect it had on her brother.

God answered our prayers, and on February 18th, Mondy was moved to a private room on the 10th floor of the UAB burn unit within the mega-complex known as the UAB Medical Center.

I had been experiencing flu-like symptoms when we left Tampa and felt worse in the wet and cold Birmingham offered. I went to the Walk-In Clinic in the UAB medical complex and they confirmed my condition and put me on an antibiotic with instructions to get rest, as if that were possible.

On February 22nd, Mondy was scheduled for skin-graft surgery, which is part of the restoration process for burn patients with third-degree burns. The process includes harvesting skin from an unaffected part of the patient's anatomy to be used on areas where skin was burnt badly; the more serious the burn, the more extensive the graft requirement.

The scheduled skin graft surgery was tentative because Mondy had developed infections beneath both arms. He was being treated with strong antibiotics, but the decision whether or not to proceed would have to wait until the morning of the 22nd. Dr. Smith decided it was too risky and the surgery was rescheduled for two days later. There was a slight unintended benefit; in typical Flores fashion, Mondy enjoyed a "fried fish platter" imported by yours truly from The Fish House Restaurant in downtown Birmingham for lunch and Frank imported Porterhouse steaks he cooked on Mondy's and Sarah's grill that evening and I was becoming concerned if the feasting would cause nausea as a reaction to the anesthesia.

The surgery on the 24th was again postponed, this time to the 29th, which was a let-down to us. Nonetheless, Mondy consented to allow the local Fox TV affiliate to interview him as part of a special report on "burn survivors;" doing so helped occupy some of the wait time generated by the postponement.

Lifting Mondy's spirits (which lifted Sarah's and ours) were visits from family and friends, including Uncle Malio and Aunt Shirley, Uncle Gene and Aunt Sylvia, Uncle Trent, Sarah's parents, Richard and Sherry, and their friends, the Randolph's; but no visitor had the effect of putting him in a good mood more than visits from his sister and fellow jokester. Alisha was in daily contact regarding his progress and would fly to Birmingham as often as possible. While visiting, they (including Sarah) would pick up where they left off with a plethora of games and conversations common to folks in their twenties. While Judy and I didn't completely understand the particulars of what amused them so, we completely understood the benefit to Mondy and Sarah to spend some time focused on something other than the misery of being confined to a burn unit.

A potential challenging situation developed at the hospital, while my brother Gene was visiting. A fire alarm sounded, eliciting concern and some fear as everyone on the 10th floor wondered how the immobile burn patients would be evacuated. The staff tried to ease the concern, but each time the alarm resounded, everyone's concerns returned. I was engaged in my own fact-finding activity when the alarm sounded for the third time and the natives (including this native) were becoming restless. Just about that time, Gene advised me that he had located a stairwell in the unauthorized area of the floor that was wide enough to accommodate Mondy's bed, and should this or a subsequent alarm not be a false one, we were to get Mondy's bed and follow him. When Mondy was successfully evacuated, we would return to help the other patients. That's my brother, and I would not suggest to anyone that they attempt to curtail his efforts. Fortunately, all ended well and we did not need to employ his plan.

The surgery on the 29th went well. Donor skin from his left thigh and groin was harvested to replace large sections of his chest, arms, wrist, and foot, which suffered third-degree burns. Blessedly, the burns on his neck and face were of the first- and second-degree nature, which restore themselves without the need of skin grafts. In total, Mondy suffered burns on over 30% of his body.

After his surgery, Mondy prayed and thanked God for the outcome of the surgery, for not being burned more than he was, and for Sarah being, for the most part, spared. When things are going well one may tend to take their blessings for granted but when confronted with the situation in which we found ourselves, nothing is taken for granted. It is in these times when we are reminded that every blessing we have is from God and God alone and that we are completely dependent on His love, mercy and grace each and every moment of our lives. We joined Mondy and Sarah in thanking God. I had thanked God for choosing me among my family when faced with both of my bypass surgeries and wished that I could have been the one that was burned, but it would not be. Sometimes, God wants people to experience difficult circumstances to strengthen them for what is yet to come.

In addition to the restorative skin-graft surgery, an integral part of the recovery process included hydrotherapy (hydro). Each day, Mondy was given morphine in preparation for hydro followed by *versant*, a medication intended to induce him to forget the procedure. The morphine helps the burn patient deal with the pain caused by the debriding process (a "hosing down" of the burned areas to release and remove the dead cells which had accumulated during the previous twenty-four hours). "Intense pain is an understatement," we were told by the hydro technicians and the screams from the hydro wing gave witness to that fact. Mondy led us in prayer before and after every hydro session. We had much to pray over, for blessings received and for strength to endure what was to come.

Mondy's body had experienced major trauma and it was necessary to undergo transfusions to keep his blood count at appropriate levels. One day, in an attempt to distract Mondy from the task at hand, a nurse asked him *if he could have anyone's blood, whose would he choose... in other words, who was his hero?* I learned of his response later and was drawn to tears then as I am now as I report his response...he said *he would choose my blood.* It is instances such as this that confirm that **the best things in life aren't things.**

Though we attempted to convince Sarah to get rest, away from the hospital, she stayed by Mondy's bedside 24/7. Her undying commitment to Mondy was a blessing to behold and I'm convinced her attention to his every need was used by God to accelerate his recovery. The evening Mondy was transported to the hospital, it was estimated that his stay would not be less than ninety days and his need to go onto a ventilator to assist his breathing was a foregone conclusion. Though there was much ahead for Sarah and Mondy with regard to his recovery, when he was discharged on March 8, 1999, only twenty days after the burn and having never needed the assistance of a ventilator, we recognized we had witnessed God's hand at work.

Judy and I left Birmingham on March 13th as it was time for Mondy and Sarah to adjust their lives to the unanticipated circumstances they now faced. During our stay, Judy had spent 12-14 hour days and had become exhausted. As for me, my upper respiratory condition was graduating to pneumonia, according to the physician whose care I was under at UAB, dimming the prospect of Judy getting the rest she needed back in Tampa. Judy continually asked me to rest while in Birmingham, but rest did not come easily in circumstances such as the ones we found ourselves. Nonetheless, Judy is always ready to care for someone's needs, and though it was not my intention, I now filled the role of that needy someone.

As part of the healing process keloid (thick, raised) scars would form at several locations on Mondy's upper torso and arms, and over the next eighteen months, Mondy would require three "tissue expander" surgeries whereby balloons are surgically inserted beneath the skin at strategic locations near large Keloid scars and are periodically inflated to stretch the skin (similar to how a woman's stomach skin is stretched during pregnancy) which then is used to cover the area where the Keloids were surgically removed. It is a long and arduous process, but it produces a valuable outcome.

The next eighteen months were a bonding and growing opportunity for our family. We visited Mondy and Sarah for the "tissue expander" surgeries and any other time they requested our help. Alisha visited them, as well, and occasionally made the trip with us. We are—and were—most thankful for the progress Mondy was making and we valued *normalcy* much higher than we had before. Mondy expressed that his relationship with the Lord had taken on a new dimension and declared that *he could not have made it without God.* We laughed and amused ourselves, but all our lives had been changed; we all recognized the close call God graciously allowed us to escape and our lives going forward would never be the same—and that is a good thing.

THE BEST THINGS IN LIFE AREN'T THINGS

One day at a time with God's grace

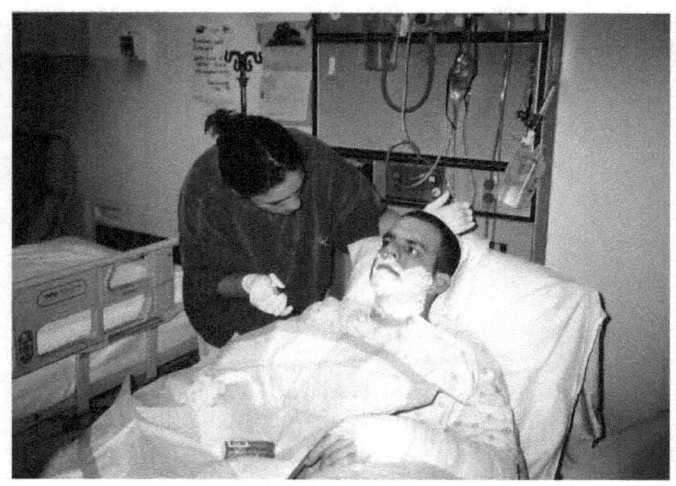

...In good times and in bad

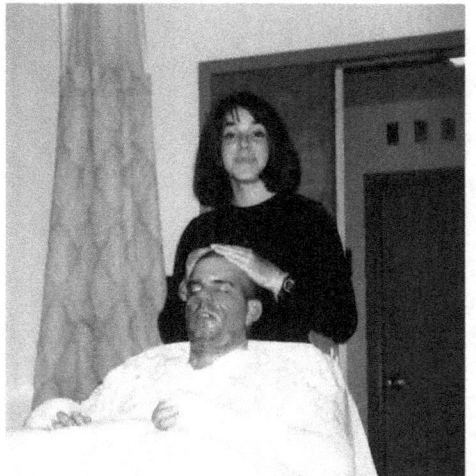

A sister's love

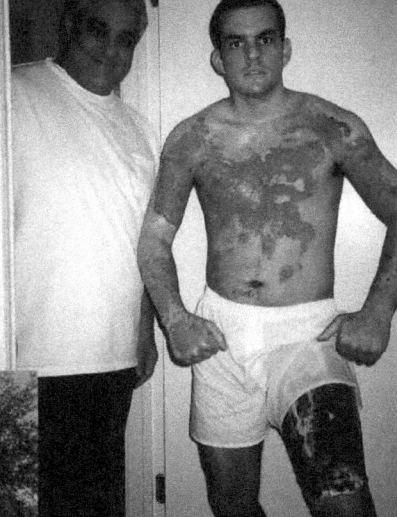

Recovering in God's strength & grace

TO GOD BE THE GLORY

NANA GOES TO HEAVEN

On June 7, 1999, four months and a few days shy of her 86th birthday, my mother was promoted to heaven. She had been active and happy before her heart gave out at St. Joseph's Hospital while in the presence of my brother Gene, who was gladly serving his part of a rotating shift staying with her during her final days.

As I look back on her life from the perspective of a fifty-four-year-old, I am encouraged and amazed by her accomplishments. At thirty-seven years of age, she had been left with the responsibility of raising four children who ranged in age from four years of age to twenty. Never did any of her children, or anyone else for that matter, hear her complain about her situation or declare that she had been dealt an unfair hand. On the contrary, she (through her actions and without intention) demonstrated a *can-do* attitude to all who knew her, but especially to her children. Shortly after the shocking murder of her husband, she took employment as a laborer within walking distance from our home and never looked back. In retrospect, it took a yeoman's effort to accomplish what she did and how she did it—without complaining or blame. But in 1971, at the age of fifty-seven, she married Claud Douglas McKay (Grandpa) and for the last twenty-eight years of her life he treated her like the queen she was. It was a delight to those who loved her that she met with the good fortune that was Grandpa, who understandably, quickly became an important member of our family.

After her promotion, Judy and I had the honor, along with my siblings, to tend to Grandpa's every need until June 28, 2006, when he joined his love and my mother in heaven. My mother and Grandpa were a wonderful blessing to our family, and though we miss them very much, it is encouraging to know that at our appointed time we will be reunited with them in Glory.

APRIL 26, 2000

I was lunching with my Pastor, Ken Whitten, and a couple of other men at Iavarone's, following our weekly Bible study, when I noticed my good friend Carmine Iavarone's puzzled look. It was Secretaries' Day, and his restaurant was jammed, so I assumed his look was related to managing the demanding crowd. But managing demanding crowds was nothing new to this seasoned restaurateur, causing me to think there was another issue on his mind. He continued to peer at our booth as his usually upbeat persona remained subdued.

I attempted to gain his attention in hopes of offering any help I could provide, but he would not make eye contact—purposely, I surmised. He paced the restaurant a couple of times as if building up to his approach of our booth. Upon arriving, he asked to speak to Pastor Whitten, feigning something about his office trying to reach him and he did all this without making eye contact with me. Something was up, I thought, though I was well aware of the many emergencies that can arise for a pastor with a flock of ten-thousand. It had to do with Carmine avoiding my eyes. Within a couple of minutes, Pastor Ken returned to our booth and asked if he could speak to me privately. He escorted me outside the building and, in his gentle pastoral manner, communicated to me that my brother Gene had unexpectedly been taken to his heavenly home. I recall feeling lightheaded as I attempted to process what I had just heard, not understanding how my younger and physically fit brother was now gone. My mind began to spin with questions.

"Surely, it must have been an accident?" I asked myself and Pastor Whitten.

"I don't know any details, but your family would like you to come home," he offered. "Would you like me to drive you?"

"No. I can drive," I responded, though I should have accepted his offer.

As I entered my vehicle, Carmine hugged me and expressed his sorrow. This time it was me who was unable to make eye contact.

I do not recall driving home, but I do recall seeing Judy at the front door ready to receive her wounded husband. Gene and Judy were very close, and I knew she was hurt as well, but Gene was my best friend, confidant, business associate, fellow bike-rider and walker, and former teammate as well as my loving brother. I was, indeed, wounded and needed the comfort she offered. She knew it mattered little at that moment, but she nonetheless cited special moments we had shared with Gene and how I was honored to have introduced him to our Lord and Savior, and most importantly, that we would be reunited. I was comforted by all she said amidst the awful pain I was suffering from his loss, but even so, I remained confounded by his sudden departure at the age of fifty-two.

Additionally, the idea of being reunited with loved ones was beginning to wear a little thin with the losses of my mother and lovable sister-in-law, Rosie, in the previous nine months, though I was aware enough to be thankful that my son was spared death when accidentally burned just over a year earlier.

Judy explained that the details were sketchy but that Gene had been found deceased in his San Antonio hotel room by a Siemens executive and the hotel manager, upon entering the room at the request of the Siemens executive who properly assumed something was wrong when Gene did not appear for a scheduled meeting that morning. From what they could gather, he experienced a heart attack after completing his morning walk but before he dressed for the meeting he had called.

This event led me to personalize the Bible passage in James 4:14: *Whereas you do not know what* will *happen tomorrow. For what is your life? It is even a vapor that appears for a little time and then vanishes away.* (NKJV)

PROMOTED TO HEAVEN

Caterina Flores McKay
10/8/1913 - 6/7/1999

Claud Douglas McKay
2/23/1922 - 6/28/2006

Gene Marcelino Flores
10/24/1947 - 4/26/2000

Gene's family accepting posthumously the Boys and Girls Club of America "National Bronze Medallion" award for "Gene's exceptional devotion and exemplary service to boys and girls"

BLESSINGS DISGUISED AS CALAMITIES

Supply, Inc. continued to be a cash cow even during bad economies aided by the fact that the company had no outside debt—the only debt was to Judy's Trust, a situation set up for financial planning purposes. Without being actively involved in the day-to-day activities of the business, I earned more during the time we owned Supply Inc. than I had cumulatively earned during my entire life, confirming the fact that God can (but doesn't always choose to) provide more than we could ever produce on our own.

However, our money machine would not last forever. As a result of management decisions (allowed by me) to expand into markets disassociated with coal mining, key members of Supply Inc's workforce became unsure of their future and decided to go into competition against us. On the day of Mondy's last "tissue expander" surgery, I received word that our top salesman was resigning to enter into his own mining supply business. This announcement was only the tip of the iceberg as key resignations followed when the owner of our new competitor's business was able to hire his former coworkers.

Though there were legal remedies I could have pursued to stave off this insurrection, I chose not to employ them, but rather to continue with the mining supply business as long as it remained profitable and shift our focus to the residential window business. Concurrent with this decision, I decided to charge the window business their proportionate share of the "market rent" for our warehouse, which motivated them to seek a less expensive location post haste. Meanwhile, we received a very attractive rental offer from an Arizona-based medical products distributor that mitigated our losses from the operating companies and which resulted in piquing my interest in the income-producing commercial real estate business. In time, both operating businesses would not muster enough sales to warrant their continuation, leading me to shut them down and remain in the commercial real estate business in Alabama.

By the first day of 1999, my family and I were unaware we had been willingly lulled into a fantasy land that had commenced on December 19, 1970, when Judy and I were married, equating to twenty-seven years and twelve days—quite a stretch of blessings and marital bliss as most would agree. Prior to January 1, 1999, aside from my heart issues and the normal challenges associated with raising a family, any and all issues we experienced were external and could be remedied without bruising the core of our family. Things were about to change.

The first day of 1999 began with the news brought by Mondy that Sarah had miscarried their first baby and our first grandbaby. Within sixteen months of that sorrowful event, our family would experience Mondy's and Sarah's burn accident, the death of my mother, the death of Judy's and my sister-in-law Rose, the death of my brother Gene, and the loss of our business in Alabama.

Our Christian worldview allowed us to manage our way through those days, knowing that God would not put more on us than we could handle with His help and that better days would surely follow—if not on earth, then in heaven. We know God is sovereign, therefore, we recognized all these events had taken place for a reason and it was our responsibility to trust and obey and leave the future in His hands—and that's what we did. We did not always like the hand that was dealt to us, but we never doubted the Dealer.

Blessings are often disguised as calamities, and it can be difficult to distinguish one from the other while engaged in the heat of the battle. A case-in-point was our business in Alabama. One could have easily become bitter by the collapse of a vibrant business, but (and in no small part, due to) the experience of Mondy's burn, Judy and I viewed the collapse as a blessing we would have otherwise missed. If our business would have continued to succeed, Mondy would have managed it and would have possibly made Birmingham his and Sarah's permanent home. Even if he would have worked there for twenty or so years before deciding to move back to Tampa, he may have been reluctant to leave a proven means of supporting his family to begin a career in some unknown field in his mid-forties—not that it could not be done, but one's inclination would be to hold on to the *bird in the hand*. Under this scenario, a profitable business would have provided increased monetary wealth at the expense of missing the untold memories that have been generated by Mondy and Sarah while raising their family in Tampa. Money for memories—that's a trade I don't care to make. Thus, our business failing in Birmingham resulted in our money machine converting to a memory machine, and that's a trade I'll make all day.

More importantly, Mondy is the first to point out that his burn experience contributed to a shift of his focus to eternal matters, and while we all would have preferred that he would have gained that realization while reflecting beneath a shade tree, we yield to the sovereignty of God with the confidence that someday we will see God's purpose in this and other matters we would have orchestrated differently.

(MY) GIRL MEETS BOY

Alisha possesses a combination of intelligence and drive that allows her to accomplish about anything to which she sets her mind. Conversely, she needs to be challenged and is bored by the mundane, as was the case while employed by Chase Mortgage Corporation.

Her ultimate life's ambition has always been to be the wife and mother she had seen modeled by her mother. When she was approximately six years old, she mildly shocked our career-minded neighbor and her friend when she expressed this sentiment in response to the neighbor's inquiry as to what she wanted to be when she grew to be a woman. The surprised duo looked to me for comment and I proceeded to support Alisha's response by adding that not everyone was capable of taking on such a tremendous responsibility. She did not require my support because she was experiencing the benefit of someone executing that responsibility at its highest level, and though she may have been a little young to articulate why she aspired to be like her mom, she recognized the importance and quality of her mother's position and desired to replicate what she saw.

So, in 2001, while she focused, from 9 to 5, on providing prospective homeowners financing, her overall focus was on meeting the man God would provide to reach the fullness in life she desired. She had dated young men at Samford and UCF, but they had not met her standards, and for that, I was pleased.

Then, in early 2002, with a twinkle in her eyes, she told her mother and me that she had met a nice young man at a church-sponsored Super Bowl party. Her description revealed that her impression of this young man was more than casual.

"How could this be?" I mused silently, but quickly answered my own question as I recalled my feelings when I'd first met her mother forty-one years earlier. She continued to describe John David Cordova unsuccessfully suppressing her enthusiasm. She initially put me at ease by communicating that John was gainfully employed and added spice to her portrayal by relating that he had come to know our Lord a few years earlier through the influence of her "uncle" and my good friend, Frank Venezia.

I'm always amazed at how God orchestrates matters. Frank accepted Jesus as his Lord and Savior in our home in 1980, and twenty-two years later, my daughter was relating to me (in that same home) that this nice young man she met had been spiritually mentored by a person I had mentored in that same regard. Notwithstanding, that information was insufficient evidence for me. I know several Christians whose company I expect I will only enjoy once we're in heaven.

They dated, and before long, I met John and could readily understand Alisha's attraction to this young man—a term I don't use lightly. John is a handsome man, and his handsomeness is trumped by his refined demeanor and social ease. Nonetheless, his appearance and persona added to his résumé but there remained insufficient evidence from my perspective. Alisha is my only daughter, and my bar for who is the correct mate for her is quite high—for her good *and* for the good of the man, as well. I was pleased with what I saw, but before I could *buy in,* I needed to understand John's heart and soul. I'm well acquainted with folks who appear to be top-notch while things are comfortable, but when challenges arise—and they always do—they morph into who they really are and it is often not a pretty sight.

Providing input on someone's character is not a perfect science, but as Alisha's father, it is my duty to make available my best assessment of someone's character if she's becoming serious about that someone *and* if she desires my opinion. Alisha has always valued my opinion and her questions to me concerning what I thought about John made it clear she coveted it in this instance. I am fully aware that developing an accurate assessment of someone is not an easy task considering many are skilled in rhetoric and pretense and adequate time to observe their actions is generally shorter than ideal. However, assessing people is a gift I've had since I was a youngster and one I have honed over the years.

As is typical in such matters, Alisha and John could not see enough of each other. The events and activities they enjoyed pointed favorably as they continued in the very important process of learning each other's likes and dislikes. Their blissful relationship led them to the conclusion that they were made for each other, but before they went any further, John wanted to meet with me to gain my blessing on their intention to wed. I was honored that he took this approach and my meeting with John supported my growing opinion that he was a quality young man and that he and Alisha would be a good match for each other. John did a masterful job of expressing his willingness to be the best husband and father he could be, and it was obvious to me that he held my daughter in the highest esteem. Because she felt that way about him, and because their faith in God was the foundation of their relationship, I knew they were on solid footing. The one thing I expressed to John and wanted him to understand was that marriage is nothing like he (or anyone) thinks it's like. Theirs would have its own uniqueness which would include some wonderful experiences but would also include some tough challenges. I went on to explain that one's *personality* is on display when things are going well, but it is a person's *character* that is revealed when times are tough. (I could not be sure he understood the essence of my comments at the time, but I have witnessed his capability to navigate through tough times since and can attest to the fact that John David Cordova is a man of exceptional character.)

John and Alisha exchanged nuptial vows on Saturday, November 9, 2002, at Seminole Presbyterian Church in Tampa. Wes Searcy, her youth pastor and his wife, Colleen, made the trip from Texas as Wes presided over the ceremony and Colleen stood as Alisha's matron of honor. It was a beautiful event witnessed by friends and family, and then celebrated with a wonderful dinner reception before the newlyweds departed to North Carolina for their honeymoon. Mr. and Mrs. John David Cordova moved into their newly-constructed home upon their return with an enthusiastic outlook on life.

A "*GENERAL*" CHRISTMAS *CONVERSATION*

During 2002, Judy and I attended Saturday evening services at Idlewild. On the Saturday evening before Christmas, Judy and I were invited to a Christmas party at the home of our friends Lenda and Vince Naimoli. The timing was perfect since the party began at 7 PM and church generally concluded by 7:15.

After the service, Judy and I waited to speak with Pastor Whitten, as we often did, before heading to the party. While we waited for the popular minister to meet and greet members of the congregation, we engaged in a conversation with a couple we knew casually. The couple expressed to us how much they were enjoying the Christmas holidays, and especially, the visit from San Antonio, Texas by their daughter and son-in-law.

Their son-in-law was a fighter pilot in the US Air Force. He was a captain expecting to become a major within the next six months and was "dreaming" about being transferred to MacDill Air Force Base in Tampa. MacDill Air Force Base was home to Central Command (CENTCOM in Air Force parlance) for the war against Al Queda and the rest of the militant Muslim world seeking to extinguish the brand of freedom exported from the United States throughout the world. The general in charge of the war effort was the well-liked, tough-minded, field-tested general named Tommy Franks. I had casually met General Franks at Malio's restaurant on several occasions over the preceding couple of years and found him to be quite personable. Additionally, Malio had developed a friendship with the general. As our acquaintances described their desire to have their fighter pilot son-in-law and their daughter return to Tampa, I pondered whether or not General Franks involved himself with such detail while in the midst of this huge campaign versus terrorists in the Arab world. Nonetheless, I considered their situation in the light of my two kids and decided to offer what help I might be able to provide through my friend Malio as a conduit to General Franks. When I mentioned to the couple that I could possibly get a message to the general, their jaws dropped, knowing General Franks required no approval to transfer their son-in-law if he so desired. With a genuine appreciation of my offer, their son-in-law (who during our conversation walked up and introduced himself to Judy and me) jotted down the pertinent information regarding his desire and gave me the information, which I promised to deliver to Malio no later than Christmas Day.

Moments later, we arrived at the Naimoli home, exchanged a few pleasantries with some guests then made our way outside around the pool. As we nibbled on some delicacies,

I looked over the crowd to see who I knew and asked Judy, "Is that General Franks?"

She replied, "I believe it is."

I ushered Judy toward the area where General Franks and his wife stood with the intention of reintroducing myself to him, and if the opportunity presented itself, discuss with him the transfer request info I carried in my coat pocket.

As I approached the general, he extended his hand to shake mine, which I had already extended.

"General," I said. "We've met before at Malio's."

He immediately acknowledged our previous meetings (whether he remembered them or not). I introduced Judy to him and his wife, and in return, he introduced his wife, Kathy. We chitchatted for a few moments before I decided to bring up the transfer matter. I began introducing the topic by expressing to the general that I did not believe in coincidences. He said he did not believe in coincidences either, but what he did believe in was (he said no more but gave an assuring smile and pointed his finger toward the heavens). I concurred with his implication of God's involvement in our lives and began to explain the situation I had experienced just thirty minutes earlier. As I told him, that I had been conversing with a captain in the Air Force after the church service at Idlewild, he emoted a prideful smile causing me to pause and ask the reason for the smile.

"Our boys work so hard and are so dedicated," he responded, "it gives me a wonderful feeling when I hear stories such as the one you're telling me."

I proceeded to communicate to him that this fighter pilot was stationed in San Antonio, Texas and was interested in relocating to CENTCOM at MacDill Air Force Base for professional as well as personal reasons.

His smile grew broader as he asked for specifics on the captain and said, "This is what I like to do, assist these young men who are working so hard and are so dedicated to protecting our way of life."

You could sense the genuine concern and admiration he had for his troops and his desire to assist them in any way he could. In connection with the difficult task facing the military, he told us that he occasionally takes Kathy with him on trips to military installations because she enjoys being around and hugging these young men who have been absent for some time from hugs from their spouses and mothers. It was a special moment to hear from the lips of the general of his interest—and that of his wife's—in our fighting corps. Given his position, he and Kathy could have easily isolated themselves from the everyday soldier and immerse themselves in the luxury and trappings of being the nation's top general, yet it was apparent their interests lay with our frontline troops. It certainly made one feel proud to be an American and secure in the protection managed by Gen. Tommy Franks.

Judy and I commented on the way God had orchestrated this evening on behalf of the fighter pilot stationed in San Antonio. Before they prepared for their trip to Tampa, God had already arranged for his wife's parents to attend Saturday night service, even though they generally attended Sunday morning. Additionally, He arranged for the Naimoli party to include both the General and Mrs. Franks and us, and furthermore, paved the way for our meeting and discussion (approximately 350 people had attended the party, yet we had spoken to no more than forty of them). What it boils down to is that God is working in our lives even as we read this account, but we often don't realize it.

After relating the story to him, Pastor Whitten said it best when he said, "I'm going to sleep well tonight knowing that God is in control of everything." My sentiments, exactly.

(In late 2003, it was reported by the fighter pilot's father-in-law (Woody Luke) to Judy and me that his son-in law was finishing up training at the base in Monterey, California and would soon be transferred to CENTCOM Headquarters at MacDill AFB in Tampa as requested the previous December.)

GROWING FAMILY

Blessings abounded with the steady addition of grandchildren. Armando Flores IV and Vincente Marcelino Flores were born in Birmingham in 2000 and 2001, followed by Tampa-born Christiano DiDio Flores in 2004, Mia Joy Cordova, and Jennifer Kaylee Flores in 2005, Olivia Grace Cordova in 2007, and capped off with the birth of Giana Faith Cordova in 2009. Our growing family gathered at our home just about every weekend and practically all holidays, except for when Mondy, Sarah and their children would visit Sarah's family, generally in Colorado or South Carolina. Amidst these births, we encountered yet another bomb. However, this bomb made the bomb regarding my career seem like a small, wet firecracker.

THE BOMB

April 1, 2004 began as a lazy day. If my mother had still been alive, she would have undoubtedly called with a fabricated story describing a sad situation only to spring "April Fool" at the appropriate time. She got a thrill "catching me" as she put it. Over the years, I was often able to detect her ploy, but would play along, enjoying the enjoyment she experienced leading me on. This April 1st, the sad situation would not be fabricated.

That afternoon, Grandpa and I installed a ceiling fan for my sister. The fan had been given to her by Mondy III and Sarah. When I returned home, I was greeted by Mondy IV who was being cared for by his *abuela* (grandmother), while Sarah took both his brothers for a "well" visit at the pediatrician.

Judy took a phone call from Sarah, and overhearing Judy's portion of the conversation, it became obvious that Sarah had been confronted by a serious situation and was engaging our assistance. She had been unsuccessful at contacting Mondy, who was playing golf, and needed our assistance in the interim.

"Yes, Papa and I will meet you at the emergency room at St. Joseph's and Papa can help you with Christiano while I take care of Vinny and Mondito (ages 2½ and 4). We'll see you there," Judy concluded with apprehension in her voice.

On the way to the hospital, she called Alisha and calmly but fearfully repeated to her what she had already told me.

"They think he has some kind of heart problem and want the pediatric cardiologist to look at him."

Alisha arrived at the hospital shortly after we did, followed by Mondy, who was still wearing golf shoes and a visor. Judy returned home with Mondito and Vinny while Alisha and I ministered to Sarah, then to Sarah and Mondy, even though we ourselves were in need of ministering as we continued to receive sketchy and perilous reports.

Amidst an ugly and tragic experience, it was a beautiful thing to see Alisha's relationship with Mondy and Sarah produce comfort as she prayed, hugged, and attended to their every need and as they (we) became increasingly bewildered and surprised as more information spelled out the fact that eight-week-old Christiano was fighting for his life as he labored for every breath due to a condition we would later find out was called Transposition of the Great Arteries (TGA).

I went home to be with Judy and the boys and was soon replaced at the hospital by Alisha's very capable husband, John (John and Alisha had been married only sixteen months, but John had already become an integral part of the family due in large part to his mature, caring, and loving demeanor.)

John and Alisha stayed with Mondy and Sarah and provided updates on Christiano's (and Christiano's parents') condition.

Eight and one-half pound Christiano remained in "very critical condition," and the plan was to stabilize him over the weekend in hopes of increasing his strength to a level that would improve his chances of withstanding the increasingly-risky surgery on Monday (April 5th).

TGA open heart surgery is generally performed on infants under two weeks old. Christiano was intubated (breathing tube), subjected to five IV lines from which medicine was administered, and underwent a heart catheterization in attempt to relieve a buildup of lactic acid.

The answer to the question often asked the doctor and staff was always the same, "You have a very sick baby."

This response, while accurate, had the intended effect of preparing Sarah and Mondy, as well as the rest of us, for the worst.

Christiano had spent the first eight weeks of his life battling to breathe, and now his battle had escalated to the ultimate battle—for his life.

One got the impression from hearing reports from Sarah and Mondy that they had developed a confidence in Dr. Morell's plan of action for Christiano. Everyone we spoke with regarding Dr. Victor Morell had glowing reports of his capabilities and was lamenting the fact that he had been selected to head up Pittsburgh's children's cardiac hospital and would be leaving Tampa to assume that role in May. We were grateful to God that he had placed us in such capable hands as we experienced firsthand that God does miracles through others.

CHANGE OF PLANS

The next morning, all plans from the previous evening were discarded when Dr. Morell met with Sarah and Mondy and sought their approval to do the surgery that morning. Christiano's condition had not improved sufficiently and there was no guarantee that he would survive the weekend. Not only did Dr. Morell want to do the surgery that morning, but he wanted to combine two procedures (generally performed utilizing two open-heart surgeries) into one because Christiano's condition did not allow the luxury of the safer alternative.

Sarah and Mondy assessed the facts, and realizing they did not have a clear alternative in the matter, granted approval. With that approval, the watch began.

PCICU

The acronym PCICU stands for Pediatric Cardiac Intensive Care Unit. Twenty-four hours earlier, we hadn't known what PCICU meant, but our family was to become involuntary experts.

Family and friends visited the PCICU waiting room providing comfort to Sarah and Mondy and the rest of us. Sarah's mom, Sherry, was on a flight from Gulfport, Mississippi and that very thought gave Sarah much-needed support. The Venezia family was *en route* from Birmingham to Ft. Lauderdale to meet their daughter Alyssa's birth mother and half-siblings but redirected their route to visit us in our time of need. This was no easy decision for them because, almost a decade earlier, Mari and Frank had stood in the same shoes Sarah and Mondy stood that day and they sincerely hoped and prayed for a different outcome from the one they experienced that June day in 1994.

On June 11, 1994, in the very wing of St. Joseph's hospital where they later comforted Sarah and Mondy, Mari and Frank had been forced to make the decision to terminate life-support and offer the organs of their beloved son, Frankie, to improve the life of a stranger as they said goodnight to him for the final time. The tragic loss of their fifteen-year-old son had been the result of a jet-ski accident in a northwest Hillsborough County lake where Frankie and some friends had been celebrating the end of the school year.

As the Venezias arrived around 10:30 on the morning of April 2nd, they joined us as we witnessed Sarah and Mondy walking alongside Christiano's bed as the medical staff transported him to the operating room. We experienced some of the pain Sarah and Mondy endured as they escorted, and subsequently, released their youngest son into the hands of what we earnestly prayed was a capable hospital staff, but the full pain of these circumstances is reserved for the parents. The sight provoked tears from many of those present who consider the Floreses dear, but especially from Mari and Frank as they fought off the grim reminder from a decade earlier.

The group of family and close friends gathered in the waiting room to be with Sarah and Mondy during the four-hour procedure. We prayed for God's management over the entire event, and of course, for a totally successful outcome.

A GREAT BIRTHDAY GIFT

Around midday, John and I picked up Sarah's mom from the airport and transported her immediately to the hospital to be at her daughter's side. As they embraced, you could see the look of comfort on Sarah's face that only a mother's presence can provide.

A member of the surgical team met with Sarah and Mondy approximately every forty-five minutes and delivered an update on Christiano. All the updates provided temporary comfort to our group until we received the news we had been waiting for: that the procedure had been successful and that Christiano would be returned to his room in the PCICU. There was, however, one caveat. Because of the trauma Christiano had endured, Dr. Morell made the decision not to close Christiano's chest for a few days, because he felt the swelling of his internal organs (primarily his heart) associated with the surgery would cause undesirable pressure on Christiano's already fragile heart if confined to the space available in Christiano's eight-week-old chest cavity.

Sarah and Mondy (and the rest of us), accepted Dr. Morell's logic and agreed with Sarah and Mondy that God had provided, through Dr. Morell and the hospital staff, a wonderful gift to Mondy and Sarah on Mondy's 29th birthday.

ONE DAY AT A TIME

We were told that Christiano's post-operative recovery in the PCICU would be anywhere from three to four weeks and that we should measure his improvement on a week-to-week basis rather than on a day-to-day basis.

Again, the hospital staff was correct with their advice.

All patients in the PCICU are listed as *critical* and some are listed as *very critical*. Christiano was listed as *very critical*.

Christiano entered the hospital on April 1st at 8 lbs. 6 ounces and, one week later, he weighed in at 7 lbs. 1 ounce—a 16% decrease. That's equivalent to a 150-pound person losing 24 pounds in a week.

Christiano's breathing was managed by breathing equipment. He was medicated intravenously and nourished through the feeding tube inserted through his nose into his stomach. Everything that could be monitored was being monitored with devices hooked up all over his tiny body from his neck to his heel. It was a long weekend, and before long, weekdays and weekends became indistinguishable.

Having cleared the hurdle of the TGA surgery, an anxious family became focused on the fact that Christiano's chest remained open. It was difficult to think of anything else, but Dr. Morell continued to remind Sarah, Mondy, and the rest of us that closing the chest prematurely would indeed prove to be counterproductive. No one liked the "Maybe tomorrow" answer we received each day, but we were continually re-consoled by Dr. Morell's logic, and more importantly, by our belief in God's sovereignty.

Christiano continued to battle and on Wednesday, April 7th, the chest-closing surgery was performed successfully.

Everyone was, of course, elated with this milestone accomplishment even though our elation was tempered by the warning the hospital staff rendered that it would not be uncommon for Christiano to suffer a setback as a result of that day's surgery.

Christiano's condition remained *very critical*, but he continued to battle all obstacles.

Sarah and Mondy continued to maintain their 24-hour vigil with Christiano; Mondy took the day shift and Sarah took the night shift. Meanwhile, Mondito and Vinny were cared for by Judy, Sarah's mom and sisters, and Jen and Heather, who alternated coming back and forth to Tampa for that purpose. It was indeed a team effort supporting Sarah and Mondy during those days. Sarah's family traveled from Mississippi, South Carolina, and Colorado.

Even though Sarah and Mondy were blessed with all this help, the grueling schedule they maintained was wearing on them (and the rest of the family). Christiano's slightest improvement was cause for immediate elation, and the slightest complication sent everyone reeling in the opposite direction.

Such was the case with his breathing tube.

Each day, we waited with bated breath for the news that his breathing tube would be removed and each day we did not receive that news. We masked our disappointment to each other. It seems elementary now that removing the breathing tube prematurely would have placed additional and unwanted stress on Christiano's already weakened system, but we were nonetheless anxious and praying for that event.

On the morning of Easter Sunday, April 11th, Sarah and Mondy informed the family of the plan to remove the breathing tube later that morning.

We met Sarah and Mondy at the PCICU in hopes of celebrating yet another milestone in Christiano's recovery, and at noon on that Easter Sunday, Christiano's breathing tube was removed. Even though we were given the (expected) warning to expect possible setbacks, we celebrated the moment and gave thanks to God for all that Christiano had accomplished thus far.

In one of their many acts of caring and support, Malio and Shirley brought to the PCICU a complete Easter dinner from the Columbia restaurant. The main course of *paella* was augmented with the Columbia's famous "1905 salad," Cuban bread and butter, and capped off with *flan de leche*. There was enough of the delicious meal to feed the appreciative and delighted PCICU staff.

Earlier that day, as I sat in the PCICU waiting room, I observed a man who had been escorted by his sister into the room. His sister left the room and he and I were left alone for a few minutes, during which time this individual continued to weep. After he refused my offer to provide him a drink, he proceeded to explain his reason for being at the hospital.

He had been awakened that morning by a phone call from the Hillsborough County Sheriff's office advising him that his sixteen-year-old son had been injured in an automobile accident and was being transported to St. Joseph's emergency/trauma center via "medi-vac." He indicated things did not look good, and later that afternoon, his worst fears were confirmed when the medical staff at the hospital asked him to consider donating his son's organs.

It was difficult on that Easter Sunday *not* to make the connection between this man's painful experience as he agonized over the *involuntary* choice of terminating his only son's life so that his son's organs could save someone else's temporal life with the *voluntary* choice made by our heavenly Father to offer his only son Jesus' life so that many lives would be eternally saved—an incomprehensible act of love.

WHAT HAVE YOU DONE FOR ME TODAY?

With the breathing tube removal not yet twenty-four hours past, we were asking ourselves, "What improvement would God provide today?"

During the previous eleven days, baby Christiano had staved off death and successfully endured a heart catheterization, open-heart surgery, thoracic closing surgery, and was now breathing on his own.

Sarah and Mondy, as well as the rest of us, were indeed grateful for all of Christiano's huge improvements, but nonetheless, our human nature cried for more and more to happen quickly. Even though the IVs from Christiano's neck and arm were removed on the Monday following Easter, Sarah and Mondy had a difficult time coping with Christiano's fidgetiness. We learned that day that one of Christiano's lungs had collapsed and that he was possibly fighting off an infection. Christiano's apparent discomfort caused Sarah and Mondy to become uncomfortable which, in turn, was transmitted to the rest of us.

Even though we had enjoyed great successes with regard to Christiano's health and were forewarned to measure Christiano's success week-to-week as opposed to day-to-day, we spent most of April 12th down in the dumps. Twelve days in the PCICU was wearing on Christiano and his family.

On Tuesday, April 13th and every day after that, Christiano continued to improve, and by Friday, April 16th his once-collapsed lung was once again functioning fine.

THE SMILE

On Sunday, April 18th, I was the second person to receive a smile from Christiano. At age eleven weeks, Christiano demonstrated his understanding of discretion when he issued the first smile of his young life to his mother. Later, we commented on the fact that no one recalled Christiano smiling prior to that day, which we interpreted as an indication of his struggle to breathe prior to his surgery.

GOING HOME

We were told that if Christiano could be weaned off the remaining support apparatus (except for the feeding tube and pump), he would be sent home for the balance of his recovery. In anticipation of that event, Sarah's mom flew back to Tampa to relieve Heather, Sarah's sister, who had been part of the local support group for several days.

Mondy had not worked since April 1st, leaving all his business matters in the capable hands of his friend and partner, Matt Shaw.

Previously, Mondy had enrolled in a one-week real estate course. If he decided not to attend, he would have to wait a year before the course would be offered again in Tampa or attend later in the year in Orlando, which of course, meant being away from home, travel, et cetera. He and Matt discussed the matter and decided that it made sense for Mondy to bite the bullet and attend as previously planned. This, of course, meant that Matt would continue to manage their business until his return on Monday, April 26th.

Mondy was, is, and will always be very grateful to Matt for his support during his time of need.

HOME SWEET HOME

On Tuesday, April 20th, Christiano was released from the hospital after a twenty-day ordeal that clearly demonstrated the fight this infant possessed. Certainly God has great plans for his life.

As I took inventory of the events of the previous three weeks, I was reminded of how blessed Sarah, Mondy, and the rest of us were to have been spared the outcomes others experienced. It is, and will always be in this life, a mystery as to why, under a sovereign

God, some are spared and others are not. What is no mystery to those who know God is that God never makes a mistake, even when the outcome is different from what we desire.

In the comfortable confines of Sarah's and Mondy's new home in Odessa, Christiano improved day-by-day. Christiano weighed 8 pounds, 1 ounce on his first day home from the hospital, and one week later, he was 9 pounds, 2 ounces. Even with this tremendous improvement, Christiano was at 3% on the height scale and negative on weight. He clearly had a ways to go.

His appetite continued to improve, and on May 5th, Christiano weighed in at 9 pounds, 15 ounces; on May 10th, 11 pounds, 2 ounces. His periodic doctor visits indicated that he was improving at a wonderful rate and the only lingering condition at his July 20th doctor visit was a slight heart leakage, which the doctors indicated was nothing to be concerned with at this juncture.

Even though there would be additional checkups for Christiano, he was pretty much out of the woods in relation to the TGA condition for which he was admitted into the hospital on April 1, 2004.

We had all experienced a modern-day miracle and are grateful to the Provider of all miracles.

THE BOMB

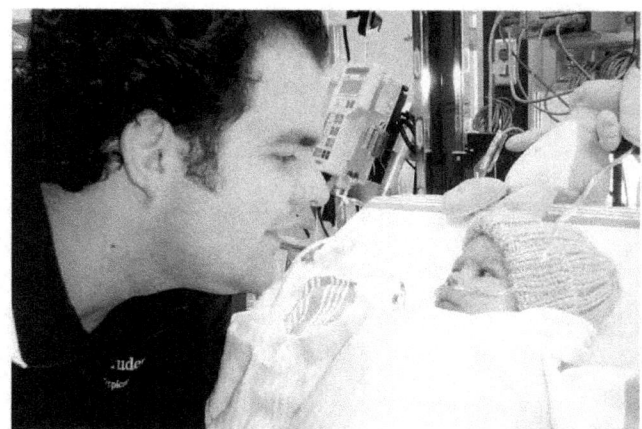

Intimate moment between father and son

Christiano in the loving arms of his mother

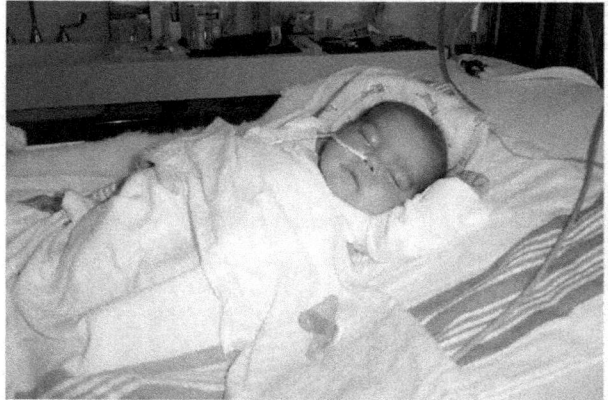

Christiano in God's hand

Me holding our 'Little Miracle'

Christiano stealing my heart - What a blessing!

TO GOD BE THE GLORY

REFLECTIONS

When Mondy and Sarah relocated to Tampa with their two baby boys in 2001, Mondy had to decide quickly what he was going to do to earn a living for his growing family. He was not looking for a job; he was deciding on a career. He discussed the matter with me, and I sensed he knew the importance of making the correct decision as his responsibility now included four people in three short years. He had decided that he preferred to work with his mind rather than his back. His narrowing process left him deciding from three offers he'd received: one in banking, one in the stocks and securities business, and the one he decided on, commercial real estate marketing, investment, and sales.

I was confident that he would choose to go into either banking or stocks and securities, if for no other reason that both of those professions offered salary and commission while his commercial real estate offer was 100% commission. It's not the first time that he has surprised me, nor do I expect it to be the last. What I did know was that he was very intelligent and was very committed to his family, a prescription for success. However, at that time, his work experience consisted of restaurant waiting and management, and warehouse labor and trucking, including 18-wheelers. That said, he faced significant challenges which could have been mitigated by a professional training program (such as I'd had when I switched from coaching to sales some three decades earlier) and close (initial) management supervision. He had neither. So, Mondy was either going to become a "Roads Scholar" (not to be confused with Rhodes Scholar) or would have to find another way to feed the three hungry mouths waiting for him at home. My money was on the former.

He worked and studied diligently and was able to shorten the normal earnings dry period. Soon, he earned national recognition for his achievement and later partnered with his friend and colleague, Matthew B. Shaw, and successfully expanded into the investment aspect of the business. During this time, Mondy became a licensed broker and maintained his affiliation with a leading national firm.

A favorable and unconsidered consequence of Mondy's career decision was that we have been able to discuss various deals he is working on and I have learned a lot about commercial real estate and gained an interest in investing in some of his projects (along with some of my friends who understandably enjoy the returns from the investment over interest in the investment itself). It is while discussing his deals that I developed a tremendous respect for his ability to identify potential investments, calculate their current and future values, and articulate to the layperson the anticipated returns over time. I recognize that all successful professionals must possess this ability, but I've dealt with business executives all of my adult life and I have learned over those years that the qualities possessed by the *crème de la crème,* and those are the qualities that make up his personal portfolio. I'm proud to share the same name with him, and though I know it's an impossible wish, I nonetheless wish that my father/their grandfather was here to enjoy my children as I do.

Very early during his now-eighteen-year career, I asked Mondy how he came about his career decision, and he quickly retorted, "I didn't want a boss and I didn't want to be cooped up in an office." As they say, the apple doesn't fall far from the tree.

FORTY YEARS LATER

Friday, April 28, 2006 was a mild day in New Orleans and local leadership was hoping *Jazz Fest* would jump-start the tourist economy still reeling from the massive blow that had been delivered by Hurricane Katrina seven months earlier. If hotel and rental car availability was any indication of a "juiced" economy, things were looking up. My contribution to reviving the Big Easy's economy was a few days away as I was making the short trip to Baton Rouge to meet up with friends and former LSU teammates, circa 1962.

The last time I'd made this trip was over forty years previously and prior to the existence of Interstate 10 in Louisiana, cell phones, and satellite radio. Now, I used all three. With the cruise control set at 74 mph, I comfortably motored west on I-10. As I whisked past the St. James Parish exit, I was reminded of how the weekend had come about.

In January 2005, Dickie Granier, (originally) from St. James Parish, Louisiana and current resident (since 1970) of the Denver area, was in Tampa to celebrate his nephew Jay's wedding. Dickie's nephew, Jay, is the son of Dickie's sister, Janet, and her husband, Jerry Boza, who was my childhood neighbor and friend. (As an aside, Jerry had received his dental training in the late 1960s at the LSU Dental School in New Orleans, a year behind my friends and former teammates, David Strange and Mike Vincent.) While visiting my home, Dickie lamented the fact that he had lost contact with our good friend Robbie Hucklebridge since our days at LSU. I queried Dickie about his efforts to contact Huck and he convinced me that he and several others had made numerous unsuccessful attempts to reach him. I offered to assist in this search and a half-day effort the following week yielded Robbie's unlisted phone number at his residence in Palestine, Texas.

Dickie and I caught up with Huck via a couple of three-way telephone conversations, and in short order, Huck suggested that we meet while that option was still available. Dickie and I concurred, and shortly thereafter, friends' names began to surface. While we could have met anywhere, we decided to meet in Baton Rouge during LSU football's open week. The open week was by design because we wanted the "get together" to be a meeting of friends rather than a football thing.

Then came Hurricane Katrina and plans across the Gulf Coast were altered, ours included. Dickie and Huck put their heads together and suggested the weekend of April 28, 2006 as the new date.

From the outset, there was a desire expressed by those who said they would be coming, to see, hug, and catch up with guys with whom they had developed a special bond some forty years earlier but had allowed the hustle and bustle of our culture to suppress taking action to meet. Dickie and Huck led the charge to meet and others enthusiastically followed.

While I was confident there would be others, the expected attendees (of which I was aware as of 4/28/06) included Butch Chaney, Malcolm Hodnett, Raymond Loup, Doug Moreau, Ruffin Rodrique, Donald Schwab, David Strange, Gene Sykes, Milton Trosclair,

Billy Truax, Dickie, Huck, and me (David Poché was a late cancellation due to the illness of his eight-month-old granddaughter).

This group represented a wide scope of personalities, but also possessed a common trait of concern and loyalty toward each other.

Raymond Loup, who lives in Brusly, on the west bank of the Mississippi River, was expecting my call as I approached Baton Rouge. We scheduled lunch at Ruth's Chris Steakhouse, a questionable choice for two guys who between them had experienced five open-heart surgeries including a heart transplant, but rest assured, we made wise menu selections as we both ordered the well-marbled rib-eye, shoestring potatoes, Caesar salad, and passed on dessert.

Before meeting Raymond, I had some time and decided to visit Tiger Stadium. I was hoping to see the old locker room, the field, and the bleachers, which those of us who violated rules were summoned to run as penance for our transgressions.

As I approached the receiving area adjacent to the players' entrance, I thought I saw Jim Smith (the locker room manager back when I was authorized to use this entrance) or his ghost. As I came closer, I realized that Jim and this sentry did not share facial characteristics, but their torsos were interchangeable. The sign on the players' door clearly stated it was for the use of current players only.

For a person who, for the most part, adheres to the axiom, *Never accept "no" from a person who can't say "yes,"* I erred when I asked if it would be okay to tour the facility. Jim's replacement responded in accordance with the authority vested in him and very politely said *no*, and that permission could only be granted from the football headquarters located down the street and around the corner.

Balancing my interest in visiting the facility against the understandable need for security, and I'm certain, the countless requests of this nature they must receive, I thanked the sentry, walked out of receiving, delivered a subtle misdirection (in the event he was watching), and walked through the unlocked Current Players Only entrance and into the facility. (Having former East Baton Rouge District Attorney, Doug Moreau, as a personal friend also entered into my decision.)

The entire facility had been tastefully modernized and many photos depicting key Tiger football events adorned the walls, but otherwise, the structure was much as I remembered.

Raymond arrived at the restaurant ahead of me, and when the hostess showed me to the table, I saw Raymond for the first time in forty-two years. I could have easily picked him out of a crowd; he hadn't changed much physically, even though he had undergone two cardiac bypass surgeries followed by a heart transplant five years prior. He could have been the national spokesman for heart-transplant procedures. His full head of hair remained brown, his physique, athletic, and his eyes sparkled, leading one to pose the questions, "Whose heart did he receive and are there any more?"

Previous phone conversations had us somewhat up to date, but over lunch, we were able to "fill in the blanks," including details regarding our families, especially grandchildren.

After lunch, we located three-hundred yards east on Constitution Avenue to the Holiday Inn that would serve as the unofficial weekend headquarters for the out-of-town contingent.

Slowly but surely, the group began to form: Huck, Hodnett, and Bain Slack from Texas; Ken Johnson and Trosclair from Alabama; Larry Sessions from Utah; Granier from Colorado; Raymond; and me. Moreau, Strange, Sykes, and Truax were expected soon.

We rearranged the lobby furniture to accommodate the growing group and engaged in small talk while individually whispering, "Who's that?" as new arrivals identified themselves, questioning the association between the name and face they just announced with the name and face stored in our memories. Raymond reminded me that when former Tigers, politicians, or boosters were introduced to us back in the day, we'd snickered and considered them near-death candidates, and they were probably younger than we were at the time.

That put things into perspective in a hurry.

Then, in walked Gene Sykes. Everyone tried to put a name with the face while we attempted to determine if the face belonged to someone we expected. Contrived smiles accompanied by purposefully slurred enunciation of possible names gave way to secondary questions and comments intended to validate who was who. Then Gene tried a soft, "Huck?" Huck smiled affirmatively, and another was brought into the fold.

No sooner did everyone (except Gene) sit when Gene suggested the group relocate to the Caterie, a nearby sports bar featuring $1.25 longnecks. The group's reaction mirrored the response of the Boston Philharmonic Orchestra when the conductor gives the queue for all to rise. In unison, the entire group rose, and all but Raymond and me, followed the pied piper to the Caterie. Raymond and I waited at the hotel for Doug, who was on his way.

Doug advised David of the venue change. We then left directions at the front desk for Billy, and off to the Caterie we went.

The conversations from the hotel were seamlessly transferred to the Caterie where David joined in. Though we had conversed sporadically via the telephone, I hadn't seen David in twenty-five-plus years and prior to the advent of his matching white hair and mustache. I gathered from the reaction of others that it had been longer than that for most of them. The fact of the matter was that, with few exceptions, most of these men hadn't seen each other since leaving LSU.

David had been billed as somewhat reclusive in recent years, but you couldn't have proven the premise that evening. He immediately caught up to the group's speed and began offering his rapid-fire comments on whatever topic was on the table.

Billy arrived and the tempo of stories increased, one tale sparking another.

It began with an all-time favorite about the *running the hounds* story where a group, while guests of Boo Levert at his family's Rienzi Plantation in Thibodaux, were offered the opportunity to run the hounds, which had been interpreted by some, myself included, to be accomplished on horseback. To our surprise, the Lafourche Parrish Sheriff was using Boo's guests to maintain the effectiveness of the Parrish's bloodhounds for apprehending escaped criminals. The look on our faces transitioned from confusion, while the Sheriff registered our scents (by rubbing towels around our necks and armpits), to bewilderment, when our comfortable head start on the bloods evaporated before our very eyes causing concern, then fear, and finally, panic as the prospect of reaching the safe haven (a metal structure) seemed doubtful.

Someone then suggested crayfish and the group broke camp and relocated to Phil's Oyster Bar & Fish House. The accommodation at Phil's allowed us to mingle more freely and visit with recent arrivals. The stories continued, altered to fit the occasion as a good story should. One of my personal favorites was delivered initially by David regarding walk-on athlete, Lonny Myles, whose confidence about being able to play at the major college level was bolstered as he observed the physiques of Mike Duhon and Mike Pharis dressing in the LSU locker room (recollection of the two Mikes' physiques is why this story gets retold as it was skillfully done by Bain over the weekend).

Apparently, Lonny's bolstered confidence transferred with him off the field because after becoming a very good receiver at LSU, Lonny became—and is—the city court judge in Zachary as well as a successful attorney (not a conflict in smaller Louisiana towns).

Another classic is *riding in Gene's convertible (on the Mississippi River Bridge)* and no one tells it better than its main character, Gene Sykes. One Saturday night (actually Sunday morning) when team members were restricted to East Baton Rouge Parish and had a midnight curfew, Gene, in his new convertible, was racing east on the bridge he wasn't supposed to be traveling on, with usual suspects, Butch, Dickie, Huck, Milton, and George O'Neal. Somehow, Gene managed to run up and under a propane truck heading in the same direction, causing the convertible to turn on its side while still engaged with the truck attempting to make it to *tierra firma.* Generating sparks dangerously close to his payload, the nervous truck driver managed to keep his vehicle in the outside lane as the car he was involuntarily towing alternated bouncing off the roadway and the side of the bridge.

Once the vehicles came to a stop, the assessment was mixed. The good news was that everyone was alive, though the occupants of the convertible sustained numerous injuries, the seriousness of which was too soon to diagnose. The main concern was the absence of Butch. Among the flashing lights of highway patrol cruisers and ambulances, authorities learned of Butch's absence and began combing the levees and shoreline for him.

Shortly thereafter, a car with friends drove by the accident scene and stopped as they recognized Gene's car.

"Where are the guys who were in this car?" asked a concerned friend as he made his way towards the ambulance.

"Who are you?" inquired the LHP officer.

"Butch Chaney. I know these guys." It was a welcome response to the group who had been searching for him.

Things quieted some as the evening matured and groups of three and four formed around trays of crayfish and raw oysters. General stories yielded to personal accounts of family and friends.

Saturday's flexible itinerary called for a noon tour of the recently-completed LSU football facility followed by a "crayfish boil" at Phil's.

Doug picked me up at the hotel and I had the privilege of visiting with his brother Al who would spend part of the day with the group. Al was a friend to most of the group from way back.

It was considerate of Doug to coordinate the tour of what can only be described as "a state-of-the-art" football complex.

Dr. Sam Nader, LSU's Assistant Athletics Director, was gracious in allocating his time to lead our group through a comprehensive walk-through of the complex. The facility includes literally anything one could fathom and lacks absolutely nothing. It was the brainchild of former coach Nick Saban and benefits current coach Les Miles, his staff, and players.

Coincidently, Les Miles was leaving the facility when he noticed (Doug) our group and was kind enough to spend a few minutes sharing his football vision with what I'm confident looked to him like the AARP chapter of former Tigers.

Things picked up at the "boil" where they had ended the night before. Chuckles developed into laughs, and laughter soon became roars as stories and narrations continued.

The group increased throughout the afternoon with the additions of Lucien Branch, Butch Chaney, Boots Garland, C. J. Gaudin, Charles Haynes, Donald Ray Kennard, George O'Neal, Ruffin Rodrique, Donald Schwab, Derwood Thomas, and Jim Turner.

With such an influx of people, old stories—with a little twist perhaps—were reborn as they were recounted by another narrator. The group received the stories as if they were heard them for the first time.

The recent additions brought their own tales and laughter abounded.

Crayfish, oysters, and beer were consumed throughout the afternoon, and out of nowhere, revelry was put on hold when Gene asked to read the following poem:

Around the Corner

By: New York American columnist Charles Hanson Towne

Around the corner I have a friend

in this great city that has no end

Yet days go by, and weeks rush on

and before I know it a year is gone

and I never see my old friend's face

for life is a swift and terrible race.

He knows I like him just as well

as in the days when I rang his bell

and he rang mine. We were younger then

and now we are busy, tired men.

Tired with trying to make a name,

tired with playing a foolish game.

"Tomorrow," I say, "I will call on Jim

just to show that I'm thinking of him."

But tomorrow comes and tomorrow goes

and the distance between us grows and grows.

Around the corner, yet miles away.

"Here's a telegram, sir. Jim died today."

And that's what we get and deserve in the end.

Around the corner, a vanished friend.

It was good that Gene introduced a sobering moment to our gathering, for it was obvious to all that life is more than laughter and slaps on the back—much more.

While C. H. Towne's poem focused on the importance of seeing friends, I could not help but think of the many other important things around the corner. Is there not a sibling, a cousin, an uncle or aunt worthy of a visit? Maybe reconciliation is what's needed. What about a son or daughter, mother or father, or anyone else with whom things aren't as they should be? Are we waiting for them to initiate the move? Are we immobilized by pride? Time, once our ally, may now be our enemy.

The weekend in Baton Rouge was intended to be a respite from the grind, a vacation from reality, and as such, life's pains were not to be discussed. Now that we are back into reality, it is my wish that the sentiment I share is received in the humble and helpful spirit which I intend.

The importance of the poem was soon compartmentalized and the subject at hand returned to what it had been before Gene asked for our attention.

As time seemed to vanish, discussions regarding supper settled on one of Baton Rouge's finest Italian restaurants, Ruffino's. Securing seating for approximately twenty diners on a Saturday night considering the influx of people as a result of Hurricane Katrina would require inside dealing—a situation managed flawlessly by Ruffino's operator, Ruffin Rodriquez, Jr.

Everyone who was going went to Ruffino's, except me. I followed Raymond across the Mississippi River to his home in Brusly to meet his wife and soulmate, Mardell. We'd spoken over the telephone, but I wanted to take the opportunity to meet this person who had been by Raymond's side as they successfully navigated through his heart challenges, a situation not unfamiliar to me.

After the brief visit, I headed to Ruffino's and found myself in a nasty torrential downpour, the type that convinces motorists to pull off to the side of the road because the visibility is nil. I often, as I did that evening, view cars pulled over as an opportunity to travel easier because of the diminished traffic.

That line of thinking resulted in a very stressful trek to the restaurant, especially as I crossed the bridge. So heavy was the rain that even eighteen-wheelers had pulled over before crossing the bridge. I nonetheless found a like-minded trucker to run interference in the blinding rain. I stayed twenty-five to thirty feet behind the semi as we negotiated the winding entrance ramps whose signs were unreadable due to the deluge. Lane demarcations and the bridge sides were invisible as sheets of rain traveled horizontally. At times we moved at less than ten miles per hour as the bridge's flexibility was tested.

My mind flashed back to Gene's experience some forty-four years prior. Was I involved in the making of another tale? Hopefully not, I prayed. Managing to exit the bridge safely was a huge relief, though the balance of the way to Ruffino's was fraught with torrents causing flooding at the lower sections of I-10.

I sat in the maxed-out parking lot for ten minutes and decided the rain was not going to let up, so I made (what was in my mind's eye) a dash to the entrance through three inches of moving water. I was drenched as I joined our contingent who, oblivious to the storm, were having a grand time.

The strapping and handsome Ruffin Rodriguez, Jr. visited our table to meet his dad's friends and former teammates.

Having observed friends in the high-end restaurant business for many years in Tampa has allowed me an insight into discerning those who are capable of juggling the many demands placed on this type of a restaurant operator, and unmistakably, Ruffin Jr. is a natural.

With hungry, waiting patrons asking, "How much longer?" and kitchen and wait staffs operating at full capacity, he exuded an *Everything is under control* persona and looked into the eyes of each person with whom he spoke, providing the feeling of special attention they relished, the mark of a professional. However, to foster repeat diners, this attribute must be in addition to a pleasurable dining experience. The crowded foyer accurately told the story.

Fun conversation prevailed throughout the evening, though some of the stories were becoming quite familiar (if you know what I mean). One of the funnier comments heard over dinner was, "We ought to do this every forty years."

While we dined, Ruffin Jr. escorted a couple to our table, loosely introducing the man so that we could make the connection. The white hair and mustache should not have been enough disguise for the trim, hip (sandals, jeans, stylish "Florida type" casual, untucked shirt) gentleman accompanied by an attractive woman. We squinted at each other and his quizzical smile provided positive ID for Mike Vincent, former teammate and current family dentist in Baton Rouge.

His smile widened as we identified ourselves, and as I made my way around our table to hug Mike, he uttered, "Florees, you still in Florida?" This was followed by a pause, and then, "How come nobody told me about this meeting?" I'm certain Mike did not intend to put anyone on the defensive, but I must admit I felt a little uneasy not having an adequate response to his question. I was hoping the knowledge of our meeting would not offend anyone (certainly anyone interested in joining us was welcome), but I still don't have an answer on how that could be accomplished. Nonetheless, I intend to call Mike and catch up with him. I wished he would have been notified in advance.

Apparently, our festive (and possibly boisterous) dinner tickled the curiosity of others in the restaurant because a woman, dining on the other side of the room with her husband and two other couples, attempted to get our attention (a formidable task) as we were bidding each other farewell. Finally, the curious and unwavering woman garnered our attention and explained that she and her friends were observing the good time we enjoyed and were trying to determine the reason for our meeting.

Without hesitation, Donald responded, "We're the Duke Lacrosse Team."

Amidst an eruption of laughter by those who'd heard Donald, she repeated his retort across the room for the benefit of those at her table who were attentive to her effort.

We spent the next few minutes repeating good-byes and promising to stay in touch and visit, knowing the probability of visiting was remote once we returned to our real worlds. Giving priority to the message of C. H. Towne's poem would be required.

After breakfast, I headed east on I-10 through New Orleans and to Exit 5, Gulfport, Mississippi, where I wanted to gain a first-hand view of Hurricane Katrina's wrath. It was humbling to witness the destruction nature can deal. Being Sunday, the clean-up and rebuilding efforts were minimal, but it was obvious that much progress had been made and that much more was needed. I also stopped in Pass Christian, Mississippi, on my way back to New Orleans and the report there was much the same.

I could be sure I was either in New York or New Orleans when the parking attendant at the Royal Sonesta Hotel on Bourbon Street in the heart of the French Quarter informed me that parking was thirty-two dollars per day as he artfully waited for his tip after moving my bags from the trunk of the car onto the sidewalk in the underground garage—a distance of approximately four feet.

I was pleased to see that the hotel had either been spared destruction by Katrina or they'd done a marvelous job of repairing the damage it may have sustained. Regardless, the accommodations were very nice.

While my bags were being taken to my room, I walked the three blocks to the Acme Oyster Bar and limited my intake to two-dozen oysters (one raw and one baked) on the half-shell, preserving my appetite for Brennan's that evening. You just can't top a Louisiana oyster.

As I walked the streets of the French Quarter, I could not help but notice everything was the same as it was forty years prior when I walked these same streets with my LSU buddies and friends visiting from Tampa. Barkers were still barking their specialties...Dixieland and jazz music, nude women dancers and men disguising themselves as women dancers, fortune tellers, retail shops hawking everything from tourist T-shirts and trinkets, voodoo paraphernalia to "backdoor items" including but not limited to every kind of illegal drug and service imaginable. Indeed the streets had not changed but they "looked" different to me. I no longer viewed them as a source of fun and entertainment. Why? Because while the streets had remained the same, I had **not**. (2 Corinthians 5:17...*if anyone is in Christ, he is a new creation. The old has passed away; behold, the new has come.*). Indeed, I **am** a new creation and as I reflect on my life before my salvation, I am truly humbled and forever grateful to my God for His protection, mercy, grace and love as He was seeking me and I was running from him, living my life to satisfy my sinful, fleshly desires with little or no regard for Him or His Word.

Feeling like this begs the questions, "Why did I choose to stay in the French Quarter, and will I stay there again?"

My lame response is that I had been led to believe that the accommodations were superior (hurricane damage the least) and because of the delectable restaurants; and as to the second part of the question, no. Not unless there is a ministerial opportunity.

I was granted a late checkout Monday, which allowed me a needed sleep-in before visiting the areas touted as the worst in terms of Katrina damage.

Following a hearty breakfast of andouille sausage, eggs, and a biscuit, I traveled to St. Bernard Parrish and the Ninth Ward via St. Claude Avenue, northeast of the French Quarter. The devastation was immense and, as aptly reported, will require vast effort and extensive resources to restore what was damaged. It was depressing to see people sitting on porches of uninhabitable houses, FEMA trailers in front, smoking cigarettes or whatever, and playing board games seemingly with no apparent option on how to reestablish their lives.

As for the ongoing debate on whether or not New Orleans was worth all that is required to resuscitate her, I believe her rich history and equally rich culture, coupled with its critical industrial assets warrant the required effort *only* if the resultant New Orleans can be significantly less vulnerable to weather events and political corruption. The political corruption issue may appear to be junior to making the huge improvements required to remedy the weather event vulnerability, but I assure you that is not the case. In fact, New Orleans' notorious political corruption is, in my opinion, the single greatest contributing factor to those improvements not already being in place. Regardless, accomplishing one without the other will be grossly expensive and ultimately futile.

As I contemplate the possibility of mitigating the corruption in New Orleans politics to a level commensurate with that of other large cities, I'm reminded of what a politician and friend told me a long time ago, "There are two things you don't want to see being made: politics and sausage."

Good luck, New Orleans.

My nonstop flight to Tampa left on time, and as always, I was looking forward to returning home where my best friend—my wife—waited for my arrival.

CIGAR CITY BIBLE STUDY GROUP

I've known John Reaves since he was twelve years old and attended Palma Ceia Playground under the supervision of my good friend and playground director, John Oliva.

One could easily see that young John Reaves was a gifted athlete, a bright young fella and a handful to manage. He was full of energy and always tested rules and regulations, but in a playful manner if you follow my drift. He became a stellar four-sport athlete at Robinson High School before lending his athletic ability as an All-American drop-back quarterback to the University of Florida, then leasing his talent to the Philadelphia Eagles, Cincinnati Bengals, Minnesota Vikings, Houston Oilers, and Tampa Bay Buccaneers of the NFL before capping off his career with three seasons with the Tampa Bay Bandits of the USFL.

However, behind the façade of the successful athlete was a man who suffered much tragedy early in his life and was challenged with its demonic after-effects, which often manifested itself with poor judgment that led to bad behavior. Sometimes he would manage his demons and sometimes his demons would manage him.

John Oliva and I stayed in touch with John Reaves throughout his career and beyond, and over the years we gladly assumed the position of his co-mentors, which just sort of morphed upon us, I believe, because he correctly knew we loved him, though often it was in the form of tough love.

Early 2007 found John, once again, testing rules and regulations, but this time those of the City of Tampa. TV and news outlets covered his encounters with the Tampa PD and a few mutual friends of John Oliva's and mine contacted us asking if we were aware of John's current legal challenges, but I believe their primary interest was to seek out the "scoop" from John Reaves' perspective. At that time, neither John nor I had heard from JR, but we decided it was time we did. JR reluctantly agreed to meet us as he astutely contemplated that we would employ our tough-love technique.

JR was stubborn, and understandably did not want to be chastised, so it took a while before we were able to convince him that we were meeting with him not only to deal with his current issues, but more importantly, to help him over the long haul. We suggested that we meet weekly to review how things were going and what things we should consider going forward. It was during the "going forward" portion that we agreed we should study the Bible to add structure to our meetings and, of course, to gain the knowledge God has revealed regarding how to be the father, husband, brother, son, businessman, and friend He has created us to be. Of the three of us, JR possessed the most biblical knowledge and we suggested he take the lead in our studies.

As the weeks went by, matters improved and JR once again began to manage his decision-making, which yielded positive results as he/we employed many of the principles we were studying from the Bible.

In time, friends we asked to visit our study did so and decided to keep coming, and others asked if they could visit, so we developed two qualifying requirements: 1) you must be a sinner, and 2) we don't do denominations (our sole source is the Bible [*sola scriptura*]). With that, we named our group Cigar City Bible Study Group and met for years every Wednesday at the Oliva Tobacco Company in the heart of West Tampa before relocating in 2018 to Speedline Athletic just down the street to accommodate the increased size of our group.

Soon after its formation in 2007, Cigar City Bible Study Group was blessed with the addition of Tim Paskert. Formerly an atheist, Tim is a long-time executive in the TV industry, but his regenerated heart is with the Lord. He and his wife Chandra have produced a wonderful Christian movie, *The Glass Window*, and together are spearheading an effort to create a children's home. Additionally, Tim has authored books now available on Amazon; but our group's greatest blessing has been Tim's teaching and pastoring us each week. Week after week, the Holy Spirit speaks to our group through the vessel that is Tim Paskert.

John Reaves was promoted to Heaven August 1, 2017, and though we sorely miss him, he is not forgotten. It was because of his struggles ten years earlier that our group was founded, and the group remains a living example of how God transforms lives and transitions troubles into triumphs. Because JR was transparent with his struggles, others followed his lead, and today we enjoy a vibrant group of men who seek the Lord's direction and not the world's for their lives including some you have "met" earlier in Mis Memorias – Greg Bonfe, Ron Brown, Ted Cannella, Ernie Casares, Pete Dearolf, Steve Malzone, Richard Martinez, John Oliva, Lou Piniella, John Reaves, Danny Someillan, Trent Stallings, George Turnpaugh.

Thank you, John, and glory be to God.

THE FOURTH CORDOVA SISTER

Our daughter beautifully describes how her and our families were blessed with the addition of *the fourth Cordova sister* by creating the following narrative.

Unbeknownst to anyone, the Lord had additional plans regarding the size of our family.

THE REDEMPTIVE DETOUR

During the fall of 2014, when we joined a ministry called Safe Families for Children, adoption was not on our radar. Safe Families, in short, places children whose parents are in crisis with host families, for a brief and fixed amount of time, anywhere from a few days to a few months at the longest.

Before we became a part of Safe Families, I felt God tugging at my heart as a result of casually reading through the book of James. I came to James 1:27, "Pure and undefiled religion in the sight of our God and Father is this: to care for orphans and widows in their distress...." Now, I've read this verse before. But this day was altogether different. I might as well have seen my name written with a comma before it! I thought surely not adoption. Adoption is fine, noble even, but you have to really "have a heart" for that. Also, it can be emotionally messy, risky even. And how would that disrupt our current family? Isn't that primarily for couples who are having trouble conceiving on their own? Also, God,....I'm sure you've noticed how we have our hands more than full with these three little girls?? It might even be called irresponsible! We already have 3 weddings to pay for! But the strange new heaviness would not be dissuaded by my good logic. I began looking for ways to care for the orphan without turning our lives upside down. We hosted foreign exchange students who "needed a home," but it didn't scratch the itch.

One night I received a call on my cell phone. It was Safe Families for Children. They were asking for a character reference for a friend who was looking to join the organization. I tried to contain my excitement as the voice on the other end of the line spelled out what the mission of the organization was. It was precisely the kind of ministry I was looking for but didn't know existed! After prayer and consideration, John and I applied, partly because of the lack of long-term commitment, and the nice neat parameters that protect the host family from any real inconvenience (God was chuckling).

After we were approved, I started watching my emails closely, anxious to experience our first placement, and our kids were asking incessantly when their new playmate would arrive. On a Sunday morning, we got an email about a 15-month-old baby girl who needed a home for two weeks while her parents looked for more permanent housing, as they had just moved from out of town and their housing had fallen through. We went back and forth about whether I should respond that "yes," we could take her. Finally, with fear of the unknown—15-month-olds can be a handful!—we said yes.

About four hours later, Khloe arrived at our house, asleep in her car seat. We signed a few papers and Ms. Debbie from Safe Families drove off and there we were.

We ended up having Khloe for only one week during that first stay, but she had already worked her way into our hearts. I told John on the day she was reunited with her family, that somehow I felt like she belonged with us. This was fully illogical, because she had a mom and dad and a semi-stable living arrangement at the time. Ordinarily upon returning her, that would be the end of our contact with the family, but because Khloe had made such an impression on us and because of some needs that the family had, we continued to stay in touch.

Many, many times over the subsequent months, I whispered vulnerable, private prayers to God. *Why is she still in my heart? Is she going to be ours? Are you moving in this situation? It is impossible that she would be ours. But you are the God of the impossible.*

Not long after Khloe went back home, her mother (Laura's) health began to decline, and in time, Khloe's father exited the picture. Laura was in a great amount of pain and visited many hospitals looking for answers and relief.

Finally, in January 2016, a group of doctors at Tampa General told Laura she had a year to live, due to liver failure. She spent as much quality time as she could with Khloe during 2016 but was often too sick to care for her. As a result, Khloe spent many days and nights with us and with John's mom, Glenda and his step-dad Tommy. During this time, Laura expressed her desire for our family to care for Khloe after she passed away.

I would be remiss not to mention how John's mom, Glenda, cared for Laura in her illness. Laura, fiercely independent, would be the first to tell you that she was not always "easy" or "a pleasure" to deal with. But Glenda would not quit. Even when we urged her to! She poured out the hard, ugly, messy kind of love that we usually reserve for our dearest friends and family to a woman that she had never laid eyes on two years prior. She transported her to countless doctors, dressed her wounds, bought and delivered groceries to her, all the while enduring an occasional tongue lashing, to be sure no good deed was left unpunished.

As her illness progressed, Laura began to open up to Glenda about her fear of dying, and lack of peace regarding her 'final destination.' In December of 2016, when her death seemed imminent, my mom suggested and organized a prayer meeting on behalf of Laura. So, while Khloe napped, our family, my brother's family, my parents and my in-laws got on our knees and begged God for Laura's salvation. We wept as we fervently prayed that we could one day tell Khloe with assurance that she would see her mama again in heaven. We also had several other friends who were faithfully praying for Laura to make peace with God.

Laura had long since held me at arm's length, and I can only imagine it was partly due to the pain of watching her daughter call me "mama," and living the life that should have been hers, if circumstances had taken a different path. But that's where this story changes.

In early January something extraordinary happened to Laura. She made the comment that she wanted to "do something, to tell everyone what God did in her life," but feared that her limited time would keep her story from going out. The following is what I wrote in

Khloe's journal about exactly what happened to her mom. Our family believes God is honored by our sharing what He did in Laura's life.

"Dear Khloe, the most amazing thing has happened! Mommy Laura knows Jesus now! I want to tell you all of the things she said so we can always remember and praise God for this wonderful miracle. "Surely the arm of the Lord is not too short to save, nor his ear too dull to hear." Isaiah 59:1 Mommy Laura wanted to talk to you on the phone the other night, so we called her and you talked with her for a few minutes, after that, she and I started talking on the phone and she began telling me that she was at peace and she had this dream... I couldn't understand every word, but she got my attention when she said, "He washed all my sins away!" I was speechless as she went on.

She said she was praying and she fell asleep and she was still praying in her dream. She was standing on a box and off the box was a thread, she stepped off the box onto the thread (which she referred to as a thread of faith) and she began to walk on it. Nothing was underneath her, but she wasn't afraid. She followed the thread, which was winding here and there, and as she walked, what was a "dull backdrop," opened up into a beautiful, lively and infinitely peaceful place. She repeated several times that it was infinite. She said it was "infinite, infinite, infinite."

She said she saw flowers more beautiful than anything she's ever seen on Earth and colors she can't describe and that cannot be created by the colors we know and understand. She also saw plants and said that all the creation was worshiping! (To me it sounds a lot like Psalm 148:7-9: "Praise the Lord from the earth, you great sea creatures and all deeps, fire and hail, snow and mist, stormy wind fulfilling his word! Mountains and all hills, fruit trees and all cedars!")

She said it made her think of the verse that says, "the rocks will cry out." (Luke19:40) She asked me if it was bad that she was now looking forward to "going" and I told her absolutely not! The people who are most in love with the Lord are longing to be with him. She asked what if I haven't read the whole Bible? I assured her that was okay! She also asked what if I sin right before I die and don't have a chance to confess it? I explained that Jesus' blood is sufficient for our past, present and future sins and that Jesus said "my sheep hear my voice and I know them, they follow me. I give them eternal life and no one can snatch them away from me. My father who has given them to me, is greater than all, no one can snatch them out of my father's hand." (John10:27-28)

She mentioned that upon waking from her dream, she felt as though she had been "dipped" and she wanted to be baptized and said how wonderful that must feel. Then she mentioned one of my favorite things. She said that God helps her with her physical pain, she said she could feel Him there with her, holding her hand, so that she didn't feel alone! I thought that was so tender and precious. She said that she never knew this was possible, that she traveled around her whole life looking for something and she finally found it, right at the end. She said she wanted "to do something," to "tell everyone" and that she was starting over new, like a "blank slate." She said that she wanted to "make God proud, like a father." I thought this was so profound because from what I know, she never had a father or a father figure in her life. She said she believed in God before, but she said it was like she was window shopping, and now it's like she was inside experiencing everything for herself!

Then she mentioned the verse "for now we look through a glass, darkly......" I couldn't believe her Bible knowledge, I quickly spoke the phrase into my phone and it is 1 Corinthians 13:12, I read the verse in its entirety to her. "For now we look through a glass, darkly, but then face to face. Now in part but then I shall know even as I am known." Your mom spent many many hours in the back of seminary classes to keep warm through the northeastern winters, but it seems as though she gained more than shelter during that time. She told me that she used to be concerned about you growing up in a "religious" home because she wanted you to decide for yourself what you believe, but now she was so happy and grateful that you will be raised to worship the awesome one true God!!

I thought I was dreaming as she was telling me all of this on the phone! At one point I said to her "you can't help but think this was all part of His plan from the beginning." And she stopped me and said "you can't help but think? You can't help but know!" She said they (her and your biological father) saw an ad on the back of a paper for a job in Tampa and two days later they drove thousands of miles down here with you! They spent two nights in a motel before they were going to be out on the street when they found and called Safe Families.

Part of this conversation took place that evening on the phone, and partly the next day at the hospice house where you and I went to visit her. While we were there, she mentioned two different times to her nurse what a great family you were going to and how much you and the other girls looked alike. She said to you, "aren't you lucky, you get to have two mommies!" She said she was always so afraid that someone was going to try to take you away, but now she wasn't. Now she was happy for you and at peace with you coming to us. She told me that she knows we will all be together in eternity. She said that it took getting to that place in her life in order to believe and that she realized that in the long run, this life is so short and insignificant, and that eternity is what matters! She said it will be as if this life never happened.

I mentioned to her about an illustration about us making a tapestry but we are so close to it that we can't see its beauty or understand God's hand, but he has an infinitely greater perspective and standing a mile away from it, it is beautiful and makes perfect sense.

She agreed and said she always thought we were like silkworms... making a tapestry but not knowing what we are making. She asked me if I thought she could look down from heaven, I said I don't know. She said, "but there will be no tears in heaven and if I look down I would have tears." Then she said, "maybe in heaven we will have a much greater perspective and see the end, and therefore those things wouldn't bring tears."

I think that is incredibly thoughtful and astute, and being that our glorified bodies will be perfect, I tend to think she is right! She talked about now understanding why I wanted to tell her about the Lord and that while she was standoffish to me in the past that we were now on the "same page." Your mama is feisty! She didn't like one of the social workers at the hospice house. She told me after the woman left how rude she thought she was. She then said, "another great thing about this way of life is when people are rude to me, I just pray for them!"

Again, she left me speechless. What wisdom! Khloe, as you grow up, I believe one of the great gifts your mom will have given you was the story of her redemption and the sure hope that you will see her again. Until then, Papa and I will carry on your mama's legacy and raise you to love and worship the one true God.

When she went home from that last stay at the hospice house, her health took an even more drastic turn for the worse. During those last weeks before her death, we shared several moments that I will never forget, and will always be grateful for. Any animosity between the two of us had been replaced with love and tenderness. I'll share just one moment. I was sitting next to her on her bed, holding her hand. She said to me, "We are special." I asked her what she meant. She said, "We're special, because He loves us." Now, here's a 34-year-old woman, who's dying an unusually cruel death and leaving behind the only thing that had ever brought her joy, and she's professing that she feels special because God loves her. One might assume she may have a different perspective of God. But she was making assessments about her circumstances based on what she knew to be true of God, instead of making assessments about God based on what she knew to be true of her circumstances. "So we fix our eyes not on what is seen, but what is unseen. For what is seen is temporal, but what is unseen is eternal." (2 Corinthians 4:18) No self-help book, no psychologist, no drug for that matter could have given her this perspective. Nothing short of this mysterious and intimate encounter she had with God Himself, could have transformed her outlook.

Khloe is working through her mom's death in what seems to be a very healthy and positive way. For several months she talked about her every day, but not in a sad way. She still shares memories or tells us what her mom "used to say." It is beyond evident that Laura and Khloe loved each other with a deep and abiding love.

While we decided against bringing her to the funeral, we did release balloons with messages on them including *"Dear Mom, it's good that you're in heaven; Happy Birthday; and I love you; also, I love you so much that you are at heaven. Love, Khloe"*

Almost 10 months later, the long awaited day finally arrived. Surrounded by family and dear friends, the court system recognized what God had orchestrated long ago. November 30, 2017 will always be celebrated in our family.

I wasn't sure how much she understood at first, but a few days after the adoption,

John asked Khloe her full name. She said Khloe Hope Cordova, then she said quietly, almost to herself, "I'll always be a part of your family, I'll be a part of your family forever." Turns out she understands after all.

THE REDEMPTIVE DETOUR

Khloe with mother (Laura)

Precious Baby

(Safe Home) for Khloe

Adoption day...All because of God's providence

Cordova sisters-Khloe, Mia, Olivia & Giana

TABLE FOR FIVE

It was four days before Christmas that brisk December day in 2005 and five good friends met to enjoy lunch together at Tampa's Palm Restaurant. Esquires John Cummings, Mac Greco, and Bennie Lazzara were joined by Lou Piniella and me. Lou was particularly grateful to John and Bennie for the assistance they'd provided with a minor matter and wanted to express his sentiments over lunch.

The mood at the Westshore Mall restaurant was irresistibly festive among the hustle and bustle of Christmas shoppers looking for just the right gift for that special loved one.

It was unusual for us to meet for lunch at 11:30, but we did so to accommodate barristers Greco and Lazzara who were meeting a plane leaving at approximately 1:15 PM bound for the north Florida town of Starke. I say approximately 1:15 PM because Mac and Bennie were the only passengers on the private aircraft that awaited them. We essentially had the eatery to ourselves at half-past eleven, but before noon, the table for five we occupied was in the middle of a packed restaurant.

The relaxed tempo began to build as the pleasantries we exchanged transitioned into war stories we'd all had heard before but still enjoyed hearing again. Hand gestures accompanied the testosterone-fueled tales garnished with hearty laughter that did the soul well. Speaking of souls, the group graciously granted my request to bless the bountiful fare being prepared for our consumption which served as a brief intermission to the entertaining reminiscences.

Utilizing good judgment, all the other diners at our table ordered fish entrées and salads, leaving me to question my judgment in choosing the New York strip with shoestring potatoes. I tasted theirs and concluded I'd made the right choice.

The lunch was thoroughly enjoyable and a welcome crown to men who feel as these impromptu, yet delightful, dinners have been earned after many years in productive careers. It was only in this regard that young John Cummings was but an observer.

We concluded lunch vowing to see each other at a Christmas Eve celebration in three days and made our way to valet parking. It was while waiting for Lou's car that I experienced a most precious, though not uncommon, encounter. A well-dressed executive-type accepted the valet stub for his late-model German luxury sedan and stared at me as he approached. He was curious enough to ask if he knew me. Not recognizing the face, I extended my hand and announced my name.

The question mark (look) on his face smoothed to a joyful glow as he boldly said, "Sure! You're Gene's brother. My name is Dennis Noto."

I did not know what was to follow, but I knew it was good.

"Gene," he said, "is responsible for me having the quality of life I enjoy. He encouraged me to attend the Friday morning Bible study with him at Palma Ceia, and through his mentoring and interest in me, I came to know the Lord Jesus and how he expects me to live my life. As a result, I love my wife more and she loves me more. I love my kids more, and our family is happier. I've learned to balance my family and my work and I'm doing better than ever at both. My life is better than I ever thought it could be because of your brother."

"Stop," I said. "Would you repeat, word for word, what you just told me to my friend?" As I directed him to Lou, who was engaged in conversation with someone, I said. "Lou, this is Dennis; Dennis, this is Lou."

He proceeded to say that he knew both of us from our days at Jesuit but that we probably did not remember him because he was behind us. He then recounted verbatim what he had just communicated to me regarding Gene.

As was the case with me, this was not the first time Lou had heard someone share the impact Gene had on their life. I could not have been prouder.

Lou and I discuss many topics while riding around. Legacy is one of them.

This brief encounter led us to focus on what is eternally important, and for a few moments, we discussed the difference between an *important* legacy versus one that is *popular*.

After that experience, I am further committed to focusing on matters with eternal implications.

The spirit *is* indeed willing, but the flesh *is* weak. (Mathew 26:41b)

HELL'S CANYON

Florida possesses some of the best fishing this planet has to offer. Anglers from around the world visit the *Sunshine State*, especially during its mild winters, to take advantage of Florida's double-play—wonderful weather and outstanding fishing.

An additional magnet for anglers is the fact that no matter where you choose to cast your line in Florida, first-class accommodations are nearby.

Some, however, can't see the forest for the trees. That would have been me in January of 2006 when I organized a fishing expedition to the Great Northwest; Hell's Canyon to be specific.

Hell's Canyon is North America's deepest canyon, trumping the Grand Canyon, and is well known for its outstanding salmon and steelhead (trout returning to their spawning origin) fishing in the Snake, Salmon, and Clearwater Rivers. Tucked in the wilderness between Idaho, Oregon, and Washington, it is truly an outdoorsman's dream.

Other than methods employed by Lewis and Clark some 200 years ago when they were contracted by the United States government to produce maps of this region, Hell's Canyon is only accessible by single-passenger, light aircraft, helicopter, or preferably by jet boat.

My friend, George Turnpaugh, has been organizing fishing trips to the canyon and other remote locations since 1984. He originally organized these trips as a marketing tool with his key customers and over the years, the trips have expanded to include friends and family—his and his friends' families.

I'd heard of the good times at these excursions through several friends and acquaintances over the years, but the fishing, camping and fellowship stories in Hell's Canyon abounded throughout 2005, and though unaware, my interest was being piqued. Contributing to my growing interest were reports I heard from Pastors Singletary and Zeller, Tony Dungy, and my longtime friend, Abe Brown.

Concurrently, Family First, an organization on whose board I have served for many years, was considering fundraising options which included the possibility of a celebrity Hell's Canyon fishing trip with popular and NFL Hall of Fame football coach Tony Dungy and/or well known MLB manager Lou Piniella, both supporters of Family First's mission and Tony Dungy being the organization's lead spokesperson.

I was discussing the matter with George Turnpaugh when he suggested a warm-up trip for Lou to gauge his enthusiasm. Dungy was already an avid and willing participant. George, Lou, and I met for lunch and the January trip was on.

Lou immediately warned me regarding the toughness of this trip and I immediately retorted, challenging his personal toughness. "If Anglos Lewis and Clark made the trip on horseback and mule pack," I argued, "how could Latins Piniella and Flores not be up to the challenge with the assistance of jet aircraft and car rentals?"

He quickly countered, "They made their trip in August."

Throughout the two weeks prior to the trip Lou gently and considerately issued additional caution about the anticipated difficulty of the trip, but I received his sincere warnings as a duck's back receives water.

What made the trip to be even nicer was George's suggestion that we fill the remaining roster spots with whomever we desired. This worked out especially nice for me since my son was able to make the trip.

The final travel group from Tampa consisted of longtime friends Pieter Dearolf, Cary Gaylord, Bennie Lazzara, in addition to Mondy III, Lou and me. At the last moment, Bennie was required to deal with a pressing conflict and had to miss the trip. He was quite disappointed, as were we.

GETTING THERE

Wednesday, January 18, 2006 was a crisp Florida day allowing us to wear light jackets as we departed TIA for Spokane, Washington, our trek's departure point for the surface portion of our trip to the canyon.

After a comfortable evening (except for me) at the Red Lion Inn, Mondy, Lou and I followed George's Dodge quad-cab pickup, transporting Pete, Cary, Homer Gonzalez (George's brother-in-law), and, of course, our host, George.

We stopped for breakfast at the Top Notch Café in Colfax, Washington, about an hour south of Spokane and about halfway to Lewiston, Idaho, where George garages his jet boat and other trip essentials. In Lewiston, we purchased fishing licenses and visited an "outdoors outfitter" so Lou could outfit himself with the latest cold-weather and fishing fashions. His claim that Tampa did not offer appropriate gear for a trip to the canyon proved to be partially correct—at least for someone interested in setting the dress standard for George's canyon trips.

Our relaxed pace resulted in a slight panic for George who thoroughly understood the peril of attempting to reach the campsite after daylight. With that in mind, George assigned Mondy, Lou, Homer, and me to the first jet boat trip with him as pilot, leaving Pete, Cary, and, soon-to-arrive son-in-law, Stephen Schmeltekopf, Stephen's friend, Josh Morton, and Josh's dad, Troy, who were arriving from Denver and Dallas, respectively.

George maneuvered his new jet boat down the Snake River against the current like the professional he is. Just beyond some aggressive rapids, about eight miles from where we disembarked and from the nearest telephone, George handed the piloting duties to his normally very able brother-in-law, Homer, as we traveled at near full speed to maximize what daylight remained for the second trip.

During that transition, all hell broke loose when Homer's fishing apparel hooked on to the steering apparatus sending the vessel into a violent 360-degree spin with an additional 180 degrees causing us to grab whatever was near to keep from being tossed into the perilous, quickly-moving, 38-degree water.

George had just made his way toward the front of the boat to speak with us when the spinning began. Since the rest of us were sitting, thus giving us a lower center of gravity, George was the most vulnerable to being spun overboard.

I witnessed George adroitly drop to the deck using the centrifugal force generated by the boat's spinning to press him to the vessel, thus allowing him to maneuver his way to the steering mechanism. In the brief but harrowing interim, Homer was able to free his garment and kill the power, leaving us emotionally sapped while we contemplated what just happened.

Homer's sincere apologies were unnecessary as it was apparent that he had done all he could to right the ship, and, as he so simply stated, this was his first time piloting the new boat which featured *rudder steering* in contrast to the conventional steering wheel with which he was familiar on George's previous boat. Nonetheless, it happened so quickly that the only thing I recall thinking was how to assist Mondy (as if I could have) and watching George frantically fight to save himself and gain control of his vessel. As a testament to thickness of blood, Mondy (later) told me his only thought during the spin was how he was going to assist me.

We were informed by George, and the following day by our fishing guide, Jason, that it was highly unlikely that any of us would have survived falling into the frigid water considering the immediate state of immobility we would have experienced after our multilayer of clothes absorbed the water. Consensus was that the estimated time before our lives were taken by shock, hypothermia, or both was ten to forty-five seconds.

With that uninvited reality check behind us, we took a deep breath and resumed our trip to the east bank of the Snake River in Hell's Canyon, Idaho.

Within twenty-five minutes, George placed the nose of his watercraft onto the beach of the campsite, barked commands for us to quickly disembark and unload the cargo, which included our individual gear among the food provisions acquired earlier in the day, so he could hastily depart to pick up the remaining campers threatened by rapidly dissipating daylight.

In the meantime, we relocated the offloaded gear and provisions from the beach up the moderate incline to the campsite and tended to the most pressing order of business—starting the campfire.

Within a couple of hours, George arrived with the rest of the group. We helped them bring the rest of the cargo to the campsite as we introduced ourselves, exchange pleasantries, and discussed supper options.

As daylight gave way to starlight, George and Homer fired up some lanterns to provide enough light to prepare dinner in the large, well-stocked "kitchen" tent before placing items to be cooked on the charcoal fire tended to by the efficient Homer Gonzalez who was in between preparing a mixed green salad, setting out potato salad, and mixing a batch of brownies to be cooked in a Dutch oven, over the fire. What was remarkable about the dinner effort was that George and Homer were able to prepare a feast for ten while the rest of us got in their way asking question after question: *Where's the other cheese? Where are the paper towels? Where do we go to use the toilet? Do we have salt 'n vinegar potato chips?* To say that George and Homer are gracious hosts is an understatement.

The mid-thirty-degree temperatures of the afternoon transitioned to mid-twenties shortly after dark, and as the temperature dropped, staring at the campfire (nature's TV, per George) in the comfortable chairs became increasingly popular. This setting later became fodder for stories.

The grill accommodated ten 16 oz. steak burgers allowing each of us to select anything from (Pittsburgh) rare to well done. Some of our group had seconds—either partial or a full additional 1lb. burger. That, my friend, is a lot of beef, especially without the solace of an elongated "whisper flush" Kohler. I took the aforementioned accommodations into consideration when I finished only ¼ of the scrumptious brownie dessert.

While we ate in the quiet of the wilderness, without TV, radio, or even the hum of a refrigerator motor, I read Psalm 104 to our group against the running water of the Snake River. To listen to King David's expression of God's creation in that setting, "He stretches out the heavens like a tent and lays the beams of his upper chambers on their waters…," took on a special appeal.

After dinner, and in the bone-chilling night, we told jokes and traded stories around the fire for a while, and at approximately 8:30 PM, I initiated the exodus to the tents to get rested for the big day of steelhead fishing and canyon exploration that lay ahead. Shortly thereafter, tent-mates Mondy and Lou followed.

As we chose our tent positions, both the oversized sleeping bags and the stand-up tent began to shrink in my eyes. While I had a full 6½ feet clearance to the top of the tent, I noticed Mondy's and Lou's clearance tapered down to 1½ feet where their torsos met the outside walls of the tent. It did not seem to bother either of them. The same was not true for me.

We unlayered to our thermals in preparation of retiring to our minus-twelve-degree-rated sleeping bags as Mondy controlled our only source of light, the oversized law enforcement-grade Mag-Lite he brought on the trip.

I was "bagged" first and was becoming disenchanted with the idea of camping. We were told it would take thirty minutes before we would feel "warm as toast" in the bags, and as far as I was concerned, the clock hadn't started ticking yet as I lay shivering in the frigid Idaho night.

We were laughing (mine required effort) as Lou and Mondy made final preparations before sleeping and I was fighting off thoughts of claustrophobia, a lifelong condition that I had no inkling could be "tent-induced." Silent prayer interrupted by jokes my tent mates made to soothe what they accurately sensed was becoming an uncomfortable situation for me, was how I fought off the building anxiety.

I've heard people, even some to whom I am close, describe the fear and sense of helplessness brought on by anxiety, but I never understood what they attempted to communicate until that night beneath the starry Idaho sky. There is, indeed, a distinction between hearing and listening.

I guess we're good at shutting out feelings that are foreign to us; or, at least, I am.

CONTRIBUTING FACTORS

For me, the evening before the trip included eating richly—make that richly overeating—at Tampa's Capital Grille resulting in, for the most part, a sleepless night.

The next evening, we traveled diagonally across the U. S., and even though the flight was uneventful, 7+ hours in the compressed cabin of a Northwest Airlines jet would not be my choice for a pleasant evening. Add to the flight a temperature decrease of fifty degrees and an altitude increase of 5,000 feet between Tampa and Spokane, plus a large chef salad topped with Dungeness crab at midnight (3am ET) and you have a second consecutive night of less than restorative sleep.

On Thursday, surface travel 2½ hours on windy two-lane state highways with a greater than 5,000 foot drop in altitude, followed by an hour ride in frigid temperatures in the mid-thirties. Then, to the camp on the active Snake River, a ride that featured the aforementioned life-threatening jet boat spin experience and you have the makings of an anxiety episode.

TIME TO SLEEP

Zip-zip-zip was how Lou described what he heard as I frantically announced my departure from the tent. Lou later added he was glad I successfully freed myself from the sleeping bag and tent because the commitment in my voice convinced him I was exiting, and not being able to open the tent would not have stopped me. He was right.

Mondy asked if there was anything he could do for me as I stood outside the tent in mid-twenties temperatures contemplating my next move. I asked him to get me a couple of pain pills I'd packed, hoping they would relax me. I took the pills with a twenty ounce bottle of water—my fourth in the past three hours. Mondy provided much comfort to me as he assisted my efforts to re-enter my bag and he and Lou engaged me in conversation to steady my nerves. About thirty minutes later, we offered each other "good night" again and Mondy shut off the flashlight.

Zip-zip-zip was how Lou described what he heard as I expressed I was—again—exiting the tent, this time because "nature" was calling. The reason generated a roaring laugh from Lou and an attempted muted laugh from my son, balancing his natural urge to express deference toward his dad. Their laughs made no difference to me; I had urgent business at hand. The facilities, as it was, were thirty to forty yards from our tent, but it wouldn't have mattered if they were half that distance—it was time to perform. With Mondy's trusty flashlight, I located an adequate spot approximately eight feet from the tent, dropped my new thermals, assumed the position (none too soon) and accomplished what could only be described as a grown man's result—you would've had to have been there to understand. My wife's thoughtfulness in packing "baby wipes" was highly appreciated. Within minutes, I was being re-bagged by my son and consoled by Lou as he sympathetically communicated his disappointment for my attempt (because I was back so soon) by saying, "You must have misfired."

"Misfired, hell!" I said. "You're camping with a new man. I took care of business and couldn't have asked for more success."

They both erupted with laughter, and each time Lou asked for a specific location of the deposit, Mondy held his stomach as he doubled over in laughter. We bantered about for twenty minutes or so before calling it an evening (again) as Lou asked which way to leave the tent should he develop the urge during the night.

I told him, "Head toward the campfire, but to be safe, make sure you're wearing your boots."

Mondy laughed himself to sleep as I pondered what the night held.

I talked to myself in an attempt to manage the anxiety. *They do this all the time. Lewis and Clark didn't have the equipment or the provisions we have... or did they? I don't want to be a burden on Lou and Mondy, and most importantly, I don't want to embarrass Mondy.*

My self-talk proved to be moderately effective, but it had no effect on my bladder, which was processing the eighty-plus ounces of water I'd downed in the previous three hours.

A slower-paced *zip, zip, zip* caused Lou to ask where I was going. The pain pills and the self-talk allowed me to doze for short periods, but my bladder demonstrated the dependability of Big Ben waking me every fifty-five minutes with a plea for relief. During one of my relief periods, Lou asked that I be accurate because he heard water close to the tent. I explained that my accuracy was not an issue and reminded him I was bedded down in the same tent. I told him he was either hearing a mountain stream or a bear was emptying his bladder by his side of the tent. Mondy laughed as we all recognized Lou's attempt to help me through the night.

I generally miss 6 AM, but I was looking for morning with great anticipation on January 20, 2006. My 5:55 AM bladder call took me from my doze while Mondy and Lou provided a snoring symphony. Upon re-entering the tent, I made every attempt to be very quiet so as not to disturb my tent mates. Lou began to rustle and Mondy remained in the delta zone. Lou said he usually makes a couple of potty trips, if not three, during the night but that it was so cold he couldn't motivate himself to get up once. "What does motivation have to do with it?" I thought, as he made his way to relieve his bladder.

"Where did you make your deposit last night?" he inquired as he carefully chose each step.

"By the baby wipes," I responded.

"I already passed the wipes," he said with a hint of concern.

"Then check your boots," I said, laughing simultaneously with him as Mondy joined the laughter.

"This couldn't have been you," Lou said. "It had to be a bear."

We were taking turns making Mondy laugh when I responded, "If it was a bear, I think he used baby wipes."

In a very rugged and uncomfortable setting, it was comforting being with my son and Lou.

CONQUER THE SNAKE

Apart from George advising us of the possibility that fishing the Snake River may be impeded by muddy water resulting from a problem with the dam upstream, I had made up my mind that I was spending the balance of the evenings of this trip in a hotel, motel, or whatever—as long as it had heat and a conventional bed. Lou and Mondy concurred, though each of us was concerned about offending our friend and host. Lou summarized our feelings when he said, "I'm praying for muddy water."

After a hearty fireside breakfast, we boarded the jet boats and set out to conquer the Snake.

The entire Friday morning yielded only one steelhead hooked—and none boated—even though we would have had to release the one hooked anyway because it was *wild* as opposed to *hatchery* (the only kind allowed to be kept). We nonetheless enjoyed the morning exploring the pristine Oregon terrain along the Salmon River, which included an abandoned mine and observing wildlife including eagles, sheep, and the like.

At lunch back at camp, George polled the group as to who wanted to relocate to Lewiston and fish the Clearwater River for larger steelhead and who wanted to remain at camp with an abundance of provisions but with no means of communicating with the rest of the world until the jet boat returned Sunday morning. The vote had a clear geographical component: the five-man Florida contingent opted to fish the Clearwater (lured by sleeping in a hotel), and the four men from Colorado and Texas gave the Floridians a taste of *how the west was won* by opting to stay and camp on the Snake. I petitioned God's blessing on them as we jet-boated away and couldn't help but think that if it were up to people with my grit to explore this country, we might still be at Plymouth Rock, if not Europe. I provided myself solace by recalling God's Word as spoken by King Solomon in the book of Ecclesiastes, Chapter 3, *There is a time for everything, and a season for every activity under heaven.* My season for the *canyon* had passed.

HELL'S CANYON

Snake River, Idaho 2006

Fishing gang from Tampa(Pete,Me,Mondy III, Lou,Cary & George) conquering the snake

Mondy and I after our near death experience in the Snake River, Idaho

Snake River accommodation-5 star rating on tripadvisor

THE CLEARWATER RIVER

Saturday morning, we met our fishing guide, Jason, and his mate at the insane hour of 5:30 AM for breakfast, then headed for the Clearwater.

Fishing guides, like most of us, live in their own universe, and as such, have their own idiosyncrasies. Jason was no exception. We were instructed by Jason to hide our *secret bait* from other anglers who, he was convinced, were out to uncover his coveted technique of catching the elusive (to this point) steelhead. That bit of instruction was the butt of a few snide remarks while we floated the river without success.

Jason was, indeed, a top-notch guide, and before long, we got into some nice-sized fish, some weighing in at 15 to 17 pounds. Catching fish and spending time in an area and a climate unfamiliar to us was fun, but the most fun was in the fellowship and barbs between good friends, and for me, the added benefit of being with my son.

That evening, as was the case for all our civilized evenings, was spent at the best restaurant we could locate doing what we do best—deciding between rare and medium rare and telling jokes.

Sunday morning, George needed the assistance of two men to join him back to the camp to retrieve Homer, Stephen, Josh, and Troy, as well as the camping gear and surplus provisions. This is when being young and fit is an advantage to those wanting to accompany George as well as to those preferring to remain behind and sleep in. Mondy III and Cary met George at 6:30 AM in the lobby.

Pete, Lou, and I met at a more civil 9:30 and enjoyed a leisurely breakfast at Shari's Pancake House before canvassing Lewiston's hot (according to Lou) real estate market. Afterward, we retreated to our rooms to watch the NFL Conference Playoff games before traveling to Spokane in preparation for Monday's 7:00 AM departure.

ON THE ROAD AGAIN

On the way to Spokane, Mondy expressed having had a nice time with George and Cary on their mission to break camp, notwithstanding missing the opportunity to sleep in. We enhanced the trip by visiting the campuses of The University of Idaho in Moscow and nearby Washington State University in Pullman. Both universities were distinct, yet similar, and WSU was of particular interest to Mondy and me because of our fondness for our friends and distinguished Cougar alumni, Jack and Molly Thompson. We capped off the trip with a delicious meal at Clinkerdagger's Steakhouse in downtown Spokane, while Toby Keith entertained his fans at the arena across the street.

We again experienced significant changes (improvements) in altitude and temperature as we backtracked cross country to Tampa and were again blessed with uneventful flights. As we scattered to our families, I'm confident the rest of the group shared my sentiment: Thanks, George for a wonderful time, and isn't it nice to live in Florida?

SIXTIES

I've been told that, statistically, if you live through your sixties you will make it to and possibly through your eighties; a prospect that has some built-in negatives if quality of life deteriorates beyond what is normal. Nonetheless, the probability quotient for me living through my sixties was considerably low since I was packing 100+ extra pounds at 365. An interesting side note is that I felt rather healthy and was not apparently restricted.

I was intrigued and motivated by my son's success in shedding some unwanted pounds. Mondy III had been married for about eight years, was the father of four children, and through not paying attention, he managed to peak at 235 pounds before deciding to deal with the issue. Over the next eighteen months, I observed him eating less and exercising more, resulting in his losing fifty pounds and achieving an impressive 185-pound physique, which he entered into various triathlons and later into *Tough Mudders* competitions in Florida and Colorado.

I thought to myself, if my thirty-one-year-old son, operating with 50% of my DNA, was able to lose fifty pounds, why couldn't I do the same? So, with that as my initial motivation, I considered the best methods for me to shed a few pounds. Not being a proponent of gimmick diets, I decided to attempt to lose the extra pounds the old fashioned way—eating less.

If I am anything, I'm a realist. If I had been unable to lose weight and keep the pounds off in the past, how was I to be successful in the future? I was, am, and had been a believing Bible student since 1980 and was aware of God's promises to those in His flock who seek His strength in battling problems of all kinds, addictions included. My excessive eating was nothing short of an addiction, and I was confident that I could not be victorious without God's assistance. I knew great effort would be necessary on my part, but I knew that without God's power, my success, if any, would be as it had been in the past—short-lived. So, recognizing my inadequacy in this matter, I asked God for the strength to lose whatever amount of weight He deemed correct and to guide me through the process, and just as important, to give me the discipline to maintain my weight at that unknown (to me) number.

At first it was quite a challenge, because I had slipped into the habit of eating whatever my heart desired whenever the desire was awakened. The combination of no restrictions and no conscience I had created was a proven formula to gain weight and maintain it, as well. Utilizing that formula, I'd managed to grow to 365 pounds without drinking soft or hard drinks; I was a pasta, bread, and steak man, always closing the session with desert led by New York cheesecake with strawberries to ensure I was taking in the nutrition offered by the strawberries hidden by thick whipped cream (my mouth waters as I strike the keyboard).

But after a few months of battling my addiction utilizing the strength God offers, my intake requirements seemed to decrease and I was developing a level of comfort in reducing quantity without giving up quality. The Lord allowed me to eat the same variety of foods I had previously enjoyed and blessed me by giving me satisfaction with about half the volume I was previously consuming. With His strength, I was losing two pounds per month, on average, until that calculus totaled 110 pounds in early 2013. I know that I had no chance of losing that much weight and developing a different perspective toward food on my own. I recognize this matter will always be a day-to-day battle and my success is dependent upon my dependence on the Lord's strength and not mine.

Early during this weight-loss endeavor, I had introduced bike riding in an attempt to attain and maintain some muscle tone while improving my cardiac function. It worked. My heart rate went to about 50 bpm as my blood pressure improved to about 120 over 70, and in the process, my atrial flutter condition vanished. My buddy Lou joined the bike riding with the same objective and we periodically traveled to the Upper Trail and Starkey Park to add some variety. Sometime later, Tony G caught the bug and joined us and suggested we add Flatwoods (east of USF) to our riding venues. Our bike riding morphed into an exercise/social time for the three of us as we often capped off the sessions with a visit to one of our favorite restaurants.

February 15, 2013 was to be one of those outings. In late February, I prepared the following recap of this particular outing as a means of communicating to family and friends the unexpected life-changing experience that occurred that day.

MERCY AT FLATWOODS

Friday afternoon, February 15, 2013 was a chamber-of-commerce-dream day in the Tampa Bay Area, featuring a bright sun under clear skies, a light breeze, and a high of 70 degrees with low humidity. Why would three childhood friends from West Tampa resist nature's invitation to go biking and fellowshipping? So, off to Flatwoods Bike Trail went Tony Gonzalez, Lou Piniella, and me as we had many times before.

We are blessed with self-directed schedules, which permit such excursions and are motivated to improve our overall health. Tony's and my additional focus is on maintaining cardiovascular health post bypass surgery and Tony also seeks to strengthen his core following lower back surgery. As for Lou, he just tries to work off some banquet food and stay on the safe side of Type-2 Diabetes tendencies. The common denominator is the fellowship.

Tony and his family were living with fresh wounds, having lost their twenty-year-old grandson, Sebastian Gonzales-Vargas in an auto accident in Peru two days after Christmas 2012. This tragedy exposed a tenderness and vulnerability within Tony I had not previously known, which has taken his stature with me to a new level. He succinctly describes life now as a combination of *God and time*.

Previous to this tragedy, the conversations in which we engaged during our bike rides usually began with our faith, then family, followed by a digression to sports, then politics, and then (if possible to digress from politics) to finances. The finance topic manages to bore me most since it has little to do with the rest of our lives, considering the Lord has chosen to bless our three families far beyond our needs, and in my opinion, deep into our wants. Since the tragedy, we stay in the faith and family categories longer, though the "pull" of the world somehow manages to lead us into the counterproductive bowels of politics and finances eventually.

As we negotiated the twelve-mile course, we engaged in gentle criticism of those we passed and gave kudos to those who passed us, especially when they were in our age group, though we generally tempered our appreciation by commenting that their equipment was superior to ours, clearly displaying our faulty logic. In addition to our harmless conversation, we lacked adherence to course protocol by riding three abreast, thus occupying the entire course and impeding those serious cyclists timing their rides. Occasionally, these serious cyclists would murmur something as they passed us and we would wait till they could not hear us before issuing a retort. If a safety-minded organization wanted to create a training film on improper course practices, they could do no better than filming us. The only redeeming characteristic of our group is that we were committed helmet wearers and advocates, though that commitment took us a while to grasp.

As we entered the ninth mile of our ride, we were well into our finance discussion and cruising between 14 and 15 mph with the aid of a slight tailwind when inexplicably Lou and I bumped handlebars causing both of us to attempt to correct the situation which resulted in me taking a spill that included breaking the fall with my helmeted head on the tarmac propelled by my 250-pound body. Tony recalls untangling my left leg from the bike frame carefully so as not to cause unnecessary moves to my unresponsive limbs. My awareness kicked in at this point as both Tony and Lou came to my side to assess the situation and take whatever action was required.

I heard the concern in their voices as they observed me lying motionless on the tarmac, sans control of my body. As I lay there, my peripheral vision allowed me to view my arms but my attempts to move them were not met with any success. I could only take abbreviated and periodic breaths, so I had to use each word carefully for fear of suffocating. I asked them if my feet were moving and they reluctantly told me that they were not. I could feel the understandable anxiety they were experiencing as they frantically communicated with 911 and park personnel, but strangely enough, at the same time, I was experiencing a seemingly inexplicable peace, the kind of peace that comes from God alone.

In John 14:27, Jesus says, "Peace I leave with you; My peace I give to you; not as the world gives do I give to you. Do not let your heart be troubled, nor let it be fearful."

As I lay on the tarmac, God allowed me to experience the fulfillment of one of His countless promises firsthand. In Hebrews 13:5, He promises, "I will never leave you or forsake you," and certainly He was true to His Word. He met my immediate needs. I needed peace and I needed faith, and the Holy Spirit graciously supplied both. He enabled me to trust His Sovereignty, and because He is incapable of error, I was able, through faith, to put the entire matter into His Hands, thereby experiencing a peace that passes all understanding (Philippians 4:7). I promised Him that I would never second-guess His decision and it would be my desire to glorify Him in whatever final condition He decided for me.

With that communication behind me, I turned my attention to Tony and Lou, who were continuing to do everything they could to get the EMS (emergency medical service) unit to our location. After communicating the essence of my conversation with God, I asked them to allow me to lead us in prayer, during which I asked them to try to relinquish any feelings of guilt they were experiencing and to accept the fact that I was fine with the outcome whatever it might be. Lou was less amenable to the request as he focused on the immediacy of the issue; I appreciated his sentiments and assured him that I was not "quitting," but that I recognized that the One in control was not visible but was nonetheless in control. He acquiesced, but continued to bark commands to get help and get it quick. Tony, on the heels of the devastating loss of his grandson, Seb, methodically worked toward the same end under his fresh understanding that the outcome was not in our hands.

What I did not share with them was that I recognized that I was in a quadriplegic state and that I had no idea what to expect. My suspicion that they recognized the same thing was verified when they later told me my color was turning progressively grey and ashen as I lay on the tarmac with no movement other than the movement on my face associated with my shallow breathing and sparse conversation.

Then, as we waited for the EMS vehicle, a wonderful event took place. My right arm flinched once, then twice. I tried to move it again, but without success, so I tried my left arm—again, no success. But while my left arm did not respond, my right flinched again, seeming to suggest that I was getting a delayed reaction. Tony tested my sensitivity to touch by running his fingernail up and down my torso, trying to determine how low these delayed commands were reaching. By the time EMS arrived, I was able to raise my arms up and away from my chest and was told my foot was starting to move, though I was not commanding it to do so; perhaps it was an extended delay from when I'd first tried to move it. I remember thanking God for seemingly upgrading me to a paraplegic.

How to communicate my situation to Judy and my children had been on my mind from the very beginning and I asked Lou and Tony to contact Mondy III and have him communicate the matter to Judy. Alisha, John, and their family were on a Disney Cruise, so communication with them would be on a need-to-know basis until they returned (Alisha did not care for this decision, but it was nonetheless the best decision given the totality of the matter). To complicate matters further, I had 6 PM dinner plans with Malio, which obviously would garner concern, so I asked Tony to cover that base, as well.

At the Trauma Center, I recognized the feigned composure Judy and Mondy III maintained as my boarded, braced, and strapped body was off-loaded from the EMS vehicle and transported inside.

After a myriad of tests and procedures, it was determined that admission to the hospital was necessary due in large part to my unstable gait attributed to the weakness in my legs. CAT scans, MRIs, X-rays, blood work, and assessments of every nature filled the weekend, and it was determined that my accident had caused severe spinal cord damage rendering me a *temporary* quadriplegic.

While I was not surprised by the news, I was nonetheless startled when that announcement was made to us by neurosurgeon, Dr. Steven Tresser. The mercy that God had bestowed upon me was medically confirmed, though confirmation for me was not necessary. The related diagnosis was that I had a pre-existing cervical compression condition (stenosis) which was also no surprise and was probably caused by football-related neck trauma and aggravated by a bull-fighting neck injury (foolish, in my case) sustained in Spain at the age of twenty-seven.

Considering that I had heretofore been asymptomatic with regard to this preexisting condition, and according to both the neurosurgeon and neurologist that the recommended decompression surgery was without a doubt necessary, I can only view the accident as a blessing revealing the need for this corrective measure.

While I would have preferred an email to advise me of this fact, I am totally thankful to a merciful God for bringing this matter to my attention in this manner. I was reminded by Tony that, during the previous thirty days, I'd experienced two falls while loading and unloading my bike on his truck, which tells me I missed a couple of the "emails" I just indicated that I preferred.

I'm confident that *time*, as it always does, will dull the vividness of this merciful experience, but I'm more confident that the portion of this event I'll forever remember is the unmerited favor and mercy that God provided me that afternoon at Flatwoods and my renewed and enhanced desire to live in appreciation of His grace.

FLESH VS. SPIRIT

I was duly advised that spinal cord injury rehabilitation was both slow and arduous. While I was immersed in rehab, I developed a new appreciation for the terms *slow* and *arduous*.

It has been six months since that day at Flatwoods when a bicycle accident left me quadriplegic for twenty minutes before I experienced God's grace in greatly improving my condition to where surgery and rehab would allow me to regain some portion of the health and mobility I enjoyed before the accident that afternoon February 15, 2013.

When I recall using a walker, a shower bench, and being tethered to a catheter (to mention a few of the required aids) during the early days after February 15, 2013, the improvement I have been graciously allowed is great. But, when I allow my *flesh* an opinion on the matter, that great improvement can be mitigated, and if left unchecked, my *flesh* can even attempt to convert my immense gratitude into a whine. How is that possible? How can a person lying on his back on the tarmac at Flatwoods without the use of any part of his body beneath his chin give the entire matter over to his Lord with no clue or expectation that his condition would improve? Then, six months later ask the same Lord why the recovery process is *so* slow and *so* arduous.

No doubt that the grace required to give the entire matter to God when the accident took place was instantly provided by God. Immediately after the accident, I recollect experiencing a seemingly-inexplicable peace, the kind of peace that comes from God alone.

So that explains "turning the matter over to the Lord," but what about doubting God's rehab timetable? Doesn't questioning why the recovery process is so slow and so arduous seem double-minded? Certainly, it does, and this is one reason why otherwise grateful people complain about the timing of blessings bestowed upon them.

God forewarns of this eventuality when He tells us in Romans 8:5-6, "Those who live according to the *flesh* have their minds set on what the *flesh* desires; but those who live in accordance with the *Spirit* have their minds set on what the *Spirit* desires. The mind governed by the *flesh* is death, but the mind governed by the *Spirit* is life and peace."

The insatiable appetite of the *flesh* can only be controlled by a *Spirit-governed* mind. The choice is mine, and I have chosen to allow the *Spirit* to govern my mind and reign in my life.

BLESSING OF BLESSINGS

As I reflect on my life, I can clearly see God's hand in the many key events that ultimately provided the framework for my life. Occurrences that seemed isolated or independent at the time can now be viewed as contributing factors to significant events, illustrating to me that every person's life can be used by God to bring about His glory—and this is why we were created. Not that God orchestrated each event but that He orchestrated some and allowed others within the framework of our free will to accomplish His purpose. It is humbling to consider the privilege it is to be used by our Creator to be a willing contributor towards the accomplishment of His Plan.

I'm confident that all earthly events will be understood once we're in heaven, but until then, we'll just have to be satisfied to operate under the comfort that God makes no mistakes and trust His love and goodness. In that category, I place (chronologically) the murder of father, my two heart surgeries, the miscarriage of Sarah and Mondy's baby, Mondy's burn, Christiano's life-threatening heart surgery, my brother Gene's premature death, the uncertain health situations within our family, and most recently, my bike accident which resulted in my spinal cord injury, but which also ushered me into a new dimension in my life. Hoping the improbable hope that there will not be others, I'm fully cognizant that it is only in heaven that these types of events are nonexistent.

Interspersed among those events are a category of events that are easier to understand and accept, and with the benefit of hindsight, have now been made clear to me. The list (again chronologically) include the circumstances resulting in me attending Jesuit High School, meeting Judith Kay Stallings, Carmine's and Malio's catalytic roles in the initiation of two of the three major events in my business career, Mondy and Sarah's relocation to Tampa due to the failure of our Alabama business, the spiritual connection between Frank

Venezia and me, and the subsequent spiritual connection between Frank and John Cordova years before John and Alisha would meet and later marry. Paramount among these events is—and will always be—meeting Judith Kay Stallings because of the spiritual example she provided then and provides now as my wife, in addition to being the person whose company I most enjoy.

As documented in the sections of my memoirs where I specifically mention Judith, she has always been a wife, a mother, a lover, a friend, a rock, a confidant, supporter extraordinaire and continues to be to this day, but where I benefit the most from my association with her is her ability to maintain the long view—the eternal perspective. My life experience for the first thirty-five years centered on getting results and getting them quickly and she has always had the ability to see things from an eternal perspective and has been instrumental in assisting me in adjusting my focus from the temporal to the eternal.

That adjustment changes everything. You see and treat people differently, you use your time and choose your life's activities differently, you use the resources God has provided differently, your appreciation for what God has done on the cross and in your life takes on a different meaning all because of your new understanding of how this earthly visit relates to eternity. That is why, in a life that has been replete with blessings, I easily refer to meeting Judith as my *blessing of blessings*.

In this fast-paced, high-tech culture in which we live, the urgent often takes precedence over the important. Not to fall prey to that dilemma, I often express to Judith how I feel about her and the tremendous value she has added to my life. I have communicated my feelings regarding Judith to my children as well, but I recently wanted to ensure that they comprehended exactly what I meant, so I prepared and sent them the following letter:

JUDITH K FLORES
(YOUR MOTHER, MY WIFE)

August 24, 2013

Dear Mondy and Alisha,

Though you will learn much in the years to come, both of you are seasoned parents, and therefore, I need not express my opinion to you as to the quality of mother you have, even though I possess a well-developed opinion. Let it suffice to say that, while I've witnessed many mothers, I've never witnessed one who could match yours.

I am, however, uniquely qualified to opine as to the quality of spouse which your mother has been and is to me.

As your mother and I joyfully build our forty-third year of marriage, it is my desire to share my reflections on what makes her the same superior spouse she is to me as she is a mother to you.

It's really quite easy to understand, though not as easy to accomplish. It centers on her freedom (John 8:32). She is *free*: free from guile, free from vanity, free from ostentation, free from what this world offers. At the core of her freedom is her unshakeable desire to be the truest *follower* of Christ she can be. She is committed to *doing* the Word, not merely hearing it. Out of her desire to follow Christ emerges the selfless person she is and the reason she is considered unique to all who know her. And therein lies the reason she has been the type of mother she is to you while being the type of wife she is to me.

Included in most (Western) wedding covenants is the mutual promise of the bride and groom *to be true to each other in good times and in bad, in sickness and in health; and to love and honor each other all the days of their lives.* I can unequivocally say that Judith K. Flores has not only beautifully upheld her end of our marital vow, but she has also deepened its meaning, and while she has been great during *good times and in health*, she has been magnificent during *challenging times and in sickness.*

To say that God blessed me with my wife is the understatement of understatements. Let it suffice to say that while I've witnessed many wives, I've never witnessed one who could match mine.

Papa

A PANGOLIN

Today I carried a (facial) mask that I did not own a week ago to pick up my vehicle from a repair shop, which took my credit card payment over the telephone so that I would be protected from them and they would be protected from me. I never saw a person, and as promised, I never came into contact with another human being. How did they know it was me picking up my car and not someone else, perhaps a thief? I suppose the cameras throughout the parking area were supposed to make me feel secure; that could be why they're called security cameras.

On the way to get my vehicle, my son (he also had a mask he did not own a week ago) and I drove by our friendly Asian family-operated pharmacy to pick up a prescription for his wife. He followed the instructions on the locked door and phoned the pharmacy which he stood in front of, only to learn that the product he sought would not be available until the following day. He did all this without coming into direct personal contact with anyone and abided by the Federal Government's "social distancing" protocol. He wiped his hands and credit card and we were safely off to retrieve my car.

The evening before, my wife and I ordered our supper in from a local seafood establishment which also was abiding by the federal protocol, we knew our prepaid meal was delivered to our front door when the delivery person abided by his end of the rules by ringing our doorbell and pointed to our package from a distance of not less than six feet away. He wore a mask. The evening news reported *ad nauseam* how many new Covid-19 cases and deaths there were in the world, in the USA, in the reigning national "hot spot" New York State with 161,807 cases, and 7,067 deaths including New York City's contribution of 87,028 cases and 5,150 deaths as of April 9, 2020.

What was going on? Were we in World War III? Had there been another attack on New York? The current number of deaths (7,067) was more than twice that of the 9/11 attack when US-trained, Middle Eastern (primarily Saudi) terrorist pilots orchestrated an attack on our country by crashing our commercial aircraft into both towers of the World Trade Center. This was followed by crashing another one of our aircraft into the Pentagon in our nation's capital and a fourth aircraft into a field in Pennsylvania after a group of US heroes stormed the terrorist-controlled cockpit causing it to abort its mission to crash into the White House. No, nothing like that; we are dealing with a virus that purportedly originated in a "wet market" in Wuhan, China, where the virus was transmitted from an unidentified species, possibly a bat or a pangolin (a strange-looking animal sometimes called a scaly anteater) to a host animal whose meat was sold in the open-air, dirt-floor market. The virus then spread to other parts of China, then exploded by means of international air travel to most countries throughout the world that now join the USA in counting "cases" and "deaths."

So, are we fighting a virus that innocently emanated from a piece of meat in that Wuhan wet market, or are we being introduced to WWIII, or what a WWIII would look like? Bullets and bombs are passé; it's now ventilators, social distancing, and PPEs (personal protective equipment), which explains why I carry a mask (which I'm told by some talking heads serves no purpose other than to remind me not to touch my face.

What I do know is that both our national and international *idols* are "frozen in time" as the Wuhan virus, sorry the Chinese virus—oops, sorry again—the Coronavirus (or COVID-19) has flipped the script on this country—and dare I say, the world—like nothing before.

Hollywood is now limited to buying Louis Vuitton essentials online; what a downer. Three-quarters of the fun is having other celebs see you in the boutique. They will just have to suffer until the LV boutiques are allowed to open under federal guidelines for social distancing, praying there will not be a requirement to wear masks, which would also impede their fun.

Sports has also taken a shot to the jaw and is now at a standing eight-count with wobbly legs. This virus has given "Fantasy Football" a new meaning.

The LSU All-American and Heisman Trophy recipient, Joe Burrow, is heavily touted to be the #1 pick in the NFL draft later this month only to be selected by a team that is unable to practice and follow federal guidelines for social distancing at the same time. However, don't be dismayed, we have been told that the NFL, MLB, NBA, and NHL players, coaches, and executives will be paid their full multimillion-dollar salaries while they continue to burn the midnight oil to see if there is enough money left for vendors, parking attendants, groundskeepers, court, and ice crews (including Zamboni operators).

Looks like there will be plenty of time for the sports world as well as the Hollywood celebs to shop online for the New Spring Collection of the Louis Vuitton essentials. Can you imagine what it would be like to implement social distancing with last year's fashions?

On a more serious tone, since prognosticators have said the number of deaths from this pandemic may exceed that of the 1918 Spanish Flu (50 million deaths worldwide with about 675,000 in the United States), my purpose for inserting this information in my memoirs is to memorialize April 9, 2020 as the day that some news sources say this pandemic will become the most devastating event in human history, resulting in an altered culture that is difficult to describe but will be very different from what we have come to expect as "normal" and what has now been referred to as a "new normal." The prognosticators add that not only will millions die from this virus, even though the infection rate should slow down as summer arrives, but it will return this winter with a vengeance fueled by cold weather and spread by a population not sold on quarantining, social distancing, wearing masks, and anxiously waiting to re-invite restaurants, bars, gyms, hair salons, movie theatres, sports, and the like back into our lives. Can it be that all of this is the result of the innocent mishandling of a bat or a pangolin in a Wuhan wet market, or is this something far more sinister?

OBJECTIVES, THEN AND NOW

When I was in my twenties, I recall that my objectives were to achieve at a level that would make my wife and family proud and to earn at a level that would allow me to attain a peaceful and comfortable life, thus demonstrating to my friends that I had *arrived*. These objectives reflected just about everything that was going on in my head.

As I ponder on the young man who sought these objectives, I sometimes question how my vision of what I desired could be so shallow and, dare I say, *selfish*. Where was my concern for others? Were the poor, the infirm, the homeless, not to mention widows with whom I had an "up close and personal" experience, present in my consciousness? How does a person who was given so much in terms of help and opportunities manage to focus on no one but himself? Was I given that help and opportunity with no responsibility of repayment? Without a rudder, a vessel will travel wherever the current dictates and the current of the culture in which I lived directed me to look out for myself, so I did.

I did not recognize it at the time, but as God sought me, He introduced many lessons into my life, which eventually drew me to His offer of salvation and redemption and altering my objective in life from one of serving myself and my desires to one of serving Him and His desires. The bonus for me in this new direction is that, since His plan for my life is perfect, seeking and attempting to carry out His plan provides the peace and comfort I desired when I was in my twenties, immeasurably enhanced by replacing the *temporal* peace and comfort I sought with the *eternal* peace and comfort He provides, knowing I will spend eternity with Christ in the heavenly realms. God's plan for my life provides the rudder I lacked and thus allows me to navigate my life through those prevalent counter-currents that is our worldly culture.

So, my life continues to be accented by God's help and opportunities, but now my responsibility is crystal clear in that I am to share with all those God puts in my path, for His purpose, the offer of salvation and redemption as part of the team He has put together for this purpose. This charge God has put on me I gladly accept, and while the sharing of His offer is often not popular, He comforts me with the knowledge that my only responsibility is to deliver His "good news" and leave the outcome to Him.

It is my hope and desire that all who read *Mis Memorias* ascertain the unspeakable joy and value of allowing the Holy Spirit to guide them to live their life for the greater glory of God.

Ad Majorem Dei Gloriam

CHILDREN AND GRANDCHILDREN

Proud Abuelo

Cousins Mia & Christiano

Me & Abuela with grandchildren

Abuela with Olivia, Giana & Mia

Abuela, Alisha & the girls 2009

Me with grandkids 2011

Flores boys at Citrus Park

Me enjoing ice cream with grandchildren

Christiano rests on Abuelo while Jenna loves on him

Our family-noche buena 2008

Khloe, Giana, Christiano & Vincent

Me, Christiano & Mia celebrating our birthdays together

Alisha with daughter Khloe

Mia & Khloe's graduation with John, Alisha, me & Abuela

Our family dining at Iavarone's

West Point Cadet-Elect Armando Flores IV receives charge from his dad at church service.

A Flores III family

Cadet AF IV, cousins Giana, Mia & Khloe, sister Jenna & cousin Olivia

Cordova Family

Our Grandchildren

Our Family

Our Grandsons

Me with our granddaughters

Me with our grandsons

GOLDEN YEARS

Armando Flores Jr

Mondy and Judith Sunset

Me and Judy North Carolina

My bride, Judith Kay

Me and Judith Kay

ABOUT THE AUTHOR

Armando Flores Jr graduated from The University of Tampa before joining Xerox Corporation as a sales representative in 1969. He held various managerial positions in sales, marketing, and administration, and was named branch manager for South Florida in 1976, a position he held until joining Jim Walter Corporation where he served as vice president and group executive until his retirement in 1989.

Mr. Flores has received various academic, athletic, and business honors including membership in the Jesuit High School Athletic Hall of Fame, The University of Tampa Athletic Hall of Fame, Who's Who in American Colleges and Universities, and Who's Who in American Executives.

He has served on the board of the Florida West Coast Chapter of the Fellowship of Christian Athletes and the Board of Trustees of The University of Tampa. He is past president of the Carrollwood Village Homeowners Association and has served as a board member of The University of Tampa Alumni Association, Tampa Alpha Chapter, and the National Football Foundation and Hall of Fame, Inc., Tampa Chapter, the board of Family First and as a commissioner on the state of Florida's Judicial Nominating Commission for the Second District Court of Appeal.

Mr. Flores is a managing member of Flores Holdings, LLC, a Tampa based investment company.

Mr. Flores and his wife, Judy, are members of Idlewild Church. They have two adult married children, eight grandchildren and live in Tampa. He was born in Tampa on February 1, 1945.

CPSIA information can be obtained
at www.ICGtesting.com
Printed in the USA
BVHW051319140521
607268BV00006B/1470